Irish Lives and Times

A LIVING HISTORY FROM NEWSPAPERS OF THE DAY

THE FAMINE YEARS
1845 to 1852

Gerald Reilly

The Raleigh Press, Publisher

Copyright © 2015 by Gerald Reilly

All rights reserved. No part of this publication may be reproduced, distributed, or transmitted in any form or by any means, including photocopying, recording, or other electronic or mechanical methods, without the prior written permission of the publisher.

For permission requests, please contact the publisher.

The Raleigh Press
Cataumet, Massachusetts

publisher@theraleighpress.com

ISBN: 978-0-9892753-2-3

Printed in USA

SELECTED HEADLINES

1845

THE NEW LORD MAYOR'S EQUIPAGE	12
AGRARIAN OUTRAGE IN TIPPERARY	14
FIRING AT PRINCE ALBERT	17
MILITARY FLOGGING—RUMOURED DEATH	17
ORANGE OUTRAGE	19
MURDER OF A MAGISTRATE IN CAVAN	23
THE DISEASE IN POTATOES	27
REPEAL DEMONSTRATION IN MAYO	28
O'CONNELL TRIBUTE	34
LECTURE ON SLAVERY	37

1846

DREADFUL ACCIDENT—COACHMAN KILLED	44
IRISH FAMINE—MR. O'CONNELL'S MOTION	50
MURDERS IN TIPPERARY	50
COMMUNICATION BY TELEGRAPH	53
LAUNCH OF THE IRON STEAM SHIP	56
COCK FIGHTING	56
DEATH FROM STARVATION	60
COW STEALING	64
FAMINE RIOT IN DUNGARVAN	72
PROGRESS OF STARVATION	78

1847

MILITARY SHEEP STEALERS	84
A CORPSE FOR SALE	90
FOOD RIOTS IN THE CITY	92
HEALTH OF THE LIBERATOR	102
THE DISCOVERIES OF 1846	102
THE FATE OF EMIGRANTS	104
DELETERIOUS FOOD FOR THE PEOPLE	108
DEATH OF MR. O'CONNELL	109
THE YOUNG IRELANDERS	121
MORE PRIEST-HUNTING	128

1848

THE POOR LAW	138
REGULATIONS FOR EMIGRANT VESSELS	142
THE ARCTIC EXPEDITION	144
PEDESTRIANISM	146
SUSPENSION OF THE HABEAS CORPUS ACT	155
REBELLION—MUSKETS—PLANS &c.	158
MILITARY OCCUPATION OF CORK	164
THE AFFAIR NEAR BALLINGARRY	166
FIRE-ARMS AND PIKES FOR SALE	168
THE ARREST OF SMITH-O'BRIEN	174

1849

AN EMIGRATION MARRIAGE	188
VICEREGAL COURT	192
AN OLD OFFENDER	197
THE OLD STORY OVER AGAIN—DEATH	202
THE STATE CONVICTS AND THEIR DOOM	204
THE CHARGE OF SHOOTING AT HER MAJESTY	209
THE QUEEN IN DUBLIN	212
ATROCIOUS MURDER IN LONDON	218
CHARLES DICKENS ON PUBLIC EXECUTIONS	234
STARVATION IN KILRUSH	236

1850

DISTRAINING IN ULSTER	244
EVICTIONS IN TIPPERARY	247
CONVENTION OF AMERICAN WOMEN	249
FORTUNATE ESCAPE	250
ATTACK UPON HER MAJESTY THE QUEEN	251
FEMALE ADVOCATES AT THE BAR	252
HIS GRACE THE DUKE OF DEVONSHIRE	254
THE NEW CARDINALS	256
THE "N0-POPERY" MOVEMENT	262
DREADFUL SHIPWRECK—LOSS OF NINETY	264

1851

RUINOUS FIRE AT HUTTON'S COACH FACTORY	270
IMPERIAL PARLIAMENT	272
THE NEW PENAL LAW	274
DISCOVERY OF CANNIBALS AT BORNEO	288
DR. FREW IN TROUBLE	289
THE MINISTERIAL JEWS' BILL	296
PRIVATE THEATRICALS AT DEVONSHIRE HOUSE	302
ENGAGEMENT WITH SLAVERS	308
MORE EVICTIONS IN CONNEMARA	320
EXTRAORDINARY SUICIDE BY A LADY	321

1852

THE IRISH PEASANTRY	333
LIGHTING ENNISCORTHY WITH GAS	334
MYSTERIOUS DEATH OF A FEMALE	335
DESTRUCTION OF LAGOS	340
PERVERSION TO POPERY	347
LOSS OF THE BIRKENHEAD	352
COMPLETION OF THE SUBMARINE TELEGRAPH	356
THE SLAUGHTER AT SIXMILE-BRIDGE	364
FUNERAL OF THE DUKE OF WELLINGTON	388
THE CROWBAR BRIGADE	392

INTRODUCTION

Irish Lives and Times is a living history of Ireland and her people during the famine years of 1845 to 1852 that was written as it happened. This anthology of articles and advertisements was recreated and reprinted from the newspapers of the day and depicts events and characters in mid 19th century real time.

The people that comprise these stories and the authors, or correspondents, experienced together the outrages, the famine and the disease that made daily existence in Ireland, at that time, as terrible and awful as Europe had ever seen. A correspondent might be an eye witness, a compiler of rumors, or a religious firebrand with an agenda, or, as indicated by "our own correspondent", someone with a more structured arrangement with a particular newspaper. Some of these correspondents regularly vented religious or political sentiments that veered far from objectivity.

The Irish peasant was dependent on the potato as a source of food, and, although Ireland had endured famine before 1845 and suffered from famine after 1852, the blight that occurred during these years delivered a blow unlike any other. The peasantry were defeated by nature but also by their colonial lords and laws, which lay the blame for the calamity on Providence and the cure on self reliance. Help yourself and God will help thee. However, the destitute and devastated peasants were rendered incapable of bettering their lot by calculated schemes directed to their detriment.

Violence was endemic; turbulence was the order of the day. Ireland was a militarized state with the British army garrisoned throughout the island supporting a ubiquitous constabulary. The people had stones and pikes but these were no match for the red-coated ranks of soldiery with rifles and bayonets.

Politics was about religion, land and class. It was often violent and always exclusionary. The Protestant Ascendancy was reviled as absentee landlords. Estates remained in families for generations, and, even during the famine, food from these estates was shipped from Ireland to England and the Continent as the feeble native creatures suffered and died on Irish soil.

Evictions, or "exterminations" were common as landlords sought to better their own situations while dealing more suffering to the decimated peasantry. Entire villages were turned out of their cottages and left on the cold, wet road as their homes were torn down in front of them. Or, they were forced to tear down their homes themselves in order to qualify for measly benefits from the poorhouse.

The young emigrated. Those who stayed were old and infirm and the task of tilling the land and providing food for themselves was not possible when their sons and daughters were in America and Australia. But the ships the emigrants sailed away from home in were often times death traps themselves with regulations just beginning to be established.

Capital punishment and transportation were regularly employed tools of the law. Executions would take place just a few days after a guilty verdict. And a sentence of seven years in Australia was not uncommon for relatively minor crimes.

Pictures of all this are limited. Photography did exist but it was primitive and travel through the country was difficult and dangerous, so, photographers were few. Artists drew scenes from being present at an event or from stories they were told about an event, or, from their own imaginations.

Some of the realities of life in mid 19th century Ireland had nothing to do with class or famine but were simply the state of life and science and culture at the time. Medicinal remedies were the stuff of quacks or established firms that offered one pill cure-alls. Ads touted glass windows, oil lamps and beaver hats. How many horses pulled the car carrying your coffin to the cemetery mattered. Mourning establishments offered four horses as an impressive option. The Duke of Wellington had twelve.

Railways, the electric telegraph and steamships were changing communications. News that previously might have taken days to travel, now took seconds. Ironically, mail that might have been delivered overnight now took train rides that meant a three day delivery schedule.

Spelling was inconsistent from one article to the next and even in the same article a person's name might be spelled different ways. Commas were used indiscriminately and abundantly. When we recreated an article, these variations were sometimes corrected and sometimes ignored.

This is not meant to be a comprehensive history of the period but rather a selected narrative related day to day as the next issue was published. The stories are in chronological order and they are reported as they happened. The repetitive nature of some articles indicates the constancy of similar occurrences and bespeaks the story of the day and the history of the time.

To be Sold,

THE INTEREST in a SMALL FARM of about Eight Acres of Prime Land, on which is a good DWELLING-HOUSE, and a COTTAGE adjoining, with Car and Cow Sheds, &c., and walled-in GARDENS, situate at NEWTOWN, within One Mile of the Quay.

The Interest would be Sold for a moderate sum.

For particulars apply at the Office of this paper.
Waterford, Sept. 29, 1848.

Jameson's LL Whiskey
FIVE YEARS OLD !!!

THOMAS MURPHY

ACQUAINTS his Friends, and all parties desirous of having REAL OLD WHISKEY, that he has in Stock a large quantity of this prime article.

His COFFEES, ground in a *New Patent Mill*, must ensure a confidence with the lovers of good Coffee.

His ALES, PORTER, & CIDER, in Wood and Bottle, will be found second to no house in the Trade.

Every article in the GROCERY & SPIRIT TRADE.

☞ *All country orders will have the best attention.*

MURPHY'S WHOLESALE & RETAIL
GROCERY WINE AND SPIRIT STORES,
8, PATRICK-STREET, WATERFORD.

A Respectable Lad will be taken as an Apprentice.

Leper Hospital.

THE TRUSTEES give Notice that they will receive TENDERS from Persons desirous to CONTRACT for the supply of the following Articles from the 14th Inst. to 15th January next :
BREAD, per 4lb Loaf.
BEEF per lb.
MOULD & DIPPED CANDLES per lb.
SWEET MILK per Gallon.
WHITE AND YELLOW SOAP per Cwt.

Sealed Proposals to be left with the Steward at the Hospital, on or before the 13th day of October.

Waterford, 6th October, 1848.

SHOCKING MURDER OF THREE BAILIFFS!!!

The following is an account of the murder which we briefly noticed in our second edition on Monday night last :—Mr. Dalton, rate collector of the Tipperary union, after frequent useless efforts to obtain the poor-rate due of a farmer named Brien, at Ballydoura, near Bansha, county Tipperary, on the estate of the Rev. Mr. Ashe, was obliged to execute a warrant of distress at the suit of the guardians, and placed three keepers named Regan, Walsh, and Dwyer on the premises last Saturday, shortly after which they were warned off, but refused to leave their charge. Next morning, while walking on the farm, they observed several men, three of them armed and disguised, approaching the house, and the keepers retreated, fastening the door against the intruders. This defence was of little avail, for the windows were burst in, and one of the keepers, who endeavoured to defend himself with a spade, was shot on the spot, while the second was felled to the ground with a scythe, and the third took refuge in the chimney. One of the party ascended the roof, and shot the man in the chimney, who fell upon the floor, and was there cut and quartered with the scythe! The third keeper was dragged outside the door, and two shots were fired at him, after which the miscreants cut the throats of their victims with the scythes, and so mangled their remains as not to leave a vestige of the features, and the heads were hanging by the skin only to the trunks.

An inquest was held, and the verdict was—"Barbarously and brutally murdered by some person or persons unknown."

DISCOVERY OF PIKES !

From private information received by Constable Harty on Tuesday evening, he proceeded to the residence of a man named Ready, on the Miller's Marsh, a lime burner, where he succeeded in finding three pikes, which were concealed in the bottom of the kiln. Ready was soon afterwards apprehended, who gave security in the sum of £20, to be forthcoming when called upon.

Reprinted from The Waterford News, Waterford, October 6 & 13, 1848.

THE EMIGRANT SHIP.

Her anchor is heaved,
Her sails unfurled,
From her prow the cleft waves flee;

And she speeds her way
To the western world,
Oe'r the bounding Atlantic sea.

She is freighted with treasure,
More priceless, far,
Than gold or diamonds are;

Her decks are crowded
With life and breath,
And hearts and hopes are there.

Hearts which, ere long, may be crushed,
And hopes to be quenched
In despair's gloom,

For the land of promise
May only yield to the seeker,
A lonely tomb.

There are smiles, bright smiles,
On the young child's face,
As it gazes on sea and sky;

But stern sad thoughts
On the fathers' brow,
And tears in the mother's eye.

Recreated from The Belfast News-Letter, Belfast, January 7, 1845.

1845

Selected Headlines

THE NEW LORD MAYOR'S EQUIPAGE	12
AGRARIAN OUTRAGE IN TIPPERARY	14
FIRING AT PRINCE ALBERT	17
MILITARY FLOGGING—RUMOURED DEATH	17
ORANGE OUTRAGE	19
MURDER OF A MAGISTRATE IN CAVAN	23
THE DISEASE IN POTATOES	27
REPEAL DEMONSTRATION IN MAYO	28
O'CONNELL TRIBUTE	34
LECTURE ON SLAVERY	37

THE NEW LORD MAYOR'S EQUIPAGE.

We have viewed the equipage of the Right Honourable the Lord Mayor, which will be used for the first time in the civic procession this day, when the inauguration of his lordship will take place, and have seldom noticed more perfect specimens of Irish art. It may be premised here that the workmanship and materials are all of home production, and it is but justice to add that where a Repealer was found competent to supply materials, &c., he had a preference of the work in all instances. The "turn out" is on the whole, one of great elegance, and such as cannot fail to attract and justify the admiration of the public.

THE STATE COACH.

The coach, built by Messrs. Hutton, of Summerhill, is perhaps, one of the most finished pieces of workmanship imaginable, considered in its chaste and beautiful designs, and its correct and elegant proportions; for its *tout ensemble*, it appears to us perfect, and as a specimen of Irish manufacture a credit to our country and its artizans.

The body is strikingly graceful in all its parts—is painted a rich purple, relieved with gold, in such a manner as to throw up the colour in high perfection. The city arms are painted in the collar of SS., and the Lord Mayor's in a riband, surrounded by the civic crown, with the supporters, emblematical of peace and justice; the quarters present the collar of SS., with his lordship's crest in the centre, and the civic crown at the top, painted by an eminent Irish artist. The upper parts are highly ornamented. In front is a pair of court lamps of superb workmanship. The body is hung on a carriage on the C and under spring principle and is painted white, picked out tourquoise, relieved with fine lines of gold colour, and so highly varnished as to give it the appearance of porcelain.

A Salisbury boot in front supports a hammercloth to match the colour of the body, trimmed with lace and olives, and highly gilt crests and collars; behind are standards richly carved.

The dress chariot is painted similar to the coach, and is a strikingly handsome carriage. His lordship's arms are painted in mantels on the doors; it has carved standards and hammercloth, with fluted corners, trimmed with lace and fringe of blue and white.

Both carriages present a striking proof that Irish manufacture requires only encouragement to carry the highest degree of perfection.

HARNESS AND HOUSINGS.

The harness has been made at the establishment of Mr. D. Alexander, of Clare street, and is all Irish materials and workmanship of the first style. There are three rows of sewing on the bridle eyes and housings; the hame tugs and breechings neatly lined and stitched, fully ornamented; all the other straps and shield pieces with double rows of sewing, with state and round reins; the bridles very tastefully executed, with fronts and ear bands covered in diamonds, with blue and white ribbons and rosets, with streamers to match. The ribbon dressing of the horses' manes and other parts of the harness are most tastefully executed. The mountings and crests, also Irish workmanship and manufacture, beautifully executed by Mr. Byrne, of Bride-street, are of prince's metal; head or fly terrut with the Irish harp and crown in centre, and a plume on top, swivels and bradoon hooks chased, and of a new scroll pattern ornaments, terminating with flower shamrock, the bits embossed with the Arabian crest and motto; draft eye of hames *fleur de lis* pattern, rein ring chased, and tug ornaments to match, with links and angles to correspond; housing, terrut button, crupper, and end loops handsomely chased; the bearing rein-hook or pillar representing the crest, which is an eagle's head, ducally crowned between two wings; all the housing furniture, with chaste escutcheons, forming rose, thistle, and shamrock, the crest as stated, with garter and motto (*Corde Manuque*); the tug buckles, trace squares, and all the small work chased to correspond, and all of which are got up in a superior manner, indeed, and much to the credit of the manufacturers, as nothing superior could be produced in any country.

THE LIVERIES.

The state liveries of the Lord Mayor are rich, yet chaste, consisting of fine white cloth trimmed with the richest military gold lace, with flaps highly ornamented, and bullion spring buttons, being lined with Irish tabinet; the aigulettes are remarkably beautiful. The undress liveries are of blue cloth, manufactured by Willams, and edged with narrow gold lace. The surtouts are drab cloth manufactured by Read. Mr. Jeremiah Reilly, of Dawson-street, has had the making of the livery, and it is no exaggeration to say that he has turned it out in a manner not to be surpassed by a Stults or a Nugee. Mr. Morgan, of Grafton-street, has furnished the hats in a style worthy of the reputation of his establishment.

MENDICITY INSTITUTION—NEW YEAR'S DAY.—The inmates of this valuable institution, amounting to three hundred persons, were absolutely regaled with a good substantial dinner of the best boiled beef and mutton, which was supplied by Mrs. Fannin, of Leeson-street, and several benevolent ladies and gentlemen, who kindly contributed for that purpose. The long-tried utility of this charity, and, if possible, the more than usual benefit it bestows on the poor of our city until they can obtain work or admission to the poorhouses, is daily proved by the interest manifested towards it by the friends and subscribers.

What can be more consoling to the humane and charitable mind when we know that no human being (no matter what statement is made by them to the contrary) is refused admittance or can want food if they only present themselves for admission. The idle and the sturdy beggar is alone to be met in the streets to impose on the charitable and kind hearted. It is only to be regretted that this invaluable charity is not more frequently visited by the wealthy and humane of our city.

SEASONAL BENEVOLENCE.—It affords us much pleasure to notice an act of bounty most seasonable at this period of year. Mrs. Colonel Arthur ordered meat and clothing for two hundred of the poor on her father's estates at Bracklin, which, in pursuance of her direction, were distributed on Tuesday last.—*Westmeath Guardian.*

MURDER.—On the night of the 27th December, about eight o'clock, William Stapleton, of Lorha, heard some person pulling the thatch off his house, when he made a stab of a pitchfork through the part, at the same time ordering his son John to light a candle and proceed to the yard. Stapleton followed his son immediately, and discovered his brother-in-law, Michael Phelan, outside, armed with a pistol, the contents of which he lodged in the body of John Stapleton, who fell to the ground and died. Land is the cause. Michael Phelan has been fully committed for this offense.—*Nenagh Guardian.*

EXTRAVAGANT LABOUR.—A man named Matthew Lalor, a workman in the employment of the Rev. Mr. Meigham, P.P., Pastorville, Gurtnahoe, Tipperary, recently gave proof of the most extraordinary capability as a labourer, by digging out of the drills, untouched by the plough, no less than six barrels, and nine stone of potatoes within the short space of one hour, in the presence of several witnesses.

Recreated from The Freeman's Journal, Dublin, January 1 & 2, 1845.

AGRARIAN OUTRAGE IN TIPPERARY.
GALLANT CONDUCT OF A REPEALER.

We find the following in the *Limerick Reporter* of Saturday:—A most respectable gentleman, and an Inspector of Repeal Wardens in the town of Tipperary writes as follows;—The peace of our hitherto peaceable district was attempted to be disturbed on Christmas Eve, which has proved a source of great regret to our Repeal Warden's Society, as, since the Repeal agitation commenced in this parish, *we have not had one agrarian outrage*.

A farmer, named Dillon, who lives near Ballyglass, and who is, I believe, driver to Mr. O'Brien, has had some dispute about land with a Widow Hastings, who held the land before Dillon got it. Dillon was attacked by four men on his way home, one of whom snapped a pistol at him—the cap went off, but it missed fire. Dillon was accompanied by an honest Repealer, named Farmer, from this town (Tipperary), who laid the fellow that missed fire prostrate.

Dillon then drew out a pistol (for he is permitted to have arms for his protection on account of this cursed land dispute,) when the other three decamped, leaving the prostrate ruffian a prisoner to Dillon and Farmer, who marched him into town amidst the joy of the honest Tipperary Repealers, who are now so well instructed as to look for the amelioration of their grievances by moral force, and not by shedding the blood of their fellow-man. The doctrine, "He who commits a crime lends assistance to the enemy," &c., is the *most conspicuous motto* in our reading room; and we never fail to inculcate the wholesome lesson at our *weekly meetings*.

Much credit is due to Dillon and his Repeal assistant, Farmer, and we trust that the ruffian assassin, whose progress they have arrested, will be punished as he so justly deserves. We are delighted to be able to say that in Ireland there does not exist a more respectable, efficient, and better organised staff of Repeal wardens than those of the town of Tipperary and district, and which is in a great measure owing to their zealous and indefatigable inspector, Mr. David Ferguson.

Recreated from The Freeman's Journal, Dublin, January 2, 1845.

LOST,

ON Saturday, the 4th instant, about Half-past Six o'Clock, a new Silk Umbrella, never used—Dropped from Summer-hill, by Upper Gloucester-street, Marlborough-street, through North Earl-street, down Sackville-street to Lower Abbey-street. It was enclosed in a Calico Case. If a conscientious person has found it, to be left with the Porter of the Metropolitan Church, Marlborough-street, which will be thankfully acknowledged.

JOYCE'S CAPS.

SHOOTING SEASON, 1844.

SPORTSMEN are respectfully informed that JOYCE'S Anti-Corrosive Percussion Caps and Wadding may be had, as usual, of all respectable Gunmakers and dealers in Gunpowder throughout the United Kingdom, Colonies, &c.

To prevent accident and disappointment from the use of spurious imitations, Purchasers are requested to observe the name of F. Joyce, the Original Inventor and Sole Manufacturer, on each sealed packet, without which they are not genuine. This precaution is rendered necessary by some unprincipled individuals having imitated the Labels and Wrappers.

Chemically-prepared Gun Waddings, of a superior description.

A liberal profit to Exporters and the Trade.

Warehouse, 55, Bartholomew Close, London, Manufacturer of Military Caps to the Hon. East India Company, and to her Majesty's Board of Ordnance.

GOVERNESS.

WANTED, a respectable, Middle-aged Person (a Roman Catholic), to take the entire charge of Four Young Children.

Application, in person, to be made at the Office of this Paper, from Twelve till One each day.

Reprinted from The Freeman's Journal, Dublin, January 7, 1845.

REPEAL—GROCERS' ASSISTANTS—REPEAL.

At a General Meeting of this Body, held in Bentley's Rooms, 161, Chapel-street, on Sunday, February 2, 1845.

Mr. BERNARD BRADY in the chair,
Mr. JOHN FEGAN acting as Secretary,

It was moved by Mr. John Faris; seconded by Mr. Patrick O'Hagan:

Resolved—That we, the Grocers' Assistants, viewing with indignation the manner in which Ireland and the Irish have been treated by English misrulers and mal-legislators who, upon each occasion and every opportunity, have harassed an inoffensive and moral people—not content with having deprived them of their just *rights*, for which we hereby pledge ourselves never to cease *agitating* until we shall have restored to us our native *parliament* in its ancient and pristine *authority*.

Moved by Mr. Mathew Fegan; seconded by Mr. John Egan:

Resolved—That for the better carrying out of the foregoing resolution, we deem it incumbent on every *member of this body* to be identified with the present movement in the cause of their oppressed country, and to aid our *beloved Liberator* in his struggle for domestic legislation.

Moved by Mr. James Dolan; seconded by Mr. Patrick O'Reilly:

Resolved—That never, at any time, was our confidence in the Liberator greater or more unbounded than at the present—for him who withstood the menaces of a twilight proclamation—for him who, boldly confronted by lying accusers—meekly awaited a judgement pronounced to have been a *mockery, a delusion, and a snare*—for him who, for his country and its people, patiently endured an unjust imprisonment of three months, and who now gloriously resuscitates our hopes that our country will soon be a nation. Fully confiding in him as our Leader, Martyr, and Liberator, we hereby tender unto him the implicit confidence of this Body; at the same time pledging ourselves to use our utmost strenuous exertions for our country's nationality under his *great guidance*.

Moved by Mr. John Fegan; seconded by Mr. Edward Lunney:

Resolved—That fully believing the Bequests Act to be an attempt to subjugate the Irish Church, with a view to enslave its people, we are of opinion that any reformation cannot amend *the act*, and that anything but its total *repeal* cannot allay our just suspicions, or subdue our determined hostility.

Moved by Mr. Matthew Fegan; seconded by the Liberator:

Resolved—That the marked thanks of this meeting, as likewise of this body, are pre-eminently due and hereby given to Mr. Bentley for the kind and courteous manner he has always granted the use of his Rooms, and his patriotic exertions in the cause of his country.

BERNARD BRADY, Chairman.
JOHN FEGAN, Secretary.

Mr. Brady having vacated the chair, and Mr. Dolan being called thereto, the marked thanks of the meeting were accorded to Mr. Brady for his very proper conduct as chairman, and his patriotic exertions on every occasion.

JAMES DOLAN, Chairman.
JOHN FEGAN, Secretary.

N.B.—The Committee will meet at 34, Stafford-street, every Sunday, from Eleven to One o'Clock, to receive the Reports from the persons appointed to collect the Subscriptions of the Body.

Recreated from The Freeman's Journal, Dublin, February 3, 1845.

MORE NOSE-BITING.—George Travers was charged with biting a piece from the nose of a person named Thomas Darbishire. Complainant said he was at the house of Mr. Thomas Simpson, publican Halliwell, on Thursday, the 13th instant; prisoner was there also. There was a fight took place concerning a penny which had been lost on the floor, that caused the complainant to strike prisoner, who afterwards got hold of his nose. He did not know then that a piece was off or not. They were friendly shortly after, but he was sure prisoner had done it.

Mr. M. H. Richardson appeared for the complainant, and called John Ainsworth, of Halliwell, who said he was in the house at the time the fight took place; he separated them, but could not see whether any blow was struck or not. He did not see any biting. When the fight was over he washed complainants face, and then he saw a piece was taken off. It was not done before they began to fight. He gathered the piece of nose off the floor that was bitten off. It was about the size of a bean. Samuel Bleakley said he was there before the fight took place. Darbishire struck first.—Fined 5£., or in default to be committed to the New Bailey for two months.—*Bolton Free Press*.

Recreated from The Freeman's Journal, Dublin, February 24, 1845.

RATHER AWKWARD.—On Sunday week, while the Duke of Hamilton was leaving Hamilton for London, his Grace's carriage was arrested by a messenger-at-arms, who stated to the noble duke that he wished to take his valet into custody, at the instance of a young woman whom he had seduced, and whom, with his child, he was leaving without support. His grace instantly ordered his servant to deliver up his keys, and told the officer that he was at liberty to take him into custody, which he accordingly did. In the course of the day the valet found security and set off to join his master.—*Greenoch Advertiser*.

Recreated from The Freeman's Journal, Dublin, March 1, 1845.

REV. C. GAYER v. THE KERRY EXAMINER.

(*From the Kerry Examiner of 25th February*, 1845.)

"Since this action was brought against us, as we before stated, our attention was directed to the articles complained of, and on the 4th instant we published our sentiments on those articles, and we then freely and unhesitatingly admitted and expressed our regret, that in the excitement of the moment we had used language towards the Rev. Mr. Gayer, which on cool reflection we could not have penned, and we then undertook to give any further apology that could be considered reasonable, and such as an independent, editor and a gentleman could publish.

Our article, it appears, has not been considered sufficient, and we now again freely and voluntarily assert that by our articles of the 22d and 26th of November last, on which the reverend gentleman grounds his action against us, we never meant to charge him with either *deliberate* falsehood, hypocrisy, fraud, or imposture; that our animadversions were solely made in reference to certain proceedings reported in the *Belfast Chronicle* to have taken place in that city; that all we meant to convey was, that Mr. Gayer was labouring under a delusion when he stated that 800 persons at Dingle changed from the Roman Catholic to the Protestant faith; and which statement we then most unqualifiedly denied, and still deny. Mr. Gayer referred to Dingle *only* in his advertisement published in the Edinburgh paper, and to Dingle therefore the articles complained of could alone have referred when we undertook to deny the statement of Mr. Gayer, that there were in Dingle 800 converts from the Catholic church.

That we were right we still firmly believe, at the same time that we regret our manner of denial was not less calculated to hurt the feelings of the rev. gentleman."

Recreated from The Freeman's Journal, Dublin, March 7, 1845.

FIRING AT PRINCE ALBERT.

We received late last night, from an occasional contributor, a statement to the effect that, yesterday, a few minutes after one o'clock, as Prince Albert, attended by his equerries and grooms, was riding up Constitution Hill, in the Green Park, on his way to Hyde Park, his Royal Highness met a man mounted on a grey horse, who got upon the footpath for the apparent purpose of leaving room for the royal party to pass; that within a few seconds "a slight report, similar to that produced by an air-gun, was heard from close behind;" that on looking round, the Royal party observed that the man on the grey horse was going off at full speed. Pursuit was made, it is said, by some of the attendants, but without effect; and that, subsequently, some policemen of the A division were put upon the alert, his Royal Highness proceeding on his ride in Hyde Park.—*Morning Herald of Wednesday.*

MILITARY FLOGGING AT THE ROYAL BARRACKS—RUMOURED DEATH OF THE VICTIM.

Considerable sensation prevailed in the neighbourhood of the royal Barrack, and indeed in all other portions of the city yesterday, in consequence of a rumour that prevailed relative to the death of an unfortunate soldier named Patrick Rice belonging to the 73d regiment, and who it was stated died from the effects of a flogging which he had received the previous day (Thursday) by order of a court martial.

A reporter belonging to this journal proceeded to the barrack in order to ascertain the correctness of the statement, but he was refused any information on the subject, although he applied in every quarter likely to be informed on the matter; and indeed there could be no doubt that the parties to whom he addressed himself were perfectly cognizant of the facts which he subsequently obtained from a quarter that reliance may be placed on.

The facts of the frightful affair are, as far as could be collected, as follows, but from the mystery observed of course the whole facts have not transpired:—Patrick Rice, a private in the 73d, was, it is said, a person addicted to intemperance, and he was several times punished for the vice. Some time since he made away with and sold his "*kit*," which, as every one is aware, contains all a soldier's necessaries; and for this offence he was sentenced to receive 150 lashes! He was not in good health at the time, it is said; but on Thursday he was pronounced well enough to receive his sentence.

He was accordingly taken to the riding school, where he received 100 lashes (some say he got the 150), after which the wretched man was carried to the hospital in a state bordering on insensibility. A person who stated himself to have been a bystander informed our reporter that the sight was horrible, and describes the howling of the unfortunate man as truly appalling. Of course, when taken to the hospital "every care and attention" was paid to his case; but he became so bad that the rumour was spread abroad on yesterday that he had died of the injuries he had received.

This rumour, however, was unfounded; but a person, who stated that he saw the man yesterday at 4 o'clock, asserts that hardly any hope was entertained of his recovery, and that at the time he was writhing under his agony, being insensible to every thing save the pain he endured. Such are the facts communicated to our reporter, and which are believed to be true; but if not minutely so, the parties who ought to give the details (as they are truly known to them), but who refused; have only to blame themselves, if the matter appears more terrible than the truth. The result is looked to with the most intense anxiety by the public.

Recreated from The Freeman's Journal, Dublin, March 14-15, 1845.

FINE ARTS.

PARTICULAR NOTICE.

The late WILLIAM PARKER's Valuable Collection of Paintings also, his very Choice selection of Silver and Copper Coins and Medals, Coin and Medal Cabinets, &c., &c.,

WILL BE SOLD BY AUCTION in the Gallery of the Royal Irish Institution, COLLEGE-STREET, on TUESDAY, the 18th MARCH 1845, and two following days, commencing to the minute at One o'Clock each day.

The Nobility and Gentry, the Admirers of the Fine Arts and the Public generally, are most respectfully informed that the *selected portion* of Paintings, the property of the late Mr. PARKER, will be submitted to their notice on the above days, by order of the Executors, without any reserve whatever.

The Paintings are chiefly First-class, in a high state of preservation, and include specimens of the most esteemed Ancient and Modern Masters, viz.:—

P. P. Rubens,	L. Giordano,
Salvator Rosa,	Rosa da Tivoli,
Quintin Matsys,	Mignard,
Linglebach,	Zuccarelli,
Rembrandt	Jordeans,
Watteau,	Dusart,
Rottenhamer,	Gabrielli,
Roberts,	Weenix, &c.

The whole of which may be Viewed on Saturday the 15th and Monday the 17th March, and as each day's Sale is allotted in the Catalogue, a punctual attendance thereat is respectfully requested.

☞ Catalogues may be had on the 13th instant, in the Office of

JOHN LITTLEDALE, Auctioneer,
11, Upper Ormond-quay.

TWENTY MILES IN FIFTY-SIX MINUTES!—On Friday last, the 8th instant, a match against time came off near Aylsbury. Mr. T. White, of Walton, backed his mare to do 20 miles within an hour, to be ridden. He stood to win 50l. or lose 20l. He has won. The mare did the distance with four minutes to spare. She was ridden by a light weight. She did it with ease. What next?

Reprinted from The Freeman's Journal, Dublin, March 14, 1845.

STATE OF THE COUNTRY.

(*From the Roscommon Journal.*)

This county has never been in so disturbed a state, owing unfortunately to the wretchedness of the peasantry, and their anxiety to raise food for the support of themselves and their starving families. Many a time and oft we told the landed proprietors of Roscommon that their depopulating system, and anxiety to clear their lands in order either to occupy them themselves or let them in large tracts to some rich grazier, would create a reaction on the part of the oppressed, the result of which we have now to deplore.—Rents were easier got in from extensive farmers than from the poorer classes, and consequently suited both the absentee landlord, and his equally non-resident agent to have as tenants men from whom they could receive the price of their lands without any trouble or inconvenience although they well knew that the greater portion of such monies were wrung from the sweat of the poor by such men in the way of conacre, at the enormous rate of from nine to ten and often twelve guineas an acre.

We deprecate as much as others the foolish and disgraceful conduct of the poor in resorting to illegal and unconstitutional means to try to reduce the price of conacre in this county. They have had recourse to the very means of adding to their present miseries, by disgracing the hitherto peaceful character of their county, and heaping enormous taxes on themselves, without in the slightest degree rendering themselves the least benefit. In their wild and criminal practices they have annoyed and outraged the feelings, the properties, and the houses of many of their best benefactors, their most charitable neighbours, and their hitherto best friends. They have turned up the lands of gentlemen whose benevolence assuaged the miseries of the poor, and whose charities wiped the tear from the eye of the widow and the orphan. Such conduct is well calculated to drive from amongst us those who heretofore supplied the place of the absentee, and whose conduct and humanity checked the cruelties of the oppressor, and put to shame the acts of those who sympathised not, nor cared not for the wretchedness they themselves had created.

Every town and almost every village in this county is now a military station, and we understand that we are to have an addition to our police force of 150 men, with another stipendiary magistrate, the expenses of which the misguided have to place to their own conduct. Emissaries, spies, and hirelings are of course active in their vocations to trade upon the duplicity of their victims, and ultimately to trade on their lives and liberties, by betraying them and sending them as convicts from their native country to spend the remainder of their existence in misery and slavery. Would to God that something may be done to put an end to the deplorable state which this part of the country is at present in, and that we may shortly see peace, order, and tranquility again restored.

(From the Tuam Herald)

On Wednesday last the Hon. M. French, R.M., accompanied by a large police force, under the command of J. Irwan, Esq., S.I., proceeded to the lands of Closhrue, the property of the Rev. John O'Rorke, and arrested four persons charged with forcible possession by having tilled a portion of land from which they had been evicted last spring. After the sheriff had delivered the possession of the cabins and lands to the bailiffs of the Rev. Mr. O'Rorke, and had retired, the people re-entered their houses and have since occupied them, but the land remained waste until Monday last when they sowed some oats, for which they have been arrested and still remain in custody.

An officer and twenty-five men of the second Dragoons arrived in Dunmore last Friday night, we understand to be permanently stationed there.

ORANGE OUTRAGE.

COUNTY OF ANTRIM.—On last Monday the Orangemen of forty lodges, armed with guns, and bearing flags and banners fired several shots when passing the Catholic chapel of Rasharkin, through which village they marched. At some little distance from Rasharkin they halted; and after drinking copiously, firing shots, and creating much alarm among the peaceable inhabitants of the locality, returned to their homes, attacking the houses of Catholics on their way, and abusing and beating such Catholics as they met.

A stipendiary magistrate, two captains of police, and one hundred of the constabulary were present, for what purpose we know not, as no effort seems to have been made to dissuade these misguided men from their lawless outrages. Such are the facts sent to us. We await more detailed information from our own reporter who is now in that district.—*Belfast Vindicator.*

Recreated from The Freeman's Journal, Dublin, April 1, 1845.

HOUSE OF LORDS—THURSDAY.
Their Lordships met to-day, for the first time after the Easter recess.
The LORD CHANCELLOR took his seat on the Woolsack at five o'clock.

MATRIMONY.
AN English Gentleman, age 24, without fortune, though possessing an equivalent, is desirous of forming an alliance with an Irish Lady, about his own age, of good appearance and amiable disposition, possessed of about 5,000*l*. It is hoped that no Lady will reply without sincere intentions, as the Advertiser is actuated by no other principle.
Address M. O., General Post Office, Dublin.

Reprinted from The Freeman's Journal, Dublin, April 5, 1845.

FATHER MATHEW.

Father Mathew's success in Youghal, yesterday, was most triumphant. The number of postulants was over 3000. Mr. C. W. Smyth, the proprietor of the Youghal coaches, requested Father Mathew's acceptance of a coach-and-four to Cork, at any time, for himself, or for any of his friends. Father Mathew, as may be supposed, returned his warmest thanks for this liberal offer, which he declined.

Reprinted from The Cork Examiner, Cork, April 14, 1845.

ROBBERY.

On the night of Friday last a gentleman, at present sojourning in this City, was robbed of a sum of money amounting to 56£, by a Cyprian of the name of Maria Kelly, in a house of ill-fame in Morgan-street. Immediately after, the circumstances being reported to Constable Crowley, (78), at the Tuckey-street station, that active officer, acting on a mere description of the person of the offender, proceeded in quest of her, and after a lengthened and fatiguing search he succeeded in arresting a woman whose appearance answered the description given, and who afterwards turned out to be the identical party who had committed the robbery.

On being brought before the Bench of Magistrates she was identified, and fully committed to take her trial before the Recorder at Sessions. Subsequently the greater portion of the money was discovered by Constable Crowley, buried in a corner of a field off the Dyke walk, a few inches beneath the surface. The present is not the first nor the twentieth occasion that this indefatigable officer has signalized himself in bringing to justice and ridding the city of infamous characters, discovering and restoring to the owners stolen property, and on more occasions than one, risking his life in the protection of premises when in a state of conflagration.

Recreated from The Cork Examiner, Cork, April 23, 1845.

DUBLIN POLICE.

CURIOUS CASE OF LUNACY.—Leonard Palmer, described in the charge sheet as a gentleman whose residence was in Cork, was brought before the magistrates of this office, charged by police-constable 75 B, with being a dangerous lunatic. From the evidence adduced it appeared that the constable found the prisoner wandering in Dawson-street upon the preceding evening, and that from his appearance he considered him to be out of his mind. He took the gentleman into custody, and conveyed him to the station, where he was searched, and on his person found the large sum of £44 17s.

Mr. Palmer appeared quite indignant at his position. He stated that he drew £100 from the Bank of Ireland upon the day before—that he had served four years in her Majesty's navy, and was quite capable of taking care of himself.

Mr. Tyndal stated that the prisoner had been repeatedly brought before him on charges similar to that preferred by the constable, and on those occasions he had been accused of spending his money very foolishly. There could be no doubt that he (Mr. Palmer) had a perfect right to do as he liked with his own, but still there was a degree of moderation to be expected from a person of his description. He (Mr. Tyndal) wished to know if the prisoner had any friends?

Mr. Palmer said he had no friends whatever, but he was endeavouring to gain them by distributing his money in the manner described by the police-constable. Her Majesty owed him two pounds, and he wished Mr. Tyndal would induce her to pay it.

Mr. Tyndal—You are acting rather unwisely in giving your money away in such an indiscriminate manner.

Mr. Palmer said he thought it was an admirable manner to make friends for himself. After many years' experience he discovered that no friendship was sincere or lasting unless it was purchased.

Mr. Tyndal having consulted with Dr. Ireland, who was in attendance, decided on discharging Mr. Palmer, his conduct not being in any way indicative of dangerous insanity.

Mr. Palmer left the office, accompanied by his brother.

☞ On Sunday last, JAMES SCANLON, who three or four months ago had joined the ranks of the "perverts", was received back into the bosom of the Catholic Church at the Chapel of Doon, (near Ballybunnion) by the Rev. Mortimer O'Sullivan. The man expressed in the presence of the entire congregation his heartfelt sorrow for the scandal he had given by his apostacy which he had unfortunately fallen into in the expectation of being raised from poverty to affluence.—*Kerry Examiner*.

AGRICULTURAL REPORT FOR APRIL.

About the middle of the past month, the most important business of sowing Spring seeds was all but finished, and that under circumstances as favourable as could be desired. Land of every description being in a most excellent state for the reception of seed, having been mellowed by the frosts of March and the heat of the sun in April, it became dry, but not bound, easily broken by the harrows, without running into clods. Thus the lateness of Spring weather has been less felt than was anticipated; and now a most beautiful and promising braird changes the aspect of the fields from red to a lively green.

In Potato planting considerable progress has been made, and for which the timely showers of the last few days are of incalculable benefit for the preservation of the sets, and for the easier preparation of ground yet to sow, which may be now made ready, and sown, with sufficient moisture for insuring a braird, if planted with healthy seed.

Recreated from The Cork Examiner, Cork, April 28, 1845.

WILL OF THE LATE MARQUIS OF WESTMINSTER.—Probate of the will and six codicils of the Most Honourable Robert, Marquis of Westminster, late of Eaton Hall, in the county of Chester, who died on the 17th of February last, was granted on the 15th instant to the Most Honourable Richard, Marquis of Westminster, the son, one of the executors, a power to be reserved to the dowager marchioness, the executrix, to prove hereafter. The personal estate in England and within the province of Canterbury, sworn under 350,000£. Bequests to his wife an annuity of 6,500£ in addition to her property under settlement; devises and bequeaths his estates at Westminster and the manor of Ebury to his eldest son, the present marquis; to his son, Thomas, Earl of Wilton, he devises his estates in the counties of Chester, Flint, and Denbigh, to be freed from any incumbrances, and bequests to him the presentation to the rectory of Prestwick, Lancaster. To his son, Lord Robert Grosvenor, his Moor Park estate, and a legacy of 170,000£. Leaves the pictures, &c., in the gallery and elsewhere, at Grosvenor House, together with the Nassuck diamond, weighing 357 grains, the magnificent brilliant earrings, weighing 223 grains, and the round brilliant, weighing 125 grains, as heir-looms. Also the pictures at Eaton Hall, as heir-looms with that property. Bequeaths to the present marquis the furniture and other moveables at Eaton Hall, and also the family jewels, and appoints him residuary legatee.

Recreated from The Freeman's Journal, Dublin, May 19, 1845

DEPARTURE OF A CONVICT SHIP FOR NEW SOUTH WALES.

The transport ship, Radcliffe, sailed on Saturday from Kingstown for Sydney, New South Wales, with 250 persons under sentence of transportation, who were collected from all parts of the country. Captain Webster and two companies of the 11th regiment were in charge (as military escort) of the ship, with a number of marines. There were also two medical officers on board the vessel. The ship went before the breeze with a flowing tide, and had her yards manned, as is usual on such occasions, the crew giving three cheers as she passed out of the harbour.

Reprinted from The Freeman's Journal, Dublin, May 19, 1845

STATE OF ROSCOMMON.

We suggested some time since the propriety of removing the police force stationed in this town, because we saw that a bad and unkind feeling existed between them and the country people, created by the manner in which the police acted during the whole of the late investigation. We feared, and rightly feared, that a pretext was only wanting for both sides to give vent to their feelings; and the conduct of some of the police on the last fair day of this town fully justified the demand then made for their removal.—They avail themselves of every opportunity to annoy and insult the people of this town and its neighbourhood, and even some of the jurors who were in the inquest have not escaped the petty annoyance which men of this class have it in their power sometimes to give. We require the police authorities to remove those men as expeditiously as possible, and restore the good feeling that ought to exist between the force and the people, by transferring a new body of men to those quarters who will discharge their duty free from local prejudices and embittered feelings. We fear the consequences that may follow if the present men are allowed to remain here, as we had reason to believe they were anxious to fire on the people the last fair day if allowed by Mr. Ceary, the magistrate who acted humanely and wisely on the occasion. It must be most irksome to the magistrates of this locality to be drawn so frequently into collision with the people, principally by the conduct of a few ill-conducted policemen under their command; and steps should be taken to remove at once from the force those men, who are ready on every occasion to transgress their duty and satisfy their perverse dispositions.

We call again on the government to remove those men, and take the necessary steps for the preservation of peace in the district.

THE QUEEN'S BALL.

The Queen gave a state ball on Monday evening at Buckingham Palace, which was more numerously attended than any former ball given by her Majesty, nearly two thousand invitations having been issued.

From nine o'clock, when the company began to arrive, until eleven, the visitors continued to arrive at the Palace without intermission, filling the suite of state saloons, which were fitted up and prepared in the usual style of regal splendour.

Recreated from The Freeman's Journal, Dublin, May 22, 1845

IRISH GRATITUDE.—In consequence of some act of kindness and justice rendered by Mr. E. Jones, of this town to the poor, upwards of two hundred men from the neighbourhood of Fairymount, marched in here on Monday last, and, in a few hours, tilled upwards of three acres of potatoes for him.

REVIVAL OF ORANGE PROCESSIONS.

DUNGANNON, JUNE 3.—On the night of the second instant, a large mob of Killyman Orangemen entered this town with drums and fifes to celebrate their release from the stringent clauses of the "procession act" just now expired. The "Protestant Boys," "Boyne Water," "Croppies lie Down," and other party tunes were played, amidst tremendous yelling and shouting. Having paraded the principal streets, and finding the Catholics *obstinately* peaceable, they returned towards their favourite locality, so famous in the wrecking records of the north. This is their third visit within the last few months. Social order requires that means should be immediately adopted to prevent the recurrence of such lawless gatherings, that are alike insulting to the feelings of the Catholics and dangerous to the peace of society. The authorities did not interfere.

Recreated from The Freeman's Journal, Dublin, June 5-6, 1845.

MURDER OF A MAGISTRATE IN THE COUNTY OF CAVAN.

It is our painful duty to record the horrifying intelligence of the murder of George Bell Booth, Esq., of Drumcarbin, near Crossdoney in the county of Cavan. This awful event took place on Sunday last, shortly after two o'clock, P.M., whilst the lamented gentleman was returning home from church, accompanied in his gig by two young children, and by a third, who was riding on a pony behind him. After accomplishing his hellish purpose, the assassin effected his escape, although the highroads and by-paths were crowded with people. The details of this melancholy and formidable transaction will be found sub-joined.—

"CAVAN, JUNE 22, 1845.— A very horrible outrage occurred this day, George Booth, Esq., on his return from Kilmore Church, with his two young sons, in his gig, was shot. This was done in a very public place, at Mr. Bell's gate—I mean a back gate, that is a few perches above the front gate, and on the same side, nearer to Bingfield. He got shot through the head, and died in a very few minutes. One of the boys fell out of the gig, by which his arm was broken. You see what a state of things this country is brought to, and all by the "Molly Maguires!" This is the most daring occurrence that has taken place in this county, or any other—done in such a public place, and at such an hour—about two o'clock. It appears there was only one concerned in the affair. He got off in the direction of Hermitage, and on by Castlecosby. The police force are out. I fear there is no chance of catching the villain. I cannot conceive the cause of Mr. Booth being shot, except that he may have done some act as magistrate against some of these "Molly Men" (as they are called). This affair has caused the greatest alarm in this town. I am just told that Mr. Booth's child is not likely to survive."

The following is from a gentleman who arrived at the spot shortly after the fatal occurrence:—

"CAVAN, JUNE 22, 1845.—I have just returned from the village of Crossdoney, in the vicinity of which a most barbarous murder was committed this day. At a quarter past two o'clock, George F. Bell Booth, Esq., of Drumcarbin, was returning from Kilmore church, in his gig, with two of his children—one five, and the other six years old; his eldest son, a boy of about eleven, rode behind him on his pony. When he arrived at "The Rocks", the residence of the sub-sheriff, William Bell, Esq., he was met by a man, who walked coolly and deliberately along the road, smoking a pipe. The villain walked up to Mr. Booth, presenting a horse pistol. It is thought Mr. Booth stooped his head, and that, on his doing so, the murderer fired. The ball entered the upper part of the forehead, and lodged within the skull; he fell instantly from his gig—he was dead.

The horse, frightened by the report of the shot, ran away, throwing the two children on the road—one of them had his arm broken in the fall, or by the wheel of the gig passing over it. The body of the murdered gentleman lies in the house of the sub-sheriff, where it will remain until an inquest can be held upon it. Mrs. Bell, of the Rocks, whose carriage had just broken down, passed the murderer on foot a few seconds before he fired. On hearing the report, she turned round, and saw the body fall from the gig.

What the motive is which instigated this assassination, we cannot form the most distant idea, for a more kind tender-hearted, upright gentleman did not exist; but he was a Protestant, and a magistrate. There is as yet no trace of the murderer, who crossed into the fields and escaped. The country about is thickly planted with hedges and hedgerows, a circumstance favourable to the concealment of the assassin."—*Dublin Evening Mail.*

Recreated from The Belfast News-Letter, Belfast, June 27, 1845.

ORANGE WALK.
(FROM ANOTHER CORRESPONDENT.)

Armagh, 13th July, 1845.

Being so far on the way when I came to Cavan determined on coming here to see my sister and pay her the long-promised visit, and it being the 12th it made the day, which was remarkably fine, one of great excitement on the line of road from Clones to Armagh. When we came outside Clones within about a mile of Smithborough, a village on the road between Clones and Monaghan, we overtook at least 200 bodies of Orangemen and women, I should suppose to the number of 20,000. They walked very quietly not being interrupted by our party, and went on to a place called Lugnamullagh.

There the whole party marched into a field, each body having their colours flying and preceded by five or six fellows carrying each an old rusty gun on his shoulder, and now and then firing an odd shot in the air, but conducting themselves, as far as I saw, very quietly.

It was really a novel scene to me who never saw an Orange walk. It was really a most extraordinary scene. My mind reverted to the Tara processions, and the comparison was every way in their favour, for this was not near so large or so respectable, and really I think the Orangemen, and most particularly "the ladies," who adore the colours of the Dutchmen, bear no comparison at all to our fair sisterhood of Leinster. Although I was saluted by a great many of them in their full robes shining, imagining, I suppose, that I must be one of the *right sort*.

So far all was harmless, but I am sorry to tell you that on our arrival in Armagh the scene was mournfully changed, as the Orangemen after walking through the city at about six o'clock proceeded to march through Irish-street, a locality all occupied by Catholics and those of the *highest metal*, for on a former occasion when "walks" were usual the "boys" of Irish-street never allowed them to pass through *theirs*. When the procession reached the end of Irish-street a conflict took place between the two parties, and several persons were shot by the Orangemen, ten of whom were women. One of the men died to-day. The excitement here is dreadful. The judges and the grand jury sitting in the Court-house, still no magistrate was there to call out the police or military until the deeds of death were *done*.

I heard the Primate's first mass this day, and he spoke very impressively, and shed tears when praying for the man shot dead in the conflict, and it was most heartrending to hear the shrieks that went through the chapel when he spoke of it. Not one, rich or poor, was not moved to tears and loud cries that were difficult to suppress. His grace said he was not in possession of all the circumstances that would enable him to speak of the melancholy event, but, said he, that men all day pursuing their industrious avocations should be murdered in open day light, was difficult to be borne with.

He, however, advised his flock to bear the affliction with patience, and that the law would redress them, and to be ready to give any information which would have the effect of having the guilty brought to punishment. But the poor people have no great faith in the law, and some go so far as to say, if the clergy here and the people were pulling together, this would not have occurred. However, I hope this will open their eyes, and make thorough Repealers of his grace and his clergy both.

P.S.—The Orangemen broke all the windows of the shops in the street where the conflict took place. The windows of Mrs. Gribbins' house are all broken, and also at a grocer's, named Peter Rock's, and *two bullets* lodged in his door, that were fired at him!

We had Judge Ball at mass here to-day.

Recreated from The Freeman's Journal, Dublin, July 16, 1845.

DISCOVERY OF HUMAN SKELETONS.—On Wednesday evening last, while some men engaged in sinking a sewer in the grounds of Daniel Baird, Esq., Cassino, they came upon two human skeletons, at a depth of eighteen inches from the surface, one of which was in a nearly perfect state. The bones of both were collected, and, having been deposited in a wooden box, were re-interred in the burial ground at the Long Tower. As this part of the city, at the time of the siege, known by the name of the Windmill Hill, was the scene of some severe skirmishes between the besieged and the army of James, it is not improbable that the bones referred to were those of a couple of the combatants who fell there in one of these conflicts. Another conjecture is, the monks at the time of, and subsequent to, the days of St. Columbkill, had a burying ground in this locality, and that this accounts for the bones being found there.—There was no trace of a coffin discernible.—*Derry Standard.*

DISPUTED TITLE TO A LEGACY.—A sharp-looking young lad, apparently not more than twelve years old, was placed at the bar of the Borough Manchester Court, on Thursday, on suspicion of having stolen a pocket handkerchief from Mrs. Taylor, Great Ancoats-street. The charge having been stated, the boy, appearing to be deeply affected, said—Sir, it is my father's wiper; he died a short time ago, and that was all he left me as a legacy. Mr. Maude—Is there any mark by which you know it? Boy—Oh, surely, Sir; there's a little bit off the right-hand corner, and a small hole in the middle that a fly might creep through. (Laughter.) Mr. Maude—Why, contrasting the colour of the handkerchief with that of your face, hands, clothes, one would say, *a priori*, that it did not belong to you; if it did, we should not find it in such a state. Boy—Oh, Sir, I never uses that, Sir, I know better. I always keep it lapped up, neat, clean, and sacred, because of my father, Sir. Mr. Maude—How often have you been here? Boy (meditating)—Why, I can recollect four times. Mr. Maude—You are a sharp boy, and it is a pity you cannot conduct yourself out of prison, so you must go back for three months.—*Manchester Guardian.*

DREADFUL OCCURRENCE.—A young man, named Joseph Brammery, residing at Hadfield, in Glossop, Derbyshire, and employed at the Dinting-vale print-works, belonging to Mr. Potter, was on Saturday, the 9th ult., found in a pan containing 300 gallons of caustic lye, which was at a boiling heat. How he came in is not known, but it is supposed that he went to the top of the pan to see if the lye was boiling, and standing on the edge, must have fallen into the horrible grave.

The deceased had not been seen about the premises after 20 minutes past ten o'clock. At a quarter past one o'clock Robert Stubes went to stir up the liquor in the pan, when, to his great alarm, he discovered some of the deceased's clothes, the body being quite eaten away by the liquor. Assistance was immediately procured, and search made for the remains of the deceased. The liquor in the pan was thrown away, and at the bottom of the pan nothing but a few bones could be found, and these looking as if they had been in the ground a hundred years. The leather and soles of his clogs were eaten away; a portion of his clothes that was made of cotton had sustained little injury, and the iron and nails that had been in his clogs were found.

The deceased's teeth were discovered separate. Strange to say, the deceased's heart was found by itself, quite sound. All that was collected of the body did not weigh 7 lb., and if these parts had remained in the liquor three hours longer, not a particle would have been left. The deceased was about 17 years of age. This dreadful circumstance has caused the utmost regret to the proprietor of the print-works, who is well known for his benevolent disposition.—*Derby Journal.*

Recreated from The Belfast News-Letter, Belfast, September 9, 1845.

ARRIVAL OF THE LIBERATOR IN TRALEE.

At six o'clock the Liberator entered the town of Tralee. Thousands of people cheered him loudly as his carriage passed through their streets. He proceeded to the house of his relative Miss Connor, where he stayed for the night. He was met there by Mr. Maurice O'Connell, M.P, and Mr. Primrose. The town during the evening presented a scene of rejoicing in honor of the Liberator's visit. Bonfires were lighted in the streets.

The Temperance bands, attended by two torch bearers, were stationed in front of Miss Connor's house, and played several national airs. It may with truth be said, that the entire day was spent in successive demonstrations for Repeal, and the numbers that participated in them, and surrounded O'Connell's carriage in the various localities through which he journeyed, amounted in the aggregate to at least twenty thousand persons. As far as can be learned at present, it is likely that the Kerry demonstration will be in every respect most effective.

Recreated from The Freeman's Journal, Dublin, October 6, 1845.

DISEASE IN THE POTATO CROP.—It is to us a source of deep pain to have this day to announce the existence of the prevailing disease in the potatoes, not alone in this county, but of the neighbouring counties of Kilkenny and Carlow. This is no idle alarm, or unfounded statement. It was only yesterday that we were made aware of the fact, that, in the western portion of this county the disease exists to a great extent, whilst we know that in the county of Kilkenny potatoes, supposed from their appearance, both in the ground and after being dug, to be perfectly sound, were discovered when boiled, to be so infected that it was impossible to stand the horrid stench they emitted.

The crop in Carlow is also injured. It is now all but certain that the entire potato crop of this country is affected to a great extent, and too much precaution cannot be used to save the portion of the crop that has yet escaped. We are also given to understand that in many instances potatoes, found to be perfectly free from blight in the course of the last week, are now very much injured. The late heavy rains, it is supposed, have been attended with prejudicial effects to the crop.—*Waterford Freeman* Oct. 11.

PRESENTING GRAND JURIES IN DUBLIN— THE ROMAN CATHOLIC RELIEF BILL A COMPLETE MOCKERY.

TO THE EDITOR OF THE FREEMAN.—SIR—I wish to direct the attention of the Catholics of Ireland to the shameful bigotry manifested in the swearing in of presenting grand juries in the city of Dublin. For the last few years common decency was observed by placing upon each jury two or three Catholics, in order to save appearances; but, for the last two terms, even this petty liberality was abandoned, and not a single Catholic was sworn upon either jury. This, sir, is really shocking bigotry in the metropolis of a country, where the vast majority of the population are Roman Catholic, and where, as in this city, a great number of Catholic jurors, qualified, could be found ready and willing to act. It is still the more insulting, inasmuch as Catholic monies have to be voted away in the shape of taxation; and one would expect that, in common justice, the Roman Catholic rate-payers (who form the majority of citizens) should be fairly represented on each jury.

I do not now mean to charge the government with promoting the exclusion of Catholics—neither do I charge the present high sheriff, or his deputy, with such bigotry, but this much I do say, that it is the bounden duty of the heads of each department to see that strict and impartial justice shall be dealt out to all classes of her Majesty's subjects in this particular. 'Tis true that these abuses may be practised by subordinates, as we frequently hear of Roman Catholic names being placed at the foot of the jury list, or passed over in a variety of ways. This subject has caused much irritation in the minds of all Liberal minded men, and much surprise has been expressed that such conduct would be pursued now-a-days, when the avowed policy of the government is to put down Protestant ascendancy in Ireland.

The character of the next presenting grand jury shall be narrowly watched, and if this insulting practice shall be continued it only remains for us then to call the attention of Sir Robert Peel himself to the manner in which the emancipation act is practically carried out in Ireland.

I have the honour to remain, Sir, your obedient servant,

A CATHOLIC RATEPAYER.

THE DISEASE IN POTATOES.

We regret to find that the accounts we receive tend to confirm the apprehension that there is a considerable failure in the potato crop, and that the disease which has caused it is not on the decrease. A gentleman in the neighourhood of Dublin, on the north side, observing some time since that his potato fields showed some indication of the approach of the pestilence, cut away the stocks to the earth, leaving the tubers to still ripen in the ground. This gentleman was on yesterday digging out those potato fields which he had treated in the manner we have described, and he assures us that he has not found one single diseased potato. Here, then, is a practical proof that cutting away the stalks arrests the progress of the disease. The neighbourhood in which the gentleman who has given us the information resides, has suffered greatly from the pestilence; his own grounds manifest unerring indications of its incipient stage, and yet by the cutting away of the stalks he has made all safe, and now possesses fields of sound tubers, where he, in all likelihood, would otherwise possess but putrid masses of vegetable pestilence.

A letter received in town yesterday from the county of Tyrone, speaks very despondingly of the prospects of the potato harvest in that county. The gentleman writes, that he is himself digging several acres of potatoes, and that he finds disease to a fatal extent prevalent in *three* parts out of *four* of his produce. Such a state of facts would be frightful, but that happily the disease is very variable in its progress, seizing upon particular portions of districts and even of fields, while the rest remains flourishing and wholesome. Haply the grounds in the immediate vicinage of the gentleman thus visited may be entirely free from all disease.

We regret to find that the pestilence appears to be travelling westwards. A letter received yesterday at this office from a most respectable gentleman residing in the county Roscommon, and onw whom we know to be as far from the influence of needless alarm as he is faith worthy, thus speaks on this subject:—"I fear that the potatoes in parts of this county are affected by the disease, which has caused so much alarm in other places."

For ourselves, we would not increase by any act of ours the alarm which is felt to such an extent already, but when we hear facts communicated to us from sources on which we can rely, we feel we would not be justified in withholding them.

STOPPED BY THE POLICE.

MONEY and a GOLD WATCH, Paris made, with GOLD GUARD CHAIN attached, which were found on the 12th of July last in possession of a Person arrested while attempting to pick Pockets at Westland row Railway Station. May be identified before 11 o'Clock, A.M., on FRIDAY next, the 17th of October, in the Office of the Superintendent of the G Division.

Recreated and reprinted from The Freeman's Journal, Dublin, October 14, 1845.

SPLENDID REPEAL DEMONSTRATION IN MAYO.—THE LIBERATOR'S PROGRESS.

(FROM OUR OWN CORRESPONDENT.)

CASTLEBAR, APPEARANCE OF THE TOWN.—At an early hour in the morning the streets of Castlebar presented a most animated appearance, being crowded with masses of people, who assisted in the erection of triumphal arches adorned with evergreens and inscriptions either of welcome to the great champion of Irish freedom, or expressive of the determination of the people to struggle for Repeal. In the main-street a very beautiful arch was thrown across from Mr. Patrick Walsh's house. On this was inscribed, "No ascendancy—Orangemen, Protestants, and Catholics unite, Repeal is certain, and Ireland happy." On another stood out, in well-painted and neatly designed letters, the motto, "Liberator! may you live to see Ireland a nation!" In one of the dining-room windows of Flyn's hotel was placed an admirably executed full length oil portrait of the Liberator, and underneath waived gracefully in the breeze an immense flag with the magic word "Repeal" worked in white letters on a red ground.

Almost at sunrise groups of the peasantry on horse and foot, from the rural districts, came thronging into town, some with wands and silken banners. On reaching the bridge at Linenhall-street they were hailed with shouts which they joyfully returned. The several thoroughfares leading to the town were thronged with men hastening to the scene of action. Hundreds of the people of Ballina, Belmullet, Foxford, Newport, Burishoole, Ballymote, Keltemagh, Killala, arrived before ten o'clock, and having procured some slight refreshment they eagerly pursued their journey in the direction of French Hill, where it was arranged the cavalcade should meet the Liberator. The men of Tyrawley turned out in splendid style. They were accompanied by their band, whilst the trades of Ballina on several cars, with gay and gorgeous banners displayed, presented an animated appearance, and evinced the greatest anxiety to give the father of his country such a welcome as he deserved. About ten o'clock the spirited and ever patriotic trades of Castlebar assembled in the main-street, and formed themselves into procession order, previous to setting out for French Hill. The excellent band of the Castlebar Temperance Society, dressed in a very becoming uniform, took up their position at the head of the *cortege*. Next came the gardeners carrying a tastefully arranged and neatly decorated triumphal car, and over the canopy was a wreath ingeniously made to represent the word "Repeal." Then followed the butchers, tailors, wheelrights, carpenters, letter-press printers, weavers, shoemakers, masons and smiths, each trade carrying appropriate banners and flags, and each artisan displaying a Repeal button embedded in a white satin rosette. Next came the independent farmers of Keelogues, carrying flags inscribed with mottoes and devices expressive of their daily occupation, and their desire to regenerate their native land. The next section was composed of the public-spirited and indefatigable trades of Westport, who, at no small share of inconvenience, secured the services of the Galway temperance band, one of the very best in Ireland. In this order the procession marched to the sounds of merry music through the principal streets of the town to French Hill, where they awaited the arrival of the Liberator.

Recreated from The Freeman's Journal, Dublin, October 15, 1845.

THE POTATO PESTILENCE.

New facts concerning the spread of this calamity and its partial remedy, so crowd upon us that the work of selection for the benefit of our friends becomes no easy task. In another column we have arranged a number of accounts from various parts of Ireland, all shewing the fearful extent to which the disease has progressed, or suggesting something useful to know, under the new and sad circumstances in which the country is placed. We are forced to condense into the present article such information as we have obtained through various sources since those accounts and suggestions were put in type.

In the first place, we have the satisfaction of stating that the government is already alive to the necessity of interfering with vigour and promptitude.

A valued correspondent thus addresses us, on this branch of the subject:—

TO THE EDITOR OF THE NEWS-LETTER.—SIR,—When you afforded me an opportunity some time since, through the medium of your highly prized and widely circulated journal, of giving publicity to some thoughts on this awful calamity, wherewith I may say the world, generally, has been visited, but more particularly our own country, I did not take up your space in uselessly discussing the *nature* or *origins* of the disease, about which, notwithstanding all that has been said and written, we are as wise as ever; but taking for granted what could not be denied, that the evil existed, I pointed out what I considered as one great means of remedying it—namely, preventing the Distilleries from working, whereby an immense amount of grain would be available for human food; and I have now great pleasure in letting you know, that it is fully believed by parties who are most likely to be well informed on the subject, that Government *have it in contemplation to resort to this measure at once*. This, it must be admitted, is more prudent than the opening of ports, for while it will have the effect of preserving to our poor countrymen the only substitute for the loss of the potato, it will show to foreign nations that even in a year of scarcity we have *internal resources that render us independent of them*. I hasten to give you this information, knowing that it must be gratifying to the country, to learn that Government are so much alive to their welfare.—Yours, &c., A CONSTANT READER.

The *Dublin Evening Packet* confirms the statement of our correspondent, as follows:—

Without any intention of assuming organship with which we have so often been invidiously taunted, we can assert that the anxious consideration of our truly paternal Government, is at this moment given to the all important question of securing, during the ensuing winter months, a sufficient supply of food for the poor. However ungrateful for the benefits conferred, it may suit organs and orators of the people to represent them, the Government still will act with a view only to their good—a purpose of genuine benevolence not to be thwarted from its onward and upright course by unthankfullness, real or stimulated.

The *Cork Southern Reporter* contains the following reply to a communication of the Mayor of Cork:—

DUBLIN CASTLE, 13TH OCTOBER, 1845.

SIR—I have it in command from the Lord Lieutenant to acknowledge the receipt of your letter of the 10th, and to acquaint you that the attention of the Government has been for some time directed to the state of the potato crop in this country, and his Excellency has already caused the fullest inquiry to be made in every district in Ireland respecting the disease which is unfortunately found to exist in the potato.

His Excellency trusts that the crop may be but partially affected, and has directed that the inquiries be continued, and further information furnished from time to time to the Government both as to the present state and probable prospects of this crop.—I have the honour to be, Sir, your obedient servant,

"RICHARD PENNEFATHER."

Recreated from The Belfast News-Letter, Belfast, October 21, 1845.

THE SIMULTANEOUS COLLECTION FOR THE O'CONNELL TRIBUTE OF 1845,

WILL BE MADE

IN ALL THE PARISHES OF IRELAND, ON SUNDAY, NOV. THE 16TH.

AGAIN the Irish People are called upon to testify their gratitude to their great Benefactor—their pride in his wonderful ability, and their appreciation of his unexampled services.

They remember what they were, they know what they are.

A province of trodden slaves, they have grown into a Nation of self-respecting Freemen. The yoke of sectarian ascendancy no longer galls or degrades them; they have mastered the tyranny against which their fathers strove in vain, and filled the world with the glory of their peaceful triumphs.

To him who accomplished this mighty revolution, they feel that a debt is due, which can never be repaid.

The Catholic Noble has been enabled to raise his head proudly amongst his Peers; the Catholic Gentleman has had the way to honour and power thrown open before him; the Senate, the Monarch's Council, and the Bench of Justice have found their cherished ornaments amid a community, whose existence—almost within the memory of man—the Law did not deign to recognise. The Corporations have ceased to be the strongholds of intolerance and corruption, and have become the People's property. The Catholic Millions have seen the barrier that divided them from their Protestant Countrymen broken down, and the principles of religious equality established for ever. They have seen inequitable exactions—even more obnoxious as outrages to conscience, than as mere fiscal burthens—put an end to, and they know that a precedent has been set for the redress of similar grievances, which still press heavily upon them, and the foundation peaceably and constitutionally laid for the political regeneration of their country.

They know to whom these great ameliorations, actual and prospective, are to be ascribed, and they behold, in the events which are passing before them, a new homage to the power which O'Connell has created, and which never more distinctly demonstrated its might, than in forcing a change of tone and policy on a reluctant Ministry, who had haughtily pronounced concession at an end.

No consideration of race, or clime, or creed, has ever rendered him apathetic in combating oppression; he has laboured for the African and the Irishman alike, and the Emancipation which he claimed for the Dissenter was won before the Catholic was free.

To the illustrious man who repudiated the highest offices in his Sovereign's gift, that he might continue to labour for Ireland—whom the terrors and the blandishments of power have equally failed to detach for a moment from her service—whose fidelity has been proved in suffering, as well as in success—in the gloom of a prison, as in the presence of an applauding senate, or at the head of a victorious Nation—to O'Connell, who toils for them in advanced life with all the zeal of his youth, and all the energy of his matured manhood, the grateful Irish people are eager once more to manifest their enthusiastic attachment. They feel it is not so much their duty, as their interest, to sustain their matchless Champion, and they will do it nobly and universally now.

JOHN POWER, Bart.,
CORNELIUS MAC LOGHLIN, } Trustees.
P. VINCENT FITZPATRICK, Secretary.

Office of the O'Connell Tribute, Dublin,
October 21, 1845.

Reprinted from The Freeman's Journal, Dublin, October 21, 1845.

Daniel O'Connell - Lithograph attributed to J. O'Shaughnessy, after an original drawing by R. E. Sly. Published by T. Price, Dublin, 1844.

DARING OUTRAGE—GALLANT CONDUCT OF THE PEOPLE.

Wednesday last, in the middle of the day, two daring ruffianly Terry Alts, attacked a farmer's house, named Michael Coony, in the parish of Killuran, county Clare, while the family were out at work, not one being in the house at the time but Mrs. Coony, and succeeded in carrying off a gun. Mrs. Coony immediately gave the alarm to the men at work in the garden, who, aided by all the neighbours, pursued the scoundrels, and succeeded in making them relinquish the gun, which (though they several times threatened to fire on the people) they threw away, being closely pressed. The people afterwards gave the alarm to four police stations in the neighbourhood, when the police assisted in pursuing the villains in the direction of Ogunnello, but, unhappily, though they had been in view for a long time, without success.—*Limerick Reporter.*

CITY OF DUBLIN HOSPITAL.

THE Course of Practical, Medical, and Surgical instruction in this Hospital, will commence on MONDAY, the 27th of OCTOBER. The Clinical Lectures will be delivered on Three days in each week, during the Session, by Dr. Jacob, Dr. Benson, Dr. Hargrave, Dr. Williams, Mr. Orr, and Dr. Geoghegan; and on the Diseases peculiar to Women and Children by Dr. Beatty.

Dr. JACOB's Clinical Lectures on DISEASES of the EYE, illustrated by the cases in the Hospital, are open to the Pupils in attendance.

Sir H. Marsh, and Dr. Apjohn, the Consulting Physicians; and Dr. Wilmot, and Dr. Porter, the Consulting Surgeons, give their assistance in cases requiring consultation.

The Certificates of attendance are received as qualification by all the Colleges, Halls, and Boards.

Fee For Winter, Six Months	Six Guineas
Ditto Summer, Six Months	Four Guineas
Ditto Nine Months	Eight Guineas.

Recreated and reprinted from The Freeman's Journal, Dublin, October 23, 1845.

AGITATION *versus* HUSBANDRY.

(*From the Examiner.*)

How Ireland is to be saved from famine is the subject of anxious discussion everywhere except at the meetings of her professed friends and champions, where the failure of the potato crop is not deemed of sufficient importance to the people to call for any special notice.

My cry is, "Ireland for the Irish," says Mr. O'Connell. The cry of food for the Irish would now be rather more to the purpose. "Ireland for the Irish" will soon be a very sorry mouthful. This is no time for fooling with the wolf at the door.

It is amazing and shocking to see a people over whom the greatest calamity is impending not only amusing themselves with mountebank exhibitions, but, in running after them, neglecting the harvest, for which there is so little time and so vast a need. The *Times* reporter observes of the Sligo meeting—"It was sad enough, as one passed along the route taken by Mr. O'Connell from Ballina into the country, to see the favourable, and but recurring, opportunity given to the poor peasant for the saving of his scanty harvest, neglected and lost for ever. For miles in the rear of the procession the fields were deserted, although many a corn-stock and patch of ripening grain showed at once the lateness of the harvest, and the necessity of making every use of so rare a blessing at this period of the year, and in the district, as a cloudless sky and brightening sun. Your reporter can with confidence declare, that for fourteen miles of country, from Ballina to the procession, there were not visible along the road ten human beings engaged in any kind of labour, and that, but for the gathering at a country fair on the way, and the appearance of heaps of children left to play with the pigs and turkeys, or the occasional sight of some feeble old man, or helpless woman, peering out of their miserable huts, there would be an utter absence of life throughout the land. The pleasant sound of labour had ceased, and not a flail plied or anvil rang along that great extent of country."

And after this melancholy account of neglected industry at a time of the greatest need for it, we have this picture of the mummery preferred to it:—"The flags were very brilliant, the sashes and streamers very gaudy, and the bands very bad. All the trades of Sligo were present in body corporate. Then there was a blind harper, robed in green, with streaming hair like the minstrels of old sitting on a hack car, playing inaudible music, and a shoemaker perched with great dignity on the back of a postchaise, and dressed like 'a king', of what country, or in what era, did not, however, clearly appear—for he wore an orthodox Jewish tinsel crown, and a blue velvet cloak which might have belonged to a modern fine lady, with an unmistakable beard. There were also smiths at work on a moveable platform, making imaginary twelvepenny nails, and bakers, bootmakers, and sailors on cars or walking, &c., with their respective banners and insignia, forming altogether a very near resemblance to a procession of Odd Fellows in England."

And these thoughtless, improvident people left their labour to hear Mr. O'Connell rail against the infidel colleges, promise parliaments in College-Green, and rant of their beauteous land, the greenness of its plains, the fertility of its valleys, the majesty of its mountains, the clearness of its streams, the multitude of its harbours—anything but the disease of its potatoes, and the frightful prosect of its scarcity.

Meetings interfering with the harvest, or any potion of it, at this critical juncture, certainly deserve the name of monster meetings; and monster man must be he who, for the gratification of his own wretched vanity, could invite the people to leave labours so vitally important to listen to his harangues for the cultivation of the animosities. Such a man in a sinking ship would call the crew from the pumps to hear his instigations to mutiny.

When the pressure of want comes let the sufferers hold him responsible for what he has done, and for what, with his powers and opportunities, he has omitted to do. And let it be remembered that when redoubled exertions were requisite to make the most of a bad harvest, the peoples' friend and guide took them from the fields to the more profitable employment of listening to speeches avoiding the only topic of instant and vital importance to them.

But allusion to the prospect of scarcity might have marred the collection of tribute.

AN AMAZON.—Last night, the inhabitants of the streets in the neighbourhood of Brunswick-street were alarmed about 10 o'clock, by the violent ringing of a bell, accompanied by the shrieks of women, in every key of female terror. Guided by the noise, a number of persons were led to the Penitentiary in the above-named street, when the cause of the uproar and alarm was at once made evident. A young woman, of abandoned character, who had conceived some dislike towards the institution, had been engaged for some minutes in smashing the windows of the building, a feat which she successfully accomplished with the most complete success, the loose macadamized pavement of the street affording her an inexhaustible stock of artillery. The screams of the frightened inmates, and the continued pealing of the bell, at length brought the watchmen to the spot, but not before the damage was so extensive that the virago had no more windows to break. She was brought to the Police-office, loudly declaring that no sooner would the windows be re-glazed than she would smash them again. It appears that this woman has already signalised herself by several similar attacks upon penitentiaries, she having been, as she alleges, badly treated in one of them.

Recreated from The Belfast News-Letter, Belfast, October 31, 1845.

O'CONNELL TRIBUTE.

CRUEL PLUNDER OF THE PEOPLE.

The Repeal Journals, every one of them, have been, for the last fortnight, parading, in their utmost conspicuous advertising type, an announcement to the effect that the simultaneous collection of the O'Connell Tribute will take place on Sunday, the 16th of November next. It is notorious that the collection of this tribute is tantamount to the imposition of a tax upon the poorer classes of the Irish people, to the tune of from twenty to twenty-five thousands pounds a-year. This large annual sum—extorted as it is from the miserable means of a wretched peasantry—"a penny from the ragged man and a half-penny from the starving man"—is Mr. O'Connell's exclusive *perquisite*, if perquisite that can be called, which is wrung, by the foulest "indirection"—by priestly intimidation, from the hard hands of artisans and labourers.

At any season—even in times of teeming plenty—it is a base and dishonest trick—a most scandalous swindle—to draw so large a sum as £20,000, or more, from the pockets of a pauper peasantry, to enable a scheming politician to carry on his baneful system of agitation; but, at the present time, when nearly total destruction threatens the chief and almost only source of the people's sustenance, the attempt to collect this tax is an outrageous insult to the common sense of society. It is a shocking—a barbarous—a wanton piece of cruelty, as regards the people, and the evidence of the most abandoned and profligate recklessness on the part of the collectors of the fund, and of its destined recipient. We have no words sufficiently strong with which to record our utter detestation of the scheme and of its abettors.

We are not surprised, guessing that this odious impost was about to be immediately levied, to find that, during the recent monster meetings in the south and west, all mention of the impending famine was studiously evaded by Mr. O'Connell and his satellites. We had set this diffidence down as a lingering remnant of modesty, not unmixed with a slight dash of prudence. But we deceived ourselves.

There was a degree of unbashful villainy to which Mr. O'Connell had yet to attain, after he had concluded his "monster" tour in the provinces; but that step he has now taken. Judge with what consistency the man—the patriot—who blinks the question of the people's woes, in order that he may rob them under a more specious guise—can come forward to advise the means whereby those woes may be soothed—*at the expense of others!* Yet such was the only piece of impudence wanting to render the robbery of the poor man more wanton and shameful.

At a meeting of the Dublin Town Council on Tuesday, Mr. O'Connell moved the adoption of a proposition for the appointment of a deputation to the Lord Lieutenant, to press upon government the necessity for the immediate stoppage of distillation and brewing; the opening of the ports for the free importation of provisions, and their closure against the exportation of all kinds of food; the raising of a million and a-half on the credit of the Irish property of the Commission of Woods and Forests; and the imposition of a tax of 50 per cent. upon the income of absentees, and of 10 per cent. upon that of residents of Ireland.

The man who has the audacity to make this proposal (however well it might come from any one else in the empire) is the same man who expects to pocket twenty-five thousand pounds of the people's money before Christmas!

Recreated from The Belfast News-Letter, Belfast, October 31, 1845.

FRIGHTFUL DELUSION.

We have received more than one communication upon the subject of an awfully blasphemous mockery now put in practice by more than one priest of the Church of Rome, for the purpose of turning the terrible visitation which has befallen the poor in the partial failure of the potato crop, into a source of profit, unexampled in its barefaced effrontery, by any delusion that the annals of Popery can furnish. In a brief paragraph in a former number, we alluded to the Granard priest, who was said to be selling holy water to the ignorant people, which being sprinkled on the potato, was to avert the calamity, and preserve their sole food from contagion.

We have been favored with a letter from a highly respectable gentleman, informing us that the *Westmeath Guardian*, from whence we derived our information, was in error in attributing this monstrous outrage against common sense to a Granard priest, as he declares all the Roman Catholic clergymen there are "Gentlemen of too much integrity, charity and high-mindedness, to stoop to humour ignorance and superstition," and that it is to another district of the county of Longford the imposter belongs. The price he charges is five shillings to the farmer, and two and six pence to the cottier; and our correspondent, on whose word we can place the most implicit reliance, assures us that over 700£ have already been netted by this novel swindle.

The following is an extract from the communication:—"The plan is to bring a quart of salt in a little bag. This is passed by the clerks—for the priest is in such a great way of business, that he is obliged to employ these aids—to the priest, who blesses it. The little bag of salt is then returned to the faithful—for he must be full of faith, and he proves it by giving his money; and if a farmer, he gets this blessing cheaply, for a crown; if a cottier for half-a-crown. The salt is then taken to the field, dissolved in water, and sprinkled on the ridges, or at least on some of them, as far as it goes. The plague is immediately stopped, and the next day the faithful digs his potatoes as sound as need be.

"It is but justice to the priest and his coadjutor of the parish in which the wizard spreads forth his wand, that they have used all exertions in their power to counteract its operations, though without effect."

The following extract from a private letter, dated the 23d instant, which has been addressed from the county of Wexford, to the editor of the *Cork Constitution*, shows that this debasing superstition is not confined to one locality, but is in full operation there.—

"I am sorry to find that you are a sufferer in your potato crop. It is the only thing spoken of here. People are justly filled with alarm; but as far as our neighbourhood is concerned, I hear of no remedial measures being adopted, except by a lot of friars here, *who are selling blessed water*, which unfortunate dupes *purchase greedily to sprinkle over their fields!—Evening Packet*.

PRESENT TO HER MAJESTY.—The *Bombay*, Captain Furley, Honourable East India Company's Service, an East India trader, and one of the largest now afloat, being 1400 tons burden, arrived off Blackwall on Thursday last. She has brought a most splendid cargo, of the estimated value of £250,000, including four beautiful symmetrically formed Arabian entire horses, of a fine grey colour, and which, together with their housings, of an extraordinary, unique, and gorgeous description, valued at £1,000 per horse, are forwarded as a present to her Majesty by the celebrated Parste merchant, Sir Jamsetjee Jejeebhoy.

Recreated from The Belfast News-Letter, Belfast, November 4, 1845.

A POTATO-FED PEOPLE.

(*From the Atlas*)

A severe and widely-spread physical visitation threatens practically to illustrate an important social principle. Enlightened political economists have long inculcated the prospective utility of the mass of every population maintaining a high standard in their wages, diet, clothing, and habitations. Men ought never, if possible, to be driven up to their last resources; they ought always to have something to fall back upon—a reserved store to meet the changes of the seasons, the casualties of scarcity, health, and the fluctuations of trade and employment.

The need of this forecast is likely to be afflictively exemplified in the approaching winter by the disastrous calamity to which we have adverted. England with her wheat-fed community may find resources in her superior riches and granaries, or by taking corn out of bond, or importing it from abroad. But what is to become of poverty-stricken and potato-fed Ireland? Her famines have been frequent and most dreadful—and why? Because the national subsistence is based on one resource—upon a single root; and if that fail there is no other substitute to which the people can resort. With us it is different; if our staple sustenance is inadequate, we may be aided from abroad; but the potato-fed Irish, with wages to correspond, cannot buy from the foreigner; or, if they could, potatoes, unlike wheat, are too bulky a commodity to be imported in large quantities on an emergency. How much safer a nation, then, when bread, meat and beer form the general diet of the working classes. Then there is scope for retrenchment in periods of failure. From wheat the working-man may temporarily resort to inferior and cheaper food—to barley, oats, rye, or vegetables. He has room to fall; but he who is habitually kept on the cheapest food is without a substitute when deprived of it. Labourers so placed are cut off from every refuge. You may take from an Englishman, but you cannot from an Irishman—no more than from a naked man. The latter is already in the lowest deep, and he can sink no lower; his wages being regulated by potatoes—the chief article of his subsistence—will not buy him wheat, or barley, or oats; and whenever, therefore, the supply of potatoes fails, he has no escape from absolute famine—unless he help himself, as the Irish have done in former scarcities, to nettles, sea-weed, and sour sorrel—the last of which was found in the stomach of one poor creature who had perished of hunger!

Recreated from The Belfast News-Letter, Belfast, November 4, 1845.

PEEL AND THE PORTS.

The *Morning Advertiser* says:—"The general impression is, that the cabinet council of Friday broke up without any determination having been come to in reference to opening ports. It is whispered in the clubs, that Sir Robert Peel is anxious for further confirmation of the prevalence of the disease in potatoes, before he has recourse to the expedient of throwing open the ports to foreign grain. If this be so, there could be no more conclusive proof of his unfitness for the high office he holds. The great proof of an able statesman, is to rise with the occasion, and to act with promptitude and energy in sudden and unforeseen emergencies. While the Premier is hesitating, and balancing in his own mind, the arguments for and against throwing open the ports, the disease in the potato crop is spreading with the fearful rapidity and hurrying on the crisis of a whole nation being brought to the brink of starvation. Appalling, indeed, is the responsibility which Sir Robert Peel is incurring by his indecision. Under the fearful circumstances of the case, a single day's delay is positively criminal."

Recreated from The Cork Examiner, Cork, November 5, 1845.

THE O'CONNELL TRIBUTE.

We would call attention to the fact that a meeting will be held on Sunday, in the Chamber of Commerce, for the purpose of making the usual arrangements, and appointing the necessary collectors in the several wards, for the collection of the O'CONNELL TRIBUTE. We feel sure it is quite unnecessary to impress upon our fellow citizens the importance of supporting the Liberator in his present position of leadership, or to tell them how much the future freedom of Ireland depends on the services of that leader. Neither need we state that, now more than ever, it is incumbent on the people of this country to show to England that they are as firmly united to that great man, and as entirely identified with his policy, as at any former period of their eventual struggle for liberty. This union and identification cannot be expressed in mere words, or in the shout,—it must be demonstrated practically—even by the continuance of the tribute.

We have expressed ourselves at some length on this subject, not many days since; and now our object is simply to call attention to the fact that the meeting will be held on Sunday, and to say that it is the duty of every friend of liberty to rally round its most illustrious champion.

Recreated from The Cork Examiner, November 7, 1845.

THE PRICE OF DIAMONDS.

In consequence of the discovery of a very rich diamond mine in the province of Bahia, the supply of diamonds has been so greatly increased during the last year that the price has fallen 50 per cent., and is likely to fall still lower, so that the ladies will be enabled to indulge their taste for this kind of luxury with less damage to their husbands' purses than formerly.

Recreated from The Freeman's Journal, Dublin, December 4, 1845.

LECTURE ON SLAVERY.

On Friday evening last, according to an announcement, Mr. Frederick Douglas, a gentleman of colour, formerly a slave in Maryland, delivered the first of a series of lectures on slavery in this town, in the Independent Church, Donegall-street, at half-past seven o'clock. From an account of Mr. Douglass's life, written by himself, and published in America, we learn that he escaped from his master in the year 1838, and after working as a free labourer in the North Eastern States till 1841, was engaged by an American Anti-Slavery Society as an itinerant lecturer, an office for which he is admirably adapted. He is a Mulatto, and supposes his first owner was his father.

At the age of six years, according to his best calculation, he was sent from the estate where he was born to wait upon his master's nephew in Baltimore, and while in the service of his new master he learned to read. For this he was mainly indebted to the kindness of his mistress—a lady who was free from all slaveholding prejudices—and who continued her instructions to the poor slave till forbidden by her husband. However, by dint of perseverance, and the assistance of white little boys, he made considerable progress, and to reading added cyphering.

At the age of fifteen, he was taken from his service, and brought back to his former master, and was engaged at field labour. He was in the employment of his third master, when he planned an escape with some fellow slaves, but being detected and imprisoned, was afterwards sent back to Baltimore, whence he managed to escape in reality. The lecture of Friday evening was merely a simple narrative of all the circumstances attending his escape from slavery—his first introduction into public life, and the manner in which he had been occupied, during the last four years, pleading the cause of oppressed brethren.

The lecture was well attended.

Recreated from The Belfast News-Letter, Belfast, December 9, 1845.

RUMOURED RESIGNATION OF SIR ROBERT PEEL, AND BREAK-UP OF THE MINISTRY.

Since the foregoing was put in type, the London papers of Wednesday came to hand, containing the most important intelligence respecting the Ministry. The following is from the *Morning Chronicle*:—

A rumour prevailed in the Clubs last night (Tuesday), which we deem it right to publish, as a good deal of credit was attached to it. It is said, that the Duke of Wellington refuses to support any alteration in the Corn Laws, and that in consequence of the difficulty thus created, Sir Robert Peel has determined to resign.

It is added, in confirmation of this statement, that it was determined, at the Cabinet Council, held on Monday, that Parliament should be again further prorogued, instead of being summoned by proclamation for the despatch of business.

Concurrently with this rumour, another and more explicit report is hazarded by the Scotch papers, in consequence of the sudden departure of Lord John Russell from Edinburgh, where he had determined upon sojourning for several days longer. It is, of course, taken for granted, that this sudden departure was in consequence of a message from the Queen, demanding the noble Lord's immediate presence in London, implying the retirement of Sir Robert Peel. The mystery is thus solved by the *Glasgow Chronicle*:—

It is affirmed, that, after the meeting of the Cabinet, at which the Duke of Wellington agreed to support the Premier, in carrying any measure which he might think necessary, in order to effect a settlement of the Corn Law question; and, after this fact has been made public, by means of the article in *The Times*, the Duke was assailed by a number of protectionist Peers, and earnestly urged to recall the *carte blanche*, which, it was understood, he had given to the Premier.

What considerations they had presented to the mind of the Duke, strong enough to overcome those which had previously weighed with him in yielding to Sir Robert Peel, we know not; but it appears their pleadings had been successful, and the Duke promised them that he would immediately undo what he had so recently done. The papers inform us that a Cabinet Council was held on Friday last.

At this Council, the Duke is understood to have informed his colleagues that he had seen cause to alter his purpose as declared at this previous meeting, and that he had reverted to the position he had previously occupied of hostility to any change in the law.

Sir Robert Peel is stated to have thereupon declared, that he considered himself shut up to decline any farther attempt to carry on the Government. On the following day, he proceeded to Osborne-house, of course to make a similar statement to the Queen. Her Majesty, on her part, had lost no time in adopting the course which the exigency called for. Acting from her own impulse and judgement, or on the suggestion of Sir Robert Peel, she despatched a messenger that very night to Edinburgh, where as we have already stated, he arrived late on Monday.

Other particulars have been stated to us of less moment, but as everything is interesting connected with occurrences so momentous to the nation, we may as well mention the message received by Lord John Russell was written by the Queen's own hand; that it was brought to the Noble Lord a considerable time after he had gone to bed; that his Lordship was at first anything but pleased at the unreasonable interruption of his rest; but the mention of the Queen's name had at once banished the Noble Lord's displeasure, and roused into instant collectedness and activity both his mental and bodily faculties.

Amidst such confusion in political circles, we have only to await with patience the issue.

Recreated from The Belfast News-Letter, Belfast, December 12, 1845.

(*From the Sun.*)

Lord John Russell has resigned the task of forming an administration, and Sir Robert Peel has been again summoned. The Right Hon. Baronet left town for Windsor at two o'clock.

When Sir Robert Peel declared his inability to carry on the government we never doubted that the formation of a new administration would devolve upon Lord John Russell. Whether he could accomplish the task remained to be seen, but the gradually improving tone of all sections of the liberal party gave the strongest omens of success.

Up to yesterday evening matters went on prosperously, so far as could be judged, but difficulties arose—difficulties, caused by the timidity of some, and by the pride and obstinacy of others, which have ended in Lord John Russell's refusal of the proffered premiership.

We believe that Lord John has acted boldly, honestly, and fearlessly. He has not swerved one particle from the straight line of public principle avowed by him, and although he has for the day excluded himself from office, the Liberal cause will far outweigh the temporary disappointment.

(*From a Correspondent of the Sun.*)

Lord John Russell has, it is understood, left town this morning for Windsor Castle, to have an audience of Her Majesty.

Sir John Hobhouse and other political leaders called at Lord John Russell's residence in Chesham-Place, this morning.

(*From a third edition of the Sun.*)

The formation of a Ministry by Lord John Russell is, for the present, at an end, and the Court Newsman will announce the departure of the members of the might-have-been Cabinet, for their county seats, instead of chronicling their arrival in Downing-street. With them will go the tribe of sucking statesmen, and expectant placemen, who have haunted Brookes' and the Reform Club for some days past, full of pleasing visions of power of self-importance.

The break-down of the Whigs, in attempting to form a Government, will, we hope prove a lesson to the narrow minded aristocrats of the Lansdowne class, that they cannot move without the aid of the true Liberals and free-traders.

The desire to extend the basis of the Administration, and to give Mr. Cubden a place in it, or rather to offer him one, with some minor disputes about particular offices, have been the rocks upon which the wreck took place.

Lord John has done his duty in all, save in discarding his ancient dregs. The Whiggism of 1830 will not do in 1845.

The people have gained by the last ten days. Lord John Russell may lead the van, be he must not put his heavy artillery in the front.

Sir Robert Peel may try to govern—he can only do so by adopting free trade measures.

The Queen has been throughout in favor of the people and of popular measures; her words and actions have been most cheering, and it is gratifying to know that a Liberal Administration would have found a firm friend in her Majesty.

(*From a Correspondent of the Sun.*)

Sir Robert Peel received this morning a communication from Lord J. Russell, and immediately summoned together to his residence all the ministers in town.

After a meeting, messengers were despatched to such members of the Cabinet as are out of town, requiring their immediate return to the metropolis.

As soon as Sir Robert Peel returns from Windsor Castle it is expected a Cabinet Council will be held.

Recreated from The Belfast News-Letter, Belfast, December 23, 1845.

THE CHILD'S FIRST GRIEF.

Mamma—why don't you answer me?
Why do you lie so still?
Can't you sit up, and can't you see?
Are you so very ill?

You have been sick a long, long while;
And very, very weak;
But yet you used to always smile—
Mamma! why don't you speak?

When round the bed I used to play,
And show'd her my new toy,
She would smile on me as she lay,
And ask to kiss her boy.

Why is that shade upon her brow?
Her eyes are sunk and deep;
She is quite still and quiet now—
And yet 'tis not like sleep.

She was in Heaven, I was told,
And there she felt no pain;
But here she is all pale and cold!—
Will she not wake again?

Poor child! thy mother feels no pain;
Her spirit is at rest;
She sleeps; she will not wake again;
With angels she is blest!

'Tis sad to chill thy tender youth—
With tears convulse thy breath;
But thou must know the mournful truth—
This sleep, dear child, is Death.

Recreated from The Belfast News-Letter, Belfast, January 23, 1846.

1846

Selected Headlines

DREADFUL ACCIDENT—COACHMAN KILLED	44
IRISH FAMINE—MR. O'CONNELL'S MOTION	50
MURDERS IN TIPPERARY	50
COMMUNICATION BY TELEGRAPH	53
LAUNCH OF THE IRON STEAM SHIP	56
COCK FIGHTING	56
DEATH FROM STARVATION	60
COW STEALING	64
FAMINE RIOT IN DUNGARVAN	72
PROGRESS OF STARVATION	78

FASHIONABLE INTELLIGENCE.

WINDSOR, MONDAY.—Her Majesty, Prince Albert, and the court, honour her Royal Highness the Duchess of Kent with their company at dinner this evening at Frogmore House. The Countess of Desurt took leave of her Majesty previous to her ladyship's departure for Bristol, en route to Lord D's seat in the county of Kilkenny.

Viscount and Viscountess Dungannon are passing the winter at Brynkinalt, their seat in Denbighshire. The noble viscount and viscountess are not entertaining company this season.

Viscount and Viscountess Palmerston were expected to arrive on Monday at their seat, Broadlands, near Romsey, from a visit to the Marquis and Marcioness of Landsdowne, at Bowood.

The Earl of Dalhousie has arrived in London from a visit to the Duke of Wellington, at Strathfieldsaye, Hants.

The Chancellor of the Exchequer arrived in London on Monday afternoon, from Cambridge.

The Earl of St. Germans rejoiced the hearts of the poor of St. Germans on Monday, by distributing two oxen among them, and presenting a shilling and a peck of wheat to each poor person.—*Falmouth Packet.*

Colonel Napier and Sherman Crawford, Esq., are at present stopping at the Palace, Armagh.

The Hon. Captain Henry Handcock, 97th regiment, and the Hon. Robert Handcock, R.A., are on leave and at present on a visit with the Dowager Baroness Castlemaine, at Athlone.

Sir Robert and Lady Peel will arrive in London this (Tuesday) afternoon from their seat, Drayton Manor, Staffordshire. The hon. Baronet and Lady Peel, after staying a day or two in Whitehall Gardens, will proceed to Windsor Castle on a visit to her Majesty and Prince Albert.

Recreated from The Freeman's Journal, Dublin, January 1, 1846.

THE LINEN TRADE.
(*From the D. E. Mail.*)

A considerable degree of alarm has been excited in the North, by an order from his Grace the Duke of Wellington, which appeared in the *Mail* of Monday last, as well as in the public journals generally. It directs that the British soldiery are to be supplied with shirts of cotton, instead of linen. That this alarm is not unfounded would appear from the following data:—Assuming the British army to consist, in round numbers, of one hundred thousand men, and allowing each man four new shirts in the year, each shirt requiring three yards and a half of linen, we have fourteen yards per man, amounting in the whole to one million four hundred thousand yards, which, reckoning the usual quantity of twenty-five yards to the piece, makes fifty-six thousand pieces of linen. In addition to this, his Grace directs the substitution of some description of woolen article for the linen trousers heretofore worn by the army, the substitution being limited to the troops on home service. Now, allowing four yards per man for one-half the troops, we have two hundred thousand yards, or eight thousand pieces more, causing on the whole a lessening of the demand for our staple manufacture by sixty-four thousand pieces annually, a quantity calculated to keep three of the first-class bleach-greens going—and this takes place at a moment when, above all others, every shilling which can be poured into this country is essential for its relief. There is reason to believe that the above calculations are rather under than over the mark: indeed, it has been stated that eighty thousand pieces might come nearer it. The gallant Duke cannot be aware of the disastrous extent to which this order is calculated to affect several thousands of her Majesty's most industrious subjects. His Grace, we are bound to believe, is actuated solely by a desire to benefit the soldier, by giving him somewhat of a cheaper article; but were his Grace as well skilled in flax and cotton as he is in lines and columns, he would find, on an enquiry into their comparative qualities, that he has been misled as to their contemplated advantages. In fact, there is not a washerwoman in the army who could not set his Grace right in that particular. The Duke, though "stern of purpose," is not altogether insensible to facts, when properly brought before him; it is not, therefore, unreasonable to expect that he will pay attention to a statement so important as that given above; and it is understood that the matter is about being promptly taken up, not merely by the trade, but by many of those whose station and character *must* give the fullest weight to anything put forward by them in the way of representation or remonstrance.

The question at issue is one totally unconnected with party or politics—it involves the interest of all classes, from the nobleman to the cottager, including the landlord, the flax-growing farmer, the merchant, the bleacher, and the operative weaver. Surely a proper appeal from these cannot be made in vain.

Recreated from The Belfast News-Letter, Belfast, January 2, 1846.

The *Standard* brings us news of a warlike character from India, and of a probable war in the Punjaub. We subjoin a summary of the news:—

(*From the Overland Bombay Times of Dec.* 1.

Intelligence of a warlike character was received yesterday from the Punjaub. The Sikh Government, it appears, have become incensed at the reported intention of the British authorities to appropriate the territories on this side of the Sutlej, and have urged the soldiery to march towards the river with the view of repelling the expected aggression.

By the last accounts some cavalry had actually proceeded in the direction indicated, and though opinion was divided as to the policy of the movement, more men were expected to follow. In the meantime strong measures of defence have been adopted at Ferozepore, and as Sir Henry Hardinge may now calculate upon having a well-disciplined force of some 50,000 men at his command, there can be little fear of the result, whatever course the reckless spirit of the Sikhs may impel them to pursue.

Reprinted from The Cork Examiner, Cork, January 2, 1846

CONSTABLE CROWLEY

It will be remembered that about a fortnight since the Pawn-offices of Messrs. Hunter, Leitrim-street, and Clarke, Douglas-street, were burglariously entered at night and property to a large amount plundered therefrom. Information of the robbery having reached Constable Crowley, that active and indefatigable officer was unceasing in his exertions to discover a clue to the perpetrators of it, but in vain.

However, on visiting the City Jail yesterday the Constable's practiced eye fell on two fellows, Whelan and Wood, who are at present undergoing the sentence of the law, being convicted on a charge of aggravated assault, and on examination of whose persons several articles of the stolen property were recovered. On the evening of the same day the Constable arrested two young women, associates of theirs, in the neighbourhood of Maypole-road, of the name Hart and Reardon, in whose possession other articles of the property were discovered.

The present is not the first robbery in which Whelan and Wood have been engaged, having, on a former occasion, been convicted of sheep-stealing at Castlemartyr, and sentenced to twelve months hard labour.—Too much cannot be said in praise of the activity of Constable Crowley.

There is no man in the entire force who has rendered such efficient public service on every occasion as he has done. He has several times risked his life in endeavouring to protect property in cases of fire; whilst by his activity and acuteness he has succeeded in bringing to justice some of the most daring burglars that from time to time have infested the city; and the present discovery is an additional evidence of the consummate tact and ability which he has ever displayed on occasions of a similar nature.

Recreated from The Cork Examiner, Cork, January 2, 1846

DREADFUL AND FATAL ACCIDENT— DERRY MAIL UPSET—COACHMAN KILLED.

The particulars of the following fatal accident which happened to the Londonderry mail coach on Thursday night, have been communicated to us by James Cahill, Esq., of 79, Talbot-street, who was a passenger, and who, we are happy to say, escaped with only some slight bruises. The coach left the Drogheda terminus of the Dublin and Drogheda Railway, after the arrival of the mail train at the usual hour on Thursday night.

The vehicle was occupied by a young lady, named Knox, her father, and two other gentlemen inside, and Mr. Cahill, the only outside passenger. The coach was driven by Patrick Shanley, a well known whip, and a very civil obliging person, who was much esteemed by all who travelled on his road. Everything went on well until about two o'clock, when the vehicle had arrived within two miles of Castleblaney where it was upset, and Shanley was killed on the spot. Mr. Cahill gives a truly horrifying description of the accident. He says that at the stage before they came to Castleblaney, *four blind horses* were put to the coach, and as the night was very dark it was with considerable difficulty that Shanley managed them.

On approaching the spot where the accident occurred, there is a curve in the road, and then a straight line. Just after passing the curve there was a large heap of stones on the side of the way, and to avoid coming in contact with that Shanley kept on the opposite side, and on this portion of the road there was a deep cut of which he was ignorant. The wheels of the coach came into the cut, the leading horses plunged into the ditch and were knocked down, the wheelers fell on them, and the coach was instantly upset with great violence. It would have been completely overturned but for the ditch. Mr. Cahill who, fortunately for himself, sat behind the coachman, although he was several times during the night solicited to take the box-seat, was thrown with great force over the hedge into a ploughed field, where he lay for some time quite insensible from the effects of the shock.

On recovering he made his way out, and a shocking spectacle presented itself to his sight. All was still as death; the horses, coach and all lay there in one confused mass. The coachman was quite lifeless; the coach had fallen on and crushed him to death instantly. The guard lay against the ditch quite insensible, and not a sound issued from inside.—Mr. Cahill concluded that all was killed. He crept up the side of the coach and took down the remaining lamp; he then dragged poor Shanley out from where he lay, but the poor clay did not return even a pulsation.

His next attempt was to extricate the guard, which he did, and finding some signs of life in him he placed him in a convenient position, and proceeded to climb up the coach. Having opened the door he found the four inside passengers completely stunned. With great difficulty he succeeded in getting Miss Knox out of the perilous position in which she was placed, and the others were subsequently extricated. Messengers were sent off at once to Castleblaney, and twenty men, with the Catholic clergyman and medical doctor, were promptly in attendance. The guard recovered after some time.

The coach was taken into Castleblaney, and had not left at seven o'clock in the morning. Mr. Cahill, who returned to town last night, says that great blame is attachable to the person horsing the coach, who should not have sent out four blind animals on such a dark night, and on such a dangerous part of the road. Had the cattle been able to have seen their way he thinks it likely the accident would not have taken place. We trust the contractors will be able to show that they are not to blame in this lamentable affair.

Recreated from The Freeman's Journal, Dublin, January 3, 1846.

CROWN PROSECUTION.—Informations were on Monday evening sworn before the Honourable Mr. Justice Burton, at his residence, in Stephen's-green, against Charles Gavan Duffy, Esq., Proprietor of the *Nation*, at the suit of the Queen, for the printing and publication of an alleged wicked and seditious libel. The article on which the informations are founded, is that in reference to railroads being an incapable mode for the transportation of troops. The affidavit of proprietorship was, at the same time, sworn by Charles Vernon, Esq., the Register of Newspapers in the Stamp-office; and all the documents were subsequently lodged with the Attorney-General to decide in what way he will proceed—whether by *ex officio* informations, or indictment; and it is probable that this decision will be announced at the opening of the Court on Monday, the 12th instant, being the first day of term.—*Mail*.

DREADFUL ACCIDENT AT LEIGHLIN-BRIDGE.—An accident, attended with fatal consequences, occurred in this quarter, which has cast a gloom upon this quiet and social neighbourhood. The Honorable and Very Rev. the Dean of Leighlin was returning from Bagenalstown on Friday night, about eleven o'clock, in a phaeton; the horse became unmanageable at a most dangerous part of the road—a very steep descent, and a very narrow street at the entrance of the town of Leighlin-bridge. The horse dashed furiously down the street; and the carriage came in contact with the spud stone at the corner next to the post-office, and was broken into pieces with the violence of the shock. The unfortunate servant, who was sitting beside the Dean, was taken up insensible; he never spoke; a great effusion of blood took place, and the poor man died in a few hours. The Dean was thrown into the centre of the Dublin road, and was taken up speechless. He was immediately removed to the post-office, where every attention was paid to him at that late hour by Miss Magee. Medical aid was procured from Bagenalstown and from Carlow without delay, and by their direction the Dean was removed on a door, and thus conveyed to his own house, which is close at hand. He rallied a little, and expressed the ease and comfort he felt when again in his own quarters. He is sorely cut and bruised, and shaken, but no bones are broken, and the medical gentlemen hold out some hopes, if nothing untoward occurs. Due attention has been directed to keep down inflammation, and the patient appeared to be somewhat more at ease in the afternoon than he had been. An inquest will be held on the body of the unfortunate young man who drove the horse. He was quite sober at the time; he has left a widowed mother, and was unmarried.—*Mail*.

SUICIDE IN DUBLIN.—Mr. Nott, of the firm Nott and Son, tea merchants and brokers, residing in Dame-street, committed suicide on Friday last, at the house of his brother-in-law, Mr. John Jones, of Burton-hall, near Whitechurch, Rathfarnham. The deceased gentleman went out to Burton-hall, the country seat of his brother-in-law, Mr. Jones, on Friday, and in the course of the evening his body was discovered suspended by a cord and handkerchief from a stair-case which led into the water-closet. The body was at once cut down, and medical aid procured, but all to no purpose, as the vital spark had been extinguished for some time. Deceased was in his 58th year, and lived on terms of the greatest affection with his family and relations. Mr. Nott had been labouring under disease of the head for some time, and was heard a week since to say "that it would be no wonder if a person suffering as he was would commit suicide." There was an inquest held on Saturday evening on the remains, when a verdict to the effect that he committed suicide while labouring under temporary insanity was returned.—*Mayo Constitution*.

Recreated from The Belfast News-Letter, Belfast, January 9, 1846.

A PROCLAMATION.

HEYTESBURY.—Whereas by an act passed in the sixth year of the reign of his late Majesty King William the Fourth, entitled "An act to consolidate the laws relating to the constabulary force in Ireland," it is amongst other things enacted, that it shall and may be lawful to and for the Lord Lieutenant, and other Chief Governor or Governors of Ireland, by the advice of the Privy Council in Ireland, to declare by Proclamation, that any county of a city, or county of a town in Ireland, or any barony or baronies, half barony or half baronies, in any county at large, or any district of less extent than any barony or half barony to be therein specified, is or are in a state of disturbance, and requires or require an additional establishment of Police.

And whereas it hath sufficiently appeared to us, that the Baronies of Clanwilliam, Owenybeg, Small County and Coshlea, all in the County of Limerick, are in a state of disturbance, and require an additional establishment of Police.

Now we, the Lord Lieuetenant, by and with the advice of her Majesty's Privy Council, by virtue of the said act and the powers thereby vested in us, do, by this our proclamation, declare that the said baronies of Clanwilliam, Owenybeg, Small County, and Coshlea, and all in the county of Limerick aforesaid, are in a state of disturbance and require an additional establishment of Police.

Given at the Council Chamber in Dublin this 27th day of January, 1846.

Edward Meath. R. Keatinge. Edward Lucas.

GOD SAVE THE QUEEN.

Recreated from The Cork Examiner, Cork, January 30, 1846.

DESPERATE OUTRAGE.—On Tuesday night last, about six o'clock, as Alfred Waller, Esq., was returning to his residence near Castle Waller, Newport, he was attacked by a gang of fellows, four or five in number, who beat him in a most dreadful manner with sticks and stones, giving him three cuts in the head, breaking one of his arms, and inflicting several contusions on different parts of his body. At the commencement of the attack Mr. Waller pulled a pistol from his pocket and fired at his assailants, which, instead of frightening them, was the cause of making them lay on the heavier, until they left him for dead. He was, however, shortly afterwards discovered, unable to rise, by some of the neighbours, who removed him to his brother's residence at Castle Waller, where his wounds were dressed, and it is hoped he is now out of danger. Land, it is *supposed*, is the cause of this daring attack, as the fellows on decamping warned him to give up some ground which came into his possession about a year since.—*Tipperary Vindicator.*—[Mr. Waller was a relative of the Waller's of Finnoe, the frightful massacre of whom so lately filled the country with horror.]

COUNTY OF LEITRIM.—A few days since an outrage, which threatened the loss of life, occurred near Mohill. As Mr. William Grogan, of Currawne, (a man of peaceful and excellent character,) was returning home from the butter market, about a mile on the road, two men rushed from behind a ditch, and violently assaulted him. Grogan, an active man, having grappled with the first assailant, the other hastily came to his assistance, and fired a pistol loaded with slugs at Grogan, which grazed the corner of his left eye, and wounded him severely. The same shot also burned and made a riddle of Mrs. Grogan's cloak. There is a man in gaol for this attack and outrage.

We have received a communication from a Strokestown correspondent, announcing the melancholy tidings that Christopher Harrison, Esq., solicitor, was murdered near that place on Saturday night. A large flock of sheep belonging to Mr. Connor, near Strokestown, were forced into a pit of water at night last week, and the animals perished. Also fields have been turned up between Tulsk and Strokestown.

Recreated from The Belfast News-Letter, Belfast, January 30, 1846.

CLONMEL.

PITCHFORKS.—We have heard that three or four gentlemen were ejected at the point of the pitchfork from a hotel in Clonmel the other day. This would be a good model for the treatment of the *Times*' Commissioner.

A constable is in pursuit of the unfortunate Bank-Clerks, Power and Hearn, late of Clonmel, in America.

Masonry is still keeping society in Clonmel in a state of ferment. A lodge is established there, which is said to be "doing well" in the way of masonic propagation, even among some leisured Roman Catholics.—*Waterford Chronicle*.

Reprinted from The Freeman's Journal, Dublin, January 30, 1846.

STATE OF DUNGARVAN.

The accounts we continue to receive from Dungarvan are indeed melancholy in the extreme. Sickness, scarcity and want of employment, shed their bitterness upon the devoted heads of the poor. There are upwards of five thousand human beings, we are given to understand, in a state of want and wretchedness, requiring assistance from Government or from those whom God has blessed with means for such purpose. The poor house is crammed with women and children, in which there are also upwards of forty men, capable of work, but none to be had. The spread of fever is really alarming, induced, of course, from want, cold and hunger. Nor do the evils stop here. The Poor Law Guardians met on last Thursday when they reported that the supply of potatoes, destined for use during the season, and carefully put up, turned out on examination to be more than half rotten, and that the remainder are going fast. It is some consolation, under those melancholy circumstances, when the Government does not seem to move in the matter, that the townspeople are exerting themselves with equal spirit and benevolence. From the subscriptions raised potatoes are purchased in large quantities, and sold after by retail, at first cost, to the poor, a plan attended with much good results.

In the mean time the Board of Guardians and the inhabitants and the rate-payers of the town have addressed the LORD LIEUTENANT. The reply of his Excellency to the memorial of the Guardians, under the circumstances, is cold, heartless, and flippant. What cares this English official—this worn-out diplomatist, for the starving people of an Irish fishing town. What sympathy could he have with their misery—what fellow-feeling for their dreams? 'Tis a heartless mockery—this creating Englishmen and Scotchmen into vice-kings—Throning them in the marble halls of St. PATRICK, and giving them jurisdiction and sway over a warm-hearted people, in whose elevation they take no interest, for whose prosperity they are not proud, and for whose afflictions they do not grieve.

Here is the benevolent reply:—

Dublin Castle, 22d January, 1846.

SIR,—The Lord Lieutenant has directed me to acknowledge the receipt of the Memorial, signed by you as Chairman of the Board of Guardians of the Poor Law Union of Dungarvan, and to acquaint you that his Excellency has desired it to be referred to the Commissioners for enquiring into all matters relating to the scarcity of Provisions.

I am, Sir, your most obedient humble servant,

RICHARD PENNEFEATHER.

Recreated from The Cork Examiner, Cork, February 2, 1846.

ROSCOMMON.—On Saturday last, when a person was about setting a portion of conacre, within about a mile and a-half of Drumsna, in this county, a person, partially dressed as a female (but having a leather belt round her waist, which secured five or six pistols), presented herself, and having ascertained that the amount of rent was £6 per acre, declared that £4, 10s. was sufficient. After cautioning the tenants not to pay any more than that sum for the ground, she fired two shots and deliberately walked away.

On the following day, two persons, dressed as females, well armed, each having sword in hand, and six or eight pistols, well secured with leather belts round their bodies, presented themselves at the chapel-door of Annaduff. They stated that their object was to caution tenants of Colonel Forbes against paying any rent or arrears of rent, until the landlord or his agent would come to Augba, more, as hitherto, for the purpose of receiving it.—*Boyle Gazette.*

DARING ATTACK IN THE NOONDAY UPON A WIDOW LADY.—Upon Sunday last, Mrs. Bennet, of Monaguill, whose mansion is within five miles of this town, left her dwelling for the purpose of attending Divine worship at the village church of Ballinaclough. When about a quarter of a mile from her home, her jaunting car, which was being driven by a servant man, was stopped by two men, who deliberately came out from amongst a crowd of others on the road side, one of whom held the horse by the reins, whilst the other went up to Mrs. Bennett and snapped a pistol at her twice, but which fortunately missed fire upon both occasions. The other ruffian, who held the reins, having a "wattle" in his hand, went over and struck her on the head and about the arms. Their intended victim, however, being closely muffled, and having a large fur tippet, put up her hands to save her head from her merciless assailants, and then, ordering the coachman to drive off quickly, she escaped providentially with but little injury. When the fellow was striking at Mrs. Bennett he asked her would she discharge Henzie, a man whom she, with a stern determination to be her own mistress, kept in her employment in despite of threatening letters and shots fired into her house at night, because she considered him a faithful and trustworthy person, but who, to her labourers and others, was obnoxious. A short time ago this Henzie was fired at through the kitchen window at Monaguill house, when a ball passed through his right hand, as he was at his supper, when in the act of lifting a potato to his mouth. No discovery has, as yet, been made of the perpetrators of this daring act.—*Nenagh Guardian.*

Recreated from The Belfast News-Letter, Belfast, February 6, 1846.

DREADFUL OCCURRENCE.—On Sunday night a party of Roman Catholics who had been, it is supposed, at a funeral at Dreenan Chapel, on the road from Portglenone to Maghera, whilst passing through the townland of Dreenan, where respectable Protestant families reside, commenced singing party songs of an irritating description, and gave other annoyance, which brought them into collision with the Protestant party. A scuffle took place, and the assailants having threatened to burn the house of a man named Downey, some of the inmates fired on the crowd and killed two persons, named Higgins and M'Quillan.—*Coleraine Chronicle.*

ALTERATION IN THE GAME LAWS.—In consequence of the inadequacy of the common law, for the punishment of persons "who fire at, or kill" their landlords, we understand that Sir Robert Peel intends to introduce a clause, making such offenses (if committed by a person not being duly licensed) punishable under the game laws. Sir Robert Peel can hardly do less for the landlords, whom he has been *making game of* ever since his accession to office.—*D. E. Mail.*

ANTRIM.—Thursday last a public meeting was held in Antrim, at which Lord Massereene presided, for the purpose of having this town placed under the provisions of the lighting, cleansing, and paving Act. Resolutions were unanimously passed to memorial the Lord Lieutenant on the subject.

FULFILLMENT OF THE SENTENCE.—In reply to a memorial in favour of the culprit, Scery, condemned to death at the late commission for firing at Sir F. Hopkins, Bart., the Lord Lieutenant has pronounced that the law must take its course. The unfortunate man will consequently undergo the final sentence on Friday, the 13th inst.

Recreated from The Belfast News-Letter, Belfast, February 10, 1846.

IN reference to the letter of "P. S." which appeared in this journal, addressed to the MAYOR last week, the following order has been issued to the City Constabulary:—

ORDERS.

Tuckey Street, 9th Feb. 1846.

1st.—The Head and other Constables in charge of Stations, will in future report to the Mayor's Office, all cases of Children found straying in the City, furnishing at the same time, a description of their person, with any other information that may be necessary.

2d.—Description of Cattle found straying, is also to be furnished to the Mayor's Office.

JAMES WALKER, Sub-Inspector.

ATTEMPTED SUICIDE.

MR. RICE of the City Bridewell informed the presiding Magistrates at the Police Court, this day, that a woman named Mary Jane Thornton had attempted to strangle herself on the previous night in the Bridewell, by twisting a handkerchief round her neck, so tightly that it had to be actually cut before she could be relieved—in fact if five minutes more had elapsed before the discovery was made, the unfortunate woman would have succeeded in terminating her existence. To prevent her making any further attempt during the night, she was handcuffed behind her back, and her legs tied. No cause was assigned for the rash act.

Reprinted from The Cork Examiner, Cork, February, 11, 1846.

THE POTATO DISEASE.

Lord Cloncurry announces a fact of most painful import, and one which should be studied by the Government and legislature. That excellent Nobleman has ascertained that there is unequivocal evidence of decay in the new Crop of Potatoes, sown in November, and upon the early gathering of which so much reliance has been placed, as food for the people in the beginning of the summer:—

9th February, 1846.

MY DEAR SIR—I think it right to mention to you that I planted some potatoes last November in lazy beds—the soil rich, maiden, and dry—the seed of the best kind, mostly cut, but some whole; the kinds, purple kidneys and pink eyes. On examining them last week, I find one third decayed after making shoots. This is bad news; but it is better to give timely information.

There is in the country at this moment corn more than enough to feed our entire population; by establishing stores or granaries in the poorhouses and other places, into which the farmers could send their corn, receiving in return a note as to the quantity, it would prevent the great loss which takes place every year by want of proper corn stands or barns through the country—it would be at hand if wanted and if not it could be sold in May or June, at probably an advanced price, which would pay all expense.

Dear Sir, your humble servant, CLONCURRY.

We understand that the Marquis of Abercorn has accepted the office of Groom of the Stole to Prince Albert, vacant by the resignation of the Marquis of Exeter.—*Times.*

The Poor Law Commissioners have issued a sealed order dissolving the Tuam and Castlereagh Guardians, "for default of their duties: and if the new electoral guardians will not discharge their functions, paid guardians wil be appointed.

Recreated and reprinted from The Cork Examiner, Cork, February 13, 1846.

IRISH FAMINE—MR. O'CONNELL'S MOTION.

We give in our adjoining columns a lengthened report of the discussion raised by the Liberator upon Tuesday last on the question of Irish famine and its inevitable concomitant, disease. There never was a case more clearly and convincingly sustained—there never was appeal received more melancholy confirmation. With much of the evidence by which the Liberator sustained his case the Irish people are familiar, with the series of remedial measures which he urged the government to adopt, those who have followed his public career are well acquainted; neither will they feel surprise at the petty shifts and halting expedients to which the ministry have had recourse, and the utter absence from their contemplation of all the great measures of relief for the remedy of admittedly great distress. The measures suggested by Mr. O'Connell possessed two great merits—they were fully adequate to the necessities to which they were proposed to be applied, and they were capable of immediate application. Perhaps it was these ingredients which have caused them to be received so coolly by the English legislature. But, however this may be, they were marked by one other clement which was sure to cause their rejection in an English parliament—and that was, their *justice*. No man could deny the justice of our obtaining the expenditure of our Woods' and Forests' revenues for the sustainment of our starving people. No man questions the *justice* of taxing absentees; how, therefore, could we hope that English legislators would give it toleration? These are neither "benevolences" or "charities;" they are purely the discharge of just obligations, and were therefore sure to meet with neither support or countenance from men who always deny us what is just, and perpetually urge upon us that which is degrading.

The minister affected great sympathy for Ireland. This is the inevitable tenour of ministerial speeches for the present. The utmost anxiety was expressed—the utmost interest pretended to be felt. Mr. O'Connell, we doubt not, estimated these kindnesses at their full value—so much breath as served to give them utterance. But what was he to do? Englishmen believed them; they cried "hear, here" and gave "loud cheers", and other unerring indications that they were ready to concur in whatever the minister was pleased to suggest. Sir James Graham expressed his readiness to accept all responsibility of the occasion, and declared that no circumstances could occur which could find the government unprepared to meet them. Under such circumstances Mr. O'Connell pursued a wise course in consenting to withdraw a notion which was sure to be rejected, and in leaving to the minister the responsibility; but it is one which England should sustain, and which Irishmen are bound, vigilantly, to take care that England shall discharge with completeness and promptitude.

Recreated from The Freeman's Journal, Dublin, February 20, 1846.

MURDERS IN TIPPERARY.

We regret to have to record the barbarous murder of an industrious man, named James Keane, who resided at Gurtmore, within a few miles of Nenagh. It appears that on the night of the 5th inst. as the unfortunate man was proceeding in the direction of his home he was met on the road, at Tullaheady, by three infuriated demons, who, with savage vengeance, rushed on their victim,—felled him to the ground, and inflicted a fatal wound on the left side of his head. The heartless miscreants decamped, leaving him almost lifeless on the road side. The unfortunate man endeavoured to make the best of his way home, where he languished under the most excruciating pains from the effect of the wound until Sunday, the 8th instant, when death put an end to his torture. No cause has been assigned for the perpetration of this horrible deed. An inquest was held on Sunday on view of the body, by Michael Carroll, Esq., coroner, when a verdict of wilful murder was returned against some person or persons unknown.—*Tipperary Vindicator*.

"O'Connell Beggars", reprinted from The Pictorial Times, London, February 14, 1846.

On Sunday night last a party of men consisting of six in number, one armed with a pistol, entered the house of a man named Meara, of Gurtavalla, within half a mile of Cloghjordan. They first knocked Meara down with a stone, inflicting a deadly wound; they then, with savage ferocity struck him on the head until his brains were dashed out. The yard was full of turf mould, and from the appearance of his body, it is supposed they trampled on him. A finger and thumb on his right hand were broken; there was a large fracture on the back of his head—one on the crown, where the brains protruded—four on his face, and his forehead presented a shocking appearance. Two sons and two daughters were in the house at the time, and never attempted to save the husband and father. This foul deed was committed between the hours of 7 and 8 o'clock, and within a few yards of another house; but though the shrieks of the inmates were heard, no one came to their assistance.

Meara's family had consisted of his wife, two sons, (one of them a grown man, the other a boy), and two daughters, who were in the kitchen at the time the party were beating the father. The son attempted to get to the father's assistance, but was held by the mother. He however, succeeded in getting away from her, but when he did, they were going away.

The number of Meara's assailants was six. Meara is father to the man that killed Kennedy on last Patrick's Day, on his return from the fair of Borrisokane. Seven men have been arrested for this murder.—*Nenagh Guardian*.

Recreated from The Cork Examiner, Cork, March 13, 1846.

OUTRAGES AND ARRESTS.

Sunday last two men well armed, named James Flynn, uncle and nephew, with their faces blackened, entered the house of a farmer named William Broderick, residing at Kiltane, near Freemount, in this county, and ordered him to give possession of the land he had lately taken. One of them shot the house dog, and threatened Broderick to serve him in the same way if their commands were not immediately attended to. They then went to the house of a man named John Sullivan, a caretaker on the same lands, and threatened to shoot him if he did not quit the place the following day.

On leaving Broderick and Sullivan, the fellows said that they were "Captain Kilfoyle's men" (the leader of the gang that lately attacked the police at Kilfinnan, county Limerick). The outrages having been reported to the Freemount police, they instantly went into pursuit of the delinquents, and about one o'clock on the following morning they arrested the two Flynn's under very suspicious circumstances, they having some powder in their pockets and their faces partially blackened.

On Monday these two men were taken by Sub-inspector Wade before Sir William Becher, and the magistrate attending the Cecilstown Petty Sessions; but no person in attendance was able to identify them, and they were recommitted.

They were again brought before the magistrates on Wednesday, and Broderick, on whom the attack was made, being present, they were both fully identified out of 20 persons, amongst whom they had been placed. Informations were then received against the prisoners, and they were forwarded to the County Jail, to be disposed of at the present assizes. The two prisoners belonged to the neighbourhood in which the outrages were committed.

On Sunday evening last about the hour of six o'clock, two men with their faces blackened and well armed, one of them having four pistols strapped round his body and a gun in his hand, the other with a pair of pistols and a blunderbuss, called at the house of John Dobbins, of Elm Mount, a workman of Patrick Galvin, between Newtown and Freemount. After calling out Dobbins they desired him to go on his knees, which he at first refused, but afterwards complied, when one of the ruffians discharged a pistol at him; the powder burned his hair and whiskers. They were shown the way to Galvin's house, which is but a short distance from Dobbins', but, fortunately for Galvin he was at the time in the cow house, at the rere of the dwelling, tying up the cows, or in all probability his life would have been taken. Galvin's daughter told her father that those persons were in the house, when the poor man, frightened as he must have been almost to death, hid under a large quantity of straw until they left the house, which was near an hour.

They could get no light to search the house, or else they would have got Galvin's gun, which was laid on the table in the room. When Dobbins thought they were gone from Galvin's he went to see was *he shot*, but on the way the two fellows met him and gave him a most unmerciful beating, inflicting, with their guns, four deep cuts on his head and a severe contusion on the eye, together with bruises on the body. After leaving him for dead they went on their way towards Freemount, calling at one house to smoke and rest themselves, as if not in the least dread of being apprehended.

The police of Newtown, under the charge of Constable Brown, proceeded to the place, which is about three miles from the station. Although borrowing a horse, and the constable with another policeman getting on him, they could not come up with them; but the police at Freemount under Constable Walsh were more fortunate. They having got information that persons were firing shots, proceeded in the direction, and after a smart chase *captured* the two fellows, who have been fully identified and committed. The police acted with great energy and cleverness on the occasion. The cause that Galvin assigns for this outrage is, that he got land from his landlord which belonged to his brother, but which his brother was not able to keep. After it had been some time in his possession the brother wanted it back again; a fight on the land ensued, when Patrick was stuck with a large bayonet by his brother.—*Constitution*.

Recreated from The Cork Examiner, Cork, March 13, 1846.

COMMUNICATION BY TELEGRAPH BETWEEN FRANCE AND ENGLAND.

Amidst the many wonderful inventions of modern days, wherein the faculties of man have overcome difficulties apparently insurmountable, and made the elements subservient to his power, there are none more wonderful than that now about to be carried out by the submarine telegraphs, by which an instantaneous communication will be effected between the coast of England and France. The British Government, by the Lords Commissioners of the Admiralty, and the French Government, by the Minister of the Interior, have granted permission to two gentlemen, the projectors of the submarine telegraphs, to lay it down from coast to coast.

The site selected is from Cape Grisnez, or Cape Blanenez, on the French side, to the South Foreland on the English coast. The surroundings between these headlands gradually vary from seven fathoms, near the shore, on either side, to a maximum of thirty-seven fathoms mid-channel. The lords of the Admiralty have also granted permission to the same gentlemen to lay down a submarine telegraph between Dublin and Holyhead, which is to be carried on from the latter place to Liverpool and London.

The submarine telegraph across the English Channel will, however, be the one first laid down. The materials for this are already undergoing the process of insulation, and are in that state of forwardness which will enable the project to have them completed, and placed in position, so that a telegraphic communication can be transmitted across the channel about the first week of June.

When this is completed an electric telegraph will be established from the coast to Paris, and thence to Marseilles. The telegraph throughout France will be immediately under the direction of the French Government, as according to the law of 1837, all telegraphic communication throughout that country are under the absolute control and superintendence of the Minister of the Interior.

Upon completion of the submarine telegraph across the English Channel, it is stated that a similar one, on the most gigantic scale, will be attempted to be formed, under the immediate sanction and patronage of the French Administration; this is no less than that of connecting the shores of Africa with those of Europe by the same instrumentality, thus opening a direct and lightning-like communication between Marseille and Algeria.

It has been doubted by several scientific men whether this is practicable, and indeed, whether even the project between the coasts of France and England can be accomplished, but it has been proved by experiments, the most satisfactory in their results, that not only can it be effected, but effected without any considerable difficulty.

Certain learned and able men of science asserted that it was impossible to bring steam to such a state of perfection as to make it available for trans-Atlantic navigation; a few short months have convinced them that the dictum so boldly propounded was altogether fallacious.—*Globe*.

Recreated from The Belfast News-Letter, Belfast, April 21, 1846.

THE FAMINE IN IRELAND—PEASANTS AT THE GATE OF A WORKHOUSE.

Anonymous engraving, English School, c. 1846.

THE IRISH "FAMINE" CRY.

(From the London Farmer's Journal.)

If Sir Robert Peel had any real faith in his own anticipations of impending famine in Ireland—first made known to his Cabinet colleagues early in the last quarter of last year, and promulgated to the world immediately after the opening of the present session of Parliament—why, in the name of common sense, did he not take those timely and effectual measures, which were always within his power, to guard against or alleviate the threatened calamity.

Within the period of the present Premier's political existence, and at times when the party he owned held power, the country has, at least three times, been visited with seasons of scarcity, and on each occasion the Government of the day, with Sir R. Peel's approbation, direct or implied—certainly not without his perfect cognizance of the fact— adopted those precautions which most obviously suggest themselves to prevent the waste of every production of the soil which, to use the expressive phrase of one of our oldest friends, "the tooth of the man can play upon."

Sir Robert Peel must be strangely oblivious if he cannot remember that, in the year 1813, when, if we mistake not, he was in office, not only was the distillation of whiskey from grain prohibited in Ireland and Scotland, but even an act of Parliament was passed, prohibiting the manufacture of starch from wheat—however inferior in quality—in England. Such were the means used by former administrations—practical politicians, and, withal, the master spirits of the age, under whom the great man of to-day was content to keep a comparatively insignificant berth warm. Did not these prohibitions answer the intended purpose? Did they not at once economise the consumption of the food of the people, and benefit our West Indian colonies by causing the Irish and Scotch distillers to substitute sugar for malt, barley and oats, in producing the alcoholic article? Answer, then, Sir R. Peel—thou GREAT, yet *little*, man—why did you not, in November last, prohibit, by order in the council, the distillation of whiskey from grain, in Ireland and Scotland? Such a prohibition could not have injured anyone, for the demand for whiskey would at once have vanished before the cry for food, and barley and oat growers would have realised quite as good prices for their produce, as soon as any real lack of food became evident.

We would not rashly impugn the motives of any man—much less those of the Prime Minister of England—in omitting to adopt the palpable means of economising the expenditure of the sustenance of the masses, which we have pointed out, and which to suppose him ignorant of would be a gross insult in every point of view; but, at the same time, we should certainly like to know—how we wish Lord George Bentinck, in his place in Parliament would ask the question for us!—what *motive* Sir Robert Peel had for not prohibiting the distillation of spirits from grain in England, Ireland, and Scotland, so soon as he had any reason to apprehend a scarcity of food in the country arising from the failure of the potato crop of last year.

Recreated from The Belfast News-Letter, Belfast, April 24, 1846.

QUEEN VICTORIA'S EMPIRE.—The Queen of England is now sovereign over one continent, a hundred peninsulas, five hundred promontories, a thousand lakes, two thousand rivers, and ten thousand islands. She waves her hand, and five hundred thousand warriors march to battle to conquer or to die. She bends her head, and at the signal, a thousand ships of war and a hundred thousand sailors perform her bidding on the ocean. She walks upon the earth, and one hundred and twenty millions of human beings feel the slightest pressure of her footstep.

Come, all ye conquerors, and kneel before the Queen of England, acknowledge the superior extent of her dependent provinces, her subjugated kingdoms, and her vanquished empires. The Assyrian empire was not so wealthy. The Roman empire was not so populous. The Persian empire was not so extensive. The Arabian empire was not so powerful. The Carthaginian empire was not so much dreaded. The Spanish empire was not so widely diffused.

We have overrun a greater extent of country than Attila, that scourge of God, ever ruled! We have subdued more empires and dethroned more kings than Alexander of Macedon! We have conquered more nations than Napoleon in the plenitude of his power ever subdued! We have acquired a larger extent of territory than Tamerlane the Tartar ever spurred his horse's hoof across.—*Finch, Boundaries of Empires*.

Recreated from The Belfast News-Letter, Belfast, May 19, 1846.

THE OLD STOCK RESTORED.—The almost obsolete custom of placing in the stocks was revived in this borough (Tewkesbury) a few days back, by an itinerant musician, named Davis, being committed thereto for three hours, in default of payment of a fine of 5s., for drunkenness.—*Worcestershire Chronicle*.

Recreated from The Belfast News-Letter, Belfast, May 26, 1846.

LAUNCH OF THE IRON STEAM-SHIP "BLARNEY"—LAST EVENING.

The launch of this beautiful Iron vessel, constructed on the screw principle, by the spirited and enterprising firm of the Messrs. LECKEY, for the Cork Steam-ship Company, took place last evening at half past 5 o'clock (high water) at Hargraves-quay. The numbers attracted to witness the ceremony of the induction of the gallant vessel into her native element were very considerable, both in the Dock-yard and on the New Wall, particularly in the former, and amongst whom were many of the leading merchants of the City, especially those engaged in the export trade. The "Blarney" is a beautiful model of nautical architecture; her proportions being—length, stem to stern, 140 feet; beam 22 feet; depth 12 feet, with a measurement of 257 tons, or 330 tons burthen. Her form and appearance are faultlessly symmetrical: and, when fully completed, with her engines of 20 horse power each, she cannot fail to realise the anticipations entertained of her "clipping" qualities, as also to reflect the highest credit on the spirited firm who built her. Shortly after 5 o'clock, the measured and continued strokes of the sledges, as, one after the other, the props were withdrawn, gave note of preparation—the goodly ship the while, with her gaudy gear, vibrating as she became more and more eased, and, as it were approaching the consummation of her union with the mighty element over which she is destined to career. At length the interesting moment arrived. The silence and expectation of the beholders were broken by the loud boom of two small pieces of cannon: a third followed, and, ere yet its echoes had ceased to rumble, the good ship slipped her hold on the "dull, tame shore", and glided, amid deafening cheers, with all the grace and beauty of a "thing of life", into the green waters, a thousand tiny billows hissing before her in her progress.

After running her cable length, she was hauled in close by the dock, where she will lie until fully completed. Her estimated cost is about £6000; and she is, we were given to understand, intended for the home trade. This is the third Iron vessel built by the spirited firm of LECKEY, within a very short period—thus, introducing and extending a most useful and important branch of enterprise, and one cannot fail to reflect the highest credit, not alone of the spirited promoters of such an undertaking, but also on our city in general. We are happy to say that not the slightest accident occurred, either on shore or on the river, which, at the time, was covered by a host of small craft. After sundry cheers were given for the prosperous career of the "Blarney"—the crowds assembled quietly dispersed.

COCK FIGHTING.

This is one of those amusements which are yet followed by the lowest class of people. We have heard some curious and at the same time degrading particulars of a late occurrence in this way. The cock fighters of Cork, represented by several notorious *amateurs* in Blackpool, Fair Lane and the parts adjacent, either sent to or accepted from their fellow sportsmen in Lismore a challenge to meet near Fermoy and fight several mains of birds, staking, at the same time, sums of money on the issues. The members of the Cork party raised money *per fas aut nefas*, in every possible way, and proceeded, well supplied, to the place of meeting. After indulging in their barbarous amusement on Monday last, it was found that large sums of money had changed hands, and that the Corkmen had become losers. Coming home, they presented a rather woe-begone appearance, without money or provisions and exhausted from drink and fatigue. We hope that the police authorities, whose interference is called for on such occasions, will be careful to prevent such demoralizing exhibitions in future.

Recreated from The Cork Examiner, Cork, May 27, 1846.

Reprinted from The Pictorial Times, London, 1846.

MAJOR P. KIRWAN'S PROPERTY, COUNTY OF GALWAY.

TO THE EDITORS OF THE FREEMAN.

Sir—Some time since I read in the Freeman's Journal certain speeches and reports, which were well calculated to prejudice the public mind against my father, Major P. Kirwan, as an Irish landlord, in reference to the proceedings which he has been obliged to institute to obtain possession of the lands of Lisscananane, a denomination of his property in the county of Galway. As I find these speeches and reports have been widely circulated by the public press, I am very reluctantly obliged to submit this statement to the public—and in doing so, trust I shall satisfy every person whose good opinion it is desirable to possess—not only that my father has neither acted harshly, or from want of good feeling, in adopting the course he is forced to take in this case, but that he could not do anything else short of relinquishing his right to the property. Lisscananane contains about 570 Irish acres, 200 of which are arable, 150 of summer pasturage (under water in winter); the rest is bog.

In the year 1803, the entire lands were leased by my grand uncle to 43 tenants, which lease expired in May, 1844. The 43 tenants from time to time sublet portions of their holdings at *profit rents*, and nothing that my father (who succeeded my grand uncle in the year 1812) did, or could do, would prevent them from continuing the subletting.

Some time about the year 1832, pending the lease, my father finding the lands sublet to such an extent, and many of the under-tenants therein living in a miserable way, proposed to some of the occupiers that if they would remove to the lands of Knockdoe and Ardgaineen, other denominations of his property in the neighbourhood, he would give them land at a reasonable rent, money to build houses thereon, and permit them to cut turf on the bog of Lisscananane, as there was none upon the lands of Knockdoe or Ardgaineen. But only one person accepted that offer—all the others refused to leave the lands of Lisscananane.

Between the years 1832 and 1844 the subletting was continued; and upon the expiration of the lease in May 1844, it was ascertained there were 110 families on the lands—80 of whom held portions of it; the remaining 30 merely occupied cabins without having any land attached thereto. And not withstanding that it was well known the lease should expire in May 1844, when my father would be entitled to possession of the lands with any crop then in the ground, yet the lands were shortly previous to May 1844, fully cropped, and when the lease expired, my father instead of taking the crop, permitted those of the occupiers for whom no holdings were provided on Lisscananane, to take their crops free of all rent.

Shortly after the expiration of the lease my father had those lands of Lisscananane surveyed and parcelled out into fifty-two separate holdings, averaging about four acres each of arable and one and one-half acre of pasture (summer grazing, besides bog), upon which he intended to build so many houses at his own expense, and they were given to fifty-two families, who were selected from the old occupiers and their descendents. To seven of the twenty-eight families for whom land could not be provided at Lisscananane under the new arrangement he, at the same time, renewed the offer he made in 1832, of allotting them land at Knockdoe or Ardgaineen, but only one family would accept his offer. The same land was then offered to any six of the aforesaid twenty-eight, but was declined by all. By this it will be seen that every one of the twenty-eight families had the offer of land elsewhere. Two respectable men from the estates of landlords in the neighbourhood were afterwards thankful to be allowed to hold portions of this land.

Notwithstanding the new arrangements to which I have referred, the twenty-eight families would neither leave Lisscananane, nor allow the fifty-two families to till such portions of the lands as they (the twenty-eight) held previous to the lease expiring.

Under those circumstances, my father was obliged to bring an ejectment on the title in the superior courts, to remove all persons from those lands of Lisscananane, except the fifty-two families he had so selected as tenants. Defence was taken to it by several persons, and after my father had incurred much expense in preparing for trial, the defenses were withdrawn in July, 1845, within a few days of the trial taking place. And my father, after all such bad treatment, allowed those very persons who had taken defence to remain in possession of their holdings until the month of November, 1845, and take thereout the crops which they yielded in the interim.

In that month the sheriff went to the lands to give my father the clear possession of them under the habere which issued for that purpose; the people offered much resistance to the obtaining of it, but eventually the possession was taken.

The aforesaid twenty-eight persons shortly afterwards re-entered upon the lands, and now hold them by force against my father; he has, therefore, been obliged to bring the present ejectment to evict them, and twenty of them have taken separate defences to it. Before doing so, however, my father offered to divide a sum of £200 amongst them; to forgive them all rent due since May, 1844. All this is admitted in a report published on the subject in the *Galway Mercury* on the 29th April last.

My father has no object whatever in the present proceedings, but to provide his tenants with such holdings as he deems to be necessary to maintain them, and their families comfortably, and the average quantity of land allotted to each of the 52 families aforesaid, is not, in my opinion, more than sufficient for that purpose.

Upon the expiration of the lease in 1844, there were no improvements whatever made on the lands, and the bog annexed to them of considerable extent, on which the original 43 tenants had *only* the right of turbary for themselves and families, was in great part cut away by the under-tenants and others, and the turf sold by them in large quantities. I shall in conclusion merely refer to the fact, that some few months since my father's land agent received an anonymous letter threatening him and his son with instant assassination if any of the people were removed from Lisscananane, from which it is evident that no reasonable terms which my father could offer would be accepted by those people or induce them to leave the lands, though by so doing they would be benefited materially.

My father's state of health is such at present that he is unable to attend to business, but I am well aware of all matters relating to the subject of this statement. I am your obedient servant,

RICHARD A. H. KIRWAN.

Fitzwilliam-street, May, 1846.

Recreated from The Freeman's Journal, Dublin, May 27, 1846.

TROOPS FOR INDIA.

THE 1st division of the 32d Regiment proceeded to Cove on this morning, previous to being despatched to Ceylon, for which purpose a transport lies at present in Cove. They were escorted as far as the Packet-office by their splendid band and a numerous body of their comrades, with the soldiers of the other regiments at present in garrison, who loudly cheered them on their onward course, which was as vigorously responded to and continued by the gallant fellows on board until the vessel had almost vanished from the spectators' sight.

Reprinted from The Cork Examiner, Cork, May 29, 1846.

MURDER BY TWO ITALIAN SAILORS.

We learn that about one o'clock this morning two sailors, natives of Genoa, accompanied by two women of bad character, hired a car from the deceased (a man named Keane) in John-street, and drove along the quay to Mary-street, where they took up two other women, named Keane and Power, and put down the two in whose company they originally were. They were then driven out the Cork road, a little beyond the Manor Castle, where they alighted. The driver immediately demanded his fare, which was refused. He drove back again into town, and having informed the owner of the car what had happened, he put up the horse and car, and they both proceeded to the place where he had dropped his passengers. The fare was again demanded, but refused, and some blows were struck, and one of the sailors immediately plunged a stiletto into Keane's bosom, who fell dead on the spot. The other sailor, a powerful and athletic man, attempted also to stab the owner of the car, a man named Elliott, but he warded the blow from off his breast, the knife passing through his arm. Elliott escaped as quickly as possible, and gave the alarm at the Broad-street police station, and Sergeants Keely and Spillane, with their men, were on the spot in a few minutes afterwards. They found Keane dead, but still warm. They then proceeded at a rapid pace for some distance along the Cork road, but not succeeding in finding the parties they sought, they proceeded into town by another direction, by Barrack-street, and succeeded in arresting there the two women who were in the car. Following up the track they had thus struck upon, they traced their game through the Mayor's Walk, down by the back of the gaol, Sargeant's-lane, &c., and succeeded in arresting both parties in the neighbourhood of Broad-street. On searching the prisoners a knife covered with blood was found.—*Waterford Freeman*.

Recreated from The Cork Examiner, Cork, May 29, 1846.

HORRIBLE CASE—DEATH FROM STARVATION—A man named Fitzgerald died at Lacken, a few miles from Dungannon, on the 29th ult., from actual want and hunger. A Mrs. Tawell, who lived in his neighbourhood, says she had known himself and his family to have been fasting 48 hours, for several days in the week, and that on the day he died there was not a morsel of food under his roof, his seven children having been crowded about his death bed (unconscious that he was in that sleep which knows no waking, and that that heart which, but a few brief hours ago agonised at the sight of his famishing family, was no longer accessible or sensible to the appeals of human woe and misery), calling on their father for something to eat. Mr. D. Tallon, and Mr. J. Galway gave 2s. 6d. each to buy a coffin for him. When will such soul-sickening heart-rending scenes of woe and death cease to exist in Ireland? How long will the noblest of God's creatures, honest men, be doomed to want food, and to famish in the midst of plenty in their own nature-blessed, but misruled country.—*Waterford Freeman*.

BALLYSHANNON.—On Friday last a number of persons (principally women and children), walked through this town, preceded by a wretched looking creature, carrying a long pole, from the top of which was suspended a loaf of bread. They halted occasionally in different parts of the town, when the leader made a speech descriptive of their distress; he said the loaf at the top of the pole was to show that, although there was at present plenty of provisions in the country, they were unable to reach them, from their price and want of employment; and, in the course of a few days more, when the spring work was completed, there would be no employment for any—how, then, were they to exist for the following three months, until the growing crops were ripe? He then noticed the cruelty of certain persons, who were sending off a cargo of potatoes to Liverpool, although before another month there would be too little for town supply.

He proposed three cheers for several persons who were reserving their potatoes for the use of the town, and three groans for those who were shipping them off—the cheers and groans were deafening. The procession then proceeded to the poor house, to demand admission, but they were told by the governor that they could not be admitted without a recommendation—they returned without committing any outrage. Great fears are entertained that the vessel loading with potatoes will be attacked. A guard of police is constantly stationed on deck.—*Ballyshannon Herald*.

Recreated from The Freeman's Journal, Dublin, June 5, 1846.

DESTITUTION AT OLDCASTLE.—MR. NAPER.—At an important meeting in Oldcastle, Mr. Naper, of Loughcrew, whose affectionate interest in his tenantry, and exertions to promote their welfare are so well known, gave utterance to the following noble sentiment:—"The committee stated that in the vicinity of Oldcastle there were sixty-three families, comprising 323 individuals, in a state of actual destitution. He wished to remark that not one of those families held directly under him, although they were all resident of his property. Now, would the meeting for a moment suppose that he made this statement for the purpose of resisting their claims on him? For his part he considered himself as much obliged to look to their necessities as if they had been all their lives contributing to his rent-roll."

These remarks were the more appropriate, that at the same meeting it was stated that the agent of an estate in the neighbourhood of Oldcastle, on which there were twenty-seven families, comprising 120 individuals, in a state of the most abject misery, had refused to contribute anything to their relief, as his instructions were to relieve tenants only! The sufferers from the potato famine in that vicinity are also greatly indebted to the exertions of Mr. O'Reilly, of Baltrasna, and of Mr. T. Battersby, who, besides contributing liberally to the relief committee, have spared no labour in mitigating the extent of the calamity, and devising means to meet it.—*Anglo-Celt*.

TRALEE.—On Tuesday morning, and Wednesday evening, a large number of mechanics and labourers, followed by a crowd of women and children, paraded our streets in solemn silence. A black flag, mounted on a long pole, and having worked on it, the inscription "Employment of Food," was borne by the men at the head of the procession.—*Kerry Examiner*.

CLONMEL.—I have visited the public works here, and am happy to inform you that there is a vast number of labourers and masons employed under the Relief Committee and Board of Works, in making sewers, public roads, &c., but I regret to say that there are still a large number of tradesmen (chiefly belonging to the building line) idle, and not the slightest chance of employment for them. Grim hunger is now beginning to stare them in the face. Some of them are, perhaps, trusting to one scanty meal per day, and glad to get that same.

I have visited the suburbs of this town, and also conversed with many persons who are employed on public works. One man said to me, a labourer, "We had 6s. a week some time since—now we are cut to 5s., and the majority of us have families—and would that sum, do you think, pay rent, fuel, light, and food for us? No, no, it only keeps the life in us."—Correspondent of the *Waterford Chronicle*.

AGRARIAN OUTRAGE ON BAILIFFS.—Phillip Connors, bailiff, when assisting to dispossess, under *habere*, Daniel and James O'Brien, overholding tenants to the Rev. Mr. Harte, at Gurtroe, near Ballingarry, on Wednesday, was attacked, and so severely beaten with sticks and stones, that there is no hope of his recovery. The assailants broke his jaw and arm, and it is feared they also fractured his head. Three of the party are apprehended.—*Limerick Chronicle*.

Recreated from The Freeman's Journal, Dublin, June 8, 1846.

TRIUMPHANT DEFEAT OF THE COERCION BILL.

At last "the sad-eventful history" of coercion has reached its close. Ministers have been defeated by a majority of SEVENTY-THREE in a house of FIVE HUNDRED AND ELEVEN members. On this proud result we congratulate the people of Ireland—we congratulate the majority, and, above all, we congratulate the hardy and indomitable phalanx of the national representatives, led by the great leader, to whom victory is specially and essentially owing.

We do not detract from the just praise owing to the pure Whigs—they behaved well—nor to the Freetraders, who remembered the obligation which the generous conduct of Ireland had imposed upon them—nor even the Protectionists, who whatever their motives in the excess of their indignation and resentment, are still entitled to acknowledgement for their indirect contribution to the civil freedom of Ireland. All are worthy but beyond all, we confess our gratitude to the Irish members who steadily waged the gallant war, and with heroic determination fought every inch of ground—never yielding "one jot of heart or hope", but striking right onward with earnest will and irrefragable argument, until at length their labours had reached a glorious consummation in the total defeat—now and for ever—of unconstitutional oppression.

Much as we value the present victory, we value more the precedent which it has established in the policy of England. Coercion must be erased for ever from the active contemplation of British statesmen. This is the principle we would deduce from the overwhelming defeat of the Peel ministry. Having succeeded in carrying the greatest social reform that British minister ever conceived, in enjoying a popularity with the middle classes in England such as no minister ever enjoyed, Sir Robert falls an unlamented victim to his insane desire to forge fetters for Ireland.

Recreated from The Freeman's Journal, Dublin, June 29, 1846.

RESIGNATION OF SIR R. PEEL.
(From the Chronicle of Saturday.)

A Cabinet Council was held yesterday, immediately after which Sir Robert Peel proceeded to Osborne House, with a view, we have reason to believe, to tender to her Majesty the resignation of himself and his colleagues.

It is understood that Lord John Russell will be summoned to attend upon the Queen this day.

The Ministerial "explanations" will be made on Monday, by Lord Ripon in the House of Lords, and by Sir Robert Peel in the House of Commons.

Reprinted from The Freeman's Journal, Dublin, June 29, 1846.

THE CORN LAWS REPEALED.

The measures of Sir Robert Peel for the repeal of the Corn Laws, and the recognition of Free Trade in this country, are now the law of the land. The Royal Assent has removed them from the legislature, and given them an immediate practical operation of which the release of two millions and a half quarters of foreign corn from bond, at the low duty, will be the first and most striking evidence. The great battle of the session is now over—a battle which has lasted for five months in Parliament, and which was preceded by an agitation of thirty years, the last seven of which were marked by the dangerous machinations of the Anti-Corn Law League. To these machinations in part, but only in part, because had not Sir Robert Peel and his colleagues reasons for fraternising with the League, and had not the inscrutible dispensations of Providence in the failure of the Potato crop, furnished the minister with an unlooked for argument and pretext for his pretended conversion, the League would have been, for many years to come, the petty and inconsiderable clique which they were a few years ago. To Sir Robert Peel is the repeal of the Corn Laws as much due as to the agitation of the League. That generally sagacious general knew that he was no longer able to command the great party which he had been for ten years endeavoring to rally around him. He saw that he should either surrender his own innate revolutionary tendencies to his party, or attempt to command the votes of that party by a despotic exercise of his will. He tried the latter plan through two successive sessions, but the attempt proved a failure. He was able, it is true, to command a majority of his party's votes, but there was always a troublesome section who would not be dictated to, and who had spirit enough to denounce, as the height of ingratitude, the tyrannical bearing of a minister who owed them his proud and enviable elevation. Sir R. Peel felt that he could not carry his favorite schemes with the concurrence of this set of so called impracticables, and he began to "cast about" for men who would more willingly obey him. He conjectured that by attaching the Free Trade party to himself, he would be more certain of retaining his power, and more likely to carry out his views. He accordingly declared Free Trade, and was at once the idol of his new adherents. With the remnant of his old party and the bulk of the new, he succeeded at length, and after a hard and prolonged contest, in carrying out the measure. This feat achieved, it was natural that he should expect some favor—some gratitude—some scope for his comprehensive plan of progressive revolution; but he has been deceived in his expectations. Free Trade secured, the League has no further need of Sir Robert Peel. The Conservative party broken up, the Whigs find that he is a disagreeable obstacle in their rush to power. The country party, deceived and betrayed, will not factiously support a government, even in the good measures it may propose, knowing that evil in the main is to flow from their support. The very first test which is applied is quite sufficient, and Sir Robert Peel is no longer at the helm of affairs.

It is, however, with discarded statesmen, as with defunct heroes.—

"The evil that men do, lives after them."

The falling off of Sir Robert Peel does not merely affect his personal interests and designs, but bequeaths a legacy of misfortune to the party he has broken up. He has depraved the public confidence in statesmen, and, by consequence, in the whole system of Government and Legislation.

Recreated from The Belfast News-Letter, Belfast, June 30, 1846.

THE CORN AND COERCION BILLS—PUBLIC REJOICINGS.

Our publication of Monday evening having put our numerous city readers in possession of the merited fate of these bills respectively the important event was celebrated in the usual way that all such public benefits are hailed by the great mass of society. Shortly after dusk the streets were paraded by the various bands accompanied by lighted tarbarrels, which, in turn, were preceded by persons bearing polls surmounted by loaves of bread, emblematic of the plenty that must result from the abolition of the restrictions on foreign grain. Broken fetters also dangled from other polls, quite symbolic of the result of the fruitless attempt of our taskmasters to force new gyves for the moral and temperate people of this country. Thousands joined in the various processions; but their bearing and conduct were of the most orderly and peaceful description; and 10 o'clock witnessed the close of their jubilations.

We were much gratified at witnessing the demonstrations exhibited by the patriotic members of the Corn Market Ward Repeal Reading Rooms, which were splendidly illuminated, having a bust of the Liberator in one of the windows decorated with flowers and evergreens, their splendid flag forming a tasteful drapery. There were several tar barrels also blazing in the street.

Reprinted from The Cork Examiner, Cork, July 1, 1846.

COW STEALING.

Informations were this day granted by his Worship the Mayor and John Bagnell, Esq., against a man named Patrick Mullany, for the above offence. From the testimony of Constable Porter, it appeared, that Mr. James Adams had intimated to him last evening that a cow had been stolen from the lands of Rathpeacon on the morning of that day. The constable, in company with some of the men under his charge, immediately proceeded in search of the lost animal. After having examined several places, in which it was supposed she might be, without finding her, he went to the prisoner's house in Barrack-street, and was obliged to force open the door before he could gain admittance. In this house he found the cow, cut up in diverse pieces and shapes, and scattered about in different places. A witness identified the hide of the cow found by the constable, as having belonged to the animal stolen from Mr. Adams. After other corroborative evidence had been adduced, the magistrates decided on committing the prisoner for trial.

Mr. Bagnell remarked that Constable Porter had displayed creditable ingenuity on this occasion.

CAUTION TO COUNTRY PEOPLE.

A labouring man, apparently from the country, applied to the magistrates for redress against a fellow who had robbed him under the following circumstances. The countryman was about proceeding to London, when he met the prisoner on the quay, and inquired of him where the proper office was. The prisoner immediately volunteered to show him and also promised to get him a passage for half price, expressing at the same time great interest in the prosecutor's welfare. In gratitude for the prisoner's kindness he offered to treat him, which, having been accepted, they adjourned to a public house, when after remaining some time, the prosecutor handed the proprietor a pound in payment of the drink. On receiving the change, prisoner offered to buy him a purse in order to keep his money more securely. On getting the purse, witness handed the prisoner the balance; but, instead of depositing it in the purse, he dropped six shillings into his own pocket, and handed witness the remainder. The Magistrates were obliged to acquit the prisoner, in consequence of the prosecutor not having reckoned the money, before he handed it to the prisoner.

Scarcely a day elapses but some of those unfortunate people are obliged to pay dearly for their credulity, by the crowds of sharpers who frequent the quays, in order to practice on their simplicity; and who, particularly, in the seasons of emigration, succeed too often in their villainous designs.

Recreated from The Cork Examiner, Cork, August 14, 1846.

Employment and Food for the People.—Dungarvan, August 13.—I never thought that the prospects of the poor of this country could sink into such utter darkness, as they really have. Upon the horizon of the future there is scarcely an inkling of hope. It is truly melancholy to reflect upon the state to which the people are fast hastening. The last year was nothing to what the remainder of this, and the greater part of next year threaten to be. Parliament, if I recollect correctly, will separate on the 25th inst. The only body to which the people have a legitimate claim to look for conservative measures, will separate, leaving throughout the country in silent operation, elements that require only a very little time longer—perhaps a few months—to swell into a fierce hurricane, and sweep over the land with a fury that may carry destruction and desolation, which years may not be able to repair. Talk of war—civil, offensive, or defensive. Its raging fury falls infinitely short of the horrors that hunger will drive the people to commit.

Who can reckon upon the security for life in such a state of things? How far, then, would tenures, title, fee simples, or leaseholds avail against the ferocity of hunger-maddened wretches? Not the force of a spider-web.

The potatoes, the staple food of the country, are gone for this year. According as the new corn will be cut, it will come to market, and be sold at any price—it *must* be sold to make up September rent. The merchants will not keep it on hands if possible—they cannot afford to do so, particularly where no prospect appears to them of higher prices. The corn, then, goes to England. Good God! That food for which the hungry stomach of the poor Irishman yearns, is torn from the country, and sent into another. This is unnatural. Rents and rentals, shipping and all other trafficking, should give way to the first necessity of the country. God gave the land the power of vegetation and production, not to leave the country for foreign ports, but to feed his people. If there be an overplus, why, let it go, but let what is necessary be kept for the people whose labour produces it. Until such a state of things exists in Ireland, even where no famine is apprehended, we will be a starved and pauperised country.

To avert this fearful calamity that I have hinted at above, employment should be given the labourers. The most productive kind of labour, in every sense, is the draining and improving of waste land; which would be of service to the labourer, to the farmer, to the landlord, and to the country. More it would be a great preventative of many kinds of sickness, such as agues, some descriptions of fever, pthises, &c. For the damp of this country, arising in great part from bogs and marshy land, is the greatest enemy to health in our climate.

Let the landlords assemble in every county, and enter into *extensive* arrangements—for no other will do—as soon as possible, while they have yet time to do things effectually. As Sir R. Peel said, "the landlords can do more than Parliament."

END TO PUNISHMENT OF TRANSPORTATION.

Lord John Russell said on Friday evening in the House that Government were anxious to put an end to transportation to New South Wales. His opinion was, he said, that transportation ought to be much diminished; and with that object he intended to introduce a measure to abolish transportation for larceny, and continue it only with respect to cases where death was commuted to transportation. Thus instead of 4,000 persons being transported in the course of a year, the number would be greatly diminished. This will be a great reform in our system of jurisprudence.

DARING OUTRAGE.

On Saturday evening, as the steamer from Cove was landing her passengers at our quay, an outrage occurred that was nigh being fatal to the lives of one of our most useful citizens, Mr. Martin H. Conway and his Lady.—The circumstances are as follow.—On Mr. Conway getting on the landing plank, in order to hand Mrs. Conway on shore, a ruffian on the plank made a grab at his watch and chain, which he failed in getting; but the collision was so great that it threw Mr. Conway off his balance, and caused him and Mrs. Conway to fall into the water. The tide was fortunately very high at the time, and instant exertions being made, they were, after a lapse of a few minutes, happily landed on the quay. We are happy to say that Mrs. Conway is much recovered from the fright, which such an alarming accident was calculated to produce.

We hear many complaints of the want of sufficient convenience for the landing of passengers from the river steamers. We think this would be easily removed by having two planks—one for those in the fore-part of the vessel, and one for those in the after part. This would completely remove the cause of the complaint, and prevent ruffians from causing such accidents as the one we now mention.

Recreated from The Cork Examiner, Cork, August 17, 1846.

FASHIONABLE INTELLIGENCE.

VISIT OF HER MAJESTY TO DEVONPORT.—Her Majesty the Queen and Prince Albert, attended by their suite, will proceed from Osborne House on Tuesday next, in the Victoria and Albert yacht to Devonport, which place her Majesty will honour with her presence until the following Monday, when, if the weather be favourable for a water-excursion, her Majesty will proceed in the yacht for a short cruise off the Scill Islands, and then return to Osbourne House. During their stay at Devenport, the Queen and Royal Consort will dine and sleep on board the yacht, which will be accompanied by her tender, the Fairy.

The Queen and the Prince consort are expected, it is stated, to pay a short visit to their Majesties the King and Queen of the French, at Eu, in the course of about ten days or a fortnight, proceeding to the French coast in the Royal Victoria and Albert yacht, from Osbourne House. The Court is not expected to return to Windsor until quite the middle of October next.

Her Royal Highness the Duchess of Kent arrived at six o'clock on Friday afternoon, from her residence, Fregmore House, Windsor. Monday was the anniversary of the birth of her Royal Highness the Duchess of Kent, who completed her 60th year.

The Marquis of Landsdowne left London on Saturday afternoon for his seat, Bowood Park, Wilts.

The Countess of Charlemont has arrived in London, from Her Majesty's Marine Villa, Osbourne House, East Cowes.

The Marquis of Normandy arrived at Osbourne House on Friday, on a visit to the Queen, and had the honour of joining the royal circle at dinner. The noble marquis left on the following day.

The Hon. Cecil Lawless has taken a lodge for the grouse season in the moors of Westmoreland, where he is at present staying.

Recreated from The Freeman's Journal, Dublin, August 20, 1846.

PROGRESS OF THE POTATO DISEASE. THE CROPS, &c.

(*From the Waterford Chronicle.*)

A correspondent, on whom we can rely, informs us that not even a single field has escaped the blight in the county Wexford. Some farmers are "ploughing them out" in order to set something else; but all agree in saying that the potato crop will hardly pay for digging. The fields that were only partially *black* last week, are much worse this week. Some people, however, think that if the weather now set fine, the stalks may again get green and healthy. But this is a new conjecture. All parties are confounded. Our correspondent also informs us that the oat crop is also bad—in fact it is denominated by the farmer as "all chaff." He calculates it to be about half the usual average. Wheat and barley are considered a fair crop.

A revered correspondent writes to us from the neighbourhood of Kilmacthomas:—"The potato crop is totally lost in the Barony of Upperthird, even the small portion in the kitchen gardens are in a state of rapid decay."

(*From the Limerick Reporter.*)

The accounts we continue daily to receive, as well as our own personal observation, confirm our worst anticipation concerning the potato crop. In this state of things it becomes desirable to know how the seed is to be best preserved for the coming year. We have been informed by an intelligent farmer who speaks from his own practical experience that the best mode of saving seed is to allow the potato to remain in the ground till the first of December.—He also states that the seed is renewed and the potato preserved from decay by planting late—say from the 1st to the 21st of June—and that potatoes so planted will not be fit for use in that year (for they would be too small) but will make the best seed for the following year.

He made an experiment in some potatoes called Americans; on the 21st of June, 1844, he planted some of that description, and left them in the ground till the 1st of December, when he had them removed. They were not fit for eating, being small, but firm. He planted them in the following February, and had an excellent crop, in which there was not a tainted potato, and which kept free from rot till they were all consumed last month. But in June, 1845, he again planted a quarter of ground with these same potatoes for seed for the present year, and early in spring he put them down whole, and now there cannot be finer potatoes, not a taint in one of them, while the black track of desolation is seen on every side of him. We publish these facts for the information of our agricultural friends, leaving them to judge of their value and importance.

(*From the Limerick Chronicle.*)

Very few loads of new potatoes, entirely sound, are received to market, but the price has fallen to 5d white, and 7d cups per stone. At market last week, 607 car-loads, an excess of 27 over the previous week.

In Kerry the early and late potato crops have equally suffered from the disastrous blight. The state of Iveragh is so alarming, from the loss of the potato crop and want of employment, that the Knight of Kerry and the Rev. Mr. Tyrwitt have written to members of the cabinet on the subject.

Recreated from The Freeman's Journal, Dublin, August 21, 1846.

EMPLOYMENT IN IRELAND.

THE MARQUIS OF LANSDOWNE has, it will be seen, taken charge of a bill, prepared with a view to the proper supply of food to the Irish peasantry, under the calamity which has already befallen this country, in the failure of the potato crop. The bill evidently has reference to the creating of a new system in the development of the labour of Ireland—namely, the substitution of wages, as a means of sustenance, instead of the chance profits of the conacre crop. Great powers are to be entrusted to the Lord Lieutenant—too great under ordinary circumstances—authorizing him to make advances from the public money, to be repaid by the districts so relieved, by installments, at a moderate interest, within ten years. This scheme is not to supercede any subsidiary measures of relief dictated by the wisdom of Parliament or the benevolence of private individuals. The measure appears to us to be a timely one, and not injudiciously prepared. The employment of the poor peasantry upon public works, it is said, will tend to throw the land out of cultivation. We believe there are but too many of our poorer fellow-countrymen ready to be employed in both ways, if opportunity be given, not only here but in other lands. It is a clear mistake to suppose that the failure of the potato crop, as the Duke of Grafton has it, is owing to the imperfect cultivation of the soil in Ireland. If so, why are potatoes ruined in every quarter of the globe, and in every variety of soil?

POLICE OFFICE.—The trials which came on for hearing at this court, since Monday last, have been of little public importance. The chief cases were those of assault, and the parties principally engaged were females, of apparently quarrelsome habits.

Recreated from The Belfast News-Letter, Belfast, August 28, 1846.

MIRACLES OF SCIENCE.—At a recent meeting of the British and Foreign Institute, a model was shewn, of the new electric telegraph, by which a person, writing by the pressure of ivory keys, exactly like those of a piano forte, each representing a letter or a figure, can transmit, by means of a single extended wire, to any distance, 500 miles or 5,000, an almost instantaneous message, in words that shall be printed, by a corresponding machine, at the other end of the line, as fast as the sentence is spoken or performed as this.

Recreated from The Belfast News-Letter, Belfast, September 4, 1846.

THE IMPENDING FAMINE.

(*From the Clare Journal Tory paper*)

We feel it absolutely necessary, from the present state of the country, to call upon the government to take immediate and decisive steps to satisfy the clamours of a starving people. Provisions are rising in price every day. As for potatoes, there are very little indeed in market, and it is almost dangerous to make use of those offered for sale. Not one stone of potatoes can be obtained, without some of them being found tainted; and even those bring seven pence halfpenny. Indeed, we are strongly inclined to believe, that, for the sake of their health, the people should not be any longer allowed to use this diseased food. We direct attention to a circumstance mentioned at the late meeting in Cork, relative to a man whose death, according to medical authority was occasioned by the use of diseased potatoes. It is useless for the government to tell people now they do not wish to interfere with private trade, and will therefore leave the private trader to meet the demand. If this be the determination of our rulers, we tell them they may as well attempt to stem the tide with an egg-cup as preserve the peace of the country. Indian corn meal is now one shilling and eight pence a stone, an advance of two pence a stone within the last three days. If other provision therefore rise at this rate, we should like to know what family can support themselves, we speak not of the labouring classes alone. The oat crop is not at all productive—the yield is not anything equal to the past year, and therefore if the people are left without a supply of Indian corn meal, as they had last season, they will be totally unable to live. We think it our duty to speak out thus early, for it is by timely exertion on the part of the government that the privations can be met, and that outrages can be prevented. If the Indian corn meal is freely sold at a shilling a stone, and beyond this we consider it over its value, the peace can be preserved; but if the country be left to private trade or speculation, we may dread the worst consequences. The people are determined if such supply is not afforded them, not to allow the corn of the country to be exported and therefore, nothing but anarchy and confusion may be looked for.

About eleven o'clock on Friday night as a car, laden with corn, the property of Hugh Singleton, Esq., of Hazelwood, accompanied by two caretakers, was proceeding to the market of Limerick, on reaching a place, known by the name of Moll Ryan's Cross, situate between Knoppouge and Rathluba, the men were pelted with stones from behind a wall. While they were running to the opposite side for shelter, a shot was fired from the same direction that the stones came from, and the horse was wounded in the side by slugs. The men immediately turned the horse and brought back the load of corn.

TULLAMOORE.—On Friday last about 200 men, armed with scythes, pitchforks, &c., and fire-arms, went to a farm, held under the Court of Chancery, near Clonaslee, in the Queen's County, within a few miles of this town, and having driven off the keepers in charge of the crops, placed the grain crops on drays, carts, and cars, and carried all off, firing several shots by way of triumph. The keepers having made their way to the Clonaslee police, the constable and three men hastened to the scene; and on coming up to the Cross of Killoughy, in this county, they found a large body of men drawn up there, who told the police to "come on," for that they were ready for them, and kept them diverted by talk and threats for a considerable time, to give the party with the corn time to escape, which they did, by taking different directions. Colonel Dunne, J.P., of Brittas, having got information of the outrage, sent for the Killoughy and Mountbolis police, and went in search of the grain, but without effect; and then the business rested until this day (Monday), when constable Hill, of the Mountbolis station, with a party, succeeded in tracing the grain to a farm-yard near Mountpleasant, in the parish of Killoughy, in this county, where Mr. O'Malley and a party of police of this town, with Neal Brown, Esq., R. M., proceeded, and on the property being identified, took possession of it, and have it now in custody.—*Evening Packet.*

MURDEROUS FACTION FIGHT.—On Sunday week last, a riot occurred in the village of Kildysart, between two factions, when a man of the name of Behane was knocked down by a blow of a stone on the head, and while prostrate, he was kicked and struck again with a stone; from the effects of these he only survived two days. Dr. O'Grady, on a postmortem examination, found a great quantity of extravasated fluid on the brain, corresponding with the external wound. An inquest was held by T. Whitestone, Esq., and a verdict was found against some persons unknown. Four persons have absconded, against whom there are strong suspicions of their being perpetrators of the savage deed.

THE NAVY.—Active exertions are at present being made in Bristol, in order to procure men for the navy. Naval officers, and hardy looking tars, accompanied by a brass band, have been perambulating the streets, in order to *induce* men to enlist. This is another "sign of the times." The services of sailors are now solicited, instead of the men being dragged from their ships, and wives, and families, by means of the infamous press-gang system. There is, too, we apprehend, as marked an improvement in their treatment when on board, as in the means adopted to get them on board. Other improvements in the navy still remain to be effected.

Recreated from The Freeman's Journal, Dublin, September 16, 1846.

THE IMPENDING FAMINE.
STATE OF THE COUNTRY.
(*From the Limerick Reporter.*)

This (Tuesday) morning, about eight o'clock, as a bread wagon belonging to Mr. John Norris Russell was passing in the neighbourhood of John's-square, its progress was arrested by a party of persons, principally boys. Two young men having charge of the wagon resisted the aggression, but were ultimately overpowered, when the wagon was broken open, and rifled of something about a dozen loaves.

The outrage was thus far checked by the timely interference of several sensible persons that were attracted to the scene. The mayor was also immediately on the spot, and strongly remonstrated with the people against such conduct; apprehension having been felt, and rumour afloat, that "a rise out" was in contemplation, Colonel Mansel and a party of the 8th Hussars shortly joined his worship.

The bread-wagon, by this time, was allowed to proceed unmolested, minus the few loaves; and the mayor, on horseback, accompanied by Colonel Mansel and the Hussars, proceeded round the town, and down William-street, followed by a large crowd, which greatly increased in its progress.

The Mayor addressed the crowd at the corner of William-street, impressing upon them the necessity of abstaining from any outrage on person or property, and requesting their immediate dispersion, telling them that he had only just returned from Dublin, where he had been during the past week, in communication with the government, and that matters were in proper training for the setting of such public works on foot as would shortly insure them employment. The crowd immediately separated, and the city has since been quiet.

Recreated from The Freeman's Journal, Dublin, September 17, 1846.

DISGRACEFUL ATTACK ON LORD DE DECIES.

[FROM A CORRESPONDENT.]

On Wednesday last the Adjourned Road Sessions was held at Clashmore, for the barony of Decies within Drum, in the county of Waterford; and the Magistrates, having finished business about five o'clock, left the Court-house to proceed to their respective residences, when a large mob of about at least 3000 persons commenced throwing stones at Lord Stuart De Decies, the lieutenant of the county.

The Dragoons charged them, under volleys of stones, and must have wounded several of the rioters. One man had his ear and the side of his face cut off. Lord Huntingdon, Sir Richard Musgrave, Thomas J. Fitzgerald, Simon Bagge, and Richard Power Ronayne, Esqrs., magistrates, rushed amongst the mob, and did all they could to stop the throwing of stones, and but for their interference, the Dragoons would have fired, as they could not stand the stone throwing, *particularly from the Church-yard*. Nothing could equal the fury of the mob against his Lordship and Sir Henry W. Barron, who fortunately was not at the sessions. Several of the Dragoons were severely hurt.

We are happy to say his Lordship escaped unhurt—but for the Dragoons he would most certainly have been murdered.

It is most extraordinary why his Lordship should have been selected for such a murderous attack, for he is a kind and very indulgent landlord, and sets his ground for the value to the occupiers, and has 60 men employed at Ballyheeney, draining, at which they earn 1s. 6p. a day, besides employing about 300 men on other parts of his estate.

There is but one feeling prevailing among all well disposed persons, that this was a most disgraceful and undeserved attack on a good resident landlord and magistrate, who is daily doing acts of kindness for the poor.

Recreated from The Cork Examiner, Cork, September 25, 1846.

THREATENED INVASION OF THE CITY.

INFORMATION of an authentic nature reached authorities of the city, this morning, that a large multitude of people were collecting at Carrignavar, as a centre, for the purpose of proceeding to Cork, to pillage the stores and shops containing provisions.

The Chief Magistrate immediately took due precautions to prevent their approach. An arrangement was concerted with the Commanding Officer of the Garrison by which an adequate force is kept under arms, ready on the first intimation of the populace coming near the town, to be posted at the different approaches, and disperse them.

These people must be actuated by the greatest infatuation to attempt the sack of any portion of this City. In reference to the matter, we have received the following communications:—

We received the following this morning from a city correspondent:—

"EIGHT O'CLOCK, A.M.—I am just informed by a person from the place that the labourers from all surrounding country, from Carrignavar to Ballyhooly, are assembling at Ballynerdan, near Dunblog, and are preparing to march into Cork by the Ballyhooly Road. God grant there may be no outrage. They want employment, and that their miserable wages should be raised, by the farmers, from 6d. to 1s. per day."

[FROM OUR CORRESPONDENT.]

CLONMEL, 29TH SEPT., 1846.—A mounted orderly galloped through this town at 7 o'clock this evening, on his way to the Barracks; and, on inquiry, I have learned that he was the bearer of a requisition from the resident Magistrate at Dungarvan, to the commanding officer here, for a troop of Dragoons to proceed at once to that place. The letter further stated that a collision had taken place there between the military and the people, in which three of the latter were seriously wounded, one of whom died since. It appears that the people had openly expressed their determination to revenge this injury; that they had dispersed for the purpose of collecting arms, with which they intended to attack the military this night, whose position is very critical, as their force is not sufficient to oppose the numbers of people who are expected to assemble. There is no disposable force here at the present to forward—one of the troops of the 8th Hussars stationed here having marched to Carrick-on-Suir on yesterday, in anticipation of an outbreak taking place there. I am informed that the Commanding Officer did not think it advisable to send the remaining troop, but he sent off an express to the Colonel of the 8th Hussars, at Cahir, for aid and advice; but as there is only one troop there at present, it is not likely that the Colonel will send it, as by doing so he would leave that place defenseless. If the Government do not come forward speedily to the rescue of our famishing population, and adopt some determined and energetic measures for affording them food and employment, it requires no prophetic spirit to tell the frightful calamity which will befall this unfortunate land and its degraded and impoverished people, maddened as they are by hunger and despair; and should a famine outbreak take place, I doubt if England has sufficient military force at her command to suppress it, as their operations will not be confined to *one* district or locality, but will require to be extended over the kingdom at large. I am therefore satisfied that 60,000 men would not suffice for that purpose. Besides, flour and meal is more digestible food than iron or metal. It is therefore time not only for the Government but the landlords, merchants, and men of property in general, to be up and stirring in the cause of their suffering countrymen, if they have any desire to protect *their properties*, and preserve the peace of the country. A troop of the 8th Hussars arrived yesterday in Clogheen, to relieve the 1st Royal Dragoons. This being the only Cavalry Regiment in this neighbourhood, is very much harassed at present.

MALLOW, MONDAY, 12 O'CLOCK.—A body of men, in number nearly Five Hundred, marched through this Town about an hour and a half since on their way to the Workhouse. I accompanied Mr. Winn, P.I., and Mr. Robert Barry, Clerk of the Union, to the Workhouse; we found on our arrival the master endeavouring to appease the poor creatures who were divided into sections, scaling the inner walls, Mr. Winn stood on the wall and said "what do you want?" he answer was "we want something to eat, we are starving." Mr. Winn—"you shall get plenty to eat." on which the poor fellows gave a hearty round of cheers. Mr. Winn "Where do you come from?" Answer, *una voce*, "from Rahan." Mr. Winn, the Clerk, the master, the Schoolmaster, the Porter and myself, then assisted in taking down the names of the parties, their age and place of residence. There were only nine from Mallow; one poor man, named Batt Twoomey, of Ballinvuskig, declared to me in the most solemn manner, that for three weeks he lived on a drop of sour milk and had not half a stone of black potatoes for that time. I asked him where he got the milk, he told me that his wife begged in Mallow, a distance of three miles.

Another man, Leahy, said that the Board of Works commenced operations this day in Rahan, and that they only employed 40 men at Sevenpence a day! ! GOOD GOD, is Seven-pence per day sufficient to feed a family of seven or eight individuals, while Indian Meal is 1s 9d per stone? Alas! but they are Irish.

MALLOW, MONDAY NIGHT.—After I had left the Workhouse this day, I understand that there were over three hundred additional applicants, making in all about 700. Some got 1 lb of bread each, and as a sufficient quantity of bread was not in the house, the others got stirabout. In the evening about 300 went for dinner, and got none; they went away quietly—a person who was present said to me "It was heart-rending to see the poor fellows *fainting*." It is expected that a much larger number will visit the Workhouse to-morrow.   R.B.B.

Recreated from The Cork Examiner, Cork, September 30, 1846.

OLD CHAPEL-ROAD, DUNGARVAN, A SCENE OF THE LATE FOOD RIOTS.

Reprinted from The Illustrated London News, 1846.

FAMINE RIOT IN DUNGARVAN.
Fatal Collision with the Military.

Dungarvan, Monday Night.—I have only time to inform you that upwards of three thousand labourers from the surrounding districts assembled in Dungarvan to-day, seeking for work and a proper rate of wages.—They were dressed in flannel jackets and corduroys.—They walked in procession.

The military were under arms. The Riot Act was read. There was awful excitement in town all day. The Dragoons cleared the town, and on coming to Carroll's public-house, near the Christian schools, they were pelted fearfully with stones, which were answered by a discharge of musketry from the Dragoons. About 27 shots were fired—wounding a great many—*two* fatally.

Great credit is due to Mr. Howley, for his humanity and superior tact in the management of the forces under his command.

Tuesday Morning.—I understand a great many are badly wounded—one man died last night who was wounded in the upper part of the thigh, the bullet passing through the *scrotum*, lacerating it fearfully. The Treasury Minute regulating wages is the cause of all.

In haste, B.

Recreated from The Cork Examiner, Cork, September 30, 1846.

Food riots in Dungarvan reprinted from The Pictorial Times, London, October 10, 1846.

LORD JOHN RUSSELL'S LETTER TO THE DUKE OF LEINSTER.

From the *Evening Post* of yesterday we take the following important document. Would we could say it was as full of hope, as it is of cold, heartless philosophising. LORD JOHN RUSSELL leaves everything to the Irish Landlords, and refuses to interfere with trade. The old Whig cry! His advice to the Irish people is to be estimated at its value. When men are starving—to tell them to be clean and well-conditioned, is peculiarly cheering and useful.

Before giving the letter, we have to express our acknowledgements to the Editor of the *Constitution*, who kindly lent us his copy of the *Post*—our's not having arrived, by some Post Office *mistake*, such as generally occurs in cases of importance. We had literally to transcribe the letter.

Downing-street, October, 17th, 1846.

MY DEAR DUKE—The Royal Agricultural Society, of which you are the head, sent a Deputation not long ago to the Lord Lieutenant, representing, that, instead of public works of an unprofitable nature, the Baronies should have the power of undertaking Works of a useful and profitable nature. It had been our hope and expectation, that Landed Proprietors would have commenced Works of Drainage and other improvements on their own account; thus employing people on their own estates, and rendering the land more productive for the future. In that case, it would have been only the surplus labour which would have been employed on roads, and other Works not immediately profitable.

The act, however, was put in operation in the Baronies, in a spirit the reverse of that which I have described. It was taken for granted that the Public Works were the chief object to be regarded, and Proprietors began to calculate, that as so large a sum was to be repaid from their estate, they should not be able to commence, or even to continue, private enterprises for the improvement of their own lands.

When the case was brought before the Lord Lieutenant, we lamented the wrong direction in which the Act had been turned, but admitting the necessity of the case and anxious to obtain the willing co-operation of the landlords, we authorised the Lord Lieutenant to deviate from the letter of the law and give our sanction for advances for useful and profitable works of a private nature. But, after having incurred this responsibility, I am sorry to see that in several parts of Ireland, calls are made upon Government to undertake and perform works which are beyond the power and apart from the duties of Government.

For instance, it seems to be expected that we should not only pay at an unusual rate of wages, but that we should maintain in this time of scarcity, the usual price of food. A moment's thought will shew that this is impossible. A smaller quantity of food is to be divided among the same number of human beings. It must be scarcer; it must be dearer. Any attempt to feed one class of the people of the United Kingdom by the Government, would, if successful, starve the other part—would feed the producers of the potatoes which had failed, by starving the producer of the wheat, oats, and barley, which had not failed. All that we have undertaken with the regard to food, therefore, is to endeavour to create a provision trade at fair mercantile prices, where no provision trade has hitherto existed, where, without assistance none might be willing to undertake a new and unpopular occupation.

But that which is not possible by a government is possible by individual and social exertions. Every one who travels through Ireland observes the large stacks of corn which are the produce of the late harvest. There is nothing to prevent the purchase of grain by proprietors or by committees, and the disposal of those supplies in shops furnished on purpose with flour at a fair price with a moderate profit. This has been done, I am assured, in parts of the Highlands of Scotland—where the failure of the Potatoes has been as great and as severe a calamity as it has been in Ireland.

There is, no doubt, some inconvenience attending these modes of interference with the market price of food.—But the good overbalances the evil. Local Committees, or agents of landowners, can ascertain the pressure of distress, measure the wants of a district, and prevent waste or misapplication. Besides, the general effect is, to bring men together, and induce them to exert their energy in a social effort directed to one spot; whereas the interference of state deadens private energy, prevents forethought—and, after superceding all other exertion, finds itself at least unequal to the gigantic task it has undertaken.

There are other questions, however, extending beyond the exigency of the day, which, it seems to me, demand the attention of the Landed Proprietors of Ireland, much more than that of the Government.

It has been calculated that one-fifth of the cultivated land in Ireland has hitherto produced potatoes. After the present lamentable failure, what course is to be taken? Some men of science deem that the Potato can no longer be relied on as an article of food; others say that time may remove the disease. The Editor of the *Gardiner's Chronicle* states that the explanation of the Potato disease, founded on the hypothesis of some unknown miasma, cannot be accepted as satisfactory; but, neither can it be rejected, seeing how signally all other explanations have failed. Seeing, then, that science furnishes us with no means of estimating the effect of the prevalent disease upon the Potato plant in future years, it would be impossible for the government, with any propriety, to give advice to the Owners or Occupiers of land in Ireland.

It is clear, however, that potatoes cannot be relied upon, as they have been hitherto. A cottier cannot hope to be able to pay a large rent for conacre, and the farmer cannot hope to obtain the cottier's labour, by allowing him land for potatoes which may, probably, fail. It is, therefore, a most important question for the people of Ireland, in what manner the deficiency of food is, in future, to be supplied.

The nature of the grain or root which is best adapted for this purpose—the course of husbandry which ought to be followed—the means of procuring seed. All these are important problems to which the attention of the Agricultural Society of Ireland cannot too soon be directed.

One thing is certain—in order to enable Ireland to maintain her population, her agriculture must be greatly improved. Cattle, corn, poultry, pigs, eggs, butter, and salt provisions have been and probably will continue to be, her chief articles of export. But, beyond the food exchanged for clothing and colonial produce, she will require in future, a large supply of food of her own growth or produce which the labourer should be able to purchase with his wages. In effecting this great change, much good may ultimately be done. But unless all classes co-operate and meet the affliction of Providence with fortitude and energy, the loss of the potato will only aggravate the woes and the sufferings of Ireland.

Such, then, is the great lesson which, by the influence of the higher classes, and of such good landlords as yourself, may be taught to the Irish people. They should be taught to take advantage of the favourable condition of their soil and surrounding sea; to work patiently for themselves in their own country as they work in London and Liverpool for their employer; to study economy, cleanliness, and the value of time; to aim at improving the condition of themselves and their children.

I would here conclude this letter which is already too long; but I cannot do so without expressing my conviction that there is every disposition in persons of property in Ireland to meet their difficulties fairly, and to submit to any sacrifices which the public good may require.

I remain, my dear Duke, yours very faithfully,

J. RUSSELL.

To His Grace the Duke of Leinster.

Recreated from The Cork Examiner, Cork, October 30, 1846.

EXPORTATION OF GRAIN.

The following letter has been received by Sir Benjamin Morris Wall from Mr. Redington, in reply to the memorial forwarded to his Excellency from the Waterford Board of Guardians, praying that government would issue an order to prevent the exportation of grain, flour, &c., from this country, and that the distillation of spirits from grain should be stopped:—

"Dublin Castle, 29th Oct., 1846.

"SIR—In reference to the memorial signed by you as Chairman of the Waterford Board of Guardians on the 22d instant, I am directed by the Lord Lieutenant to state, that the suggestions therein contained shall not fail to receive the fullest consideration of government. I have the honour to be, Sir, your most obedient servant,

"T. N. REDINGTON.

"Sir B. M. Wall, D.L., J.P., Waterford.

Reprinted from The Cork Examiner, Cork, November 2. 1846.

THE FAMINE MONGERS.—FURTHER CORN IMPORTATIONS.

LIVERPOOL, TUESDAY AFTERNOON.—All of a sudden the famine-mongers seem to have discovered the truth of what we have all along stated, and it is now admitted there is to be no famine at all. This sudden change of opinion is only to be accounted for in the fact of the speculators having had the market in their own hands for a time sufficient to have served their purposes. The corn market to-day has been miserably dull, as will be seen from our report.

Even in the present early stage of importation we continue to receive large supplies. The Liverpool bill of entry for yesterday and to-day announces the following in the port:—

Forty-two thousand bushels of wheat.
Twenty-one thousand bushels of Indian corn.
Eleven thousand one hundred barrels of flour.
Seven thousand six hundred bushels of barley.
One thousand bags of peas.
Besides other provisions.—*Morning Herald.*

Reprinted from The Cork Examiner, Cork, November 6, 1846.

STATE OF THE COUNTRY.

(From the Kerry Examiner.)

RIOT AT THE TRALEE WORKHOUSE.—On Tuesday morning last, a body of unemployed labourers, amounting to over one hundred, proceeded from this town to the poor house, where they demanded a breakfast. The unfortunate men were in a state of great excitement, and refused to listen to the remonstrances of G.D. Stokes, J.P., W. Denny, J.P., J. Drummond, R.M., and Mr. Hackshaw, C.I., who were in attendance. It was, therefore, deemed necessary to call out the military and police. After some show of opposition, a few of the ringleaders having been taken into custody, employment promised, &c., the wretched men agreed to leave the house. Great excitement was caused amongst the poor seeing the prisoners marched to gaol.

A wall was levelled on the property of Mr. C. Minchin, of Rutland, on Friday night. Report stated that he reduced his labourers' wages to 6d. per day, and that all left his work in consequence. His steward yesterday (Monday) spoke loudly in the street to some gentry of the kindness of his master, whom he said was falsely maligned as he gave 8d. per day, and the overseer said that that was *fine* wages at such a season. Mr. Minchin has not contributed to the Shinrone relief fund.

Near Kylepark, on Wednesday night, the house of a man of the name of Michael Cahill was entered by four men, two of whom were armed, and having demanded what firearms were in the house, they obtained a gun which they carried off, first striking Cahill a blow on the head with a pistol, from the effects of which he has since perfectly recovered.

We understand that in consequence of serious riots apprehended in Castleisland, the police and a party of the military marched for that town yesterday (Monday) morning.

Recreated from The Freeman's Journal, Dublin, November 12, 1846.

MORE STARVATION.

William J. Maher, Esq., one of our County Coroners, held an inquest at Corbertstown, in this county on view of the bodies of four individuals, found drowned in a dyke on the townsland of Webbsborough, on Sunday last. It appeared from the evidence at the inquest that the mother and three children had been in that neighbourhood for some days in a state of very great destitution. On Friday last they had been relieved at the house of Hugh Muldowney, a respectable farmer living in Corbertsown; they were subsequently seen loitering on the road at Webbsborough—the mother, about 30 years old, appeared to be in an unconscious state, probably from mental anxiety and hunger. The bodies were brought to a house on the road side, the nearest that could be procured, by the police—they presented a truly heart-rending spectacle; partially covered with filthy rags saturated with mud, and frozen, having been exposed to the inclemency of the weather. The hand of one child, and part of the foot of another, had been devoured, probably by rats. Doctor Gwydir, of Freshford, made a minute *post mortem* examination of the bodies of the mother and eldest daughter, a child about nine years old. The Doctor was unable to detect in the stomach or the bowels of the mother a trace of food having entered for more than twenty hours before death. The child's stomach contained a very small quantity of half-digested potatoes. The following was the verdict of the jury:—

We find that deceased and her three children's deaths were caused by drowning, and we find from the *post mortem* examinations made by Doctor Gwydir on two of the bodies, that they were in a state of hunger bordering on starvation, but how the bodies came into the dyke of water, whether by accident or design on the part of the mother, we have no evidence to show.—*Kilkenny Journal.*

Recreated from The Cork Examiner, Cork, December 4, 1846.

PURCHASE OF FIRE-ARMS.—The purchase of fire-arms in this town by the country people, who manifest the greatest avidity to possess themselves of weapons, continues unabated. The mania has, it appears, extended to the north—and in Cavan and Fermanagh the sale of guns and pistols was never so great as at the present time.—*Tipperary Free Press.*

TEMPLEMORE—CAPTURE OF ROBBERS.—The house of a man named John Stapelton, of Knocks, near this town, was attacked by four armed ruffians on the night of the 1st instant, who broke open a drawer and took therefrom 20£ in notes; it was reported to the police at ten o'clock, who divided themselves into three small parties and searched the town and suburbs—two of the three came in contact with the four lads in a public house, regaling themselves with meat and punch for which they gave a three pound note to change; the police kept them at the point of the bayonet until the head constable, with another man, arrived. The fellows made the greatest resistance possible, so that it took more than 40 minutes before the police could succeed in handcuffing them. There was a loaded pistol got, nineteen pounds fifteen shillings and sixpence, in notes and silver, and plenty of powder, slugs, and blank cartridges made up; they are men of the worst character, one of them having been tried for the murder of his own nephew about two years ago at Nenagh assizes. The names of the ruffians are Michael Whelan, Timothy Grace, Thomas Maher, and Phil Kennedy, stout able fellows. They were this day committed to Thurles by the magistrates and sent forward under a strong escort of constabulary.—*Nenagh Guardian.*

Last week some persons entered a farmer's cowhouse near Boyney, where a cow was fastened by the head with an iron chain to the manger; they severed the body from the head, leaving the head, and carrying off the remainder.—*Ballyshannon Herald.*

Recreated from The Freeman's Journal, Dublin, December 7, 1846.

PROGRESS OF STARVATION.

DEATH BY DESTITUTION AT MARYBOROUGH.—On Saturday last a labouring man, named Wm. Fitzpatrick, died at Ter-lane, Maryborough. From the evidence given at the inquest an intelligent jury found for their verdict that the deceased died of want and destitution. Language is inadequate to describe the horrifying misery with which the deceased was encompassed. The night he died, we understand, there was neither fire nor candle-light in the wretched hovel—no drink to allay the death-thirst of his parched lips but cold water; while his bed was a wisp of straw, on a damp floor, with little or no covering. It appeared that his wretched wife had neither food nor covering for her four children. They were unanimous in their verdict that the deceased died of want and destitution.—*Leinster Express.*

DEATH FROM HUNGER.—Again has starvation sent another victim to his account in this unfortunate county. Mr. John Atkinson, coroner, held an inquest in Ballina, on Tuesday, on view of body of Hugh Daly. Dr. Whittaker, who made a *post mortem* examination of the body, gave it as his opinion that deceased died for want of sufficiency of food.—*Mayo Telegraph.*

RUMOURED OUTBREAK IN KILKENNY—We have heard that private letters reached town yesterday, stating that an outbreak of rather a serious nature took place in Kilkenny city on Saturday. The accounts which reached us are rather vague, but from what we could learn of the rumour it appears that a very large number of people collected in the town and attacked some flour mills and baker's shops. The military were called out, and after charging the people with fixed bayonets, order was in some measure restored. The accounts state that the people were fired on from the mills and bakers' houses, but it is not reported that any person was killed. The military did not fire, but dispersed the people with the bayonet without doing any injury. Mr. Carter, a gentleman connected with the Board of Works, escaped (by the fleetness of his horse) from an attack made on him by the people. The state of feeling in the town and districts about it is said to be very excited in consequence of the occurrence alluded to.—*Freeman.*

Reprinted from The Cork Examiner, Cork, December 9, 1846.

SKIBBEREEN.

We have little space to allow us, as we would wish, to refer to the second letter of our Special Reporter, and an important meeting of the Relief Committee of this afflicted town. If the letter be appalling in its details, the meeting is infinitely more appalling in its statements. What are these statements?

Disease and death in every quarter—the once hardy population worn away to emaciated skeletons—fever, dropsy, diarrhea, and famine rioting in every filthy hovel, and sweeping away whole families—the population perceptibly lessened—death diminishing the destitution—hundreds frantically rushing from their home and country, not with the idea of making fortunes in other lands, but to fly from a scene of suffering and death—400 men starving in one district, having no employment, and 300 more turned off the public works in another district, on a day's notice—seventy-five tenants ejected here, and a whole village in the last stage of destitution there—Relief Committees threatening to throw up their mockery of an office, in utter despair—dead bodies of children flung into holes hastily scratched in the earth, without shroud or coffin—wives travelling ten miles to beg the charity of a coffin for a dead husband, and bearing it back that weary distance—a Government official offering the one-tenth of a sufficient supply of food at famine prices—neither mill nor corner store within twenty miles—every field becoming a grave, and the land a wilderness!

The letter and the report will prove that, even in a single feature of the many horrors that have given to the district of Skibbereen an awful notoriety, we have not in the least exaggerated.

Greatly pressed as we are for space, we cannot avoid calling the earnest attention of every friend

OLD CHAPEL-LANE, SKIBBEREEN.

Reprinted from The Illustrated London News, 1846.

of humanity to the noble exertions of Dr. Donovan and the Catholic Clergymen of the town; nor can we refrain from alluding to the liberality of Sir Wm. Wrixon Becher, who has not only given a large subscription to the funds of the Relief Committee, but made such abatements in the rents of his tenantry as will, we trust, enable them to pass through the ordeal of this year, and prepare for the next.

It will be seen that the Committee are about commemorating, in an enduring form, the splendid liberality of a worthy man—Mr. Daniel Welpy, whose conduct may well put the haughty, heartless aristocrat to the blush.

At length, an official inquiry is being set on foot as to the number of deaths, and the amount of destitution; but not before all men have united in heartily execrating the criminal apathy and fatal policy of the present Government.

Recreated from The Cork Examiner, Cork, December 18, 1846.

ATTEMPT TO MURDER.

ATHLONE, MONDAY, DEC. 21.—I lament to have to communicate to you that an attempt was made to murder the Messrs. Longworth, of Glynwood, last evening, but providentially the assassins failed in their deadly purpose. Mr. John Longworth, who is a deputy lieutenant of the county, was returning home to Glynwood, about four miles from the town, so early as four o'clock in the evening, when they were fired at in the avenue of their own demesne. Mr. L. was driving his own carriage, a servant sitting behind; but most fortunate the shot did not take effect upon any of the parties, nor did any of them pursue the assassins, as from the thickness of the plantation it would be worse than useless, and none of the parties were armed. When the shot was fired, the horses under the carriage, being high spirited, ran away at full speed, and but for this occurrence, it is more than probable a second shot would have been fired with more deadly effect. No one can assign the slightest reason for this diabolical attack. There are not better landlords or more excellent resident gentlemen in any county in Ireland.—They keep packs of hounds, and contribute in every way to the amusement of the gentry, as well as to the employment and relief of the peasantry in their neighbourhood. The country is in a most awful state. I fear that many of us will be provided for before the winter is well over.—*Saunders.*

(From the Limerick Chronicle).

There are computed to be fully three thousand tons of Government provisions stored up in charge of the Commissariat in this district, and laying by for some weeks, which no entreaty or inducement can unlock. Were only one-third of this vast quantity sold out to the Relief committees for distribution, the fearful pressure on the local market which merchants, with all their exertion, are unable to meet, would be so reduced, as to abate an incalculable mass of misery and discontent. Under the present exorbitant prices of food, and unexampled deficiency of produce, many a poor family is ground down to the last stage of mortal suffering, and sinking fast into an early grave. Who can disguise the appalling fact, that not a day has passed of this month without hearing that a fellow-creature has perished of absolute hunger?—and the victims of death are fast increasing. The Coroner's inquests proclaim this awful accusation, by the verdicts on record. Such an indulgence, then, as we now earnestly implore from the Government, could but lightly, if at all, disturb the rapid profits of the regular traders, who, it is obvious, have more orders than they can execute; and if some partial relief is not conceded from the source we mention (for where else can the people, under such a visitation, look for it) famine and disease will make "rich church-yards," and the natural conclusion of the country must be, that Lord John Russell is sustaining a mercantile monopoly in the bread of life at the sacrifice of thousands of the Queen's unfortunate subjects in Ireland, whose spectre forms now begin to startle the passer-by, as they totter in the cold street.

THE ELECTRIC TELEGRAPH was put to new use on Thursday. Mr. Hudson, "the Railway King," gave, as Mayor of York, a grand entertainment in the Guildhall of that city. While the wine circulated, a message arrived by Telegraph announcing that the Mayor of Newcastle was entertaining a large party in that town (80 miles distant), and that they were about to toast "the health of the Lord Mayor and prosperity of the city of York." The announcement was received with cheering, and the good folks who sent it were informed by the same swift messenger that the Yorkists were in return drinking "to the health of the Mayor of Newcastle and Prosperity to its town and port."

Recreated from The Cork Examiner, Cork, December 28, 1846.

STATE OF THE COUNTRY.

FAMINE and outrage still form the sad burden of Irish intelligence. In the poorer and more barren districts deaths by starvation are of such frequent recurrence, that some of our more eloquent contemporaries tell us, that coroners and coffins are as much wanting as food for the people. The descriptions of the distress in those districts are so ghastly and appalling, that it is impossible to read them without shuddering. Much has been recently done with a view to alleviate this terrible distress in some degree, but we fear all efforts, however strenuous, must fall far short of effectual and general relief. Even in the heart of large and opulent towns, there is a dreadful amount of human misery meeting the eye at every step. The workhouses are full to overflowing, and even already there are but few vacancies for new-comers except those caused by the deaths which, in large numbers, daily take place within the walls. We have the testimony of the medical men of our town, that fever is very prevalent here, chiefly introduced by the starving wretches who hourly swarm into our streets from the country. If such be the condition of the towns, what must be the state of the rural districts. Famine and disease are not, unfortunately, the only evils of the time. The catalogue of outrages in most of the country papers is quite long and as frightful as that of the woes of an unprecedented privation. Attempts to murder, robberies of firearms, and plunder of property, form the staple of each day's news. With respect to the so called mania for firearms, it is impossible to gather from the accounts of our contemporaries its true aim. Some assert positively that the purchasers are of the lowest and poorest class, and that their object is not the protection of food, but the unlawful means of procuring it; others, on the contrary, insist that the increased briskness of the gun trade is caused by the demand made by the farmers, who have still some store of food to guard from the attacks of the necessitous. The truth, perhaps, lies midway between both statements. Firearms are bought for both purposes. Certain it is the demand for firearms in Ireland has furnished certain hard-hearted writers in the London press with a strong argument, which they were not too slow to seize, against the extension of English charity to Ireland. We are gratified to perceive, however, that a large and honest portion of the London press has taken a noble and more Christian view of the whole Irish question than the journals to which we allude; and we quote, elsewhere, with pleasure, the language of the London *Standard* and *Sun*, as a true index of the mind of the better class of thinkers in England on the subject of Irish distress. Meanwhile, we are not idle at home. Every method, within the power of the wealthy and influential to devise and put in operation, is being tried; and we doubt not that partial success at least will crown their benevolent exertions.

Recreated from The Belfast News-Letter, Belfast, December 29, 1846.

(*From the Mayo Constitution.*)

MORE DEATHS FROM STARVATION.—The long feared crisis of starvation has arrived. Each week we have had to record the deaths of our fellow beings who have been victims to the monster, hunger. Last week we recorded *nine* deaths; this week we have to add *six* more to the fearful catalogue. The rapid ravages of hunger were frequently foreboded by us; but without creating an effort to stay them. We now again declare that the deaths which have occurred are but the mere shadow of the great coming event, which, unless provided against, will be fearful, but we think the opening of the government food depots might tend to check it, as we have found that in almost every case the poor creatures, the members of whose families have been starved to death, might have been able to procure food for some time to come, had provisions been sold at reasonable prices and in small quantities.

Recreated from The Freeman's Journal, Dublin, December 31, 1846.

THE FAMINE.

From north to south, from east to west,
Through our afflicted land,
Gaunt Famine stalks with dismal mien,
And spreads its wasted hand;

For direful Pestilence hath smote
The people's humble food,
And hunger, with its wolfish pangs,
Is raging in their blood!

And Manhood's boasted strength is past—
His wonted vigour fled,
His childhood's feebleness returns—
Despair weighs down his head,

All hope, all energy is lost—
Still through affections claim
He staggers to his task,
Till life forsakes his famished frame.

If for our sins, this heavy blow,
A judgement dread, is sent,
Oh! may it bear a happy fruit,
And teach us to repent!

To mend our lives,
In after time our children this to tell,
Tho low the stroke, yet by God's grace,
At last it ended well!

Recreated from The Belfast News-Letter, Belfast, February 5, 1847.

1847

Selected Headlines

MILITARY SHEEP STEALERS	84
A CORPSE FOR SALE	90
FOOD RIOTS IN THE CITY	92
HEALTH OF THE LIBERATOR	102
THE DISCOVERIES OF 1846	102
THE FATE OF EMIGRANTS	104
DELETERIOUS FOOD FOR THE PEOPLE	108
DEATH OF MR. O'CONNELL	109
THE YOUNG IRELANDERS	121
MORE PRIEST-HUNTING	128

MILITARY SHEEP STEALERS.

In the course of last week a gentleman residing in the vicinity of Middleton, near Killea, (Mr. Welland) engaged a prize ram for breeding purposes for £20 which, with two sheep, was left out at night to pasture in a field about a mile distant from Middleton. On missing them one morning, information was conveyed to the police, who made every effort to discover their whereabouts, but with no success. The secret, however, soon transpired. A knife, lost by the depredators, was found, and, on its being shown by the police to a butcher resident in Middleton he instantly identified it as his property, which on the previous evening he lent to a few of the soldiers of the 47th Regt., a company of which is at present stationed in Middleton, with a view to the *protection of property*, as well as the preservation of the peace of the country. The constabulary instantly proceeded to Thomas Street, Middleton, where the military are quartered, and on examination discovered portions of the carcasses of the slaughtered animals safely deposited in a coal hole. Suspicion strongly attaching to three of the gallant corps, they were arrested and taken before the sitting magistrates, who decided on receiving information against them; and now they await their trial at the ensuing sessions in durance.

It is to be regretted that the conduct of a few scoundrels should have the effect of bringing into disrepute a gallant body of men, such as unquestionably is the 47th Regt., who, since the unhappy occurrence, are denominated by the people here—"the 47th sheep stealers."—*Middleton Correspondent.*

A Fast Day.—A clergy man in a neighbouring parish, belonging to the Archdiocese of Tuam, announced on Sunday week, from the altar of his chapel, that the following Wednesday, Friday, and Saturday, would be fast days of strict obligation upon one meal. One of his congregation with great truth exclaimed—"Father Charles, you need not take the trouble to tell us that—sure every day now is a fast day with us, and we're fortunate and happy the day we can get even one meal for our families."—*Galway Mercury.*

Upset of the Enniskillen Coach.—The opposition night coach, which left the Imperial hotel, Sackville-street, on Thursday evening for Enniskillen, on arriving within about four miles of Navan, was overturned by the endeavour to avoid some carts which were passing along the road. Fortunately no injury was sustained by the passengers, among whom was a female, an "outside," who had a narrow escape. After about an hour's delay, the coach was re-adjusted by the united efforts of the sufferers. Owing to the depth of the snow on the road between Drogheda and Navan, the Enniskillen mail was also detained three hours beyond its time.

Fatal Conflict.—A raffle for a horse skin, was being held on Saturday night, in the house of a man named John Sheehan at Leamybrien, about six miles from Dungarvan, on the road leading from that town to Waterfrord, being within a few miles of Kilmacthomas. The police of the station Leamybrien, having received information that one John Coghlan, against whom there was a warrant for murder, was at this raffle, proceeded in a body to the number of six, to Sheehan's house. On reaching it, four of the police entered, when the lights were all put out in the kitchen, but there was a light in the room which one of the police took up into the kitchen, when it was quenched by some of the persons in the house. It would appear that about eighty persons assembled there. Immediately on the extinguishing of the light, a fearful scuffle ensued in the dark, between the four police and the people, in which some of the police were disarmed. The police succeeded in getting out of the house, when they (the police) were immediately followed by a number of men with sticks, out of the house, and a desperate conflict took place, terminating in the shooting of two unfortunate men, Coghlan and Mooney. An inquest was partially held on the bodies, at the scene of the conflict, on Sunday morning, as far as seeing the bodies. It was terminated in Dungarvan, on Monday evening, about six o'clock. Mr. Gamble was the coroner. Verdict, justifiable homicide.—*Waterford Chronicle.*

Recreated from The Cork Examiner, Cork, January 1, 1847.

LEITRIM.—A great number of people are dying here; some days it is not unusual to see from this neighbourhood, and including the poorhouse, twelve funerals. The number on last Monday was fifteen.—*Ballinasloe Star.*

A memorial to the Lord Lieutenant has been sent from the Ennis relief committee, declaring "the conduct of the suffering poor of that locality, has been patient and exemplary in the highest degree, but there is a point beyond which endurance cannot be expected, and that the quietness and submission, hitherto so exemplarily manifested, must cease if provisions are not supplied at rates nearer to the means of the poor."—*Clare Journal.*

To the list of deaths by starvation it becomes our unpleasant duty to add one. Pat Hackett, a poor man of large family, was working on the Fahy road till last Saturday; he was in great poverty, but sad as was his condition he did not reveal it, through a mistaken idea of shame. On Sunday last, he fell ill, and died immediately through inanition. There is no blame attached to the authorities, as no money was due to him. Many a person though is going down into the grave "unchronicled and unknown."—*Ballinasloe Star.*

DEATH BY STARVATION.—Within a few miles of this city (Armagh,) there has fallen a victim to starvation. Deceased was of the name of Tomlinson, of the neighbourhood of Tartaraghan; and it appeared on the inquest held on the body by George Henry, Esq., coroner; that he and his wife and three children had existed for some months past on miserable food given them by the farmers of the place; that for days previous to his death, the whole family had nothing to eat except raw kale and turnips, without a particle of meal or other food; and, further, that he died begging a drink of water with meal in it, he was a man of only 45 years of age, strong and healthy previous to this winter.—*Armagh Guardian.*

EMIGRATION FROM SLIGO.—This week several poor creatures left this port for England, there to take shipping for America; they were nearly all destitute of clothes, money, or sea stores, and how they will be able to make their way to the United State is, indeed, a mystery. But the fact of the people leaving the country in the very depth of winter, on the eve, too, of a festival most sacred and holy in the estimation of the pious Irish peasantry, affords lamentable evidence of the appalling destitution which prevails. The dread of starvation has forced those poor people to brave the perils of the deep, at a time when emigrants never before attempted to cross the Atlantic. Since October last, upwards of three thousand souls left this port for America. Judging from this circumstance, we may safely predict that emigration will be enormous during the ensuing spring.—*Sligo Champion.*

DEATH FROM DESTITUTION.—Mr. Richard Keough, one of the coroners of the county Roscommon, held an inquest at Killanvoy, on the body of Patrick M'Keon. After the examination of several witnesses, the jury returned a verdict—"That the death of the deceased was occasioned through want and hunger."—*Athlone Sentinel.*

Recreated from The Belfast News-Letter, Belfast, January 1, 1847.

DEATH FROM STARVATION.

Churchtown Dec. 29th, 1846.

SIR—Political economy is doing its bloody work—slowly, steadily, but not the more surely. One day we read of 47 deaths from starvation in Mayo, ratified by the solemn verdicts of so many coroners' juries. Another, we read of frightful destitution in Skibbereen, dreadfully augmented by fever and dropscal complaints. Not a single day passes by without abundant evidence of the total inadequacy of the present government, to wield the destinies of this great empire, or to preserve from *actual starvation* the great majority of this long misgoverned and unfortunate country.

Were you to seek for an exception to the general distress prevailing over the face of the country, could you discover one spot before another not entirely suffering through the dreadful ravages of the famine, you may fix on this parish as a resting place—as an oasis in the desert. True, our people are not *all* employed—true, the rate of wages allowed is *not* entirely sufficient for the support of the working man himself; but, ere this, we have had no reason to complain of any death *immediately* caused by starvation. This was a proud, triumphant boast; but now, Sir, we can no longer make a similar boast—one of our people—one of God's poor people—has already gone to his account, a victim to Whiggery, before that just and awful God, who on the last day will see no distinction between the lord and his vassal—the beggar and the prime minister—before the Court of Justice where paltry special pleading on Bourke's political economy will not avail.

Yes, Sir, a poor fellow, named Courtney, after working a few days on the public road, badly fed and worse clothed, caught cold. Little though his earnings were, 10d. a-day, doled out with a niggard hand, still it kept him alive till sickness prevented his being able to work, and, horrid to relate, he was obliged in his pitiable state to depend for *several days on cabbage to support existence*, till death more merciful than our rulers, came to the rescue, and took him to himself. He has left a wife and six children in a most miserable state. How else could they be? The lowest price of meal and flour here is 2s. 8d. per stone. Good God! How could any man with 10d. per day support a wife and six children on this paltry stipend?—eight persons depending for support on 5s. for seven days, not minding any wet days on which they may not be able to work;—1 1-14th pence per day, equivalent to seven and a half ounces of flour! Think of a working man—yes, or an idle man,—living on seven and a half ounces of flour every twenty-four hours. It is absurd—it is horrifying—it is more than dreadful to contemplate; but why pursue it further? It is done enough before. The Irish are the most patient people on the face of the globe. Cast your eyes over the wide world, and can you discover another people suffering so much, and bearing those suffering so patiently? The people heretofore had some hopes; they are now beginning to give themselves up to despair; and I would remind our rulers that if the bounds of discretion be once set at defiance—they may find it more difficult, nay, more expensive, to restrain a frantic multitude, maddened into despair, than now to feed a hungry, a quiet, but a *feeling* people.

Your obedient servant, O.

BENEVOLENCE OF LADY HEADLEY.

IN this season of calamity and distress, when disease and famine, as in rivalry, sweep along, when strong men fall on the roadsides, struck down by the hand of hunger, and when the shadows of future events are borne upon us so ominously and so darkly, it is an agreeable task to record the energetic endeavours of kind hearts to alleviate, at least, the misery of our fellow-men. Our County of Kerry is blessed with a gentry, good and well meaning, but there is one, Lady Headly, with whose name charity and benevolence have ever been synonymous, and whose memory will remain stamped on the hearts of the people. She is giving at present, weekly support to *all* the poor in her neighbourhood, and has distributed large quantities of bedding and clothing.

Recreated and reprinted from The Cork Examiner, Cork, January 1, 1847.

OUTRAGES IN DROGHEDA.—Outrages and attacks on the bakers' bread-carts and baskets are becoming frequent here. The constabulary force are almost fatigued to death with extra duty, as escorts to the bread, flour, and other provisions leaving town.—*Argus*.

RURAL DEPREDATIONS.—A farmer's house in the neighbourhood of Ballymayer was attacked, a few nights since, by a party of men, some of whom were armed. The party was, however, repulsed without having effected their object. A correspondent also acquaints us that some alarm for the safety of property begins to be felt in the neighbourhood around Dungannon. The petty thefts committed at night are frequent, and the people are, in consequence, becoming more apprehensive and watchful. The inhabitants of some of the townlands sit up by turns for the purpose of protecting their property. In other localities, one or two individuals of a family sit up all night for the same purpose. It is added that plunderers are constantly on foot, many of them armed. We are informed that there has been another robbery committed on an oatmeal-laden vessel, in the Bay of Carlingford. We defer entering into particulars, in expectation of procuring a full statement from the sworn informations.—*Newry Telegraph*.

FOOD RIOTS IN DUBLIN.—On Friday morning, a body of men, passed down Summer-hill, and stopped at the corner of Lower Gardiner-street. In course of a short time two bread carts were passing, when a portion of the men, armed with large wattles, singled themselves out, stopped the carts, while the rest deliberately plundered them of their contents. The bread-shop of Mr. Jeffers, Church-street, was attacked, but being near the station-house, a sufficient force arrived in time to prevent depredation. Several bread carts have been stopped in the outlets and plundered of their contents. About mid-day, a party of fellows entered a baker's shop in Marlborough Street, but the police appearing they left it without committing any depredations, and proceeded over Carlisle-bridge. In the evening, six men rushed into the shop of Mr. Halahan, baker, 128, Great Britain-street, and were forcing their way behind the counter, when he produced a pistol and threatened them. They said they did not want to use force, whereupon he gave them four loaves. About the same hour, Mr. Manders's bread-shop, in Moore-street, was entered by twelve men, who demanded bread. On being refused it, they became violent, and said they would come again to-morrow, but went away without doing mischief. In the course of the evening, a large body of police had to go down to the neighbourhood of Patrick-street, in consequence of intelligence being received that parties were attacking the bread shops there. Next day, several bread-carts were plundered, north and west of the city. A few persons were apprehended by the police, brought before the magistrates of the head-office, who ordered them to be bound in their own recognizances to keep the peace.—*Packet*.

Recreated from The Belfast News-Letter, Belfast, January 12, 1847.

LIVERPOOL.—On Friday the Catholics of Liverpool intend to hold a meeting at the Concert-hall, Lord Nelson-street, Mr. Richard Sheil in the chair, to raise funds for the support of the famishing people of Ireland, and on the following Sunday sermons would be preached in all the Roman Catholic Chapels of Liverpool, and Birkenhead, for the same object.

UNCHARITABLE DISTINCTION.—We regret to hear that a clergyman has announced his intention to preach a sermon in behalf of the *Protestant* portion of the starving Irish. We refrain from giving the name, as we sincerely trust that there has been some mistake in the matter—the charitable spirit and liberal character of the rev. gentleman have hitherto secured him the esteem of a large majority of the people of Exeter, and we should be sorry to mar that feeling without the strongest proof of the alleged fact.—*Western Times*.

Recreated from The Cork Examiner, Cork, January 18, 1847.

MORE TRUE NOBILITY.

I have been some time expecting to see some public acknowledgement of the very munificent donation lately given for the relief of the Poor of Thurles, now 8,000 on the poor roll. As no one else has undertaken to perform this duty, I beg to announce, through your respectable journal, that the Viscount Chabot, lord and proprietor of the soil, has contributed the munificent sum of £10!! His son, Count Jarnac, "Charge d'Affairs" to the French Embassy in London, following the splendid example of of his noble sire, has contributed the bountiful sum of £5!! Thus a Viscount, and a Count have by their united efforts made up £15!! What care need the 8,000 paupers of Thurles have about famine after such generous, noble efforts, as this to relieve them.—Correspondent of the *Tipperary Vindicator*.

Recreated from The Cork Examiner, Cork, January 20, 1847.

THE DISTRESS IN THIS TOWN.—Notwithstanding the existence of a union workhouse, a charitable society, soup-kitchens, and munificent private subscriptions, not to speak of many other agencies, there is in this town a greater number of beggars and of really destitute people than, we are certain, ever crowded it at any former period. The streets are thronged with them, and every humane institution is filled to inconvenience. This is a sad truth. There is, however, one other fact also worthy of record, which is that the accumulation of all this misery has not been able to shut up one public house. Some three months ago, there were 625 spirit-shops in this town, and to this day they remain in all their opulence and glory.

SINGULAR CASE—MARRIAGE ACT.—Two persons named Robert Breadnell and Sarah Ann Bright, residing in Gilford, were married on the 15th of December last, in the district registrar's office, Banbridge. A few days afterwards, a person from Gilford called upon the registrar to say that these two persons had contracted an illegal marriage, as the parties were too nearly related, Sarah Ann Bright being *mother-in-law* to Robert Breadnell. This information the registrar, Mr. Scott, laid before the registrar general, when he received instructions from him to have the parties prosecuted for contracting an illegal marriage, they being within the prohibited degrees, and also for making a false declaration. A warrant was accordingly issued for their apprehension, when they were brought up for examination before Capt. Jenkins, R.M., and were committed to jail to take their trial at the Downpatrick assizes.

Recreated from The Belfast News-Letter, Belfast, January 26, 1847.

BALLIDEHOB—JANUARY 26, 1847.
TO THE EDITOR OF THE CORK EXAMINER.

SIR—In passing through the village of Keelbronoge this day, about midway between Skull and Ballidehob, I observed some of the inhabitants, complete moving spectres, endeavouring to redig potato ground. They told me a sad tale of their lamentable condition.

The first house I entered was that of the Widow Regan—*she lay on the floor a corpse for the last five days*, unattended by any, save her only son, who lay beside her, a young and able-bodied man *just expiring*. I viewed the dying and the dead with a feeling of commiseration. No neighbour attended to mourn their desolation—they lay alone in their abject misery.

In the next cabin I visited, *a dead body intercepted my entrance*—the wife of the dying man I have alluded to. *She was unburied for the last five days*. Her decrepit father, who was endeavouring to nail a few boards together, said, with a groan, "Where can I find a coffin for this woman's husband? he must be dead by this time." The wretched man was on his way to eternity himself.

I next went to the house of Charles Crowley. His son was crying at the door; he told me his father expired that moment. I asked *was there any house in the village without a corpse?*—the reply was, *very few*.

I then went to what I considered the most respectable house in the village. The door was closed; I rapped, but heard nothing for a considerable time; at length a woman crawled to the door, and, after much exertion, opened it. *I had to pass over the dead body of a young woman*. I went towards the fire-place, and saw the man of the house, John Coughlan, *in the agony of death*—his son, at the other side, apparently contending with each other for the first opportunity to get rid of their mortal sufferings. His wife and child were in a dark corner. My feelings at the time were so paralyzed, I could not ascertain whether they were living or dead.

This devoted village is a perfect charnel-house. Though the day was unusually bright, a murky cloud of pestilential vapour overshadowed it.

The last wretched man was under the protection of the Board of Works; he continued crawling to his employment until his wasted limbs were unable to carry him; his family were languishing at home in unknown misery, incapable of rendering him any assistance. A wet floor is now covered with the dying and the dead, and in all probability, will be their common grave.

I hastily quitted this death-stricken village; but just at the moment the bodies were about to be taken to some burial place altogether; the living being too few to compose separate funerals, the friends exhibited no signs of grief; they appeared rather tired of their existence—it seemed to me they envied their departed relatives; but it will be of short duration, a few weeks, and all the inhabitants of this grave-yard village will disappear.

In the name of the dying and the dead, how are the living to be treated? Will they be allowed to drop imperceptibly into eternity, until the entire country is reduced to a frightful waste? Where is our boasted protection of life and liberty? The Irish labourer is at perfect liberty to work on one of the government roads, and support *nine in family with eight pence a day, till he dies at his work*, when the family may entomb themselves in their hovel, and moulder there for eternity. This is the *liberty* we enjoy in Ireland.

If the most insignificant creature in her Majesty's service received but an insult, whilst in the discharge of his duty, what a warlike display of horse and foot would be exhibited! Placards posted on every Police Barrack, offering large rewards for the apprehension of the dangerous outlaw. The same protective government will not interpose when famine and fever are united, and determined to annihilate what was once "a bold peasantry, their country's pride." It is obvious our rulers are determined to hand us over to insatiable death; they are content with their visionary road relief, but fatal experience has proved the fallaciousness of their opinions.

I could point out to Lord John more misery in the village I travelled this day than it would be possible for him to conceive. Callous and impenetrable the soul must be that would look on without soul-cutting emotions on the scenes which I have but imperfectly described. Cold and unsympathising must our English statesmen be who could abandon us in the day of calamity and death, should they not save us for their own sake? Do we not merit the protection of honest subjects? Suppose we were only useful at such a place as Waterloo, or the Indias, are we not worth at least something to exist upon? When we ask for bread, they gave us stones to break, until our nerveless hands are unable to wield the hammer. Let not the Premier delude himself with the futile consolation of having done his *duty* to her Majesty's Irish subjects, he has only protracted their blighted existence by the shadow of Government relief.

I have combated my feelings for the last three weeks, and would have retreated, if I did not consider my presence here of some advantage to the dying.

JEREMIAH O'CALLAGHAN.

Recreated from The Cork Examiner, Cork, January 29, 1847.

YOUGHAL INQUESTS.— DEATHS FROM STARVATION.— A CORPSE FOR SALE.

On Friday last, D. Geran, Esq., Coroner, held an inquest at Youghal, on the body of a boy seven years old named Wm. Miller. The corpse was taken by the Police *while exposed for sale.*

Mr. John D. Ronayne being sworn, deposed as follows.—I am an Apothecary in the town of Youghal; was in my own shop about one o'clock in the afternoon of Wednesday, the 27th inst., a man, now in court, whose name I don't know, came into my shop, and asked me *did I want to buy a corpse?* I asked was it a man or a woman? He first said it was a man, and then that it was a boy. I asked the age, and he said, seven or eight years old; asked was the boy coffined and buried? and he said he was; asked where the boy was from? he said from the West, asked was he his own child? he replied not; at this moment I was called into my house, and on my return back to the shop the man was gone. In the interim, I saw a Policeman passing bye: I called him, mentioned the circumstance, and described the man who was in my shop. In about ten minutes after the Policeman returned with the prisoner, and asked me was that the man that offered to sell the body? and I said it was. In about three hours afterwards the same day, I saw the body of a boy about seven years old in the Police Barrack, Youghal. I never knew anything of the kind to have occurred in Youghal before, nor even knew of the sale of bodies there.

Michael Mangan, Sub-Constable, sworn.—I was passing the town of Youghal at midday on the 27th inst., another Sub-Constable gave prisoner in charge to me; observed a woman, now in court, standing close by—she had on her back a basket and a cloak over it; asked what was in the basket; she said "nothing;" removed the cloak, and took a little straw out of the mouth of the basket; and there found, doubled together, the dead body of a boy, about seven years old; the man and woman were arrested, and brought to the Barrack; did not know them; while under way to the Barrack the male prisoner wanted to state something to me; cautioned him not to do so, as I would bring it in evidence against him; on coming into the barracks; took the basket, with the corpse in it, off the woman's back; the male prisoner began to state a second time why he brought the child for sale; was cautioned against doing so, but persevered. He stated that the child was sickly some time before he died; that it was want that *compelled him (prisoner) and his wife to offer for sale the dead body*; admitted the child did not belong to himself; that he was an illegitimate child for the last six years, and that his mother went to England.

Richard Ronayne, Esq., M.D., sworn—On Monday last was called on to make an examination on the body of a male child, apparently between 7 and 8 years of age—went to the Police Barrack at Youghal, was pointed out this body, doubled up in a blanket, and covered with straw; there were no marks of violence on the body; on opening it found the contents of the chest and abdomen perfectly healthy, but there was *not a particle of food in the stomach or intestines*, nor a particle of adipose or fatty mater; from all these circumstances, together with the extremely emaciated appearance of the child, is of opinion he *died from hunger.*

The Coroner asked was there any more witnesses, and none appearing.

Thomas Miller, the person charged, asked permission to say a few words.

The coroner cautioned him against saying anything that would incriminate himself.

Miller, a poor emaciated looking man, who was in custody of the police, then came forward and stated—I lived with Mr. Gaggan, of Greenland for the last ten years; and since the potatoes failed I got 8d. per day, and that was not able to support my family, being six in number. When the public works commenced Mr. Gaggan knocked off all his men but two. I went then to the public works, earned about *five shillings a week, and that would not give my family a meal a day when things got dear.* I had to break off from work from want of food; I went to beg for food among the neighbours, and sent my wife to be taken in my place for a couple of days at the works—she was refused. I went back to the works again on the following Monday, *and was without food from Monday morning till the following Thursday on the works*; I used to take a drink of spring water sometimes and *faint every night with weakness*, and then turn into bed, not having light or fire, and I left the work on Friday to go a second time a begging. I went to Ballymacoda, to the relief committee, the gentlemen were coming out, I saw there Mr. Fitzgerald and Mr. Egar, the rector of the parish. Mr. Fitzgerald asked me why I was not at work? I said I was not able, Mr. Egar looked at me, and said "I was not able to work from starvation." Mr. Egar rode on, and told me to follow after; I followed, till he came to a house where he sold bread at half price, at Ballymacoda; he told me to rap at the door; the woman came out, and Mr. Egar ordered me 2s. worth of bread; I got it and went home. Having so much to share among my children on Friday, I went to the works on Saturday. I was paid my wages on the following Wednesday, 4s., and of this had to pay 3s. 6d. to Pat Griffin, of Ring, who passed his word for meal for me the week before. I had only 6d. left going home, and took with me the worth of it in bread. I shared the bread among my children, *and God knows how little of it I left myself*; the day following I saw the children had nothing, till my wife went when the tide was out to cut Doolamaun (sea weed) off the rocks; she brought it home, boiled it, put a little salt on it, *and on this we were living for days before the child, William Miller, died.* I went to work again, on last Tuesday morning, and on returning in the evening the child was dead. The statement I am ready to make on oath; and if you doubt me, ask the Rev. Mr. Egar, of Lisquinlan, or Mr. Fitzgerald, of Ballykennily, and with the exception of the charge now against me, nothing was ever laid before to charge me.

The prisoner's wife, a wretched, care worn looking woman, with an infant at her breast—said—The reason I was selling the child was *from want*, and I would do anything to keep the life in my children and in myself; and this I shall publicly say, however I may be punished by law. A couple of days before the child died, I went to my master's son, John Gaggan of Greenland, for a few turnips to eat; he said the last of them were in the boiler for the horses; I went then and stole a few slices of boiled turnips for the children; Mr. Gaggan saw me, and told me never to do it again. I was not able to sweep the house from weakness, and would eat the cat through hunger.

The Coroner addressed the jury, and told them that exposing for sale a dead body was an indictable offense that would come before another tribunal. It was for the jury to enquire how, and in what manner, the boy Wm. Miller, came by his death. The principal evidence was that of the Doctor, and upon his testimony the jury should return their verdict.

The jury, after a short consultation, returned a verdict—*Death by Starvation.*

Same day, inquests were held on the bodies of Margaret and Patrick Croneen, a mother and son, who died at the Windmill, near Youghal. It appeared on evidence that the parties lived for days upon *turnips*, and latterly on the *putrid remains of a pig*, that died on the premises of a neighbouring farmer, and for days before death they had nothing to eat.

The jury at once returned their verdict, finding that Margaret and Patrick Croneen *died from starvation.*

Recreated from The Cork Examiner, Cork, February 3, 1847.

BREAD RIOTS—CAPTURE OF THE RIOTERS AND ATTEMPTED RESCUE.

On this morning, about half-past nine o'clock, a notice was brought to the Tuckey-street Guard house, stating that a large mob, numbering from 800 to 1,000 persons had gone to the Workhouse, with the intention of attacking that establishment, and plundering the provisions contained there. A party of police, under the command of Sub-Inspector Walker and Head-Constable Condon, was immediately ordered out, and proceeded quickly to the scene of the anticipated riot. It appeared, from the evidence of Head-Constable Crowley, delivered before the magistrates this morning, that he had also proceeded with a detachment of police to the Workhouse, but, on his arrival there, he found that the mob had left it a short time previously without committing injury or violence. After leaving the Workhouse, the mob came down Douglas-street, and attacked the shop of Mr. Barry, baker, out of which they took a quantity of bread. They then proceeded down White-street, and up George's quay, where they met a bread cart, which they rifled of the greater portion of its contents. Head-Constable Condon and the party under his direction met the mob at Parliament-street, and followed them into Prince's Street. They then attacked the shop of Mr. Thompson, baker, Prince's-street, and, notwithstanding the opposition of police, carried off a large quantity of bread, after demolishing several panes of glass, and committing other injury. A party of 300 or 400 separated from the main body, and walked quickly up Prince's-street; accompanied by Head-Constable Condon and his party. On entering Patrick-street, they ran quickly towards the Parade; and on getting into North Main-street, they rushed into the shop of Mr. David Walsh, broke the glass in the window with their shovels, and attempted to obtain possession of the bread in the window. The police arrested two of the most prominent actors in the outrage, named Daniel Wallis, and a man named Casey, at present living in Blackpool, but originally from the parish of Macroom. The prisoners were taken into Mr. Walsh's shop, when the mob attacked the police with their spades and shovels, and swore they would not leave the place until their comrades were liberated. Several of the police were struck with stones, and also beaten with the spades of the rioters. At this time the riot had assumed a most serious aspect, the mob appearing determined to rescue the prisoners. Head-Constable Condon took a bayonet from one of the policemen, and with a few of the party, charged the mob with drawn bayonets down the North Main-street, over North-gate Bridge, up Shannon-street and Clarence-street. The rioters then retired towards Blackpool, and the constabulary returned into town.

Upwards of a dozen prisoners were brought up this morning, charged with breaking glass in the bakers' shops, and running off with the bread exposed for sale there. Some of them were sentenced to terms varying from a fortnight to a month's imprisonment.

Up to the hour of one o'clock the bakers' shops on Patrick-street, and the other principal streets of the city remained closed for fear of a second attack.

Recreated from The Cork Examiner, Cork, February 5, 1847.

FOOD RIOTS IN THE CITY.

On Saturday a deputation, consisting of the principal Master Bakers in the city, waited on the Magistrates at the Police-office, and stated that in consequence of the present alarming height to which the disturbances in the city have risen, they should be compelled to close their shops and sell no more bread unless the court would ensure to them the protection of the military and police force. The court requested the deputation to attend at the office at 3 o'clock, at which time they would be able to enter into such arrangements as to secure to their body the required protection. At the hour appointed, the Mayor, Mr. Fagan, and Mr. Lyons, together with Col. Beresford and Captain Price, County Inspector, were in attendance, and it was then agreed on that a party of the military should assemble at Tuckey-street guard-house every morning, at 11 o'clock, and then in company with a body of the police force, to patrol through the city until night, the shops of the bakers not to be opened until after the hour first mentioned. The deputation then withdrew, declaring themselves satisfied with this arrangement, which was carried into effect for the first time this morning.

Recreated from The Cork Examiner, Cork, February 8, 1847.

THE CONDITION OF IRELAND.

The more we study the appearance of all human things around us, the more we are appalled. If we look to the past, our only wonder, in studying its history, is, that the crisis had not arrived sooner. If we look to the present, we behold only shifts, expediences and temporary palliatives—if we look to the future, we discern only shadows, clouds and death in the mortal perspective. From the bosom of the land a voice is hourly lifting itself up in most unutterable desolation. The country this moment is literally the role of the Prophet, which was "writ within and without, and was filled with mourning and lamentation and woe." The change wrought in the appearance and manners of the people is most remarkable, and must strike any observer with peculiar force. Study the faces of those who, rejected and flung off the supporting land on which they were born, throng crowded streets of thickly peopled cities, and how actually inhuman have grown all the lineaments of the human countenance? Then listen to the voice of those *men*—it is not the sorrowful but manly expression of a distress, calamitous and inevitable in its nature, but which might be met by the wisdom of our legislation, or the superfluous riches of the great of the land, or the sympathising benevolence of a Christian people—no, it is the utter debasement of mental and physical prostration—the whine of unredeemed mendicancy—the beggar's wrongs and the beggar's sores put into a hideous agglomeration and hawked before the public eye. Did these men serve a long apprenticeship to oppression, and endure a weary load of life, lashed by the law of lords and the lords of land—that it might all issue in this picture of abomination? Are *these* specimens of the manly and heroic Irishman, whose courage was proverbial, and whose personal and military bravery were acknowledged in every battle field in this contending world? How much must the iron have entered into the soul of Ireland when she thus pictures herself before nations? "It is Greece but living Greece no more."

Who now shall lead thy scattered children forth,
And long accustomed bondage uncreate?

As we look on those miserable multitudes that cumber the fair earth, we cannot help the internal longing that springs within us, we trust from no irreverend spirit, that they had died as became freemen, in the bold assertion of the eternal rights of man and human nature, against tyranny, oppression, exaction, monopoly and the law of their masters—instead of being whipped into slaves and beggars, and lashed into a submission and bondage as unholy in the ways and means of its cause, as it is now bloody in all its detestable effect. After all, the brave death of a freeman and the reverence of posterity *are* noble, and we look upon the *living* hideousness of Ireland this moment, with every ennobling spark within her bosom quenched, and the light of hope as it were darkened for ever.

Recreated from The Cork Examiner, Cork, February 12, 1847.

MURDER OF HUSBAND AND WIFE.

A double murder, which could not be exceeded in atrocity in the most savage country, was perpetrated in the town of Askeaton upon Saturday night last. The unhappy victims were David Fitzgerald and his wife, an industrious and unoffending couple. The murders were committed with Fitzgerald's own hatchet, which was found covered with blood, and we learn from one who visited the awful scene upon Sunday morning, that the spectacle was most revolting and hideous. The gashes upon the faces of the unfortunate victims, their brains protruding, and the floor of the house was literally deluged with blood. The fatal blows must have been rapidly inflicted, and with deadly force, as no alarm was heard, although the house was in the centre of several others, and within ten yards of the Police-barrack, and at a very early hour of the night as Fitzgerald or his wife had not undressed or retired to bed. Robbery is supposed to have been the object that led to this horrifying crime, as Fitzgerald's house was found unlocked and apparently rifled. A man named John McCarthy, who worked as a journeyman weaver with Fitzgerald, and who was at Fitzgerald's house on Saturday night, was suspected and surrendered himself to the Police.—*Limerick Chronicle.*

Recreated from The Cork Examiner, Cork, February 12, 1847.

(From the Tralee Chronicle.)
ASSES USED FOR HUMAN FOOD.—A man of the name of John Goggin, caretaker to Mr. Crosbie, living at Ballinfriar, came into the Ardfert committee-room, and stated, that on the previous day he was requested (and he complied with their request), by two of his neighbours, namely, Thomas O'Brien and Denis Flynn, to shoot their asses, with a view that they may feed themselves and their families. And they did so, to save themselves even for a short time from the horrors of actual starvation, by devouring this loathsome and disgusting food.

Reprinted from The Freeman's Journal, Dublin, February 12, 1847.

DRAWING-ROOM AT DUBLIN CASTLE.

HIS EXCELLENCY THE LORD LIEUTENANT held his second drawing-room for the season at the Castle, on Thursday evening, when a large proportion of the nobility and gentry now in the metropolis paid their homage to her Majesty's representative. The presentations were numerous. The following is a description of a few of

THE LADIES' DRESSES.

The Ladies Harriet and Kathleen Ponsonby—Corsage and train of richest pink and silver poplin, lined with flounce, trimmed with tulle and silver, the corsage with draperie of tulle; petticoat of white tarlatau with Limerick lace flounces, looped with bouquets of pink and white roses, with diamonds. Head-dress—Plume of ostrich feathers, point lappets; ornaments, diamonds.

The Lady Mayoress—Corsage and train of emerald velvet, berthe and sabots of the finest Honiton lace; rich white satin petticoat, tastefully trimmed with lace and white satin ribbands. Head dress—Feathers and lappets; ornaments, pearls.

Lady Hervey Bruce—Corsage and train of the richest velour poplin, brocaded in silver, tastefully trimmed with silver lace; petticoat of white moire silk, flounces of deep Limerick lace. Head dress—Lappets, ornaments, and magnificent diamonds.

Mrs. Langley, Brittas Castle—train and corsage of superb lavender satin, richly trimmed with real black lace and no ends of satin ribband; dress of black lace, with two deep flounces, over rich black satin; magnificent black lace berthe. Demi head dress—Lappets and plume of ostrich feathers; ornaments, jet.

Mrs. Leckie, Ballykealy—Magnificent Limerick lace train and corsage, expressly for the occasion, lined with rich maize glace silk; dress of rich white, with handsome flounces of Limerick lace; berthe to correspond, trimmed with flowers. Head dress—Plume of ostrich feathers, with real lace lappets; ornaments, diamonds.

Mrs. Maberley—A superb dress of Brussels lace, with two deep flounces over rose de China satin; corsage and train of black velvet, lined with rose de China satin and trimmed with a deep border of Brussels lace, confined by bouquets of Chinese roses; berthe, sabots, and lappets of Brussels lace. Head dress—Wreath of diamonds and plume of Aleppo feathers.

Mrs. Goodrich Shedden—Corsage and train of a splendid moire antique, pink watered ground, with large damasked white flowers, lined with white and trimmed round with white open gimp, the body trimmed a Pantique with point lace; petticoat of white net over rich white satin, with a deep flounce of lace festooned, and headed with pink quilled ribbon and large rosettes. Head dress—White ostrich feathers, point lace lappets; bandeau and ornaments of diamonds.

ERRONEOUS REPORT.—We can state upon the best authority, that Miss Susan Cashman was not married a few days back, as reported in the *Albion* of yesterday, and moreover, that the nuptials of the lady cannot take place for some time.—*Liverpool Times.*

Recreated from The Belfast News-Letter, Belfast, February 16, 1847.

HENRY STREET.

THE LATE ROBBERY IN HARDWICK-PLACE.—On Saturday, Police Constable Nowlan 151 D, arrested two women named Mary Boylan and Ellen Donnelly on some petty charge, and on conveying them to the station-house, he found on them six forks which were a portion of the property stolen from Mrs. Irvine, Hardwick-place. The prisoners, it appears are sisters of Donnelly, the man who was sentenced to 15 years' transportation on Thursday last at the commission for the robbery. The prisoners communicated something which perhaps will lead to the recovery of the plate stolen, and which up to the present has not been recovered.

Reprinted from The Freeman's Journal, Dublin, February 16, 1847.

DEATHS FROM DESTITUTION IN THE CITY—CORONER'S INQUESTS.

Yesterday Dr. Kirwan, one of the city coroners, held an inquest at No. 6, Hendrick-street, on view of the bodies of John and Ellen Mulherin (husband and wife), the latter having died on Sunday, the former on Saturday evening.—It was said that the unfortunate creatures died of starvation, and this caused considerable alarm and excitement in the neighbourhood.

The bodies lay in a small hut in the yard of a house where the family of deceased, consisting altogether of six individuals, resided, and for which a rent of 8d. per week was paid. It was one of the most frightful habitations—if it could be called by such a name—ever beheld. There was not a particle of furniture in it save an old cracked table. A person could not stand upright in it, and the walls were quite wet and covered with filth.

The floor was composed of soft mud at least two inches deep, and in the right-hand coroner (observable only by strong candle-light), lay the lifeless figure of the unfortunate man, while opposite in the other corner lay the corpse of his wife; and two more horrifying and ghastly spectacles could not be imagined.

The bodies were stretched on litters, which at some remote period might have been composed of straw, but in the present instance the worst dunghill in a stable was superior to them; and in this cheerless abode resided the deceased with four children, the eldest about 14, the youngest 2 years. With the exception of a few rotten rags there was no other covering; and although the deceased parties were hardly 40 years of age, their pale, emaciated, and haggard appearance proclaimed them at least over 60. They were natives of the county Leitrim, and came to Dublin about a year ago.

Recreated from The Freeman's Journal, Dublin, February 16, 1847.

THE IMPERATIVE NECESSITY OF A UNIVERSAL AND ENERGETIC POPULAR AGITATION.

(From *Howitt's Journal*.)

We had hoped that the time was come when the frightful mass of Irish misery before our eyes would rouse England, not only to acts of present benevolence, but of future and permanent justice. We did hope that now all party feeling would perish in the gulf of national destitution opened at our feet; that all temporizing would cease; that all good men, of all ranks and opinions, would unite to prevent the recurrence of such a spectacle as this winter has unfolded, of a portion of the richest, the wisest, the most benevolent nation in the world, presenting a scene of horrors such as no other nation in the world can parallel. But our hopes were in vain; the measures proposed by ministers in Parliament show us too plainly that neither Parliament nor ministers are prepared to go to the bottom of the Irish evils, and to apply to them a real and sufficient remedy.

The evils that exist will, therefore, continue to exist; the calamities, the famine, the perishing of whole families of starvation, and in utter nakedness, on their own hearths, will be but postponed, to revive in future winters with aggravated horrors.

The sore that goes down to the very bone of Ireland is only to be plastered over; it is not to be probed, and thoroughly cleansed, and healed. We are to have palliatives, not remedies; we are to have quackery, and not a cure.

We call upon the people of England to awake, arise, and prevent this mischief. We call upon them, as they value the name of the Englishmen—as they wish to be real men and Christians—to stand forth as one man and one mind, and declare that this system of fatal procrastination shall end.

It is you, people of England, that must answer to God and man for the future fate of Ireland. It is you that must now say whether the evils that bear down that wretched country, and that rob the poor man of this, to help—and vainly help, under present circumstances—to keep it on the mere surface of existence, shall be put an end to, or should be left to an indefinite period and an augmented malignity. From both God and nature you have now had warning; and woe to you, and to us all, if you do not take it!

What are the remedies proposed by Lord John Russell? To grant money to the Irish landlords, to improve their estates, and to give some undescribed modification of the present absurd Irish Poor Law. A more wretched farce was never attempted to be played, instead of a great, a wise, and successful political deed done.

What and who are these Irish landlords? Are they men who have ever shown, as a body, any disposition to improve their estates? There are some few brilliant exceptions; and these exceptions don't want help—don't want your money. Their improvements have enriched them, and rendered eleemosynary aid needless. Such are Lords Lansdowne and Fitzwilliam,—Wallscourt, Lord George Hill, of Gweedore, etc. But the body of the Irish landlords are, without question, the most reckless, the most proud, the most hardened and thriftless race of men in existence.

We rejoice to see that now nearly the whole Press of England has come to this necessary discovery, and avowal of it. These landlords have lived amongst their starving neighbours, and on their starved estates, for ages, without an attempt to improve them, and to employ the people. From the invasion of Strongbow, the Irish landlords, have done nothing, or next to nothing, towards enclosing their wastes, draining their bogs, and cultivating their estates. They have neglected the very fisheries, and instead of busy fishing-towns, have vast extents of solitary coasts.

They have done nothing; but lie like big dogs in the manger, idle themselves, and preventing others from doing anything. Hence, nearly half of Ireland is a bog, or a desert. There are four and half million acres of waste. From time to time they have had large grants from this country to aid them in their difficulties, but when did they ever repay a penny of it? From time to time we have been called on to send government help to the poor Irish; and where has the cash gone to? To Paris, or Vienna, or Rome, or Naples, the very next summer. To swell that beggarly state which Irish landlords maintain in rivalry to each other, while their neighbours are living in cabins worse than dog-kennels, and on offal that they would not give to their hounds.

Countrymen! we do not want a landlord's measure; we want a people's measure. We do not want more money flinging into that gulf where it yet never did any good, and out of which it never rose again—the maw of an Irish landlord; we want money bestowing on the people of Ireland; we want land bestowing on the people of Ireland; and that money must come out of the pockets of the Irish landlords; and that land is lying all over Ireland ready for occupation, but still unoccupied; ready for culture, but uncultured; ready for draining, but undrained; ready to make a busy and happy people, but lying a dreary desert in the midst of a famishing nation.

Countrymen! you must take that land—it is yours and God's—and give it to its true owners—the Irish people. Let the cry of O'Connell be realized—let "Ireland be for the Irish". These Irish landlords tell you that these lands are theirs. It is false: they are God's and Irishmen's. Where are their titles? They are certain musty parchments—if they have even these. But the title of the Irish people is the right to live! Life, and not yellow crumbling sheepskins, are the grand title to the land, and that title must be asserted—ay, asserted by the people of England.

We must tell the Irish landlords and the world, that, whatever titles their fathers had in the land that has never been cultivated, is now become void. They have lost the whole by neglect of occupation. They have neglected to fulfill the conditions on which they received it—that they should occupy and cultivate it, and make it of benefit to the commonweal.

We have invaded many nations in many regions of the earth, and seized on them, and driven out the aborigines; and justified ourselves by the declaration that the only true title to land is occupation—not merely wandering over it. We must put that doctrine in force at home; and every acre of land, not merely such as is not worth 2s. 6d. per acre, as Lord John Russell says, but all that has not yet been occupied, must now be occupied by and for the people.

With you, then, Englishmen, it rests, whether Ireland shall now be dealt with effectually or not. If you are not up and determined, you will leave ages of misery to your children, and pauperism to Ireland. You must turn out, and call public meetings in every town, and pour petitions, and those strong ones, into Parliament by thousands, that Ireland may have an effective Poor Law—that Irishmen may have the waste lands, and that England may cease to be at once a great foolish pelican, feeding her Irish children out of her own life's blood. Now is the day and the hour for doing what must be done, if we do not desire again and again to witness the existence of far more misery than we now affect so deeply to deplore.

William Howitt.

Recreated from The Northern Star, Leeds, England, February 20, 1847.

EXTRA
SHORT NAPPED BEAVER HATS
Of a Rich, Brilliant and Permanent Black.

GENTLEMEN who usually prefer wearing a Beaver Hat because of its peculiarly agreeable and easy feel to the Head, as well as for its good substantial wear, are respectfully informed, that

WOOD & SON,
69, PATRICK STREET,

Can with the greatest confidence (from their practical knowledge as one of the oldest manufacturing Houses in Ireland) strongly recommend their present Stock of BEAVER HATS for
COMBINING BEAUTY WITH DURABILITY, the Naps being the very shortest that can be made consistent with Elegance and Wear, and the Colors being of a beautifully Bright and " Fast Dyed" Black
WATERPROOF FELT JERRY HATS
In a most Tasteful Variety of Shapes.

Reprinted from The Cork Examiner, Cork, February 22, 1847.

LANDLORDS
CULTIVATION OF THE LAND.

The observations of Mr. LABOUCHERE in the House last week, in relation to the non-cultivation of land in the county of Mayo, and the letter read by the Right Hon. gentleman, ascribed the fact to an organised system on the part of the farmers, have given rise to the following resolutions adopted by the Catholic Clergy:

"Resolved—That we have read with the utmost astonishment the report of a speech ascribed to the Secretary for Ireland, imputing to the people of Mayo a deliberate determination of leaving their fields untilled. That whilst we acquit the right hon. gentleman of any wish to misrepresent, we have no hesitation in ascribing the calumny of which he was the unconscious dupe, to some of those cruel proprietors and members of relief committees who, after stripping the tenantry of the last grain of oats or insisting on its consumption, left them without the means to seed the ground, and then turn around on the unfortunate victims of their cruelty, and impute to them an imaginary conspiracy among the beggared tenants, of the utter desolation of whom their own heartlessness will have been the cause.

"Resolved—That in the late instructions forwarded to relief committees there appeared a similar cruel delusion, these instructions assuming that there are many persons able, but unwilling, to assume the labours of agriculture; whereas to leave the unfortunate tenantry without seed, which they are unable to purchase, and yet to refuse them labour or gratuitous relief, would be to expose them to certain starvation.

"Resolved—That the system of cruel and wholesale evictions for rent and arrears of rent, so remorselessly practised during this awful crisis by many heartless landlords, is crying to Heaven for vengeance on the heads of that devoted race; and that we cannot command language sufficiently strong to mark our reprobation of those who avail themselves of the obsolete cruelties of the joint-lease system in driving from their homes solvent and honest tenants, unless they also pay the rents of others, with whom they happen to be bound in a lease of a joint tenure.

"Resolved—That after the evils to which such landlords have brought the country, it is passing strange that the legislature is imposing no check on their future career of similar injustice, by protecting the rights of the tenant—nay, that they are receiving every encouragement to turn the country into a desert, by setting seed for green crops, to feed bullocks and other beasts of the field; whereas, neither the government, nor the legislature, nor the landlords are supplying seed for corn, the necessary food of man; whence the people are drawing the obvious conclusion, that whilst provision is being made for feeding cattle—they, the noblest of God's creatures, are unheeded and doomed to perish.

"Resolved—That we adjure the higher classes to pause and not pursue a course which must terminate in their own ruin, and the government to take timely precautions to see the fields sown with corn; otherwise we tremble at the consequences of a series of famines, which will waste the country, and leave it a bye-word and a reproach to the rulers of this great empire.

"Resolved—That we have abundant evidence of the bigotted intolerance of the present government, in their exclusion of the Roman Catholic curates from relief committees, whilst others, who have neither knowledge of, nor sympathy with the suffering poor *are made prominent and confidential members.*

Recreated from The Cork Examiner, Cork, March 15, 1847.

FASHIONABLE INTELLIGENCE.

The Marquis of Stafford has purchased the Ondine schooner of the Hon. Mr. Ponsonby, of the Royal Yacht Squadron, and is expected to become a prominent member of the yachting fraternity.

The Earl and Countess of Warwick have lately been entertaining a small party at Warwick Castle; the circle including the Countess Dowager of Clonmel and the Ladies Scott, &c. The Countess Dowager of Clonmel has since returned to Eaton Place for the season.

Lord and Lady Stanley are expected to leave London at the close of next week for Knowsley Hall, Lancashire, where they will remain with the Earl of Derby until after the recess. A large party is to assemble at Knowsley, on the 29th inst., to celebrate the birthday of Lord Stanley.

Sir Robert and Lady Peel entertained the Earl of Aberdeen, Sir James Graham, the Right Hon. H. Goulburn, the Right Hon. Sidney and Mrs. Herbert, Sir George Clerk, Sir Thomas Freemantle, Sir Frederick Thesiger, Mr. Caldwell, Mr. Young, Colonel and Lady Alice Peel, Mr. F. Peel, and a select party, at dinner, on Wednesday, at their residence in Whitehall gardens.

Recreated from The Freeman's Journal, Dublin, March 22, 1847.

DISMISSAL OF THE LABOURERS.

We regret to learn from the voluminous correspondence that reached us yesterday, from every part of the country, that the government has persevered in enforcing the order for the immediate and almost simultaneous dismissal of 140,000 labourers, without making any other provision for their sustenance. Lord John Russell expressly stated in parliament that employment on the public works would be continued *until* the temporary relief act would have been brought into operation. The relief act is not yet in operation yet the people have been disbanded.

The temporary relief act has, indeed, become law, but in no one district in Ireland has it yet been brought into operation and yet in every district have the labourers been dismissed! Even in Dublin, the headquarters of the Relief Commission—the residence of the official printer—the requisite forms for arranging the preliminaries could not be supplied to the relief committees yesterday, they not having been yet printed. When will they be supplied to the relief committees in the rural districts? But even were the forms ready—the districts defined—and the committees named, a week or more must elapse before food could be distributed. Surely, surely, our foreign masters, when dispensing our own money to our own poor, ought to have acted with more humanity and justice than to check the supply of one class of sustenance before another had been provided. The feelings which have been excited throughout the country by this unaccountable, and almost reckless, proceeding, are of the most bitter character. Some of our correspondents write with no ordinary apprehensions of the consequences to the ill-fated people who have been dismissed, and to the peace of the district upon which they have been thrown as destitute wanderers. So far as our accounts reach, we rejoice to see that the people, guided by their faithful pastors, have conducted themselves in the most peaceable and orderly manner. A few cases of petty depredation have been reported to us, but they form the exception. One of the worst features of this ill-judged proceeding is the fact universally stated by our correspondents that no tillage labour seems to offer for the dismissed, owing to the difficulty of providing seed. In the absence, then, of the relief to be provided under the temporary act, the people must undergo the most heartrending privations. They will be driven, too, in the absence of employment, to brood over their misfortunes, and with what result to the country Heaven only knows.

Recreated from The Freeman's Journal, Dublin, March 23, 1847.

CONVERSIONS TO THE CATHOLIC CHURCH.

The continual accession of distinguished members of the Church of England to the Catholic Church is one of the most remarkable signs of the times. Scarcely a day passes that one or more conversions of eminent Protestants, generally ecclesiastics, or the relations of ecclesiastics, are not announced. This state of things naturally fills the minds of the Catholics with joy and hope; and the least confident among them begin to think that there is nothing so very extravagant in the prediction made by Mr. O'Connell some years since, that some of those then living would see high mass celebrated in Westminster Abbey.

IRELAND—MEETINGS OF THE CATHOLIC CLERGY TO DEFEND THE PEOPLE FROM CALUMNY—The weather is encouraging in Ireland; the heavens are serene and pure, the wind is dry, and in that unfortunate isle is called to mind the old proverb which says that a peck of March dust is worth a bushel of gold. From this there might be hope for Ireland; yet, notwithstanding the fineness of the weather, the soil remains untilled. The labourer has nothing to sow, and hunger has derived him of strength—his calumniators, the landlords, say that he wants will, that there is a conspiracy against cultivating the soil; but the Catholic clergy assembled in many places to defend the people from this calumny. The FREEMAN'S JOURNAL of the 11th brings us the resolutions passed at the meeting of Catholic clergy of the Deanery of Castlebar, and the number of the journal of the 16th contains those agreed to at the meeting of the deanery of Westport. They fling back to the authors the accusation of a conspiracy against the cultivation of the soil, on the part of the Catholic people, and prove that it is mainly attributable to the want of seed and the means of present support the non-tillage of the land is owing.

STATE OF THE COUNTRY.
(From the Sligo Champion.)

Deaths from starvation are of daily occurrence throughout this county. In the remote districts the sufferings the people are enduring beggar all description. The following statement respecting the condition of the inhabitants of a single parish, Kilfree—will serve to shew the extent of the misery which now prevails. Our correspondent thus writes:— "Since my last communication to you our distress is hourly increasing; dysentery and fever are spreading wider every hour, and many of our people are dying of starvation. A son of James Walsh, of Cairns, has been starved to death, as also the daughter of James Casey, of Gurlygana, and the three children of Daniel Dyer, of Kilmore. On Sunday, the 14th inst., the child of Mrs. Fahily, was found in a helpless state at the chapel door of Kilfree. He died in the arms of the person who was bringing him to the fever hospital. What will become of us? THE LANDLORDS ARE DISPLAYING NO BENEVOLENCE NOR COMPASSION. One of them has served a number of processes upon his tenants. And to add to our misfortunes 450 men have been dismissed from the public works, many of whom have not a morsel to eat nor the means of procuring it; some of them have all the members of their families labouring under fever." So much for the state of one parish; Ahamlish is in an equally deplorable condition and along the mountains of Tireragh, and about the bogs of Liney, famine, fever, and dysentery are killing hundreds of human beings, whose deaths have never been noticed, and whose dreadful sufferings are not even heard of.

EMIGRATION.—The cost of a passage in the forcastle from Cork to America is raised to 4l 10s and 5l that is 20s to 30s over the usual charge.

Recreated and reprinted from The Freeman's Journal, Dublin, March 30, 1847.

THE LATE MURDERS IN KILKENNY.

We deeply regret to have to record the following outrage connected with the late atrocious murders of Mr. Prim and constable Yeates. Our readers will remember that in our last we gave a report of an inquest on the body of a man named Roe, who had died of a wound which he acknowledged to have received from Mr. Prim, when engaged with the assailants who have escaped in the murderous attack on the gentleman. Well, on the day after the inquest (Thursday last, we believe) the deceased prisoner's wife brought a hearse for Roe's corpse, but was informed by the police that she could not get it until the following morning at six o'clock. At the appointed hour two men appeared at the police station, and claimed the body, saying they were Roe's nearest relations. On their making this statement, the constables allowed them to take it, enclosed as it was in a shell, which had been ordered by the coroner. The men who, it has since turned out, are inhabitants of the neighbourhood in which the murders were committed immediately carried off the corpse to the spot where Mr. Prim had been murdered, and there, with the assistance of several others of the country people, dug a hole, flung the corpse into it and threw a quantity of large stones and lime on top of it.

This was conduct for which we will offer no palliation. We have given the above facts as they reached us; but we must also add that we have been informed that the people, who, as stated before, held the late Mr. Prim in very great esteem, were provoked to this outrage on Christianity by Roe's wife having stated she would have as good a coffin for her husband as Mr. Prim had. The peasantry also felt very indignant at seeing a grand hearse brought in for the body of one of the murderers of a gentleman to whom they had been so much attached, and hearing the woman boast that she would have a fine funeral for him, being very naturally under the impression that part of the stolen money would defray the expense of such burial. We do not wonder at this; but as we said before, we cannot excuse men for having acted in such gross violation of the rules of common decency.

It was apprehended that a collision would have taken place between Roe's friends and the Kells people; but we are happy to say that no such disturbance has taken place.—*Kilkenny Journal.*

EXTRAORDINARY AND PROVIDENTIAL ESCAPE.

As the down mail from Thurles to Cork was on its journey between Thurles and Cashel, on the night of Tuesday, the 30th March, the coachman by some accident fell off the box without the knowledge of the only outside passenger; and the guard being alarmed at the fearful pace the horses were going, called to the driver to slacken his speed, but to his surprise received no answer until he had roused the only passenger outside, who sat behind the coachman, and was informed by him that they had no driver. The guard, since ascertained to be John Connolly, at the imminent risk of his life, got over the roof (on which there was a great quantity of luggage), and when he saw there was no means of stopping the horses, jumped from off the box on the back of one of the wheelers, and by great exertions succeeded in arresting the further progress of the team after they had ran over two miles; and had it not been for the courage and presence of mind, regardless even of life of this experienced guard, now 14 years on the road, loss of life would, in all probability, have been the result.

He succeeded in taking the coach and passengers safely into Cashel, and delivered his mail; on doing which he procured the aid of a doctor, and both returned on a car in quest of the coachman, whom they found seriously injured, but it to be hoped not fatally.—*From a Correspondent.*

Recreated from The Freeman's Journal, Dublin, April 1-2, 1847.

HEALTH OF THE LIBERATOR.

The accounts of the health of our illustrious countryman continue good. One of our letters says that Doctor Oliffe not only calculates on his perfect recovery, but that he will enjoy many years of life, and be qualified fully to resume his public labours as the result of his visit to Italy. Another correspondent thus writes from Paris, March 28:—

The Liberator's reception here has been most enthusiastic, and all that was anticipated from the journey already begins to be realized. Ireland will be taught by Catholic Europe to set additional value on the champion of her faith and rights, who is regarded by the highest intellect and worth of the world as far and away the first man of his age. The address delivered yesterday to O'Connell, he properly designates as the most important demonstration of Catholic opinion that ever he has witnessed. Thousands of the *elite* of Parisian society have been anxiously entreating to be allowed to behold him who they revere and honour so greatly, and the first nobles of France have gone away in rapture on being allowed to salute him and press his hand. The necessity of guarding him from the effects of over excitement has, however, restricted the privilege of *entree* to a comparatively small number of the distinguished applicants. Paris, has "pronounced" magnificently the estimate formed of O'Connell by its mighty population; and the same may be predicated of all the other places through which he proposes to pass to the capital of Christendom.

The Liberator starts for Orleans this afternoon, and will, it is expected, reach Rome about Low Sunday.—*Freeman* of Friday.

☞ In consequence of the severe duties of the Roman Catholic clergy of this town attending the sick, the religious ceremonies of the past (Holy) week were omitted.—*Tralee Post*.

THE DISCOVERIES OF 1846.

We apprehend that there can be no doubt, that the year 1846 will be memorable to the end of time, for the remarkable extensions, or new applications, of human knowledge, which will come before future historians, as rendering illustrious its narrow limits. Most evident is it, that we are now living in the days predicted by the Hebrew prophet:—when "*many shall run to and fro; and knowledge shall be increased.*"

1. Foremost among these may be placed, the use of ether, inhaled for the facilitating surgical operations. Like all other appliances of this kind, it meets with failures and even evil results, in a few cases. But, for *one* fatal result, and *five* failures, we have *five hundred* instances of vast benefit; in many of which, beyond all doubt, lives have been saved, which would otherwise have been lost. Without describing it as infallible, or in *all* cases safe, or to be relied on, there can be no doubt that this discovery has conferred vast benefits on mankind.

2. The substitution of a new explosive material—the gun-cotton—in place of gunpowder, is another remarkable event. The extent of its utility is not yet ascertained.—Whether it will be largely adopted in warfare is still a point on which no decided opinion has been formed. But of its great utility in all blasting and mining operations, not the slightest doubt can exist. It is both cheaper and more powerful than gunpowder; and the absence of smoke gives it a decisive advantage. There can remain no question, that in all works of this description the new agent will rapidly supercede the old one.

3. The third discovery of 1846 is perhaps even of greater importance than either of the former. We allude to the lately patented process of smelting copper by means of electricity. The effect of this change will be quite prodigious. It produces in less than two days, what the old process required three weeks

Recreated from The Cork Examiner, Cork, April 5, 1847.

to effect. And the saving of fuel is so vast, that in Swansea alone, the smelters estimate their *annual saving in coal at no less than five hundred thousand pounds?* Hence it is clear that the price of copper must be so enormously reduced as to bring it into use for a variety of purposes, from which its cost at present excludes it.

The facility and cheapness of the process, too, will enable the ore to be largely smelted *on the spot*. The Cornish mine-proprietors are anxiously expecting the moment when they can bring the ore which lay in the mine *yesterday*, into a state to be sent to market *tomorrow*; and this at the very mouth of the mine. In Australia, also, the operation of this discovery will be of the most importance. Ten thousand tons of copper ore were sent from Australia to England last year, to be smelted at Swansea; and the result was only 1,600 tons of copper. But Australia in future will smelt her own copper, by a 36-hours' process; saving all this useless freight of the 8,400 tons of refuse; and saving also the cost of the old and expensive process. In a few years, Australia will send to market more copper than is now produced by all the rest of the world. But if our future penny-pieces are to bear any proportion to the reduced cost and value of the metal, they must be made of the size of dinner plates.—*Morning Herald*.

Recreated from The Freeman's Journal, Dublin, April 5, 1847.

RELIEF DELAYED—RIOTS AT YOUGHAL.

A FEW posts ago, we spoke of the atrocious precipitation of a Government which had dismissed twenty percent of the labouring population from the roads, without providing simultaneously the relief, in daily food, contemplated by the recent temporary Act. The inexorable order has been obeyed. But the daily rations to the disemployed are not forthcoming; and they are starving all over the country, and beginning to be mutinous.—The reproductive farm-work, to which the ministry, with a late—too late recognition of a necessity and a truth—bids them turn their spades and shovels—is not now to be had. The time is gone by. The opportunity was lost three months ago, while the people were sweating their unhappy souls away on those infernal high roads, which for many a long day to come shall remain as vestiges of LORD JOHN RUSSELL's Whig wisdom—preserving "the memory of his immortal services". There is no farming work to be done. The farmers everywhere say that, in the absence of the potato culture, they want few or no hands at this advanced period of the year. In most of the counties of Ireland this is the fact and the story. We have before us official and other information from the counties of Meath, Waterford, Clare, and Kerry, from which we gather that the employment of the dismissed labourers in agricultural work is entirely out of the question. Our blundering and botching government are once more at fault. There is no work for the people. Where is the food, at least, which should have been, under the Bill just passed, ready to diminish the misery of disemployment? It is not ready; and will not be ready these three weeks. Government Officials have got directions and formularies to observe; and will not move to the rescue of the people *selon les regles*—or not at all. At this moment, Commissioners and Committees are exhorting each other to haste, complaining of each other, and ready to go together by the ears. Let them take care a more formidable third party do not rush into the contention, striking both to the ground in a general tumult. We direct attention of all concerned to the movements of the starving people at Youghal, as they appear in the letter of our correspondent, MR. O'BRIEN. The untaught peasantry have no respect to the sacred regularity of official preliminaries. Being very degraded, they only understand that they are starving—that they want bread for themselves and the children at home.

Recreated from The Cork Examiner, Cork, April 9, 1847.

FURTHER REDUCTION OF LABOURERS ON THE PUBLIC WORKS—DETERMINATION OF THE LABOURERS.

On Saturday morning last the labourers who had been dismissed from the Public Works, on the previous evening, in the districts of Whitechurch and Carnavar, to the number of near 130, came into town and surrounded the residence of Mr. R. Brash, Assistant Engineer of the barony of Cork.

Mr. Brash seeing the assemblage of people, went out and spoke kindly to them; expressing a hope that they had not come to give him any annoyance, or create a disturbance.

Their spokesman stated that they had not come with any such intention, as they knew he had always acted kindly and humanely towards them. But they came for advice to know what they were to do now that the works were suspended.

Mr. Brash advised them to apply to the Relief Committees; as they were empowered by law to provide for the destitute and unemployed.

The men declared that not one of them had the means of providing a day's subsistence for their families; that they would apply to the committees, and that, if they did not get immediate relief, *they would help themselves, as they preferred being hung or shot to being starved!*

It is melancholy to think what may be the fate of those unfortunates, as the relief measures are not in forwardness in these districts.

The people, up to the present, have been orderly and well-conducted—no case of outrage or insubordination having occurred. It is now fearful to anticipate what these hitherto honest, industrious, and hard-working peasants may be driven to by the pressure of misery and starvation.

We would earnestly entreat the Relief Committees to be up and doing. Using the means which the law provided to avert famine, disease, and death, which must result from the suspension of the Public Works, and the supiness of Relief Committees. Of one thing we would have gentlemen be sure—these people will not suffer themselves to be starved to death; and who can blame *them?* The Government and the Relief Committees must divide the responsibility of all that occurs. Do not, we say, drive these and other wretched men to desperation, or you may find them more dangerous than you now imagine. Again, we say, be warned. We give the advice in all sincerity; for we have heard something of the expressed determination of these people.

Recreated from The Cork Examiner, Cork, May 5, 1847.

THE FATE OF EMIGRANTS.

The fate of the ship lately lost upon the coast of Scotland, leads to the most gloomy misgivings, with respect to the character of the vessels, which have been pressed for the first time into a dangerous voyage, by the extraordinary demand for a passage to America from this country. At this moment it appears that vessels sail from the various small inlets upon the Irish Southwest coast, each bearing away its crowds unnoticed, but for the most part of a description, that no one, who was not flying from death, would dream of putting his foot in. Not a creek but sends out its contribution of these into the ocean, frequently under the command of Captains, who never tried it before.

The *Times* lately contained an article, upon the necessity of exacting some proof of capacity and skill, from the men intrusted with the lives of so many persons. But to say nothing of fitness or experience, in the commanders, qualifications of which they are mostly destitute; or of the dangers, which the passengers incur, of being suffocated over water, from want of room, the size, construction, and age of the Ships, cause one to shudder for their seaworthiness across remote and perilous waters. The danger of their foundering at Sea is apt to be lost sight of, in the fears of the coast; but no one can doubt the frequency of a catastrophe, which none survive to tell.

The passengers in such craft, too often console themselves with a belief in the caution of the Captain, whose foot is on the same plank, for life or death. But they should not be so forward to measure their confidence by the conduct of a man whose habit is daring. He also follows a lucrative profession; and his rashness or ignorance may easily account for his courage.

We see no immediate check to this danger, except from the active inspection of emigrant ships by the local officers appointed to that duty. Nothing should be left undone to smooth the path of the poor emigrants, for none deserve it better. Unfortunately it avails little to plead the cause of those, who have no power to benefit or hurt, and even whose misfortunes occur unseen. Still it evinces a shameful disregard for life, to push out such multitudes upon the deep, without taking strict precaution for their transit over it.

Recreated from The Cork Examiner, Cork, May 12, 1847.

CITY OPPOSITION TO OUTDOOR RELIEF.

We perceive, by the report of the meeting of the Local Board of Health held yesterday, that the Mayor expressed his intention of calling a Public Meeting, in compliance with a requisition signed by some of the citizens, to petition against Out-door Relief. We know not the names of those attached to the requisition, nor any more of the matter than what we have seen in the report alluded to, but we have no hesitation in adopting the emphatic denunciation of Dr. LYONS against an intended opposition so inhuman and so cruel. The Workhouse is filled beyond what prudence would suggest as safe to the health of the inmate, or that of the city. At most it can shelter but a few *hundreds* more—while every lane in the city has its hundreds of starving poor—while every parish in the city swarms with THOUSANDS of destitute men, women, and children.—What, then, is to be done? Are the citizens of Cork, who can appear at a public meeting, to protest against giving relief to their *fellow-citizens*, because they are poor—because they are wasting away—because they are helpless, and at the mercy of the rich? Can it be possible that any man will publicly come forward, and oppose the *only* species of relief that can save thousands from death by starvation? Or; if they oppose Out-door Relief, *what relief are they to substitute for it?—What is their plan?*—who is to put it forth?

We write in haste; and shall, in the absence of fuller information as to the intended opposition, refer the reader to the emphatic observations of Dr. Lyons at yesterday's meeting of the Health Committee.

Recreated from The Cork Examiner, Cork, May 14, 1847.

THE COURT.

The Queen and Prince Albert, accompanied by the Prince of Wales, and the Princess Royal, and the Prince of Leiningen, arrived at Buckingham-palace, at ten minutes before six o'clock, on Tuesday afternoon, From Osbourne, Isle of Wight. Her Majesty and Prince Albert, accompanied by the Prince of Leiningen, honoured the Italian Opera-house with their presence in the evening.

Mr. Hugh and Lady Charlotte Montgomery have taken a mansion in Curzon-street, for the season.

Charles Powell Leslie, Esq., M.P., has arrived in Berkley-square, London, from Glasslough.

George Joy, Esq., has arrived at his seat, Woodtown House, county Dublin, from Galgorm Castle, County Antrim.

The Earl and Countess of Caledon have arrived on Carlton-house-terrace, from Caledon-park, county of Tyrone, for the season.

Recreated from The Belfast News-Letter, Belfast, May 14, 1847.

RIOTING IN SOUTH STAFFORDSHIRE.

Birmingham, Wednesday Evening.—The outrage which took place in Walsall on Monday, in consequence of the influx of Irish Labourers, has been followed by similar outbreaks of popular violence in the mining district. Near Wolverhampton about 1,000 miners and others met yesterday, and drove every Irishman from his employment. If they hesitated for a moment they were attacked with sticks and assailed with volleys of stones. Some of the men have been seriously hurt; one poor fellow was so stunned by a blow he received that it was feared death would ensue, but he is now recovering. The police, to the number of about fifty men, under the direction of Colonel Hogg, deputy chief constable, endeavoured to persuade the mob to disperse, and in some cases succeeded; but the assaults on the poor Irishmen were continued by the great majority of the rioters; and many of them had difficulty in escaping with heir lives. Many women were conspicuous amongst the crowds urging on the mob, and encouraging them in their violence.

To-day immense crowds of miners and others, to the number of between 1,000 and 2,000, again met on the Bilston and Willenhall-road. They attacked numerous of the Irish labourers, but the presence of the police awed them from further violence. Their appearance, however, was so threatening, that the authorities have deemed it necessary to take every precaution for preserving the public safety, and have accordingly put themselves into communication with Colonel Arbuthnot, the military commandant of the district.

Yesterday, at Wednesbury, another body of miners, numbering about 1,500, perpetrated similar outrages.—One man had his eye knocked out, several had their skulls nearly fractured, many were beaten till scarcely able to stand, and it was with difficulty some of them escaped with their lives. Two of the ringleaders have been apprehended by the police.

The whole of this populous district is in the most unsettled and excited state, and the contagion seems spreading, for accounts have been received this afternoon of similar proceedings at Stafford and in the Potteries.

The causes of this outbreak are somewhat deeper than at first appeared. The miners work only about three days a week, refusing to do more; and the coal and iron masters being thereby subjected to great loss and annoyance, have employed many Irishmen, who do not ask for holidays, and do the work equally well. This, we believe, is the real cause. The result of these tumults will, if persisted in, have a most disastrous effect on the iron trade, which is at the present moment in a very favourable condition. The miners threaten to strike on Saturday next, and there is reason to believe that it will be general, the amount of misery it will entail on the district will be incalculable.

Very few of the Irishmen have dared to return to work; such as have, being escorted by armed police to the places where they were employed.

Recreated from The Cork Examiner, Cork, May 17, 1847.

OMINOUS SIGN OF THE TIMES.

We have heard of a fact, which speaks more eloquently of the wretched and truly deplorable condition of our ill-fated land, than all the laboured essays or discourses which could be composed on the sad subject. The Cork Patent Saw Mills at King street, the largest establishment of the kind we believe in the land, have been at full work, with from *sixteen* to *twenty* pair of saws going at the same time from morning to night, for the last six or eight months, cutting planks for coffins ! The other orders to the same establishment were planks and scantlings for the furniture of berthing in emigrant vessels, and for the erection of Fever Sheds in all parts of the county !

Reprinted from The Cork Examiner, Cork, May 21, 1847.

WIDE STREET BOARD—*Friday.*

Mr. Michael Collins waited on the board, and said, gentlemen, some officer from this board has interfered with my business, for which I seek redress at your hands. I have been carrying on business for a long time on the Grand Parade, and driving a very good trade—indeed notwithstanding the general depression of the times my business is as good now, as it ever was for the last 25 years (oh, and laughter). In the course of my business it is requisite for my customers to send or bring cars to my door, to get either wine, rum, hollands, &c. (laughter); and on the preceding Saturday, when there were some cars there, I saw, having got out of a sick bed for the purpose, a man with a red cape, aided by a man in the employ of Mr. W. Fitzgibbon, who struck one of the horses in the head with a stick, attempting to send the horses and cars away, although they were at the moment waiting to be loaded with some of the various goods of my establishment.

Now, I, who never in the course of my life summoned any person, or received a summons, was fined, whilst in Dublin, for having a truck before my door; and now I demand that no horse or car be molested, whilst waiting for orders at my establishment.

Carey, the officer of the board, was then brought in and interrogated; but no charge was proved against him.

The Chairman intimated to Mr. Collins that he should get all possible protection in the prosecution of his trade, and that if anybody, except an authorised officer, attempted to molest a horse and car at his door, he would be liable to prosecution.

Mr. Westropp said, that he would suggest, nevertheless, that some third person should be got for the purpose of bringing both parties together on friendly terms, as it be of mutual advantage to both parties, as each had the opportunity of giving annoyance to the other.

Mr. Collins then withdrew, the Commissioners expressing their astonishment at the flourishing state of his trade.

Dr. Keough was next introduced, and he said he had to complain of a great nuisance, it was that the people of the Chamber of Commerce were in the habit of throwing filth before his door.

Mr. Reeves—They have been in the habit of throwing a great deal of that commodity upon us from time to time (laughter).

The Doctor observed that he meant the servants of the Hotel-keeper.

The Board having recommended the Doctor to prosecute the parties, he withdrew.

Two or three humble vendors of baskets came before the board, and besought in the most touching terms, the restitution of some of their goods, which had been seized, as a nuisance, on Daunt's-square. One of the petitioners, in the most ingenious manner, accounted for the baskets being on the pavement, which she attributed solely to the well known power of the laws of gravitation. After some merriment the matter was referred to his Worship the Mayor.

SOLDIERS IN CLOYNE.

We have letters before us complaining very bitterly of the grievous hardship occasioned by about 60 men of the 67th Regiment now billeted on the industrious but struggling householders of Cloyne.

Our correspondents also speak of the ill conduct and continued drunkenness of the soldiery. Rows and disturbances are of frequent occurrence, and, in some instances, assume a very dangerous aspect. On Saturday night last, one of the men brought out his bayonet into the street; and but for the interference of his Sergeant and the Head-Constable of the Police, bad work might have happened.

Surely, the Authorities might find some empty house, or houses, which could be used as temporary barracks; instead of rendering the presence of the military a burden and an annoyance to the peaceable inhabitants.

Recreated from The Cork Examiner, Cork, May 24, 1847.

SHAMEFUL IMPOSITION.
DELETERIOUS FOOD FOR THE PEOPLE OF THE WEST.

SOME gentlemen came to this office, last Saturday, for the purpose of shewing to us samples of damaged Indian Corn, from which meal was then being ground in an establishment of this city; samples of which meal were also shewn to us. The Corn was discoloured, and greatly deteriorated in value—fit, we should say, only for feeding cattle. *But the meal was most offensive in smell, and quite unsuited for human food.* Not only did it seem, if used, prejudicial to health, but, in such a sickly time as the present, positively destructive to life.

We were informed by the gentlemen who exhibited these samples—gentlemen in whom we place full reliance—that this villainous trash was intended for sale in a certain town in the West of this County, the name of which is one of those unhappily but too familiar to our readers. The names of the parties who ordered this stuff to be ground for *human food* were mentioned to us; and we must confess we heard them mentioned with a feeling of shame and sorrow—and particularly, in one case, with surprise.

We shall not mention these names *at present,* trusting that this notice will be sufficient to deter the parties in question from persevering in the cruel and inhuman intention of selling such deleterious stuff, as good food, to poor people already heavily visited by famine and pestilence; which latter must be aggravated by the reception, into the stomach, of any quantity of the meal exhibited to us, and of which we now possess a sample.

Bad Indian Meal is easily known by its *smell.* We would have our Western readers be on their guard.—Desire of gain induces "honourable men" to do extraordinary things.

Recreated from The Cork Examiner, Cork, May 24, 1847.

O'CONNELL.

The public mind yet feels intensely the shock it has received by the national bereavement. Our faculties are so steeped in sorrow that we have had neither inclination nor calmness sufficient to arrange matters for a public demonstration every way worthy the man lost to Ireland, and of the nation which he raised. The year '47 may indeed be marked in black. Human and superhuman ills have come upon us thick and heavy. The wrath of Heaven and the injustice of man have been both signally demonstrated. The land and the people have been struck with calamity. The poor and the humble have been first worn away to skeletons from want of food, and then mowed down in whole battalions by a murderous plague. Upwards crept the slaying typhus, and the good and merciful and loved of the land have been stricken with death during their merciful ministering.—These were home sorrows and individual evils which we bore up against with as much resignation as generally falls to our poor humanity. But in O'CONNELL the land has lost its great father and benefactor, the people a protector, counsellor, and bold, unflinching advocate; and every man, as it were, a personal and most beloved friend.

There is at this moment only national mourning in this ill-starred country, but we are not amongst those who give way to gloomy anticipations for our future progress in nationality and rational freedom.

We have lost O'CONNELL, but not the spirit of the man, nor the energy of his teaching. The land and the people, regenerated by the genius of universal emancipation which he evoked, cannot go backwards. The young blood of Ireland so often appealed to, and stirred to its depths by the words of the dead orator, cannot freeze into icy indifference whilst Ireland demands "the hearts and hands of free-born men." The more aged and sober-minded, the personal and political friends and fellow labourers of the LIBERATOR, who have been schooled so long in his tactics—with matured minds and manly independence—never could submit to any future tyrannical dominancy over their country—but above all, the public opinion of the day and the enlightenment of the popular mind could not brook the revival of any obsolete and governmental policy for Ireland. Whilst then we mourn over the departed veteran of Irish freedom, we have also reliance on the calm determination and cool energies of a people who have been taught wisdom by a most sorrowful experience, and who have learned from a disastrous history, that they have nothing to *hope* from the justice of England, but *everything* from reliance on themselves.

We are to take it for granted that there will be no future individual leader of the Irish people. Times and circumstances forced O'CONNELL into that national position. He was every way qualified, by his high physical and moral attributes, as well as by his consummate wisdom and prudence, for so elevated and perilous a duty. The one great object of his mission he achieved in the emancipation of the Catholics of Ireland, the other he has not lived to witness the triumph of, but he has educated the Irish people so that its attainment can only be a question of time. To achieve this, all we want is *unity* and *action*—a proper organisation of ALL the people of this country, and the determined and honest working of the men qualified by position, education and popular respect, to lead the movement in favour of all and every measure having for its object the real independence and true liberties of their country. Let the leaders of the Irish people be but true to themselves, to honour, freedom, and the old Ireland, and they have at their back, to aid them in a struggle so glorious and to cheer them on to a decided victory, some millions of as honest and true hearted men as ever strove for liberty, or laboured for the land they loved both wisely and well.

Reprinted from The Cork Examiner, Cork, May 28, 1847.

DEATH OF MR. O'CONNELL.

THE rumour of Mr. O'Connell's death, to which reference was made in our last, has since been fully confirmed. It is with no ordinary feelings we take up the pen to comment on the decease of a man, who, for a considerable portion of the life of the present generation, has been more prominently before the public, as a political character, than any other individual in civilized society. The death of such a character is an event involving, not merely a retrospect of the deepest interest, but a problem of prospective inquiry of the utmost importance, both to the internal condition, and external relations of these realms; and, even as a matter of personal history—of the history of an eminently distinguished man, whose biography is a mingled tissue of good and evil—

"A heterogeneous mass of glorious blame"

—the subject is fraught with the most powerful excitement to the public journalist. The acts, opinions, and speeches of Mr. O'Connell have, for a long period of years, exercised the abilities of the press to such an extent, as to render the task of approving or condemning them, when occasion required, a very considerable item in the duties of a public writer; and now that, to this extent, our "occupation's gone," even we, who have consistently, ceaselessly, and religiously, opposed his principles and condemned his motives, from the earliest hour in which we began to form an opinion upon the leading questions of Irish politics, cannot pretend to reflect upon his death, and the circumstances connected with it, without a deep impression of the solemnity of the occasion.

We have resigned our warfare with all that is mortal of Mr. O'Connell, but never shall we cease to bear our testimony against the evil doctrines which he has bequeathed, as a fatal legacy, to the country in which their operation, during his lifetime, was so baneful and deplorable.

Recreated from The Belfast News-Letter, Belfast, May 28, 1847.

RELIEF DEPARTMENT.

The following circular we extract from the *Clare Journal* of Monday, bears date the 2d of June, which we suspect should be the 2d of July:—

RELIEF DEPARTMENT.
Office of Public Works.
2d July, 1847.

SIR—I am directed by the board to inform you that the whole of road works in your district must be discontinued, unless under special authority, subsequently to this date, there being no funds available for their completion.

You will also discontinue all persons, whether assistant engineers, overseers, check-clerks or other persons acting under your directions, from Saturday, 10th inst. In the interim they may be employed in preparing the information called for by the circular of the 29th June (100), storing implements, and arranging all instanding claims, whether for temporary damages, for land or quarries connected with the road works, or for implements, &c., and the greatest vigilance must be used on your part to see that no claims are made for work done of any kind which has been already paid for. The repairs of implements as previously ordered, must be discontinued, and no claims for work subsequently to the 3rd inst., will be admitted.

In your office you may retain one clerk, but no more unless under special permission.

BY ORDER,

Jos. C. Walker, Secretary.
John Hill, Esq., Ennis.

Recreated from The Freeman's Journal, Dublin, July 1, 1847.

THE CROPS—THE POTATO.

The accounts relative to the crops continue to be of the most cheering description. The potato crop especially, about which so much anxiety has very naturally been felt, is represented as the most promising that has been seen for several years. There are, to be sure, statements or rumours, that in some few places the disease has re-appeared; but even supposing that those isolated statements were well founded, as far as they go, the positive and well authenticated accounts from almost every district in Ireland, describing the sound healthy appearance of the crop, and the joyous prospect of a bountiful return, afford a certain ground for hoping that the apprehensions entertained by some on the subject, will not be realised to any extent.

The intelligence from England, Scotland, and the Continent are also most encouraging.

Reprinted from The Freeman's Journal, Dublin, July 1, 1847.

STATE OF THE COUNTRY—FEVER.

A correspondent writing from Ardfert says:— "Fever goes on apace, cutting down the population rapidly: and by the decree of the relief committees, and the Relief Commissioners, the turf harvest has been entirely neglected, and very probably the wheat and corn harvests will, by the same politico economic scheme be equally neglected."

(*From the Sligo Champion.*)

Many persons have remonstrated us for making known the real state of the town. It is said that such announcements have a tendency to injure the trade of the locality, by keeping strangers out of Sligo. Although we have as much interest as any one else in the prosperity of our town, we think we would not be justified in concealing from the public its present deplorable condition.

Fever has been raging for a length of time in this unhappy borough, and we cannot say the disease is assuming a milder form. The contrary is the fact. The hospitals are full, and night and day numbers of persons in all stages of fever may be seen lying at the gates, exposed to "the pelting of the pitiless storm," for perhaps, in memory of man, there never was severer weather in the month of June. On Wednesday last we counted twenty fever patients lying upon damp straw, by the road side, upon the Mall.

A similar scene may be witnessed every day by any one who will risk his life by going to see it. We have been informed by the medical officers that the disease is not only increasing but that it is assuming a more malignant character. The type of the fever is much worse than it was a month ago. In fact we are plague-stricken, and there is not in Ireland, or perhaps, in the world, a more unhappy or dangerous spot than Sligo at the present moment.

Recreated from The Freeman's Journal, Dublin, July 2, 1847.

HARVEST PROSPECTS—THE POTATO, &c.

We copy the following from the *Cork Examiner* of Monday:—

Killarney, July 1st, 1847.

My Dear Mr. Maguire—Having just heard of your laudable desire to ascertain the state of the crops in this county, I am enabled from personal observation, as well as from the undoubting statements of the Catholic clergymen of this Decanate, to inform you that crops of all kinds, cereal and vegetable, are most flourishing here, and the potato throughout a diameter of 20 miles does not present a *single solitary stalk* on which the most scrutinising eye could discover either blot or blight.

It is moreover truly cheering to add that the breadth of cultivated land equals, if not exceeds, the average extent.

I remain yours very faithfully, T.J. O'Sullivan.

P.S.—Dysentery, which in winter and spring heaped up mounds of dead bodies, has entirely disappeared, and the fever at present prevalent, is of a *very mild* type.

We (*Clare Journal*) regret to learn from the subjoined letter, written by an experienced agriculturist, that the disease has again made its appearance in this county:—

"Sir—Like most people connected with farming, I have carefully watched the growth of the potato crop this season. The stalks at times presented some unusual appearances, but upon the whole have got on pretty well until now, when, I am sorry to say, the *disease* has fairly made its appearance upon the potato stalks.—Your obedient servant, J. F. Clarke."

THE IRISH RELIEF FUND.

It is highly creditable to the committee who had undertaken in Dublin the administration of the fund for the mitigation of the destitution in Ireland, that they dispensed the munificent sums placed at their disposal with a degree of economy and judgement which most effectually promoted the objects of the benevolent donors, the sum of nearly 60,000£. having through their excellent arrangements and personal superintendence been distributed at an expense of less than 500£., and the labours of the committee in this pious and charitable work extending over a period of six months ending on the 30th June. This statement must be particularly gratifying to the kind hearted contributors to the funds, as proving that no part of their benevolent subscriptions has been squandered in unnecessary expenses, or diverted from their legitimate purposes, which, on the contrary, have been materially aided by the discreet and prudent course adopted in their distributions.—*Morning Herald*.

Recreated from The Freeman's Journal, Dublin, July 7, 1847.

THE TWELFTH OF JULY.

We are induced to make one effort more to endeavour to dissuade those Protestants, in Belfast and its neighbourhood, who propose celebrating the approaching anniversary by a public procession, from a step in every way so ill-advised, injudicious—nay, absolutely indefensible—taking the present melancholy situation into account. Their best and most influential friends—the bulwarks of the cause they profess to hold so dear—set their faces against any obtrusive display of loyalty in such a calamitous season as this; every truly rational man, here, as in other principal Protestant districts of Ulster, (witness the excellent example of Newry, Armagh, Loughgall, &c.) condemn it; good sense is utterly opposed to it. If, however, young and thoughtless persons *will* persist in their silly intention, we may as well warn them now, that we should not be surprised if their conduct, in such circumstances, should lead to the re-enactment of the Processions Act next session.

Recreated from The Belfast News-Letter, Belfast, July 9, 1847.

(*From the Westmeath Independent.*)

A most daring and malicious attack was made on the butcher that supplies the meat to the troops stationed in Boyle and Strokestown. At about a mile from Boyle, at a place called Knockarush, a man asked for a seat on a car that was conveying the meat, and after walking along side of it for some time, he told the butcher to stand, as there were two comrades of his had sore feet, and give them a lift; he refused, when the ruffian drew out a pistol and told him to obey. On his comrades coming up, they turned the horse to the right about, and commenced distributing the meat to different houses on the road, and took the horse about a mile out of his course, and when parting, fired at the horse and wounded it in the groin; the man picked up most of the meat on his return. No clue has yet been obtained of the perpetrators!

Recreated from The Freeman's Journal, Dublin, July 12, 1847.

THE TWELFTH OF JULY IN BELFAST.

This ever-memorable anniversary was celebrated by the Orangemen of Belfast and the surrounding districts, in the usual way, by a procession; and we have much gratification in announcing, that, in this quarter, the day passed off without the slightest disturbance.

At an early hour yesterday morning, the members of the various lodges in town assembled quietly at their rooms; where, after arraying themselves with their insignia, they proceeded, without music, but with colours and characteristic decorations, to the appointed places of rendezvous. One of these was York-street, where a very large concourse assembled; and, having formed into procession, they marched to the Linen-hall. Here they joined the main body of the district; and having been marshalled according to their numbers, the whole body, comprising thirty stand of colours, proceeded, shortly after ten o'clock, on their way to Ballylesson. All the arrangements were carried out in a remarkably quiet and peaceable manner. There was no music—no shouting—no irregularity, all seemed determined to act up to the spirit of that admirable role of their institution, "giving none offence."

The appearance of the men, as they walked through the town, was pleasing. They were all well-dressed, and respectable-looking; and though, perhaps, nearly one-half of the members did not turn out on this occasion, the procession was imposing in point of numbers.

After passing the Malone turnpike, the Protestant band, which occupied the van, and who wore their handsome uniform, struck up their favourite airs; and their example was followed, along the line, by the drummers and fifers connected with each lodge; who made the hills and dales resound again with the sounds of those instruments, which are associated, in the minds of so many, with the pleasing scenes of bygone times. As the procession wound past the Botanic-garden, and through the picturesque scenery of Malone; its appearance was highly animated and spirit-stirring. The colours waved proudly in the breeze; strains of martial music aroused and delighted all hearts; and the steady deportment of the Orangemen was not the least gratifying circumstance to the eye of the spectator.

On reaching Ballylesson, the lodges debauched on a field, kindly granted for the occasion. Other bodies, from Derriaghy, Lishern, and the County Down side, successfully came in, until there were, in all, about 50 lodges on the ground, comprising probably about 3,000 members. Of spectators there was, at least, three or four times as many; and, as usual, the fair sex appeared in large numbers, to cheer their husbands, brothers, and, no doubt, lovers, with their smiles and beaming looks. A gayer or more cheerful spectacle than was presented, when all were assembled, perhaps never met the eye. Throughout the immense mass of people the sounds only of innocent mirth and amusement were heard; and all the arrangements were so admirable, that there was no confusion or disorder.

A platform was created in the field. The vast audience having drawn near it, and arranged themselves in order around it, the Rev. Mr. Brown, of Carryduff, preached a most eloquent and impressive discourse. This being concluded, the lodges marched round the field, and then separated, at an early hour, to go home. Those belonging to the district of Belfast reached town before six in the evening. On arriving at Donegall-pass they separated—one division proceeding to Cromac-street, and thence to their lodge-rooms; the others, marching through the principal streets to Talbot-street, at which they dispersed. As in the morning, there was no music while the procession passed through the streets; neither was there any disturbance or rioting. During the course of the day we did not observe a single person belonging to the institution intoxicated. Great credit is due to the authorities of the town, for the prudent precautions they adopted in order to prevent a breach of the peace. Bodies of the police patrolled the town in various parts; a troop of dragoons were stationed in the old House of Correction; and parties of military were placed in Townsend-street, and in the large school-room, Rosemary-street, ready for any emergency.

We observed with much gratification that Major-General Bainbridge, with his aide-de-camp, was on horseback during the afternoon, evincing a most creditable anxiety for the peace of the town. Lieut-Col. Williams, also, as well as several of the magistracy, were indefatigable in their exertions. Messrs. Lindsay and Armstrong were, as usual, most efficient. In answer to inquiries at a late hour last night, we were informed that there was not a single case of riot or intoxication, arising from the celebration of the anniversary, entered on the books at the police-office.

THE WEATHER—THE CROPS.—Since our last, the atmosphere has become considerably more humid than it has been since the commencement of the month, and on Saturday evening one or two very heavy showers descended, which had the effect of laying some of the heavier crops of wheat and barley in exposed situations. The weather, however, has been extremely sultry, and the ripening process must be going on with extreme rapidity. Nothing can exceed the luxurance of all the crops, both white and green, except upon the poorest soils. Potatoes continue to look extremely well. The fall crops appear in the best condition, and not withstanding the uncertainty of the weather, hay-making proceeds with activity.

Recreated from The Belfast News-Letter, Belfast, July 13, 1847.

FUNERAL OF THE LIBERATOR.

Sad, solemn and impressive—beyond all human power to describe, and almost beyond human conception—was the scene witnessed in our city yesterday—Ireland's last tribute of respect to her departed Liberator. Everything wore the appearance of mourning. It was impossible to pass through our streets without feeling that a great event was about to take place, and that event one of sorrow. In the countenance of every one there was depicted a heart-home grief. Not alone in the line of procession, but through the city generally, the shops were closed. The bells of the different churches tolled knells to the memory of the illustrious dead, and these were in fact the only sounds that broke on the solemn stillness; there was even in the most youthful and unthinking of the congregated masses, an appearance of solemnity well befitting the occasion. Every possible mark of outward respect and affectionate grief was demonstrated, and the demeanour of all proved that mourning was not put on as a mere holiday garb. Never before had so many persons assembled in public to behold a spectacle or rather to pay tribute of devotion and respect among whom there was such unbroken silence.

Men knew that he was dead, and yet it is only within the last few days that the fact has been realised to their minds. On the arrival of the body the melancholy truth burst for the first time upon the nation in its full intensity, and of the effects of that knowledge our streets afforded ample proof to-day. Each man felt the death of the Liberator as a family bereavement, and accorded a child-like devotion to the memory of him who loved Ireland, with more than a father's love. Rich and poor—old and young—men of every class and creed joined in the tribute. Never was a people's gratitude and a people's sorrow more unequivocally expressed; never was such expression more undividedly deserved.

From an early hour in the morning vehicles of every description continued to pour into the city; the several railway companies caused special trains to run on their respective lines for the accommodation of parties wishing to take part in the funeral, and the various coaches from the provinces for several days came fully loaded with persons from the most remote districts desirous to participate in the concluding honours to him whom they loved in life.

At eleven o'clock the hearse, drawn by six horses, arrived, and was admitted within the barrier. The canopy was tastefully ornamented; large velvet banners drooped from the side of each horse; the centres consisting of escutcheons of O'Connell. Its appearance was neat, elegant, and impressive—the ornaments most appropriate, and it passed along amidst the most silent and anxious attention.

MONUMENT TO O'CONNELL.

To-day a national meeting is to be held, at one o'clock, in the Royal Exchange, to consider what is the most fitting monument Ireland could raise to commemorate the principles, virtues, and deeds of O'Connell. We have no wish to anticipate the decision a meeting of such paramount importance may come to. Sure we are it will be worthy of the country. The monument, whatever it may be, will tell future generations that the men among whom O'Connell lived were deserving of being his cotemporaries. There will be no petty measuring of means. The conception will be grand, even though time should be required for its completion.

THE FUNERAL.

Yesterday was a day memorable for history, and consecrated to sorrow. On yesterday the earthly remains of Him who has left behind a name which time will only render more precious—a name bound up indissolubly, and for ever, with the most glorious struggles and brightest traditions of our land—were deposited, amid mourning and lamentation, in their last sad resting place. O'Connell slumbers in his tomb. After "life's fitful fever" the great man sleeps well. His ashes repose where he willed they should lie—among the citzens of Dublin—among the generous and faithful men who stood by him with courage and devotion throughout all his trials and sufferings—who bore him onward with a noble enthusiasm through the world of difficulties he successfully encountered—and shared in the mighty triumphs he had won. Among such a people his sacred ashes are deposited; and they will treasure them throughout all time, as the holy relics of one whose fame "will never perish", but pass down through all succeeding generations with ever increasing veneration and renown.

Deeply as he had been venerated when living, it was when the day of his final rest had come that the attachment of the people displayed itself in all its affecting intensity. It was when they saw the bones of him they loved so well, and who loved them with a love surpassing that of all others, that the kindliness of the Irish nature burst forth, and vented its regret in silent but profound sorrow. It was an affecting spectacle to hear them, as we have heard them, utter a simple and heartfelt prayer, and reverentially bow, as the sable hearse rolled slowly on; and scarcely less affecting to hear them recount his services and his triumphs, ending, with a mournful exclamation, that "the likes of O'Connell would never again appear on the world". And, in all their native simplicity and tenderness, they spoke the language of truth, and confirmed the certain judgement of history. Never again will the world behold such a man. The greatest, not of Irishmen, but the foremost among the sons of men, was consigned yesterday to his last repose in the Cemetery of Glasnevin.

O'Connell will sleep in Glasnevin; but his spirit will never sleep. It will be abroad—not only through Ireland, but through the world—to mould the thoughts of men, and direct them to the accomplishment of mighty issues by the simplest, although the grandest and most irresistible means that ever genius and wisdom placed in the hands of men to protect or recover their liberties.

THE ORIGINAL MARBLE BUST
OF O'CONNELL,
BY JONES.

THE Friends and admirers of the late lamented individual, are invited to an inspection of the above inimitable work of art, together with a specimen of the beautiful small copy, manufactured by Copeland and Garrett, a supply of which will shortly be ready for sale, at the moderate price of 10s. 6d.

To be seen at Cranfield's, 23, Westmoreland-street, where a book is open to receive names.

NATIONAL MEETING.

O'CONNELL MONUMENT.

IN compliance with Requisitions addressed to me from numerous Cities, Towns, and other localities, in and out of Ireland, calling upon me to convene a National Meeting to take measures for the erection of a Monument to the memory of the Liberator of his Country, DANIEL O'CONNELL, I hereby appoint THIS DAY (FRIDAY), the 6th of August Instant, for that purpose, the Meeting to take place at One o'Clock, p.m., at the ROYAL EXCHANGE.

MICHAEL STAUNTON,
Lord Mayor of Dublin.
Mansion House, August 6, 1847.

Recreated and reprinted from The Freeman's Journal, Dublin, August 6, 1847.

FUNERAL OF MR. O'CONNELL.

Dublin, Thursday.

The internment of Mr. O'Connell took place this day. His remains were removed from the Roman Catholic church in Marlborough-street to the cemetery of Glasnevin. They were brought along a line of road which must be at least eight Irish miles, and were made the leading attraction of a funeral procession, such as never before has been exhibited in Ireland. This procession was so arranged as to pass through the finest portions of the city, and to afford to the greatest advantage a view of that which was really a spectacle of what may be deemed "a national mourning;" for wherever it passed all business was suspended; the shops closed, and the windows occupied by those who seemed to take a deep interest in the scene before them. The enmity which hundreds entertained against Mr. O'Connell appeared to have been forgotten; and the only recollection of him that predominated was that he had been possessed of pre-eminent talents, and had attracted towards his country a large portion of the regards and interest of Europe. This might be considered as the cause why his funeral procession was the most extraordinary exhibition that has ever taken place in Ireland. The mourners were to be reckoned by the thousands; and more actually took part in the ceremonies of the day than there were persons to look at them. There were various con-fraternities, many trade associations, the representatives of corporations from all parts of Ireland—Catholic clergyman, and Catholic bishops, from the most remote parts of the kingdom; the commissioners even of the smallest towns; the members of the temperance societies, and in addition to these testimonies of democratic, or Roman Catholic sympathy, there were to be seen the carriages even of persons connected with the government and the law.

It may be added, that this procession, greater than the greatest of those political demonstrations in which the deceased so much delighted, passed off without the least disorder occurring to mar the solemnities of the day, or the slightest disturbance breaking forth amongst those thousands who had crowded together to manifest their grief and to exhibit their respect for the departed.—*Morning Herald.*

Dublin, Aug. 5.

To-day the mortal remains of the Great Agitator of Ireland were consigned to the grave, and a vault in the cemetery of Glasnevin now encloses the body of the man whose political career has for so many years excited the attention of all Europe. Perhaps no funeral was ever more numerously attended, in Ireland at least, than that of Mr. O'Connell was to-day, for at the lowest computation not less than 50,000 persons left their homes to follow in the funeral train, besides twice as many more who thronged the windows and roofs of the houses on the route which was pursued by the procession. Some persons, and principally those who differed from the political creed of the deceased, attended from a respect to the memory of a great and illustrious countryman; the remainder, who formed the great mass of the people—those whose hearts he had gained over, and by whose aid he had raised himself to power—the stepping stones of his greatness—these, the middle and lower classes of the Irish people, attended him to the grave with hearts overflowing, and vieing with each other in a sad species of enthusiasm in paying homage to the memory of their beloved leader.

On the preceding day Dr. Miley delivered a funeral sermon over the remains, at the chapel, Marlborough-street, to a crowded audience. The rev. gentleman in the course of his sermon became so intensely affected, that the tears flowed down his cheeks, and his auditors, influenced by his example, participated in his feelings.

The London Illustrated News, London, August 14, 1847.

From an early hour this morning numbers of persons congregated in the neighbourhood of the chapel, which contained the remains, and amongst the rest, "the maim, the halt, and the blind," who cared little for the pressure and violence of the crowd, provided they could obtain the earliest glance at the coffin which enclosed the body of O'Connell. At twelve o'clock the procession set forth from the above chapel, and thence proceeded through the principal streets of the city, attended by an immense concourse of people. It was about one mile and a half in length, and was composed of various associated trades walking on foot, followed by Mr. O'Connell's triumphal car, which conveyed him from the Richmond Penitentiary to his residence in Merrion-square after his acquittal by the House of Lords. The coffin was laid on a large rather plain, and open hearse, and which was itself covered with rich Genoa velvet and gilt ornaments. The members of Mr. O'Connell's own family, the Lord Mayor, clergy, magistracy, gentry, and citizens followed.

After the procession had passed through the appointed route, and arrived at Glasnevin Cemetery, the usual service was read over the coffin, which was then consigned to a magnificent vault especially prepared for its reception in the very centre and most elevated portion of the burial-ground by the Cemeteries Committee, who have spared no expense to bestow, both on the ceremonial and on the grave, the most gorgeous appearance which the most liberal expenditure could present.—*Times*.

Recreated from The Freeman's Journal, Dublin, August 7, 1847.

DREADFUL ACCIDENT.

Another instance of the imprudent use of fire arms occurred yesterday, at Dollymount wall, off the North Bull. Three lads, belonging to the humbler classes—two of whom were brothers—went out to amuse themselves at Dollymount, taking with them a short fowling-piece, for the purpose of firing at a mark. The two brothers, having bathed, were proceeding to dress, when their comrade, who was about twelve years of age, took up the gun, under the impression that it was not charged, levelled it at one of his companions, who was a few years younger than himself, and fired. The gun was loaded with large duck shot, and the charge took effect in the left cheek of the unfortunate boy, inflicting a very severe and dangerous wound. The sufferer was immediately conveyed to one of our city hospitals, where he now lies in a most precarious state. The lad who fired the gun was taken into custody by the police of Clontarf station.

Some measures should be taken to prevent the recurrence of accidents of this nature. Numbers of young and inexperienced persons, with fire arms, are to be seen, particularly on the Sabbath, parading about Clontarf strand, and the other suburbs of the city. Even yesterday we observed several individuals carrying fowling pieces in a very careless and reckless manner in the vicinity of the place where the accident occurred. The authorities should look to this.

TO THE PUBLIC.

ON MONDAY, the 16th inst., the LOUGHREA and TUAM DAY COACHES will run Daily (Sundays excepted) to and from the Railway at Enfield; and in about a fortnight or three weeks it is expected the Loughrea will be extended to Galway. It is also intended to extend the Boyle Coach to Sligo.

A Coach leaves Athlone at 8 o'clock every Monday, Wednesday, and Friday, and arrives at Enfield in time for the 3 o'clock Train; it returns on Tuesdays, Thursdays, and Saturdays, on the arrival of the 12 o'clock Train.

A Coach leaves Longford every Morning at 8 o'clock, and arrives at Enfield in time for the 3 o'clock Train; it returns every Afternoon on the arrival of the 12 o'clock Train.

Seats Let in Dawson-street, and Railway Office, Broadstone.

48, Dawson street, August 9, 1847.

VALUABLE COSMETICS.

H. P. TRUEFITT, Son and Successor to the original and celebrated P. Truefitt, Sen., 20 and 21, Burlington Arcade, Piccadilly, London, is desirous of Introducing to General Notice in the Provinces, the following invaluable appendages to the Toilet, which have been long in use on the Dressing Tables of the Fashionable World in London.

The TINCTURA, or LIQUID HAIR DYE. Dying the Hair has hitherto been a most uncertain and unsatisfactory operation, but by this valuable discovery Grey or Red Hair is infallably and permanently turned to Brown or Black, Full instructions for applying the dye will be found on each Bottle. In cases at 5s., 10s., and 21s., each.

The MEDICATED MEXICAN BALM, for strengthening and beautifying the Hair, far superior to Bears Grease or the compounds sold under that name. In bottles from 2s 6d. Upwards.

TRUEFITT'S FLORAL EXTRACT, a fragrant and refreshing Hair Wash of the most grateful qualities. It renders the Hair delightfully soft and glossy, and is the most *recherche* article for the Toilet ever produced. These are all packed in external cases for protection in travelling.

Sold by Truefitt, 20 and 21, Burlington Arcade, Piccadilly, London, *and by no other house in that locality*—pray observe the numbers particularly.

Agent for Dublin: Mr. RICHARD WORN, 17, Dawson-street.

TO THE LOVERS OF THE FINE ARTS.

MICHAEL GAFFNEY,
77, ABBEY-STREET,

BEGS to inform his Friends and the Public that he has for Sale a Print of the only Genuine Likeness of the late DANIEL O'CONNELL, Esq., M.P.; also a splendid Engraving of the LAST SUPPER, by Waggoner, of Germany, with a collection of beautiful Engravings, too numerous for insertion, which he will dispose of on very moderate terms.

Prints framed on the most moderate terms.

Reprinted from The Freeman's Journal, August 2-10, 1847.

TERMINATION OF THE RELIEF SYSTEM.

On this subject, the following circular, conveying important information, has been issued to the inspecting officers of the unions:—

RELIEF COMMISSION OFFICE, DUBLIN CASTLE.

6th August, 1847.

SIR—The relief commissioners have received many communications from committees remonstrating against closing temporary relief in their respective districts on the 15th of August. The objections advanced are—1. That the harvest will not be in full operation by that period. 2. General want of means of the poor. 3. That the poor law guardians have no funds.

With regard to the first, the commissioners wish it to be understood that they do not consider the actual state of the harvest in the precise locality to be the only datum for discontinuance of relief to the able-bodied, since it is clear that the reduced prices of provisions, together with the general, if not local, increasing demand for labour, must afford means of earning a subsistence to many who are now depending on public support. That this is the case, and that many who ought not, have been still lingering on the gratuitous relief, has been proved in several places by very light tests. Many have given up the rations for themselves and families, rather than perform three or four hours' labour, and others rather than enter the poorhouse.

Temporary Relief Act was passed, not as a remedy for any embarrassments in the union, nor for any general poverty in the country, but solely to replace for one season the food of which the people were deprived by the failure of the potato crop, and the operation of the act was to be discontinued as the different crops of the ensuing season should come forward and provisions become more abundant.

As these are gradually in the course of being realised, the commissioners feel that their functions must close, and the poor law guardians must make the necessary efforts for such partial early collection as may be sufficient to meet the first emergency.

There are still some remote districts where the relief may be continued by special permission after the 15th of August, for limited periods, on account of the peculiar extent of distress in them, added to an unhappy neglect of that cultivation which might have provided an earlier and more general stock for the support of the people, but even in these the scale must be very mush reduced.

The period for the revision of the lists, in reference to individuals only, is now passed, and they must be reduced by classes even where relief is allowed to be partially continued.

It must be recollected, that nothing but compelling men to make greater efforts for self-support, and to avail themselves of means that are really within their reach, will prevent the great amount of disastrous results that must otherwise ensue from a sudden stoppage, on a great scale, at the end of September, after which *all advances under the Temporary Act must cease.*—(By order of the Relief Commissioners).

R. Hamilton.

Recreated from The Freeman's Journal, Dublin, August 11, 1847.

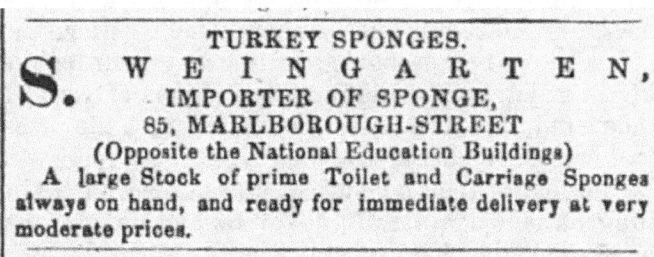

Reprinted from The Freeman's Journal, Dublin, August 19, 1847.

PRIESTLY INTOLERANCE.

COACHFORD PETTY SESSIONS.—BUCKLEY *v.* REV. WM. M'CARTHY.—The prosecutor being examined by Mr. Thomas Ware Croker, solicitor, stated as follows:—

Witness is a young man in the employment of the Rector of Donoughmore, the Rev. Mr. Cotter, as colporteur or distributor of Bibles and Testaments; was proceeding alone on Friday last, on his peaceful mission, when he met Mr. William M'Carthy, a Roman Catholic priest, who, after passing him, rode back and inquired what he had in the bundle? Witness said, "Bibles and Testaments, Sir." The priest then induced deponent to produce all his books, and, as soon as he got them together, he flung them in witness's face, dashing them about the road and saying, "I left the house this morning to horsewhip you;" the priest then called a man to hold his horse, and jumping off, he ran to witness and struck him several blows across the face and neck, and when the lash of the whip came off, he struck witness with the leaden end about the head, which, but for the hardness of his hat, might have killed him, and the man who held the horse, instead of coming to witness's relief, flourished his stick in a threatening manner.

The priest then laid hold of witness by the breast, and made two attempts to trip him, by putting his leg behind witness; he then let him go, and drew back to strike him another blow, when witness ran off without hat or books, calling out "murder," being in great fear of his life; the hat was afterwards recovered, but Buckley was informed that the priest had caused the books to be burned on the road.

The bench then consulted, and agreed on taking informations against Mr. M'Carthy, and ordered that he should give bail to stand his trial at the next quarter sessions in Cork.—*Cork Constitution.*

Recreated from The Belfast News-Letter, Belfast, August 17, 1847.

FAMILY MOURNING ESTABLISHMENT.

THE Proprietor of the above Establishment begs leave to call attention to its great utility. It has ever been a source of inconvenience and regret on an occasion when mourning has been required, that its purchaser has at such a time been compelled to the painful necessity of proceeding from shop to shop in search of each distinct article of dress. This may be completely obviated by a visit to the
FAMILY MOURNING ESTABLISHMENT.
where every description of
WIDOW'S SILKS,
PARAMATTA, ZEMALINE, CASHMERE,
4-4, 5-4, & 6-4 CRAPE,
without a fold,
GLOVES, HOSIERY, &c. &c.
can be bought on the most
REASONABLE TERMS;
and where everything necessary for a complete outfit of
MOURNING
may be had and made up, if required, by
EXPERIENCED ARTISTES,
with the strictest attention to taste, elegance, and economy.
WIDOWS' AND FAMILY MOURNING
are always kept made up, so that the Ladies may, by a note descriptive of Mourning required (either for themselves or household), have it forwarded to them in Town or Country immediately.
Every description of Silks, for slight or complimentary Mourning; Printed Muslins, Goats' Hair, Barege, and Evening Dresses in the greatest variety.
THE MILLINERY ROOMS
contain a beautiful assortment of Millinery, Head Dresses, Flowers, Crape and Muslin Collars, Berthes, &c., &c., with every description of Jewellery for Mourning.
99, GRAFTON-STREET.

DEVONSHIRE CIDER.

WE have just received per Ceres, from Paignton our last Cargo of the above for this Season. The quality is very superior and terms liberal.
The early orders of the Trade are requested.
JOHN GILBRT & SON.
Office and Stores, 25, Upper Jervis-street,
19th August, 1847.

Reprinted from The Freeman's Journal, August 19, 1847.

THE YOUNG IRELANDERS.

We have learned, "more in sorrow than in anger," that a number of misguided youths in this town, diseasedly emulative of the questionable reputation of the Young Irelanders in the other provinces, held a meeting, for the purpose of organizing an "affiliated" Confederation Club. In what entry, or nameless crypt, this meeting took place, we have not been informed; neither can we give our readers any information respecting the names of the orators, or the nature of the oratory. We have reason to believe, however, that the majority of the meeting was composed of young persons, who have no visible occupation, and who wish to cut a short way to fame, without the trouble of earning it by close application to a legitimate study or avocation. We are inclined to think, that this juvenile body will occasion more perplexity to anxious fathers and respectable mothers than to the state at large. We shall watch their proceedings, however; and, should they be guilty of any overt act of indiscretion beyond their present folly, the public shall be duly informed thereof.

Recreated from The Belfast News-Letter, Belfast, September 10, 1847.

OPPOSITION TO THE PAYMENT OF RENT—THE POOR LAWS.

A landlord in the neighbourhood of Clara, having intimated to a tenant in comfortable circumstances, after repeated applications for payment of his rent, that he would enforce it by distress of his property. On the night of the day on which this conversation took place, nearly one thousand persons assembled, cut down and carried away large quantities of grain crops; while these unlawful acts are nightly increasing, and every fraudulent means are resorted to by the tenantry, to defraud the landlords of their rights, the government are about to enforce the repayment of the advance, made to relieve the people during the late famine, not withstanding the urgent reasonable appeals that have been made to them by the landlords, to postpone the repayment to a future period, as under the present exigencies of the country, they are unable to meet the increased taxation. In addition to repayment of the famine loan, the boards of guardians of the several unions throughout the country, are called upon to make provisions for affording outdoor relief, a system which it is to be feared unless the greatest prudence and caution is adopted, will not only in many places be destructive to property, oppressive to the ratepayers, but be productive of deleterious effects upon the poorer classes, as it will tend to demoralize and create a spirit of indolence. It is quite impossible that these excessive demands can be met. The Boards of Guardians generally, are in a state of bankruptcy. With reference to those in our district, the greater portion of them are heavily in debt. In Nenagh there is not as much in the hands of the treasurer as would purchase a cwt. of oatmeal; large sums are due to the contractors, some of whom have expressed their inability to give further supplies unless their demands were paid. The unions of Tulamoore, Roscrea, &c., are in a similar state; and as regards the Parsonstown Union, the board is nearly 3,000£ in debt. A few days hence the accounts were made up, and it was found that a sum of *one thousand and eight pounds, seven shillings, and two pence*, was due to the bread contractor! The guardians have not a shilling to their credit, and the provincial bank refuses to make any advance. A new rate has been made, but no measures have yet been adopted to enforce it; indeed we fear that the great majority of the ratepayers will be unable to pay it. If the rate is not paid, the guardians will be obliged to close the workhouse, and if such a course has to be adopted what is to become of the large number of decrepid and infirm creatures who now have no other asylum to seek refuge in? In order that the difficulties may be met, some active and vigorous steps must be immediately taken to obtain a loan.—*King's County Chronicle.*

Recreated from The Freeman's Journal, Dublin, September 18, 1847.

THE TIPPERARY TENANT LEAGUE.

We cannot permit such a demonstration as that which took place in the county of Tipperary, a few days since, to lie on record, without expressing our sentiments regarding it. The meeting, which was a sort of "monster meeting", in its way, was held in the open air, at Holycross, on *Sunday* last, a fact which proves that the place is a very *un*holy cross, indeed. We pass over the flagrant desecration of the Sabbath, thus perpetrated in the face of the Christian world, because every Ulster reader will pass his own condemnation upon it, without needing our suggestion. The meeting was convened under Young Ireland auspices, who it thus appears, have as little respect for the Lord's days as their elder compatriots of the O'Connell school. By turning to the brief account of the proceedings, which will be found elsewhere, it will be seen that the Tipperary League coolly demands for the occupying tenant a right *in perpetuity* to his holding, as long as he pays his rent; and this is called the tenant right of Ulster! It is, in fact, a demand that the whole soil of Ireland shall be transferred from the landlords to the people, the former being generously allowed, in exchange, the nominal title, and whatever premium upon their capital (which is the land) the latter may choose to afford them. We can imagine what amount of premium the "Tipperary boys" would be disposed to allow, when the rental of Ireland would come to be fixed by Messrs. Doheny and Lalor, at a Holycross conclave. This is the first practical step in the march of anti-rent agitation. The landlords are, indeed, kindly called upon to *co-operate* in the goodly work of handing over their estates to the "finest peasantry;" but the inference is, that if they do *not* co-operate, the estates will be seized whether they will or no, and the long-sighed-for consummation will be achieved. We owe this delightful state of things partly to Conciliation-hall, and partly to the "Confederation", for it is now a race between these parties which shall be first "in at the death". We shall remember this to the latter when they make their *debut* in Belfast. The calling of the demand of the Tipperary League "The tenant right of Ulster" is not only an abuse of words, but a falsehood in point of fact. It would be impossible *now* to establish the Ulster tenant right in the other provinces. That right is simply the maintenance of a *custom* which has survived to the present time since the Plantation. It is coeval with the original title of the colonists themselves, and was given to them as a compensation for leaving a rich, enlightened, and prosperous country, to come to a province laid waste by fire and sword, and peopled with the enemies of the state and of its religion. It is a right totally independent of the landlord's right, and was always so recognised. It is simply a substitute for that compensation for improvements upon a farm which ought to be the right of every improving tenant in giving up, or being obliged to leave, his holding; but it is not a perpetuity or fixity of tenure. It is evidently not this description of right which the Tipperary men covet. They want to be masters, not tenants.

Recreated from The Belfast News-Letter, Belfast, September 24, 1847.

A NEW PENAL SETTLEMENT.—The Commander of her Majesty's ship Bramble has taken possession of New Guinea in the name of her Majesty, which circumstance is strongly confirmatory of the reported intention of the British government to found a penal settlement in that vast island.—*South Australian Register.*

No trace whatever has been had to the recovery of the 7,500l. bank notes missed in the packet of the National Bank.—*Limerick Chronicle.*

By the death of our distinguished and gallant countryman, Lieutenant-General Sir Henry Sheehy Keating, K.C.B., his estates in the counties of Cork, Limerick, and Tipperary, devolve on his eldest son Captain James S. Keating, late Royal Dragoons. His remains will be interred in the family vault at Dromcologher, in this county, of which the late general was a native. Sir Henry Sheehy Keating was married to the sister of the Rev. Joseph Singer, F.T.C.D.—*Limerick Chronicle.*

Reprinted from The Freeman's Journal, Dublin, September 24, 1847.

WHAT ENGLAND HAS DONE WITH HER VAUNTED MILLIONS FOR IRELAND.

Mr. Edward Wilmot Chetwode has addressed the following letter to the *Evening Mail*. It will be remembered that Mr. Chetwode is a Protestant gentleman of ability and patriotism, and a Federalist, we believe, in political opinion.

If government is not ignorant itself of the state of things in Ireland, and of the worse prospects before us, it must be afraid to grapple with the ignorance of the people of England and with the mercantile calculation which is involved in the common English answer to our renewed claims on charity this year, viz—"if the loan of £8,000,000 or £10,000,000 last year has done you no good, what can you expect this year?"

The result of either ignorance or fear on the part of government, at the present crisis, must involve it in the further guilt of waiting till famine, and, it may be plunder and bloodshed, shall have awakened the English public, and till outraged humanity shall call on the government no longer to remain inactive.

If it does not intend to await this still more cruel point it must at once begin to act—it must tell the English public what their £10,000,000 have done, and what they have not done. In a mercantile view they have done nothing; but in the view of humanity, they have prevented some new millions of deaths, for the last few months; but death stares our millions in the face again; our own resources are nearly exhausted, and after, perhaps, some plunder and some bloodshed, the wider work of famine will again set in—the crisis demands action or ensures guilt, the heavy guilt of delay.

Has England forgotten how she ought to meet a foreign foe, if landing on the coast of Ireland; and is not our present famine a stronger enemy than were a few French ships in Bantry Bay? Would she hesitate one hour in adding even a hundred millions to the national debt under the former supposition, and does she now talk of the small loan of last year as the *'ne plus ultra'* of her power? Government must tell the English public that the *land* of Ireland cannot keep the people of Ireland alive, and the government ought not to fear to broach the bold principle that *property must support poverty*—that the whole property of a country ought to be taxed to support the poverty of a country, especially when the land, which never should have been required to do this work *alone*, is unable to perform the unfair task. Free trade, which has dealt so heavy a blow on our land, demands that *this burden shall be placed on property at large*.

The same God who lends his ear to the landowner lends his talent to the capitalist, and adds the same condition of stewardship to both. Let this position once be established (and I know no policy which would cast more credit on a fearless minister)—and then the course for unfortunate Ireland is clear. Either the Union has made her one with England, or it is an empty name—and if she be one with England, English wealth should be taxed for Irish poverty.

And I would ask, is there any one argument which is offered in favour of a well-managed estate paying for the paupers of an ill-managed estate in the same parish, which does not also apply to the claim of the pauper of Ireland on the wealth of England, and if the estate of England has had the management of the estate of Ireland for the last forty seven years, how much stronger is our present claim?

Statistics of the Electric Telegraph.—The total extent of telegraph in England is nearly 4000 miles, representing an outlay of about £300,000. The staff of *employes* may be taken at upwards of 800 persons.

Two of the Sisterhood of Mercy have arrived in Nenagh to open the convent founded for them by the Right Rev. D. Vaughan who held a conference at Nenagh on Tuesday.

The Great Britain, outward bound for Melbourne, was spoken with twenty three days out from Liverpool, and will a six day's sail of the Cape of Good Hope—all well.

Reprinted and recreated from The Cork Examiner, Cork, October 22, 1847.

CHANCERY.
(*Before Master Murphy.*)

On Saturday, Messrs. Ardill and Gresson, solicitors for the receiver, laid statement of the facts before the Master. By said statement, it appeared that five tenants on the estate of the lunatic, scituate in the King's County and Tipperary, were in arrear, and they refused to pay their rent. And, it appeared also, that a combination existed amongst all the tenants of the estate not to pay. The plan suggested by the receiver was, to have notice to quit served on said tenants, as a warning to the other defaulting tenants that, if they would not pay, they should be dealt with in a similar manner.

Mr. John McGrath appeared on behalf of Capt. Rochfort, a party beneficially interested in the estate, and the brother-in-law of the lunatic. He said that the tenants selected on this occasion, and for the purpose of eviction, were five of the poorest tenants on the estate, whose yearly rent in the aggregate did not amount to a sum of 30£. He was instructed by Capt. Rochfort to oppose such a proceeding. The people on whom notice to quit was sought to be effected lost their entire property when they lost their potato crop; and these were not times to hunt such poor people from their dwellings merely that their condition might be made an incentive for others to pay. He thought that the rich combinators should be looked to rather than the poor, who had been deprived of their property by the awful visitation of Providence, which is now afflicting this land.

Master Murphy very humanely recommended that the tenants should be processed, and a notice to quit served at the same time, not for the purpose of doing anything which might be considered harsh and unreasonable, but for the purpose of showing that the laws should be vindicated, and giving them an opportunity of coming into court with such proper explanations as they had to offer for the conduct complained of. He said he invariably found the tenants disposed to pay when they saw a judicious line of proceeding adopted.

A novel case of summary ejectment occurred at Chester on Wednesday. A house in the occupation of a Mr. Crawford, which was required for the purpose of the new station in the course of erection, was attacked by a number of railway workmen while a guest was sitting down to dinner, and in the course of two hours the building razed to the foundation. The occupier had several notices served on him, which were treated with contempt, therefore, the adopted mode of ejectment.

Recreated from The Freeman's Journal, Dublin, November 1, 1847.

"ATROCIOUS MURDER."

Under the above head a correspondent of the *Limerick and Clare Examiner* gives the following brief but horrifying account of a most savage act of assassination stated to have been perpetrated on Friday last. We should observe that the correspondence is anonymous, being merely signed "A Subscriber":—

"Fortanne More, Oct. 29, 1847.

"DEAR SIR—At eight o'clock this morning a most cruel murder was committed within a quarter of a mile of my house. The victim was Mr. Michael Walsh, steward to Charles George O'Callaghan, of Ballinahinch. He was on his way to Ennis, to arrange some business with Mr. Enright, and had not proceeded more than half a mile from his own house when he was shot dead, and his brains dashed about the road."

The *Limerick Chronicle* states it has received the following from a county Clare magistrate :—

"SCARIFF, SATURDAY.—Another of those horrible murders which disgrace our unfortunate country has just been committed on the public high road, leading from Killaloe and Scariff, to Tulla and Ennis in this county. The unfortunate victim was Michael Walsh, steward and care-taker to Charles G. O'Callaghau, Esq., of Ballinahinch. This respectable man, when on his way to Ennis this morning, at the hour of eight o'clock, on the public high road, near Fort Anne, was fired at from behind a wall, and shot dead. One ball entered his mouth, and took with it the roof of his skull. The second entered his head. Both shots were heard distinctly by persons immediately near, but no clue has been obtained of the perpetrators."

Reprinted from The Freeman's Journal, Dublin, November 2, 1847.

EXTERMINATION IN THE COUNTY LEITRIM.
TO THE EDITOR OF THE FREEMAN.

Sir—Permit me through your valued journal to give to the public a brief account of the most heartless extermination with which this part of the country has ever been disgraced. On the 29th instant the sheriff, with a detachment of military from Mohill, and fifty police from the surrounding stations proceeded to the townland of Leganomer, in the parish of Aughavess, in this county, the property of Major Ormsby Gore, Porkington, Wales, for the purpose of dispossessing the tenants on that farm—fifty-five human beings were left houseless on that night. The places they used to call their homes were burnt to the ground. The number of dwelling houses burnt was ten, together with the office houses attached to each. Mr. Henry Fry, of Carrigallen, who did business under Mr. Dix, for Major Ormsby Gore, to his credit be it told, refused to set fire to the houses, saying, "Major Gore did not employ him for burning houses." Now, had those poor people been exterminated for non-payment of rent there might be some palliation for the cruelty, but such was not the case; for of three half-years' rent due the 1st of September, 1847, they offered to pay one year's rent (the custom in this county being, that one half-years' rent should remain unpaid) which Mr. Lawder refused to accept, saying, "He would take no receipt from any tenant holding under *twenty* acres of land." But as none of them came up to that standard, they were all cleared away.

I send you the names of the heads of families dispossessed, with the number of family:—

1. John Grant, four in family, held eight acres of land, a very solvent tenant.
2. John Quinn and wife, two in family; himself aged 87, was dragged from his sick bed, and laid on a wad of straw, to see the house in which these 87 years were spent burned.
3. Thomas Currin, six in family, held six acres of land.
4. John Currin, eight in family; a solvent tenant holding thirteen acres, of which he lately purchased seven acres for the sum of 20l.
5. Brien Currin, eight in family, held four acres of land; solvent.
6. Pat. Donohue, seven in family, held five acres of land; Pat Donohue being in Scotland earning the rent, his wife and five children just recovering from fever, refused to leave the house, but the fire being applied, she was forced to depart.
7. Thomas Quinn, four in family, held seven acres and a-half of land.
8. John Quinn, four in family, held seven acres of land; his family recovering from fever, could scarcely crawl out before the house was burnt.
9. Laurence Quinn, four in family, held six acres of land.
10. Widow Quinn, eight in family, held seven acres of land.

It was a most heartrending scene to witness on the day after the burning, the smoking embers of the consumed village, the fragments of broken furniture scattered around, as it was rescued from the flames, and the sorrowful looks of that group of old and young as they gathered around me to tell the sad story of their misfortunes. They said "We all lived in peace in this village; we were never at law with each other. Our forefathers lived here for generations past. You would say, if you saw it before this ruin came, that "it was a nice little village;" and so, I am sure, it was. Another said, "Do you think does the law sanction such cruelty?" But I will not detail any more of that affecting conversation which left on my mind one impression stronger than the rest, and it was a horror for the laws that would permit, nay, sanction, such extermination. I wonder if such a scene were enacted in the north of Ireland, would Lord Clarendon have reason to congratulate the Synod of Ulster on the peaceful effects of its teachings.

I will communicate to you the result of next week's burnings when they take place, for the truth of what I have stated I can give fifty vouchers if necessary.

AN OBSERVER.

On Wednesday last Mr. Neal M'Corniskin, was killed at Ture Bridge, county Donegal. The occasion of the accident was the furious driving of two other persons in carts, which upset the one wherein he and his little daughter, who escaped, were seated. An inquest was held, when a verdict of accidental death was returned.

A party of armed men entered the house of James Misogue, of Coolderry, on the 27th instant, and by presenting pistols, and threatening to take his life, made him deliver up to them a blunderbuss with which he was in the habit of protecting at night his little property.

Reprinted from The Freeman's Journal, Dublin, November 2, 1847.

ANOTHER DREADFUL MURDER.

STROKESTOWN, TUESDAY NIGHT.—As Major Mahon was returning home from a meeting of the board of guardians of Roscommon union, on this evening, he was *shot dead* by an assassin, about four miles from Strokestown. The melancholy occurrence took place about twenty minutes past six o'clock in the evening. Major Mahon has been in possession of the Hartland property for a couple of years. The tenants owed three year's rent, amounting to thirty thousand pounds. At first, the tenants refused to pay rent, till the land, or give it up. Last year, however, a large portion of them agreed to leave the country; and Major Mahon, at his own expense, chartered two vessels, and sent a number of the tenantry to America. Long, however, before this occurred, it was well known in the country that Major Mahon was a doomed man. His name stood first upon the list of twelve gentlemen, all of whom have been doomed to death on account of their refusal to continue the conacre system. The failure of the potato crop saved them for a time. As Major Mahon has been taken off, there is little doubt that the other gentlemen will soon follow. Major Mahon, within the last few days, was publicly denounced, in one of the reports to head quarters, as an absentee, and one who refused to contribute to the local subscription of the neighbourhood.—*Correspondent of the Evening Mail.*

ANOTHER ACCOUNT.—Major Mahon, of Strokestown, fell by the hands of assassins this evening. He had lately succeeded to a property so over-peopled that, if left unaided, the population would have starved. He, therefore, laid out £6,000 last year in assisting a large number to emigrate; many more solicited to be so favoured, but more could not be done. On Tuesday he had driven into Strokestown, and called at his agent's office, to lay out plans for the employment of men upon a large scale. He proceeded to Roscommon, where, for want of funds, the poorhouse was in danger of being closed, and his wish was to keep open everything that could benefit the poor. Returning from this charitable duty, he was marked by two assassins, who fired at him a little after six o'clock in the evening, at about four miles from Strokestown. One piece missed fire, but the other took effect, lodging a heavily loaded discharge in the breast; the victim exclaimed, "O God!" and spoke no more.—*Ibid.*

Recreated from The Belfast News-Letter, Belfast, November 5, 1847.

FASHIONABLE INTELLIGENCE.

WINDSOR, WEDNESDAY.—Lord Camoys has arrived at the castle, and has succeeded the Earl of Morley as the Lord in waiting to the Queen. Colonel Berkeley Drummond has also arrived, and has succeeded Mr. R. Ormsby Gore as the Groom in waiting to her Majesty.

The birth-day of her Royal Highness the Princess Sophia was celebrated here to-day, by the ringing of bells and the firing of cannon as usual. Her Royal Highness this day entered her 70th year.

The intense fog has confined her Majesty and the royal family within doors to-day. But the prince, accompanied by Sir Charles Wood, Lord Camoys, and the Marquis of Exeter, went out to shoot in the preserves round Norfolk Farm. His royal highness and party left the castle at half-past ten, and returned to luncheon shortly after two o'clock.

Arrangements have been made for celebrating the birth-day of his Royal Highness the Prince of Wales, on Tuesday next, by a grand public dinner, at the Royal Adelaide Hotel, no less than thirty-six of the royal tradesmen and principal inhabitants of the town having enrolled their names as stewards. A quantity of game and venison will be forwarded to Mr. Oliver, the proprietor of the hotel, from the castle, as well as a liberal supply of fruit from the royal gardens, at Frogmore, by command of her Majesty.

Recreated from The Freeman's Journal, Dublin, November 6, 1847.

SOUTH DUBLIN UNION

NOTICE—ELECTION OF WARDMAID.

THE Guardians of the South Dublin Union hereby give notice that they will, on THURSDAY, the 11th November next, proceed to Elect a Suitable Female, whose duty it will be to take charge of the Female Paupers' Clothing, and to assist the Matron generally.

Salary £8 per annum, with Rations and a Furnished Apartment.

Two Sureties in £10 each will be required for the faithful discharge of the duty.

Applications for the office, accompanied with testimonials of character, and naming sureties, to be forwarded to the Board at or before Four o'Clock, p.m., on Wednesday, the 10th instant, and Candidates to be in attendance the following day at One o'Clock.

By order,
MARK BYRNE, Clerk of the Union.
Workhouse, James's-street,
Oct. 29, 1847.

NOTICE.
BARRACKS.

Office of Ordnance, London, 25th Oct., 1847.

WASHING AND REPAIRING BEDDING, EMPTYING PRIVIES, REMOVING PRIVY SOIL, ASHES, AND OLD STRAW OF THE SOLDIERS' BEDS, AND SWEEPING CHIMNIES.

THE Barrack-Masters at the several Barracks in Ireland, will receive Proposals from such Persons as may be disposed to enter into Engagements for Washing and repairing Bedding, for Emptying Privies, Removing the Privy Soil, Ashes, and Old Straw of the Soldiers' Beds, or for Sweeping Chimnies, at each Barrack, for Three Years, from 1st January next.

Particulars and Printed Forms of the Proposals may be had upon application at the Barrack Master's Office. Each Proposal must be Sealed up and Endorsed, "Proposal for Washing Bedding," "Repairing Bedding," "Cleansing Privies," or "Sweeping Chimnies," (as the case may be) and handed to the Barrack-Master on or before Tuesday, the 7th of December next.

☞ No Proposal will be attended to which is not made on one of the Printed Forms to be had from the Barrack-Master.

By Order of the Board,
R. BYHAM, Secretary.

FASHIONS FOR NOVEMBER.
(From the *London and Paris Ladies' Magazine of Fashion*.)

For promenade and carriage dresses the handsomest materials are used either plain or broche; in shapes of the same colour the mixture of tints is only adopted in full dress. For redingotes the tints of scabious, olive green, violet, aile de mouche will be very fashionable. Sevillien fringes rival those a la guimpe in trimming as flounces, which are frequently in four, five, and six rows from top of the skirt to the bottom; they are also placed en tablier or double echelle on each side the skirt, a very thick round braid of soft silk is also much used, forming patterns in the soutache style on redingotes of cachemere, or pekins. Another new trimming is formed of velvet and gimp. Black lace will be as fashionable as ever, and galons polonais and epingle for dresses and manteux. Deep blue and ecrue are the favourite colours for cachemere dresses, ornamented with velvet or gimp; the corsages en blouse very high, the sleeves wide at the top and narrow at the wrist, the skirts very full, some have mantelets wadded to match. Great simplicity is observed in all toilettes that are not decidedly full dress. A warm and comfortable addition to the winter dress are the little circassienne vestes; the corsage formed so as not to increase the size of the waist, and left open or crossed at pleasure; the sleeves wide, reaching to the elbow; they fasten in front by means of brandenbourgs or nœuds of ribbon; they are made of velvet, trimmed with black lace or rich gimp, for evening wear, also of pink or blue satin, with fringes or white lace, and more en neglige of molleton cachemere-gris, lined with pink or cerise silk.

Manteaux are made of velvet, satin, or cachemere, embroidered or trimmed with fringe, deep blue violet ramona, and black; of the latter the majority are made: they are longer than those of last winter, particularly those intended for walking or neglige; the form is pretty and comfortable; one of the prettiest trimmings for pardessus and mantelets consists of application of velvet on satin de chine. The form of bonnets differ but little from those worn during the summer, the fronts a little less open, the crowns round and low, and the bavolets not separate from the bonnet. Coloured blonds are much used to ornament them, and orange is a favourite colour, and velvet flowers for satin or velvet bonnets; also foliage of various vegetables, carrot leaves, &c., and taffetas pinked and made to imitate flowers. Capotes either resemble bonnets, except in having coulisses, or they are of the form styled bonne femme, with the crowns demi bombes, and are pretty, covered with a fauchon of lace.

Reprinted from The Freeman's Journal, Dublin, November 6, 1847.

MORE PRIEST-HUNTING.

With mingled pain and disgust do we draw the serious attention of the public, and in a special degree of the spiritual superiors of the zealous MR. COWEN of Bearhaven, to the details of the miserable, trumpery case, upon which a host of legal gentlemen were engaged—against a hunted, tortured, broken-hearted Priest, who happens to be cursed by the neighbourhood of Protestant Clergymen, who, disdaining the *honourable example* of Christian tolerance and Christian charity, set them by their brethren throughout the country, turn religion into a farce, by their revolting traffic—stirabout for creed—and debase a starving population into a race of swindling hypocrites. Heaven knows, it is with pain and disgust we witness a Protestant clergyman—a Minister of Religion and a Priest of Peace—feeing counsel and a host of attorneys to prosecute and punish a Catholic clergyman—aye, a *brother Priest*—for having, in the discharge of his duty, as a member of the Relief Committee, turned away from a meal depot that Protestant Clergyman's steward and dependent, who, though in possession of sufficient worldly means for their sustenance, were placed on the list of the destitute, and consumed provisions of the starving! Because the precious pair of porridge-perverts were turned out of the depot, rather roughly, by the indignant Priest, counsel and attorneys are to be feed, in the aid of the public prosecutor, by this Protestant Curate, who should rather have turned the pair of mean wretches from his employment, than backed up their malignant hatred with the aid of English gold. Imagine, English reader, the zealous, apostolic, evangelical Mr. Cowen, who deliberately swears, that the creed of more than half the population of the Christian world, is damnable, suffering *his steward*, to whom he *allows five shillings a week, besides a farm, and a milch cow*—English reader, we say, only think of this high-souled minister of Religion suffering this steward of his *to be placed on the relief-list*, AND EAT THE RATIONS OF THE STARVING POOR! This is the first prosecutor, PATRICK SULLIVAN. Let us come to the next prosecutor, SYLVESTER SULLIVAN. SYLVESTER is also in the employment of the REV. MR. COWEN, from whom he receives *"his weekly hire, a farm, and two milch cows"*; and this Priest-prosecutor swears that he also *"was on the list for rations"*—that he also consumed the food intended by English bounty for the relief of the fever-stricken destitute! The steward was put off the list twice by the REV. MR. HEALY, who would have acted culpably, and even criminally, if he had not done so;—hence the ire of PAT SULLIVAN, and his precious brother in the Gospel, SILVY! Independently of this unblushing *robbery* of the destitute—for, in reality, it's consumption by a person with a farm, a cow, and five shillings a week, is nothing less—the evidence of TIMOTHY RAHILLY, a witness brought up for the prosecution, is most damnatory; for he distinctly swears that if Sullivan had stated a certain fact, which he did on oath, he must have sworn falsely!

We would ask ARCHDEACON KYLE, DEAN NEWMAN, or any of the respected Protestant Clergymen who have been so active in this City in the administration of relief to the poor—*the Roman Catholic poor*—what is their opinion of the conduct of this hair-brained Curate, who not only swears that the religion of the majority of his Countrymen is damnable and idolatrous, but knowingly suffers his well paid dependents—his own servants—to be placed on the paupers' list, and filch the food of those who were dying of utter starvation?

God forbid that we, who are of the creed anathamatized by a raving fool, should we take *him* as a type of the Irish Protestant Clergyman. We well know that the ferocious zeal with which he has hunted an impoverished half-starved Priest, is revolting to the Christian feeling of his respected brethren who live in charity with their neighbour, and obey the command of the Divine Founder of the Christian Religion, by doing unto others as they would wish to be done by.

But, we solemnly say, such mischievous firebrands, such hot-headed, stupid bigots as are typified by this eighteen-months-old Curate, should be rebuked by their spiritual superiors, who must be more or less responsible for all the antics and mountebank tricks played off by those clerical idiots. Every Christian man would wish to live in unity with his fellow-man. GOD himself has said that it is sweet to see brethren dwell together in unity. But how is it possible that the unity, so necessary for our distracted and much-afflicted land, can be established, or can be perpetuated, if ignorant and hungry men are to be ensnared from their faith and their altar by the silver of JUDAS and the porridge of ESAU? How is it possible to avoid strife and heart-burnings, when the accursed system of appealing to the low animal wants of the starving wretch, is that adopted for teaching the holiness of religion and the loveliness of charity?

We do solemnly call upon the spiritual superiors of this foolish man, to express their censure of the conduct which he and his fellow-labourers in the field of perversion and hypocrisy have been pursuing, to the injury of religion, and the extinction of all feelings of charity and good will.

Mr. LITTLE, R.M., deserves our notice—public notice—Government notice. He should have sat rather with the prosecuting bar, and held a brief, than taken his seat on the bench. We regret to be compelled to say it, Mr. LITTLE is not fit to sit as a judge. There are certain qualities eminently required for a judge, which Mr. LITTLE eminently lacks. Presumption, passion, bias, arrogance, are none of these; and these, unhappily, Mr. Little may safely lay claim to. We are not going back to old cases; we write on this case before us—a case in which, we regret to say, Mr. LITTLE has comported himself with a total absence of temper, dignity, discretion, and impartiality. We know that what we write will meet Mr. LITTLE's eye; but we have a duty to discharge, and that duty we shall discharge at all times.

Recreated from The Cork Examiner, Cork, November 8, 1847.

An incident took place yesterday in the office of Mr. Murphy (one of the Masters in Chancery) which strongly illustrates the disastrous effects of the utter insecurity of life and property in this country. A fee simple estate, consisting of 288 acres of prime feeding land, with an excellent dwelling-house, advantageously situated, in the county of Roscommon, was put up for sale at £10,000 for the first bid, being scarcely one-half of the estimated value of the property. While the sale was proceeding, a gentleman got up, and addressing those about him, spoke of the dangerous neighbourhood in which the estate lay, remarking that it was close to the spot where only the night previous Major Mahon fell by the bullet of the assassin. The announcement created a powerful sensation in the office, and a chilling silence of a minute or two succeeded. The Master at length interposed, and having severely reprimanded the speaker for his intrusive observations, ordered the sale to proceed. But it was to no purpose. The blow had struck home; and after an offer of £2,599, or something like four years' purchase, the sale was indefinitely postponed.—*Times Correspondent.*

MURDER OF MAJOR MAHON.—The scene of this cruel deed was about four miles from Strokestown House, the residence of Major Mahon. It is called the Khyber Pass, and a police station had been lately placed in the vicinity, owing to the many outrages previously perpetrated there. Two assassins lay in wait for their unconscious victim, who was accompanied by Dr. Shanly, and they both fired together. Major Mahon was shot dead, and Dr. Shanly lightly wounded.

The news of Major Mahon's murder was welcomed by lighting bonfires throughout the parish of Ballykilcline, where is situate a Crown estate, the tenants of which have successfully resisted the payment of rent during the last ten years.

Recreated from The Cork Examiner, Cork, November 10, 1847.

THE RETURN.

All hail! all hail, my native land,
I gaze on thee once more;
How swiftly o'er the heaving wave
My bark flies to the shore;

But many a day, though far away
Beyond the bright blue sea,
My soul on Fancy's angel wing
Returned home to thee.

A cold, cold blank was in my heart
Since first the roving gale
Had wrenched me from the hearts I loved,
The glen, the grove, the vale,

When all the joyous moments passed
Of childhood's sunny prime,
And sped me o'er the ocean's breast
To yon cold cheerless clime.

Oh, how my bosom leaps with joy
As every scene appears,
The craggy cliff I used to climb
In boyhood's happy years,

And e'en the wave that broke just now
In yon familiar bay
Brought back methinks the sound I heard
In childhood's happy day.

Recreated from The Waterford News, Waterford, November 24, 1848.

1848

Selected Headlines

THE POOR LAW	138
REGULATIONS FOR EMIGRANT VESSELS	142
THE ARCTIC EXPEDITION	144
PEDESTRIANISM	146
SUSPENSION OF THE HABEAS CORPUS ACT	155
REBELLION—MUSKETS—PLANS &c.	158
MILITARY OCCUPATION OF CORK	164
THE AFFAIR NEAR BALLINGARRY	166
FIRE-ARMS AND PIKES FOR SALE	168
THE ARREST OF SMITH-O'BRIEN	174

ECCLESIASTICAL.

CATHOLIC CHURCH.
THE PRIMATE TO THE BISHOP OF ARDAGH.

My Dear Lord,—I have the honor to submit to your lordship's consideration a communication which I lately received from the Holy See, of which I gave you a correct copy, and after you have read it, I hope that you will favour me with a line on the subject:—I have the honor to remain, with the highest respect, my dear Lord, your obedient servant,

W. Crolly.

To the Right Rev. Dr. O'Higgins, Ballymahon.

MOST ILLUSTRIOUS AND REVEREND LORD.—

The rumors that have for some months back been in circulation through the public journals of England, relative to the pursuit of political parties with which some ecclesiastics are carried away, and the abuse of some of the Irish churches, for transacting in them secular affairs, or adding towards their transaction; and also regarding the murders which are said to be repeated through Ireland, and are imputed to the clergy; as if they were previously planned, on account of the imprudence of some, in their preaching, or an indirect encouragement from the pulpit, or at least a wicked approval of them—such rumors ought, no doubt, to excite the solicitude of the Sacred Congregation.

Although the Sacred Congregation could not, on any account, persuade itself, that what is so ostentatiously proclaimed is true—both that ecclesiastics forget that the House of God should be the house of prayer, and not an office for traffic, or secular business—and that they, the ministers of peace and the dispensers of the mysteries of God, should not engage themselves in secular concerns, and should have a horror of blood and revenge; yet it has deemed it a most important duty, to seek reasonable and full information on all things, that it may be seen what credit is to be given to such public defamations.; whereof I have come to the resolution of addressing this letter to your Grace, in accordance also with the opinion of our Most Holy Father, Pius IX., in order that you would be kind enough, at your very earliest convenience, to satisfy this our most reasonable solicitude, admonishing, in the meantime, all the clergy that, always seeking the things that are of Jesus Christ, they devote themselves with cheerfulness and zeal to the salvation of the faithful committed to their care, and that, as soldiers of God, they should not implicate themselves in secular affairs, and should earnestly take care that from no quarter their ministry be despised, and that those who are against them having nothing wherewith to approach them.

In the meantime, I pray God long to preserve your Grace in health and happiness. Of your Grace the most obedient servant,

J. Ph. Card. Fransonius, Praef.
Alexander Barrabo, Pro. Sec.

From the office of the Sacred Congregation of the Propaganda Fide, Jan 3, 1848.

To his Grace the Archbishop of Armagh, Armagh.

THE BISHOP OF ARDAGH TO THE PRIMATE.

Ballymahon, January 29th, 1848.

My Dear Lord,—I have the honor to acknowledge the receipt of your Grace's note of the 27th instant, together with a copy of a letter from his Eminence Cardinal Fransonius, dated the 3rd of this month. On the subject referred to in that letter your Grace desires to have a line from me; and in compliance with your request I beg to say that I believe your Grace is now bound to make known to the Propaganda Fife that a most wicked and diabolical conspiracy is being carried on by almost all the English and Irish press against the Catholic hierarchy, the Catholic priests, and the Catholic people of Ireland; that Lord Minto was sent to Rome to deceive the Holy See, and that the means he and his friends use are notorious calumnies against us all.

I think also the Cardinal should be informed that, under the name of legal right, the body of the landlords of Ireland are literally starving the poor, and doing so without a single remonstrance from our Lord Lieutenant, or his employer, Lord John Russell, and that neither ever published a single word in vindication of the Archbishop of Tuam, the Bishop of Elphin, and other Irish ecclesiastics, notwithstanding that they demonstrated the charges made against them and their priests to be premeditated slanders of their enemies. Of course you will further state that whilst the whole of the English and Irish government press publish daily every sort of ruffian libels on ourselves and on our clergy, they scarcely ever publish our defense. I think, too, the Propaganda ought to be solicited to send over to Ireland some intelligent, pious, and independent Italian ecclesiastic, with instructions to go from diocese to diocese—visit our priests and our poor—see matters with his own eyes, and report to Rome without consulting the feelings of any party, religious or political. I have myself publicly suggested that England should send honest Protestants among us to ascertain the truth; and if this be done, and that the Propaganda send the ecclesiastic referred to, Rome will be soon enlightened—the conspiracy blown up—the real friends of order, justice and mercy made known to the world, and the intrigues of the unprincipled exhibited to the execration of every lover of truth.

For my own part, I have for the past two years constantly gone through the most afflicted portions of this diocese, preaching patience and resignation to the persecuted and half-starved people, and my reward is, to be involved, in common with my brethren, in the infamous calumnies that are heaped on our heads.

Our Viceroy, too, has proclaimed portions of the diocese as free from agrarian outrage as the streets of London; and yet he calls himself our friend and protector! The people are dying everywhere from cold and hunger, and still he refuses to apply in their favour the laws or other means at his disposal! Were Rome to know (and, please God, she shall know) how we are persecuted, she would look on our forbearance almost as miraculous. If we write a line in an honest journal to repudiate calumny, and bring public opinion to bear constitutionally upon our heartless rulers, we are at once gazetted by the infidel press as the disturbers of that peace which we alone are preserving.

As for my priests, they never directly or indirectly denounced any landlord or other citizen from their altars, nor have they up to this been accused of doing so. Their flocks are patient and resigned, with death staring them in the face, and neither they nor myself shall ever seek redress except by those peaceful and constitutional means to which every subject of the empire has an unalienable and undoubted right.

Finally, I say, let effective means be taken to enlighten Rome on every detail of this infamous anti-national and anti-Catholic conspiracy, and the enemies to our creed and of our race will be humbled, and some little justice done to poor, calumniated, and persecuted Ireland.

I have instructed Dr. Cullen to furnish to the authorities in Rome an authentic copy of my letter to Mr. John O'Connell. I have the honor to be, my dear Lord, your obedient servant,

W. Higgins.

To the Most Rev. Dr. Crolly, Primate of all Ireland.

Recreated from The United Irishman, Dublin, February 12, 1848.

FOREIGN FRUIT OF EVERY DESCRIPTION.

NEVER was *Finer* or *Cheaper* than at the present time, owing to the immense Arrivals in Liverpool, from which Port the Subscriber has now received the largest and best selected Stock that can be possibly piled together in any one Establishment, including

Prime Almeria Grapes (large Amber.)
Ditto Malaga, ditto (Green, most tender.)
Large Black, ditto.
Sweet St. Michael and China Oranges.
Fine Large Bitter Seville, ditto (for Preserving.)
Ditto, do. Messina Lemons.
American Newtown Pippin, and other Apples.
New Spanish Chesnuts.
Ditto, French Walnuts.
Kent Cobb Nuts and Filberts.
Extra Eleme Figs (from the London Market.)
Fancy Cartoons and Boxes—French Plumbs.
New Barbary Dates (Abd-el-Kader's favorite.)
Chrystalized Fruits (in Casquets assorted.)
The Finest Muscatel Raisins (Layers,) in Packages from 3lb. to 26lb. each.
New Jordan, Valencia, and Bitter Almonds.
Ditto Soft Shell, ditto.
Very large Spanish and Portugal Onions, &c. &c., with a great Variety of well-known genuine Old Liqueurs.
Town and Country Orders promptly attended to.
N.B.—A Constant Supply of beautiful *Camelia Bouquets* from the best Green Houses in the vicinity of Dublin.

JOHN HUGHES, Proprietor
Of the Home and Foreign Fruit and Liqueur
ESTABLISHMENT,
40, Westmoreland-street,
(Near Trinity College.)

Reprinted from The United Irishman, Dublin, February 19, 1848.

ANOTHER CRUSADE FOR POOR RATES.—On yesterday (Friday) a formidable military and civil force, consisting of a troop of Scots Greys, two companies of the 40th regiment, and a large body of police, under command of J.B. Kernan, Esq., R.M., accompanied by Mr. Patrick Martin, poor rate collector, and Mr. G. M'Donnell, collector of the public cess, proceeded to the lands of Rosshill, two miles from town, to distrain for poor rate and town taxes. They succeeded in their mission, and returned to the town with thirteen cars of prime upland hay, nine carts of oats in sheaf, three cows, one heifer, one calf, and a box cart, which were distrained for poor rates, and two cows and a heifer, seized for public cess. Upon arrival at the market square at five o'clock, the auctioneer proceeded to sell, and although fair prices were obtained, we are of opinion a very small sum (if any) will go to the credit of the defaulter, who is indebted for poor rate 67£, and 36£ for town taxes.

The outstanding poor rate is now over 12,000£, and the commissioners have given positive instructions to have it collected with all possible despatch.—*Galway Vindicator.*

The *Ballyshannon Herald* states that threatening letter have been sent to the poor-rate collectors in that union.

Recreated from The United Irishman, Dublin, February 19, 1848.

THE ENEMY IN AFRICA.

The English Government have just succeeded, as they say, in crushing another nation. The Caffre war, which has cost, in one year, more than a million of money to the tax-payers of Great Britain and *Ireland*, is over; the chiefs are prisoners; the warriors are slain or scattered; and the red-coated robbers have their will of South Africa, to convert, plunder, and civilize it to their hearts' content. So, at least, the Minister has declared; but we have some hope that his announcement is premature. If the Caffres can hold their ground but a little longer, we predict that they will be left in possession: there will be need of the British forces in Europe: and the first good shock the "empire" gets will shake loose her possessions from pole to pole. We live in hope of seeing that day, and soon.

In the meantime there is one other tongue added to the polyglott litany of curses that rise morning and evening against the name of Britain.

A column of 150 feet in height is about to be set up in Calcutta, to commemorate the victories of the Punjaub. The column is to be crowned by a figure of Britannia, supported by two *native* soldiers. What a compliment to the Sepoys!

Recreated from The United Irishman, Dublin, February 26, 1848.

March 4.

Foreign News.

REVOLUTION IN FRANCE.

ABDICATION OF LOUIS PHILIPPE.
Flight of the Royal Family.
PROCLAMATION OF A REPUBLIC.
ACTS AND PROCLAMATIONS OF THE NEW GOVERNMENT.

The French people have made another glorious three days' work of Revolution: they have abolished the treacherous monarchy of July, 1830, and all monarchy in France, henceforth and for ever. The tyrant is now a wanderer over the face of the earth; his throne is in ashes; and France is a REPUBLIC. Long live the Republic!

The Poor Law.

PAUPERISM AND THE POOR LAW.—A Roundstone correspondent of the *Galway Vindicator* writes as follows:—"The poor laws, as administered in this quarter, have now become grievous, and are a total failure for any mitigation of the daily increasing calamity now witnessed in Connemara. The constant crusades against the poor farmers for rates have made them all beggars, and the abject poor are still getting no food to support existence. As for the out-door relief, they are left without any. In this electoral division there are from twenty to thirty daily famished from want; their bodies left where they fall, without any interment. Many are eating dog's, horse's, and foal's flesh; and dogs are feeding on the corpses of the unburied dead. Mr. Martin gave out 273 coffins heretofore mostly to wandering paupers from other districts, found dead on the road-sides in this neighbourhood—so much so, that he has not left himself a bit of timber for his own tenants. It is much feared this state of matters will wholly depopulate the district. Those now paid commissioners, inspectors, guardians, &c., are strangers, walking and talking—political gentlemen, doing nothing whatever but lending a deaf ear to the hundreds of supplicants; and in case they get cross may make things worse. The people are driven to desperation—slaughtering sheep and cattle from their neighbours, and marauders breaking into houses, stealing all within their grasp forcibly, by day and night."

RECOGNITION OF THE REPUBLIC IN IRELAND.

Roscrea, Borrisokane, and other towns in our country, were illuminated on Monday night, and immense bonfires were lighted in commemoration of the popular triumph in Paris, and the fall of the tyrant Louis Phillipe, and vehement cheers were given for Repeal!! This is the hour for Ireland to look to herself.—*The Tipperary Vindicator*.

Within the last two months you (the English government) disarmed the people, and now you ask them to arm. They may, when the time comes, with such weapons as opportunity will supply—*furor arma minstrat—but they will not arm for England*. We have one warning word for that country and its rulers. They may despise it now, but the hour will come when they will regret too late they did not hearken to it, and to similar indications of opinion in this country. It is this—"Give us back our parliament *at once*, and let every man have his own country." *Upon this hangs the salvation or downfall of England!—Limerick Examiner.*

TENANT-RIGHT MEETING.—We have been favored with a copy of the following placard, which has been posted up far and wide through the county of Down:—

ROBBERY! ROBBERY!—Men of Ulster, your sacred rights are invaded!—your properties are about to be alienated by an insidious act of parliament! Shall you tamely submit, without even a constitutional struggle, to be *robbed* actually, and unmistakeably robbed of millions of capital, which you have had always available in the recognized ULSTER TENANT-RIGHT? Be up and stirring—attend the meeting to be held in BANBRIDGE on Monday, the 13th of March. Be peaceable, but resolved!—Dated 28th February, 1848.

TENANT-RIGHT—CARRICKMACROSS.—Nearly 20,000 signatures have been already appended to the petition adopted at the baronial meeting lately held in Carrickmacross, to both houses of parliament, to legalize the tenant-right of Ulster, and to extend same to the other provinces of Ireland.—*Freeman*.

[If they think tenant-right is to be won by "twenty thousand signatures," or forty thousand "petitions," they are stupider people in Monaghan than we thought.—ED. U. L]

Reprinted and recreated from The United Irishman, Dublin, March 4, 1848.

Portrait of the Countess of Clarendon
by James Sant (British, 1820-1916)

George William Frederick Villiers
4th Earl of Clarendon
LORD LIEUTENANT OF IRELAND 1847-1852
Painted by Sir Francis Grant
Engraved by William Walker
Published 1848

BY COMMAND

OF

THEIR EXCELLENCIES THE

LORD LIEUTENANT AND COUNTESS OF CLARENDON,

And under the special patronage of Her Royal Highness

The Duchess of Kent and Countess of Dublin, and his Royal Highness Prince George of Cambridge,

THE Annual Grand, Fancy, and Full Dress CHARITY BALL, in aid of the Funds of the Sick and Indigent ROOM-KEEPERS' SOCIETY, Founded A.D. 1790, will take place

IN THE ROTUNDO,

On MONDAY, 6th MARCH, 1848.

PATRONS.

The Lord Mayor.
The Lord Chancellor.
Marquis of Waterford.
Marquis of Donegal.
Marquis of Thomond.
Marquis of Headfort.
Marquis of Sligo.
Marquis of Ormond.
Marquis of Clanricarde.
Marquis of Abercorn.
Marquis of Kildare.
Earl of Carnwath.
Earl of Meath.
Earl of Fingal.
Earl of Besborough.
Earl of Shannon.
Earl of Arran.
Earl of Miltown.
Earl of Charlemont.
Earl of Howth.
Earl of Enniskillen.
Earl of Wicklow.
Earl of Donoughmore.
Earl of Kenmare.
Earl of Clancarty.
Earl of Gosford.
Earl of Rosse.
Earl of Listowel.
Earl of Rathdowne.
Earl of Mountcharles.
Viscount Gormanstown.
Viscount Southwell.
Viscount De Vesci.
Viscount Clifden.
Viscount Lismore.
Viscount Gort.
Viscount Guillamore.
Lord Brabazon.
Lord Carbery.
Lord Muskerry.
Lord Cloncurry.
Lord Clonbrock.
Lord Rossmore.
Lord French.
Lord Dunally.
Lord Clarina.
Lord Castlemaine.
Lord Talbot de Malahide.
Lord Stuart de Decies.
Lord Dunsandle.
Rt. Hon. Sir Wm. Somerville, Bart., M.P.
Rt. Hon. Sir Edwd. Blakeney, K.C.B., G.C.H.
Rt. Hon. the Master of the Rolls.
Rt. Hon. the Attorney-General.
Rt. Hon. Sir T. Esmonde, Bart.
Hon. David Plunket.
Hon. Patrick Plunket.
Hon. Frederick Ponsonby.
Sir Compton Domville, Bart.
Sir Edward Borough, Bart.
Sir Matthew Barrington, Bart.
The High Sheriff.

PATRONESSES.

The Lady Mayoress.
Marchioness of Waterford.
Marchioness of Donegal.
Marchioness of Thomond.
Marchioness of Sligo.
Marchioness of Ormonde.
Marchioness of Clanricarde.
Marchioness of Abercorn.
Marchioness of Kildare.
Countess of Carnwath.
Countess of Meath.
Countess of Fingal.
Countess of Shannon.
Countess of Arran.
Countess of Miltown.
Countess of Enniskillen.
Countess of Wicklow.
Countess of Donoughmore.
Countess of Kenmare.
Countess of Clancarty.
Countess of Rosse.
Countess of Listowel.
Viscountess Southwell.
Viscountess Gort.
Viscountess Guillamore.
Lady Brabazon.
Lady Kilmaine.
Lady Clonbrock.
Lady Rossmore.
Lady Dunally.
Lady Clarina.
Lady Castlemaine.
Lady Talbot de Malahide.
Lady Stuart de Decies.
Lady Elizabeth Borough.
Lady Juliana Brabazon.
Honorable Mrs. D. Plunket.
Honorable Mrs. P. Plunket.
Lady Blakeney.
Lady Domville.

STEWARDS AND MANAGING COMMITTEE.

Ansell, Major A. C., 74th Highlanders.
Ansell, Major E. C., do.
Ball, J. B., Esq.
Bagot, Captain, A.D.C.
Balfour, L. T., Esq.
Barnaby, Major, R.A.
Bernard, Captain, A.D.C.
Blackburne, Major, 85th Light Infantry.
Boyce, Joseph, Esq.
Boyce, John T., Esq.
Browne, Lieutenant-Colonel.
Brownrigg, Henry J., Esq.
Burdett, Major, 17th Lancers.
Butt, Isaac, Esq., Q.C.
Cane, Richard, Esq.
Clarke, Col. St. John, K.H.
Cockburne, Major.
Conroy, Captain, A.D.C.
Connellan, J. Corry, Esq.
Cust, Captain, A.D.C.
Davis, Henry, Esq.
Dennan, John, Esq.
De Lacy, Major, 75th Regt.
Draper, Major, D.A.A.G.
Dunkellin, Lord, A.D.C.
Fane, Major, 4th Light Dragoons.
Faber, Major, 49th Regt.
Fitzgerald, Lord Otho, A.D.C.
Fitzgerald, Lieutenant, A.D.C.
Foley, Hon. St. George, A.D.C.
Forrester, Hon. Major, A.M.S.
Forster, Lieutenant-Col., K.H., A.A.G.
Fortescue, Matthew, Esq.
Frith, Colonel, I.F.O.
Greaves, Lieutenant-Col., M.S.
Gresham, Thomas M., Esq.
Grogan, Edward, Esq., M.P.
Hagart, Major, 7th Hussars.
Hallifax, Colonel, 75th Regt.
Hervey, Captain, A.D.C.
Hudson, Alderman.
Jardine, Major, 75th Regt.
Macdonald, Hon. Capt., A.D.C.
M'Cullagh, W. T., Esq.
M'Kenna, Theobald, Esq.
Matthews, W.P., Esq.
Meredyth, H., Esq.
Morris, Colonel Sir George, D.L.
O'Grady, Honble. Major, 74th Highlanders.
Paget, Lieutenant-Col. Lord G., 4th Light Dragoons.
Ponsonby, Lieutenant, A.D.C.
Ponsonby, Hon. G.
Redington, T. N., Esq.
Roe, George, Esq., D.L.
Russell, Lord Cosmo, A.D.C.
Sandes, Captain, A.D.C.
Shirley, Colonel, 7th Hussars.
Standish, Captain, A.D.C.
St. Quentin, Col., 17th Lancers.
St. Lawrence, Viscount, A.D.C.
Strangways, Lieut.-Col., R.A.
Thomas, F. E., Esq.
Tinling, Major, 74th Highlanders.
Turner, Colonel, C.B., R.A.
Turner, Major, R.A.
Udney, Major.
White Major (Town Major.)
Wilbraham, Major, 7th Depot.
Williams, Captain R.
Williams, Captain, A.D.C.
Willis, Frederick, Esq.

Family Tickets, to admit Four, ... £1 10 0
Single Ticket, ... 0 10 0
(Including Refreshments.)

Tickets to be had of the Managing Committee, from One to Four o'Clock, daily, in the Committee Rooms, No. 66, DAME-STREET.

N.B.—In order to enable the Managing Committee to provide ample accommodation, and complete their various arrangements, it is requested that persons who purpose attending the Ball may provide themselves with Tickets as soon as possible.

Master of the Ceremonies—Mr. WILLIAMS.

A Quadrille, Waltz, and Three Military Bands, will be in attendance.

The whole suite of Ball Rooms will be thrown open, and brilliantly illuminated.

Reprinted from The United Irishman, Dublin, March 4, 1848.

The Poor Law.

STOPPAGE OF OUT-DOOR RELIEF.

The following circular has been issued by the poor law commissioners:—

"Poor Law Commission Office, Dublin, 2d March, '48.

"SIR,—The commissioners have had under their consideration the subject of the duration of out-door relief at present afforded to able-bodied poor persons in unions in Ireland; more especially in reference to the labour wanted at this season of the year for the cultivation of the land, and the employment provided under the land improvement act, 6 and 7 Vic., c. 32; also the assistance afforded to the labouring classes in twenty-four unions, which comprise the most distressed parts of Ireland, by the rations given, from funds supplied by the British Association, to all children attending the public schools.

"The commissioners deem it desirable to determine or to suspend, on the 18th of March instant, all orders under the second section of the Irish poor relief extension act, authorising out-door relief to able-bodied men; and the commissioners wish to know whether, in your opinion, there would be any decided objection to this course in the union of which you are inspector.

"You will be good enough to report to the commissioners on this subject at your earliest convenience.

"I have the honor to be, sir, your most obedient servant,
"W. STANLEY, Secretary.

"To   Temporary Poor Law
Inspector of the   Union."

EMIGRATION.—At the meeting of the Kilrush guardians on Wednesday, application was made by Mr. Foley, of Bella, under the 13th section of the poor law extension act, for one-third of the expense of providing for the free emigration of 149 persons in Moyarta, as the only means at present available for them, owing to the depressed state of the country. The guardians representing the district, Doctor Foley and Mr. Thomas Gibson, said before assenting to the proposition, they should consult their constituents. Capt. Kennedy said the rate-payers could have no objection to such a course, as a great saving would be effected by it—that at 4*l.* 18*s.* 2*d.* each, per annum, the support of the 149 persons, would exceed annually the sum necessary for their emigration, which was only 748*l.* 15*s.*, of which Mr. Foley was willing to pay two-thirds; and that there need be no apprehension of such a course being acted on by the landlords as a precedent, for the principal part of them cleared their estates by *an other process.—Limerick Examiner.*

THE LANDLORD AND TENANT WAR.—On Saturday last we witnessed, with no small degree of sorrow and dismay, the wholesale leveling of TWENTY-ONE HOUSES, and the extermination of one hundred and four unhappy individuals, in the centre of this town, by a writ of *habere*. To add to the melancholy spectacle, the rain poured down in torrents the entire day, and to have looked on the hapless inmates as they issued from the homes that were being destroyed over their heads, and heard the pitiful lamentations, would have appalled the stoutest heart. It would be perfectly useless to attempt to describe the sufferings of the unfortunate creatures, endeavouring to take from the ruins of their once happy homes their miserable articles of furniture. All this happened on a market day, in a crowded town, without the slightest disturbance occurring, the poor people submitting in silence. What caused this wholesale eviction we are not at present acquainted with. We believe the property was involved in law, in Chancery, but we are not aware at whose instigation the houses were levelled, so many hapless beings sent outcasts on the world, to become a burden on the ratepayers. The greater number of persons had their rent paid, and very few were in arrear.—*Athlone Sentinel.*

TROOPS FOR ST. PATRICK'S DAY.—The following troops, composing the garrison of Dublin, will be held in readiness at short notice to turn out in aid of the civil power, should their services be required, on St. Patrick's Day:—1 troop royal horse artillery, royal artillery with field batteries, 7th royal fusiliers depot, 49th regiment, eight companies of the 55th regiment, under Colonel Warren, C.B., 74th Highlanders, 75th regiment, and 85th light infantry. The enrolled pensioners at all their stations in Ireland will be held in readiness to turn out on St. Patrick's Day, if necessary.—*Saunders.*

☞ A large quantity of of provisions, consisting of biscuit and beef, has been conveyed by escort to Clare Castle, in anticipation of an attack on Patrick's Day.—*Limerick Examiner.*

☞ The guns, pistols, and other weapons in the gunmakers' shops in this city are removed to the ordinance barracks, where ten tons of gunpowder have been this day transferred from the vendors' depot at Ballinacurra.—*Limerick Chronicle.*

☞ We have every reason to believe that the disposable force at present in Dublin, including cavalry, infantry, artillery, and police, considerably exceeds ten thousand men ! ! ! During this day large quantities of ammunition have been despatched from the magazine to the several points which are to be occupied on Friday by the military.—*Evening Mail.*

THE BANK OF IRELAND has been carefully fortified and victualled for a siege. Several pieces of cannon have been raised on the roof, which has also been plentifully stored with hand-grenades and other combustibles. The *reveille* sounds nightly a false alarm in each of the barracks, when the troops are obliged to rise and make ready for action on the shortest notice.

ST. PATRICK'S DAY IN BELFAST.—There will be 940 troops under arms in Belfast, on Friday next, including the carbineers, "buffs", and pensioners. This force will be distributed in different places through the town.—*Belfast Chronicle.*

THE LANDLORDS AND THE PEOPLE IN CLARE.—A Kilrush correspondent of the *Limerick Examiner* gives a list of one hundred and sixty-six persons ejected from the property of Mr. Westby, an absentee English proprietor, by his agent, a Mr. Marcus Kean, during the week previous. The writer adds:—"On the 13th of last month there were 19 persons evicted, in Garrantuoha, by the same man, which, added to the above, make 185 souls cast upon the world, without a home, without shelter, without friends. The friends who were left in were warned, at the peril of the agent's displeasure, not to admit to a night's lodging those who were turned out; and on the very night that there houses were thrown down, they let in some of them by stealth, but sent them out before day, lest Mr. Kean's men would see them on the land."

The following are the names of persons who died from want in the parish of Aughagour, within the last fortnight:—March 1st, Duke Dawson, interred without a coffin on the fifth day after his death; Thomas Geraghty, of Garue; March 3d, two sons of Francis Nugent, of Curdarugh, one seven and the other nine years' old; February 28th, in Srakun, two children of Bryan Scahil, also the grandfather and grandmother of the Scahils; at Leitrum, Peter Gavan, who went into a roofless cabin, where he died; at Lanmore, Peter Mullholland fell on the road from exhaustion, from which he was carried into a cabin—buried in four days after, without a coffin, in a turf bank. On Saturday last a poor woman carried her dead son in a rope to the grave; but she was so exhausted, she could not bury him. A charitable man opened a grave for the coffinless dead.—*Mayo Telegraph.*

The following is from the same paper:—Died at Kilmeena, of want, this week, Austin Heraghty. This wretched man had been deprived of his scanty allowance of meal during *seven days*, for having absented himself one day from the stone-braking depot! He was that day engaged in seeking out some asylum for the ensuing week; and when he found one, the poor, heart-broken man had to carry his sick children on *his back* to their new quarter. Tis needless to add, that he had to assist in throwing down his own cabin before he would get a morsel of food.

Reprinted and recreated from The United Irishman, Dublin, March 18, 1848.

FRAUDS ON THE JURY PANELS.—The investigation into the frauds connected with the jury system in the county of Antrim, to which we called attention in our last, commenced on Saturday, before P. J. Blake, Esq., a commissioner sent by the government to Belfast for the purpose. The chief fact elicited was that Hugh Devlin, a bailiff, was in the habit of receiving money from parties indicted for having favorable jurors summoned, and unfavorable ones omitted. He had received blank summonses, and the sub-sheriff had left it to him to select the parties. The investigation closed on Tuesday. Mr. Rea applied to have it merely adjourned, but Mr. Blake refused.

PIKES FOR THE MILLION.—The owner of a timber yard in one of the streets leading into this city has received an order for 500 pike handles, and is executing it.—*Cork Examiner.*

CORK SAVINGS' BANK.—The draw on the Cork savings bank last week amounted to the enormous sum of 10,300*l.* Up to yesterday the notices of those intending to draw sums over 20*l.* this day amounted to 3,500*l.* And it is thought that 3,500*l.*, if not more, will be drawn in sums under 20*l.*, for which no previous notice of the intention of the drawer is required. The government will be heavy losers by this panic. The bank directors do all in their power to check the growth of the feeling of insecurity that is assuming so startling a form; but in vain.—*Cork Examiner.*

WEDNESDAY.—The crush is enormous, and the run a perfect panic. The bank is literally chock full. The drawing promises to be enormous.

THE LIMERICK SAVINGS BANK.—The run upon the savings bank here yesterday was tremendous, and the notice for further withdrawals are most numerous.—*Limerick Reporter.*

THE SAVINGS BANK IN TRALEE.—The savings bank in Tralee is smashed by the defalcation of the secretary, Mr. John Lynch, solicitor. It was discovered by the run recently made on the establishment.—*Ibid.*

Tuesday evening, as a number of soldiers were passing up William-street, they commenced shouting for Repeal! They said they were the men to stand to their countrymen, and that they need not be afraid of them (the soldiery), firing on them. They gave three cheers for the success of the Confederates, and were much applauded as they passed up the street.—*Limerick Examiner.*

Weekly meetings of the citizens are about being fixed upon in this city, with a view to have every man at his post. The rifle club is receiving daily augmentation.—*Ibid.*

The petition to the Queen, the last appeal of an oppressed people, was numerously signed at the several chapels of this city on Sunday last.—*Ibid.*

Reprinted from The Freeman's Journal, Dublin, April 15, 1848.

THE BELFAST DEMONSTRATION OF LOYALTY.

WELL, we the citizens of Belfast—we beg pardon, Belfast is only a town, and its population only townsmen, but a town and townsmen which would make up, in moral and mercantile weight, half-a-dozen of the repeal "cities" of the south and west—have done our duty to the throne and to the country. Let the pikemen and riflemen of Dublin, Cork, Limerick, and the other nests of treason, look at the record of our demonstration on Saturday last, and proceed in their tactics "with what appetite they may." Here we are—a population of one hundred thousand, bating the miserable few who have pinned their fate to the sleeves of the Drennanites—resolved to resist the threatened march of revolution. Belfast—the Liverpool of Ireland—we may say the Liverpool and Manchester of Ireland combined—has declared in favour of monarchy—in favour of the existing institutions of the empire—in favour of the legislative union. And of what is this the index? Of the similar resolve of all Ulster, of which Belfast is the metropolis and representative—the guide, the guardian, and the glory. Let us hear no more, then, of Protestant defection in the north—of Orange fraternisation. Ulster, through Belfast, has declared against insurrection and disloyalty—against revolution and Repeal. Let the other three provinces unite if they will—though it is a a dream beyond the intoxicated fancies of even the *Nation* and the *United Irishman*—in summoning the friends of civil war to perfect the desolation which famine and pestilence have left unfinished—Ulster rises her impregnable redoubts along her frontier, and is ready to meet the invasion. Her true-hearted sons, of whatever creed or politics, have merged their minor differences into the swelling current of loyalty.

They have vowed to risk their lives and property in the struggle, if it should come. Men of the pike and rifle, attack us if you dare. Cowards of the vitriol flask and the soda-bottle grenade, we are ready to receive you. We have stout hands and able arms to oppose your scrap-iron and sulphuric acid; and we have, what you want, the blessing which descends on those who defend a true faith and a righteous cause.

Our anticipations of the great demonstration, of which this town was the theatre on Saturday last, have been completely realised. It was a noble assemblage. Our merchants—men who may be called the "merchant-princes" of Ireland—were there—Whig and Tory, Conservative and Liberal—vieing with one another as to who should be most conspicuous in registering his devotion to the throne and to the cause of order and law.

Our professional men came forward in a phalanx which proved that the intellectual aristocracy of the Irish Athens were not behind the representatives of the wealth and enterprise of the province. Our tradesmen and artisans mingled their cheers in the sonorous diapason of applause which followed every loyal sentiment, and every withering rebuke of the blasphemy and the treason of the rebel orators of our day. And what shall we say of the eloquence of our speakers? Search the school-boy harangues of the O'Briens and the Meaghers, the Mitchels and the Dohenys, and say if their choicest metaphors, their most picked periods, do not "pale their ineffectual fires" before the blaze of brilliant rhetoric with which our Cooke and our Montgomery have denounced the machinations of the revolutionary convention.

If there is anything which could add to the immense importance of this demonstration, it was the absolute unanimity of the vast assemblage. The affirmation which followed each resolution as it was put, was unmarred by the discord of a single negative. Amidst the mass of intelligence, wealth, industry, and enterprise concentrated in that hall, not a voice was raised to say "no" to a single proposition.

Will not this *tell* in Dublin? Will it not tell in the Imperial Parliament? Will it not give courage to the Legislature, and strength to the Executive? Will it not dash the hopes of traitors; and infuse, like a potent elixir, new hope and resolve, if such were needed, into the mass of our loyal population, bewildered as they are with lies and sophistry, with wild promises and extravagant chimeras?

There was one exception to the general harmony of creeds and classes which manifested itself at this meeting. Though ministers of every other religious denomination were present—Presbyterians, Episcopalians, Wesleyans, Unitarians—one class of the clergy was absent. Need we say what class that was? The priests of the Roman Catholic creed thought fit to absent themselves. We had thought better of some of them. We had hoped that, at least, Dr. Denvir, the Roman Catholic Prelate of the diocese, would have repudiated, in his person, on behalf of the Romanists of this town and neighbourhood, the horrible doctrines of the Irish Traitors. But, it appears, even *he* could not abide the test. He and his brethren shrunk from the application of the touchstone. They either would not, or dared not, join with an assembly whose sole declared object was to record their allegiance to the Queen, and their love of peace and order. Ah, how the white heat of a *real* crisis—of a raging political furnace—while it tries and tests the pure gold of loyalty, evaporates the dull dross, rendering it vain to seek for one precious drop amidst the cold ashes of apathy and disaffection!

And now, through the hands of the deputation which is about to proceed to Dublin, we tender to Lord Clarendon the casket of our fealty to the Sovereign whom he represents. He will understand and appreciate the value of the offering. The whole country will understand and appreciate it. It contains the death-warrant of treason in Ireland; and we leave the rest to his Excellency and the Attorney-General.

Recreated from The Belfast News-Letter, Belfast, April 18, 1848.

The Provinces.

THE FAMINE.

PLUNDER OF MEAL.—This outrage has become very prevalent within the past month—the state of the poor impelling some to the commission of offences, whilst others take advantage of the state of the times to perpetrate robberies. On the 1st instant, three carts laden with meal from Ballina to Foxford, were attacked at a village called Ouloge by about one hundred persons—principally women, and having assaulted the carriers, they succeeded in carrying off the entire of the loads, amounting to three tons weight.—*Mayo Constitution.*

DEATH FROM HUNGER.—On Wednesday last, a poor woman and her infant child were found dead in a tenantless house, within a mile of Swinford, their names unknown. An inquest was held on the bodies, when a verdict of "Death from starvation" was returned.—*Ibid.*

THE BLACK BREAD—STARVATION.—The Rev. Mr. Conway, P.P., of Partree, called at our office with a specimen of the unwholesome food given for the use of the children of his parish. The reverened gentleman assured us—and we believe him—that he has often seen the dogs refuse to touch it. No less than four deaths from starvation have taken place in the above district last week.—*Ibid.*

A poor woman fell down in Ellen-street, Limerick, on Sunday, through exhaustion, from want of food. She died on Monday morning.

Reprinted from The Freeman's Journal, Dublin, April 15, 1848.

REGULATIONS FOR EMIGRANT VESSELS.

(From the *London Gazette* of Tuesday night.)

At the Court at Osborne House, Isle of Wight, the 15th day of April, 1848, present, the Queens's Most Excellent Majesty in council.

Whereas by an act passed in the eleventh year of the reign of her Majesty, intituled "an act to make further provision, for one year and to the end of the then next session of parliament, for the carriage of passengers by sea to North America," it is enacted that it shall be lawful for her Majesty, by an order or orders in council to be by her made, with the advice of her privy council, to prescribe any such rules and regulations as to her Majesty may seem fit, for preserving order, and for securing cleanliness and ventilation on board of British ships proceeding from any port or place in the United Kingdom, or in the islands of Guernsey, Jersey, Alderney, Sark, or Man, to any port or place on the eastern coast of North America, or in the islands adjacent thereto, or in the Gulf of Mexico.

Now, therefore, her Majesty doth, by and with the advice of her Privy Council, and in pursuance and exercise of the authority vested in her by said act, order, and it is hereby ordered, that the following shall be the rules for preserving order, and for securing cleanliness and ventilation to be observed on board of any such ships proceeding on such voyage as aforesaid—

1. All passengers who shall not be prevented by sickness or other sufficient cause, to be determined by the surgeon, or, in ships carrying no surgeon, by the master, shall rise no later than seven o'clock, a.m., at which hour the fires shall be lighted.

2. It shall be the duty of the cook, appointed under the 3d clause of the Act 11 Victoria, cap. 6, to light the fires, and to take care that they be kept alight during the day, and also to take care that each passenger or family of passengers shall have the use of the fire-place at the proper hours, in order to be fixed by the master.

3. When the passengers are dressed, their beds shall be rolled up.

4. The decks, including the space under the bottom of the berths, shall be swept before breakfast, and all dirt thrown overboard.

5. The breakfast hour shall be from eight to nine o'clock, a.m., provided that, before the commencement of breakfast all the emigrants, except as hereinbefore excepted, be out of bed and dressed, and that the beds have been rolled up, and the deck on which the emigrants live properly swept.

6. The deck shall further be swept after breakfast and after every other meal, and as soon as breakfast is concluded shall be dry holystoned or scraped. This duty, as well as that of cleaning the ladders, hospitals, and round houses, shall be performed by a party taken in rotation from all the adult males above fourteen, in the proportion of five to every hundred emigrants, and who shall be considered as sweepers for the day; but the occupant of each berth shall see that his own berth is well brushed out.

7. Dinner shall commence at one o'clock p.m., and supper at six p.m.

8. The fires shall be extinguished at seven p.m., unless otherwise directed by the master, or required for the use of the sick, and the emigrants shall be in their berths at ten o'clock p.m.

9. Three safety lamps shall be lit at dusk and kept burning till ten o'clock p.m., after which hour two of the lamps may be extinguished, one being nevertheless kept burning at the main hatchway all night.

10. No naked light shall be allowed at any time or on any account.

11. The scuttles and stern ports, if any, shall, weather permitting, be opened at seven o'clock a.m., and kept open till ten o'clock p.m., and the hatches shall be kept open whenever the weather permits.

12. The coppers and cooking utensils shall be cleaned every day.

13. The beds shall be well shaken and aired on deck at least twice a week.

14. The bottom boards of the berth, if not fixtures, shall be removed, and dry scrubbed, and taken on deck at least twice a week.

15. A space of deck-room shall be apportioned for an hospital, not less for vessels carrying one hundred passengers, than forty-eight superficial feet, with two or four bed-berths erected therein, nor less for vessels carrying two hundred or more passengers, than one hundred and twenty superficial feet, with six-bed berths therein.

16. Two days in the week shall be appointed by the master as washing days, but no washing or drying of clothes shall on any account be permitted between decks.

17. On Sunday mornings the passengers shall be mustered at ten o'clock, a.m., and will be expected to appear in clean and decent apparel. The Lord's Day shall be observed as religiously as circumstance will admit.

18. No spirits or gunpowder shall be taken on board by any passenger, and if either of those articles is discovered in the possession of a passenger, it shall be taken into the custody of the master during the voyage, and not returned to the passenger until he is on the point of disembarking.

19. No loose hay or straw shall be allowed below for any purpose.

20. No smoking shall be allowed between decks.

21. All gambling, fighting, riotous or quarrelsome behaviour, swearing, and violent language shall at once be put a stop to. Swords and other offensive weapons shall, as soon as the passengers embark, be placed in the custody of the master.

22. No sailors shall be allowed to remain on the passenger deck among the passengers except on duty.

23. No passengers shall go to the ship's cook house without special permission from the master, nor remain in the forecastle among the sailors on any account.

24. In vessels, not having stern ports or scuttles in the sides, such other provision shall be made for ventilation as shall be required by the emigration officer at the port of embarkation, or, in his absence, by the officers of Customs.

And the Right Honourable Earl Grey, one of her Majesty's principal Secretaries of State, is to give the necessary directions herein accordingly.

C. C. GREVILLE.

Recreated from The Freeman's Journal, Dublin, April 21, 1848.

PIKE-DRILLING IN BELFAST.—The hydraulic treatment to which the Young Irelanders were lately subjected, instead of cooling their ardour, has it appears, had the effect of producing a species of *rabies* among them. A day or two ago, a gentleman walking with a friend in the vicinity of the town, observed about twenty of them, armed with pikes, going through a regular drill, in a field! It may be well to remind these gentry that they are liable to a penalty of seven years transportation for this offense; and, most assuredly, if they have not the fear of God before their eyes, they will be taught to fear the laws which they would like to overturn.

A "DYING" IMPOSTER.—For some time past, a fellow, whose real name is Thomas Dooly, and who comes from the county Westmeath, has endeavoured to excite the sympathy of the humane, by lying down in the streets, stretching himself out, turning up the whites of his eyes, and groaning, so as to make the people believe that he was in extreme distress or that nature was quite exhausted. It so happened that, while going through one of these exhibitions, Dr. Wheeler came up, who stated, after due examination, that he was scheming, and he was taken into custody. He was brought up yesterday before the magistrates at the Police Office, when he appeared to be stout and healthy; and was sent to the House of Correction for a month.

MELANCHOLY SUICIDE.—Joseph Wilson, a driver of the Dublin day mail-coach, on arriving in Belfast last Monday evening, and going to his residence, in M'Clenahan's Court, off Mill Street, had a dispute with his wife. He immediately left the house, and, having purchased some laudanum, under the pretence that it was for a horse that was unwell, he returned home, and swallowed the poison. Next morning, he expired. A verdict to the effect that the deceased committed suicide while labouring under temporary insanity, was returned.

Recreated from The Belfast News-Letter, Belfast, April 21, 1848.

THE ARCTIC EXPEDITION.

WOOLWICH, MAY 2.—The Mary lighter arrived to day from Deptford with a cargo of provisions for the Enterprise, Captain James Clarke Ross, and the articles were taken on board that vessel, consisting of a number of cases of prepared potatoes, boiled mutton, pork, beef, peas, and other preserved victuals, with a large supply of flour, oatmeal, and biscuits. The quantities of provisions taken on board the Enterprise and Investigator, will not only be amply sufficient for the officers and crews of these vessels, but they will also have plenty to spare for the officers and crews of the Erebus and Terror, should they be so fortunate as to meet with any of the parties who proceeded to the Arctic regions in those discovery vessels. Captain Sir James Clarke Ross is indefatigable in ensuring that every preparation is made for the comfort of his officers and crew, who are a fine body of hardy men. The vessel has been greatly strengthened by projecting timbers of considerable thickness, gradually rising from below her water line, and the interior has been fitted with pipes to circulate hot water through all parts of the vessel. A roof similar to the roof of a dwelling house is constructing at Blackwell for each of the vessels, to be put up on deck between masts, in the event of having to winter in the Arctic regions, and the Lords Commissioners of the Admiralty have afforded every facility for the comfort of every person to be engaged in the expedition in search of Captain Sir John Franklin and the officers and crew of the Erebus and Terror.

AN INQUEST was held on Wednesday at the Police Office, Belfast, on the body of James M'Gonnigal, who, it was alleged, came by his death in consequence of a drenching he got from the water-engine which was employed for the purpose of dispersing the late Young Irelanders' meeting, on the evening of the 7th April last.

Recreated from The Freeman's Journal, Dublin, May 5, 1848.

THE LOYAL MEETING AT DONAGHADEE.

The following address, to his Excellency the Lord Lieutenant, having been adopted unanimously at the late meeting of the inhabitants of Donaghadee and its vicinity, was forwarded to his Excellency by Admiral Leslie, chairman of the meeting:—

MAY IT PLEASE YOUR EXCELLENCY—We the inhabitants of Donaghadee and its vicinity, in public meeting assembled, desire to express our abhorrence of the treasonable attempts at present making in different parts of Ireland, but especially in Dublin, to array the population in armed insurrection, in order to carry, by force, a Repeal of the Legislative Union, between Great Britain and this country. Firmly believing, as we do, that the continuance of that Union is essential to peace, prosperity, and safety of the empire at large, and of Ireland in particular, we are determined to resist all attempts at its Repeal, by every means in our power.

We are convinced, that it only requires the energies and talents of the people of this country to be turned from wild theories and the strife of politics to industrial pursuits, to raise Ireland, in a short time, to the same state of agricultural and commercial prosperity which Scotland has achieved for herself, since her union with England.

We consider it to be the duty of all friends of peace and order, at the present crisis, sinking all minor differences, to rally in support of her Majesty's Throne, and of the Government and Constitution of these kingdoms, in order that a speedy end may be put to the present state of agitation, which is so seriously injuring all business pursuits in this country; and we, therefore, offer our services to your Excellency, in any way which your superior wisdom and experience may deem advisable.

His Excellency was pleased to return the following answer, through Corry Connellan, Esq., his private secretary:—

Viceregal Lodge, April 29, 1848.

SIR—I am directed by the Lord Lieutenant to thank you for the transmission of a loyal address from the inhabitants of Donaghadee, in public meeting assembled, declaring their firm allegiance to the Queen, their attachment to the institutions which secure the liberties, lives, and properties of her subjects, and their determination to maintain the integrity of the British empire.

The Legislative Union, which has now for half a century subsisted between Great Britain and Ireland, has so blended together the people of both countries, that they must forever constitute one indivisible nationality. The attempts made to repeal this Union by violence and outrage are, therefore, as obviously absurd in the end proposed, as they are wicked in the means recommended. There can be no doubt, that, if the present excitement so perversely kept up by the seditious and disaffected, should be allowed to subside, that Ireland possesses resources, physical and mental, amply sufficient, if rightly employed, to retrieve the past and secure the future.

His Excellency trusts that the precautionary measures adopted by the Government, supported as they have been by the well-disposed of all creeds and classes in Ireland, will not only prevent an outbreak, but ultimately allay agitation, and afford an opportunity for the influx of that capital, which Ireland so much needs, and which the country would assuredly obtain, if confidence were restored and tranquility ensured.

I have the honour to be, SIR, your obedient servant,

CORRY CONNELLAN.

Recreated from The Belfast News-Letter, Belfast, May 5, 1848.

PEDESTRIANISM.

FULLER AND MOUNTJOY'S FORTY-MILE MATCH FOR ONE HUNDRED SOVEREIGNS.—Few pedestrian contests have of late excited more general interest, both on account of the men engaged, and the conditions of the competition, than the forty mile match between the ancient antagonists whose names head this report.

The meeting on Monday was fixed on the turnpike-road near to Mr. Grastrex's, the Three Magpies, Hounslow Heath.

At a few minutes before twelve o'clock, the civil and lively Bob Fuller appeared at the scratch, with his more saturnine and shorter opponent. The contrast of the men's styles is well known; Mountjoy, with his head slightly inclined to one side and forward, seemed ready to "slouch" off in his peculiar style, while Bob, erect as a dart, and graceful as a greyhound, smiled cheerfully. Mountjoy was all his friends could wish him to be, but it was rumoured that Fuller had had a cold, and hence the application of a plaister and mustard poultices, of which, after the race was over, we had ocular demonstration. Still his eye was bright, his colour fresh, and his countenance pleasing.—Five to four on Mountjoy, and level seemed the order of the day. On going off old Mountjoy, warned by experience, made play and led the way at a pretty stiff pace; so strong was it, for the opening of so long a day's work, that it rather influenced the odds against him than otherwise. The old one, however, kept drawing ahead by degrees up to the 18th mile, when Fuller was three minutes and a quarter in the rear; in the 19th and 20th Bob revived the hopes of his friends by gaining one minute and fifteen seconds on his antagonist, an advantage he held by getting twenty-one seconds in the 21st and 22d, and a trifle in the 23d and 24th. In the 25th and 26th little change took place, but in the four following miles Fuller, who had shortly before seemed weak, pulled on so gallantly that he actually overhauled Mountjoy, amid immense cheering from his friends. The betting now fluctuated to two to one on Fuller, nay, three and four to one was staked, so sanguine were his supporters. Several sporting men, considering the match at an end, more especially as Mountjoy seemed flagging and dropped his arms, departed for London, and there spread the news of Fuller's victory as a certainty. In the 33d and 34th, however, "the veteran" recovered surprisingly and came out as fresh after a little jelly and tea (taken while slowly progressing) as though he was beginning his task anew. He gradually and uniformly drew on Fuller, passed him on the 36th mile, was before him in coming down the 36th and 37th, shortly after turning which poor Fuller fainted, dead beaten, into the arms of his attendants, Sam East and a friend. So suddenly did he fall that he reached the ground before a saving arm effectually interposed; he was carried into Mr. Grastrex's, where, by friction, warm tea, and the most sedulous attention, he was soon alive to a keen sense of his manfully opposed defeat. The old one "bored" on, and completed his fortieth mile in seven hours four minutes seven seconds, thus winning one of the best and most gamely contested long distance matches on record.

Recreated from The Freeman's Journal, Dublin, May 5, 1848.

ARREST OF MR. REILLY, LAST NIGHT.
On yesterday evening Mr. Reilly was arrested in Newgate, on a warrant issued for him for having, when turning into the place of meeting, on Sunday, at the head of the St. Patrick's Club, given the words "Right shoulders forward, left wheel." Though the warrant was issued at 12 o'clock, its execution was delayed till four, at which hour the several police-offices were closed, and, in consequence, Mr. Reilly had to spend the night in Chancery-lane stationhouse. Messrs. Magee and Porter were applied to to take bail, but refused. The case was brought on at the Head Police-office this morning. Three witnesses connected with the constabulary were examined, whose evidence was for the purpose of proving that the words were used, and that they were military terms.

Mr. Reilly cross-examined the witnesses on his own behalf. In reply to his questions they admitted that the meeting was not a military, but a peaceful one—that no military evolutions were practised, and that the movement of "right shoulders forward," &c., was necessary for the club to enter the place of meeting in an orderly manner. They also admitted that at funerals and temperance processions such words of command may be made use of without breach of the law. Mr. Reilly urged that the act expressly referred to meetings held "clandestinely and unlawfully" "*for the purpose of drilling,*" and could not possibly contemplate an open and legal procession to a peaceful meeting. Notwithstanding, the magistrates determined to send Mr. Reilly for trial at the commission. Mr. Reilly then traversed to the next commission, and was admitted to bail at three o'clock.

DUBLIN POLICE—Monday.
HEAD OFFICE.

CHARGE OF USING MILITARY PHRASES.—Mr. John Sheehan was charged by Inspector Campbell with having been at the head of a body of men in Dame-street, in the city of Dublin, and for having used military tactics, and training a body of men contrary to the statute, &c.

Mr. J. B. Dillon, as counsel, and Mr. Kenny, as agent, appeared for the prisoner, and Mr. C. G. Duffy was present.

The case excited a good deal of interest, as it being known Mr. Sheehan was the person who had been taken up in Dame-street for saying "Halt." The office was crowded to excess.

Inspector Campbell, sworn—I was on duty in D'Olier-street yesterday between two and three o'clock, when I saw a body of men formed at a house; they marched three deep up the street, and turned into Westmorland-street; there were from 150 to 200 men altogether; I did not count them, but, from the appearance of them in the street, I think that was about the number; followed the procession, and when it came opposite Exchange-court, the prisoner turned round, and, in a loud and distinct voice, he gave out the word "Halt," and the whole body halted accordingly; I went up to where he was standing, when some person came up from the rere, and spoke to the prisoner in a low tone, and then one of them, but I cannot say which, gave the word, "Forward," and the body marched on; when I arrested the prisoner, as I considered he was leading a body of men in military order through the streets.

Mr. Porter—How long did they "halt" in the street? About two or three minutes.

Mr. Porter—Is there any military man here to prove the case? I am not aware, your worship, but I was drilled by a military man, and I am aware the words used by the the prisoner are used by the military; I am not aware that there was any word given at the corner of D'Olier-street, as I was not within hearing of the party there; the prisoner was to the left of the body of men when they commenced marching.

Mr. Porter—Then his taking a position at the "left" was the "right" one (laughter.) It was, your worship; the people came out three abreast from the door of the house.

Mr. Porter—A good wide door that must be. Do you know if the prisoner said "left face" to his men when turning from D'Olier-street into Westmoreland-street? I do not. I was two or three perches away from the head of the column, when I heard the word "halt," and all the men in the body heard it, for they all "halted" on the moment; they went up Cork-hill and Castle-street into High-street; some of the men had ribbons and green leaves.

Mr. Dillon—Would you call a green leaf a sign?

Mr. Porter—Have you any other evidence, Mr. Campbell? No other, your worship, except as to the facts to which I have sworn.

Mr. Porter—If you were marching a body of men, and wanted them to stop, would your word be "halt?" It would.

Mr. Porter—Would "forward" be your word when you wanted them to go on? It would.

Mr. Porter—Would that be the proper military word? I don't say it would be the proper military word, but I have often heard it given by military parties; I would not use the term "march," nor can I exactly say that that is the usual military word, although I have heard it used.

Mr. Porter—So have I, but then it is "right (or left) shoulder forward—march."

Witness—I will not say it was the prisoner who gave the word "forward" to the people.

Cross-examined by Mr. Dillon—Do you know what the people were assembled for?

Witness—My opinion is, that they were members of a club, and I believe they had assembled and were going to a meeting.

Mr. Dillon—I ask you as an honest, conscientious man, do you think that they were assembled for the purpose of practising military evolutions?

Witness—I can't say they were. I believe their object was to meet in D'Olier-street, and then go to the meeting.

Mr. Dillon—And is that the whole crime? Yes; but when he put up his hand, and cried "halt," he did it better than any of our men (laughter.)

Reprinted from The United Irishman, Dublin, May 23, 1848.

EXTERMINATION IN TIPPERARY.—We believe that a larger number of persons have been this year ejected than within any similar period within the oldest remembrance. In this county the number never reached half the amount it has arrived at within the last twelve months. Almost daily the sheriff, or his deputy, is engaged in the sad and melancholy work of levelling the houses of the rural population, who have no resource except the workhouse; not even the workhouse in many unions now, as, with few exceptions, all those institutions are densely crowded. During the present week the deputy-sheriff was engaged in Borrisokane, Portrue, &c., &c. On Wednesday he ejected ten families from a place called Belleen; and it is stated that he has several other similar calls for the ensuing week.—*Tipperary Vindicator.*

Numerous complaints now lie before us (says the *Mayo Telegraph*) from unfortunate peasantry who have paid their cess, and whose cattle have been recently seized by the barony of Carra high constable, and sold in this town for the cess of others in the townland who have failed to pay their share of the demand.

In the parish of Herbertstown are two townlands namely, Ballylundas and Ballynard. On one of these townlands a farmer's house was some time since attacked by a party who succeeded in depriving the owner of a small sum of money. The sergeant of Herbertstown police of course represented the circumstance to the Sub-inspector, Mr. Carey; that official immediately communicated with the Government, and the Government, without any delay, proclaimed the district—not for legal combinations, for murder or intemperance, but for the act of one farmhouse being attacked by the party alluded to. Six police officers were sent to Herbertstown, in addition to the number (ten) already stationed there, and the constabulary of Herbertstown now number fourteen police in all. The oppressed farmers of Ballylundas and Ballynard are saddled with this most unjustifiable taxation, and compelled, under circumstances, of painful character, to pay the sum of 1s. 4d., it is said, an acre to support six police walking about in idleness.—*Galway Vindicator.*

The *Mayo Constitution* gives an account of the death of a person named White, owing to the negligence of a relieving officer of the Castlebar union, although his attention had been called to the condition of the unfortunate man by Mr. Barrett, M.D. It is to be hoped that relieving officers, who, as in this instance, suffer the destitute to perish of hunger by their gross negligence, will be made amenable to the law.

At Bruff a poor but respectable man, who was remarkable for his honesty, of the name of Murphy, was recently ejected out of his farm. He did not owe much rent; what he did owe he would be able to meet if time were allowed him; but he would get no quarter. His doom was sealed, and what has been the consequence? A total mental aberration. For several days this poor man might be seen hovering around his farm with a slow pace and melancholy aspect, til ultimately persons were *obliged to chain him, and he is now a raving maniac.*—*Limerick and Clare Examiner.*

DEATH FROM STARVATION.—On Saturday last a boy named Moran, son of the widow Moran, of Claggan, parish of Glanisland, was found dead in a field, owing to the want of food. Our informant states, that it is awful to see the numbers of dying creatures who were just lying along the ditches and about the public barrack—that Thursday last was the day for distributing relief to the poor, but, owing to the neglect of the relieving officer, no aid was given up to the hour he was speaking to us (six o'clock on Saturday evening). We hope the vice-guardians will institute an inquiry into this horrible and distressing case.

Recreated from The Irish Felon, Dublin, June 24, 1848.

THE STATE OF THE COUNTRY.

The state of the country at present is such as to afford great cause for alarm. It is impossible not to perceive that throughout a large section of the country the law is almost a dead letter, and that the poor oppressed labouring classes are driven, by the acts of a tyrannical, imbecile, and shuffling Whig government, to acts of violence and riot—nay, almost to open rebellion. This is certainly an alarming state of things. Our magistrates and would-be great men, throughout the country, who are fond of signalizing themselves when their activity is useless or mischievous—in danger, become alarmed for their houses and property. They are at present literally frightened out of their whit; and each endeavours to throw the responsibility of acting on its neighbour. The ground of quarrel between the people and the ministry is (after all that can be said to the contrary) a want of the necessities of life in the midst of abundance.

The people see hoards of food, and they now are starving. The warehouses are glutted with pieces, the produce of their own labour; and yet they have a scarce rug to cover their nakedness. They see a government rioting in every sort of luxury and wasteful expenditure, whilst they, though ever ready to labour, are denied the comforts of life—nay, even the means of existence. Neither their patience nor their sufferings have obtained for them the least respectful attention or sympathy from the government. The more tame they have grown, the more they have been oppressed—the more they have been trampled upon. No terms of pacification have been offered.

The existing legislature has not the faculty of doing anything to relieve the distress of the country, it has not the capacity to do it. It is not its interest to be honest towards the people. It is itself the evil—the thing complained of—the thing to be removed; and can we expect them to commit suicide? Will such a parliament as the present, or any reform it is likely to sanction, remove the evils which at present afflict the country? We think not. What is, then to be done?—who is to do it? Will the Whigs? Never. Would the Tories? Never.

It will require the united exertions of the leading minds amongst the Radical Reformers, backed by their followers both of the middle and working classes, to set these matters right. Any piecemeal attempt to reform the House of Commons will only make it more contemptible. It must be a fair appeal to the nation—no shuffling will suffice; and everything must stand or fall upon the principle of honesty and justice.

We hope the people will persevere a little longer in their just and righteous demands, and, in order to strengthen their cause, unite with those who are willing to place them on the same political equality with themselves; they might thus create a moral power that the Whigs would not be able to resist even by the severity of their NEW GAGGING BILL.—*Bolton Times.*

ATTACK ON THE HANGMAN AT CORK.—The wretched caitiff, whose "poverty, not his will," compelled him to fill the degrading office of "Jack Ketch," left the jail on Saturday evening, having obtained a commutation of sentence, together with a few pounds, in lieu of his services. He was not more than a few hours at large, when, being recognized, he was assaulted in the locality of the Coalquay by a large mob, before whom he retreated, followed by "popular vengeance," until, having arrived at the Tuckey-street station, he was protected from further molestation by the police. The unfortunate fellow is a native of the county Tipperary, of the name of Ryan, and was undergoing sentence of incarceration for stealing a lot of watches in the town of Youghal some months since. He is of most wretched and cadaverous appearance.—*Cork Reporter.*

Recreated and reprinted from The Irish Felon, Dublin, July 1, 1848.

WHOLESALE EVICTIONS IN THE KILRUSH UNION.

Our special correspondent brings us frightful details of the clearance system in unhappy Clare, and communicates the awful fact, that since last November one thousand houses have been levelled with the ground in the Kilrush Union.—*Limerick and Clare Examiner.*

BROADFORD.—We have been informed that upwards of one hundred tenant-farmers have received notice to quit in the neighbourhood of Broadford.—*Ibid.*

THE POOR RATE—CURIOUS SEIZURE.—The liability of property under the poor law was tested in a very curious manner on Thursday, by one of the rate collectors of Thurles union. Ten very fine fat heifers, destined for the Dublin market, to which they were to go next morning by train, were driven to pasture for the night on lands near the town. These very fine fat heifers were the property of Lord Hawarden, of Dundrum, whose love for such cattle is a matter of public notoriety. The lands on which they were temporarily located were in debt, it appears, for poor rates to the union in the sum of £35. The collector had made many attempts to seize, but all to no purpose. The moment, however, he perceived his lordship's fat heifers on the grass he drove them to the parish pound, detained them, and resolved on selling them this day (Saturday) for the rate, unless the sum due shall be paid in the mean time.—*Tipperary Vindicator.*

DEATHS BY STARVATION IN TIPPERARY.—On Saturday, James Carol, Esq., coroner, held an inquest at Ballyhogar, on the bodies of a woman named Coltins, and her infant. It appeared in evidence that the poor woman's husband held over a statute acre of ground, on account of which the family were denied relief; but being seized with fever, as generally happens in such cases, they were received into the fever hospital. It was the will of Providence that they should recover; but, when convalescent, famine completed the worst, which the prevailing epidemic failed to accomplish—the mother and child sunk down from absolute want. The jury returned a verdict accordingly.

On Thursday last ten families were exterminated from the property of Mr. Peter Conelan, who resides at Coolmore, county Kilkenny, and is brother to Mr. Corry Conelan, Private Secretary to the Castle.—*Galway Vindicator.*

EMIGRATION.

FREE EMIGRATION.—On Friday, two hundred and eighty persons from the crown lands of Ballynane, within a few miles of this town, who voluntarily resigned their holdings, were dispatched on cars to Galway, from whence they will obtain a passage to Canada at the expense of the government. Should they remain in the British dominions on their arrival, employment will be secured to them; and to such of them as choose to seek their own fortunes in other portions of America, a certain sum of money—we believe 2£. each—will be given towards enabling them to do so.—*Ballinasloe Star.*

TRALEE.—The following resolution was adopted by the Tralee Board of Guardians at their meeting on Tuesday last:—"That this Board avail itself of the opportunity now afforded of permanently providing for several inmates of the workhouse through the medium of emigration, as recommended by the Commissioners of Colonial Land and Emigration to the government; and we hereby undertake to provide the outfit and conveyance to the port of embarkation of such females as may be considered eligible and desirous to emigrate."

Recreated from The Irish Felon, Dublin, July 1, 1848.

CAUTION.

Whereas, several wicked and evil-minded persons are visiting the different parishes in this county, exciting the minds of the inhabitants, and calling upon them to form clubs and to procure arms, with a view of accomplishing their own selfish and wicked designs. And whereas many ignorant persons may be led by the arts of such persons to enroll their names, and unwittingly become parties to their acts, thereby bringing themselves into great danger, and their country into civil war, anarchy, and bloodshed. I hereby caution all those who value their own lives and liberties, and all those who have anything to lose, to refrain from the formation of political clubs in their respective parishes, or affixing their names as members thereof; and I call their serious intention to the scenes lately passing in France, where (in consequence of such clubs) the streets of Paris have been deluged with the blood of thirty thousand of its inhabitants, and the archbishop murdered in open day, while in the exercise of his pious and Christian endeavour to stop the effusion of blood.

Always anxious for the peace of this district, and for the security of the lives and property of all its inhabitants, I give this friendly caution beforehand to all my neighbours, assured that long experience will have convinced them how deeply interested I am in their welfare.

CHARLES COBBE, Deputy Lieutenant and J.P.
County of Dublin.
Newbridge, July 3d, 1848.

[This is rich. Mr. Charles Cobbe, in his "deep interest" for the welfare of his neighbourhood, calls upon "all who have anything" to lose to shun those "political clubs" which lately "deluged the streets of Paris with blood." Benevolent Cobbe, Paris was deluged with blood because of the "deep interest" which sweet-souled officials like yourself took in the affairs of all those who had "something to lose," while they forgot the very existence of those poor devils who had *nothing* to lose, and everything to gain. Make yourself not too conspicuous, O, long-headed Cobbe! for in despite of your great foresight, the working men of Ireland may rise up like their brothers in France, and the first blood that would "deluge the streets" of Dublin might be official blood. Think of this, Cobbe, and hide yourself in a pantry or such like!]

Recreated from The Irish Felon, Dublin, July 8, 1848.

Fire-Arms, all Warranted.

THE Cheapest and most Extensive Stock in the Kingdom for Sale, at the Gunmakers' Hall,
No. 34, WELLINGTON-QUAY, DUBLIN.
at the following unprecedented Prices. viz. :—

	£	s	d	
Good, well-made Rifles, warranted, Twist Barrel and Patent Britch	3	3	0	upwards.
Double-barrelled Rifles, do.	2	10	0	
Double Fowling Pieces, do.	2	10	0	
Single do., do.	1	15	0	
Imitation do.	1	0	0	
Carbines	1	0	0	
Military Muskets, with Bayonets, and Bullet Moulds to match	1	3	0	
Queen Anne, and long Duck Guns	1	2	6	
Air Guns, and Canes	3	0	0	
Screw-barrels, Pocket Pistols, with bullet moulds and barrel-key	0	11	0	per pair
Large Military Pistols, £1 5 0 to	1	15	0	
Belt and other Pistols, 1 0 0 to	2	0	0	
Six-shot Self-revolving Pistols 2 0 0 to	3	0	0	

All warranted Double Tower Proof.
With a large variety of Wash-rods, Ram-rods, Tips, and Screws, Nipples, and Nipple-winches, Bullet-moulds, Turn-screws, Shot-belts and Bags, Powder-flasks, Percussion Caps, Elly's Shot Cartridges, and a great many other Gun Implements, too numerous to insert.

Country Orders punctually attended to,
And the sum paid for either Guns or Pistols returned within ten days, if not approved of.

There are two Shooting Galleries on the premises, where all Guns and Pistols sold can be proved, or gentlemen can practise the use of either for 1d. per shot.

N.B.—Second-hand Guns and Pistols taken in Exchange, or sold on commission.

Reprinted from The Irish Felon, Dublin, July 1, 1848.

THE COERCION ACT—THE LAW OF DUBLIN.

(*From the Freeman.*)

Dublin is proclaimed, so are three of the chief commercial cities in Ireland. We are soon about to live under this severe law, which places the liberties of the subject in abeyance, and transfers their rights and privileges to the constitutional mercies of police and detectives. Now, for the first time, we are about to experience the bitterness of this persecuting law. When the metropolis of the kingdom is placed under ban, we may well say that all real freedom is extinguished, and we wait to know "what next." As it is probable the provisions of this act have passed from the public recollection, we think it right to supply an abstract to guard and guide our readers in the terrible times which appear to be foreshadowed by the present.

The essence of the act commences with the ninth section. From and after the day named in the proclamation—in the case of Dublin, for instance, on Thursday 20th inst., and thenceforth whilst the proclamation is in force—no person whatsoever shall carry or posses arms elsewhere than in his own dwelling-house. The contraband instruments include "guns, pistols, or other firearms, or parts of such"—likewise "bullets, gunpowder, or ammunition." Any open wearing or *carrying* of such arms to be a misdemeanor, and punishable with *two years' imprisonment, with hard labour.* The person exempt from this provision—that is, who may carry arms outside of their dwelling-houses, are—justices of the peace, persons in the public service, special constables, and persons released under the act.

By the tenth clause any *constable* or *other person* whatsoever may seize and apprehend any person found carrying arms, and deliver him into the charge of a policeman or special constable, in order that the offender might be brought before a magistrate or *constable*, to *search* any person "*suspected*" of having arms, or bullets, or gunpowder in his possession, and forfeit the same to her Majesty. The eleventh clause improves on the foregoing. From and after the day named in the proclamation, the Lord Lieutenant, by notice duly published and posted, may require, and doubtless will require, all persons, save those privileged, on or before a day named in the notice, to deposit at a place named in the notice, all manner of arms—to be there detained until the proclamation shall cease to be in force in the district. A valuable security is guaranteed to the depositors. They will not come under the penalty of the ninth section whist conveying their arms to the place of deposit. Every person continuing to keep arms in his possession after the day fixed for the surrender shall be punished *with two years' imprisonment.*

If the authorities *suspect* that the surrender has been imperfect in the proclaimed district, a search warrant may be issued to all inspectors and constables—to remain in force for twenty-one days, and to be renewed, if necessary, so long as the exigency may require. By this warrant, any house may be entered between sunrise and sunset, and if admission be not given within a reasonable time, force may be used for the execution of the warrant.

We trust that all will conform themselves to the "invasion," and obey the law. Such desperate courses cannot be long lived. The best way to overcome their severity is to afford no pretext for the pains and penalties any violation of the law must involve. We rely on the good sense and resolute firmness of our brother-citizens to meet this unconstitutional usurpation. The day of triumph will yet come. Let us await it like freemen, and remember, that the greatest and most lasting victories are those achieved by order. The following is the proclamation issued for this city:—

BY THE LORD LIEUTENANT AND COUNCIL OF IRELAND.

A PROCLAMATION.

CLARENDON.

Whereas by an Act passed in this present Session of Parliament, in the Eleventh Year of her Majesty's reign, intituled, "An Act for the better Prevention of Crime and Outrage in certain parts of Ireland, until the First Day of December, one thousand eight hundred and forty-nine, and to the end of the then next Session of Parliament," it is amongst other things enacted, "That whenever, in the judgement of the Lord Lieutenant, or other Chief Governor or Governors of Ireland, by and with the advice of the Privy Council of Ireland, it shall be necessary for the prevention of crime and outrage, that the said Act should apply to any County, County of a City, or County of a Town, or any Barony or Baronies, Half Barony or Half Baronies, in any County at Large, or any District of less extent than any Barony or Half Barony in Ireland, it shall be lawful to and for the Lord Lieutenant or other Chief Governor or Governors of Ireland, to declare by Proclamation, to be published in the *Dublin Gazette*, that from and after a day to be named in such Proclamation, the said Act shall apply to any County, County of a City, County of a Town, or any Barony or Baronies, Half Barony of Half Baronies in any County at Large, or any District of less extent than any Barony or Half Barony in Ireland.

Now, We, the Lord Lieutenant, do, by this our Proclamation, in the pursuance and execution of the said act, and by and with the advice of her Majesty's Privy Council in Ireland, declare, that from and after THURSDAY, the TWENTIETH DAY of this present month of July, one thousand eight hundred and forty-eight, the said act shall apply to, and be in force in and for, the County of the City of DUBLIN.

And for this our Proclamation all Justices of the Peace of the said County of the City of DUBLIN, Constables, Peace Officers, and all others whom it may concern are to take notice.

Given at the Council Chamber in Dublin, this 18th day of July 1848.

GOD SAVE THE QUEEN.

MR. S. O'BRIEN IN DROGHEDA.

The visit of this patriotic gentleman to Drogheda, announced in yesterday's Freeman as about to take place, was hailed with the greatest delight by the nationalists of all classes in that town, who received him with the warmest welcome, and evinced the utmost anxiety to testify their desire for the promotion of union among all classes of Irishmen in the cause of their common country. On arrival of the train at half-past seven o'clock, Mr. O'Brien was met at the railway station by an enormous assemblage of the trades and working classes, preceded by the splendid banners of several guilds, and having formed into a procession, headed by the temperance band belonging to the town, they preceded Mr. O'Brien and his friends through the principal streets, cheering enthusiastically as they went along for "Smith O'Brien and Repeal"—"John Mitchel"—"The Irish League"—and the patriots in prison, &c., &c. On arrival at the place of meeting, which was most judiciously selected—namely, the spacious Market-square of the town, the assemblage had swelled to the full extent of what, in 1843, would have been entitled to the designation of a "Monster Meeting." It is always difficult to estimate with accuracy the number of persons present at popular assemblies; but, judging from the closest observation, and the opinion of many persons very competent to form a correct judgement, the numbers present may, without the least exaggeration, be set down as exceeding 10,000.

Recreated from The Irish Felon, Dublin, July 22, 1848.

MR. DOHENY IN TIPPERARY— GREAT MEETING ON SLIEVENAMON.

Mr. Doheny having been bailed out on Saturday—the charge against him being one of sedition, not, as stated by the *Nenagh Guardian* and the *Mail*, one cognizable by the "treason-felony act"—remained in the capital of the north riding for a short time, and then started for the city of Cashel. Here immense preparations had been making for the great demonstration which had been advertised to take place on the mountain of Slievenamon, under the auspices of Mr. Doheny. That gentleman arrived in Cashel on this (Sunday) morning, and there having put on the uniform of the '82 Club, he, in company of his lady, started at eleven o'clock in an open barouche, drawn by four horses, for the place of the meeting. Upwards of two thousand persons formed the cortege from the "City of the Kings." Wandering their way up the side of the mountain from the direction of the various localities, might be seen the men of Cork, Waterford, Wexford, and from all sides the "Boys of Tipperary."

At two o'clock the chair was taken, when not less than fifty thousand souls overspread the summit of the mountain. Unfortunately, I happened to be late, and thus found it impossible to pierce the dense mass to come by any means within earshot of the speakers. They consisted but of four—the chairman (whose name I could not ascertain), Mr. White, Mr. Doheny, and another gentleman. Mr. Doheny, I understand, advised the people to form clubs, cautioned them to be firm, and fear not, and the "day was their own." The observations of the other parties were of the usual import.

The immense assemblage separated in the most orderly and peaceful manner.

There were no police present, except a few in coloured clothes, one of whom told me there could not have been less than fifty thousand people present.—*Correspondent of the Pilot.*

Sixteen Arrests in Cashel!—More Arrests Contemplated!—Cashel, July 15—I wrote to inform you of the fact, that there have been sixteen arrests made here this morning, and more are being made as I write. The crime with which the arrested are charged regards the rescue of Mr. Doheny. They are all fine young fellows, with their "hearts in the right place," as they humorously informed me when I had the honour of visiting their cell this morning. The attention of Mrs. Doheny and her sister towards the prisoners speaks much for their generosity and patriotism.—Correspondent of *The Freeman's Journal.*

Cashel, July 16.—Mr. Michael Doheny has just returned in triumph from the north riding, and is now setting out, dressed in a most showy military costume, green and gold, mounted on a chestnut charger, at the head of his club (*quere regiment?*) to the great rendezvous of the clubs, on the mountain of Slievenamon, where it is expected some thousands of the army of the League will assemble this day. Mr. Meagher, of Waterford, is gone with Doheny.— A correspondent of the *Evening Mail.*

GREAT EXCITEMENT IN WATERFORD.

Great excitement prevails through this city since the arrival of Mr. T. F. Meagher from Limerick, which took place on yesterday morning, at about three o'clock, A.M., when, notwithstanding the hour, he was surrounded by hundreds of the inhabitants, in addition to great numbers who accompanied him from the mountain of Slievenamon, the towns of Carrick-on-Suir, Mount Coin, and other places through which he passed. On arriving, he addressed his followers from his own residence, and in the evening spoke for nearly two hours to one of the densest multitudes I have ever witnessed, from the window of his club-room, detailing to them the particulars of his late visit to Dublin and Limerick, and exciting them to energy and perseverance.—*Freeman.*

GREAT COMMOTION IN CARRICK-ON-SUIR.

A correspondent, writing from Clonmel, under date Monday, four o'clock, gives the following version of the affair at Carrick-on-Suir:—

"The car has just arrived from Carrick-on-Suir. Awful commotion prevails in that town. The occasion is said to be this:—Some persons from Carrick, who were at the meeting yesterday, had a tricolour flag; when returning from the meeting, they were arrested by the police, and put in the Bridewell. When the people heard of it to-day, they assembled in crowds opposite the Bridewell, many of them being armed. The military were drawn out, and the riot act read, but all to no purpose. Some persons even say that the prisoners had to be let free."

Another correspondent, writing from Clonmel, on Tuesday, graphically describes bonfires which lit up the whole country, hill and dale, far as the eye could reach, and finally Clonmel itself; and adds:—

"The bonfires, and the excitement consequent upon their appearance, were caused by the intelligence received from Carrick-on-Suir, that some prisoners were arrested, but were subsequently rescued from the Bridewell keeper. The accounts received here make it appear that the Carrick people, upon hearing of some of the club's men being arrested, and the rumour that one of their priests was marked out for the same fate, rose e*n masse*, and, with arms in their hands, consisting of pikes and rifles, repaired to the authorities, and demanded the prisoners, who were at once delivered up to them. They then rang the chapel bells, and 4,000 men came down from the neighbouring hills, armed to the teeth, and remained in Carrick all night, lest an attempt should be made to arrest Fr. Byrne. The delivery of the prisoners, and the withdrawal of the few troops in Carrick, was considered as a triumph so far, and the people signalled it by the bonfires.—*Freeman.*

Recreated from The Irish Felon, Dublin, July 22, 1848.

SUSPENSION OF THE HABEAS CORPUS ACT.

LIVERPOOL, FRIDAY, EIGHT MINUTES PAST SIX P.M.

"Lord John Russell has announced that he will to-morrow, at a special sitting, move for leave to introduce a bill to empower the Lord Lieutenant of Ireland, until the 1st of March, 1849, to apprehend and detain such persons as he shall suspect guilty of treasonable designs against her Majesty's crown and government. *An order for suspending the Habeas Corpus and arrest of Smith O'Brien has gone over.*"

HOUSE OF COMMONS—SATURDAY, JULY 22.

Lord John Russell rose and said—Mr. Speaker, I never felt so deep a concern in bringing any question before this house as that which I now feel in proposing to this house to suspend for a limited time the constitutional liberties of Ireland. I feel, however, at the same time that the measure I am about to propose is not only necessary for the preservation of life and property in Ireland—it is necessary for the purpose of preventing bloodshed—but it is necessary to put a stop to incipient insurrection, and is eminently called for to secure the safety of the British Empire (hear, and cheers).

LONDON, SATURDAY, SEVEN O'CLOCK, P.M.

The standing orders having been suspended, the bill for suspending the Habeas Corpus was read the first and second time, and committed. It was then read a third time and passed, all in the space of *ten minutes*. It is to be sent to the Lords on Monday, when similar expedition will be used.

It is provided that persons may be arrested in Ireland under the provisions of the bill on the same day that it receives the royal assent in England.

Recreated from The Freeman's Journal, Dublin, July 24, 1848.

ARRESTS FOR SELLING SEDITIOUS NEWSPAPERS.

In the course of Saturday, several newsvenders were arrested and brought before the Dublin magistrates, on a charge of selling seditious publications—namely, the *Nation* and *Irish Felon*. The parties were bailed out to appear on Monday to answer the charge preferred against them.—*Freeman*.

DROGHEDA—THE PROCLAMATION.—The inhabitants of Drogheda protest against the outrageous conduct of evil-disposed persons, in combining to falsely representing Drogheda as in a state of insurrection. The inhabitants are signing a requisition to the Mayor to hold a meeting to proclaim against what they all consider an uncalled-for and trade-destroying exercise of authority.

The *Drogheda Argus* states that it is in contemplation to commemorate the monster meeting at Tara, of 1843, on the approaching 15th August.

Carrick-on-Suir and Carrickbeg have been in a most excited state since the Slievenamon meeting. The country people are really "up and stirring;" arming themselves with every weapon they can lay hold of, and eager for the word of command from Meagher or Doheny, whom the misguided people are everywhere asking for. All business has been suspended in these towns, and the inhabitants have closed their shops. The peasantry round Carrick-on-Suir are cutting down the plantations for pike handles. They carried away three cart-loads from Mr. Wall, of Coolnamuck.—*Limerick Chronicle*.

YESTERDAY (FRIDAY), Major-General Napier and Col. Doyle, acting Adjutant-General, left Limerick on an inspection of the military posts at Clonmel, Cahir, and Carrick-on-Suir.—*Ibid*.

Four pieces of artillery and a mortar-gun were added, this week, to the military force at Cork, escorted by the twelfth Lancers, from Ballincollig. The Lancers were hooted, groaned, and spit at by the crowd. The police charged, and cleared the streets.—*Ibid*.

CLONMEL.—SIGNAL FIRES.—The *Cork Examiner* states that, from all the hills in the counties of Waterford and Tipperary, signal fires blazed out in thousands on Thursday night, and before ten o'clock the roads leading to Clonmel were also illuminated. The centre and main street of that town were also illuminated, and the clubs mustered at eleven o'clock. Their rooms were opened, and speeches made of a determination to work to the last at all hazards. It was considered necessary to have the military in attendance. Sir Chas. O'Donnell, who ventured to remonstrate with the people, was rather roughly handled.

FIRST ARREST UNDER THE RECENT PROCLAMATION.—Friday, at three o'clock, a man named John Martin, twenty years of age, was arrested in Earl-street, Dublin, for having a gun in his possession. He was at once brought to Sackville-place station house, where a charge to the effect "that he was found carrying arms in the street without being duly licensed to do so," was entered against him. He was then conveyed to Henry-street police-office, but as the magistrate had retired for the day, the young man was again "marched" back to the station, where he was locked up.

THURSDAY MORNING, orders were given from the Commander-in-Chief's office to all officers belonging to regiments in Ireland, on leave of absence in London, to repair immediately to rejoin their respective regiments quartered in that country. His Royal Highness Prince George of Cambridge left by the mail train the same night for Liverpool, *en route* for Dublin; also, the Marquis of Worcester to join the 7th Hussars.

London, Thursday Evening.—A cabinet council was held at the Foreign Office on Thursday afternoon for the purpose of considering some important despatches received at two o'clock from Lord Clarendon. Lord Clarendon has addressed an urgent despatch to Lord J. Russell, which was delivered on Thursday, by special messenger, calling for additional troops, and the immediate presence of a large fleet of war ships and steamers on the coast of Ireland at different points, which he named.

The Lords of the Admiralty have given it as their opinion that Sir Charles Napier's squadron should be increased, and directions to that effect were forwarded by electric telegraph this afternoon to Portsmouth, Plymouth, and Spithead. The Horse Guards have received orders to hold themselves in readiness for instant departure, by railway, to Liverpool. The troops at Weedon, Birmingham, Manchester, and other military stations, are under similar orders. The Duke of Wellington and Lord Hardinge, on Thursday evening, tendered their services to the Government, and had conveyed to Lord John Russell their readiness to proceed to Ireland by express train for the purpose of assisting Lord Clarendon in his government of the country, should the Government desire. Lord John referred the proposal to the Home Secretary.—*Correspondent of Freeman's Journal.*

Great Excitement in Waterford.—Thursday Evening, Seven o'clock.—The city of Waterford still remains in a state of the greatest excitement. Strong reinforcements of military (3rd Buffs) and constabulary, fully equipped for a campaign, have arrived here for the preservation of the peace. The Lord Lieutenant's Proclamation, ending with the usual phrase "God save the Queen", has been posted all over the town, which was immediately posted over, with a counter proclamation, signed "Thomas F. Meagher", and ending, "God save the People".

The police, in pursuance of instructions, tore down several of Mr. Meagher's proclamation, but, in doing so, they received every possible annoyance and obstruction; they were shoved here and there by groups of idlers, hooted, and in some instances pelted. There are several smithies hard at work making pikes; and cart-loads of ash poles for pike-handles have been brought openly into town. Everything is in a fearful state; but it is a gratification to know that the Government have a strong force at their disposal in Waterford, and at hand, which would be more than sufficient to suppress at once any attempt to break the peace. Colonel Sir Charles O'Donnell left Clonmel on Wednesday evening for Waterford, to assume the command of the troops there, in case of any disturbance occurring.

Mr. Doheny Again.—We have been informed that informations were sworn at Waterford, on Wednesday last, against Mr. Doheny for delivering a seditious speech, on Sunday, sen., at the Slievenamon meeting. If this be so, and his arrest effected, he will be tried in Clonmel at the present assizes.—*Clonmel Chronicle.*

Arrival of Troops in Waterford.—Friday afternoon, the *Duchess of Kent* steamer arrived here with 400 of the 3rd Regt. (or Buffs) from Belfast. They had not disembarked at the time we were going to press.—*Waterford Mail of Saturday.*

Warrant for W.S. O'Brien.—The Freeman's Journal has put forth a placard, stating that a warrant has been issued for the arrest of Mr. Wm. Smith O'Brien.

Additional Troops for Ireland.—The second battalion 60th Rifles and 89th Regiment are under orders to proceed from the Northern District to Dublin, and to be relieved by the 33rd from Edinburgh, and 90th Light Infantry from Chatham.

Recreated from The Belfast News-Letter, Belfast, July 25, 1848.

THE APPROACHING CRISIS.
REBELLION—MUSKETS—PLANS. &c.

Without one word of unnecessary commentary or preface, we proceed to lay before the Government, as well as before our readers, the following alarming facts. We are not at liberty to say through what channel the information has reached us; but we can assure the government that its accuracy may be relied on; and we trust that, if hitherto unapprised of the circumstances we are about to mention, they will lose no time in testing the truth of the intelligence and acting as the exigency may require.

Our information is to the following effect:—Last week, eighty stand of arms were purchased by the Dr. Doyle club, of which Mr. Duffy, of the *Nation*, is president.

Twenty thousand stand of the disused military flint muskets have been purchased in London, for the use of the insurgents, and are coming over in batches.

On yesterday evening, a large van, with four horses, was publicly, and, as it happened, actually under the eye of a police inspector, laden with muskets, at the door of a gunsmith, who keeps a shooting gallery upon Wellington-quay.

On yesterday morning, Hyland, the noted "pike-maker to the Castle", left this city for Carlow, with a large consignment of pikes.

The rebels have prepared a map of the city of Dublin, subdivided into districts, in each of which the points at which the clubs are respectively to muster, and where barricades are to be thrown up are indicated. It is now arranged that, if upon the formation of the jury to try Duffy or his fellows, it shall appear probable that a conviction will be had, the clubs are to rise immediately, and prevent the trial by an anticipatory, and, as they hope, a successful outbreak.

One word we must add. The 20,000 stand of arms above mentioned will alone cost £10,000! How and whence is this money procured? How and whence are the enormous sums necessary to make the various and vast purchases of arms and ammunition for the towns and country, of which this is but an inconsiderable fraction, obtained? For this difficulty we can offer *no* solution whatever.

It can only be explained upon the supposition that the ostensible instigators of rebellion in Ireland are clandestinely backed by men of large resources. We mentioned the other day a rumour respecting a document of which the Government had information, implicating men of a station much superior to that occupied by the recognized leaders of the republican movement. We do not vouch for the accuracy of the report, but its truth would certainly explain what is otherwise inexplicable.

THE DISARMING NOTICES.

Last night's *Dublin Gazette* contains five disarming notices, fixing the days on or before which arms must be delivered up in five of the proclaimed districts, with the exception of the privileged classes, and such as may obtain licenses:—

The citizens of Cork are called upon to give up their arms on or before the 27th instant. The inhabitants of the baronies of Cork, Fermoy, and Condons, and Clongibbon, in the county of Cork, are to give up their arms within the same period. The citizens of Waterford, on or before the 27th instant also. The inhabitants of the baronies of Kilculliheen, Middlethird, and Gaultiere, in the county of Waterford, on or before the same day. The inhabitants of Drogheda, on or before the same day.

RAILWAY DESPATCH AND TELEGRAPHIC MAGIC.

His Royal Highness Prince Albert left the Euston station at nine o'clock, on Wednesday morning week, to attend the meeting of the Royal Agricultural Society, at York, at which city he arrived at forty minutes past two, thus travelling the whole distance, 228 miles, at the rate of forty miles an hour. In ten minutes after his royal highness had reached the archiepiscopal city of the north, that is to say, at fifty minutes past two, her Majesty received information in London, by means of the electric telegraph, that the journey had been safely accomplished.

Recreated from The Freeman's Journal, Dublin, July 25 1848.

O'BRIEN REQUESTS POLICE TO SURRENDER.

About nine o'clock this morning, Mr. Smith O'Brien and his comrades, Messrs, J.B. Dillon, Cantwell, and O'Donahoe, unaccompanied by any person whatsoever, rather silently dropped into the police barracks of Mullinahone, and for some time questioned the temper and feelings of the police of this station, and, as rumour states, requested of them to surrender up their arms to the people—a mandate with which the police very properly refused to comply. This circumstance having been immediately made known, the people of the town offered their services and protection to the constabulary. Nothing could possibly have better effect on the people than the absurd idea of Mr. O'Brien's having called on the police for a surrender of their arms. At this time the crowds were fast hurrying into the town—a circumstance which rendered it imperative on the Roman Catholic clergymen, accompanied by the Messrs. Kickhams, Cleary, Norton, and other inhabitants, to at once wait on Mr. Smith O'Brien, and call for his immediate removal from town, to which injunction the unhappy gentleman very calmly consented, and, accordingly, proceeded to Ballingarry, five miles distant from this.

THURSDAY, FOUR O'CLOCK, P.M.—To the great surprise of the inhabitants, Smith O'Brien and Co., accompanied by some hundreds of armed men from Ballingarry and the colliery, arrived here. The Rev. Dr. Corcoran and Rev. Mr. Cahill were at once on the spot, and succeeded in causing the Ballingarry men to return to their homes—a proceeding that left Mr. Smith O'Brien and comrades almost alone. He remained in the immediate vicinity of Mullinahone until eleven o'clock, when he pursued his course towards the direction of Thurles. I could hear that the poor deluded gentleman betrayed much uneasiness of mind at his leaving.

The Lord Lieutenant has been pleased to grant a reward of twenty pounds to Constable Williams, of Mullinahone, and five pounds to each of his men, in consideration of their determined conduct on the occasion above referred to.

Recreated from The Belfast News-Letter, Belfast, July 25, 1848.

STATE OF IRELAND.
THE APPROACHING CRISIS.
STATE OF DUBLIN.

(FROM OUR DUBLIN CORRESPONDENT.)

We are in a state of fearful excitement here. Even people who were callous about public events a few weeks ago are now seriously weighing the chances of and against a rebellion. These are now arming themselves to the teeth, in order to be in a state of defense, should things come to the worst. It is lamentable to think how many young men of promise are joining the rebel clubs, careless of all the consequences, so that they may have the glory of being participators in the struggle.

Most of them have been egged on by the inflammatory language of the paupers, and the Jacobian orators—these are the enthusiasts, or fanatics; but I fear the rest are wholly influenced by hopes of plunder. Every legal inhabitant should be prepared. Business, and trade of every kind, are getting worse and worse every day. Shopkeepers and merchants are becoming bankrupt, or are selling off and emigrating; and this state of things is the more truly lamentable, at a time when people were just beginning to recover themselves from the disastrous effects of the two preceding years.

As I travel through the city so much every day, I am in a way to hear the complaints and repinings of mercantile men, but a glance at the closed shops of ruined traders would be a sufficient criteria to judge by, even if there were not these complaints to corroborate such testimony of the general stagnation of trade. The prospects of a plentiful harvest were beginning to make people happy and hopeful; the use, however, that the disaffected threaten to make of that harvest, will, it is feared, change the blessing to a curse.

Recreated from The Belfast News-Letter, Belfast, July 28, 1848.

SEIZURE OF THE *FELON* NEWSPAPER.

On Friday evening a strong body of armed police entered the premises of the *Felon* office in Trinity street, and at once proceeded to take possession of the types, the proof press, the forms, and all other apparatus connected with the paper. They carried them away in a well-laden float to the Lower Castleyard. One side of the paper had been prepared for Saturday's publication. A dense crowd of people was collected in the street, but no manifestation of popular feeling was exhibited.

KILKENNY, FRIDAY.—Information from Callan today states that Smith O'Brien was then at Ballingarry with a rebel army of 2,000 men, armed and ready to march, some said to Kilkenny, others to Urlingford. O'Brien was dressed in rebel uniform.

NOTES OF PREPARATION IN CARRICK-ON-SUIR.—We saw a letter this day from Carrick, in which it is stated that among other extensive preparations on the part of the people in that town, twelve anvils ring night and day with the sound of the pike in defiance of all "legal consequences", and presence of police and military.—*Limerick Reporter.*

CARRICK-ON-SUIR, SUNDAY.—The state of alarm into which the inhabitants have been thrown has not as yet subsided in this town. Two or three respectable families have already left for America. God grant that we be not plunged into anarchy and confusion here. The town is filling with soldiery and police. I have every hope that the deserved influence of the respected clergy will prevail in inculcating such a course of conduct on the part of the people as will foil all the machinations of their enemies.—*Tipperary Vindicator.*

EXCITEMENT IN CLONMEL.—Within the last two days Clonmel has been filled with the most alarming rumours. The most painful anxiety is awakened, as the general feeling is, that an insurrection, with all its horrors, is at hand, and may commence before we see the light of another day. The police have removed from the barracks in the Irishtown and taken possession of the West Gate. Military are to occupy the main guard; and no doubt, every necessary preparation will be made for the protection of the town and the security of its peaceable inhabitants. It is further said that one of the leaders spent last night at Thorney-bridge, in the neighbourhood of Slievenamon, and that the Carrick-on-Suir corps are in readiness to join in the onslaught. We are informed that the riding school of the cavalry barracks is open for the reception of families, or any one who may require protection, and probably will be used should alarm and apprehension continue to prevail as they have since Sunday. A number of the inhabitants were served with notices to-day to attend before the magistrates, in order that they might be sworn in as special constables.—*Clonmel Chronicle.*

CLONMEL, MONDAY, JULY 24TH, 1848.—On yesterday, Sunday, the agent for the sale of the *Irish Felon* was arrested, and held to bail for vending a seditious publication. A large force of police came into town this day, and took up their quarters on the New Buildings at Bagwell-street. People here are expecting a reign of terror.

SLIGO, MONDAY, JULY 24, 1848.—Two respectable persons—one the Deputy Post-master—were arrested here yesterday morning, for being agents and disposing of the *Nation* newspaper. They were admitted to bail last evening. We have not the least particle of excitement in either town or country.—*Dublin Evening Post.*

Recreated from The Belfast News-Letter, Belfast, July 28, 1848.

By the Lord Lieutenant General and General Governor of Ireland.

A PROCLAMATION.

CLARENDON.

WHEREAS We have received Information that *William Smith O'Brien* has been guilty of Treasonable Practices, and has openly appeared in Arms against Her Majesty:

Now We, the Lord Lieutenant, being determined to bring the said *William Smith O'Brien* to Justice, Do hereby offer a Reward of

FIVE HUNDRED POUNDS

to any Person or Persons who shall secure and deliver up to safe custody the Person of the said *William Smith O'Brien;*

And We do hereby strictly charge and command all Justices of the Peace, Mayors, Sheriffs, Bailiffs, Constables, and all other Her Majesty's loyal Subjects, to use their utmost diligence in apprehending the said *William Smith O'Brien.*

Given at Her Majesty's Castle of Dublin, this 28th Day of *July*, 1848.

By His Excellency's Command,

T. N. REDINGTON.

Printed by GEORGE and JOHN GRIERSON, Printers to the Queen's Most Excellent Majesty.

BY SPECIAL EXPRESS.

LATEST FROM THE SOUTH.

ATTEMPT TO ARREST SMITH O'BRIEN IN TIPPERARY—SEVERAL OF THE COUNTRY PEOPLE SHOT—REPORTED WOUNDING OF MR. DILLON GREAT EXCITEMENT IN THE COUNTIES OF KILKENNY AND TIPPERARY.

Freeman Office, Four o'Clock.
We have received the following by Special Express from our Correspondent in Kilkenny:—

Kilkenny, Sunday Night.
Early on Sunday morning Sub-Inspector Trant of the Callan station, county Kilkenny, with between forty and fifty men under his command, proceeded to the neighbourhood of Ballingarry, on the borders of county Tipperary, and twelve miles from the city of Kilkenny, to assist in arresting Smith O'Brien, who, it was reported, was somewhere in the mountains of that locality, surrounded by a large body of armed peasantry. In some time afterwards a mounted policeman, Constable Carroll, was despatched from the Maudlin-street station, Kilkenny, with a despatch for Sub-Inspector Trant. Carroll rode on until he came to a part of the country between Ballingarry and a place called the Commons, when he heard several shots fired, and was soon afterwards taken prisoner by armed country people. Some of them were for shooting him, saying, as I have been informed, "if this man gets back he will hang us all," but others declared they would not take Carroll's life. I should remark that the constable was in coloured clothes. He was then brought into the presence of Smith O'Brien, who, it appears, wore a cap with a peak and silver band, and carried a stick in his hand.

Mr. O'Brien, addressing Carroll firmly said, "you are one of the mounted police?" The constable at once replied that he was, being aware that he was known to persons in the neighbourhood. Mr. O'Brien then, I am informed, turned round and asked the people about him would he give himself up? but they not having advised him to such a step he walked about for some time and then mounted the constable's horse and rode away. Carroll was detained for some time afterwards in the custody of four men.

During this period Sub-Inspector Trant and his men were shut up in a house to which they had retreated, surrounded by country people, on whom they fired from the windows. After the lapse of two or three hours Carroll was left in charge of one man, and this one allowed the constable to take his departure. In coming along the road on his way back to Kilkenny, Carroll encountered Mr. Smith O'Brien, who had changed his dress, now wearing a hat, and on horseback. Mr. O'Brien stopped him. The constable, I am told, informed O'Brien that he had no arms, remonstrated with him, and told him it was foolish to think of holding out against the force that would be brought against him, especially as the priests were exhorting the people not to join in resisting the authorities. Mr. O'Brien seemed to think deeply on what the constable had said—observed that for twenty years he had been trying to serve his country, and that if the people did not stand by him, he might as well give up.—Shortly afterwards he parted Carroll, giving him his stick, and rode off by himself. On the return of the constable to Kilkenny, orders were given to the military and police to march to Mr. Trant's assistance; and at half-past eight o'clock in the evening the city was thrown into an awful state of excitement by the moving onwards towards Ballingarry of a most formidable looking force. In the van was a troop of the 4th Light Dragoons; then followed a large body of police, then came about three hundred infantry soldiers, headed by the resident magistrate, Joseph Green, Esq., and the rear was brought up by another body of police. There were in all between three and four hundred soldiers, and about one hundred and sixty of the constabulary. A guard of the 83d Regiment kept watch on the Tholsel, and a very large number of police were under arms in the Assembly-room, it being generally supposed that Smith O'Brien would be brought in a prisoner during the night. However, shortly after the departure of the military and police, news of the safe retreat of Mr. Trant and his party were conveyed to Kilkenny, and cavalry police were despatched to recall the soldiers and constabulary who were on their way out. They were overtaken in Kilmanagh, about eight miles from Kilkenny, and returned at an early hour this morning.

Mr. Trant and his men got off in safety; but I regret to say that several of the people were killed and wounded. Amongst the latter is, it is thought, Mr. Dillon. Some accounts state that twelve people were killed, but I believe those to be exaggerated.

I have learned that there were about 300 armed men about Smith O'Brien at the time Carroll was taken, and some four hundred more on the hills near him. Catholic clergymen were seen in vain exhorting the people to cease resisting the police, whilst the shots were whizzing around them.

It is supposed that Mr. Trant proceeded to Ballingarry, under the impression that he was to find a large force there to meet him, and that the mounted policeman was sent after him to recall him on its being known that he would not be joined by the expected force. It was confidently asserted that it was owing to the interference of the Roman Catholic clergymen that the police were at length allowed to retire unmolested.

The last accounts from Ballingarry state that the military were concentrating on that point from all the surrounding districts.

(*From the Galway Mercury.*)

On Wednesday last, in pursuance of an order, as we learn, from the Castle of Dublin, a diligent search was instituted for arms in the houses of many of the inhabitants. The police were most active in the discharge of their duty in this respect, but without any greater success than in capturing one pike at the establishment of Mr. Geoghegan, T.C., gun manufacturer, where the instrument has for some time past been publicly exposed.

(FROM A TUAM CORRESPONDENT.)

Before the inhabitants could have well left their beds this morning they have been favoured with visits from Mr. Brereton, the stipendiary magistrate, and by "the gentlemen in green," in search of pikes. Two of the police were left at each door, while others went in quest of the dreaded instruments. No one was allowed to pass inwards or outwards, and I myself was detained, I may say, in custody within doors from eight til ten o'clock this morning, neither would any customer be allowed to enter my shop to purchase.

FROM OUR PRIVATE CORRESPONDENT.

London, Saturday Night.

Viscount Hardinge, who came up to town yesterday by express train, and the Duke of Wellington, accompanied by his secretary, had a protracted interview this morning with Lord John Russell and Sir George Grey. They recommended, it is understood, *that martial law should be immediately proclaimed in the south of Ireland*, and an intimation to that effect has been forwarded to the Earl of Clarendon.

Recreated from The Freeman's Journal, Dublin, July 31, 1848.

MILITARY OCCUPATION OF CORK.

On Wednesday night the troops in this garrison took possession of the city. From some information obtained by the magistrates, it was considered necessary to keep them under arms, and in readiness for an immediate turn-out. At nine o'clock a rocket was sent up from the Tackey-street Guard-house, and soon afterwards such of the people as were in the streets were astonished to behold a large military force marching in Patrick-street to the grand parade, where they took up a field position. Immediately after the Lancers arrived from Ballincollig, where they had been in waiting for the signal. The troops, which consisted of the Lancers, the 26th and 70th regiments, and a large police force, numbering, as far as could be estimated, between 500 and 600 men, remained for some time on the grand-parade, while the general, field officers, magistrates, police officers, &c., were in consultation, we believe, at the Guard-room.

The subject of the consultation, of course, was kept a profound secret, but, on its termination, a movement, or rather a series of concerted movements took place. Shortly after the first arrival of the troops on the parade, a number of people assembled, from motives of curiosity and wonder, at this inexplicable movement, and remained for some time watching the proceedings; but, as the hour became later, they gradually dispersed, and, after eleven o'clock, very few were to be seen in any part of the city, which remained in the possession of the military.

Things continued in this state until midnight, when, the order being given to re-form, the troops immediately departed, in nearly the same order as they had previously used in entering the city, the greater portion of the Lancers to Ballincollig, and the remainder, with the 26th and 70th Regiments, to the barracks. Large bodies of police, however, numbering from 70 to 100 men, continued to patrol the city till a late hour of the morning. It is quite impossible to conjecture the cause of these extensive demonstrations. We are, therefore, unable to say whether they were necessary for the peace of the city or not; but, if any formidable movements were contemplated on the part of any portion of the people, the only indication of it was the unusual tranquility which prevailed in every quarter.—*Cork Reporter.*

THREATENED INSURRECTION.

FLIGHT OF FAMILIES FROM WATERFORD AND CARRICK.—The first of the rebellion may almost be said to have commenced. Soldiers are marching and counter-marching, bugles are sounding, rumours are flying through town of the most exciting nature, despatches are arriving every hour or two calculated to alarm the people. No less than 25 families from this neighbourhood left yesterday in the *Rose* steamer for Bristol. Families are leaving Carrick and other towns in this neighbourhood very quickly. It has been reported about town to-day that some of the most extensive establishments in the city are about stopping work, and that all hands will be discharged. If so, it will entail ruin on the poor families of the artizans. In Carrick the people are terribly excited, there is nothing spoken of but war; the armament is progressing very rapidly. There can no longer be a doubt about it, the people will fight and no mistake. We have just heard that Mr. O'Brien informed the people of Carrick, on Monday night, if the Government attempted to arrest him, they would only have his lifeless corpse to take. Mr. Meagher is reported to have said—"The assistance of the people might be called into requisition in a couple of hours, provided the authorities attempted to arrest him."—*Waterford Chronicle of Wednesday* (Repeal paper).

MORE ARRESTS.

Friday morning, at two o'clock, a car, containing five persons, was stopped at the Blanchardstown turnpike gate, by Constable John Blayney and another of the police at that station, and on examining the car they found three guns, three pistols, two bullet moulds, and two pike heads, with a very large quantity of ball cartridges, loose powder, balls, caps, &c., and conveyed the car to the station house. The prisoners stated that they were going to Dunshaughlin. The party were followed by Constable James Hewston, of the detective force, which received information of their departure, but they were arrested before he reached Blanchardstown. The prisoners gave their names as M'Kenna, O'Rorke, Hayes, Lee, and Fahey, and stated that they resided in Clontarf. The prisoners were escorted into Dublin by twelve mounted and sixty foot policemen, of the reserve force, under the command of Sub-Inspector Gould, at four o'clock on Friday morning. The whole of the parties, including the carman, were committed to Kilmainham; and as a warning to other carmen, the magistrates decided upon confiscating the horse and car.

Recreated from The Belfast News-Letter, Belfast, August 1, 1848.

(From the *Pilot* of last night.)

MR. W.S. O'BRIEN—LATEST AND MOST AUTHENTIC ACCOUNT.—Versions of the affair between a party of country people and some police having been communicated to us from respectable sources, we have published them elsewhere. We now direct attention to the contents of a letter from a person who came up almost immediately after the occurrence, and upon whose correctness we place entire reliance.

Inspector Trant, it appears, with forty police, had been for some time in proximity with about three hundred country people, William Smith O'Brien at their head. Some amicable conversation must have taken place between the two chiefs, for it is positively stated by our informant that Mr. Smith O'Brien rode away on Mr. Trant's horse. A police party of twenty, under the command of Inspector Cox, marched up to join Sub-Inspector Trant's party, and these were fired on *after Mr. O'Brien's departure*, by the party he had just left. Another party of twenty police, under the command of Sub-Inspector J. Callaghan Foot, also arrived at this period, and both formed a junction with Mr. Trant's party, who immediately attacked the party which fired on Cox, killing four, and wounding ten or twelve.

The shots of the peasantry took no effect, and those that escaped the fire of the police instantly dispersed.

It is plain now the movement never had a chance. Boastful writing does not show the real tendency of public opinion, and the writing on this occasion was only calculated to alarm the government to make preparations, and thus to do away with any chance it might possibly have had, instead of rallying the people. But never had the movement any chance. The Catholic clergy, the middle ranks, all the industrious portion of the community, set their faces against it from the first. Throughout the south of Ireland the Catholic clergy have been indefatigably, and with the best effect, warning their flocks; and once more the public peace is deeply indebted to that body of estimable men.

We conclude by exhorting the deluded, for their own sake, to give up the foolish, as well as criminal delusion, and to recollect that Repeal Ireland is still unbroken, and that they have yet a country and families to save.

We know there are a great many of the young men of Dublin, and we believe the country, who entered the clubs just because others did the same, who had no participation in any plan of violence, or knowledge that they were doing anything illegal. Such cases are worthy of the immediate clemency and forbearance of the authorities, and, we are confident, will be favourably considered. It cannot be useful to society to have young men, of industrious pursuits and good habits, deprived of bread.

Recreated from The Freeman's Journal, Dublin, August 1, 1848.

THE AFFAIR NEAR BALLINGARRY.

(From the Mail of last night.)

KILKENNY, JULY 30, 1848.—I suppose you have already received some account of the affray which took place yesterday near Ballingarry, on the borders of this county, between the police and the rebels. I now send you the details, which, so far as I have been able to learn them, I have reason to believe are correct. Proclamations having been posted yesterday morning, offering a reward of £300 for the apprehension of Meagher, Doheny, and Dillon, and of £500 for that of Smith O'Brien, Sub-Inspector Trant proceeded from Callan, with a police force of between 40 and 50 men, in the hope of capturing some of the proclaimed rebels. When they arrived within a short distance of Ballingarry they were encountered by Smith O'Brien, at the head of a body of from 400 to 1,000 men. The police then took possession of a house close at hand, when the rebel leader, addressing one of the police, summoned the party to surrender. The policeman, in place of shooting Mr. O'Brien, which he might easily have done, went to the part of the building where Mr. Trant was at the time, to report the matter to his commander. Mr. Trant immediately hastened to the spot, but Mr. O'Brien had taken his departure.

Mr. Trant forthwith directed his men to fire; the engagement then commenced, and speedily terminated with the defeat of the rebels, of whom about eight or ten were killed, and several wounded. During the conflict two shots were fired at O'Brien, but neither took effect. One of the shots hit a rebel who was standing by O'Brien's side brandishing a pike. He was killed on the spot. Another party of police, under the command of Mr. Cox, and accompanied by Mr. French, the stipendiary magistrate, made up at the instant, and fired on the rebels with considerable effect—after which the insurgents fled in the greatest disorder.

Eighteen were killed altogether, and a vast number wounded. The police ultimately retired upon Callan, without suffering any loss whatever.

P.S.—O'Brien is in the colliery district, near Slievenamon, and General Macdonald close at his heels.

SUNDAY, FOUR O'CLOCK, P.M.—Great excitement has prevailed here to-day. The constabulary were called out while attending Divine service, as a rumour has just reached that Smith O'Brien was arrested, but it turns out to be untrue. The army did not attend Divine service to-day, and are confined to barracks. There are great crowds of idlers in the streets.

(From the Evening Herald of last night.)

We have just heard from the best authority the following accurate details respecting the collision above alluded to:—

Between Ballingarry and Killenaule, early on Saturday, Sub-Inspector Trant, accompanied by a body of constabulary, was encountered by a large body of insurgent peasantry, headed by Smith O'Brien. The rebel leader despatched a flag of truce inviting them to fraternise. The sub-inspector, who was in advance of a second body of constabulary, until whose arrival he was anxious to defer engaging the rebel force, proposed a parley, and entered a slated house, where he and his men remained until the expected party (Sub-Inspector Cox and his detachment) came up. This officer immediately called on Smith O'Brien to surrender upon his allegiance, which he and the rebels refusing to do, the police at once fired upon them, killing five and wounding nineteen. The remainder, including Smith O'Brien, fled to the neighbouring mountains.

As regards the movements of the minor leaders, Mr. Doheny is a fugitive in the mountainous district near Nenagh, and Mr. Meagher and Mr. Dillon have been traced to the Kilworth mountains.

Recreated from The Freeman's Journal, Dublin, August 1, 1848.

The affray at the widow McCormack's house, from The Illustrated London News, August, 1848.

AS A MATTER OF INTEREST AT THE PRESENT MOMENT, WE SUBJOIN THE OFFICIAL RETURN OF THE TROOPS IN IRELAND, FOR THE MONTH COMMENCING AUGUST 1:—

1st Dragoon Guards, Cahir.
6th Dragoon Guards, Dundalk.
2nd Dragoons, Athlone.
4th Light Dragoons, Newbridge.
6th Dragoons, Dublin.
7th Hussars, Dublin and Tipperary.
8th Royal Irish, Newbridge.
12th Lancers, Cork.
13th Light Dragoons, Longford.
17th Lancers, Dublin.

Making, in all, a force of ten cavalry regiments.

1st Foot, Parsonstown.
2nd Foot, Dublin.
3rd Foot, Waterford.
64th Foot, Limerick.
68th Foot, Mullingar.
70th Foot, Cork.
6th Foot, Youghal.
9th Foot, Dublin.
13th Foot, Belfast.
26th Foot, Cork.
31st Foot, Athlone.
35th Foot, Dublin.
40th Foot, Galway.
41st Foot, Buttevant.
43rd Foot, Templemore.
47th Foot, Clonmel.
48th Foot, Dublin.
49th foot, Dublin.
55th Foot, Dublin.
57th Foot, Enniskillen.
60th Rifles, Dublin.
71st Foot, Nass.
74th Foot, Dublin.
75th Foot, Phoenix Park.
83rd Foot, Kilkenny.
85th Foot, Dublin.
89th Foot, Kilkenny.
92nd Foot, Limerick.
19th Foot, Castlebar.
34th Foot, Nenagh.
38th Foot, Boyle.
66th Foot, Kinsale.
73rd Foot, Fermoy.
79th Foot, Mullingar.
88th Foot, Tralee.
95th Foot, Londonderry.

Recreated from The Belfast News-Letter, Belfast, August 1, 1848.

STATE OF AFFAIRS IN THE SOUTH.

Each consecutive train arriving at the Great Southern and Western Railway terminus is anxiously waited for by numbers of our fellow-citizens. The arrival platform on last evening was literally thronged with anxious groups, eager to ascertain the real state of facts with regard to Mr. Smith O'Brien and his movements. Manifold and varying rumours have been set afloat as to his *locale* and probable intentions; but, on close enquiry, few of those reports have been found correct.

Last evening's train, at half-past eight o'clock, brought up an immense number of passengers, comprising many travellers in the first class carriages, the bulk and extent of whose luggage would seem to indicate an intention not to return to the country for some time. The passengers, one and all, unite in representing the country about Kilkenny, Carlow, Thurles, Roscrea, and their several vicinities as perfectly tranquil and peaceable. It is stated that Mr. O'Brien, accompanied by a large body of the peasantry, has removed farther to the south and east, in the direction of the Glenbower Mountain. Several of the passengers confirm the statement relative to the interview between Mr. O'Brien and the commandant of the police force; and it is further stated, that whilst Mr. O'Brien was in communication with the policeman, the Rev. Mr. Corcoran, P.P., who was on the spot, contrived by admonition and rebuke to disperse the assemblage of peasantry which accompanied Mr. O'Brien, and that they returned to their homes leaving behind but very few men, who remained.

The number of troops, including police, now centered on or about the locality where Mr. O'Brien has taken up his position has been established at some 10,000 men. It has been stated to us that positive orders have been given to the troops and police, who have been ordered out on service, to enforce the arrest of Mr. Smith O'Brien, that not a shot shall be fired by either soldiers or police save in self-defense, or when fired on or attacked. We have it on good authority that the last four regiments which have arrived within the preceding few days in Dublin *en route* to the south, have been sent by orders direct from the Horse Guards.

On the departure of the 75th regiment yesterday morning from Kilkenny, the camp in the Park which that corps occupied was filled by the 9th Regiment of Foot. Three infantry regiments are expected by this day's steamer.

FIRE-ARMS AND PIKES FOR SALE IN WEXFORD.

On Wednesday evening, as we are informed, Gerald Barry, Esq., R.M., having received information that certain individuals passed through Enniscorthy, on their way to Wexford, with a vehicle containing a quantity of fire-arms and pikes intended for sale, adopted immediate measures for apprising the Wexford police. In consequence, three men—named Thomas M'Grade, Patrick Richard Kelly, and John Hughes—were arrested at one o'clock on Thursday morning, and the van in which they had conveyed the arms, and which was found in the yard at White's Hotel, placed under seizure.

The van contained about 100 stand of fire arms, consisting of pistols, muskets, fowling pieces, double barreled pieces, fuses, carbines, and blunderbusses. Two of the blunderbusses, which were large with very wide mouths, were mounted on swivels.

The van and the firearms were conveyed to the military barrack. The pikes were detained at the police barrack. They were fearful looking weapons, of different patterns, pointed as finely as could be imagined, and tapering to a fine edge on each side from the sharp central ridges on the upper and on the lower surface. Two of them were fixed on handles of different lengths—as intended for front and rear ranks. The shorter handle was about six feet long.

One, at least, of the heads was made to screw on and off, so that it might be used as a dagger. The length of all was from fifteen to eighteen inches, if not more. The extreme finish would seem to evince *English* rather than Irish workmanship. They evidently appeared to have gone under the lathe. An old gentleman who saw them, and was able to compare them with pikes he saw in 1798, said that those used in 1798 had nothing at all like the same finish. They were rude, and showed the marks of the hammer throughout. He observed, moreover, that the handles of those used in 1798 were much longer—two or three times as long—as when borne through the streets they rose as high as the drawing-room windows.—*Wexford Guardian*.

Recreated from The Freeman's Journal, Dublin, August 1, 1848.

LATEST INTELLIGENCE— AUTHENTIC AND IMPORTANT.

By the arrival of the Dublin mail, this morning, we are put in possession of a copy of the *Dublin Evening Herald* of yesterday, which contains the following important particulars:—

The Government having received information to the effect that large supplies of arms, ammunition, and food, intended for the use of the rebel army in Ireland, had been shipped from France and America, have taken effectual measures to prevent the landing of these mischievous consignments.

In addition to the fleet at Cove and the steam frigates, nine sloops of war have received orders to cruise off the Irish coast. It is right to state that the governments of the respective countries from which these supplies are coming are in no wise connected with the proceeding. These warlike cargoes are the substantial tributes of *private* sympathy.

We are glad, however, to learn that the British ambassador has apprised the American Government that all persons, whether subjects of the State or otherwise, taken in the attempt to aid the insurgents by such supplies, will be forthwith hanged by the British authorities.

It is now, upon what appear to be grounds of the highest probability, conjectured by the authorities, that Mr. Meagher has succeeded in effecting his escape from New Ross to Bristol in female apparel. Four arrests were yesterday effected at Nenagh, among which was that of Mr. Egan, formerly connected with the National Bank.

The Cork mail arrived at three o'clock this afternoon, brought no intelligence respecting the insurgents. The answers to inquiry of the guard and passengers was to the effect that all continued tranquil along the line of railway.

There is every reason to believe that Smith O'Brien is concealed somewhere between Ballingarry and Thurles. It is certain that he has not more than two or three followers with him.

TRIAL OF THE PRISONERS.—Contrary to a rumour very confidently circulated for some days, Charles Gavan Duffy late proprietor of the *Nation*, and John Martin, late proprietor of the *Felon*, together with several prisoners of minor note, will be put upon their trial at the ensuing commission, which opens on Tuesday, the 8th instant. The summonses have already been served upon the jury.

Recreated from The Belfast News-Letter, Belfast, August 4, 1848.

THE MOVEMENT IN THE PROVINCES.

(From the Tipperary Vindicator.)

INQUEST ON THE BODIES OF PATRICK M'BRIDE AND THOMAS WALSH, KILLED AT BALLINGARRY.—An inquest was held at Ballingarry, in this county, on Monday, 31st July, by Thomas O'Meara, Esq., Bouladuff, Coroner, and a jury of the farmers of the locality, on view of the bodies of Patrick M'Bride and Thomas Walsh, the two men who were shot dead by the party of police on Saturday, the 29th July, in the affray between the police and the insurgents, assembled on the Commons of Boulick.

The inquest was attended by one of the local magistrates, Mr. Going, of Ballyphillip, by Mr. Fitzmaurice, R.M., as well as by General M'Donald and officers of his staff. The coroner first took the evidence relating to the death of M'Bride, and called John M'Bride, brother of the deceased, who being sworn deposed that on Saturday last he heard his brother was shot at Farranrory, near the Commons, and went in that direction, when he met some men carrying him home on a door; asked him what was the matter with him, when he replied, "Oh, I'm killed." He said no more until he came home, when he said he was coming over the wall of the Widow Cormack's yard; the police were at the time in the house, when he was shot in the back from the house; witness stated that deceased had gone with the crowd who followed the police, and heard about half-a-dozen shots; he was a servant boy that was making hay at the side of the road, and when he saw the crowd he followed them.

Thomas Connors sworn—Was the employer of the deceased; he, with some others, were drawing hay for witness on the day in question; missed him from the meadow, and on inquiring, found that he had followed the company that passed by on the road; means the company of police; saw the police, and after that saw the people; there were not many people present; in about two hours after seeing them, saw the deceased brought back on a door, wounded by a gunshot; heard it was the police who fired on the people from the Widow Cormack's house, when the people were following on them; Cormack's is not a public-house.

Surgeon Fennelly sworn and examined—On Saturday, 10th stant, went to visit the deceased; I found him suffering acute pain in the shoulder and along the back, in the right side. On examining the body I found a circular opening over the scapula, or shoulder blade on the right side, caused, in my opinion, by a gun shot. I made a *post mortem* examination on this day, with Dr. Ryan, and found a large quantity of blood on the right side of the chest, and the right lung injured by some portions of the scapula, which was very extensively fractured. I also found a leaden bullet lodged in the shoulder. I am of the opinion that this death was caused by injuries done to the right lung, by spiculae of the fractured scapula, and which fracture was caused by a gun shot.

In reference to the cause of death of the unfortunate man Walsh, the coroner examined—

Anne Walsh, wife of deceased, who, being sworn, deposed—I recollect Saturday last; my husband went to work at breaking stones about six o'clock that morning; about twelve o'clock I saw crowds of people going to the commons, and heard some shots, but cannot say how many. I then went to the widow Cormack's house, where the shots seemed to be firing from, and saw my husband lying on the field outside the wall of the house. I was going over to him, when two guns, were put out of the highest window of the house, and some persons inside cried out to me to go back or they would let the light through me.

There was not a man near the house or any other person except myself and my husband, and another man who was lying at the wall of the house, struggling for death. The Rev. Mr. Fitzgerald then came up and I asked him to intervene to my husband's body, that I might bring it home to wake it. I have one child, and had no way of living, but as my husband earned a pound of meal a day stonebreaking on the relief works. It is Smith O'Brien I blame for my husband's death, he would not have gone there only for him.

Dr. Ryan swore that the deceased had got a gunshot wound on one side of the chest, and an aperture at the opposite side, where the bullet passed out. The shot must have been fired by some persons on a level with the deceased—that wound caused death.

The jury returned a verdict in both cases, that death ensued from gunshot wounds inflicted by some of the police, who had retired to the widow Cormack's house, and fired in self-defense.

On the suggestion of General M'Donald, Anne Walsh was called, and on being asked did she receive money from Mr. Smith O'Brien after her husband was shot, she said that Mr. O'Brien gave her a £1 note before he left, expressing the greatest sympathy with her misfortune, and telling her to bury her husband with the money.

The district throughout Ballingarry is just now extremely quiet and orderly. There are several detectives in this county at present, among whom is that very practical hunter of men, Constable Hughes, of Waterford, whose station is Nenagh.

An order of the most rigid description has been sent to all the prisons, we understand, to the effect that the political prisoners shall be kept in the closest possible confinement, and that no extern whatever shall be permitted to see them except the chaplain and physician.

Recreated from The Freeman's Journal, Dublin, August 7, 1848.

ROBBERY OF THE MAILS.—The guard of the Tralee mail (Galvin), just arrived, reports that over 3,000 armed persons were this day assembled at Abbeyfeale, where the coach was stopped and surrounded, himself attacked, and knocked off the seat by a stroke of a gun, and while on the ground over 100 guns were presented, threatening to shoot him if he dared to offer resistance. The entire of the mail bags were carried off from the box, and after much difficulty he and the driver escaped with their lives. He also states that the mail from Limerick this morning was robbed at the same place, and Purcell, the guard, badly injured. There was a party of police looking on at a distance, but were afraid to encounter so formidable a body—the fire-arms of both guards were carried off.

LORD HARDINGE'S DEPARTURE FROM DUBLIN.—Lord Hardinge left town with his staff this morning for Kilkenny. As lieutenant-general, the noble and gallant viscount takes command of the southern division of Ireland. General M'Donald continues in the command of the moveable column. Colonel Clark, late of the Scots Greys, and Colonel Pennefather, have been appointed to the staff in Ireland.—*Mail of last night*.

MORE ARRESTS.—The following persons were yesterday lodged in Newgate under warrants granted by the Lord Lieutenant under the suspension of the habeas corpus act:—Patrick Marron, editor of the *Drogheda Argus*; John Lawless, of the Sandymount Club; Michael Hanly, who is said to have belonged to one of the clubs; and James Bergin, a native of America, and a merchant, who arrived in this country a few days since. The *Mail* of last night says it understands that he has forwarded a complaint on the subject of his arrest to the American Consul in this city.

Recreated from The Freeman's Journal, Dublin, August 8, 1848.

THE CROPS—THE POTATO.

In crops, this county is abundant in promise. In some places bere-fields have been saluted by the sickle. New oats will soon be general, as also barley, and, what is better, both an excellent crop. The wheat is rapidly advancing to maturity. Potatoes are ranging in the market from three to five pence per stone, and of good quality. The growing crops are all that can be wished. The late turnip crop is satisfactory in promise, and indeed other green crops also.—The second cut of hay will prove better. On the whole, we can afford to be anything but prophets of disaster.—*Ulster Gazette.*

We regret to say that our fears respecting the potato crop are every day receiving confirmation. The blight appears as yet to have taken effect principally on the stalks, and also in many instances on the potatoes. We have examined some fields near this town, and found potatoes diseased as they were in the year before last, and accounts have reached us to the same effect from several other places.—*Tuam Herald.*

We are happy to say that the weather during the past week has been beautifully fine. The harvest operations are consequently being proceeded with in the most vigorous manner. There are some rumours of symptoms of blight having appeared in the potato, but on inquiry we find there is as yet no well-grounded cause for alarm. The other crops look well and promising.—*Athlone Sentinel.*

Letters received at our office this day from experienced farmers represent the potato blight as fast extending in this county, the disease has exhibited a virulent aspect within the last week. Other accounts state that where the blight appeared three weeks ago, a black potato has not been found, and that the stalks which seemed quite lost are grown again.—*Limerick Chronicle.*

The attention of our reporter, while recently in the country, was directed carefully to the condition of the potato crop, and he states that throughout a progress of over 150 miles through the counties of Tipperary, Waterford, and Cork, he did not see a single field that was not most luxuriant and free from trace of disease. His own observation was corroborated universally by the accounts of the people themselves, who expressed the most favourable anticipations upon the subject.—*Cork Reporter.*

Recreated from The Freeman's Journal, Dublin, August 8, 1848.

The following is a copy of some written placards which were posted about Cashel on the 2nd instant. We do not for one moment suppose it originated with any of the unfortunate madmen whose names are attached; in Dillon's signature there is internal evidence of the contrary—the signature being B. Dillon, whereas it should have been J. B. Dillon:—

£1,000 REWARD FOR CLARENDON DEAD OR ALIVE.

Now we, the undersigned, do hereby offer the aforesaid reward to any person or persons who shall, within nine months from this date, bring the said head to any of us.

WILLIAM SMITH O'BRIEN.
THOMAS FRANCIS MEAGHER.
B. DILLON.
MICHAEL DOHENY.

The Earl of Donoughmore, Lord Lieutenant of the county of Tipperary, has addressed the following important communication to the *Clonmel Chronicle*:—

"Sir—I have to request that you will make it known, through the medium of your journal, that all persons harbouring men accused of high treason render themselves liable to capital punishment.—I have the honour, &c.,

DONOUGHMORE, Lieutenant.

William Smith O'Brien, lithograph by Henry O'Neil, 1848.

THE IRISH TRAITORS.—The following are the description given of the leading traitors in the *Hue and Cry*:—

1. Wm. Smith O'Brien: age, 46; six feet high, sandy hair, dark eyes, sallow long face. Has a sneering smile constantly on his face; full whiskers, sandy, a little grey; well set man, walks erect; dresses well.

2. Thomas Francis Meagher; age, 25; pale face, high cheek bones; peculiar expression about the eyes, rather cocked nose, no whiskers; well dressed.

3. John B. Dillon, barrister; age, 32; thin sallow face, rather thin, black whiskers; dress respectable; has a bilious look.

4. Michael Doheny, barrister; aged 40; hair sandy, eyes grey, course red face, like a man given to drink; high cheek bones, wants several of his teeth, very vulgar appearance, peculiar course, unpleasant voice; dress respectable; small short red whiskers.

5. Richard O'Gorman, jun., barrister; aged 30; thin, long, dark face; large dark whiskers; well made and active; walks upright; black frock-coat, tweed trousers.

Thurles, Friday morning, half-past Six, a.m.
Immediately after I forwarded my parcel last evening, I found that the military had received a sudden route from their encampment at Killenaule, and were moving towards this place. The route reached them at three o'clock, and by half-past three their tents were struck, baggage packed on cars, &c., and the whole on the march, comprising the 85th, 74th, and 60th Rifles. They arrived about six, and at once encamped under the superintendence of General M'Donald, on the demesne of Turtulla, the residence of Mr. Maher, M.P. for this county, about a mile from town. They were accompanied by a half-battery of horse artillery, with field-pieces, and two troops of the 86th Hussars and 1st Dragoons, who were distributed through Thurles. After seeing the three regiments of artillery encamped, the general and his staff rode into town, and put up at the hotel.

The cause of this sudden movement is said to be the receipt of positive information by the authorities that Mr. S. O'Brien and his friends had left the neighbourhood of the collieries, and were at present located in the mountain fastness, known as Keeper-hill, some fifteen miles from here. Certain it is, that, on Wednesday, the police of Ballignarry discovered some of his clothes in the house of a poor woman near the commons, whom they arrested, and have still in custody. The articles found were a pair of boots and a shoe, two cloth trousers, a coat and a waistcoat, and two shirts, on which Mr. O'Brien's name was marked. These are all in the hands of the police, also a great coat belonging, it is said, to Mr. Dillon.

I visited the camp at Turtulla this morning, the appearance of which was very picturesque. The soldiers were very early astir, and engaged in cooking, loading cars, &c. A cordon of baggage drays was placed outside and around the tents, which were pressed into service some days ago, and will be detained as long as they are required. The owners are paid 7s. 6d. a day for each horse and car, with rations.

Recreated from The Belfast News-Letter, Belfast, August 8, 1848.

THE ARREST OF SMITH O'BRIEN—SOME ADDITIONAL PARTICULARS.

(*From the Reporter of the Cork Examiner*).

SUNDAY MORNING, EIGHT O'CLOCK.—Having intimated to you, in my despatch of yesterday, my intention of proceeding to Thurles, and from thence towards Keeper-hill, I accordingly left Cashel for that town at three o'clock on yesterday evening. I reached Cashel shortly after five o'clock. The town and neighbourhood was perfectly quiet. I proceeded towards the Thurles terminus of the Great Southern and Western Railway, which place I reached about ten minutes to eight o'clock. The officer on the station told me that the Dublin train would be in at three o'clock, and that the Limerick train would start immediately after. Having an anxiety to see them start I made up my mind to wait for a short period.

It was not but a few minutes of eight o'clock when I perceived a gentleman cross from the town side towards the station. I know not why, but I assure you my entire attention was instantly absorbed by him. He wore a black hat, a blue boat cloak, in which he was rather tightly muffled, and a light plaid-like trousers; he carried a rather large black stick in his right hand. He entered the office, and, as he passed me, with what feelings I cannot describe to you, I recognised the features of WILLIAM SMITH O'BRIEN.

There was at this time not more than one dozen persons in the vicinity of the station; five or six of whom were gentlemen who had engaged places in the Limerick train; the others were three policemen, and some one or two railway officers, with two fellows, rather decently dressed, whom I afterwards discovered to be "detectives".

Mr. O'Brien entered the office. I watched his movements with the greatest anxiety—he paid his fare to Limerick, got his ticket, and walked out. He again wrapped himself up in his cloak, and, folding his arms, walked across the line to the opposite side. Scarcely had he reached the other side, when I perceived the guard of the Dublin train pass from behind the office, and anxiously look in the direction in which Mr. O'Brien had gone.

Mr. O'Brien was walking slowly along the line, awaiting the arrival of the Dublin train, by which he was to start for Limerick, when this same officer, who is an Englishman, and named Huhme, stole quietly across the line to where Mr. O'Brien was, and, placing his hand on his collar, said "You are the Queen's prisoner". Instantly the two detectives called on the three policemen, and all ran towards Mr. O'Brien, each catching him by the collar as he approached him. At this moment, a young gentleman who was standing by, ran towards Mr. O'Brien, and stretched out his hand to him. No sooner did one of the "detectives", who was clad in a white overcoat, perceive this movement, than he drew from either pocket of his coat a double barrelled pistol, and, pointing each at the gentleman, exclaimed, "stand back! for by heaven, if you move another foot in advance, I'll shoot you—policemen, draw your bayonets". The latter command was quickly obeyed, and the second detective, who walked at the rere of Smith O'Brien, produced two pistols similar to those of his companion who walked in front, each pointing his arms at the heads of any person who attempted to approach them.

Mr. O'Brien, who looked as though he had only made his toilet a few hours before, was exceedingly pale. He seemed most dejected, and was scarcely able to walk, having to lean back on the policemen who were behind him, and who, in the roughest manner possible, shoved him under the neck with their open fists, whilst two others dragged him by the collar, as if he were a pickpocket, or petty thief; yet he did not appear irritated by the conduct pursued towards him by those officials, but on the contrary, smiled on them, and handing his stick to one of them, he reached his hand to another for support.

In this manner he was taken to the station, through the streets of Thurles, and lodged in the gaol of the most central town in Tipperary, escorted by five almost unarmed policemen, and two "detectives."

The only words I heard Mr. Smith O'Brien utter were, when his guards were shoving him violently, "Easy—take me easy." And these he repeated with the greatest mildness of tone and apparent suavity of temper.

As he was carried through the streets some few persons recognised him, and exclaimed "there is Smith O'Brien." A number of women quickly collected, and commenced hooting the police; but, with this single exception, there was no sympathy of excitement.

Mr. O'Brien was then taken up a narrow lane, in which the gaol is scituate; and the troops, who by this time had got the alarm, were instantly drawn across the lane, so as to prevent any approach thereto. A despatch was immediately forwarded to the encampment outside the town, when troops were instantly poured into the town in vast bodies.

On my return to the railway office, I could scarcely make my way through the streets, so filled were they with military; yet the people were unexcited.

On my arrival at the office, I perceived the same person who arrested Mr. O'Brien, dressed in a different costume, and heard him order a special train for Dublin, in which I afterwards learned Mr. O'Brien was to be conveyed. Whilst in the office, another gentleman, who, I was told, was a reporter from the London *Times*, ordered a second special train for the same city.

When leaving Thurles, all was quiet, The line near the station being guarded on both sides by strong detachments of the 8th Hussars. From what I saw of the people, I am fully convinced there was no attempt at rescue.

(FROM AN EYE WITNESS).

Thurles, Sunday.

Smith O'Brien was captured here last night about eight o'clock. He was taken in a carriage on the train for Limerick *quite undisguised*, He was arrested by two policemen. He told me he had determined to go home to see Mrs. O'Brien and his family. He said he did not wish to peril the poor people who sheltered him, but were unprepared to meet the dangers that beset him. He appeared to me quite resigned.

(FROM ANOTHER EYE-WITNESS).

Thurles, 6th August, 1848.

Smith O'Brien was arrested here last evening at the railway station. I was present at the time. It was a most distressing scene. He came to the station-house, got his ticket for Limerick, and was immediately arrested by two detectives, who dragged him down to the gaol. In ten minutes it was like a besieged town. Dragoons were galloping in every direction. The military were brought in from their encampment near Turtulla, to the number of 1,000 men.

I should have mentioned that J.R., who was standing with me, was the first to notice Smith O'Brien. He did not, however, even tell me that he saw him until he was taken.

> As a party of visitors from Kilkee were enjoying an excursion to Dunlicky Castle, on Tuesday, a young country fellow presented a gun at a lady who was in advance of her friends upon a donkey, and demanded money! The donkey boy, with great resolution, closed upon the armed ruffian in defence of the lady, and caught hold of the gun, when a gentleman of the party running up, the gun was wrested from the offender, who slunk off, but as the party were returning to Kilkee they were assailed with stones at Moveen by a gang of the country people, who insisted upon having back the gun, and a second gentleman of the party received a severe and dangerous blow from a stone on the head, under the effects of which he is still confined to his hotel. The loaded gun went off in the struggle, and the original offender, who is known, has recovered it.—*Limerick Chronicle*.

Recreated and reprinted from The Freeman's Journal, Dublin, August 8, 1848.

The following account of Mr. O'Brien's transmission to Dublin we copy from the correspondence of the *Evening Mail*, under date Thurles, Saturday night:—

On entering the carriage, Mr. O'Brien was placed in the centre seat, and in the compartment with him were Lieutenant Alexander M'Donald, with Sub-Inspector Bracken, Head-Constable Hanniver, and four constables. Mr. O'Brien was told by Lieutenant M'Donald that he must not move or speak, at the peril of his life. Mr. O'Brien, before starting, inquired of the general whether it was by his directions that he was ordered not to speak. The general replied that it was, and added—"I wish, Mr. O'Brien, to treat you with all the respect due to your station in society, and to your misfortunes; but I have a duty to perform, and my orders must be obeyed."

Mr. O'Brien replied—"I have played the game, and lost. Had I won, my power would have been unlimited, and I am ready to pay the penalty of having failed. I hope", he added, "those who accompanied me may be dealt with in clemency. I care not what happens to myself." He said that, as he was enjoined to keep silent, he would try to sleep; but he did not succeed in the attempt, and though his manner was composed throughout the journey, he moved about restlessly in his seat.

THURLES.—You have, of course, heard of the arrest of O'Brien, and his subsequent transmission to Dublin. It is not true that he himself purchased the ticket at the railway station, as reported here. It was purchased for him by a peasant who accompanied him—his only companion during his melancholy wanderings. There is every probability that he would have escaped had the train arrived at the time it was due, as he might then have jumped in without being recognised; but, unfortunately for Mr. O'Brien, the train was half-an-hour late, and his chance of escape became almost impossible.

On the arrival (adds the *Mail*) of the special train at Dublin, soon after midnight, he was at once conveyed to the Royal Barracks, where, having seen him safely deposited, Lieutenant M'Donald proceeded with despatches from his father, the general, to the Viceregal Lodge. Mr. O'Brien continued to walk for about half-an-hour in the square of the barrack, until the arrival of Town-Major White; after which the prisoner was conducted by the Hon. J. M'Donald, A.D.C., to his Royal Highness Prince George of Cambridge, attended by Town-Major White, and by the constabulary force, without the intervention of the military, and lodged in Kilmainham.

Amongst the passengers who arrived by the three o'clock afternoon train yesterday, were the lady of William Smith O'Brien and her father (Mr. Gabbett). The country in the vicinity of Thurles, Kilkenny, and the neighbouring towns, is stated to be perfectly tranquil. Accounts are said to have reached the quarters of the general commanding, that disturbances had broken out in the Limerick direction. The 75th regiment broke up their encampment near Thurles, by a sudden order, and before eight o'clock were marching *en route* for Limerick. A sergeant and a few privates of the 75th came up by the three o'clock train, being ordered to the Royal Barracks. A rumour was current amongst the few troops who came up, and also amongst the passengers, that Mr. Doheny had been brought a prisoner to Cashel yesterday morning. Many state positively that 24 of the peasantry have been taken prisoner and brought into Cashel.

SUPPLY OF POTATOES.—The supply of potatoes to our markets have been so extensive for weeks back, that the prices have come down so as to enable the poorest of our working classes to make use of them. This morning there were no less than 124 loads brought into the Coal-quay market, the price opening at from 6d. to 7d. per weight of 21 lbs., but in the course of the evening it is expected to fall at least a penny or three halfpence per wight.

Recreated and reprinted from The Freeman's Journal, Dublin, August 8, 1848.

REWARD FOR THE ARREST OF SMITH O'BRIEN.

Yesterday Huhme, the guard on the Limerick and Thurles train, was paid the £500 reward offered by the government for the arrest of Mr. William Smith O'Brien. Huhme has resigned his situation as guard on the Great Southern and Western Railway, and is about to leave for his native country—England.

Recreated from The Freeman's Journal, Dublin, August 9, 1848.

LORD JOHN'S VISIT—THE NEW INSURRECTION.

We abridge the following from the last number of the London *Tablet*:—

Lord John has made his visit to Ireland. All the world has been agog to know where his Lordship was to go—who he was to see—what he was to do—where he was to stay—and how he was to be treated. The end of all has at length shown itself, and it is of the true Whig character. The Premier has gone nowhere—has seen nobody (except in the Park)—and has done nothing.

However, the minister has left behind him something. A new insurrection has broken out—fresh meetings of men—new armings—new encampments—new pikes—a live policeman wounded—great activity—a more shifty leadership.

It cannot be repeated too often that Ireland, in its spirit and disposition, is in a state of perpetual insurrection. The bulk of the people are insurgents, and what is called "government" has no hold on their consciences no further than terror lends its way—that we there occupy essentially the position of invaders. The state of things cannot be changed by a prolongation of coercion; nor by any Whig practice of *laissez faire*, nor by any form of brutality, cowardice, or chicane. If it can be changed by anything it can only be changed by our learning the lessons of wisdom. The present military occupation of Ireland is greedily accepted by the Irish landlords as an admirable time for the extermination of their tenantry, &c.

Recreated from The Waterford News, Waterford, September 22, 1848.

AUGMENTATION OF THE CONSTABULARY.

Constabulary Office, Dublin Castle,
17th August, 1848.

Thinking it probable, from the numerous applications that have been addressed to this office by magistrates and other gentlemen, for the admission of young men into the constabulary, that the recruiting regulations are but imperfectly known to them, I request that county inspectors will direct their officers to lay before each bench of magistrates, within their respective districts, a copy of this paper, for their information, assuring them of my readiness at all times to give effect to their recommendations as opportunities occur, and expressing my hope that, with their aid, *the numerous vacancies at present existing in the force* will be speedily filled up.

I. Each candidate is required to be of good character for honesty sobriety, fidelity, and activity—a single man, or a widower without a family—capable of reading any printed or written document, and able to write a legible hand.

II. The age for admission is between nineteen and twenty-seven years, and each candidate is required to join provided with four shirts, four pairs of socks, and two pounds in money, together with a suit of plain clothes and a hat.

III. The standard height for the force is five feet eight inches, though (owing to the large number of recruits now required), for the present, young men are admitted who are *fully* five feet seven inches in height—provided they are intelligent—do not exceed twenty-one years of age—are of a stout frame of body, and are likely to grow.

IV. The recommendation of the magistrate should be sent with the candidate to the county inspector, that he may examine him, and if he find him fit, attest, and send him at once to the depot for training and instruction.

D. M'GREGOR.

DRAWING ON ENGLAND.

For many years Ireland has been drawing largely on English sympathies, and in some years not less largely on his (the Englishman's) purse.—*Times*.

Reprinted from The Waterford News, Waterford, September 22, 1848.

THE STATE TRIALS.

FRIDAY.

The proceedings of Friday commenced with the calling over the long panel; jurors being summoned to appear under a penalty of £20. In some two hours after the sitting of the court "12 good men and true" were empaneled

TO TRY WM. S. O'BRIEN

on a charge affecting his life. I shall say only this of the jury that not a single Roman Catholic sits amongst the 12, and they are all men of high Conservative principles; all with one exception being magistrates of the county. From their appearance as they sat before me in their box and attentively listened to and took notes of their proceedings, I would say they are men of intelligence; but beyond that I cannot venture to say. How or in what manner they are likely to act I shall not presume to speculate, but most assure me that they will discharge their consciences without favor, prejudice, partiality, or bias.

Recreated from The Waterford News, Waterford, October 6, 1848.

TRIAL OF W. S. O'BRIEN.
THE VERDICT.

The public will hear with feelings of astonishment and grief that, notwithstanding the many grounds which existed for anticipating a different result, the jury have returned against Smith O'Brien a verdict of GUILTY.

The jury have accompanied their verdict with an earnest recommendation to mercy.

Throughout the course of the trial there was much reason for hoping that the jury would have arrived at a different conclusion.—This hope was raised to a high pitch, when, at the close of the proceedings, by a seemingly providential interposition, the prisoner was enabled to demolish the evidence of the government witness—the informer Dobbin. But the event has disappointed expectation. The jury have pronounced Smith O'Brien GUILTY!

Of the demolition of the informer's evidence our readers will find more elsewhere. It was utter and complete. A respectable witness, a student of Trinity College, Mr. Dalton, a Protestant and an anti-Repealer, thoroughly trustworthy, though in unpretending circumstances, accidently reading in a newspaper, some days old, the evidence of Dobbin, was struck with a recollection of a singular conversation which he had had with that individual, in which he, Dobbin, had actually revealed to him his intention of "*counterplotting*" on the AVOWED basis of PERJURY.

Mr. Dalton having called at this office late on Friday night to publish a letter revealing the infamy, but without the least idea that any evidence of his could be available for the trial, which indeed he believed to be over, we immediately ordered a special engine, and though unable to have it ready for departure until half-past four o'clock on Saturday morning, we were still enabled to reach Clonmel with the witness and an eminent counsel to whom the country is indebted, Mr. O'Hea, at the hour of ten o'clock. The court had sat an hour before. The Chief Justice was completing his charge, which he had partly gone through the evening previous; but such was the importance of the new evidence announced, that after hearing counsel in chamber, and by consent of the crown, the witness was examined. Dobbin was utterly demolished, but the jury it appears thought, that enough remained to enable them to find the prisoner—GUILTY!!

Recreated from The Freeman's Journal, Dublin, October 9, 1848.

Foreman—GUILTY! (Great sensation in Court).

The Foreman handed in the following, which was read by the Clerk of the Crown:

"*We earnestly recommend the Prisoner to Mercy, the Jury being unanimously of opinion that, for many reasons, his Life should be Spared. Signed, for Self and Brother Jurors,*

"R. C. MANSEGH, Foreman."

Clerk of the Crown—William Smith O'Brien, you theretofore stood indicted—

Mr. Whiteside—I believe this is the proper time for an arrest of judgment in this case. I believe that the proper time is after conviction has taken place, and I therefore have three objections to make. The first is the speeches delivered by Mr. O'Brien previous to the 21st of July was admissable against Mr. O'Brien—on two grounds; second, that Dobbyn had not confirmed; and the third is, the admissability of the contents of portmanteau, as there is no proof tracing them to the possession.

Mr. Fitzgerald followed Mr. Whiteside for the prisoner, and was replied to by the Solicitor-General.

The Court, after viewing the arguments of counsel on both sides, overruled the application, and stated that they had reserved some of the objections raised by the prisoner's counsel for the opinion of the 12 judges.

The Clerk of the Crown asked Mr. O'Brien what he had to say why judgment should not be passed upon him?

Mr. O'Brien, in a firm, and manly tone, replied—It is not my intention to enter into any vindication of my conduct, however much I might desire to avail myself of this opportunity for so doing. I am perfectly satisfied with the consciousness of having performed my duty to my country, and that I have only done that which was in my opinion what every Irishman ought to do. I am therefore prepared to abide the consequences of my having done my duty to my native land. PROCEED WITH YOUR SENTENCE.

[The bold determined tone in which the last few sentences were uttered, and the noble posture assumed by Smith O'Brien in giving utterance to the words "Proceed with your sentence," evoked a loud expression of feeling from all present, while many a stifled sob escaped from hearts that felt the awful position in which the patriot was placed more than he did himself. After a brief interval, was

THE SENTENCE.

The Lord Chief Justice then proceeded, amid the most profound and painful silence, to pronounce the extreme penalty of the law upon the prisoner. He said—William Smith O'Brien, after a long and painful trial, a jury of your countrymen have found you guilty of High Treason. Their verdict was accompanied by a recommendation to mercy; that recommendation, as was our duty, we shall send forward to the Lord Lieutenant, to whom, as you must know, exclusively belongs the power to comply with its prayer. It now remains for us to perform the last solemn act of duty which devolves upon us. Oh! that you would feel and know that it is really and substantially as repugnant to the interests of humanity and the precepts and spirit of the divine religion which you profess as it is to the positive law, the violation of which is now attended by the forfeiture of your life. The few words you have addressed to the court forbid me any further proceeding with this subject. [Here his lordship assumed the black cap, and amid a silence at once solemn and painful, proceeded as follows:—That sentence is, "That you, William Smith O'Brien, be taken from hence, to the place from whence you came, and be thence drawn on a hurdle to the place of execution, and be there hanged by the neck until you are dead; that afterwards your head shall be severed from your body, divided into four quarters, to be disposed of as her Majesty shall please, and may God have mercy on your soul."

The most profound sensation followed the conclusion of the sentence.

Several persons then rushed forward to the dock to shake hands with the prisoner. He left the dock with a steady step, and was soon placed into the black van (drawn by two horses) which conveyed him to his cell.

Several women ran to the gates of the prison shrieking most awfully.

The excitement in the streets was intense.

Reprinted from The Waterford News, Waterford, October 13, 1848.

COLLECTION OF THE POOR-RATE.—On Monday last we witnessed a curios scene in the County Waterford—The poor rate collector accompanied by two bailiffs had seized upon two cows the property of a poor woman, for the amount of rates due by her—No sooner was the mission discovered than an immense number of women and children surrounded the bailiffs, whom they abused in no measured terms—A lot of boys drove the cows up the mountains, whence they were pursued by the bailiffs, but with what result we have not since been informed.—*Tipperary Free Press.*

EJECTMENTS.

At an early hour on Thursday morning Samuel Going, Esq., sub-sheriff, with a party of police under command of the 85th Regt. from Carrick-on-Suir, proceeded to the lands of Castlejohn, in the neighbourhood of the State Quarries, the property of John Maher, Esq., of Tullimaine, and ejected 16 families, consisting of over EIGHTY individuals, for non-payment of rent, and levelled eight houses.

It was a most pitiable sight to see so many human beings being driven from their home at such a season of the year and left without a roof to shelter them, and many with scarce a rag on them.

MURDER OCCASIONED BY JEALOUSY.

On last Monday night, about the hour of 12 o'clock, a murder was perpetrated at Cappanabawn, in the south west of this county, under the following very singular circumstances:—A farmer of the name of Dennis Long, rather comfortably situated, had reason to suspect the fidelity of his wife. As each day rolled by, fresh suspicions crowded on his mind; every trivial event was to him "confirmation strong as proofs of holy writ." He watched with the eye of a Lynx the movements of his wife and those of her paramour, who was in the employ of her husband, and who has been sent with all his imperfections on his head to meet an angry God and to render an account of his misdoings. The husband laboured incessantly to come at the real truth of his wife's iniquity, for he still had some doubts of the profligacy of his dissolute partner. In order to satisfy this suspicion, he exercised the power of his intellect in arranging the following plot which has terminated fatally. Long stated to his wife on Sunday night that he would proceed early on the next morning to the fair at Rathkeale as he had some business to transact there, and if he did not return about two o'clock in the day he would not be at home until next day. Having made the necessary preparations to prosecute his journey, he departed, and did not return at the hour appointed, which satisfied the wife and her paramour that he would not be back before the ensuing day, but he arrived sooner than was expected, and he found too truly the realization of his wife's dishonour. With the fury of a lion, and in a moment of temporary insanity, he seized a spade handle and struck Walsh a blow which killed him on the spot. The man was arrested, and an inquest was held, when the verdict was that he died from the effects of blows inflicted by Dennis Long, who at the same time was labouring under insanity, caused by jealousy.—*Limerick Examiner.*

Recreated from The Waterford News, Waterford, December 1, 1848.

FRIGHTFUL TRAGEDY.

Brutal Murder of Scores of Human Beings on board of a Steam Boat, sailing from Sligo to Liverpool.

"SENTINEL" OFFICE, DERRY, MONDAY EVENING.
For the information of our contemporaries, we subjoin the particulars of this most dreadful calamity. About 9 o'clock yesterday evening the inhabitants of this city were startled on hearing the astounding intelligence

that the Londonderry steamer, Captain Johnstone, which plies between Sligo and Liverpool, had reached our quay with a number of dead bodies on board.

Great anxiety was manifested through the city immediately after the arrival of the vessel. Thereupon we hastened to the spot, and found that the steamer, crew, cargo, and surviving passengers were in the hands of the authorities.

Fifty men of the 95th Regiment, supported by the constabulary, were present, and prevented the egress of any person from the vessel. The scene, on entering the steamer, was truly heart-rending, and such as no human being could witness without feelings of the most poignant description.

In the steerage the terrific spectacle presented itself, of 73 individuals piled indiscriminately on each other deprived of life. Though various rumours, as to the cause of death have got into circulation, instantly after the vessel arrived, it was quite apparent, from the appearance of the bodies, that death was caused by suffocation.

After the lapse of some time a respectable jury was empaneled, and they proceeded to hold an inquest on the body of one of the sufferers, a little girl of about eight years of age.

Two witnesses were then examined, at the conclusion of which, it being six o'clock, the coroner adjourned the investigation until ten o'clock, this morning.

It appeared from the evidence tendered that the Londonderry steamer left Sligo for Liverpool at four o'clock on Friday evening, having on board besides cattle, &c., nearly one hundred and fifty steerage passengers—the greater number of them were on their way to America; and, that the evening was so boisterous that none but the crew could keep the deck. The passengers were ordered below—the hatch was drawn partially across, but it appeared that sufficient space was not left for the purpose of ventilation, which caused the unfortunate people below to experience all the horrors of suffocation. One passenger, more fortunate than the rest, succeeded in gaining the deck, and alarmed the mate, when he, with some of the crew, hastened to their relief; but alas! too late, seventy-three human beings had ceased to exist.

The captain and crew have been taken into custody.

Recreated from The Waterford News, Waterford, December 8, 1848.

Matrimony.

A GENTLEMAN OF about Thirty Years of Age, and not unprepossessing appearance, tolerable Manners, and College-Educated, is precluded from accepting a Public Situation in consequence of his being still in a state of Single Blessedness, and would be most happy to find a Lady, somewhat under the above age, willing to adopt him as a Partner for Life; is not particular as to sect, but would prefer a good Christian (who has seen a little of the world), of an intellectual turn and animated Physiognomy, Agreeable Manners, and Lady-like appearance, about Middle Stature, Dark Hair and Eyes preferred, but not considered essential. It would be well if the Lady were possessed of a Competency sufficient to secure her against the effects of excessive grief in case of accident to the Companion; he is not particular as to Town or Country, but would like a good Accept, a Musical Voice, and the usual female Accomplishments.

Any Lady answering the above description, and willing to enter the Holy Bonds of Matrimony, would oblige by notifying her wishes to the address of M——y NEWS Office. The strictest secrecy will be observed and expected.

Waterford, June 29th, 1849.

Reprinted from The Waterford News, Waterford, December 8, 1848.

STATE OF IRELAND.

HOUSE LEVELLING AND EXTERMINATION.—This house levelling trade, which is being carried on in parts of Clare to a most frightful extent, did not commence in the Scariff union on any extensive scale until last Saturday, 25th instant; and it was the only ingredient that was wanted to fill the cup of misery and woe. On that day the sub-sheriff, accompanied by a large body of police from Feakle, station, proceeded to the townland of Crusderra, on Lord Norbury's property, between Feakle and Scariff, and immediately the signal for destruction was given. In less than one hour eight houses were levelled with the ground and their wretched inmates, thrown out on the roadside, were soon seen dragging their famine-stricken limbs and starving children towards the workhouse, their only home for the future.

Two other houses were levelled in a neighboring townland, and the inmates had to betake themselves to the same home as their neighbours. The sooty sticks that covered those ten houses were carefully brought home by the superintendent of the levelling process for fuel for his kitchen, thus preventing those forlorn creatures, just thrown beggars on the world, from the possibility of erecting sheds for themselves and their starvlings, even for one night.—*Limerick and Clare Examiner.*

COLLECTION OF THE POOR RATE.—Colonel Sir Michael Greagh, Bart., has arrived in town to inspect the collection of the poor rate in this locality. His first crusade is to be directed towards Spiddal, Tully (the seat of former evictions), Askawce, Letterah, Thonabrucky, and other interesting districts. A large quantity of bread is being prepared for the troops, about 700 in number, before they enter upon this arduous duty.—*Galway Vindicator.*

IRISH EXPORTS.—A great number of horned cattle, sheep, and pigs, were sent on Wednesday morning by the railway train to Dublin, for shipment to England. A number of emigrants departed also. Thus, the bulk of the population and the food of the land are daily leaving our shores.—*Limerick Examiner.*

Recreated from The Freeman's Journal, Dublin, December 8, 1848.

FAIRS.

LOUGHREA.—We have attended many fairs, but so bad a fair as that of Loughrea on yesterday (Tuesday) we never witnessed. It was a complete picture of the distress and misery of the country. Cattle were in abundance—buyers from Meath, Westmeath, and Kilkenny were numerous, yet but few sales were made, Those anxious to purchase thought the prices asked too high, and the consequence was that nearly all left the fair unsold. The number of sheep was small, and the quality very indifferent; upon the whole the fair was flat, stale, and unprofitable. The decline per head in black cattle was about 20s. under Ballinasloe.—*Galway Vindicator.*

SIXMILE-BRIDGE.—The fair of Sixmile-bridge, county Clare, on Tuesday, was the smallest that has been for some years; little business done.

THE COUNTY WATERFORD ROADS.

A gentleman just returned from Waterford describes the mail coach road from the city to Cappoquin, as loaded with heaps of stones almost all the way, making it dangerous to travel in these dark evenings and mornings. In may cases cars attempting to pass were forced on the stones from the narrowed breadth, large heaps being laid in some places 12 feet and more from the fence. Is there a County Surveyor in Waterford?—*Cork Constitution.*

[In answer to our contemporary's question, "Is there a County Surveyor in Waterford," we say, yes. Mr. Henry Owen is our County Surveyor, for which he is paid a very nice salary, besides having *four assistants*. The *Constitution* need not trouble itself about our thoroughfares, as we generally must have two or three persons killed, drowned, &c., before the roads about this city are thought of being repaired. It was only last week that we recorded the death of a young woman who was drowned at Grenagh Bridge, a mile and a half from this city, in consequence of the shocking state of the roads in that locality.—ED. W. NEWS.]

Recreated from The Freeman's Journal, Dublin, December 8, 1848.

LETTER OF AN "IRISH PRIEST"

The second letter from the "Irish Priest" has appeared, and has attracted considerable attention. The first letter was directed to the Attorney-General; but this is addressed to Lord Clarendon himself.

Here is a specimen:—"The blood boils in my veins when I think that the little gang of Orange "ruffianism" of Dublin, the descendants and the representatives, and the heirs of the principles and the spirit of the perjured, murderous, sacrilegious robber crew whose bloody hands have reddened every page of our history for two hundred years; that this sanguinary section of a sect should alone hold the scales of justice and its sword in this Catholic land of ours."

Recreated from The Waterford News, Waterford, December 22, 1848.

A GOOD AND A BAD MAN!

John Edward Redmond, Esq. of Wexford, has given a free passage to Liverpool, in his fine vessel the Town of Wexford, to three poor men, their wives, and twenty children, who had been lately turned off the estate of Sir Hugh Palliser, near Carne. The only claim they had on the benevolent Mr. Redmond (himself a good landlord) was their poverty.

A WORD TO EMIGRANTS.

(Written for The News)

An emigrant going to America, should always provide for a 60 days' passage, although he may not be half the time crossing.

Poor passengers, when they go to large English ports should be very watchful.

It is always better and safer for Irish people to embark at Irish ports.

Be careful to select a good spacious vessel, as there is great inconvenience in a small one.

And when you arrive on the new soil, get in to the heart of the country.

Do not wait to spend your last farthing in seaport towns.

Do not refuse any situation that may turn up.

Reprinted from The Waterford News, Waterford, December 22, 1848.

CHINA.—A serious affray took place at Hong-Kong, on the 15th Oct., between the boats of her Majesty's ship *Cambrian* and two Chinese junks. A Mr. Moore and some friends were going ashore from the *Tam O'Shanter*, at six p.m. on the 15th, when showers of stones were thrown at them from two junks. They lodged a complaint at the police station, when three boats of policemen were sent to the junks, but they were assailed with stones also, and were beaten off with gingals and matchlocks. The superintendent of police then proceeded on board the *Cambrian*, and requested the assistance of Commodore Plumridge, who, with the view of arresting the Chinamen without bloodshed, ordered all the boats of the frigate to board the junks. When the man-of-war's boats arrived alongside the Chinamen they were fired at, whereupon Lieutenant Lloyd gave the word, the marines of the launch sent back a volley of ball cartridge, with three cheers, the junks were boarded through the smoke, and the prisoners, twenty-two in number, were soon secured. The Chinese further resisted, by pouring hot water and molasses on the boat's crew, and by presenting bamboo spears, and bit and pinched the seamen and marines when they were captured, two of the Chinese having been killed in the boarding.

Recreated from The Belfast News-Letter, Belfast, December 22, 1848.

SHIPWRECKS.

On Thursday last—the brig *Growler*, Captain Attridge, from New York, for Waterford, with a cargo of Indian corn, was completely wrecked in Whiting Bay, near Youghal. This vessel was 29 days on the voyage, during which she experienced most severe weather, having been obliged to lie to for days in consequence of the violence of the storm. She narrowly escaped going on shore near Halifax, Nova Scotia, was beating about St. George's Channel for seven days previous to her wreck.

Barry's Cove, Dec. 16.—A French schooner, from Rochelle, bound to Waterford, laden with maize, came on shore out at Dunworley Bay. The crew, consisting of five men, with the master, were saved.

On Friday morning a foreign brig, laden with oranges and oil from the Mediterranean, parted from her anchors near Barry's Head, and drove towards the shore. The crew, in their endeavour to save the vessel, cut away the masts, notwithstanding which she was completely wrecked in Dunbogue Cove, near Kinsale, and the crew, 15 in number, drowned.

Greencastle, Dec. 16.—The barque *Grace Darling*, of Dundalk, from New York, with Indian corn, M. Doran, master, bound to Newry, was wrecked here this morning.

How Strand, Dec. 16.—The barque *Severn*, of and to London from St. John's, with a cargo of deals and sleepers, Richard Cresca, master, has been totally wrecked. The coast guards promptly rendered their assistance, and with the aid of Denett's rockets, succeeded in putting a line over her, by which means the lives of fifteen of the crew were fortunately saved. Two were drowned owing to their own neglect in not securing themselves properly to the hawser. The inhabitants seconded in every way the exertions of the coast guard to render aid.

On Thursday night two vessels were driven ashore outside Clonakilty harbour.

Newcastle, Co. Down, Dec. 17.—During the heavy gale here om Friday, the British barque *Bee*, 577 tons, Thomas Muir, master, five days out from Liverpool, belonging to Hatrush and Co., New Ross, came on shore near Dick's bay. The rocket apparatus was sent to the spot, and the first rocket fired carried the line fairly over the vessel, but the line, having been a long time in store, broke when hauled on. A communication having once been established with the vessel, by means of a large hawser and an arm chair with hauling lines, the coast guard succeeded in saving twenty lives—one man only of the vessels crew, twenty in number, being lost, having gone over with the main mast.

One of the country people was arrested on Friday by Mr. Taylor, of the coast guard, in the act of cutting a hawser which was fast to the ship. He was taken prisoner, and convicted under the Wreck and Salvaging Act.

Cooley Point, Dec. 15.—I greatly regret to say that this morning the pilot-boat *Betty Jane*, of Whitestown, which was launched in order to look out for vessels either for Dundalk or Carlingford, was overtaken by the gale, and in attempting to reach the bay, a tremendous sea on, she upset, and five out of six were unfortunately drowned.

Glandore, Dec. 16.—This morning, the schooner *King of the Forest*, of Milford, wheat and flour laden, from Marseilles for Cork, came on shore.

A schooner was dashed to pieces soon after on the rocks, close to the old signal tower on the Head. All hands have unfortunately perished. A French brig was driven on shore, and three kegs, containing about four gallons of brandy, damaged.

Nohoval Turrets, Dec. 16.—There was an awful wreck this morning in Dunboygy Cove, of a brigantine from Palermo, laden with olive oil, *shumac*, I think, and oranges and lemons, all hands lost (six men).

Recreated from The Waterford News, Waterford, December 22, 1848.

CHRISTMAS FESTIVITIES.

The Duke and Duchess of Norfolk will receive a succession of distinguished visiters at Arundel Castle, during the holidays.

The Duke and Duchess of Richmond will entertain a select circle at Goodwood, during the ensuing festive season.

The Duke and Duchess of Beaufort are receiving a select circle at Cabminton.

The Marquess and Marchioness of Lansdowne are displaying their princely hospitality at Bowood Park to a very numerous circle, among whom are the Earl and Countess of Shelburne, the Hon. Mr. and Lady Louisa Howard, the Count and Countess Flahault, &c.

The Marquess and Marchioness of Westminster have a select party at Motcombe house for the Christmas holidays.

There will be a drawing-room at the Castle on Thursday evening, Jan. 24.

Reprinted from The Waterford News, Waterford, December 29, 1848.

THE "TURNING POINT" OF IRELAND'S FATE.

That we have arrived at the very crisis of our country's destiny, at least, as regards the present generation of her inhabitants, is now the general opinion of all who have watched the progress of affairs with unbiased judgement or reflective mind. We need not quote authorities. The most stubborn enemies of all salutary concessions to Ireland's necessities are now forced into an admission of the fact, that unless our country is snatched by a saving hand from the abyss upon the brink of which she is already tottering, she must sink into irretrievable ruin. Even the *Times*—that pertinacious stickler at no distant date for the *laissez faire* system—for the "help yourself and heaven will help you" arguments applied to the Irish landlords and the Irish people *en masse*—is now swelling the indignant chorus which rises from all sides, that Ireland must be rescued from the fate which threatens her, unless the empire is prepared to see her perish of inanition. The fact is palpable. Need we assign the causes? First in the list is the destruction of our agricultural interest by the operation of free trade, in the reduction, and as will shortly happen, the total abolition, of protective duties; next we may rank the disproportionate increase of taxation in a country groaning under the accumulation of every social evil; next, the prostration of the landed interest, weighed down by the impossibility of collecting rents, the encumbrances of estates, the repayment of loans, and the maintenance of a gigantic yet inefficient poor-law; next, the redundancy of a pauper population in the room of the very flower of our industrious and skillful yeomanry who have carried to distant lands the capital, the labour, and the example for which no field was left in their native land, leaving misery, want, and despair, behind them; and we may crown the gloomy catalogue with the singular and unforeseen disaster which, for three successive seasons, diminished the peoples' food and cast them at the mercy of the imperial charity, while it cramped their energies and retarded every effort towards recovery. To remedy this dreadful state of things, many nostrums have been suggested, but the most specious is that which the *Times* has the credit of inventing—namely, the substitution of a class of English for Irish proprietors, by the compulsory sale of the encumbered estates—a measure which, it is said, will reanimate the desiccated frame of society, supply the labor market, improve the soil, and give life and spirit to our enterprises. We question, however, if this would produce the effect intended. The same causes would operate against wealthy English capitalists as against the impoverished Irish landlord. It would only be a question of time. The process of ruin would only be arrested for a given period, for no capital, however great—no energy, however determined—no enterprise, however well aimed or brilliant—could long withstand the crushing influence of enormous taxation, of unprotected agriculture, and of a redundant population.

Recreated from The Belfast News-Letter, Belfast, December 29, 1848.

TO THE MEMORY OF A YOUNGER BROTHER.

Oft tender flow'rs do quickly fade,
Their beauties soon decay;
So thou hast there been early laid—
Within that bed of clay.

Six summers' suns did o'er thee pass'
As sweetly thou didst bloom;
The seventh beheld the waving grass
Around thy silent tomb.

I thought it hard to say farewell,
When forced from thee to part;
And bitter were the tears that fell.
And pangs which wrung my heart.

The friends stood round the dying bed,
Where calmly thou didst lie;
They watch'd the breaking of life's thread,
And closed thy gentle eye.

The angels bore thy soul away
To that fair land above—
Your heavenly home—and endless day—
Won by a Saviour's love.

Though now on earth we'll meet no more,
My hope is still in God—
That I may reach that peaceful shore,
Where thou hast thy abode;

And with thee strike the harp on high,
Within Immanuel's land;
To swell the choral symphony,
As round the throne we stand.

Recreated from The Belfast News-Letter, Belfast, January 12, 1849.

1849

Selected Headlines

AN EMIGRATION MARRIAGE	188
VICEREGAL COURT	192
AN OLD OFFENDER	197
THE OLD STORY OVER AGAIN—DEATH	202
THE STATE CONVICTS AND THEIR DOOM	204
THE CHARGE OF SHOOTING AT HER MAJESTY	209
THE QUEEN IN DUBLIN	212
ATROCIOUS MURDER IN LONDON	218
CHARLES DICKENS ON PUBLIC EXECUTIONS	234
STARVATION IN KILRUSH	236

AN EMIGRATION MARRIAGE.—A Devonport correspondent sends us the following:—A young woman, aged 22, a servant, being taken ill of typhus, was removed to the workhouse at Devonport, where, by attention, she soon recovered. After her restoration to health, she expressed a desire to emigrate to Australia, if the guardians would advance the sum of £2 10s., which is necessary to be paid to the Emigration Society for outfit previous to sailing, and which money is returned them on embarking; and the guardians having received a most satisfactory character of her from the governor of the workhouse, they agreed to do so; and she accordingly went to the office to enquire about her passage. Whilst waiting there, however, she was accosted by a respectable person, who asked her business, and if she were going to emigrate? She replied in the affirmative, when he rejoined, "So am I; and if you have no objection I'll marry you previous to sailing." She replied that she was obliged for the offer, but thought it was very extraordinary and premature, seeing that he knew nothing about her; upon which he remarked that he liked her honest countenance. At length the matter was most seriously entertained, and she referred him to the service she had lately left. He at once started off to the address, and received such a satisfactory character, that, on returning, he immediately purchased the license, and the hasty couple were married on Christmas-day. It may be added that previous to the wedding he spent £20 for his wife's outfit, paid her passage, and returned the £2 10s. to the guardians, with many thanks.—*Standard*.

FESTIVITIES AT HILLSBOROUGH CASTLE.—During the past week, Hillsborough Castle, the residence of the Most Hon. the Marquis of Downshire, has been the scene of brilliant festivities. A temporary theatre had been tastefully and elegantly fitted up, under the superintendence of the Marchioness, for an amateur performance, which took place on Wednesday, under the patronage of the youthful Earl of Hillsborough, in the presence of a large number of the *elite* of the town and neighbourhood, who had been invited to witness it, and which passed off with great *eclat*, those present expressing themselves highly delighted with the performance. There was afterwards a select evening party of about two hundred, at which they had the various amusements suited to the season—dancing, Christmas tree, &c. On the previous day, the servants, tradesmen, and those connected with the Marquis of Downshire's office, were invited to witness a rehearsal of the play, and had also an evening entertainment after. It is gratifying to be able to record that the poor have not been forgotten by the noble Marquis at this festive season, who, with his accustomed liberality, caused three fine oxen, and between three and four hundred loaves of bread, to be distributed to the needy in the town and neighbourhood, for which he was rewarded by the thanks and blessings of the grateful recipients of his bounty.—(*From a Subscriber.*)

Recreated from The Belfast New-Letter, Belfast, January 2, 1849.

SHIPWRECK—THANKS.—The owners of the *Little Queen of Youghal*, Patrick Prendergast, Master, bound to Youghal, which was wrecked on Woodstown Strand, on the 18th inst., crew and passengers saved, beg to return their sincere thanks to the Right Hon. the Earl of Huntington, Gaultier Lodge, co. Waterford, for his very kind and active exertions on that occasion in rescuing the crew (five in number, and two passengers) from a watery grave, by having four lights conspicuously placed to cheer their sinking hopes; in patrolling the Strand all night, and offering any amount of money to whoever should rescue them, as well as for his hospitable treatment of the crew and passengers at his mansion for four days and nights, where they received every comfort after their fatigue and fortunate rescue.—*Cork Examiner*.

Recreated from The Waterford News, Waterford, January 5, 1849.

STEALING BREAD.

This morning three young lads were detected stealing bread from Mr. Jacob's man whilst passing along the Quay. One of them was arrested by sub-constable M'Carthy, the other two having decamped, eating the loaves as they ran along. They were poor looking creatures.

Reprinted from The Waterford News, Waterford, January 5, 1849.

CORONER'S INQUEST—FATAL ACCIDENT.

Yesterday John E. Hyndman, Esq., city coroner, held an inquest on Usher's-island, on the body of a man named Job Cartwright, late a servant in the employment of Richard Pim, sen., who it appeared had fallen over the Liffey wall while in a state of intoxication, opposite the house of his master's son, on Sunday night, about ten o'clock. It appeared that Mr. Pim, sen., dined at the house of his son, on Usher's-island, on Sunday, and from the following evidence the facts of the case will be collected:—

John Ryan stated that he knew deceased five years, and during that time deceased was groom and own man to Mr. Richard Pim; saw deceased about nine o'clock the previous night in the yard, when witness and another person helped him to put the carriage out of the yard; deceased got on the box and drove round; witness knew he had some drink, but did not think he was incapable of doing his business; in a few minutes after the yard bell was rung, and witness with the other man was called to take round the carriage, as the pole was broken, and when witness went round the deceased was standing at the horses' heads; there was no one near him at the time; deceased did not say how the accident happened; deceased was ordered to get the harness on one horse and go home, but on consideration it was thought that he was unfit to go home with the carriage and the horse; deceased then went away, and it was near ten o'clock at the time; did not see him after until he was brought in dead an hour after that.

John Roche stated that he was informed a man of Mr. Pim's had fallen into the Liffey, and he went in a boat and dragged the river; got the body in the river at about half-past ten o'clock, quite dead.

Two soldiers and some policemen were sworn, and stated that they heard a man had fallen over the wall, and they did all they could to save him, but without effect.

Surgeon Wright stated that he examined the body; there was no mark on it except some mud on the forehead; deceased did not seem to have made the least exertion to save himself; witness does not think he was in a sober state; when he got into the water he went down head foremost, and was suffocated by drowning.

It appeared that the unfortunate deceased (who was about 35 years of age), after leaving the stable yard, went over to the Liffey wall, which is very low at the place, and in consequence of his unsteady position he lurched, and fell over the wall.

The jury found the following verdict:—We find that Job Cartwright was accidently drowned in the river Liffey, last night; and the jury take leave to call the serious attention of the Directors of the Ballast Board to the wall of the river at Usher's-island, which is not high enough to protect passengers from falling into the rive there, and they attribute the death of Job Cartwright to this defect of the wall.

Recreated from the Freeman's Journal, Dublin, January 9, 1849.

At Fermoy Sessions on Saturday, Thomas M'Donnell was indicted for having, at Mitchelstown, taken and carried away Anna Maria Slark from her father, John Slark, she being unmarried and under the age of sixteen years. The jury returned a verdict of guilty, and the prisoner was sentenced to 12 months' imprisonment, and to pay a fine of £20 to the prosecutor.

Reprinted from The Waterford News, Waterford, January 12, 1849.

STATE OF IRELAND.

DEATH FROM STARVATION.—An inquest was held on Sunday, in Nenagh gaol, by James Carroll, Esq., and a respectable jury, on view of the body of Denis Brien, a miserable man, who had been an inmate of the Nenagh union workhouse, and who was committed to prison on New Year's Day by the magistrates for having left the workhouse during the Christmas holidays. He died suddenly in gaol. Doctor Neil Quin deposed that the deceased was committed on the 1st instant as "a pauper vagrant", that his death was caused by a natural decline of constitution from his previous state of destitution and misery—that they did all they could in the gaol to restore him, but it was impossible. A verdict was returned according to the circumstances, the foreman of the jury making strong observations respecting the miserable condition of the poor in the houses.—*Tipperary Vindicator.*

DEATH FROM STARVATION.—Friday evening last, a person named Mooney, found a man, whose name and place of residence are unknown, lying in the road at Woodfield, within one mile of this town, who told him he was dying with hunger. Mooney gave him some money, and another person who happened to be passing, gave the unfortunate creature some bread, which he appeared to eat. Mooney at once informed the police, and Sub-Constables Connell and Call, of the Ranemills station, went to Woodfield, where they found the poor man lying in an unoccupied house, in a state of exhaustion and unable to speak; they placed him on a car, and had him removed to the hospital, where he was immediately attended by Dr. Waters, but he died in an hour after his admission. An inquest was held before B. T. Midgley, Esq., coroner, as to the facts. Dr. Waters deposed that he was of opinion that death was caused by starvation and exposure to cold. The jury found a verdict accordingly.—*King's County Chronicle.*

OUTRAGES.—A few nights since a party of ten armed men, attacked the dwellings of Thomas Condron, and John Egan, at Tullamore, near Cloghan, in the barony of Garrycastle. The banditti broke into the houses, smashed the windows, and beat the inmates. They swore Condron and Egan to give up their farms, and also swore the other inmates of the houses not to tell of them. After going away, they fired several shots. Constable Vass, of Cloghan, aided by the English police, since arrested several persons, two of whom named Shaw and Murray, have been identified, and fully committed to abide their trial at the ensuing assizes of Tullamore.—*Ibid.*

The house of a farmer named Coffey, residing on the banks of the canal, at Gallen, near Ferbane, was attacked on Wednesday night last, by a large party who were armed with guns, blunderbusses, pistols, swords, &c. Having effected an entrance, one of the gang presented a blunderbuss at Coffey, and threatened to shoot him if he did not give up his money. He denied having any; they then ransacked the house, and found only about ten shillings, which they took away, together with five cwt. of oatmeal, a scythe, and several articles. They carried away the booty on a car which they took from another farmer; they left a sentinel on the door for more than two hours, in order to prevent Coffey or his family leaving the house to give alarm—several shots were fired. Head Constable Biard and Constable Mende were most active in their exertions to discover the perpetrators. They succeeded in capturing two notorious characters named Shaughnessey and Hughes, who were identified as being of the party, one of whom pleaded guilty at the quarter sessions in this town on Saturday last, and was sentenced to ten years' transportation. The other postponed his trial to the assizes.—*Ibid.*

CLONMEL.—JANUARY 8, 1849.—The state of affairs is becoming alarming here. There was never such gloomy forebodings of a famine. Horses and cars were being auctioned off all day on Monday in the Main-street for poor rates, and under civil bill decrees.—*Waterford Mail.*

On New Year's night two fine heifers, the property of a very poor man, named William Power, were brutally houghed, the hind legs being totally cut off, on the lands of Park, near Rathcormac, county Waterford. The cause of this inhumane outrage is, that a man named Patrick Toole was recently evicted from a farm on the Disney property for non-payment of rent, which farm was taken by a man named Connolly, who gave permission to Power to graze his heifers there a few days, and the midnight legislators having a few nights ago fired at Connolly through his bedroom window, and served him with a notice that they would take his life and the life of any person found on the lands, are determined that no beast shall be on the farm with impunity.—*Ibid.*

THE CLEARANCE SYSTEM—CAHIR.—Since our last notice of levelling on the Glengall property, the townland of Kilnabutler, was the scene of similar operations. On Friday last, the 5th instant, they levelled eleven houses containing 51 souls, leaving only two standing. The ejectments were through the Court of Chancery, viz., the following:—Widow Cleary and three children, 4; Widow English and five children, 6; Widow Sheehan and two children, 3; Widow J. Cleary and two children, 3; widow Farrell and three children, 4; Brien Hennessy, wife, and six children, 8; Larry Cleary, wife, and six children, 8; John Boyle, wife, and child, 3; P. O'Donnell, wife, and three children, 5; Con. Keefe, wife, and three children, 5; John Tobin and wife, 2, Total, 51.—*Tipperary Vindicator.*

A family named Looby, consisting of seven persons, were evicted at six o'clock on Saturday night by Mr. Going, sub-sheriff, and a party of constabulary, from off the townland of Rosegreen, the property of a Mr. Newenham, of the county Cork—they were a year and a-half in arrear for rent.—*Clonmel Chronicle.*

On the night of the 2nd instant, a cow, the property of Richard Torpy, of Currakelly, farmer, near Rathcormac, was driven out of his cow-house, killed on the road, the carcass taken away, and the hide and head left; the tongue also was taken away.—*Ibid.*

STATE OF MAYO.—Mayo, the third largest county in Ireland, has not now a population of able bodied men sufficient to cultivate four baronies out of the nine—add to this, while we write we have emigrant ships riding in our bays, taking off such of our people as yet posses the means of emigrating to the states of America; some of these might be seen in this town on Saturday last making sale of their furniture, and taking leave of their friends, prior to encountering a long sea voyage in a hard winter.

What a prospect does not this present of the future; and yet the landlords seem not to perceive their source of wealth moving away, while they themselves are falling, step by step, from affluence to beggary, from fashionable courts to the precincts of workhouses! Nay, their courtly halls, once inaccessible to the tread of the tenantry, are now occupied as auxiliary workhouses by paupers of landlord creation, and by street vagrants.—*Mayo Telegraph.*

PLUNDER.—On Friday night last four bullocks, value of forty pounds, the property of the Earl of Lucan, were feloniously stolen from his lordship's farm at Anghagoulamore.—There has been no trace as yet of the offender.—*Mayo Constitution.*

Recreated from The Freeman's Journal, Dublin, January 12, 1849.

ASSISTANCE TO EMIGRANTS.

The Marquis of Ormonde has given notice to all the small tenantry on his estates in Kilkenny and Tipperary, that he will give 25s. per head to all the members of any family holding a house or small plot of ground, provided they sell the land and level the house! Many of them are anxious, but unable, to comply with the injunctions of the landlord. Such has been the depressed state of the poor in these counties, that they are no longer able to retain house or home.   H.

Reprinted from The Waterford News, Waterford, February 9, 1848.

VICEREGAL COURT.

FESTIVITIES AT DUBLIN CASTLE.—Since the return of the Viceregal Court from the Viceregal Lodge, in the Phoenix Park, to the Castle, their Excellencies the Lord Lieutenant and the Countess of Clarendon have not allowed a week to pass without receiving several numerous parties at dinner, and on Thursday evening, as if to form a re-union of the nobility and gentry who had been presented at the late levee and drawing-room, their excellencies received about 1,600 persons at a ball and supper.

The suite of apartments comprising the drawing-room, dining-room, the round-room, and St. Patrick's Hall, had each been furnished and decorated in a style of elegance never, perhaps, arrived at on any previous festival at the Viceregal Court. Tea and coffee were served in the drawing-room; refreshments of ice and an endless variety of rare and costly viands in the dining-room; the presence chamber was appropriated for *conversazione*; St. Patrick's Hall was filled with the votaries of music and dancing; the picture gallery and the round room were furnished as supper-rooms, and the billiard-room, which formed a communication between the two supper-rooms and St. Patrick's Hall, was converted into a cool and refreshing bower.

The billiard table was not removed, but, protected by linings of timber and cloth, it bore a rich burden of flowering shrubs and plants in full blow, intertwined with delicate and creeping exotics as if growing from rocks, and shells, and moss. Underneath the table, and corresponding with the shape of the room, an oval trough, formed of zinc, twenty feet long, and about ten feet wide, was charged with water, three feet deep, in which living fishes plied their fins, several species of waterfowl gliding along its surface.

Around the walls evergreens and flowering shrubs were arranged in order; and statues, modelled from the Pantheon, were placed in the niches, as if peeping through the rich foliage in which they were partially concealed. The pedestal on which the Arcadian Shepherd, playing on his pipe, stood, rested on a self-acting musical instrument, which, having been wound, discoursed several compositions of exquisite music.

Various species of singing birds, including German canaries and piping bull-finches, and macaws of the richest plumage, placed in cages, and perched on branches, were disposed throughout; and a fountain, sprouting from the lips of a little Triton, fell on the rocks and shells, and rippling from thence through the moss, trickled down through the superstructure, into the trough which formed the reservoir. Transparencies, representing columns, and formed of green muslin, overlaid with white, the cavities of which were lighted with small gas-jets, reflected a dreamy light through the room, which was still further mellowed by a reflector in the ceiling to represent the moon at the full. The entire of this enchanting bower had all the appearance of a still evening in summer, after sun-set, with the moon careering in the high heavens.

Recreated from The Belfast News-Letter, Belfast, February 13, 1849.

STATE OF IRELAND.

DEATH FROM STARVATION IN ROSCREA UNION—MONEYGALL, THURSDAY.—We had another death from starvation in this village, which is likely to become another Schull in a short time. John Cantwell died on Tuesday morning last of mere want; and from the evidences adduced before the jury—that his house was thrown down, and he turned out on the wide world to starve and die—there was no hesitation on their part in giving their verdict.

Mary Cantwell, sister to the deceased, his wife, and a girl named Mary Guerins were examined from whose testimony it appeared he had been turned out of a house and garden, which he held from Mr. Cole Bowen, in November last, when the house was thrown down. He was in the Nenagh workhouse for six weeks, but left it, according to the first witness, because he could not use the food. He got sixpence out-door relief from Mr. Hayes, the relieving officer, the night before his death!

Dr. Bindon's testimony was to the effect that death was the result of privation of food, and exposure to the inclemency of the weather, and the jury returned a verdict accordingly.—*Tipperary Vindicator.*

CATTLE STEALING.—We are sorry to announce that cattle stealing is very prevalent in this county, and that the farmers have consequently suffered severely; the plunder of sheep has also been extensive in this and neighbouring counties.—*Tipperary Free Press.*

EXHAUSTION FROM COLD AND HUNGER.—On Friday as a poor wretched man, reduced to the last degree of emaciation, was proceeding up George's-street, he fell senseless to the ground from sheer exhaustion brought on by cold and hunger. A crowd of persons collected around him, and to all present he seemed to be quite dead. He was, however, removed to the police barrack in William-street, where every attention was paid him. Mr. Moore, governor of the city gaol, with his usual characteristic generosity, at once procured for him some refreshing draught, which had a most beneficial effect, and to which, probably, may be attributed to the poor man's existence at present. If the Limerick Union Workhouse be now full, and capable of containing no more inmates, as is stated, it is a cruel mockery to deny applicants out-door relief, and tell them to "go to the workhouse."—With guardians of the poor, magistrates, and ratepayers, the term "go to the workhouse" is a quite familiar phrase; and to such it may be necessary to state that the workhouse is said to be filled to the brim and can contain no more; so if no other provision be made for the destitute, they must lie down and die in the street from hunger and starvation.—*Limerick and Clare Examiner.*

THE SMASHING SYSTEM.—There have been twelve windows broken in the streets of Killaloe within as many days by paupers, with a view of getting into jail; but they were disappointed, partly because there was no magistrate to commit them, and partly because the shopkeepers didn't like paying for informations—they thought it enough to lose their glass.—*Ibid.*

A considerable body of farmers, comfortably clothed, came up from Kilrush yesterday (Friday) on their way to Liverpool for America. The parting scene between those hardy men and their relatives was most affecting. Many wept aloud, men kissed each other as they parted, and when the steamer left the quay a wailing cry arose from those remaining, as if they wept for the dead.—*Ibid.*

THE JEWS IN PARLIAMENT.—It is rumoured that the bill to alter the oath which prevents Jews from sitting in parliament is not likely to meet with any serious opposition.—*Observer.*

Recreated from The Freeman's Journal, Dublin, February 27, 1849.

STATE OF IRELAND.

SOCIAL REVOLUTION.—Sir John Judkin Fitzgerald, Lisheen, near Cashel, formerly an extensive proprietor in the Tipperary union, has disposed of his property. The Tipperary gentry are vanishing daily; and, as might have been readily expected, few are the tears and fewer the sighs breathed by the peasantry at the ruin which the proprietors themselves produced and the poor law completed.

IRISH RUIN.—The "Jessy" which sails from our port the 28th of this month, will contain on board some of our most wealthy, honest, and intelligent countrymen. Among the emigrants will be Terence Ryan, Esq., Cross Cottage; Joseph Gubbins, Esq., Knokalong; Mr. O'Donovan, who graduated at one of our most distinguished universities, and was intended for a learned profession; James Keating, a respectable farmer near Croom, and Miss Eliza Manahan, one of the beautiful fair ones of our city. Thus Irish capital, wealth, and intelligence quit our country, while our "paternal government" suffer the ruin of Ireland to progress to completion.—*Limerick and Clare Examiner*.

LORD GLENGALL'S PROPERTY.—The tenantry of Lord Glengall are daily quitting their holdings; since we announced the first flight to America, several others deserted, and untilled acres have been added to his lordship's *abandoned soil.*—*Ibid*.

BEANFIELD.—I regret to say that *three deaths* from *starvation* took place, on the estate of Sir C. H. Coote, in this miserable parish, since I wrote you last. On two of these unfortunates *haberes* had been lately executed, and though an application for outdoor relief was made, it was peremptorily refused. From the absolute destitution of this locality arising from *want of security in the land*, and *consequent of exertion*, until *all* was swept off by the late famine, the respected Catholic pastor of the parish is involved in great pecuniary responsibility in trying to cope with the difficulties of his position.—*Ibid*.

GLENROE—DEATH FROM STARVATION.—Mr. Bennett, coroner, Kilfenora, held an inquest on Wednesday on the body of a young man who expired from starvation at Danagh. We could not learn who this victim of hunger was; but from the circumstances connected with his death it is generally supposed that he was some poor forlorn stranger, urged by hunger and weakness to quit his home in pursuit of food. It is thus that our poor countrymen are everywhere falling by the roadside the victims of direful want.—*Ibid*.

CONFLAGRATION AT GALBALLY.—Some nights ago, the inhabitants of Galbally were thrown into the greatest consternation when the report became general that some infamous incendiary set fire to three houses, the property of the Rev. Massy Dawson. The inmates of those houses were under sentence of expulsion by the landlord, and the lands on which they resided were to have been, or were actually let to a man of the name of Blackbourne. But for a little girl, who had been in attendance on a poor old sick man, and, who perceived the flames on their first appearance, upwards of 20 human beings must have been burned to ashes.—*Ibid*.

DUNGARVAN, WEDNESDAY.—Last week 24 houses were levelled at Knocknagrana, and over 130 human beings cast out on the bleak world, By Sir John Nugent Humble, Bart. As house after house was thrown down, and family after family turned out on the road, the screaming of children, and the shrieks and lamentations of their unfortunate parents presented one of the most distressing and heart-rending scenes that has taken place in this neighbourhood for a series of years, The evicted poor creatures had no place to shelter from the cold and wet of the approaching night. The neighbouring farmers were afraid that they would incur their landlords' dreaded ire, by giving them a night's lodging. Hence they had to seek refuge within the mud walls of the ruined cabins. To prevent this last and worst nuisance, the "mud walls" were ordered to be levelled with the ground.

These poor people were under tenants to some middle-man named Shaw and others; they owed Shaw two and three years' arrears with a few exceptions. Mr. Shaw neglected to pay Sir Nugent the head rent. Hence the eviction of 24 families who paid a rack rent to the middle men, and paid it punctually, too, until the failure of the potatoes. But the condition of these creatures has lately been so extremely miserable that their extermination was almost a natural consequence.

Sir Nugent gave each evicted family one pound, and the sooty and rotten roofs of their houses; but unfortunately the "tax-gatherers" seized on these and the little manure heaps some of them had gathered. These evictions caused a great sensation in this town, the inhabitants of which will now be saddled with the support of these poor people in the workhouse.—Correspondent of the *Southern Reporter*.

AWFUL DESTITUTION.—Moycullen is in a most destitute state. There are three or four burials every week in the graveyard of persons who die of starvation. Two persons named Cunlish and M'Donagh died of starvation in that district this week.—*Galway Vindicator*.

AWFUL MORTALITY IN NENAGH UNION WORKHOUSE.—In the Nenagh union workhouse last week there were no less that fifty-one deaths!!

Recreated from The Freeman's Journal, Dublin, March 6, 1849.

To the Editor of "The Waterford News.

DEAR SIR—I beg to call the attention of the Sanitary Committee, through your very popular journal, to the filthy state of several dirty places in our city, amongst which I may mention Little Barronstrand-street, High-street (near Keyser's-street), Jail-street, Garter-lane, &c.

These places are in the most fearful condition—full of fish offal, nasty dirt, and even excrament.

I do think, sir, that a smart fine ought be imposed on those who fling out their filth opposite their doors regardless of the public health.

In several towns in the surrounding counties persons have been fined for similar offences.

I think, sir, that every one who is able at all should see about whitewashing his concern be that great or small. As Waterford has been so fortunate as not to have cholera within its walls, that's no reason that its walls should be neglected.

Yours very truly, WATCHMAN.
Waterford, Thursday.

WEST OF ENGLAND
Fire Engine.

T. S. HARVEY

HAS the pleasure of informing the numerous FIRE POLICY HOLDERS in the WEST OF ENGLAND INSURANCE COMPANY, that the Directors have kindly acceded to his request, to be furnished with a FIRE ENGINE for the protection of the large and increasing amount of Property Insured in this Office.

A NEW and POWERFUL ENGINE has just arrived direct from the Makers in London, amply supplied with Hose, and every necessary convenience.

The STATION-HOUSE is in MEETING-HOUSE LANE, THOMAS'S-HILL, and the ENGINEER, ROBERT SCLANDERS, resides close at hand, No. 3, WELLINGTON-STREET, THOMAS'S-HILL.

55, Merchants' Quay,
4mo., 3, 1849.

Reprinted from The Waterford News, Waterford, April 6, 1849.

DUNGARVAN.

(From our own Correspondent.)

PAUPERS.—It is melancholy to reflect on the deplorable condition of our poor people. On Monday night 150 to 200 creatures who were seeking admission to the workhouse, on "out-door relief" had to sleep in a *field* near the establishment, having no place to shelter them!!—What country on the face of the globe, except ill-governed and oppressed Ireland, could present such a sad spectacle? Two hundred individuals in the land of their birth and toil, sleeping out in the open air for want of a home or house, from which they have been so cruelly and unwisely driven by the very class who should have been their guardians and benefactors. Mr. Fitzmaurice, the relieving officer, has been engaged for the last three days giving these starving people "out-door relief." But this relief is so miserably small (one penny a day each) that it is only protracting a starving existence.

SQUADS OF PAUPERS.

A friend who has just returned from Carrick mentions to us that he met several "squads of paupers" in the most wretched condition, on the road between this and Carrick. Some had fires by the ditch-side, round which sat their unfortunate families! Are these heart-rending scenes ever to have an end?

About eight o'clock on last Sunday evening a poor woman, named Johannah Reardon, from Tramore, whilst gathering grains of Indian corn on Merchants' Quay, had a narrow escape of being bitten by a horse, and when endeavouring to escape, fell over the Quay. The tide being out, her head was very much cut, it having come in contact with the sharp stones that lay in the mud. The police brought her to the poor-house hospital, where she was well attended to by Mr. Fardy, the master, who at once sent for Dr. Elliot. We understand she is going on favourably.

A clergyman from the village of Moycullen, about four miles from the town of Galway, addressing Mr. Anthony O'Flaherty, the Member for the town, says of his own parishioners that they are dying at the rate of twelve a week of hunger, and that there were, at the time he was writing, (Wednesday last,) 220 more lying sick of every disease, most of them without a fire, bed, or any covering save the tattered rags on their backs.

STATE OF THE COUNTRY.—Whatever way you turn the first prominent object that rivits your attention is a funeral. This is a sad picture, but it is not overdrawn—it is stern truth. Another inference of the decline of the country is furnished by the fact that one seldom sees a spade—that, too, has almost vanished with the hardy population which prided in yielding it.—*Clonmel Chronicle.*

HORRIBLE.—At the meeting of the Tralee board of guardians on Tuesday, Mr. John Twiss, of Haremount, related to us the following horrifying circumstance. A farmer named Daly, of Killakeen, in the parish of Dysert, in the previous week lost a mare by fever. In two hours the skin was taken off, the entrails and head were seized by some squalid wretches, and devoured! This occurred within a musket shot of Mr. Twiss's house. Mr. Twiss informed us also that a poor man, in his locality, who had succeeded in procuring a coffin for his brother, was obliged to leave it on the road within two miles of the hovel where the dead man lay, and died on the spot, the victim of that exhaustion and physical debility which what is called out-door relief is every day producing, and which had already, bit by bit, crushed the life from the once vigorous frame of his brother. They were both buried next day in some humble grave.—*Tralee Chronicle.*

AN OLD OFFENDER.—A decent looking old man, dressed as a farmer, whose name was Brennan, was charged with being drunk, and found in the company of bad females.

Mr. King, in fining him 1d. and 1s. costs, said it was a shame for a man of his years, who could be a father or grandfather of a family, to be found in the company of bad characters.

Brennan—'My con'shins, gintlemin, I never tasted a drop these sevin years afore; 'an I took a little drop too much that night.

Have you the money to pay the fine?

Brennan—Not a hape'ney—I lost it all.

Mr. Newport—If you went to your landlord, Dr. Elliot, wouldn't he give it to you?

Brennan—Ah! I'd be ashamed to go to the gintlemin.

Mr. King—Mr. Newport says he will pay the fine for you, if you'll pay him again?

Brennan—Oh! leave that to me; faith it's I that will [laughter].

The fine was paid, and Brennan left the court grinning with joy, and snapping his fingers at the policemen.

HEALTH OF WATERFORD.—We learn, with delight, that this city was seldom more free from sickness of any and all kinds than she is at the present moment. When we behold the condition of other towns, some of them quite at hand, have we not ample reason for thanking God for his merciful protection? We think, however, that we are much indebted to the gentlemen who commenced the sanitary measures in due time.—If we had some employment by which our poor people could earn nutritious food, Waterford would have no need to complain.

ROYAL SOCIETY.—THE EARL OF ROSSE, as president of the Royal Society, gave his annual soiree to the members and fellows of that institution on Saturday last at Somerset House, London.

THE POOR DROPPING DEAD IN FIELDS AND ON HIGHWAYS.

A Correspondent of the *Freeman*, writing from Killiamore, in the Ballinasloe union, in the county of Galway, under date May 6, says:—

Allow me to give a few details, all of which occurred in this town and neighbourhood within the last few days:—

Patrick Walsh, found dead by the Ballycrussane police in a heap of straw at the rere of their barrack.

Patrick M'Donagh, found dead by the said police in a fir bush in a field opposite their barrack.

Mary Mulloy, found dead, by said police on the public road.

John Quirk, found dead by the relieving officer on the public road.

Whelan found dead by the relieving officer in an open field.

Patrick Lyons, found dead on the public road.

Mrs. Grimes found dead in a heap of straw at the rere of this town, and a son of hers found dead the day before on the public road.

Laurence Kelly found dead in a field.

Patrick Cain, dropped dead in a field at heathlawn, near this town.

Tom Clary, found dead this morning in the ruins of a deserted house.

I have now to give you a list of no less than five human beings of the same family who on yesterday fell victims to starvation in this parish—

Owen Moran crept into his brother's house and died; the same day his brother, Larry, was found dead in a field; the same day his sister, Mrs. Whelan, with her husband and child, found dead in a deserted forge. What a sad spectacle! The two brothers, the sister, the brother-in-law, and child all dead the same day.

Recreated from The Waterford News, Waterford, May 11, 1849.

LORD JOHN RUSSELL.

Lord John is past the prime of life, considerably under the middle size, with a forehead more remarkable for its lowness than any other characteristic. Though the body be small yet the head is large, and not at all in proportion to the diminutive physique of his lordship; and in particular the extraordinary length of his cranium—a bald furrow running lengthwise over the whole ridge—will attract attention. Still more, if his lordship should for a moment be roused out of his usual musing attitude, his hat over his brows, and his head sunk on his breast—his insignificant features are redeemed by a remarkably penetrating eye sunk deep in his forehead. Those who are familiar with the portrait of Lord Nelson——with his thin wasted features, and grave and mildly melancholy expression of countenance—will have no very unfaithful idea of the aspect and bearing of the present premier of England.—*Hogg's Messenger.*

Reprinted from The Waterford News, Waterford, May 11, 1849.

Dr. Franklin, in speaking of education, says—"if a man empties his purse into his head, no man can take it from him."

The landlords in Clare who turned out their tenantry some time since to starve, are now suffering for want of them to till their land. In few instances only tenantry can be obtained.

A bailiff was murdered by a party of men on Thursday night, about a mile from Frankfort, Tipperary, and his comrade was almost killed.—The cause was, for having arrested a man under a civil bill decree, and conveyed him to gaol.

Lord Eglington's *Flying Dutchman* won the Derby at Epsom on Wednesday by half a length. 26 horses started.

Reprinted from The Waterford News, Waterford, May 25, 1849.

NATIONAL MEMORIAL.

The following has been sent through all Ireland for signature:—

To his Excellency the Earl of Clarendon, the Lord Lieutenant, &c.

MAY IT PLEASE YOUR EXCELLENCY.—We, the undersigned inhabitants of Dublin, desire, most respectfully, to represent to your Excellency the general feeling of this city, with regard to Wm. Smith O'Brien and the other state prisoners at present confined in Richmond Bridewell.

The high personal character which these gentlemen bear, their long sufferings in prison, and their serious pecuniary losses, have excited lively and universal interest in their fate among all classes of society. And men who are unalterably opposed to all their political opinions are most sincerely anxious that their lives should not be wasted in painful exile or protracted imprisonment.

The sincere humanity and respect for property which they are known to have exhibited under trying circumstances, have deepened this sympathy in their favour. And we are thoroughly convinced, and can therefore most respectfully and most confidently represent it to your Excellency, that it will meet the general wishes of the country—now restored to profound peace—if their sentence be commuted to the smallest punishment your Excellency may deem fit.

Trusting that your Excellency will take the prayer of this memorial into your gracious consideration with that humane spirit which will meet the wishes of the country, and which you have hitherto evinced towards them, your memorialists as in duty bound will ever pray.

Recreated from The Waterford News, Waterford, May 25, 1849.

AN IMPORTANT FACT!—The Duke of Wellington rides every day to and from the House of Lords, in his favourite blue frock coat, and white duck trowsers.

Some of the Cork Insurance Offices have got instructions to charge an additional rate of premium on the lives of medical men and clergymen.

Constable O'Malley found a gun and two pistols concealed in an old wall at Ballinareena. The gun was newly stocked by a house carpenter.

Quinlan (Cud), late of the 84th Regt., who was sentenced to be hanged at Clonmel for murder, is to be transported for life.

Mr. John Murphy, coppersmith and bell founder, of James-st., on Saturday obtained a verdict of £150 damages in the Exchequer court against Mr. James Kennedy, his father-in-law, for board and lodging of defendant's wife.

RESTORING A HUSBAND.

A Mrs. O'Brien, potato huxter very meekly and modestly appeared before the bench to solicit a restitution of conjugal rights. Mr. O'Brien who, it appears, is rather rakishly and intemperately inclined, was in the habit of taking money by force from his better half whilst plying her vocation on the quay. She called the civil authorities and had him consigned to a dungeon. She felt lonesome on Saturday night, and on Sunday thought he was punished enough.

Magistrate—And I suppose you thought yourself punished enough too?

Mrs. O'Brien—Indeed I did, your worships; but he threatens not to come out now to vex me!

The magistrates ordered the husband to be restored to the owner.

There was nothing of interest on Tuesday.

THE SLAVE TRADE.—On the 2d of March, H.M. brig *Philomel* captured, after a most exciting chase for ten hours, 110 miles south-west of Ambriz, a large schooner, with 600 slaves on board.

ATTEMPTED ASSASSINATION OF HER MAJESTY.

On Saturday, the anniversary of the natal day of our gracious Sovereign, as the royal cortege was proceeding to Buckingham Palace, after the Drawing Room, she was fired at by one of the many loungers who on public occasions are always to be found in the Park anxious to get a glimpse of royalty. That assassinaton was not the object as the heading to the *Observer's* reports might seem to indicate, will, we think, be apparent to all who read the details of the atrocity, together with the examination of the culprit, as subjoined from our contemporary. That there does not exist a man on British ground who would not stake his life to preserve that of her Majesty we firmly believe—that there is not an Irishman, under the canopy of high Heaven who would molest her sacred person we would stake our existence. No bullet was found after the shot was fired, and had the weapon been loaded her Majesty's equerry, it will be seen, according to all rules of projectiles, would have received its contents.

London, Sunday, Afternoon.

According to information received this afternoon, it appears that Prince Albert was not with her Majesty when the attempt was made. Her Majesty was taking an airing with the Royal children, and was not the least alarmed. After arriving at the Palace the Queen walked in the garden with Prince Albert. The prisoner has stated that the pistol was not loaded with ball or shot, and his object was to gain notoriety and some temporary relief, he being out of employment. Her Majesty is perfectly well, and the inquiries at the Palace have been very numerous.

Reprinted from The Waterford News, Waterford, May 25, 1849.

THE STATE PRISONERS.

(*From the Evening Freeman of Saturday.*)

We are informed, upon good authority, the arrangements are already completed by the government for the deportation of the state prisoners. The convict ship by which it is intended they shall be despatched is now lying in an English harbour. We understand it is the intention of the government to send the Irish convicts in her. She will carry a large number of English convicts. This intelligence, which reached us through a private channel, is confirmed by the following paragraph from a Portsmouth paper:—

"The convict ship *Mountstuart Elphinstone*, having embarked yesterday about thirty prisoners from the hulks at this port, sailed at an early hour this morning for Moreton Bay, Australia. She calls at Portland for a few more prisoners. There is a rumour that the Irish rebel leaders are to take passage in her. This is certain, that a stricter system is enforced in her than has ever before been observed, and that there are certain reserved berths on board unoccupied."

EVENING FREEMAN OFFICE,
Half-past Three o'Clock.

It will be seen by the following letter, just received by the committee, that the Lord Lieutenant has appointed Tuesday next, at half-past three o'clock, for the presentation of the memorial. This will afford some additional time for obtaining further signatures, and for the arrival from the country of gentlemen who are to be the deputation:—

Viceregal Lodge, June 2, 1849.

SIR—In reply to your communication of the 1st instant I beg to apprise you, for the information of the committee, that his Excellency the Lord Lieutenant will be prepared to receive the deputation of the memorialists on behalf of William Smith O'Brien and the other state prisoners contained in Richmond Bridewell, at half-past three o'clock, on Tuesday next (June 5th), at the Viceregal Lodge.

I have the honour to be, Sir, your most obedient servant,

J. CORRY CONNELLAN.

The *Packet* of Saturday evening, after quoting the intelligence respecting the state prisoners published in the morning *Freeman* of that day, said—

Since the above was in type, we have been informed that an official letter has been addressed by Sir George Grey to Sir Lucius O'Brien, instructing him that a transport ship with 250 convicts on board, was about to sail from Portsmouth for Ireland, in order to convey the state prisoners to Van Diemen's Land. This letter was received yesterday by the Dowager Lady O'Brien, who immediately proceeded to Richmond Prison and communicated its contents to her son and his fellow-prisoners. They heard the pronouncement of their doom with calm fortitude.

It is expected that they will be conveyed, in the first instance, per steam ship, to Spike Island, to be transported thence to the penal settlement selected as the scene of their punishment.

Although it may be too late, after the receipt of such an official communication, to endeavour to alter the determination of her Majesty's advisers, we still think it right that they should be informed of the impression that exists among all creeds and classes against the banishment of these gentlemen, misguided and guilty though they have been. It is, we have the best reason for believing, the general opinion that they might be sufficiently punished by imprisonment in any of her Majesty's fortresses at home—such as has been the doom of the English Chartists, who were far greater criminals in intent—witness the hand-grenades and the horrible fireballs seized in the heart of London. We would be the last to give circulation to this opinion if we were not convinced that there could be no danger whatever involved in such a proceeding, and we would not at any future time counsel their liberation, unless bail, the most solvent, and to such an amount as would be deemed ample security, would be given for their future good conduct.

We do think their imprisonment would have this advantage. It would not be dwelt on, as assuredly their banishment will, by thousands of Irishmen with exasperated feeling.

We, their uncompromising antagonist, have now done our duty. It remains for the government, with the knowledge of these facts, to do theirs.

DISTRESS IN IRELAND.

LORD JOHN RUSSELL—THE REV. MR. ANDERSON.

In the London journals which reached us yesterday we saw, the words "Distress in Ireland," in large type, immediately succeeded by the words "Lord John Russell rose," &c. &c. We read on with avidity, and said, as we re-assured ourselves that the Premier had risen to address the house on "Irish distress," conscience has at last asserted its prerogative, and the minister, coerced by its goadings, is about to propose some plan for the alleviation of the appalling misery which oppresses and decimates this land! But, alas! it was *not* for this purpose the Premier interrupted the ordinary proceedings of the house. Far different were his objects. He had discovered an error in *one* of the cases incidentally used in a recent letter from the pen of the humane Rector of Ballinrobe, in illustration of the dire sufferings of the people, and it was to proclaim the "falsity" of the isolated case used to illustrate the general distress, and *not* to propound remedies, that the Premier manifested such haste to call attention to "*distress in Ireland!*"

Recreated from The Freeman's Journal, Dublin, June 4, 1849.

STATE OF THE TIMES.

A farmer of six acres of land, in the parish of Youghal in the Nenagh Union, gave up his holding last week to qualify himself for relief in or out of the workhouse.

Mr. Hunt, of Limerick, attorney, agent of an extensive property in the parish of Youghal, was engaged Thursday in getting up the houses and lands of a number of persons who abandoned their tenements in order to get relief out of the rates. Over twenty families left their houses on this occasion.

I beg to inform you of the awful and terrific state of this locality particularly the parish of Clonrush. Mr. Waley, of Dublin, has, on this week, evicted fifty families, consisting of about 400 persons, who are evermore added to the pauperism, though once respectable and some of them even aboriginal inhabitants of the parish.—*Tipperary Vindicator.*

Recreated from The Freeman's Journal, Dublin, June 5, 1849.

FASHIONABLE INTELLIGENCE.

DEPARTURE OF HER MAJESTY AND THE COURT FOR WINDSOR CASTLE, FOR ASCOT RACES.—Her Majesty and the Prince Consort, accompanied by the royal children, and attended by Viscountess Canning, the Earl of Listowel, the Maids of Honour in waiting, and members of the household, left Buckingham Palace on Monday afternoon, escorted by a party of the 11th Hussars, for the Paddington terminus, when a special train conveyed them to the Slough station, where a party of the 2d Life Guards escorted the august party to the Castle. Her Majesty will give sumptuous banquets in St. George's-hall to her distinguished visitors, and will honour the course with her presence, it is expected, accompanied by her illustrious guests on the days of the races. The court will return to London on Friday.

Recreated from The Freeman's Journal, Dublin, June 6, 1849.

STATE OF IRELAND.

TOOMEVARA!—LIVING AMONG THE DEAD!!—The condition of the wretched people of this ruined village continues as deplorable as ever. We do not know what movement the board of guardians has made in their regard; but we have heard that a person of the name of Wilson, who has been stopping in Toomevara at Donoghue the bailiffs house for the last few weeks, and who is said to be an agent on the Massy Dawson estates, besought the Rev. Mr. Meagher, P.P., to advise the people to leave the village and proceed to the workhouse; but the fact is that the establishment contains, by some hundreds, more inmates than the sealed order of the commissioners permits; and we do think that the best thing that could be done for the miserable poor of that most wretched district is to procure house accommodation for them forthwith, as in the event of a change in the weather it is impossible to say what may become of them. They are all congregated in squalid huts near the Chapel walls; some of them have got into the graveyards adjoining, where they have endeavoured to make huts for themselves also, but their condition in the churchyards can better be imagined than described; it is enough to state that nothing can possibly be more afflicting in every sense of the word.—*Tipperary Vindicator.*

DEATH FROM STARVATION.—On Sunday evening a man of the name of Egan died of starvation in William-street. He was one of the witnesses in the prosecution of the parties who were found guilty of the diabolical attempt to assassinate R. U. Bayly, Esq. He received from the crown £20; which he lavishly expended in England and then returned to this country a beggar. The unfortunate man's body presented a frightfully emaciated appearance, and indicated that he died from want of the common necessaries of life.—*Armagh Guardian.*

NENAGH PRISON.—This prison is fearfully crowded with destitute persons committed for most trivial offenses. Over 700 prisoners are now in gaol, and yesterday (Tuesday) 50 vagrants from Thurles were added.—*Tipperary Vindicator.*

EVICTION.—On the 1st inst., six families, numbering thirty individuals, were evicted from their holdings, at Cloneyharp, near Thurles, and their houses were levelled.—*Armagh Guardian.*

THE OLD STORY OVER AGAIN—DEATH.

Alas! alas! as our week's labours progress, our hearts are only more and more sickened by the same fearful cry which has so long appalled the public—death, death, death.

Truly did the Rev. Mr. Anderson declare in his painfully eloquent letter to Lord John Russell—"I can with truth assure your lordship, that independently of what I daily witness myself, every one I meet, in every grade of life, has something so mournful to relate, that *no language can depict* the miserable condition of the *whole* west of Ireland. The police themselves can well attest it, for they are discovering dead bodies amongst the walls of ruined habitations, or rather hovels, and find them the frightful prey of rats and scarecrows! Thus it is, my lord, that the f*amine progresses*—and, oh! how awful the prospect for at least two or three months to come."

Similar in tone, and fearful foreboding are the resolutions passed at a public meeting in Ballintubber Abbey on last Saturday, "We owe it to our feelings as men and Christians," say those who attended that meeting, "*to make one last effort to save the lives of thousands in this district now actually sinking under all the horrors of hunger.*"

Recreated from The Freeman's Journal, Dublin, June 7, 1849.

DEPUTATION TO THE LORD LIEUTENANT.

TUESDAY.—This day, at half-past three o'clock, the deputation appointed to present the memorial praying for a commutation of the sentence on William Smith O'Brien and his fellow-prisoners, waited on the Lord Lieutenant, at the Viceregal Lodge.

The memorial having been read to his Excellency by the Lord Mayor of Dublin, Lord Clarendon read the following brief reply:—

"My Lord Mayor and Gentlemen,
From the moment the sentence of the law was pronounced upon the prisoners, on whose behalf you have addressed me, I have felt bound to give the most anxious consideration to the unhappy condition in which they were placed, so far as I could pay regard to their situation, consistently with the obligations imposed on me in the exercise of those powers and prerogatives of the Crown with which I am invested.

I have felt deeply concerned for the unfortunate situation of men whose lives are forfeited to the offended laws of their country, but an imperative duty compels me to look to the nature and character of the crime of which they were convicted—to the circumstances proceeding and attending it, and above all, to the consequence which might have resulted from its temporary success.

I cannot disregard matters unfortunately too notorious: the disturbance of the public peace—the dislocation of society for many weeks throughout an extensive district—the armed opposition to the constituted authorities of the realm—the serious loss of life among the poor, misguided followers of the prisoners—the utter havoc which seemed, for a brief time, impending over many parts of the country from their wild and desperate proceedings—their avowed rebellion and treason against her Majesty, and her rights to the Crown and Sovereign of Ireland.

I fully appreciate the motives of humanity which have prompted this appeal, but in reply to it I have at present only to assure you that the government, in performance of its duty, can have no other desire than that justice should be administered without any severity beyond that which the interests of society demand."

The deputation, who were pleased with their courteous reception, then withdrew, the interview not having lasted more than fifteen minutes.

Recreated from The Freeman's Journal, Dublin, June 8, 1849.

THE STATE PRISONERS.

Thursday Mr. Marquiss, the governor of Richmond Bridewell, received a notification from the Lord Lieutenant that the sentence of death, which had been passed on the state prisoners, Messrs. Smith O'Brien, Thomas Francis Meagher, Terence Bellew M'Manus, and Patrick O'Donohoe had been commuted to transportation for life.

No orders had been received up to last night in reference to the removal of the state prisoners, although it was confidently asserted through town yesterday, that they were removed at an early hour yesterday morning. A considerable number of persons on the Circular road, near the prison, during last evening, trying to ascertain something in reference to the prisoners.

The committee who have acted with so much zeal and effect in getting up the memorial in the state prisoners, considering that its prayer was not complied with, have resolved to continue their exertions until they lay the memorial at the foot of the throne.

Reprinted from The Waterford News, Waterford, June 8, 1849.

THE STATE CONVICTS—AND THEIR DOOM.

The law is at length about to be vindicated, and the interests of society avenged, upon the misguided men who, in the summer of last year, sought to organise a rebellion against her Majesty's Crown and Dignity in Ireland. The memorial on their behalf, which, it appears, was signed by nearly one hundred and fifty thousand persons, of all parties, classes, and creeds in the country, was on Tuesday presented to the Lord Lieutenant, and, as will be seen, without avail. His Excellency's reply was distinguished as much by its courtesy and kindly feeling as by its firmness, and it amounted to a positive refusal of the prayer of the memorial, assuring the deputation that "justice should be administered, without any severity beyond that which the interests of society demand." In another country, or another age, or coming from the lips of another man less guided by pure motives, humane feelings, and thorough sincerity, we should consider such a reply a too evasive and elastic one, which might mean the infliction of any punishment between the extremes of the utmost severity and the most culpable indulgence. We have instances of both degrees already in treatment of State and other prisoners. We find the good and pious man, who became amenable to the laws while simply obeying the behests of conscience and duty languishing in a dungeon; and we have seen the crimes of traitors rewarded by honours, and their losses made good by indemnity bills. But there is no reason to fear that Mr. Smith O'Brien and his accomplices will endure more or less than the amount of punishment due to their crimes, that punishment which, if the original sentence had been carried out, might have terminated their existence by a disgraceful death, has been commuted to transportation for life; and, perhaps, as we write, the unhappy victims of their own deluded imaginations and perverted aspirations are now on their way to the cheerless and hopeless exile which awaits them. All must lament the infatuation which hurried men of high standing, polite education, and perhaps keen sensitiveness to the taint of disgrace, into such a position as now ranks them with vulgar caitiffs and felons of the darker shades of crime; but none who calmly reason upon crimes and their consequences will say that their doom has not been deserved. Were guilt of great magnitude to escape with impunity, merely because its perpetrators were men of gallant bearing, heroic fortitude, and amiability of disposition, then, indeed,

"*Would vice be honoured, virtue vice obey*;"

and the very foundations of the moral world would be upheaved in a chaos in which mankind could not live or breathe. It is, therefore, necessary, in estimating the true deserts of these men, to keep steadily in view the *consequences* of their crimes, so clearly and succinctly enumerated by his Excellency—"the disturbance of the public peace—the dislocation of society for many weeks through an extensive district—the armed opposition to the constituted authorities of the realm—the serious loss of life among their poor misguided followers—the utter havoc which seemed for a brief time impending over many parts of the country, from their wild and desperate proceedings—their avowed rebellion and treason." That so many as one hundred and fifty thousand of our countrymen should have forgotten these things, in their anxiety for the pardon of the criminals, seems strange to all who do not recollect the proneness of the public mind to forget *public* injuries, and only to remember private virtues, and more so to those who seem to forget that to vast multitudes, unhappily, these men leave our shores with the departing *prestige* of martyrdom. We cannot but feel satisfied with his Excellency's determination in rejecting a petition on behalf of criminals, who, so far from acknowledging their guilt, still glory in it, either too weak or too wicked to make even this poor atonement to the violated laws of their country.

It appears, however, that the memorialists are not content with the mild and courteous refusal of the Lord Lieutenant. The *Freeman's Journal* informs us that "The committee, who have acted with so much zeal and *effect* (?) in getting up the memorial on behalf of the State prisoners, considering that its prayer was not complied with, have resolved to continue their exertions until they lay the memorial at the foot of the throne." We predict, however, that, until Mr. Smith O'Brien and his fellow-convicts *lay their contrition at the foot of the throne*, the step will be premature.

FATAL ACCIDENT.—CORONER'S INQUEST.—An inquest was held yesterday, at the house of a man named Jefferson, in John-street, before J.K. Jackson, Esq., and a jury, upon the body of a woman named Campbell, the wife of a weaver, who came by her death in the following circumstances:—

The deceased, with her husband, who resided in Ballymacarrett, came into town on Wednesday afternoon for the purpose of seeing her sister previous to the departure of the latter for America. They stopped at Jefferson's house to get some refreshment, and after eating their dinner, sent out for two pints of whiskey and a gallon of porter. The usual consequence of overindulgence arose. A disturbance took place between the husband and another man who was in the room, and the husband ordered deceased to go down stairs, while they remained inside to settle the difference. She went down, until she got to an awkward turn in the staircase, when, missing her footing, she fell to the bottom, fracturing her skull. She lingered till eight o'clock in the evening, when she died. The jury returned a verdict of "Accidental death."

Recreated from The Belfast News-Letter, Belfast, June 8, 1849.

HER MAJESTY'S SUMMER CRUISE.—It is said the services of the Royal yacht Victoria and Albert will be brought into requisition some time towards the latter end of July, when it is confidently asserted that her Majesty, Prince Albert, and the Royal children, will proceed in her to Scotland.

WATERFORD POLICE OFFICE.

WEDNESDAY.

The magistrates present this morning at eleven o'clock were, the Right Worshipful, the Mayor, and Dr. Mackesy.

SHOPLIFTING.

Constable Barrett brought up a female, who gave her name as Biddy Hanlor, and stated that she came from the county Limerick, charged with having some calicoes, and other goods, supposed to have been stolen.

The prisoner stated that the articles found on her were her own property.

The Mayor—Where did you get those articles?

Prisoner—I bought them in the town of Limerick, your worship.

The Mayor—I am certainly of opinion that you must have stolen those goods; however, it is very fortunate for you that no person is coming forward to prosecute; under these circumstances I very reluctantly must discharge you, but you will not be permitted to remain in town, and you must be put outside of the city by the police. I cannot allow a suspicious character of your description to remain in Waterford.

Prisoner—I intend to go home, to-morrow, your worship.

The Mayor—I will not permit you to remain, you must be put over the bridge at once.

Reprinted from The Waterford News, Waterford, June 8, 1849.

STATE OF IRELAND.

The Clearance System.—We regret to state that this horrible system progresses with the certain destructiveness of the plague throughout the country. No part of Tipperary is exempt from its influence; and all manner of landlords appear to be bitten by the mania to get rid of the poor Irish tenant, who, when the land yielded fruit, toiled like a galley slave for those who now turn upon, and treat him with the basest ingratitude. We have heard that no less than FOUR HUNDRED AND FIFTY notices of ejectment have been served on one or two properties not many miles from Borrisokane; and we learn that THREE HUNDRED miserable beings were sent on the world from a property near Clonmel; that five houses were levelled and forty persons were turned off on the lands of Knocknaclara—thirty-six persons off the lands of Knockakelly, near Slievenamon—one hundred and six off the lands of Ashgrove, near Caher, under the Court of the Chancery ! ! !—forty-four off the lands of Barnclough, twenty-three off another property, seventy-eight off another, and twenty off another! Good God where is this sweeping system of wholesale extermination to end! Here are SIX HUNDRED AND FORTY-SEVEN HUMAN BEINGS sent on the bleak ocean of a cheerless world to swell the tide of misery which swallows up the substance of every struggling man in the community! We challenge the world for a parallel to such scenes.—*Tipperary Vindicator.*

Daring Outrage.—On Tuesday last three armed ruffians entered a field where three men were ploughing for Lord Dunally, and from which a man named Mara was dispossessed some short time ago. They desired the ploughmen to quit the field at once; but they having refused to do so, or to comply with the intimidating mandate, a shot was then fired, one of the workman named Rigney had a providential escape. Another shot was also fired, whereupon the ploughmen untackled their horses, and quitted the field.—*Nenagh Guardian.*

Mutilating Cattle.—On the night of the 4th instant, some evil-minded fellows, who appeared to be armed, entered some fields at Toomavara, where a large number of cattle, the property of different persons, was grazing. The fields are the property of the Rev. Massy Dawson. The ruffians cut off the tails of two cows, the property of Michael Boland, of Poulakers, and off two cows belonging to Phillip Burke, of Granne. A cow, the property of a man named M'Donnell, was dangerously cut in the back and sides with some sharp instrument, and also the horn of a heifer of his was cut and mutilated. These cows are rendered perfectly useless to the owners for the present, for they will not give milk, neither are they salable.

The *Nenagh Guardian*—Tory and landlord organ—from which we quote, goes on to say:—

"The cause of this outrage is, to prevent parties from bringing their cattle to graze on those fields, and to let Mr. Dawson see the vindictive spirit which exists against him in the 'Terry Alt camp' for having exercised his just rights!!!"

The County Galway Gaol.—During the last week there were fifty convicts removed from this prison for transportation; and there are upwards of seventy more under like sentence. The total number of prisoners now in custody is 681, one hundred and thirty of whom are in hospital.

Incendiarism.—On Thursday 10 stacks of oats the property of John Maher, Esq., were maliciously burned at Tullamaine.—*Tipperary Free Press.*

Recreated from The Freeman's Journal, Dublin, June 12, 1849.

DUBLIN, Monday Morning.

[FROM OUR OWN CORRESPONDENT.]

Countermand of the Order of the Removal of the State Prisoners.—As I apprised you in my last, the State prisoners were to have been removed by the Trident war steamer from Dublin to Cove, there to be placed on board the convict ship for Australia. The commander of the Trident had received orders to proceed from Kingstown to the entrance of the harbour at the North Wall, in order to take Mr. Smith O'Brien and his fellow prisoners on board on Saturday night, and have all in readiness for sailing at daylight yesterday (Sunday) morning.

The prisoners had received the necessary official initiation representing their intended removal, and they had, in consequence, made all needful preparations on Saturday evening. A large body of mounted police were ordered to be in attendance at Richmond Bridewell; but about nine o'clock counter-orders were issued to the commander of the Trident, as well as to the police, and the State prisoners have since remained in the old quarters.

It appears that Mr. Smith O'Brien took steps to protest against the commutation of his sentence to transportation for life. A copy of the order for his detention in Richmond Bridewell was required from the Government, and his agent was referred to the Crown-office of the Queen's Bench, where a copy of the order of that court was obtained, to the effect, that Mr. Smith O'Brien and his fellow prisoners should be kept in safe custody until removed by due course of law. Subsequently notices were served, on behalf of Mr. Smith O'Brien, upon the Under Secretary, the High Sheriff of Dublin, and the Governor of Richmond Bridewell, warning them to hold their prisoner in safe keeping until he should be removed "by due course of law." It seems that none of the other state prisoners adopted this course; but Mr. Smith O'Brien, it is stated, has obtained high legal opinion that no commutation of the sentence for high treason can take place unless the prisoner should be a consenting party.

At all events, there has been a suspension of the order for the removal of the state prisoners to the convict ship; and it is now difficult to speculate upon the course that may be adopted regarding them.

Mr. Meagher, M.P., father of one of the state prisoners, sailed from Kingstown yesterday afternoon for London.

Recreated from The Morning Chronicle, London, June 12, 1849.

THE STATE PRISONERS.

A paragraph in the government organ of last night, the *Evening Post*, would lead its readers to believe that the state prisoners have protested against any commutation of the sentence of death passed on them at Clonmel. If that was the impression intended to have been conveyed to the public by that paragraph, we are enabled in the most positive manner to contradict that statement.

It is quite true that the state prisoners have refused to assent to the course proposed by government of sending them beyond the seas; but it is totally untrue that they in any way claim or insist that the capital sentence should be carried out.

The question at issue between the state prisoners and the government is not whether their sentence should be carried out, but whether, that sentence having been commuted to imprisonment, they should be imprisoned in this country or Van Diemen's Land.

Recreated from The Freeman's Journal, Dublin, June 13, 1849.

THE STATE CONVICTS—THE ROYAL CLEMENCY REPUDIATED.

We recollect the story of the poor Frenchman, whom Lindley Murray tells us once cried out, "I will be drowned, and nobody shall save me!" Change the word, and this is now the outcry of the convicted Irish traitors—"We will be hanged, and nobody shall save us!" They have, one and all, rejected the proffered mercy of the Crown in commuting the extreme sentence of the law to that of transportation for life. Mr. Patrick O'Donohue has written a formal piece of impertinence "to his Excellency the Lord Lieutenant, the Attorney-General for Ireland. T. N. Redington, and Wm. Kemmis, *esquires*", (imagine "His Excellency the Lord Lieutenant, esquire!") informing them, that, lest his silence should appear to give consent, he is not a consenting party to the commuted sentence being carried into execution, the same being, as he is informed by eminent counsel, "unconstitutional and contrary to law." Mr. Meagher, it appears, has also forwarded letters to the same effect, to the same quarters; and we perceive by the Parliamentary reports that Mr. Smith O'Brien, who is well-versed in the tactics of pseudo-martyrdom, has presented a petition to the House of Commons through Mr. Mousell, objecting, "on legal grounds", to the sentence of transportation contrary to his consent. It is eminently ridiculous to find these convicted transgressors and defiers of the law insisting upon constitutional and legal rights, and demanding a decision upon the predicament in which they have placed the Government, on legal grounds. They stand upon the law—and not merely upon Irish law—but upon that English law which they have so often ridiculed, and evaded, and affected to despise. They insist, forsooth, upon the completion of the original sentence. They demand a martyr's death by the rope of the hangman in preference to an exile in Van Diemen's Land. Smith O'Brien, at least, was not always so enamoured of the grisly tyrant, especially when he ducked aside from the policeman's bullet under the Widow M'Cormack's cabbages; nor could his fellow-traitors be suspected of any particular desire to wear a hempen cravat when they pleaded not guilty to the capital charge of treason, and wearied out the patience of all, and the lingering sympathy of some, by their contumacious obstructions to the course of justice. But their present procedure is so palpable and transparent a dodge, that we are surprised any sensible man, much less a sensible journalist, could affect not to see through it; and yet we find our respected contemporary, the *Evening Packet*, gravely asserting that the first and most palpable of the two courses open to the Government is, "to permit the voluntary expatriation of the prisoners on parole", a course that would at once relieve the Executive from all difficulty, and be gratefully appreciated by the country, as an act of *considerate* clemency." Now, we beg to know, in the first place, what right have these convicts to any further "considerate" clemency than that which has been proffered to them? It was extreme considerateness in the Government to cancel the capital sentence, and it is because these men audaciously and contumaciously, and what is worse, maliciously, spurn the mercy of their Sovereign, they are to be considerately let loose to plan fresh treason against Britain with D'Arcy M'Gee in New York, or to conduct a descent upon England with the Red Republicans of France? In the next place, we ask, upon what grounds is it assumed that "the country" would gratefully appreciate the voluntary expatriation on parole of this dangerous knot of traitors? The country—at least the loyal portion of it—is not quite so sympathy-smitten with traitors and treason, or so abandoned of common sense, as this comes to. The hesitation, however, of the Government is ominous. Either they should at once carry the commuted sentence into execution, and ask for a bill of indemnity, or they should give the convicts the full benefit of "the law" upon which they insist. The sight of the scaffold would soon test the sincerity of the martyrs.

Recreated from The Belfast News-Letter, Belfast, June 15, 1849.

THE CHARGE OF SHOOTING AT HER MAJESTY.

CRIMINAL COURT—LONDON, THURSDAY.

Before the Lord Chief Justice Wilde, Mr. Justice Patteson, and Mr. Baron Rolfe.—

Immediately after the learned judges had taken their seats on the bench, William Hamilton, aged 23, described as a bricklayer was placed in the dock, and charged with having "in a certain public place, called the Green-park, a loaded pistol, which he did point, aim, present, and discharge at and near the person of our Sovereign Lady the Queen, with intent to break the public peace and alarm our said Lady the Queen."

The Attorney-General, Mr. Bodkin, Mr. Wells, and Mr. Clarke, appeared for the prosecution. The prisoner was not represented by counsel.

The indictment having been read over by the clerk of the court, the prisoner, who was attired in the garb of a bricklayer's labourer, such as a white fustian jacket and trousers, was called upon to plead, when he did so in a subdued tone of voice, pleading guilty.

The prisoner was then asked if he could state any reason why the judgement of the court should not be passed upon him, but he made no reply.

The learned judges then consulted together for a short time, when the Chief Justice passed sentence upon the prisoner in the following terms:—"Prisoner, you have pleaded guilty to an offence created by an act of parliament, of the 5th and 6th Victoria, and your crime consisted in the fact of your having discharged a pistol loaded with gunpowder at or near the person of her Majesty, with intent to alarm her. This is the offence to which you have pleaded guilty, and although in some cases, it may be desirable that all the particulars under which a charge is preferred should be made public, yet your case is so simple and clear that it is not an inconvenient circumstance that you should have pleaded guilty to the charge made against you. The case against you was perfectly clear, and the offence imputed to you is that of having offered a gross insult to her Majesty. There is no ground for supposing that you intended to do her Majesty any personal injury; indeed the weapon you used appeared hardly capable of doing mischief. The manner in which it was loaded also tended to confirm that impression, it being the opinion of persons well conversant with the nature of fire-arms, from the sound of the report and other circumstances, that the pistol was merely loaded with powder, and that no ball had been placed in it. There appears, therefore, to be no manner of doubt that you are free from the guilt of intending any personal injury to her Majesty, and it is also equally clear that you had no associates, but that it was your own individual act to commit this gross insult upon her Majesty. It is difficult to imagine what motive you could have had for the commission of this act, and it appears only to be attributable to an unfortunate desire to obtain notoriety and attract public attention for a short period, without any intention really to injure her Majesty.

"As, therefore, notoriety was your only motive for committing this mischievous act, it is necessary that you and others of similar propensities should be taught that such notoriety is very short-lived, and it is speedily followed by a sentence involving a considerable amount of degradation and suffering. The sentence upon you, therefore, is, as a punishment for your offence and as a warning to others, that you be transported beyond the seas for the term of seven years."

The prisoner, who heard the sentence with apparent indifference, and without making any observation, was then removed from the bar.

Recreated from The Freeman's Journal, Dublin, June 16, 1849.

THE MARTYRS.

Nearly every one is aware that these ill-fated men are now breasting the billows towards the penal spot to which they are destined. The people, we may remark, have been somewhat disappointed; for nearly every one of every creed and class, imagined that they would not have been sent out of the country before the arrival of the Queen. They are, however, gone; and gone at a time just when a gleam of hope, of confidence, of prosperity—shall we say?—was beginning to smile on the old land of their birth!

We feel for their fate. But we deeply feel and most truly regret the sad fate of our learned young Citizen and friend—THOMAS FRANCIS MEAGHER. Eschewing politics altogether, we may now remark that we never did business for a more off-handed or a more honourable man. What an affliction, what a reverse of fortune expatriation must be to him, in the prime of youth, and manhood, and genius, and affluence!

He is gone! Never more to see parent, friends, relatives, the domestic hearth, or his "dear old land!" He is gone! after having loved Ireland "not wisely but too well!"

Reprinted from The Waterford News, Waterford, July 13, 1849.

HORRIBLE.—Mr. Gilbert Lloyd, of Millview, Kanturk, made application to the magistrates on Saturday to have the dogs of the neighbourhood logged, as he stated that his men found the *leg and arm of a corpse* near his house after being devoured by dogs, and he, in person, was compelled to force away some dogs on yesterday from *another corpse, after devouring the head and neck, and destroying the entire body.—Cork Examiner.*

Reprinted from The Waterford News, Waterford, July 27, 1849.

THE QUEEN'S VISIT.

A Royal standard will be hoisted at Duncannon Fort while the squadron will be passing our harbour, and the heavy ordnance of the Fort will fire a salute.

An address has been drawn up by the Archbishop of Dublin, and submitted for signature to all the Irish Catholic Prelates, to be presented to her Majesty.

Her Majesty will hold a full-dress levee and drawing-room at Dublin Castle in the course of next week.

The Marquess of Waterford is to be in Dublin during the Queen's stay.

All addresses are to be either sent to the Secretary of State for presentation, or to be addressed to her Majesty at the levee.

It is said her Majesty will visit the Giant's Causeway on the 14th inst.

Triumval arches are to be erected in Dublin. £50 was expended in the purchase of Blackpool ginghams, which will be afterwards handed over to the Ladies Clothing Society for the benefit of the poor.

The Queen will wear a dress of rich blue Irish tabinet on her entry to Dublin.

Tents will be erected in Phoenix Park for the encampment of troops during the royal visit.

The public institutions in Dublin will be visited by her Majesty.

The Corporation of Limerick will dine at the Mansion House, Dublin, they have been invited by the Lord Mayor.

All the public institutions in Dublin will be lit with gas on the night of her Majesty's arrival.

The Queen's private carriage is an open barouche, of light and elegant construction, capable of containing two persons only. It is painted royal blue, and lined inside with royal blue tabinet. It will be drawn by four horses only, with postillions and outriders dressed in the private livery of her Majesty.

ACCIDENT AT A CATHOLIC CHAPEL.

Sunday night great alarm was created in parts of London in consequence of a catastrophe at a Roman Catholic chapel. During the last five weeks a spacious building in Charles-street, Drury-lane, formerly a coach-factory, has been opened as a Catholic chapel. Dr. Farre, one of the priests, was announced to preach Sunday night, which drew an overflowing congregation. The large number of persons caused one of the posts near the pulpit to fall out of perpendicular. On this being noticed by some of the congregation, they thought the lower part of the premises was on fire, and immediately the cry was raised. The consternation which ensued it would be impossible to describe, for the front windows being opened, and the crowd below hearing the alarm, shouted out also that the building was in flames, and cried to the people above to make their escape. Dr. Farre in vain called to them to keep their positions but they crowded upon the stairs, and the result was that it fell, with a tremendous crash, throwing 100 persons in confusion on each other. The noise caused the persons at the other end of the chapel to press towards the doors and as fast as they reached they kept falling upon those below. The cries of the latter were truly distressing.—The cry of the fire was still kept up; and two of the congregation, who were nearest the pulpit, immediately leaped out of the window, a distance of 40 feet. They were obliged to be removed to hospital. Fire-engines were brought to the spot, but they were unable to get to the chapel until the arrival of a strong body of police. A frightful scene then presented itself. On the lower landing of the stairs were nearly 100 persons, piled upon each other, and working with all their strength to get away. Inspector Marsh, with a strong muster of police, immediately set to work, and succeeded in pulling the people out. About 20 persons had to be conveyed to hospital on stretchers and in cabs. No person has died as yet.

Recreated from The Waterford News, Waterford, August 3, 1849.

ARRIVAL OF THE QUEEN'S SERVANTS, CARRIAGES, AND HORSES.

The City of Dublin Steam Packet Company's vessel, the Royal William, Captain William Williams, arrived at the North-wall, Dublin, at eight o'clock on Wednesday morning, from Liverpool, having on board three of her Majesty's carriages, twenty-four horses, and seventeen servants. *Packet.*

Reprinted from The Waterford News, Waterford, August 3, 1849.

FASHIONS FOR AUGUST.

BALL DRESS.—Robe of white cartelane muslin or crape, over white satin. The skirt of the dress is made with a broad hem and two tucks, each surmounted by a narrow wreath or cordon of wheat ears, intermingled with blue and red cornflowers. The corsage rather low, and the crape or muslin laid in perpendicular folds. In the centre of the bosom a large *bouquet de corsage*, composed chiefly of coquelicots, daisies, and other wild flowers. Short sleeves, rather wide, gathered on the outside of the arms, and tucked to correspond with the skirt of the dress; each tuck being surmounted by a very narrow cordon of wheat ears and corn-flowers. The hair plaited and fastened closely at the back of the head, where it is confined by an ornamental comb with a gold top. The head is encircled by a wreath of wild flowers, namely, coquelicots, daisies, wheat-ears, and grass, the whole most tastefully intermingled and mounted very fully. A large hand-bouquet of the same flowers. Short white kid gloves, confined at the wrist with jewelled clasps. Pocket-handkerchiefs richly embroidered in an open-work pattern.

In evening dress, ribbon sashes are fashionable. The ribbon should be very broad and tied in front, the ends sufficiently long to hang nearly to the bottom of the dress.

Recreated from The Belfast News-Letter, Belfast, August 7, 1849.

THE QUEEN IN DUBLIN.

ARRIVAL OF HER MAJESTY AND PRINCE ALBERT IN KINGSTOWN.

The various rumours and announcements which were in circulation on Sunday, relative to Queen Victoria and the Prince Consort in the harbour of Kingstown, created a number of conflicting opinions amongst thousands of all classes, who continued to pour out from the city since an early hour in the morning. It was generally known to the Dublin public that her Majesty's yacht, accompanied by the flotilla, cleared out of Cork harbour on Saturday morning at 10 o'clock. It was also known that the royal yacht, instead of carrying on for Dublin, bore up for Tramore Bay, the weather having become somewhat rough, and a strong head wind having sprung up.

Under those circumstances, it was of course impossible, during the earlier part of Sunday, to state with any certainty the exact time at which her Majesty would be likely to reach Kingstown. However, between the hours of three and four o'clock the lookout, stationed at Killiney Head, and several of the gentry residing in the neighbourhood, could perceive, by the assistance of telescopes, the leading vessels of the royal flotilla well round Wicklow Head. The ships approached rapidly, and proved to be the Sphynx, the Stromboli, the Lucifer, and the Trident, forming the advanced squadron of the flotilla. These vessels arrived off Killiney Bay, and lay to awaiting the coming up of the royal yacht and the rest of the fleet.

About seven o'clock her Majesty's yacht bore into sight of those who stood on the lower ground of the piers.—The masts of the royal yacht, which led the squadron, soon became perceptible at Kingstown. The royal yacht first entered the harbour of Kingstown, having at a short distance behind her, and on her quarter, the Fairy and the Vivid. Every steamer in the squadron wore her full suit of gala flags. As the royal steamer approached within 100 yards of the jetty, she there came to moorings amidst a salute of cannon from the ships and yachts at anchor in the harbour, as also from the club-houses on shore. The cheering too was rather enthusiastic. Soon afterwards her Majesty came forth in person from the round-house cabin and approached the quarter-gangway of the yacht, where she stood for some moments. The parties in the boats cheered loudly, and the cheering was taken up by several on board and transferred across the water. Her Majesty bowed repeatedly in acknowledgment of the cheering, waving of hats, &c., that greeted her from the boats. The Queen wore a large plain Dunstable straw bonnet.

After having remained a few moments in the sight of the assemblage her Majesty retired to the deck, or round-house cabin. Immediately after Prince Albert was recognised as he issued from the cabin, and the cheering was repeated. The Prince advanced to the side of the vessel, and gracefully acknowledged the cordial reception accorded to him.

The town was partially illuminated after dark, and some of the hotels were decorated with devices and transparencies.

THE LANDING—MONDAY MORNING.

At ten o'clock the Queen and Prince Albert were seen stepping on the gangway. The Queen was attired in a dress of brown and white spotted muslin, with a visite of pearl-coloured silk and Limerick lace, and a white crepe bonnet. She looked young and animated, smiled, and acknowledged repeatedly the plaudits of those who had the privilege of being near her. She is very like her portraits. His Royal Highness Prince Albert was dressed in a dark-coloured frock coat, and drab trousers. The Prince of Wales, the Princess Royal, and two other of the children were walking immediately after their august parents. Amid enthusiastic plaudits, the royal cortege reached the platform of the railway. The royal standard was immediately hoisted when the royal visitors began to ascend the staircase leading to the terrace. When her Majesty descended to the starting platform she was greeted with loud cheers from the gentlemen who were located there. They next entered the royal carriage.—The Albert engine preceded as a pilot, and the Cyclops engine drew the royal train. The engines were tastefully festooned with evergreens and flowers, and the Cyclops had the royal standard and union jack flying. The royal train went at about half speed. It stopped at Sandymount-lane, where her Majesty's carriages were waiting with outriders, under the command of Major Turner, master of the horse, &c. A group of elegantly-attired ladies greeted the approach of the royal train. A spacious platform was constructed at Sandymount-avenue, to enable the royal party to alight from their carriages in the most convenient manner.

At half-past ten o'clock the word of command was given to receive her Majesty with all the honours due to royalty—the trumpeters' shrill blast rung in the ear, and a vociferous and general cheer, waving of hats, &c. welcomed the royal party as they passed along the platform towards the carriages. The carriage in a few minutes moved slowly on, amidst deafening cheers. The red liveries of the postilions and outriders, the glittering uniforms of the soldiers, and the flags and banners which floated in all directions, contrasting with the corn fields and the green grass of the surrounding meadows, rendered the scene pictorial in a high degree. The Prince of Wales and the Princess Royal were seated in the Queen's carriage, and Prince Alfred and the Princess Alice were in a carriage with the maids of honour. Amongst the carriages immediately succeeding that of her Majesty was Lord Clarendon's private carriage. The high sheriff preceded her Majesty to the city gate from Sandymount-avenue. Some of the gentlemen of the county of Dublin who joined the procession were on horseback, wearing a red scarf each; and the gentlemen of the city of Dublin were also mounted, and ornamented by blue scarfs. A long train of carriages followed the royal party.

ENTRY THROUGH THE CITY GATE.

The royal cortege having passed through Upper Baggot-street, arrived at the Bridge, on the city side of which the grand arch and gate were erected. It was a splendid piece of architecture—127 feet in width, and 92 feet high, consisting of a great arch and wings. The great gate on the centre was 20 feet wide and 35 feet high. It was constructed of wrought iron, and had the letters V.R. on the one compartment, and on the corresponding one A.C., the whole exquisitely decorated with roses and floral wreaths, and surmounted by an immense shamrock branch. Over this stood an architrave ornamented with artificial flowers and laurels supporting the royal arms, with the city arms on either side. The whole was capped with an imperial crown of beautiful workmanship, ten feet in diameter. The inscription on the face of the arch was *Cead Mille Failte*. The side arches were admirably decked with evergreens and heaths, interspersed with roses and the choicest productions of the *parterre*. On the approach of the Queen's carriage, the royal standard of England was hoisted on a flag-staff on the summit; and, from each point on the top, flowing garlands gracefully waived in the breeze. Four City Heralds, or "Beef-Eaters" occupied the pediments at each side, and were attired in grey frocks, of an antique fashion, and with the city arms emblazoned on their points, and red caps and hose. The royal *cortege* having stopped at the bridge, an equerry rode up, and demanded admission for her Majesty into her ancient loyal city of Dublin—the gate was instantly thrown open by the City Marshal, Mr. Thomas Reynold.

Reprinted from The Waterford News, Waterford, August 10, 1849.

THE QUEEN'S VISIT.

(*From the Times.*)

While Ireland has, for years and years, been fretting and chafing for a separation from England, every accident of weal and woe has shown that her only chance of prosperity and safety is bound up in her close connexion with England. Arrayed against England, she has found only defeat and humiliation—leagued with England, sustenance and sympathy. At this moment the Sovereign of the empire goes as the ambassador between two of its constituent nations to extinguish the embers of a flickery jealousy and ratify an amnesty of attempted wrong. The Queen is at this moment the representative of English feeling and forgiveness. She embodies the sentiments of the majority of the English people towards Ireland. Like her English subjects, she entertains the greatest interest in behalf of her Irish people, and the deepest commiseration for their present distress. It is not often that Sovereigns have an opportunity of exhibiting that benign compassion which becomes them better than their sceptered sway; but it can never happen that an opportunity thus seized should be entirely fruitless.

There is one material advantage, less striking indeed, than the sentimental one which we have named, attending the Queen's visit. She will draw in her train an imitative host of tourists and travellers. She will make Ireland fashionable; Limerick, Kilkee, Galway, Killarney, and Wicklow will share the attentions of the holyday traveller with Edinburgh, Malvern, Matlock, and Ullswater. Ireland will soon be to Englishmen what Wales has long been to Lancashire and Cheshire—the usual summer tour. It will soon be as rare to find a man who has not lounged about Sackvill-street, or steamed down the Shannon, as it is now to find one who has not climbed up Snowden, scudded along Menai Strait, or sailed upon the English lakes.

All this will not be without value. It will break down the strong barrier of ignorance and prejudice; it will teach Englishmen what are the real capacities and the real grievances of Ireland; it will teach Irishmen the values of English opinion and reciprocal good offices; it will teach both that neither of them can do without the other; it will unveil many a case of petty tyranny and skulking oppression, of fraud which was successful, and violence which was triumphant, until both were revealed to the keenness of English curiosity, and punished by the flagellations of English publicity.

THE VICEREGAL LODGE.—Precisely at twelve her Majesty entered the gate, and in a few seconds afterwards she was received by his Excellency, by the Countess of Clarendon, and the entire suite of his Lordship's household. Her own state officers were in attendance a few moments afterwards to wait on her Majesty. On leaving the carriage she was at once conducted to the state apartment, and immediately after the royal standard was hoisted on the Viceregal Lodge, and guns belonging to the magazine in the Park fired a royal salute in honour of her arrival.

The Earl and Countess of Clarendon had entered the Lodge about an hour previous to arrival of her Majesty. There was a grand banquet given yesterday evening at the lodge; tents were erected on the lawn for the accommodation of the officers and band and the men composing the guard of honour attending her Majesty during her stay here.

THE ILLUMINATIONS.—On Monday night the entire city was brilliantly illuminated. The public buildings and the great number of private establishments displayed loyal devices in gas, and variegated lamps, and the appearance of the streets was on the whole exceedingly beautiful.

Reprinted from The Waterford News, Waterford, August 10, 1849.

THE PROCESSION AT THE GRAND TRIUMPHAL ARCH IN UPPER BAGGOT-STREET, AT THE ENTRANCE OF THE CITY OF DUBLIN.—(SEE PAGE 84.)

Reprinted from The Illustrated London News, London, August 11, 1849.

Reprinted from The Illustrated London News, London, August, 1849.

HER MAJESTY'S LEVEE.

Her Majesty and his Royal Highness Prince Albert, attended by his Excellency the Lord Lieutenant, and the principal officers of her Majesty's and the Viceregal Courts, arrived at the Castle, at two o'clock, and were received with hearty cheers by the vast multitude of persons assembled in the vicinity of the Castle-yard.

The lines of carriages conveying company during the afternoon seemed interminable, and the streets in the vicinity of the Castle were filled with spectators, the passage for the carriages being kept open by police. There were upwards of four thousand noblemen and gentlemen present at the Levee, independent of the deputations.

HER MAJESTY'S DRESS at the levee attracted the highest admiration. She wore a robe of exquisitely shaded Irish poplin, of emerald green, richly wrought with shamrocks in gold embroidery. Her hair was simply parted on her forehead with no ornament save a light tiara of gold studded with pearls and diamonds.

Recreated from The Waterford News, Waterford, August 10, 1849.

KILCASH, AUGUST 15, 1849.—FATAL ACCIDENT.—On Sunday last a labouring man named Patrick Morrissey, living at Ballyboe in the county, was proceeding to Clonmel, when meeting with a friend on horseback, who offered him a ride, Morrissey accepted the invitation and they had not proceeded far when the horse, not willing to be over-burdened, jumped up and threw both riders, when, most melancholy to relay, Morrissey was killed on the spot.

AN ELOPEMENT CURIOUSLY PREVENTED.—A singular instance of popular morality was displayed a few days since in a city in the South of Ireland, to which we do not desire to refer particularly, but which is remarkable for the strength of its military garrison, and the beauty of its fair daughters. A lady, highly connected, and married to a respectable gentleman, conceived the romantic and very novel idea of eloping from her husband, and with a son of Mars. The lady and her husband had been staying at a fashionable watering-place; but suddenly pretending that she stood in desperate want of a particular article of female dress, she left her unsuspecting lord, and returned to ____. She then ran into her house, picked up a few "necessaries", ran back into the street, and got on a car with her military Paris, and was dashing off to the railway station, when a young lady, a relation of the adventurous Helen, recognised her as she was flying off on the "wings of Love", and called on the virtuous populace to arrest her flight. The populace, moved by the appeal, quitted their various occupations, flang aside the implements of their craft, and rushed after the car, which they soon overtook and stopped. They then seized the lady and bore her off, in spite of her struggles, and took the military hero into custody! Thus the affair rests at present; but whether the lawyers are likely to be benefitted by the mad freak of this lady, remains to be seen.—*Cork Examiner.*

TUESDAY EVENING.—a pony, whilst passing round by the Scotch Pill, got stubborn, and backed into the mud, when the rider had a narrow escape from being buried beneath. Ropes were got round the animal, and after a good deal of exertion he was extricated.

A GOOD LEAP.—On the same evening, a man named Rogers was arrested by two policemen for being slightly intoxicated. They brought him down to the Tower gate, and while waiting to be let in, he ran from the police into the hulk opposite, leaped into the river on his head, and swam (with all his clothes on) about half way across, when he was picked up by the ferry-boat, and landed at the Ferrybank side. He was arrested again the same evening.

☞ We entirely agree with the remarks in the *Mail* in reference to the opening of Oliver's-Lane. It has always been a receptacle of filth, and a fruitful source of disease. The widening of this lane, in short, would not only improve the sanitary condition of the neighbourhood, but would open a direct passage to Cathedral-square and Beresford-street.

☞ The only daughter of Mr. G. Cowley, a farmer, residing at Kilsby, has eloped with, and got married to, her grandfather's groom. She is 26 years of age, and possessed of considerable personal attractions, together with £6,000 or £7,000 in her own right. She had the principal part of her wardrobe and jewellery removed for the occasion, besides £900 to defray the expense of the nuptials, and the subsequent tour.

☞ The body of Catherine Dillon, executed in Limerick, was conveyed to her late residence at Cappamore, where she was waked that night, and the internment, which took place the next day was attended by hundreds.

Recreated from The Waterford News, Waterford, August 17, 1849.

ATROCIOUS MURDER IN LONDON.
(From the London Papers of Saturday.)

One of the most appalling and cold-blooded murders that has probably been heard of since that perpetrated by the notorious Daniel Good was discovered yesterday afternoon to have been committed at No. 3, Minver-place, New Weston-street, near the Skin Market, Bermondsey.

The following are the particulars connected with this atrocious affair, as far as the police authorities were enabled to learn up to eleven o'clock last night:—

A gentleman of the name of Patrick O'Connor, residing at 21 Greenwood-street, Mile-end-road, left his home on Thursday, the 9th instant, at half-past seven o'clock in the morning, and was last seen passing over London Bridge at five o'clock the same afternoon. From what has since transpired there is not the least doubt that the unfortunate party proceeded from there to the house where he met with the fearful death about to be narrated.

The house which has been the scene of such a dreadful tragedy, is one of a newly-built and apparently respectably tenanted row, consisting of six rooms, two kitchens in the basement, with parlours and a floor above them, and is approached from the street by a flight of several stone steps.

The house in question was taken by the supposed murderers at midsummer last. The parties who tenanted the house subsequently to that period were a man named Manning, and a woman, a native of Sweden, who is stated to be young, and of great personal attractions. Their conduct since they have been in the house had been such as to cause suspicion in the neighbourhood. The man had formerly been a publican at Taunton, and was unfavourably known to the police, from his having been in some way connected with some robberies on the Great Western line of the railway, which were the subject of a trial at the Central Criminal Court a few years since. Some acquaintance, it would appear, existed between the female and the murdered man, but of what nature cannot at present be ascertained, she having, when speaking of him, alluded to him as being her guardian.

Shortly after the time the deceased was seen passing over London-bridge, a cab was noticed to drive up to the door of the house in Minver-place, out of which a man alighted supposed to be the deceased. His not returning home that night, and several days having elapsed without any tidings being heard respecting him, caused a deal of anxiety among his friends; and on one of his relatives inquiring at Manning's house whether the deceased was there, the female answered the party, and denied that he had been there on the day he left his home or since. Bills were thereupon printed and sent round to all the police stations in town, giving a full description of the missing man, and offering a reward of £10 to any person giving information as should lead to his discovery.

Nothing however was heard of him until yesterday when he was found under the circumstances subjoined. But during the interim it would appear that Manning sent to a broker and disposed of the whole of his furniture, which was removed on Tuesday last. He then went and slept for two nights at Mr. Bainbridge's, 14, Bermondsey-square, and, on leaving, said he should send his wife to look at the apartment; this, however, he never did, neither of the parties has been seen in the neighbourhood since.

The police, unable to gain any tidings of the missing man, entered the house, searched the garden, and the various rooms, but could find nothing to excite their suspicions, until their attention was directed to one of the stone flags in the back kitchen, which being rather loose, induced them to remove it. They found the earth underneath had been recently laid in, and upon removing it to the depth of three feet, they found a layer of slaked lime, and beneath it, to their horror, a portion of the back of a naked man. Upon removing the coat of lime, they found the unfortunate man with both of his feet tied together with strong cord, and a dreadful wound in the head, clearly indicating that a bullet had either passed through or lodged in the cranium.

Whilst the body was removed, a messenger was sent for the attendance of a surgeon. Mr. Lockwood, of Guy's hospital, quickly arrived, by which period the body was taken out of the ground, when that gentleman, found a bullet in the head, which he succeeded in extracting. The lime was carefully washed off the unfortunate man, and the body taken in charge by the police until an inquest is held. The friends of the party having been sent for, they at once identified the body by a set of false teeth the deceased wore.

Information of the discovery was forthwith forwarded to Mr. Evans, the superintendent of the M division of police, who immediately obtained a description of the supposed murderers, and sent a copy round to every station in London.—At the same time messengers were despatched to the various railways and steam-boat piers, to make inquiries as to whether any persons answering the description of the Mannings had been seen to leave London, so that they might be searched after. Up to eleven o'clock last night not the least tidings could be heard of either party.

The police have likewise been despatched to make inquiries of the different clothes dealers, to learn whether they had purchased any of the clothes worn by the deceased on the day he was murdered. His dress on that day consisted of a black dress coat, light plaid trousers, black silk stock, and Albert boots. It is understood that on the day he visited the house of the Manning's he must have had a considerable sum of money in his possession, all of which the murderers must have taken away.

To show that the murder must have been long planned, and robbery contemplated, it is only necessary to state that as soon as the poor fellow met his death, the female who passed as Mrs. Manning, there is no doubt went to Greenwood-street, Mile-end-road, the late residence of the deceased, and stole his watches, several articles of jewelry, a considerable sum of money, and it is believed, a quantity of railway scrip.

The deceased was in his 50th year, and was unmarried. He was a guager in the Customs at London Docks, where he has for some years received a salary of £300 a year. He was supposed to be in possession of nearly £4,000 in foreign railway bonds and securities, which was well known to Manning and his wife, who were frequently in the habit of visiting him at his lodgings, No. 21 Greenwood-street, Mile-end-road.

Manning is described as being about 30 years of age, and has a peculiar mark over his eyes. When last seen, he was dressed in black cloth trousers and invisible green coat.

The female is stated to be 27 years old, and remarkably good looking.

Mr. Hitchcock, who resides next door to where the tragedy was enacted, states that on the day the murder must have been committed, not the least disturbance was heard in Manning's house, neither was there anything resembling the discharge of fire-arms, nor at any subsequent time, leaving a strong impression in the mind that the deceased had been inveigled into the back kitchen, and there shot with an air-gun.

Recreated from The Freeman's Journal, Dublin, August 20, 1849.

ATROCIOUS MURDER—
FURTHER AND LATEST PARTICULARS.

In addition to the foregoing particulars we are enabled, from inquiries made by our reporter on the spot, to add the following particulars:—From the appearance of the pit into which the body was placed, there can be no doubt that it must have taken several days to have had it in readiness. It also appears that some of the flags in the passage of the basement floor were taken up, apparently with the intention of placing the body there, but from the narrowness of the passage it was impossible to bury it in that spot. In the back room of the upper floor (the house consisting of a basement, ground, and first floor, with two rooms on each), there are marks as if certain spots had just been washed with soap and water, and in the ceiling of this room there is a hole, as if a bullet had penetrated it, and from these appearances there is little doubt that the deceased must have been shot and murdered in this room, and the body, being afterwards stripped, was taken down stairs and buried in the back kitchen or cellar. Although the body lay in lime there is not the slightest appearance of decay or dissolution upon it, and, in the language of a medical student who viewed it, "it smelt quite sound."

It appears that the unfortunate deceased cohabited with Manning's wife, with the knowledge and consent of the husband, and that he was frequently in the habit of visiting her when her husband was at home; the crime must therefore have been committed not from feelings of jealousy, but from motives of cupidity. Manning, who was employed some time ago on the Great Western Railway, and who was implicated in the robberies which took place on that line, is described as "a fellow fit to do anything." It also appears that a person named Massey had lodged in the house, and that on this day three weeks he removed his luggage, consisting of three boxes and a carpet bag, having been removed by a carman of the name of Reed, of Long-lane, Bermondsey, to the house No. 14, Bermondsey-square, which he left a few days afterwards, and has not since been heard of. It is surmised from the circumstances that Manning and his wife contemplated the perpetration of the murder for some time, and in order the more effectually to accomplish their diabolical intention they gave their lodger Massey notice to quit. These facts were ascertained through the indefatigable exertions of Sergeant John Henhinick, of the M division, and the premises were thoroughly ransacked and examined by Sergeant Barry and police-constable Balls, who have all day been busily engaged with pick and spade in digging up the garden and the basement floor of the premises. Three buttons, no doubt belonging to the top coat of the deceased, were found in the back room of the top floor, and additional evidence that the deceased must have been murdered there. A shoemaker in the neighbourhood, who was in the habit of making boots and shoes for Manning and his wife, gives a vague description of both, saying that the male was a course, rough-looking fellow, and his wife was rather an engaging woman. During the day immense crowds of people visited the house in which the body was found, and the discovery has created the greatest excitement in the neighbourhood. As yet Manning and his wife have not been apprehended.

Recreated from The Freeman's Journal, Dublin, August 20, 1849.

THE CHOLERA.—PHOENIX HOTEL, D'OLIER-ST. AUG. 22.—The cholera, I regret to say, has been very fatal here for the last few weeks. Stand on the Carlisle bridge for an hour and you may be astonished to see the number of funerals that will pass during that time. On Sunday I visited Glasnevin, and there were at that hour (three o'clock) about half a dozen parties digging graves. And outside the church-yard there were five or six hearses "waiting for their turn" to deliver up their dead.

Recreated from The Waterford News, Waterford, August 24, 1849.

THE MURDER OF MR. O'CONNOR.

(*By Electric Telegraph.*)

EDINBURGH, WEDNESDAY.—This morning, at ten o'clock, Maria Manning was brought up from Calton Hill gaol for examination before Mr. Sheriff Arkley, charged with the murder, or participating in the murder, of Patrick O'Connor. After being cautioned, the prisoner was asked what she had to say to the charge. She replied that she had nothing to say, whereupon she was remanded back to prison to await the arrival of officers to convey her to London. It is expected that one or more of the metropolitan police will arrive here this morning, with authority to receive her into custody.

Mrs. Manning is described to be a remarkably fine woman, and it is said that correspondence discovered in her boxes discloses familiarity with persons far above her own station in life. She is a woman of very violent passions, and Manning's brother states that while she lived at Taunton she more than once attempted to stab him with a knife during family quarrels.

Manning is still at large; but there is great reason to hope that ere long he will be in custody. The police authorities believe that he is lurking in the west of England, and two or three officers have been sent down in that direction.

It was several times reported during yesterday that he had been seen in London; but the officers do not attach any credence to these statements. It is quite certain that he left town by the South-Western Railway on Wednesday morning, the 15th inst., and it is fully believed that he is now hiding himself in some of the villages or towns on the west coast of England.

The furniture purchased of the supposed murderers by Bainbridge, the broker, is advertised for sale by auction to-day. It consists of articles of the commonest description.

A great crowd of spectators awaited the arrival of the various trains at Euston-station yesterday, under the impression that Mrs. Manning would arrive in town from the north.

Recreated from The Freeman's Journal, Dublin, August 24, 1849.

DUNGARVAN—CHOLERA.—We are most happy to learn that cholera has taken its departure from Dungarvan. We are most sanguine that September will chase it out of every town and hamlet in Ireland. The people of Dungarvan, as well as those of other towns whom this scourge visited, owe a lasting debt of gratitude to the Catholic clergy for their unswerving zeal, immense courage, and untiring exertions.— In Dungarvan, as in Waterford, night and day they have been on duty; sometimes sitting for hours in the most wretched; the most desolate hovels.—There are other philanthropic lay gentlemen in our city whose efforts in behalf of sanitary measures deserve much commendation.

THE CHOLERA.—It is a fact worthy something more than a passing remark that though the cholera of 1848-9 has been more prevalent and destructive both on the Continent and in England than it was in 1831-2, it has excited much less alarm.—At its last appearance it was a novelty. No epidemic of equal importance had been known in England since the plague of 1665. Not that the two visitations can be properly compared, with reference to their effects. The average annual number of deaths in what are called the metropolitan districts is about 50,000; and in the cholera of 1832 (it broke out at Sunderland in October, reached London in February, 1832, and ceased there in the following November) only increased this number to 65,000. A return of the plague as destructive, in proportion to the population, as that of 1665, would have raised the deaths for the year to about 500,000.—*From the Globe.*

Recreated from The Waterford News, Waterford, August 24, 1849.

NEWTOWN (KILMACTHOMAS), August 23.

We have had a change of delightful weather for the last few days, and kind and maternal Nature has treated us this week with those serene and lovely autumnal days that spread so much beauty and repose on the face of creation, and which administer so much joy to the contemplative eye of the beholder. Reaping is going on on a large scale here, and a large area of corn will be cut down in this district before next Sunday. The country is literally inundated with reapers, whose wages range from 10d. to 1s. a day, and diet. After the vast devastation which famine and its usual attendant (fever) have made for the last five years among our rural labourers, it is astonishing to see what multitudes of them throng our streets when there is any demand for their labour.

I fear some potato gardens present symptoms of the blight. I have seen some tubers slightly affected; but if the disease sets in this year, it will be quite partial, and far from being at all fatal. One thing is certain, that the fatal malady is fast disappearing, and, like most chronic diseases, it cannot leave us at once. Report speaks of three days' racing again at Ballydurn.—*Correspondent.*

A LADY ATTORNEY.—Of late there have been frequently paragraphs about lady physicians, bu the following, from the *Gloucester Journal*, seems something new : " The business in the Nisi Prius Court (at the asizes) was unimportant, and 'dry as a remainder biscuit after a voyage,' but there was a first appearance of a very novel kind. This was nothing less than a female attorney; and a *fair* one too. The lady is a daughter of a deceased Warwickshire attorney. She gave her evidence with great precision, and *au fait* in legal matters, and talked of abstracts, deeds of covenant, release mortgages, and other things too dry to excite the curiosity even of ladies, as 'glibly as maids of fifteen do of puppy dogs,' while she handled the deeds themselves with the peculiar dexterity which lawyers only exhibit. One of the counsel fairly confessed that he was afraid to ask her many questions, for he found she was getting beyond his depth in legal matters, and he felt his wisest course was to retreat. Some discussion took place sotto voce on the question whether there was any legal obstruction forbidding a lady to become an attorney, and the leaders on both sides were agreed that there was no proviso against it.

Reprinted from The Waterford News, Waterford, August 24, 1849.

THE MURDER OF MR. O'CONNOR.

EDINBURGH, THURSDAY.—Yesterday morning Maria Roux, or Manning, who was apprehended on the previous day, was placed at the bar of the Edinburgh Police-court, according to the usual form observed in all such cases. She walked into the dock with a firm unfaltering step, and during the whole time she was at the bar her countenance did not betoken the slightest symptoms of agitation or alarm. Ever since her apprehension, indeed, she has conducted herself in a manner that shows she is determined to brave all consequences, and not give the slightest hint or indication that may, at a future period, tell against herself or her alleged husband and confederate in the murder. She was very neatly dressed, and from her easy and graceful manner she is evidently a person who has mixed a good deal in society. She is not, however, by any means what may be styled as beautiful, as some of the papers have asserted. There is a kind of dogged expression about her face, which, when conjoined with her bold and somewhat callous manner at the bar of the police-court, and during the reading of the very serious charge against her, led not a few of the on-lookers to say that she was just such a woman as could assist in the devising and carrying out of such a deed as that in which unhappily, she is said to a lesser or greater extent, implicated.

Recreated from The Freeman's Journal, Dublin, August 25, 1849.

ARREST OF MANNING.

(From the London papers of yesterday.)

SOUTHAMPTON, WEDNESDAY, 8 p.m.—The South Western Company's steamer Courier has just arrived here bringing the intelligence of the arrest of Frederick George Manning, last night at Jersey, on a charge of murdering O'Connor. Manning was apprehended whilst in bed, at half-past nine o'clock last evening, (Tuesday) at a public house in St. Helier's, by the chief of the police of the island, in conjunction with Messrs. Langley and Lockyer, officers of the metropolitan detective police. The intelligence has been received here officially by Mr. Whicher of the detective force, who has been in Southampton several days engaged in looking out for Manning, and who has searched every steamer arriving at or departing from Southampton. Manning is to arrive in Southampton on Monday evening next by the steamer, being detained in Jersey for the necessary warrant for his removal to England.

Manning confessed his guilt to officers upon his apprehension, adding that he was instigated to the deed by his wife, and affirming that Mrs. Manning fired the pistol shot at the unfortunate O'Connor. Manning moreover stated, that it was his intention to have surrendered on Wednesday if he had not been captured.

Recreated from The Freeman's Journal, Dublin, August 31, 1849.

EXTRACTS FROM OLD "NEWS-LETTERS."

As there is now a lull in the stormy strife of general and local politics, and as the public journalist has consequently more space to spare for the amenities of his arduous profession, we propose to indulge our readers, from time to time, during the parliamentary recess, with a few backward glimpses into the social history of the past century. We, therefore, now start with a volume exactly one century old, and proceed with our gleanings:—

ATTEMPT FOR THE DISCOVERY OF THE NORTH-WEST PASSAGE.—In the *News-Letter* of Jan. 5, 1749, we have the account of "A new Attempt for the discovery of a North West Passage to the South Seas and the East Indies," by which we learn that "About the year 1730, Arthur Dobbs, of Lisburne, in the county of Antrim, Esq., Member of Parliament for Carrickfergus, a Gentleman of Learning and Fortune, having drawn up for his Own Satisfaction some reasons for the Probability of a N. W. Passage to the South Sea, through Hudson's Bay, as also the Advantages that would attend such a discovery, communicated his papers to Colonel Bladen, one of the Lords of Trade and Plantations, with a view of engaging the South Sea Company in the undertaking." The matter lay over till the Summer of 1737, when Mr. Dobbs induced the Hudson's Bay Company to fit out two sloops, which went no farther than latitude sixty-two degrees thirty seconds, and returned. Mr. Dobbs next applied to Sir Charles Magee, Horace Walpole, and others, who laid the scheme before the king in 1739, and two other vessels were fitted out, under the command of a Captain Middleton, who sailed from the Thames in May, 1741; wintered in Churchill river; was frozen up till July, 1742, when he proceeded as far as latitude sixty-five degrees, ten seconds North, where he named a high point of land Cape Dobbs. We need not trace the history of this celebrated expedition. It is enough to say that, finding no passage, Captain Middleton returned in September, having been out two years and three months. Mr. Dobbs always asserted that the frozen straits in which Captain Middleton (who was suspected of being a secret agent of the Hudson's Bay Company, who threw cold water on the expedition) said he was embayed, was only a chimera of the Captain. We allude to the matter because we think it is not generally known that the idea of a North-West Passage, upon which so much money, and labour, and we fear life, have since been expended, originated with an ancestor of the Dobbs family in this neighbourhood.

Recreated from The Belfast News-Letter, Belfast, September 4, 1849.

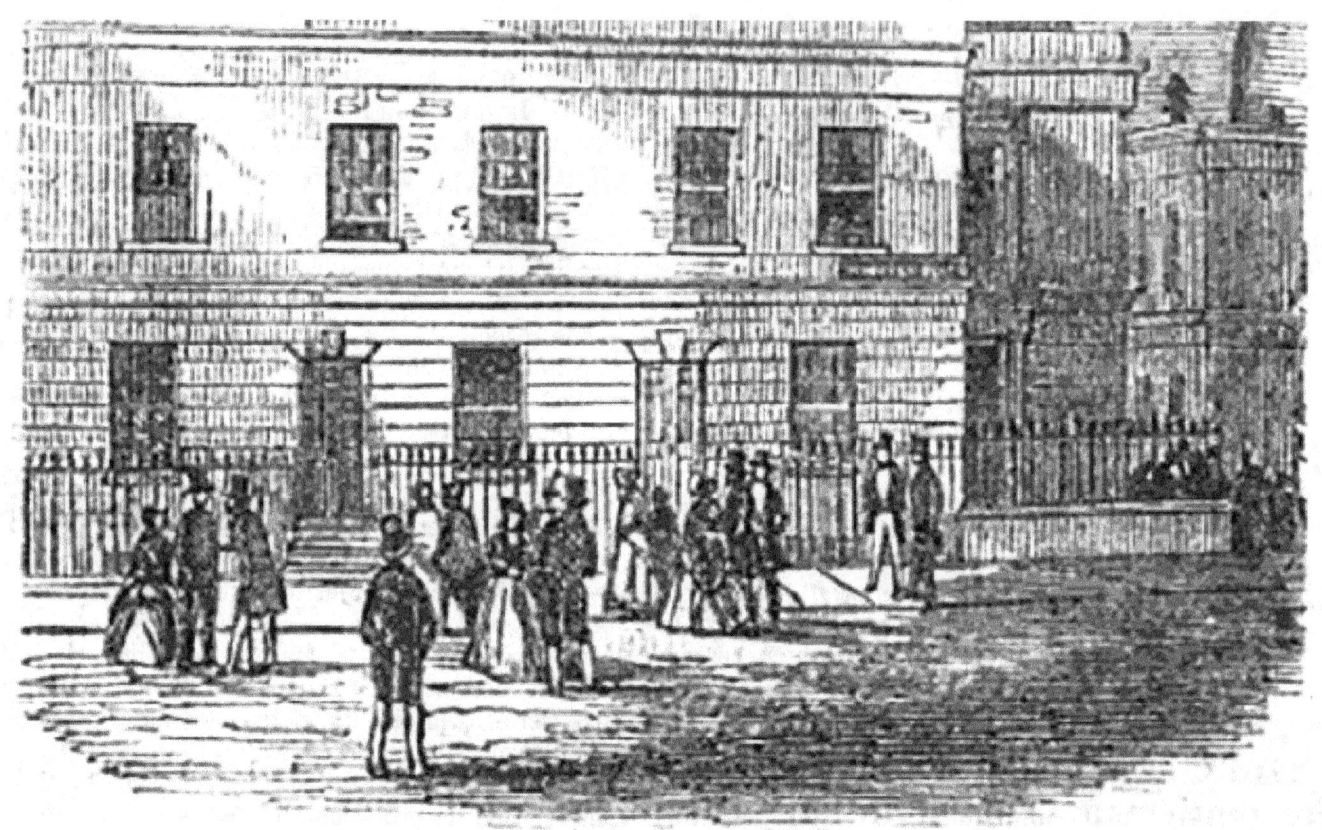

NO. 3, MINVER-PLACE, THE SCENE OF THE MURDER.

Printed and published by W. M. Clarke, London, 1849.

THE BERMONDSEY MURDER.

Mrs. Manning has somewhat recovered the excitement she displayed on the fact being made known to her of her husband's arrival at Horsemonger-lane gaol after being examined at the police-court on Saturday. The coolness and general levity of her conduct, however, excites considerable observation, if not surprise. She often confesses much concern about Manning, and when speaking of him remarks, "Ah, poor boy, he ought not to have been taken." Scarcely a word escapes her lips in reference to the part she is supposed to have taken in the dreadful crime. All her thoughts apparently are devoted to dress. Having obtained permission of Mr. Secher, the police magistrate, for some satin dresses and bonnets, found in her luggage when apprehended, to be returned to her, she has been employed most of the time since her last appearance at the police-court in preparing her attire for the next examination.

She has been very busy in adding a double fall to her bonnet so as to screen her, as she says, from the vulgar gaze of the mob. She makes but little complaint of the restrictions imposed upon her; indeed she has often expressed her self satisfied with what the prison authorities had done for her, saying, "I have plenty of room, plenty of air, and plenty of food, and am not without society." She expressed a desire to see Mr. Moxey, the superintendent of the Edinburgh police, but being told that that gentleman had left the metropolis to attend his duties in Scotland, she became rather disappointed and observed that "She wishes particularly to have thanked him for his gentlemanly conduct," adding that "I intend to go again to Scotland as soon as I have got over this difficulty, and I will call and see him." During the whole time she has been in the prison, it has been generally observed that she relies much on the belief that she will succeed in satisfactorily clearing away all suspicion of her being concerned in the murder of O'Connor.

The appearance and conduct of Manning have undergone a great change in prison. Yesterday he seemed depressed in mind. On Sunday night he expressed a wish to have an interview with his wife, but Mr. Keene, the governor, informed him, as on the previous occasion when he made a similar request, that it could not be granted.

Mrs. Manning attended Divine service in the chapel at Horsemonger-lane gaol on Sunday, both in the morning and afternoon. Her husband was not present at either service. Both the prisoners have had several interviews with their professional advisers, preparatory to their being brought up for final re-examination on Thursday next. Manning still asserts his innocence, and upbraids his wife as the sole perpetrator of the deed. The police are actively engaged in making inquiries after the air-gun or pistol from which the bullet found in the deceased's head was fired; and it is believed that a clue has been found which will fix the recent possession of an air-gun on Manning.

An air-gun, wrapped in a baize cover, was left by a man answering his description at a shop in Cheapside on Wednesday, the 8th, and taken away again on Thursday morning. The shopkeeper states, that the person who left it appeared to be in a state of great agitation, and said that he would call for it again, which he did.

Since the examination of Manning, the house No. 3, Minver-place, has undergone another minute search, by order of Mr. Evans, the superintendent of the M division of police. The whole of the back kitchen was dug up some distance below the depth where the body of O'Connor was found, but nothing material was discovered. Inquiries are now being made of most of the marine store dealers in the metropolis respecting the crowbar which Manning bought of Messrs. Evans, the ironmongers, in King William-street, and which is missing. It is evident that a weapon of that description must have been employed in raising the Yorkshire flagstones and picking up the hard soil under them.

It will be recollected that a dress was found by Inspector Haynes in one of Mrs. Manning's boxes, the front and left shoulder of which bore marks of blood. This confirms the admission made by Manning when apprehended at Jersey, that Mrs. Manning invited O'Connor downstairs to wash his hands, and when reaching the bottom of the staircase put one arm round O'Connor's neck, and with the other shot him through the head. The stains on the dress have been examined by Mr. Odling, the surgeon, of the Borough, and that gentleman is of the opinion from experiments he has made that they are marks of human blood.—*Times* of Yesterday.

Recreated from The Freeman's Journal, Dublin, September 5, 1849.

STATE OF THE POTATO.

Kerry.—The weather for the last ten days has been rather changeable, but still sufficiently favourable for harvest operations, which are actively progressing. We occasionally hear complaints of disease having appeared in potatoes in some districts, but the consequent failure is very limited. We have not heard of the complete destruction of any one crop in an entire field in any quarter. A few unsound potatoes here and there are the only proofs of disease. The evil is, therefore, very partial, and is as nothing compared with the general crop, which is not only healthy but of unusual bulk, as regards the size of the potatoes. We have seen some surprising instances of their great size.—*Kerry Examiner*, September 14.

Armagh.—During some few days this week we had un-genial and what may be termed unseasonable weather. There were some slight thunder claps on Monday, accompanied and followed by light and continuous showers, and on the following day there were heavy showers, which seriously impeded the progress of harvest operations. The weather being dry on Thursday and the greater part of the following day, the farmers availed themselves of the opportunity, and made great progress in cutting down several crops. As far as we have learned as yet, the standing cereal crops have sustained no serious injury, and the potatoes in this quarter have escaped unscathed by an atmospheric visitation. Withered stalks, which many folks ascribe to "the olden blight," are either the effect of frost or of natural decay, owing to the near approach of the root to maturity.

There is a great deal of harvest work to be done as yet; and therefore, farmers are particularly sensitive as to the prospects of the weather.—*Ulster Gazette*, Sept. 15.

The Potato.—We regret to say that our accounts this week respecting the potato are most unfavourable. The disease so long lurking in the stalks has at length attacked the tubers, and within one short week, so rapid has been its progress, that in some cases one half of the crop has been found damaged. The disease has progressed more among the white kind than the red. We have seen some fields examined so lately as yesterday, and the tubers, in many cases, presented a mass of putrescence. This is deeply to be lamented, and were it not for an abundance of cereal crop, and the prospect of a good return from turnips and other green crops, the consequences would be alarming. It has been recommended in some well informed quarters to dig out the potatoes, and separate the sound from the diseased. The latter may be used by cattle, and the former pitted in fresh dry earth.—*Downpatrick Recorder*.

DEPARTURE OF THE LORD LIEUTENANT FOR KILLARNEY.

Tuesday morning, half-past eight o'clock, his Excellency the Lord Lieutenant and the Countess of Clarendon, accompanied by Lord and Lady Craven, Captain H. Ponsonby, Mr. C. Connellan and suite, left the King's-bridge terminus of the Great Southern Railway, on a pleasure excursion to the Lakes of Killarney. The noble party were taken to Mallow in a special train. Mr. Murphy, the superintendent of the railway police, accompanied the viceregal party as far as Mallow, where the train arrived at half-past 12 o'clock. Carriages were in readiness to receive his Excellency and suite, who at once drove off for the romantic scenery of the lakes. We understand that the Lord Lieutenant will return to town at the end of the week.

Recreated from The Freeman's Journal, Dublin, September 18, 1849.

WORKHOUSE EMIGRATION.

This morning twenty-three orphan girls, who had been prepared by the Vice-Guardians for emigration to South Australia, left this city by Bianconi's car *en route* for Dublin, from whence they will sail on to-morrow for Plymouth, where the ship *Panama* awaits to carry them, with others, to their destination. They were selected by Lieutenant Henry some time since. It was cheering to see the comfortable appearance of these young women, &c. When we consider that these poor girls should spend their lives in the workhouse, we think that the step they have taken is far preferable; besides it is a considerable savings to the rate-payers.

The Vice-Guardians of the New Ross Union have also prepared eighteen girls for the same destination. They will depart to-morrow morning.

Recreated from The Waterford News, Waterford, September 21, 1849.

ENTERTAINMENTS AT LISMORE CASTLE.

On Tuesday night last the Duke of Devonshire entertained a large party at Lismore in a magnificent style. About 120 persons were present. Everything was on a princely scale, and the supper consisted of all the delicacies of the season. Dancing was kept up till five o'clock in the morning, when all left with regret, but well prepared to meet the pitiless storm of rain which assailed them on leaving the Castle of their hospitable and noble host. The exterior of the Castle had a most imposing effect, being brilliantly illuminated; both the avenue and the terrace on the north front were lighted up, about 200 lamps spreading their bright light during the entire night.

Reprinted from The Waterford News, Waterford, October 12, 1849.

Important.
NOTICE TO BOSTON EMIGRANTS.
TRAIN AND CO.'S NEW LINE OF REGULAR PACKETS, FROM CORK TO BOSTON.

FIRST OF THE NEW LINE.
To Sail Punctually on the 15th JULY.
The Splendid American Packet Ship,
ST. PETERSBURGH,
Wm. J. Howard, Commander, 2,300 Tons Burthen.

THE above magnificent Packet is the First Regular Liner, and in every respect the finest Vessel that has ever entered Cove for the conveyance of Passengers. She is coppered and copper-fastened; remarkable for strength, size, and swiftness; furnished with new Patent Ventilators, and improved Kitchen-ranges for Cooking; worked by a full and efficient crew, and commanded by an able and humane Capt. Her height between decks are more than eight feet high, and the berths are of the most improved description, being permanently prepared with that regard to the comfort and health of passengers, observable in each of the celebrated Line of packets belonging to her owners, Messrs. Train and Co., of Boston.

The Chief Cabin of this Packet has been fitted out for a select number of Passengers, at moderate rates. This will be found a rare opportunity for respectable families intending to emigrate. Respectable parties of limited means can secure Private State-rooms in the Second Cabin, at slightly advanced rates.

Medicine and attendance of a duly qualified Surgeon gratis.

Each Passenger by this conveyance over 12 months, will be faithfully supplied during the passage, with provisions according to the following scale, as regulated by the American law:—
15lbs. of Bread, 10lbs. of Oatmeal, 10lbs. of Peas and Beans, 10lbs. of Pork (free from bone), 1 pint of Venegar, 10lbs. of Rice, 10lbs. of Flour, 35lbs. of Potatoes, 60 gallons of Water.

For Passage, which is upon the most advantageous terms yet offered, apply to
E. S. PLYNN,
Merchant's-Quay, Cork,

Reprinted from The Waterford News, Waterford, September 29, 1849.

VERDICT OF GUILTY AGAINST BOTH PRISONERS.

The jury having answered to their names,

The Clerk of the Arraigns said—Gentlemen of the jury, how say you, is the prisoner at the bar, Fredrick George Manning, guilty or not guilty?

Foreman—GUILTY.

The Clerk—How say you; is the prisoner at the bar, Maria Manning, guilty or not guilty?

The Foreman—GUILTY.

The prisoner, Mrs. Manning, here exclaimed with violent gesticulation. "I will not stand here—I have not had a fair trial!" and one of the officers in attendance was compelled to remover her to the front of the dock, and remained stationed close behind her for a few minutes.

Mr. Streight then asked the prisoners whether they had anything to say why the sentence of death should not be passed upon them in the usual form? A pause of a few seconds followed, and Mr. Harker, the crier of the court, was about to make the usual proclamations for silence, when, the female prisoner, whose extraordinary command of feeling had been conspicuous throughout the trial, and who had maintained a stolid indifference up to this moment, advanced to the front of the dock, and, placing her hands on the bar, in a voice which was at first overpowered with intense emotion, which she attempted to subdue, proceeded to address the bench with a broken English accent. The report of her address was, as nearly as we could understand, or hear it, "My Lord! I have been treated most cruelly in this country. I am a foreigner, and I have been denied justice. There is no justice or protection here for any foreign subject in this country. I have received no protection or justice from the prosecutors, from the jury, or from the Court. I am, therefore, convicted unjustly this day in court. It could have been proved by my counsel and solicitor that money was sent to me from my own country, from abroad, to the Bank of England, to show that those shares which were found upon me were bought for me, with my own money; and that witnesses could have identified those shares if they had been called; and when I am charged with taking the life of Mr. O'Connor, I say that he was much more than my husband to me. I had known him ever since I was in this country. I have known him for seven years. He was to me a brother and a father, and the best friend I had in the world. He wanted to marry me, and I ought to have married him when I was a widow. I can never forget his regard for me; and the letters that he wrote will prove the respect and regard he had for me; and I consider that I, a foreign woman, have had to fight against my own husband's statement which he has made against me, and against the judges and those who have conducted the prosecution. I complain of the judges themselves. I have not been treated like a Christian, but like a wild beast of the forest; and all the judges, and the jurors, and the counsel will have it on their consciences that the verdict which has been given against me is an unjust one, for I am not guilty of the murder of Mr. O'Connor. How should I wish to do so? I could not attempt the life of a man who was my most honoured friend on earth, and who would have made me his wife when I was a widow. If I wished to take anybody's life, why should I not take that of my husband, who is the greatest enemy to me in the world? Because it pleased my husband, from his jealousy, to kill Mr. O'Connor, I am dragged to this bar. I wish I could better explain myself in the English language, but I cannot."

Mr. Harker having made the usual proclamation for silence,

Mr. Justice Cresswell then proceeded to pass sentence upon the prisoners:—George Frederick Manning and Maria Manning, you have been convicted of the crime of murder—Maria Manning (in a loud voice, and with great earnestness)—"I have not, my Lord. I will not stand here to hear that said." The prisoner then rushed hastily towards the back part of the dock; upon being brought back to the front of the dock by Mr. Cope, the Governor, she said—"it is a shameful thing—you ought to be ashamed of yourselves, all of you; and (addressing the barristers in the front of the dock) you and the judges too."

Mr. Justice Cresswell then proceeded—You have been convicted by a patient and intelligent jury, and you have been defended by counsel. Whatever assertions you may make—whatever indignation you may express, and really or affectedly feel, and manifest with respect to the course of the proceedings this day—depend upon it that others will judge very differently; and I doubt if there is one who has heard this trial who is not as well satisfied as I am that the result of it is the only one which is consistent with justice. [His Lordship having put on the black cap, then said]—Having given you this warning and advice, which I pray you once more to receive in all humility, it remains for me but to pronounce the dread sentence of the law, which is, that you be taken hence to her Majesty's gaol for the county of Surrey, and thence to the place of execution, and that you there be severally hanged by the neck until you are dead, and after death that your bodies be buried within the precincts of that gaol in which you shall be confined after the passing of this sentence; and may the Lord have mercy upon your souls!

Mr. Streight—Amen.

Mr. Justice Cresswell—This court does now commit you to the gaol of the county of Surrey, there to remain in the custody of the sheriff of the county until your execution takes place.

Maria Manning—My Lord, you have given me an unjust judgement.

Mr. Justice Cresswell—Remove the prisoners.

Upon the turnkeys removing her from the dock, she exclaimed, "Base and shameful England;" and indignantly threw into the body of the court some piece of rue which she held in her hand, a quantity of which is usually placed in the front of the dock.

The male prisoner left the dock without saying a word.

The prisoners having been removed from the bar, the court was adjourned at a quarter past seven o'clock.

Recreated from The Cork Examiner, Cork, October 29, 1849.

STATE OF IRELAND.

THE WEST OF CLARE.—The whole west of Clare is in an awful state. In Killand, Dumore, Doonbeg, Tullig, Kilballyowen, Rehy, Newtown, and Rahanisky, the inhabitants of entire villages are huddled together near the ditches, partially covered by a few old sticks and porous sods, drenched with wet, and dying as fast as hunger, cold, and damp can sap their constitutions.

They are the last victims of eviction—the latest draft of occupiers encircled in the exterminator's far-spreading net, and cast out a prey to death on the wild bleak hills, or bleaker bogs, where alone they are allowed to tarry before translation to the churchyard or the workhouse! Hundreds are so circumstanced.

The union asylum could not receive them all; the exterminators expel too fast for its accommodations. The long and dreary nights of winter, the frequent storms, the drenching rains, the bitter cold, the damp ground, the bedless sleep, the meagre food, and scanty covering, will answer all the purposes of an intramural pestilence. If the central asylum is a huge tomb no longer, the grave will receive its complement just as well without.—*Limerick and Cork Examiner.*

Recreated from The Freeman's Journal, Dublin, November 2, 1849.

HOW THE LANDLORDS GET ON.
(*From the Dundalk Democrat.*)

The entire surface of this island is owned by about ten thousand persons, some of whom never visit, and what is worse, never think of it only when they want money. Their forefathers received these estates in many instances as the reward of treachery to the Irish, or for adhering to the cause of some English adventurer, some cut-throat or perjured villain who perpetrated crime, the enormity of which was sufficient to damn a dozen worlds. And these estates having come into the possession of some of the forefathers of the present proprietors in this way, the owners now think that they may re-enact the same crimes as their wicked forefathers have done. How else can we account for the awful sights witnessed in the South and West, the extermination of tens of thousands, the legal murders, that is murders which "the law" cannot punish, because it is "law" made by the landlords, and because the landlords are the murderers. How else can we account for the robberies according to "law" which these wicked landlords are perpetrating; carrying off by force the crops which the farmers, at enormous cost of labour and money, have grown upon rack-rented lands; and leaving the tiller of the soil to live on rotten potatoes, or make the best of his way to the workhouse. Yes, truly, these descendants of drummers and freebooters are in their own way laying the country waste, and carrying on a war more destructive to the native Irish than was the bloody campaign of Cromwell. Such scenes were never before witnessed in any civilised country. A defenceless people, who have ploughed the land and sown it, proceed to cut their corn, and they are pounced upon by a crowd of profligate ruffians who carry it off the land, leaving the rightful owner to discuss in his own way the rights and duties of landlords.

In this way the ten thousand proprietors, or nearly that number, exercise their sway over millions of human beings.

What have the landlords ever done for the country? Have they ever identified themselves with their interests, or joined with the people to build a prosperous nation in which they might rest with gladness, and witness a happy people prospering in arts, in industry, and in the progress of civilization? We may safely answer that the present generation of them have never done anything for Ireland. Idlers and vagabonds many of them are, creatures who, it would seem from their conduct, think they have a license from heaven to oppress, scourge, and exterminate from the country all who are, as they imagine, in their way.

Is it any wonder when such characters are the owners of the soil—when many of them are grand jurors—when, in fine, they are often our law makers, and those who deal out "the law", that the whole country presents a spectacle unknown in any other part of the world?

HEARTLESS TYRANNY.

We can only find room for the following extract from the letter of our Kilmacthomas correspondent:—" In Wetherstown, in this parish, an extermination of the most barbarous description that ever disgraced human nature, occurred the other day. In act of obtaining possession, *two bed-ridden cripples were launched out on the street*, and their screams and moans were enough to convulse the heart with horror, and would commisserate into sorrow the most savage mind. The felling-stroke of the exterminator is progressing with alarming velocity in this parish." Who is the landlord in the above case?

Reprinted and recreated from The Waterford News, Waterford, November 9, 1849.

'BRIDGET O'DONNELL AND CHILDREN' from The Illustrated London News, December, 1849.

EXECUTION OF MANNING AND HIS WIFE FOR THE MURDER OF MR. O'CONNOR.

Tuesday morning having been appointed for the carrying out the sentence of death passed upon the above criminals, the excitement which appeared to prevail to witness the awful ceremony seemed to be of the most intense description.

During the whole of the night an immense crowd was assembled around the gaol, and as nine o'clock, the hour for the execution, approached, there could not have been less than fifty to sixty thousand persons present.

THE CULPRITS' LAST MOMENTS.

We are indebted to the chaplain of the gaol for the following account of the conduct of the unfortunate convicts on Monday night, up to the moment when they are launched into eternity:—

He saw the unhappy woman shortly after eight Monday night and remained with her until after ten, and during that time she again made a statement about the murder having been done by a young man from Guernsy, and other statements altogether inconsistent with the facts of the charge against her, and to which, as matter of course the reverend chaplain attached he says, not the slightest importance. She declared that she was away from the house when the murder was committed, that she did not know such a crime was intended, and that she was ignorant that it had taken place. She did not receive any apparent benefit from his spiritual instruction, nor indeed has she through her whole captivity, and conducted herself and wished to be believed altogether innocent. She offered no explanation, as to how she became in possession of the murdered man's keys, although she said she forgave her husband. She immediately proceeded to her husband's cell, and remained with him in prayer until one o'clock in the morning. He seemed resigned, but he was extremely restless and petulant. Both husband and wife seemed most anxious to know what were the statements made by the other, but, looking upon them as strangers, he did not feel disposed to be communicative on the point. His petulancy rendered it necessary for the chaplain to extend his patience to the utmost. When he left him, Manning said he wished to see him at five in the morning. Manning, it appears, passed a very restless night, as also did his wife; they both rose early, and having partook of breakfast, Manning sent for the chaplain between six and seven. He found him more composed than the preceding night. He subsequently visited Mrs. Manning, and importuned her, as she was about to appear in the presence of God, before whom there could be no disguise, and that as the opinion of mankind availed her nothing, now that she was about to quit this world, to tell him if she had any request to prefer, or anything to say or unsay. She said she had not, and requested him to write to two ladies (whose names the chaplain declined to mention), to beg their acceptance of her kind and heartfelt thanks for their condescension in making efforts to save her.

At a quarter past eight they were brought into the chapel, Manning being brought in first. They were placed on a seat immediately before the pulpit, male and female officers being placed between them. Manning looked intently at his wife but said nothing. The sacrament was then administered.

As the chaplain was about to enter the vestry the prisoners appeared to be communicating with each other. Manning, who was the first to do so, crossed over to his wife and kissed her three times. They spoke in a low tone, and Mr. Freshfield, who stood near, understood Manning to urge his wife to confess, saying, "Do confess." They were then taken into separate apartments on either side of the chapel, where they were pinioned.

Mrs. Manning solicited that a black veil might be bound over her head, and that she might be led blindfold to the scaffold. This was acceded to, and Mr. Davis, the surgeon, and another person, led the unhappy woman out of the chapel. Manning, who had been led out of the chapel some minutes before his wife, and who stood on the spot where his grave had been dug [when our reporter left the gaol] where he was met by the sheriff, the chaplain, the governor, and other officers of the prison. Manning said to the chaplain, "I was petulant last night—I hope you will forgive me and make allowance for a person in my situation." The chaplain gave him his forgiveness, saying that in the discharge of so sacred and awful a duty it was sometimes necessary to be firm as well as to be kind.

The procession then moved slowly on, and up the stairs of the lodge to the fatal spot. Calcraft went first, then came the chaplain, followed by the wretched man Manning, who ascended the stairs with a firm step, but appeared pale and emaciated, and seemed to be crying. He was dressed in black, with a long frock coat. The rope having been adjusted, and the cap drawn over his face, the female partner in his crime was brought forth, and, like himself, walked with a firm step. She was attired in a black satin dress, tightly bound round the waist, with a long white collar fastened round her neck. On advancing upon the drop she observed her husband, and, as if acting upon the impulse of the moment, she seized his right hand and shook it for several minutes.

The chaplain asked the female when the fatal noose was in course of adjustment, if she had anything more to say. She replied firmly, "Nothing, except to thank you for your kindness."

The hangman then hurriedly completed his deadly preparations, and having as suddenly disappeared, in the next instant the slam of the drop was heard, and the dread sentence of the law had been accomplished. Manning gave a few convulsive jerks, and all was over, but his wife had a long struggle with death, and it was some moments before the immortal spirit left her body forever, and passed the threshold of eternity. A slight shudder—a murmured expression of horror—escaped the multitude, the terrible drama closed.

No sooner had the drop fallen than the intelligence of it was conveyed by carrier pigeons, while, within a quarter of an hour afterwards, the sad tidings of their terrible end had travelled far and wide through the very same electric wires that had been used to bring one of them to justice. At the very time these wretched beings were descending to their graves the sun shone out with unusual warmth and splendour for this period of the year, falling directly upon the lifeless bodies as they swayed to and fro in the keen morning air and lighting up the white caps that concealed their features.

Recreated from The Waterford News, Waterford, November 16, 1849.

THE PROSELYTIZING IN DUNGARVAN.
(From our own Correspondent.)

The poor Catholic children who attend the Protestant infant school get some bread and milk every day they make their appearance at the school, and MEAT *on every Friday!* To make a poor hungry Catholic child eat meat on Friday, against the holy principles of its religion, and the sacred duties of its conscience, is deemed a work of charity by the supporters of this Protestant infant school! Out on such *charity!* It is a vile kidnapping corruption. The poor children, when commencing prayer, through a long observed custom, make the sign of the cross on themselves, and whilst their little hands are being raised to make the sign of the salvation, the school-mistress strikes it down with true Protestant indignation. By the bye this lady has but one eye, and is beautifully pockmarked!—a true type of her proselytising creed!

Reprinted from The Waterford News, Waterford. November 23, 1849.

CHARLES DICKENS ON PUBLIC EXECUTIONS.

TO THE EDITOR OF THE TIMES.

SIR,—I was a witness of the execution at Horsemonger-lane this morning. I went there with the intention of observing the crowd gathered to behold it, and I had excellent opportunities of doing so, at intervals all through the night, and continuously from daybreak until after the spectacle was over. I do not address you on the subject with any intention of discussing the abstract question of capital punishment, or and of the arguments of its opponents or advocates. I simply wish to turn this dreadful experience to some account for the general good, by taking the readiest and most public means of adverting to an intimation given by Sir G. Grey in the last session of Parliament, that the Government might be induced to give its support to a measure making the infliction of capital punishment a private solemnity within the prison walls (with such guarantees for the last sentence of the law being inexorably and surely administered as should be satisfactory to the public at large), and of most earnestly beseeching Sir G. Grey, as a solemn duty which he owes to society, and a responsibility which he cannot forever put away, to originate such a legislative change himself. I believe that a sight so inconceivably awful as the wickedness and levity of the immense crowd collected at the execution this morning could be imagined by no man, and could be presented in no heathen land under the sun. The horrors of the gibbet, and of the crime which brought the wretched murderers to it, faded in my mind before the atrocious bearing, looks, and language of the assembled spectators. When I came upon the scene at midnight the shrillness of the cries and howls that were raised from time to time, denoting that they came from a concourse of boys and girls already assembled in the best places, made my blood run cold. As the night went on, screeching, and laughing, and yelling in strong chorus of parodies of negro melodies, with substitutions of "Mrs. Manning" for "Susannah", and the like, were added to these. When the day dawned, thieves, low prostitutes, ruffians and vagabonds of every kind, flocked to the ground, with every variety of foul and offensive behaviour. Fightings, faintings, whistlings, imitations of Punch, brutal jokes, tumultuous demonstrations of indecent delight when swooning women were dragged out of the crowd by the police with their dresses disordered, gave a new zest to the general entertainment. When the sun rose brightly—as it did—it gilded thousands upon thousands of upturned faces, so inexpressedly odious in their brutal mirth or callousness that a man had cause to feel ashamed of the shape he wore, and to shrink from himself, as fashioned in the image of the Devil. When the two miserable creatures who attracted all this ghastly sight about them were turned quivering into the air, there was no more emotion, no more pity, no more thought that two immortal souls had gone to judgement, no more restraint in any of the previous obscenities, than if the name of Christ had never been heard in this world, and there were no belief among men but they perished like the beasts. I have seen, habitually, some of the worst sources of general contamination and corruption in this country, and I think there are not many phases of London life that could surprise me. I am solemnly convinced that nothing that ingenuity could devise to be done in this city, could work such ruin as one public execution, and I stand astounded and appalled by the wickedness it exhibits. I do not believe that any community can prosper where such a scene of horror and demoralization as was enacted this morning outside Horsemonger-lane Gaol is presented at the very doors of good citizens, and is passed by, unknown or forgotten. And when, in our prayers and thanksgivings for the season, we are humbly expressing before God our desire to remove the moral evils of the land, I would ask your readers to consider whether it is not a time to think of this one, and to root it out?—I am, sir, your faithful servant,   CHARLES DICKENS.

Recreated from The Waterford News, Waterford, November 23, 1849.

LORD CLARENDON'S SECRET SOCIETY IN DUBLIN.

Lord Clarendon has been holding communication with an illegal society in Dublin for upwards of ten days. The Grand Orange Lodge, with its *secret signs* and *pass-words*, has been plotting with his Excellency during the whole of that period. This may seem strange, but it is a fact. Were any other *illegal* assemblage of delegates but Lord Clarendon's pet "grands" to meet in Dublin, and hold, by means of secret signs and pass-words, private cabals, all the authorities of the city would be at once put in harness to exercise the city of such dangerous Catalines,

Reprinted from The Waterford News, Waterford. November 30, 1849.

FIRE.

On yesterday morning a rick of hay belonging to a farmer named Walsh, residing at Grantstown, was discovered to be on fire. The fire-bells were immediately tolled, and the alarm became general.

The first persons we noticed on the spot were—Mr. W. H. Harris, T. S. Harvey, agent to the West of England Insurance Company, Capt. Gunn, Mr. P. Gallway, Mr. Hayes, and several others belonging to the West of England, Sun, and National engines; they, however, proved of little avail. A large body of police was marched to the spot on the first alarm, who rendered every assistance in their power.

The hay is supposed to have been set fire to, as a stack of corn at some distance was on fire at the same time, and a piece of burning rag was found at the other side of the haggart. There was a member of the family waking in the horse at the time.

We are happy to state that the fire did not extend to any other part of the premises. Various reports are current as to how the hay got on fire.

—A woman, giving her name as Margaret Keeffe, and who states that she is from Abbeyside, (Dungarvan) surrendered herself on yesterday, afternoon, to the police. At the time Mr. Tabiteau was investigating the circumstances, she stated that she and another woman, of whom the police have got a description, maliciously set fire to the out-house, hay, and corn, on this morning, in consequence of Walsh refusing them a lodging.

Reprinted from The Belfast News-Letter, Belfast, December 4, 1849.

DIGESTION.—The construction of the digestive apparatus of man, as well as his instinctive propensities, point to a mixed diet as best suited to his wants. With the exception of bread, which contains *gluten*, a vegetable principle analogous to *gelatin*, and whose chemical constituents are, in a great degree similar, a diet composed altogether of vegetables, is not favorable to the full development of either his mental or bodily powers. On the other hand, a completely animal diet seems equally unfit, and, when carried too far, interferes in a remarkable manner with the faculties and functions of man. My readers will remember that I before alluded to the *gastric juice* as the solvent of the food that enters the stomach.

Now it is remarkable that the *gastric juice* of dogs and other carnivorous animals produce little or no effect on *vegetables*, but readily dissolves flesh and even bone, while the same fluid in ox or the sheep, makes no impression on *flesh*, but acts energetically on vegetables. The *gastric juice* in man, on the contrary, is able to dissolve both flesh and vegetables, indifferently and, evidently, it is by a well-regulated admixture of both, judiciously apportioned to the tastes and habitudes of the individual, that health is best preserved, and the *full* development of the mental as well as the bodily powers secured.—*A Doctor in the Commercial Journal.*

Recreated from The Waterford News, Waterford, December 14, 1849.

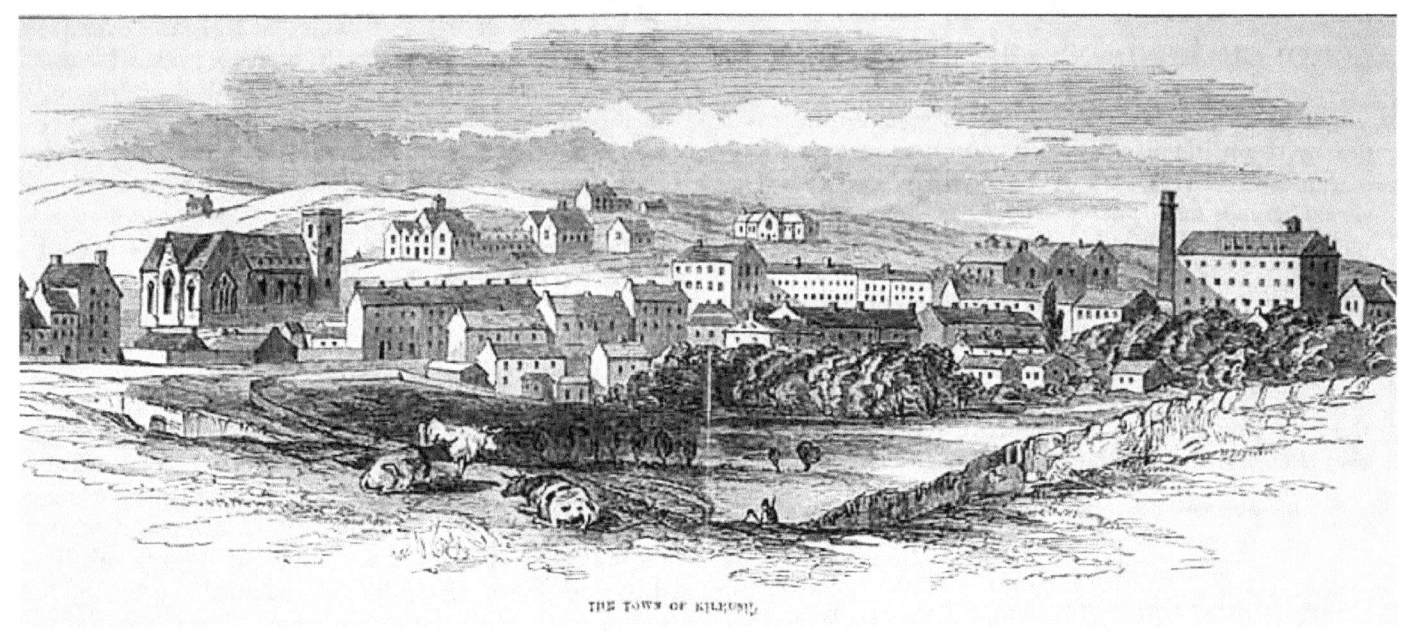

Reprinted from The Illustrated London News, London, December 15, 1849.

STARVATION IN KILRUSH.

We have been favoured with the following highly important correspondence which has taken place between the Rev. Mr. Kelly, P.P., Kilrush, and the Lord Lieutenant on the subject of the distress and starvation in that wretched locality.

The simple statement of facts contained in the good priest's letter is more eloquent and impressive than a more elaborate description. We regret that such an appeal did not eventuate in something more substantial than the mere expression of sympathy. His Excellency transfers the public responsibility of providing against the starvation of so many thousands to the Poor Law Commissioners, who will transfer it to the guardians, who will in turn hand the complaint and complainants to the gravedigger:—

VERY REV. MR. KELLY'S LETTER TO LORD CLARENDON, LORD LIEUTENANT AND GENERAL GOVERNOR OF IRELAND.

Kilrush, Dec. 13th, 1849.

MY LORD—Fully sensible of your pressing engagements I am unwilling to trespass on your Excellency; yet, from the heartrending scenes which have occurred in this district within the last few days, I feel it a duty briefly to offer our distressed situation to your Excellency's consideration.

In this union (Kilrush), the poorest in Ireland, during the summer months 30,000 persons—half the present population—received outdoor relief. Of these nearly 20,000 have been within the last year thrown houseless and homeless on the world. I shall not harrow your Excellency's tender feelings by a description of their miserable state—whole families huddled together in miserable huts—in appearance more like corpses from the sepulcre than animated beings. Several philanthropic Englishmen have visited the district, and saw with their own eyes our situation, who, I presume, have already given your Excellency a faint idea—yet the cup of our misery has only within the last fortnight been filled up. Not a single ounce of meal or any outdoor relief has been given for the last ten days. Our poor-house contains over 2,000 inmates. Of these 900 are children of a delicate frame and constitution. Yet the young as well as the old are fed on *turnips* for the last week. Thousands from the neighbouring parishes, deprived of outdoor relief, crowd about the union workhouses—there disappointed, they surround the houses of the shopkeepers and struggling farmer; their lamentations, their hunger shrieks, are truly heartrending. Yet, my lord, I am gratified to say, that no property is touched—no threats held forth.

I know whole families in this town to lie down on their bed of straw, determined rather to *starve* than *steal*. It is true, that no means are left untried to alleviate their miseries but many, very many charitable persons, of whom it may be said that if they could coin their heart's into gold they would give it to the poor in their present extreme necessity. Yet what avail their efforts to meet the present awful visitation? It was determined that a public meeting would be held to address your Excellency; yet, when a report—alas! a true report—has reached, that *thirty-five paupers* from Mayarta parish, who travelled some 15 miles in the hope to be relieved at the workhouse, *were all drowned* whilst crossing a narrow ferry, I considered it my duty not to lose a moment in communicating to your Excellency our awful situation, which may be imagined but cannot be described. *One week more and no food*. The honest peaceable poor of this district fall like leaves in autumn. I feel in thus addressing you I have taken a bold step, yet your sympathy for the poor has encouraged me.

Never—never be it said that during your Excellency's administration half the population in a remote and wretched district were suffered to starve.

I write in a hurry—I write in confusion. At this moment my house is surrounded by a crowd of poor persons whose blood has become water, seeking for relief, which, alas! I cannot bestow. Anxiously and confidently expecting at your Excellency's hands a remedy.

I have the honour to be, my lord, your Excellency's most obedient and humble servant,

TIMOTHY KELLY, P.P., KILRUSH.

HIS EXCELLENCY'S REPLY.

DUBLIN CASTLE, DECEMBER 18th, 1849.

SIR—in acknowledging the receipt of your memorial, the Lord Lieutenant has directed me to state, that his Excellency has received with deep regret, the intelligence of the melancholy loss of life which has occurred at the Ferry of Kilrush, and of the destitution stated to prevail in that union.

He regrets that the guardians have not put rates in course of collection, from which funds could be afforded for the relief of the poor, the responsibility of providing which rests with that body.

Your communication has been referred to the Poor Law Commissioners.

I am, SIR, your most obedient humble servant,

T. N. Reddington.

Recreated from The Freeman's Journal, Dublin, December 24, 1849.

HOPE.

Hope on, hope on, though all seems dark,
And clouds obscure thy way;
Though bitter tears and sorrows mark
Thy rising every day;

Though pain and care oppress thy heart,
And troubles cross thy mind.
Still cherish hope within the heart,
There's happiness yet to find.

Hope on, hope still, though sad the hour,
Though storms may swell thy breast.
Though gloom surround and darkness low'r,
Thou shalt have future rest;

Though grief should point her piercing dart,
And plant its barb in thy mind—
Still cherish hope within thy heart,
There's happiness yet to find.

Recreated from The Waterford News, Waterford, February 8, 1850.

1850

Selected Headlines

DISTRAINING IN ULSTER	244
EVICTIONS IN TIPPERARY	247
CONVENTION OF AMERICAN WOMEN	249
FORTUNATE ESCAPE	250
ATTACK UPON HER MAJESTY THE QUEEN	251
FEMALE ADVOCATES AT THE BAR	252
HIS GRACE THE DUKE OF DEVONSHIRE	254
THE NEW CARDINALS	256
THE "NO-POPERY" MOVEMENT	262
DREADFUL SHIPWRECK—LOSS OF NINETY	264

TENANT RIGHT.

New Lodge, Garristown.
December 26th, 1849.

DEAR SIR—In compliance with the wishes of many of the guardian of the Dunshaughlin union, I forward you a copy of the petition for "tenant right" adopted by them lately. They consider that public opinion should be kept alive on the subject as much as possible, and would feel obliged if you would be kind enough to insert their petition at the earliest date your convenience would admit of.

I have the honour to remain, Sir,

Very sincerely yours, J. Markey.

TO THE RIGHT HON. AND HONOURABLE THE KNIGHTS, CITIZENS, AND BURGESSES IN PARLIAMENT ASSEMBLED—THE PETITION OF THE GUARDIANS OF THE DUNSHAUGHLIN UNION—

SHEWETH—That poverty and destitution are increasing in an alarming degree in this country, in consequence of the great bulk of the labouring population falling on the rates for support. Industry is paralyzed, employment and improvement at an end, public confidence shaken, and nothing but ruin staring us in the face. It is the deliberate opinion of this board, that this deplorable state of things is the result of the present high rental, and the insecurity of tenure in this country.

Petitioners beg leave to call the attention of your honourable house to the fact of your hon. house having withdrawn the protection in the shape of duties on foreign production which protection enabled the landlords of this country to pay a rental which it would now be impossible to meet, and ruinous to attempt.

Petitioners, therefore, most earnestly implore your hon. house to enact a law of "Tenant Right," founded on the following propositions, which will give the landlord a fair value for his land, and secure to the tenant his outlay and occupancy:—

"That Griffith's valuation, when revised according to the present corn and provision averages, be declared the letting value in all instances, and that the tenants in possession get the preference on said terms.

"That a revision take place at the expiration of every seven years, and the rent raised or lowered accordingly for the next ensuing seven years; but that the revision shall be guided solely by the corn and provision averages of the past seven years, and shall not take into account any improvements effected on the land by labour or capital. That the tenant shall never be deprived of his occupancy, except for non-payment of rent; and in case a year's rent was suffered to be due, that the landlord should be empowered to dispose of the occupancy to the highest and fairest bidder—sufficient notice of same being given, reserving to himself the arrear due, and handing the balance, if any, to the tenant. That, in order to encourage employment, the outlay of capital, and consequent improvement, and in lieu of compensation for same, the tenant shall possess the right to dispose of his occupancy whenever he may think fit, which will be a stimulant to the judicious outlay of capital, as on that will solely depend his hope of remuneration from a discerning public."

Petitioners beg leave to submit to your hon. house that Griffith's valuation is the most perfect document of the kind that has ever appeared; that he is a disinterested party; that it was made at a time and for a purpose that places it above all suspicion and peculiarly adapted to the present emergency, on account of its extraordinary excellence as a relative standard. It would consequently have the effect of establishing a uniform system, and put an end to all the odious distinctions and recriminations of the present individualised mismanagement. It would, in fact, create a great national system founded on the Divine precept of doing unto all men as they would be done by. It would also encourage the employment of labour, as it would be the means of keeping down the rates.

Such are the great and simple principles on which we most respectfully demand the verdict of your hon. house. The time for temporising is past; any attempt at such must only end in the most signal failure.

Thousands upon thousands of our countrymen await in the most intense anxiety the result of your deliberations, ready with joy to start in the race for prosperity and freedom—if, in the recognition of these their just and reasonable demands, you bid them hope—or, in the event of their rejection, to seek beneath the star-spangled banner of the west for that encouragement and protection which the impolicy of their own rulers deny them.

And petitioners will pray.

MISCELLANEOUS NEWS.—The death of the late Mr. A. B. Bleasley, county Monaghan, continues a subject much discussed in his neighborhood, in consequence of reports which appear to have been circulated from a horribly malicious motive. Though attended by two respectable medical gentlemen in his last illness, letters by some person unknown insinuated mysteriously that he had been poisoned, and continued to spread the accusation till it was deemed necessary, first, to hold an investigation, and afterwards the district coroner caused the body of the deceased to be exhumed, and the stomach sent to Dublin to be analysed by a chemist.

It was next found that the expense of the analysis in Dublin would exceed the amount which the coroner was legally allowed to pay, and so the stomach has been transferred to Dr. Hodges of Belfast, who has not yet furnished the report of his analysation. The (to all appearance) malicious accusations insinuate that the deceased was poisoned by the nearest member of his own family.

The *Cork Examiner* says that the board of superintendence of Cork Prison requires the turnkeys to discharge the debasing office of inflicting chastisement, by whipping, upon young persons convicted of turnip stealing and other petty larcenies, and that two who refused to comply with the order were punished by a fine.

EXTERMINATION IN WEXFORD.—We have received a letter from Ferns, dated Monday night, December 31st, in which the writer states that on that day a number of men, sent by a Mr. Donovan, had been levelling with "pick and crowbar" an entire street in Ferns, and when our correspondent was closing his letter the last of forty houses was *on fire!* It belonged (our correspondent adds) to a poor widow of the name of Byrne. It is thought that one of Mr. Donovan's levellers set it on fire as she would not surrender. Some of these poor people say they never gave possession, and it is pretty certain that no notice was ever sent to the workhouse.—*Freeman.*

LANDLORD AND TENANT WAR.—On the night of the 22nd instant, as Terrence Foran, a driver on one of the estates of H. D. Carden, Esq., was returning to his home between Mountmelick and Maryborough, he was fired at by a man who concealed himself between two bushes on the road side. The shot did not prove fatal. Two slugs being lodged in his arm and shoulder. Foran is at present under the care of Dr. Jacob, in the county infirmary. Three men, named Garret Kelly, William Kelly, and John Keating having been arrested on suspicion of being implicated in this outrage; they were remanded until next Monday, for further examination.—*Leinster Express.*

Recreated from The Nation, Dublin, January 5, 1850

House of Correction.

WANTED, TWO ACTIVE and EFFICIENT MEN to act as TURNKEYS in this Prison.

Applications, and Testimonials of Character, to be lodged at the City Gaol before 12 o'Clock on MONDAY, the 28th inst.

Waterford, January 24, 1850.

FOR SALE,

THE FINE A. I.

BRIG, "MARY,"

Register 108 Tons, New Measurement,

BUILT at Bras D'or, Cape Breton, for Private Use; launched in November, 1846; registered April, 1847; is in very superior order, as regards Hull, Rigging, and Sails; carries a Large Cargo, say 160 Tons dead weight; sails remarkably fast, and is a first-rate sea boat.— Length, 70 feet; breadth, 20 feet; depth, 12 feet; can be sent to sea without any outlay, except provisions; now lying at the Quay, opposite Little George's Street, Waterford.

Apply to

R. F. SWEETMAN.

23 Jan., 1850.

Reprinted from The Waterford News, Waterford, January 25, 1850.

THE HORRORS OF KILRUSH.

A Catholic clergyman, in a letter to the *Limerick Examiner*, says:—The part of the union of Kilrush with which I am officially connected—Moyarty and Kilballyowen—extending from Loophead to the Ferryboat Pass, (notorious for the drowning of forty paupers coming here from Kilrush), is a promontory between the sea and the Shannon, 20 miles long and about 3 broad. Its population in 1841 was 13,000—it is now cut down to 9,000. Of this amount 1,700 are on the relief list. For the last month, since the stopping of out-door relief, they are living on turnips principally—most of the poor creatures on a meal a day, and longer, sometimes, without a morsel at all. The poor people are worn out to skeletons, with yellow skins. The other clergymen of this parish and myself see them daily dying of cold and want, and the many diseases that attend famine. In two townlands near each other, eleven persons died of want since the beginning of December last. On last Thursday I met four pauper families returning from Kilrush to Kiltulig, a distance of 21 miles. They travelled all night on Wednesday, so as to be in time, according to the directions of the relieving officer, for the sitting of the board on Thursday, to have their names called. After remaining the whole day, they were told that their ploughland would not be called until some other time. They had only one halfpenny worth of bread for the 42 miles. It was truly pitiful to see the old, hardly able to carry themselves, endeavoring to bring the young children on their backs.

Mr. Major stated—"That there must be something radically wrong in Kilrush Union—that in every part of the county with which he was acquainted, there were evident signs of returning prosperity, even in the worst parts of those districts; but in this Union our fellow creatures are reduced to a condition unexampled in any time or country. The poor presented a spectacle of wretchedness that would be unsupportable to the feelings of men if they were not, as appeared to him, beginning to forget that these poor people were their fellow-creatures. In the whole course of my life I never witnessed such patient agony. I protest that I thought the sufferings of the poor in this Union beyond human endurance." And while the Assistant Barrister sat in the court-house, the coroner sat in the market-house, holding an inquest on the body of "Bryan M'Mahon," who lay four days unburied, midway between the "great man's gate" and the workhouse; not three hundred yards from either; and within a stone's throw of the court-house. What were the facts? The wretched father, John M'Mahon, had his house twice levelled by the mild "Marcus;" wandered from place to place; at last, driven by hunger, entered the work-house, remained fourteen days; some of his children got the small-pox—fled from it, returned to Kilrush, starved—was ordered 14 days relief, five pounds of (contractor's) Indian meal per day for seven in family!!—eat a part—paid his rent with more; the fourteen days expired; his relief(?) was stopped—his child then died, he and another child lie dying at this moment.

A coroner's jury have returned a verdict that another person, a man named O'Brien, died, in Kilrush Union last week of starvation.

LANDLORD AND TENANT WAR.

EXTERMINATIONS IN THE KING'S COUNTY—A correspondent writes to us as follows:—Jan. 23d, 1850. In my last, I promised to send you a list of the evicted on Mr. Cassidy's estate: I now fulfil my promise. They are as follows:— Widow Walsh, seven in family; Widow Walsh, six in family; Catherine Walsh, six in family; John Byrne, three in family; Michael Walsh, four in family; Bridget Walsh, widow, six in family; Edward Walsh, three in family; James Reid, ten in family; Michael Fitzgerald, two in family; Widow Williams, four in family; James Cavanagh, three in family; Dan Carey, jun., six in family; Dan Carey, sen., five in family; Margaret Loghnan, five in family; John Delany, six in family; Joseph Jennings, three in family. Total seventy-seven. The above had their homes thrown down and were sent homeless wanderers. The following are those who had their houses taken possession of, but let in again as caretakers, at one penny per week—William Spain, six in family; Michael Spain, five in family; Larence Spain, six in family; Thomas Corcoran, six in family; Michael Read, jun., five in family; William Pardy, eight in family; Michael Read, sen., four in family; Elizabeth Jennings, six in family; Total, forty-six. Ejected in all, 125. Of the forty-six who were let in as caretakers, some were compelled to go as bailiffs next day, on their first and second coming, else the house would be tumbled about their ears. The case of Williams is the worst of all—lying in a fever bed, and dragged out in the presence of a large crowd of people, sheriff, police, &c.

THE POISONING OF MR. BLEAZBY.

The *Armagh Guardian* has published the verdict of the coroner's jury as follows;—"The late Arthur Bernard Bleazby, late of Glenaul, came by his death by poison called arsenic having been administered into his body as said jury believes by the hands of Sarah Maria Bleazby (his wife) and that William Gordon, her steward, was accessory thereto, and that both said individuals are guilty of the murder of said A. B. Bleazby." The coroner's warrant was immediately issued for their arrest. They have both been committed to the county gaol.

ATTEMPTED MURDER AND ROBBERY.

The *Nenagh Guardian* states that on the 22nd inst., Mr. Kennedy of Hollymount, county Tipperary, while riding near Charleville, in the King's county, was waylaid in a narrow lane by two men, one of whom presented a pistol and demanded his money. Mr. Kennedy grasped the pistol which went off in the struggle, wounding him slightly and his horse. Mr. Kennedy's foot slipped, and having fallen, was obliged to give up his purse to his assailants.

REV. MR. O'REILLY OF CAVAN, cautioned the people against Ribbon societies on Sunday last, and on the same evening the police searched a party in a public house for Ribbon documents, and arrested one of them.

Recreated from The Nation, Dublin, February 2, 1850

RETALIATION IN ULSTER.—*The Northern Whig* says:—A man named M'Kergar, near Belfast, whose character is highly spoken of, held, under Mr. Shaw, of Ballytweedy, a farm in the town of Carnmavey, parish of Killkead, six or eight miles from Belfast; and it appears that he and his ancestors had occupied the farm for several generations back. He had lately got into some arrears of rent, and an ejectment was sued out against him. He disposed of his crop, and handed over the proceeds to the landlord, leaving only £10. due, and hoping that he would be permitted to retain possession; but he was disappointed, and was turned out. The farm was let to a new tenant, who was put into formal possession, and was about to enter upon actual possession, with his family; but, on the previous night, the house and office-houses were burned to the ground.

The *Tuam Herald* says:—Within the last few days, no less than twenty families, on the Killaloonty property, near this town, have been dispossessed of their houses, by order of the Court of Chancery. The peculiar hardship of this case is that the tenants so ejected were paying at the rate of £8. per acre, for the land held by them, and that their houses were built solely at their own expense, notwithstanding which, and being up to this distressing period most punctual, they are mercilessly thrown upon the world's wide waste with their helpless families.

A MAN KILLED LEVELLING HIS OWN HOUSE.—The *Kilkenny Journal* states:—A poor man named John Hickey, a tenant of P. R. Welch, on the lands of Newtown Welch, came by his death under the following melancholy circumstances, on Tuesday last:—He received from his landlord £5 for parting with his little holding of 4 1/2 acres, on the condition of pulling down his own house, and while engaged in this hard, heart-breaking operation, the walls of his cabin fell upon him, crushing him to instant death.

DISTRAINING IN ULSTER.—We (*Londonderry Standard*) learn that in the neighborhood of Quigley's Point, on the shore of Lough Foyle, on Saturday last, Lucius Carey, had occasion to distrain, for payment of rent, a horse, cow, and heifer, belonging to Michael Bonnar, a tenant of lands near to Redcastle. Bonnar prevailed on the bailiff to leave the premises, by promising that he himself would take the animals to Mr. Carey and settle with him. This he did not do; and, on the bailiff returning, he found that the horse and cow had been driven away, and the heifer slaughtered, one quarter of which was boiling in a pot in Bonnar's house and, as if in utter recklessness, the fire had been fed with a spinning-wheel, and flax produced from three gallons of seed. On Monday, Peter Anderson, an under-tenant on the farm occupied by the late Mr. Arthur Leper, of Three Trees, had three cows and a calf distrained for rent, by order of Mr. James M'Conalogue, Receiver under the Court of Chancery. While the care-takers were on the premises, a crowd of persons appeared on the ground, and, on the caretakers approaching to ascertain who they were, they made off. The care-takers followed a short way, and, on their return they found the cattle were driven away. They went in pursuit, but in vain, and, on again returning, they found that Anderson's cart had disappeared.

WORKING OF THE POOR LAW IN LIMERICK.—A poor man recently died in Newcastle of starvation, and the guardians of that union attributed his death to the refusal of the Poor Law Commissioners to allow them to give out-door relief. They then renewed their application for such permission, but were again refused. Since that, another inquest has been held, and the following verdict returned:—"We, the jury on the coroner's inquest, held on the late Charles M'Carthy, having duly heard the evidence ad-

THE VILLAGE OF KILLARD.

Reprinted from The Illustrated London News, February 9, 1850.

duced on that occasion, find that deceased came by his death from gradual hunger, though having duly received the quantity of meal allowed by the Poor Law, for himself, his wife, and children; and that this hunger was occasioned by the incompetency of the legal provision, and all having to give 3 lbs. from said limited quantity of meal, as weekly rent for his lodging, and we recommend, that the guardians do henceforward make some allowance for rent to the destitute, who may be houseless, on out-door relief.

Recreated from The Nation, Dublin, February 2, 1850

BREAKFAST, LUNCH, AND DINNER BREADS of extraordinary excellence, made from superior French Flour, are now on sale at the Establishments of

O'CALLAGHAN AND CO.,
37, AUNGIER-STREET,
152, CAPEL-STREET,
41, HENRY-STREET,
13, WILLIAM-STREET,
13, MERRION-ROW.

Those breads are fermented on a new principle, which perfects the process in a much shorter time, ensuring a particular sweetness which the old tedious system could never produce.

Reprinted from The Nation, Dublin, March 9, 1850.

STATE OF THE KANTURK UNION.—We have received the following from a Kanturk correspondent:— "The number in the workhouse and its fourteen auxiliary houses is very near 6,000; receiving out-door relief 16,000, applicants for and in want of relief 18,000; so that we have 40,000 of in-door paupers, out-door recipients, and applicants for relief in their rack-rented and distressed union. Nearly half the workhouse inmates are either sick or in a convalescent state. The bread boxes which convey the bread from the workhouse to the auxiliaries return with dead paupers crammed into them to be coffined at the workhouse, and thrown into watery pits with only a little clay shovelled over them. Unless this union get a liberal share of the government loan, few souls of the 40,000 will be alive next harvest."

Recreated from The Nation, Dublin, March 9, 1850.

MATHEW COLLINS,
CHIMNEY SWEEPER
To the Royal Bank of Ireland, the National and Provincial Banks,
13, SOUTH KING-STREET,
(Near Stephen's-green.)

MATHEW COLLINS will not be accountable except for orders left at his own residence, as persons in his line are in the habit of going in one another's name, particularly as there is a party of the same trade in the street.

He cautions the Housekeepers not to employ Men Chimney Sweeps from the streets in his name. Those who seek employment by knocking at hall-doors, please give them no answer, except they are all well known in person, or by persons answering the door.

M. C. has a Machine for Cleansing Crooked Chimneys, by a ball and rope; also can supply any house with a boy, by giving two days' notice, for examining Smoky Chimneys, by the wind blowing down them or the smoke returning, which Chimneys are always in the habit of doing.

M. C. engages to cure Smoky Chimneys in Country or City.

1,000 Barrels of the best description of Soot for Manure, to be Sold either by the Sack or Cart Load.

A CARD.

MR. PATRICK BROPHY,
IRISH AND BRITISH
LAW, LAND, PARLIAMENTARY
AND
GENERAL AGENT,
OFFICE, 38, LOWER ORMOND-QUAY.
DUBLIN.
RENTS COLLECTED.
LIFE AND FIRE INSURANCES EFFECTED.
ABSTRACTS OF TITLE PREPARED
AND INVESTIGATED.
RENTALS PREPARED, AND LOANS ON
REAL ESTATE NEGOCIATED.
Proceedings conducted in the Equity Courts, and before the Commissioners for the Sale of Incumbered Estates.
Petitions and Memorials to the Crown, for Patents, Renunciations, &c., prepared and forwarded.
Appeals to the House of Lords, and Privy Council, Election and other Petitions to Parliament prepared and conducted.
RECEIVERS', TRUSTEES', AND EXECUTORS' ACCOUNTS ARRANGED AND PASSED.
ESTATES SOLD BY COMMISSION,
And all descriptions of Law and Land Agency transacted in all parts of the Empire.

Reprinted from The Nation, Dublin, March 9, 1850.

METROPOLITAN NEWS.

SANATORY MEASURES.—At the last meeting of the Sanatory Association, a letter was read from Dr. Willis, of Ormond-quay, approving of the proceedings of the Sanatory Association generally, but pointing out one error which they should have avoided, and which should not be again committed. This was, opening and cleaning out filthy sewers in crowded localities during the heat of summer. It should be done only during the winter months.

Reprinted from The Nation, Dublin, April 6, 1850.

EVICTIONS IN TIPPERARY.

The *Tipperary Vindicator* says:—"Two thirds of the land in the North Riding of Tipperary, held by the tenant farmers, will change occupiers this year. Never were such shoals of ejectment notices levelled against the unfortunate tenants as the landlords are issuing for the coming quarter sessions in Thurles and Nenagh. "The razed village of Toomevara presents a melancholy spectacle to the eye of the tourist. The long line of destroyed habitations which formed the principal street of the unfortunate place, remains as they were eleven months ago. The huts which were built against the chapel walls have been tumbled down under the vigorous blows of sundry bailiffs, and their inhabitants scattered far and wide over the country.

"The village of the Silvermines has lately undergone the ordeal of the destroying system. Very many of the houses have been tumbled down; and like Toomevara, this once gay and happy hamlet presents a gloomy picture of woe and desolation."

A DEFENCE FUND.—The *Dondalk Democrat* suggests to the tenants to subscribe to a common fund for defending ejectment processes. We are certain, it remarks, "that if the tenants defended these actions, not more than one-fourth of them would be decreed. We have been told that one proprietor in this county (Louth) has given orders to have sixty of his tenants proceeded against by civil bill, and we are certain that others will follow the same course. Ejectment decrees will also be sought for on a large scale by several rack-renters, to hunt out the plundered populations from their homes."

An incendiary fire occurred last week on the property of Mr. Munce, near Killough, county Down. The reason assigned is, that he had taken several small farms, which were unoccupied.

BY APPOINTMENT.

M. FARRELL,
FANCY BREAD AND BISCUIT BAKER TO HIS EXCELLENCY THE LORD LIEUTENANT.

THIS Establishment is conducted strictly on the principle of the most eminent London, Paris, and Continental Houses in a similar line.

Farrell's Celebrated Wine and Oyster Biscuit, so well known in Burton Bindon's, Duke-street, and the principal Hotels and Taverns in the City of Dublin, also at various Grocery Establishments and Officers' Messes throughout reland.

FARRELL'S APPROVED INFANT BISCUIT POWDER.

The Proprietor to prevent mistakes by Parents, Nurses, &c., requests it to be particularly observed that it can be procured at no other house in Dublin but at

FARRELL'S, 30, GRAFTON-STREET.

It may be had there, and there only, in its genuine purity.

MUFFINS.

These delicious articles, which have met with immense public patronage at

FARRELL'S, 30, GRAFTON-STREET,

continue to be supplied to the Nobility, Gentry, and the Public generally, made up in the same Superior Style of Material that has rendered the article the foremost in its line.

Soda Bread, Rusks, and Fancy Bread of all kinds to be had always ready.

Mrs. Mary Woodhouse, of Poulton, who died last week, at the age of eighty-nine, has left the following offspring :— seven sons and daughters, 59 grandsons and daughters, 72 great grand-children, one great-great-grand child; total, 139.

It is stated that great excitement was momentarily caused in Waterford on Good Friday, on seeing, as it was thought, a man hanging from the yard-arm of a Portuguese vessel. It transpired, however, that it was a national custom, there being nothing more than a stuffed figure to represent Judas Iscariot.

On Saturday night a dreadful accident occurred near Newtownhamilton, county Armagh. A farmer after seeing his cattle all safe at night, went away, leaving a coal of fire after him by accident. When he awoke in the morning the premises, with three cows and a horse, were burned to ashes.

KILRUSH WORKHOUSE.—A correspondent of the *Limerick Examiner* says—"The Union Workhouse contains about 8,000 inmates. Nearly one third of this number is under medical treatment. The expense of giving the poor wretches the comfort of a fire is an unwarrantable indulgence; therefore they are not left a spark to heat drink for the dying. The luxury of a little butter mixed with stirabout, which, in the utter impossibility to procure milk, was given to the paupers for some time past—this of course is a shocking abuse, and on the extraordinary plea of its being productive of disease, it is made the subject of a board room sitting, the result of which is, to reduce the quantity to one-half the usual amount. Over forty are turned out from it each week to the dead house. That is, 160 each month, or 1,920 per year."

DESTITUTION ON THE NORTH.—At the Newry board of guardians a case of the destitution of a family that had seen better days, was brought under consideration Saturday. Doctor Davis, who had visited them, stated that he could not have believed, unless he had witnessed it, that there were any persons in Newry so awfully destitute. The three younger children—two of them were girls and the other a boy—aged, respectively, ten, eight, and six years, were completely naked, and, reduced to mere skeletons. The older children appeared to have got little food, but they had scarcely any clothing. When he desired one of them to stand up, she declined doing so, as was supposed by Acting Constable Williams, because she had not sufficient clothing.

PAUPER GRATITUDE—The following letter was recently addressed by some female emigrants to the guardians of Newcastle union:—

"**GENTLEMEN**—We take the liberty of writing these few lines to you, thanking you sincerely for your kind benefits towards us. We thank God for having such a favourable opportunity of doing some good for ourselves. We hope the Great God and His Blessed Mother will be our guide by sea and land. We never can return thanks to you, gentlemen, for your kindness towards us. May the blessing of the Almighty God and the orphans attend you and your families both day and night, not forgetting our worthy master, and our kind and affectionate matron. We remain with the most grateful respect," &c., &c.

A SMALL TITHE AGITATION.—At the Trinity parish vestry in Cork on Monday, the Rev. Mr. Williamson in the chair, when the motion against Ministers' money was introduced, the chairman refused to put it, and warned the meeting that he would not leave the chair, except by force, and then they should take the consequences. They were then about to adjourn to the school-room, when Alderman Hodder said if they went to the school-room they should be punished for it.

A MILLTOWN MALBAY correspondent writes—A few days ago, the bailiffs of an absentee landlord came on part of his lands, near Milltown, and dispossessed a poor man named Malone, having seven in family dependent on him for support. He had but the cabin he lived in, as he had given up his land, and his poor family are now thrown out on the road-side without any shelter from the inclemency of the weather. His forefathers were in possession of the place for the last 160 years. Is it not a cruel thing that no resource is left the poor tenant? I have known many more tenants who expended up to 180£ on part of the lands, in building lodges; and half of them were forced to fly, as they would not get an abatement. They were paying 2£ 10s. per acre, and now it is set for 1£ 5s. to the new tenant.

Recreated from The Nation, Dublin, April 6, 1850.

CONVENTION OF AMERICAN WOMEN.—A number of the women of Ohio, who are "dissatisfied with the present position of their sex," have signed a call for a convention of females to meet in the town of Salem, Ohio, on the nineteenth of this month. The purpose of the convention is stated to be, in the words of the signers, "to concert measures to secure to all persons the recognition of equal rights, and the extention of the priviliges of governmen without distinction of *sex* or colour :—To inquire into the origin and design of the rights of humanity, whether they are coeval with the human race, of universal heritage, and inalienable, or merely conventional, held by sufferance, dependent for a basis on location, position, colour and *sex*."

HOLLOWAY'S PILLS AN INFALLIBLE CURE FOR FEMALE COMPLAINTS.—Women at different periods of life are subject to complaints which require a peculiar medicine to remove, and it is now an established fact that there is none so suitable as Holowny's Pills—their purifying qualities render them invaluable to the maiden, the mother, and the middle-aged; they are searching, cleansing, and yet invigorating, so that females of all ages may take them with perfect safety; and it is truly astonishing to find the benefit that is derived by taking a few doses, which speedily remove every species of irregularity in the system, and establish health on a firm basis.

Reprinted from The Waterford News, Waterford, May 31, 1850.

POLICE OFFICE—MONDAY.

(The Mayor presided.)

CHILD FOUND.

Costable Horan stated that he had, at an early hour on Monday morning, found a fine female child on the Tramore road, near this city (the child, only a few days old, was in the arms of a woman in court).

The Mayor ordered it to be taken to the union.

WINDOW BREAKING.

Mr Grady, relieving officer, complained against a pauper named Kiely for breaking his windows on Sunday evening. Prisoner was let off with a reprimand.

ARMS.

An old Frenchman, in broken English, applied for his gun which had been taken from him by the police when "goen' out shoot de crows." He said he thought the gun was as free here as it was in France.

The Mayor ordered him his gun.

TUESDAY.

Magistrates present—The Mayor, Mr King, Mr Dobbyn, and Mr Tabiteau.

GOING TO JAIL A BOON.

A decent but poor-looking woman (with a child in her arms) named Rourke, was charged for street begging. The woman stated that she was totally destitute.

Mr King said that the magistrates would send her to jail for a short time through charity.

Woman—Thank your worship.

WATERING THE STREETS.

TO THE EDITOR OF THE NEWS.

SIR—Permit me, through your influential journal, to ask the Corporation why it is that the streets are not regularly watered? In all directions large clouds of dust were flying on Monday, yet, sir, no watering-cart did I see? Having suffered so much last summer, I think we ought to be very careful as to watering, cleansing, and ventilating this year. It is possible that we would have no sickness at all last summer if our city had been as it ought to be—clean.

Respectfully, M.

Waterford, June 5.

Reprinted from The Waterford News, Waterford, June 7, 1850.

FORTUNATE ESCAPE.

DUNGARVAN, JUNE 18.

On this evening three young ladies took it into their heads to take charge of a horse and gig belonging to their papa, to take a drive some distance into the country for recreation. The horse took head, and ran off in full speed; Miss Godkin acted as driver on the occasion, and showed great courage and presence of mind though in the midst of danger. The other young ladies were determined to jump off the gig, but most fortunately a young lad came up at the time, and rendered every assistance by stopping the horse. It must be stated to his credit, were it not for his exertions the ladies would have been precipitated into a deep dike on the side of the Military-road filled with large stones, and in all probability would have cost them their lives. I would most humbly suggest to the fair ones, in future that they ought to wear "a neat stiff tommy with a high collar, black stock, and a copper-colored hat." This dress, I presume, may be the means of giving a more masculine air, and a more commanding attitude to the ladies assuming the dignity and pomposity of an Arabic chieftain or warrior, to check a restive horse. This is the third time within the last fortnight that life has been endangered in this locality, in consequence of ladies attempting to manage these restive animals.

ROBBERY IN CHURCH.

DUNGARVAN, JUNE 16TH.

On Sunday a woman of the name of O'Brien robbed another woman named Mary Hayes, by cutting the pocket, containing 7 shillings, off her side with a scissors, in the Chapel of Dungarvan. The times are very alarming, most particularly when these deluded and misguided creatures commit such acts of wickedness in the house of the Lord. When the congregation is most intense in offering up praise and adoration to Him who holds in His hands the destinies of all nations; this unfortunate creature assumes all the sanctity and devotion of the primitive Christians, but like a painted sepulchre fair without and foul within.

Constable Mathew Dwyer having received intelligence of the robbery, detected the delinquent in the Chapel, wherein she was most attentively listening to the Christian Brothers lecturing on the principles of morality and Christian virtue. I am particularly informed this is the third time that a similar robbery has been committed in this Chapel, by some more of the party with whom the prisoner is connected, and the sooner we get rid of such notorious characters the better.—*Correspondent.*

Recreated from The Waterford News, Waterford, June 21, 1850.

BOOKBINDING.

M. CALDWELL,
No. 31, SOUTH FREDERICK STREET,
Bookbinder to the Royal Dublin Society, &c.,

RESPECTFULLY intimates to his Friends and the Public that he continues to Bind in every variety of style—namely: Morocco, Russia, Patent and Classic Vellum, Velvet, Silk, Law, Fancy and Stained Calf Cloth, &c., which he executes with elegance and expedition, on Moderate Terms.

ANTIQUE OR MODERN.

NOVEL, RARE, AND ELEGANTLY DESIGNED
FINE GOLD BROOCHES,
BRACELETS, SOLITAIRES,
CHAINS, RINGS, STUDS, VEST
BUTTONS, PINS, &c.,
To be had on Moderate Terms,
IN THE
LONDON JEWELLERY, WATCH,
AND
PLATE SHOWROOMS,
GRAFTON-STREET,
(Near Trinity College).
GARDNER.

Reprinted from The Nation, Dublin, July 6, 1850.

ATTACK UPON HER MAJESTY THE QUEEN.

It is our painful duty to announce that a cowardly attack was on Thursday made upon her Most Gracious Majesty the Queen by a man who until within the last four years held a commission in her Majesty's service.

About twenty minutes after six o'clock last evening her Majesty, accompanied by three of the royal children, and Viscountess Jocelyn, Lady in Waiting, left Cambridge-house, Picadilly, where her Majesty had been calling to inquire after the health of her illustrious uncle. A crowd had assembled without the court-yard to witness her Majesty's departure, and as the royal carriage passed out of the gates a person respectably dressed, advanced two or three paces, and with a small black cane, which he held in his hand, struck a sharp blow at the Queen. The blow took effect upon the upper part of her Majesty's forehead, and upon her bonnet, which being of light texture was driven by its force. The act was witnessed by a great many persons, and a rush being made, the delinquent was instantly seized, and one person, unable to restrain his resentment, dealt the man a blow in the face which drew blood at once. But for the timely arrival of the police, he would have been still more roughly handled.

Her Majesty betrayed no feeling of alarm, and immediately after the occurrence drove up Picadilly, on her return to Buckingham Palace, the spectators cheering her loudly as she passed along.

When the prisoner was brought to Vine-street station, Inspector Whall, the officer on duty, received the charge. On being asked his name, he replied, without hesitation—"Robert Page," describing himself as a retired lieutenant of the 10th Hussars, and adding that he resided at No. 27, Duke-street, St. James. Evidence of several witnesses having been taken, the prisoner was asked what he had to say to the charge. He replied that it was true he had struck her Majesty a slight blow with a thin stick, but he added emphatically, in allusion to the witnesses, "those men cannot prove whether I struck her head or her bonnet." The prisoner was then conducted to one of the police cells, the charge being entered upon the police sheets as follows:—"Robert Page, aged 43, retired lieutenant, charged with assaulting her Majesty the Queen by striking her on the head with a cane, in Picadilly, at twenty minutes past six on Thursday, the 27th inst."

On being searched there was found upon the prisoner two keys and a pocket handkerchief. No money or weapon of any kind was discovered.

After the prisoner had been placed in a cell Mr. Otway, superintendent of the C division, despatched Mr. Inspector Field, the chief officer of the detective force, to search his lodgings. Mr. Field there ascertained that the prisoner had lodged on the third floor (an elegant suite of apartments) of 27 Duke-street, during the last two years and a half; that he was a man of regular habits, and paid his bills with great punctuality. His father was described to be a man of large property at Wisbeach, where he formerly carried on business as an extensive corn factor. A large number of papers and documents was seized by Mr. Field, but nothing has yet been discovered which could by possibility explain the motive of the rash act.

The prisoner was to have been brought up for examination at the Home-office yesterday morning.

A reference to *Hart's Army List* shows that the prisoner entered her Majesty's service as a cornet, by purchase, in the 10th Hussars, on the 5th of February, 1841. He was promoted to the rank of lieutenant on the 22d of July, 1842, and retired, by sale of his commission, a short time previously to the embarkation of the regiment for India in 1846.

The prisoner is a respectable looking man and slightly bald. He wears mustacheos, but has not a very military appearance.

Recreated from The Freeman's Journal, Dublin, June 29, 1850.

EVICTIONS ON THE CLANRICARDE PROPERTY.

TO THE EDITOR OF THE NATION.

Sir.—In your perambulations it may be possible you have visited Loughrea, an old town, with long-stretching suburbs to nearly all points of the compass, situated on the shore of a lake of the same name; once the stronghold of the bold Mac-an-Earlias, (the sons of the Red Earl of Ulster, DeBurgo) who braved English rule for better than half a century, fighting side by side with the Celtic chieftains, O'Flaherty, O'Halloran, and Mac-Neeveen, but whose proud castle now shows no more trace of where it stood, than does old Ilion's towers. On this old battle-field stood, some years ago, long-stretching suburbs, inhabited by a hardy, laborious population, amounting to thousands, all of whom are nearly swept from off the face of the earth; some hundreds of both sexes have fled to America; some hundreds have died of famine and in the poor-house; but all who remained alive—(and better far would it be for many of them, they were in their last resting-place)—have been expelled within the last month from their miserable residences. In fact, two whole streets, with the exception of a few houses, have been razed. Oh, what sight in a Christian land!—Nearly an English mile in each street, while nothing to meet the eye but blackened gable ends, standing forth in melancholy but bold relief! To see at night the unfortunate beings huddling together under the bleak and blackened walls they once called home, amidst the wailing of young children, mothers, aye, and grandmothers, is a sight to stir the heart of the most obdurate. But, alas! not a voice is raised—not a remonstrance—no rebuke to the tyrant oppressor—no sympathy or feeling for subdued, suffering humanity—is to be heard on the part of cleric or layman. All is passing off as quietly as if nothing extraordinary occurred; hundreds of human beings, stamped, as we are taught, with the image of the Divine Redeemer of mankind, are flung houseless and homeless on the world, to rot or die without observation! whilst a palace on Carlton Terrace, and its grand saloons, was partly supported by the sweat and labour and health of these unfortunate victims!

A Loughrea Man.

Recreated from The Nation, Dublin, August 3, 1850.

FEMALE ADVOCATES AT THE BAR.—A momentous question has been raised and decided this week at the Guilford assizes; no less a matter than the right of the fair sex to aspire to forensic honors and emoluments. It was decided in the negative, though not without the mature deliberation of a moot-point so important demanded, the court having taking days to make up its mind. On Tuesday Mrs. Cobbett presented herself, duly armed with a brief and other papers, and prepared to address the jury, and conduct a case in which she had her husband for a client. Every gown masculine in the court rustled with apprehension at this prospect of intrusion of gowns feminine upon their legal monopoly.

The Lord Chief Baron, with the politeness which became a judge sitting on the "civil side," delicately expressed a doubt of the lady's competency to act. Mrs. Cobbett, with a degree of ready wit and legal acumen that deserved better success than she met with, argued in the first place that as man and wife were considered in law to be one, she had a perfect right to appear for her husband, who was a plaintiff in the case. The judge, still dubious, asked her whether she could state any precedent in support of her claim; a difficulty which the lady promptly met by counter-questioning his lordship, whether he knew of any precedent against it? Seriously embarrassed, sensitively alive to the awful load of responsibility he incurred by deciding such a novel case, the Lord

Chief Baron despatched a note to his brother Erle, who was sitting on the crown side. Brother Erle's reply intimated his participation in the doubts of the Lord Chief Baron, and that learned judge, like Mark Antony, unable to say no to a woman, postponed his decision till the next day. The next day Mr. Justice Erle, who appears to be of sterner stuff than the Lord Chief Baron, intimated to the fair aspirant that her claim could not be admitted. It must be a difficult thing, indeed, to say no to a woman. The Lord Chief Baron could not do it; and though Mr. Justice Erle undertook the arduous task, it was only as delivering the message of another. He blandly told Mrs. Cobbett that the Chief Baron, not himself, ruled that no gown, even though it were made of silk, had a right to appear at the barristers' table, except such a one as was surmounted by a horse-hair (or whalebone) wig, and concealed no petticoat under it.—*Daily News*.

EXECUTION OF EDMOND CHRISTOPHER.—The unfortunate man, Edmond Christopher, was executed in front of our County Jail, about one o'clock on Saturday. Unfortunate, we repeat, but only in a worldly sense, for we are now fully assured the man was innocent of the crime of which he suffered an ignominious death. In our last publication we were betrayed into some remarks, on the authority of our messenger, touching this man, which we regret. During the whole term of his imprisonment, and especially since the awful sentence of death was passed on him, we are informed that his conduct was not merely exemplary, but most Christian-like, and in perfect keeping with the holy and heroic fortitude which so gloriously marked his last moments.—The Rev. M. Flynn, P.P., of Ballybricken, chaplain to the prison, with his truly zealous curates, assisted by Mr. Hearn, of the Christian Brothers, were unremitting in their attention to him—one or the other of them was constantly with him from the time sentence was passed till the trying moment of his execution. And it is also our pleasing duty to remark that the humane and excellent Governor of the Prison, Mr. Triphook, constantly visited him. The Governor is a man of heart and feeling, and by his kind and charitable attention, as far at least, as was consistent with his duty, served to mitigate his sufferings and greatly sustained him in the trying ordeal to which he was necessarily subjected. The heroic fortitude manifested by this poor man, his resignation to the will of God, and reliance on his mercy, throughout this dismal tragedy is beyond all description.

When the appointed hour arrived—the Sheriff, accompanied by the Governor and the other officers of the law, came to his cell, where he had been for some hours previously engaged in prayer and preparation with the assisting priests, he at once cheerfully stood up and said "welcome be the will of God," and walked between the two clergymen calmly, firmly, and unassisted to the place of execution. He shook hands with the executioner, and when that official endeavored to excuse himself, he quietly remarked, "I do not blame you, this painful duty should be discharged by some one." He was then pinioned, and the true Christian fortitude which sustained him all through did not forsake him now. He ascended the scaffold with a firm step and with astonishing self-possession, proclaimed his innocence saying, "I do so, that no disgrace may be attached to my children," he besought his family and friends not to think ill of his prosecutors, to forgive them as he did, for he believed they were influenced by no personal feeling, but laboured under some mistake. It is but a matter of justice to say that no men could have made greater exertion to avert the late legal murder than did Counsellor Meagher, and Mr. Henry B. Godkin, of Dungarvan, at Christopher's trial, in this city. Four memorials, we learn, were since forwarded by Mr. Godkin to government, on the unfortunate man's behalf.

Recreated from The Waterford News, Waterford, August 16, 1850.

HIS GRACE THE DUKE OF DEVONSHIRE.

We are exceedingly happy to read the following in the *Limerick Vindicator*. It exactly corresponds with what we have heard on the subject:—

"A respected correspondent informs us that his Grace the Duke of Devonshire arrived in Lismore only on Friday, not on Wednesday as was expected. Nothing could exceed the enthusiastic welcome which the inhabitants of every class gave to the noble duke. Every house was illuminated—the Very Rev. Dr. Fogarty's residence most brilliantly—even the convent of the Presentation Nuns, who, within the walls of their secluded retirement, joined in the general demonstrations of the people outside. The *religieuses* of this institution are most grateful to his Grace for substantial proofs of his liberality, and their joy at the noble Duke's approach in the vigour of health, and in the enjoyment of that happiness which they so frequently invoke upon his head, was sincere and heartfelt. The Very Rev. Dr. Fogarty, the venerated Roman Catholic pastor of Lismore, went out in his carriage, followed by the entire population, and, having met his Grace, bade him welcome in cordial and eloquent terms, and in his own name and on the part of his entire congregation also. For several days preceding, the very rev. gentleman had urged on his parishioners the many and strong claims which the good Duke of Devonshire had on their gratitude and love; and the appeal was not made to unwilling ears, for there was scarcely an individual in the ancient city that did not join in the general acclaim with which his Grace's advent was joyously hailed. When evening fell, every part of the town glittered with illuminations and fire-works, and, as we have stated, the house of the very reverend pastor and the Presentation Convent were particularly conspicuous. Over ten thousand people had collected in the streets of Lismore, and his Grace, impressed with so many touching testimonies of esteem, left the castle and walked through the streets, conversing gaily with the crowds as he passed along. Hissing fire-works, blue lights, rockets, and various curious pyrotechnic contrivances shot up around from the windows of the houses in the various streets, and from the flagged ways. For an hour and a half his Grace continued conversing with the people, and then returned to the castle highly pleased and gratified at the enthusiastic and warm reception he had experienced."

Recreated from The Waterford News, Waterford, September 27, 1850.

MURDER OF A LANDLORD.—A correspondent of the *Freeman* writes the following particulars of a murder committed on the borders of Westmeath, at a place called Rathue, situated about five miles from this town, in a peaceable part of the country, on yesterday afternoon (Monday), between the hours of four and five o'clock in the afternoon (occurring on a public road leading from this to Phillipstown and Edenderry). The gentleman that fell a victim to the assassin was Roger North, Esq., of Kilduff House, King's County, a magistrate and landlord in said county. He was shot dead, within one mile of his home, as he was proceeding home on his return from inspecting some cattle, one or two of which was sick, on a farm of his (Garryduff), nearly two miles from his residence. Some persons have been arrested on suspicion. It is considered he was murdered owing to his having lately used some of his tenants on his Rathue property with coercive severity.

EVICTIONS IN KERRY.—A Ballybunion correspondent of the *Limerick Examiner* furnishes an account of wholesale evictions in the county Kerry. Off Mr. St. John Blacker's property *fifty-eight families—three hundred persons*; Lord Burgess's property, *twenty-five families*; Miss Hearn' property, several families, "and more to follow," together with a middleman named Julian, and *sixty families* who held under him—*two hundred* individuals.

Recreated from The Nation, Dublin, September 28, 1850.

FORTUNATE ESCAPE OF UPWARDS OF FIFTY FEMALE CHILDREN.

Dungarvan, 24th Sept., 1850.

A horse with a car belonging to Thomas Traher, having taken head, about the hour of four o'clock in the afternoon, on Friday the 20th instant, when upwards of fifty of the children who attend the Presentation Convent School of this town, were leaving and destined for their respective homes. The restive animal took flight and ran through the street amongst these poor children; they on beholding such impending danger, ran in all directions, bawling and screaming; more of them were not able to run, from their extreme youth, came in contact with the car— and most providentially—they did not suffer much, except two of them, whose legs and arms were much injured. And, were it not for a number of labourers that were employed in cutting a sewer to the street wherein the wheels were caught, in all probability very few of them would escape with life.

It is most painful to see numbers of country rusties coming into market, sitting leisurely on their cars, or standing to the rere of their old *truckle*, smoking their pipes and whistling—whilst the lives of the children of the town are in danger by their carelessness and inattention. Had this unfortunate man attended to his business such accident would not have occurred.

A BOLD STROKE FOR A HUSBAND AND A FORTUNE.— The following singular advertisement appeared a few days ago in the columns of a London paper:— "To Elderly Gentlemen.—A young lady of highly respectable connexions, rather above the middle height, of an amiable disposition, agreeable temper, &c., is desirous of forming a matrimonial engagement with a gentleman (from decided preference) some twenty or thirty years her senior. To one of sensible mind whose tastes and disposition resemble her own, and who could conscientiously, having no fortune of her own, offer her to share with him the refinements and luxuries of life, in exchange for the cheerful society and undivided affection of a confiding wife, this advertisement, which is of no common character, may be appreciated; but it will require an explanation before it can lose the truly unfeminine cast it must acquire in the eyes of its readers. It is requested no gentleman under fifty, and none from idle curiosity, will respond to this, since a more careful investigation will be made and courted, and inviolable secrecy imposed and relied on ere an interview be granted. Address, with real name, &c."

Recreated from The Waterford News, Waterford, October 4, 1850.

PETTY SESSIONS—THIS DAY.
Magistrates on the bench, The Mayor, Wm. Morris Samuel King, Joseph Tabiteau, R.M., Esqrs., and Sir B. M. Wall.

Mr. Walter Phelan applied to the bench on behalf of several respectable citizens concerning the New car stand at the Scotch church, and requesting it may be altered. Granted.

Three young men were arrested on last night for having a double barrelled gun in their possession. To be tried under the arms act.

John Bryne was summoned by R. H. Smyth, Esq., Solicitor, Beresford-street, for having besmeared his hall door on the 24th ultimo. John Downey proved the case. Mr. L. Stephens requested the bench to punish the fellow for this dirty act. To be imprisoned for a month with hard labour.

After a great number of drunken cases were disposed of the court rose.

Reprinted from The Waterford News, Waterford, October 4, 1850.

THE NEW CARDINALS.

(*From a Roman correspondent of the Times.*)

ROME, SEPTEMBER 30.—In the Consistory of this morning his Holiness named Dr. Wiseman cardinal, under the title of Archbishop of Westminster. The consistory of this day is one of the most remarkable in modern times, from the circumstance of 10 out of the 14 cardinals having been chosen from foreign states, and only four of them being Italians.

As the nomination of an English cardinal is of rare occurrence, I may venture, perhaps, to describe the ceremonies which accompany his elevation. This morning a Consistory was held at which the Pope announced to the cardinals present his intention of conferring a mark of favour upon various bishops and prelates whose qualifications he briefly noticed. The cardinals expressed their assent, and his Holiness then proceeded to publish the names and declare the formal nomination of the 14 cardinals according to their rank and seniority. Three messengers were sent to announce the intelligence to each of the four cardinals at present in Rome, and other messengers will start in the course of a few hours to convey the news of their promotion to the cardinals residing in foreign countries. These messengers are chosen from among the noble guards of the Pope, and are followed by young prelates whose mission to the new cardinals is of a more formal character. As soon as Dr. Wiseman received notice of his elevation he placed himself, according to the usages, upon the threshold of one of the state rooms at the Palace of the Consulate where his receptions take place, to receive the congratulations of the cardinals and ambassadors, who send their attendants for the purpose. This visit, styled from its hurry the *visita di calbre*, occupied two or three hours. This afternoon each of the new cardinals will proceed with the blinds drawn to the Vatican, where his Holiness will give them the red *beretta* or cap, after which Cardinal Wiseman, in the name of the others, will return thanks, standing, for the honour bestowed upon his colleagues and himself. As they leave the Pope's apartment they will receive from an attendant the red *zucchetto* or skullcap. They will afterwards go home with the carriage darkened as before, and during the next three days they must remain always at home. This evening the cardinals, ambassadors, and nobility, Roman and foreign, present their congratulations in person to each of the new cardinals. The Bishops of Andria and Gubbio reside in the House of the Theatines, at St. Andrea della Valle, and ladies will not be able to attend their reception, but the cardinals who reside in the city usually request one of their own family, or some lady of rank, to receive the Princesses and other ladies who may wish to be presented on the occasion. Our countrywoman, the Princess Doria, will do the honours for Cardinal Wiseman, and the Princess Massimo will receive for Cardinal Roberti. On these occasions there is generally a grand display of the diamonds of the noble Roman families, and curiosity is attracted by the brilliant jewels of the Torlonias, and the splendid heirlooms of the Doria, Borghese, Ruspigliosi, and others.

On the mornings of Tuesday and Wednesday the Roman princes will visit the new cardinals in state, the rule being that no two princes be present at the same time, in order that the rank and precedence which etiquette obliges them to respect may be duly preserved. The generals of the religious orders will likewise attend to offer their respects. The great ceremonies, however, are reserved for Thursday morning. At an early hour the new cardinals take the oaths in the Sistine chapel, whilst the other cardinals assemble in the Sala Ducale, or hall of the Consistories, near the chapel. The new cardinals are introduced, and, kneeling, receive the red hat from the Pope, with an admonition that its colour is to remind them that they are to be ready to shed their blood, if necessary, for the church. They are then embraced by their colleagues, and take their places among them. The *Te Deum* is afterwards sung, whilst the new cardinals are prostrate on the floor. At this public Consistory all may be present, but a secret Consistory is afterwards held, in which the Pope declares the mouths of the new cardinals closed, so that they are incapable of voting upon matters appertaining to the judgement of their colleagues, until by another act, at the end of the Consistory, their mouths are declared to be opened.— Between the closing and opening a considerable time may elapse, during which the candidates can vote for the election of a new Pope in conclave only. At this secret Consistory each Cardinal receives a sapphire ring, for which he pays 500 crowns, for the benefit of the missions to Asia, China, and other countries, and a title or church is assigned to him. I believe that Cardinal Wiseman will receive the title of St. Pudentiana, who is stated by ancient authors to have been a granddaughter of the celebrated British chieftain Curactacus, and whose church is said to contain memorials of the earliest days of the preaching of Christianity in Rome.

In the afternoon of the same day the new cardinals will visit St. Peter's in state, followed by the carriages of their colleagues and other personages. In the evening a curious ceremony will close the solemnities of their promotion. The keeper of his Holiness's wardrobe will bring the red hat, which was placed on his head in the morning, to each of the cardinals, who will receive it in full costume, standing near the throne erected for the Pope in every cardinal's residence. Complimentary addresses are made by the keeper and by the cardinal, who then retires, puts on a simpler dress, and returns to attend to his visitors. Refreshments are handed round, and at a suitable hour they retire, and all is over.

Recreated from The Freeman's Journal, Dublin, October 10, 1850.

THE CATHOLIC CHURCH.

RESTORATION OF THE ENGLISH HIERARCHY.—We are authorised to state, that on the 30th ult., the most memorable Consistory for England, perhaps in history, took place at Rome, when his Holiness proclaimed the restoration of the hierarchy, and conferred on Dr. Wiseman, the two-fold dignity of Cardinal Archbishop of Wesminster. His Eminence the Cardinal Archbishop will arrive in London about the middle of November next.—*Catholic Standard.*

Reprinted from The Freeman's Journal, Dublin, October 14, 1850.

THE CARDINAL ARCHBISHOP OF WESTMINSTER.

(*From the Catholic Standard.*)

Dr. Wiseman has been elevated to the Cardinalate under the above title, and may now be legitimately regarded as the head of the English hierarchy. The other changes cannot long remain a secret, when the leading diocese has thus been so prominently settled. Westminster was only a cloister for abbots and monks up to Henry the 8th's day, who pillaged the saintly inhabitants and gave up their property to a reforming bishop and canons instead. Mary turned back to, and Elizabeth deflected the old abbey from its original uses, but allowed the bishopric her father had founded to die out, and it has not been restored till the Roman consistory called it, the other day, into being with the same fiat which restored the hierarchy of England, and conferred the cardinalate upon one of her most gifted sons. Since the death of Cardinal Pole in 1558, his eminence will be the first of that dignity who has appeared in this country, and in announcing his return to take possession of his new see, in the middle of next month, we are only sorry that we cannot remove the beastly statues out of the venerable abbey, and make its fretted roof ring with the song which they have often re-echoed, in celebration of so joyous an event as the advent of a cardinal archbishop to our shores.

Recreated from The Freeman's Journal, Dublin, October 15, 1850.

FATAL EFFECTS OF A BEATING—JEALOUSY.

CARRICK-ON-SUIR, 23RD OCT., 1850.

On Sunday the 13th instant, as Michael O'Connell, a servant boy to a farmer named Coady, of Ahermr, was attracted by the shouting of persons early in the night in his mother's yard, when he went to learn what the cause was he saw six young men, who, when they got him amongst them inflicted several blows on his head. Coady and his family on hearing the blows rushed out, and they saw the six boys run off through the fields. O'Connell was carried into the house and in a short time got a fit of convulsion, he continued so ill for four days that Coady thought it necessary to get him into hospital; he subsequently brought him to Carrick on Friday, and applied for admission at the poor-house, but could not obtain it until the next day (Saturday), when the poor boy had to walk into town again; he was then admitted by the guardians, placed in the infirmary and showed symptoms of insanity till Monday morning when he died. Mr. Chaters (Coroner), held an inquest on the deceased on Wednesday last, when the following verdict was returned:—"That Michael O'Connell came by his death from the effects of wounds inflicted on his head and temples, by persons as yet unknown."—Three boys have been arrested on suspicion, and, who, from the evidence given on Wednesday, were fully committed to stand their trial at the next Assizes. The only cause of this diabolical murder was, it is said, jealousy about a young woman.

Recreated from The Waterford News, Waterford, October 25, 1850.

A LOST CHILD.

A little boy about four years' old, with an immense old *felt hat* on his head and minus of shoes, stood before the bench as a "deserted child." As no one appeared to know him, and he not knowing the whereabouts of his parents, he was transmitted to the poor house.

Reprinted from The Waterford News, Waterford, October 18, 1850.

THE LAND QUESTION.

The rack-renting landlords, the tyrannical exterminators, and the sleek, cunning dodging landlords are making sad havoc, just now, amongst the tenant farmers. They are proceeding with their robberies of the poor as if there were no God looking on them, and that the devil and his works were only to be worshipped in this world. The landlords of Ireland are, at this moment, committing more crime than could be tried and punished in twelve months by all the judges in the land, and yet they are unpunished, because they are protected by their own laws, made to suit the criminal works they pursue through the country.

Every class is suffering from the conduct of those insatiable monsters. The tenant farmer is their first victim, next the labourer; and then the pressure of poverty comes upon the shopkeeper, the tradesman, and all professional men.

It is because we know all this that we have often pronounced landlords and landlordism, as they are, to be the enemies of the country.

O'Connell committed a great error when he spent his valuable time in striving to conciliate them, and get them to work for the welfare of Ireland. Had he endeavoured to destroy their infamous power, and succeeded in laying it prostrate, he would have done more to liberate the people than in gaining emancipation.

The Tenant League, however, is labouring to effect what he has left undone. That body, backed by the people's sympathy, support, and contributions, together with the aid which a host of tenant-right representatives will give to the cause in parliament, will win a law which must have the effect of putting an end to the wicked powers which the landlords now possess, and which they used in scourging, robbing and exterminating the people.—*Dundalk Democrat.*

Recreated from The Waterford News, Waterford, November 1, 1850.

MOVEMENT OF THE CHURCH IN THE METROPOLIS AGAINST PAPAL DOMINATION.

SIXTY-NINE clergymen of the Church of England, including six canons of Westminster, the principal of King's College, and the rectors, curates and minsters of many of the most notable places of established worship in the metropolis, on Friday presented to the Bishop of London an address, asking for counsel under the extraordinary circumstances of the usurpation, by a Roman ecclesiastic, of the title of Archbishop of the English city in which the sovereigns of England are crowned, the Parliament of England sit, and the laws of England are administered, the city of Westminster. They solemnly protest against this act of religious invasion, of outrage to the British constitution, and of indignity to the British crown, and crave directions how to vindicate the rights of their Church and country.

The Bishop of London sent the following reply:—

Fulham, Oct. 28, 1850.

REV. AND DEAR BRETHREN—The sentiments expressed in the address which you have presented to me are in entire accordance with mine, and I am persuaded that they will be responded to by the unanimous feelings of Protestant England.

The recent assumption of authority by the Bishop of Rome in pretending to parcel out this country into new dioceses, and to appoint archbishops and bishops to preside over them, without the consent of the Sovereign, is a schismatic act, without precedent, and one which would not be tolerated by the Government of any Roman Catholic kingdom. I trust that it will not be quietly submitted to by our own.

Hitherto, from the time of the Reformation, the Pope has been contented with providing for the spiritual superintendence of his adherents in this country by the appointment of vicars apostolic, bishops who took their titles as such not from any real or pretended sees in England, but from some imaginary diocese *in partibus infidelium*. In this there was no assumption of spiritual authority over any other of the subjects of the English Crown than those of his own communion. But the appointment of bishops to preside over new dioceses in England, constituted by a Papal brief, is virtually a denial of the legitimate authority of the British Sovereign and of the English Episcopate; a denial also of the validity of our orders, and an assertion of spiritual jurisdiction over the whole Christian people of the realm.

Rome has more than spoken; she has spoken and acted! She has again divided our land into dioceses, and has placed over each a pastor, to whom all baptized persons, without exception, within that district, are openly commanded to submit themselves in all ecclesiastical matters, under pain of damnation, and the Anglican sees, those ghosts of realities long passed away, are utterly ignored.

You will do well to call the attention of your people to the real purport of this open assault upon our reformed Church, and to take measures for petitioning the Legislature to carry out the principle of the statute which forbids all persons other than the persons authorized by law to assume or use the name, style, or title of any archbishop of any province, bishop of any bishopric, or dean of any deanery in England or Ireland, by extending the prohibition to any pretended diocese or deaneries in these realms.

That it may please the Divine Head of the Church, who is the true centre of unity, and the only infallible judge, to guide and strengthen us in these days of rebuke and trial, to open our eyes to the dangers we are in by our unhappy divisions, and to unite us in one holy bond of truth and peace, of faith and charity, is the earnest prayer.

Your affectionate friend and bishop,

C. J. London.

Recreated from The Belfast News-Letter, Belfast, November 1, 1850.

THEATRE ROYAL--THE OPERA.

Last Saturday evening was the concluding night of Miss Catherine Hayes's engagement at our theatre on this occasion. The audience in point of numbers, and in the brilliancy of the dress circle, seemed to exceed the many splendid houses which our fair and accomplished countrywoman has gathered round her by the spell of her genius, and the enchantment of her melody. To all who were present any detail must be needless of the overflowing crowds, the joyous excitement, and irrepressible enthusiasm that characterised the scene presented in the interior of our theatre on Saturday evening—whilst to those who did not enjoy this rich national treat, we must leave imagination to supply what we feel it vain to attempt conveying by mere description. It was literally a "command night" of the majesty of genius—the homage of music-loving people to the embodied spirit of the melodies of our land. Wreaths of laurels, garlands of flowers, and richest bouquets were showered in profusion at the feet of the fair artiste, and the word applause is but a weak and meaningless term for the fervid and tumultuous bursts of rapturous greeting and laudation that pealed from every part of the house in her honor.—*Freeman*.

POLICE COURT--YESTERDAY.

Two young chaps were charged with stealing a pair of fowl from Mr. Short in William street. Committed for trial.

A man named Sinnott was charged with being drunk, and knocking his head against the walls in John-street. Fined as usual.

Reprinted from The Waterford News, Waterford, November 8, 1850.

THE WATERFORD POOR HOUSE.

In the Waterford poor-house, which gives shelter to a thousand unfortunates, every one—save infants, or the helplessly old or infirm—is engaged in some profitable employment. Every article of clothing or bedding, used by the paupers, is manufactured in the house. I visited every department of the building, and found the inmates, generally, looking cheerful and healthy, as they pursued their avocations. Here are produced frieze cloth, which makes jackets for the men and boys; tweeds for trousers; ducks; caps for the men; straw bonnets for the women; clogs—that is, leather shoes with wooden soles; shirts, sheets, blankets, (warm, soft, and fleecy enough to enwrap the Prince Patrick), knit quilts, knit shoes, linsey, linen, handkerchiefs, shawls, shoes, stockings, &c. The wheat is ground and the bread is baked in the workhouse, and the result is, that the 4lb. loaf, of excellent quality, as I ascertained, only costs the union 3d. Boys and girls, who were as ignorant as Ojibbeway Indians of any useful handicraft before they entered the workhouse, are being taught to be shoe-makers, tailors, and spinners. Health rules are paramount in the establishment, disease being almost unknown. When the cholera ravaged Waterford last year, the workhouse passed almost scathless through the frightful ordeal.—In the principal workhouse and four auxiliaries, there are two thousand five hundred people; and in the week preceding my visit, only two deaths have occurred.

The poor-law rating of the union is only 3s. in the pound, and Mr. Stark tells us that the admirable arrangements originated with, and are carried on, under "the personal and constant inspection of Mr. John O'Connor, the assistant guardian, to whom great credit is due for the result." We believe him, and we dare say, both paupers and rate-payers echo his sentiments.—*Stark's Tour in Ireland*.

Recreated from The Waterford News, Waterford, November 15, 1850.

LORD JOHN RUSSELL'S LETTER TO THE RIGHT REV. THE BISHOP OF DURHAM.

My Dear Lord—I agree with you in considering "the late aggression of the Pope upon our Protestantism" as "insolent and insidious", and I therefore feel as indignant as you can do upon the subject.

I not only promoted to the utmost of my power the claims of the Roman Catholics to all civil rights, but I thought it right, and even desirable, that the ecclesiastical system of the Roman Catholics should be the means of giving instruction to the numerous Irish emigrants in London and elsewhere, who without such help would have been left in heathen ignorance.

This might have been done, however, without any such innovation as that which we have now seen.

It is impossible to confound the recent measures of the Pope without the division of Scotland into dioceses by the episcopal church, or the arrangements of districts in England by the Wesleyan Conference.

There is an assumption of power in all the documents which have come from Rome—a pretension to supremacy over the realm of England, and a claim to sole and undivided sway, which is inconsistent with the Queen's supremacy, with the rights of our bishops and clergy, and with the spiritual independence of the nation, as asserted even in Roman Catholic times.

I confess, however, that my alarm is not equal to my indignation. Even if it shall appear that the ministers and servants of the Pope in this country, have not transgressed the law, I feel persuaded that we are strong enough to repel any outward attacks. The liberty of Protestantism has been enjoyed too long in England to allow any successful attempt to impose a foreign yoke upon our minds and consciences. No foreign prince or potentate will be permitted to fasten his fetters upon a nation which has so long and so nobly vindicated its right to freedom of opinion, civil, political, and religious.

Upon this subject, then, I will only say that the present state of the law shall be carefully examined, and the propriety of adopting any proceedings with reference to the recent assumptions of power deliberately considered.

There is a danger, however, which alarms me much more than any aggression of a foreign sovereign. Clergymen of our own church, who have subscribed the thirty-nine articles, and acknowledged in explicit terms the Queen's supremacy, have been the most forward in leading their flocks, "step by step, to the very verge of the precipice." The honour paid to saints, the claim of infallibility for the church, the superstitious use of the sign of the Cross, the muttering of the liturgy so as to disguise the language in which it is written, the recommendation of auricular confession, and the administration of penance and absolution,—all these things are pointed out by clergymen of the church of England as worthy of adoption, and are now openly reprehended by the bishop of London in his charge to the clergy of his diocese.

What, then, is the danger to be apprehended from a foreign prince of no great power, compared to the danger within the gates from the unworthy sons of the church of England herself?

I have little hope that the propounders and framers of these innovations will desist from their insidious course. But I rely with confidence on the people of England, and I will not bate a jot of heart or hope so long as the glorious principles of the immortal martyrs of the Reformation shall be held in defence by the great mass of a nation which looks with contempt on the mummeries of superstition, and with scorn at the laborious endeavours which are now making to confine the intellect and enslave the soul.

I remain, with great respect, &c., J. RUSSELL.

Downing-street, November 4, 1850.

Recreated from The Waterford News, Waterford, November 15, 1850.

VEGETABLES
FOR THE USE OF HER MAJESTY'S SHIPS AND VESSELS
AT
WATERFORD.

NOTICE is hereby given that Sealed Tenders will be received by me ON THE 28TH INSTANT from parties willing to enter into contract for the supply of such quantities of vegetables as may be required for the use of Her Majesty's Ships and Vessels at Waterford between the 1st January 1851 and the 31st December 1854, both days inclusive.

A copy of the conditions of the proposed contract may be seen on application at this office. No Tender for the supplies at Waterford will be received at the Admiralty without having previously passed through my hands unopened.

The quantity of vegetables supplied during the last twelve months was 1934 lbs.

ARTHUR LAMBE,
Collector.

Custom-house, Waterford,
13th November, 1850.

Reprinted from The Waterford News, Waterford, November 15, 1850.

EEL AND HOT MUTTON PIES.

BY the advice of his numerous Friends, M. FARRELL, 30, GRAFTON-STREET, BAKER IN GENERAL TO HIS EXCELLENCY THE LORD LIEUTENANT, has commenced to make the above Articles at the low price of Two Pence each, and engages to have them constantly hot from noon each day to 9 o'clock in the evening.

Reprinted from The Freeman's Journal, Dublin, November 16, 1850.

THE "NO-POPERY" MOVEMENT.
PUBLIC MEETING AT YORK.

On Wednesday afternoon a large and influential meeting was held in the Guildhall, called by the Lord Mayor, for the purpose of adopting an address to her Majesty, expressive of indignation at the late aggressions of the Pope of Rome, and to pray that steps may be taken to prevent any encroachments on her Majesty's supremacy.

The Lord Mayor took the chair.

Mr. T. Barstow proposed the adoption of the following address, which he proceeded to read:—

"TO THE QUEEN'S MOST EXCELLENT MAJESTY.

"We, your Majesty's loyal and devoted Protestant subjects, inhabitants of the city of York and its vicinity, humbly approach your Majesty with dutiful affection to express our deep concern and indignation at the late attempt of the Bishop of Rome to exercise a spiritual despotism in this your Majesty's independent realm of England.

"The Bishop of Rome, in defiance of your Majesty's undoubted supremacy, has with daring presumption parcelled out the whole kingdom into pretended dioceses, and usurped your Majesty's exclusive prerogative of conferring titles and appointing authorities—ecclesiastical as well as civil.

"We deem this act of aggression to be an invasion of the rights of your Majesty's crown, an inroad upon the provinces of the English Protestant church, a violation of the constitutional laws of the realm, and an infringement of the rights and liberties of your Majesty's Protestant subjects.

"We therefore, humbly, but earnestly, entreat your Majesty to vindicate your royal authority, and, if needed, to call upon the legislature to enact such laws as may be effectual to repress this or any future act of Papal encroachment upon the rights, laws and liberties of England.

"And your petitioners will ever pray," &c.

Recreated from The Freeman's Journal, Dublin, November 16, 1850.

DUBLIN POLICE—Yesterday.

EXTRAORDINARY CASE OF DESERTION.—Michael Bayley, a smart-looking soldierly cut of a man, apparently in the prime of life, was brought before the bench as a deserter.—The prisoner had on that morning gone to a constable of the E division stationed at Portobello Barracks, and voluntarily surrendered himself as a deserter from the 86th regiment (now in India, but having a depot or head-quarters at Portsmouth).

Bayley stated in the office that he was a native of the county Carlow, had enlisted (being at the time under the required age) in the 86th in the early part of the year '31, and deserted from it in the latter end of '33, upwards of seventeen years ago. On being asked if he had enlisted in any other regiment since, he replied in the negative. To interrogatories as to his means of supporting himself during his long period of desertion, he stated that he was by trade an organ builder, and had spent ten years in China following his business. He was accompanied by a fine boy of five or six years old, who, he stated, was his son, born in China, and that his wife, the child's mother, was dead. The little fellow, who possessed a most striking oriental countenance, with extremely piercing black eyes, wept bitterly when about to be separated from his father on the committal of the latter as a deserter being made out.

The unfortunate parent entreated that the child might be sent with him, but the magistrates told him that they had not it in their power to comply with his request. They assured him, however, that due care should be taken of the boy.

The prisoner was then committed to be forwarded to the head-quarters of his regiment, and his child sent to the South Dublin Union, with a letter from the bench to the guardians for his admission to the workhouse.

THE BOROUGH RATE—ASSAULT ON BAILIFFS—John Lawler and Thomas Slevin were charged by two "Court of Conscience" bailiffs—to wit, Timothy Fagan and Mathew Lacey—with assault and rescue, under the following circumstances:—From the deposition of the complainants it appeared that on the 16th inst. Fagan, who was the principal bailiff, with Lacey as his assistant, acting on a warrant, signed by Sir Timothy O'Brien, President of the Court of Conscience, proceeded to the shop of James Lawler on Patrick-street to collect an amount of borough rate due by him. They found Mrs. Lawler in the shop, and demanded the rate from her. She refused to pay it; on which they went into the parlour for the purpose of distraining for it. Soon after they had entered the apartment the prisoners accompanied by three other persons, followed them, and commenced a violent assault upon them. While Fagan was in the act of seizing a sack of flour he was himself seized by Slevin, who smashed his hat in the first instance, and then punished him severely with his clenched fists. At the same time Lacey was undergoing still more severe usage at the hands of Lawler, who cut his mouth, tore his shirt, nearly strangled him by twisting his neckcloth, besides leaving sundry records of "hard hitting" on his countenance. The property seized for the rate was rescued, and the bailiffs were forcibly ejected from the premises.

The prisoners were ordered to be committed for trial at sessions, but were subsequently admitted to bail.

Recreated from The Freeman's Journal, Dublin, November 19, 1850.

BALLYMONEY.—The town of Ballymoney is to be lighted with gas this week. The cost will be something under £2,000, which must strike our readers, as particularly economical. The light is to be admitted into 120 houses. The Earl of Antrim, in the most liberal manner, gave free ground for the works, and took shares to the amount of £250.—*Derry Sentinel*.

Recreated from The Belfast News-Letter, Belfast, November 19, 1850.

HORROR AT KILRUSH—DREADFUL SHIPWRECK AND LOSS OF NINETY LIVES.

A Kilrush correspondent, whose letter is dated on Thursday, has sent us the following dreadful particulars:—

The splendid barque, Edward, Captain Wilson, commander, bound for New York, took in passengers at Limerick, 207; crew, 17. She was for some time delayed at Carrigaholt, taking in a fresh supply of water at Scattery Roads. Left Carrigaholt on Monday morning, the 11th, with a fair slant of wind; but after a couple of hours' sailing, the wind blew W.N.W., getting very thick. The Captain then steered for Galway, hoping to gain that port before rough weather set in. At noon, he could take no observation, owing to the thick haze and squalls. A 'Look-out' was ordered to the maintop-sail yard, to direct the man at the helm. They then endeavoured to regain the Shannon, but could not see a rope's length in advance of them. About ten o'clock P.M., they found themselves in smooth water, and were disposed to cast anchor, but were then apprised of their position, by one of the passengers, who informed the Captain that they had just passed a ledge of rocks called 'Dhuggernach,' and were right under Sikes' Lodge, Kilkee.

Contrary to orders, the carpenter cut the stopper, and let go the anchor—it partially checked the vessel for a few minutes; but the sea washing heavily over her, the main and mizzen masts fell over on the rocks—the canvas had been previously blown away. At this time she became perfectly unmanageable—it blew a hurricane, and before eleven o'clock she was in pieces!

Forty-five bodies have been picked up—all more or less bruised or disfigured among the rocks.

Were the Humane Society, for the Protection of Life, aware of the dangers that Richard Russell, Esq., of Limerick, encountered, and his two companions—M'Carthy, the Coast Guard, and a shoemaker of Kilkee—they would certainly award them collars of gold, for their invaluable assistance on that terrible night. They, under Providence, saved those who escaped destruction. The truly gallant Captain (Wilson) stood by his vessel while a stick remained together. He saved life while he could; and his last burden, off the last plank, was an old woman he carried on his back to shore.

When the roll was called, at the Police barracks, ninety-six were missing; but I know one or two were put to bed in the village, and Father Kenyon's brother had gone at the time to Kilrush.

A portion of the stern remained fastened in the rocks, to point out where the catastrophe occurred; but not a plank is left whole—not a spar or cordage left together. The beautiful vessel is now in small pieces scattered round the Bay of Kilkee!

It is feared other vessels were wrecked on this coast the same night. A vessel laden with corn is reported off Liscannor, without a soul on board.

Recreated from The Nation, Dublin, November 23, 1850.

HORRIBLE OUTRAGE.—About an hour of nine o'clock on Friday night week, an armed party, consisting of over fifteen men, well armed, and obeying the commands of a "captain" with military precision, attacked the house of a man named John Martin, care-taker on the lands of Rapla and South Hill, the property of Mr. Vincent, of Dublin.

The marauders had been lying in wait for a bailiff who had been placed in care of corn seized for rent on the farm of one of Mr. Vincent's tenants, named Meara, and who had entered Martin's house a few minutes previous to the attack. The door was opened for them by Martin's wife, whom the first of the ruffians struck with his gun on the head such a blow that the poor woman was stunned and felled to the earth.

The party rushed in, to the number of eight or nine, and seizing the obnoxious bailiff, beat him with the butts of their guns and with spade handles in a most brutal manner, cutting his head, and inflicting many severe bruises on various parts of his body. In the frenzy of the moment (the party being half intoxicated) one of the fellows cried out, "shoot him," but the captain interposed, and cried out "no, no, beat him well," and his obedient underlings amply fulfilled his directions in that respect.

Five of the party remained outside to guard, and one of them having cried out "he is coming," the strictest silence was observed till Martin, who had been absent, entered the open door, when he was immediately seized upon and beaten similarly to the unfortunate bailiff.

They even beat the children, and the woman on recovering from the swoon into which she had been thrown by the first ruffian's blow, was again laid hold on, nor did her cries that she was pregnant save her from a repetition of blows, the unfortunate assailants exclaiming, "we will not spare woman with child, or child in the cradle." When the captain drew off his men, the inmates of the house summoned the courage to go abroad, the corn that had been under seizure was gone.—*Limerick Reporter*.

Recreated from The Nation, Dublin, November 30, 1850.

THE SUBSCRIBER, desirous to avoid creating the jealous feeling ever inseparable from the practice of Mercantile Houses giving Christmas Presents, yet most anxious to prove to his numerous kind Friends and Customers a just and grateful appreciation of the liberal support with which his ESTABLISHMENT has been honoured, will, from the Present until New Year's Day next (both inclusive), dispose of his large and elegantly-assorted Stock of Watches, Jewellery, &c., by RETAIL & WHOLESALE Prices.

R. K. GARDNER,
WAREROOMS near Trinity College,
GRAFTON-STREET.

Reprinted from The Freeman's Journal, Dublin, December 24, 1850.

CHRISTMAS DAY.

To-morrow, being the anniversary of the Nativity, we will observe the time honoured custom of not publishing the FREEMAN'S JOURNAL on that day. The other part of the ancient custom—the "bidding" all "a *merry* Christmas" on its eve, we must omit; for, though time was when Christmas brought universal joy and gladness to every hearth in Ireland—as in all other Christian lands—that is true of Ireland no more.

We heartily *wish* to all such mirths as can be their's—but *bid* to all "a merry Christmas" we cannot—we dare not. The pauper pest-house is no place for mirth; yet thousands who last year sat around their own hearths 'midst good cheer and joyous friends, now await within those jaws of death a passage to untimely graves. The memory of "the levelling" cannot cause mirth; yet the return of Christmastide brings to thousands and tens of thousands the memory of that which saw the rooftree burn under which they and their fathers were born, and beneath which they and their children assembled last year to celebrate the festive night. We will not mock then, by "bidding" all a merry Christmas now. The time to do so may not, however, be far distant. We are not without hope. The rooftree of the Irish peasant may yet become as sacred as the castle of the peer. Then we will "bid" our friends a merry Christmas, in the full assurance that the fruits of industry will gladden the dwelling of every Irish peasant.

Meantime, let those whom God has blessed with worldly blessings open their hearts and purses today, and in the name of HIM whose name we all bear, "bid" the poor around them be "merry" on HIS day.

Recreated from The Freeman's Journal, Dublin, December 24, 1850.

On Saturday last Dr. M Neill, of Liverpool suggested to his congregation that the only punishment he could suggest for Roman Catholic priests was—*death!!*

Reprinted from The Freeman's Journal, Dublin, December 24, 1850.

THE REQUIEM OF YOUTH.

Oh, whither does the spirit flee
That makes existence seem
A day dream of reality,
Reality a dream?

We enter on the race of life,
Like prodigals we live,
To learn how much the world exacts
For all it hath to give.

The fine gold soon becometh dim
We prove its base alloy;
And hearts enamoured once of bliss
Ask peace instead of joy.

Spectres dilate on every hand
That seemed but tiny elves;
We learn distrust of all, when most
We should suspect ourselves.

But why lament the common lot
That all must share so soon;
Since shadows lengthen with the day,
That scarce exist at noon.

Recreated from The Waterford News, Waterford, January 24, 1851.

1851

Selected Headlines

RUINOUS FIRE AT HUTTON'S COACH FACTORY	270
IMPERIAL PARLIAMENT	272
THE NEW PENAL LAW	274
DISCOVERY OF CANNIBALS AT BORNEO	288
DR. FREW IN TROUBLE	289
THE MINISTERIAL JEWS' BILL	296
PRIVATE THEATRICALS AT DEVONSHIRE HOUSE	302
ENGAGEMENT WITH SLAVERS	308
MORE EVICTIONS IN CONNEMARA	320
EXTRAORDINARY SUICIDE BY A LADY	321

ANOTHER YEAR FOR IRELAND!

A new year dawns this day for Ireland. To those who give a serious thought to the fortunes of this country, the commencement of another year has in it something that is peculiarly solemn and saddening. Prosperous nations look forward to the advent of a new year with hope and confidence, anticipating some addition to their glory, whether in arts or arms, in letters or in science.

But Ireland, alas! is the NIOBE of nations, her bright hopes destroyed, her days darkened with sorrow and despair. Does she look back, what is there in the retrospect to cheer? Half a century of provincial slavery, rendered more intolerable by contumely and neglect—half a century of deepening misery, beginning with the loss of freedom, and ending in famine, pestilence, poverty, and dismay. Dark, indeed, is the retrospect, and only less darkly lowers the unknown future.

We are now standing on the threshold of a second half century of English rule; and well might the soul of every Irishman be filled with despair, if he did not trust in the abiding mercy of God, and in the power of Him in whose hands are the destinies of nations and of peoples. One half-century of English rule has reduced a fine country, and a gifted and spirited race, to a condition which appalls the heart of the philanthropist, and baffles the wisdom of the statesman.

If the coming half century shall bear no other fruits to our children and our children's children, than those which our fathers and ourselves have gathered from that which has just expired, who is there wicked enough to pray to Heaven that that rule may long continue? Is there a *man* in the land who does not feel in his heart of hearts that something is wanting in Ireland, and that something, for which he longs instinctively, is *liberty*?

The path which this country has to travel, is rough, and full of difficulties. There is no going back; it is our destiny to advance. To falter is to fail, to pause is to perish—to push resolutely onwards, is to succeed. We have much need of success; therefore, let us onwards! Let our every conquest over difficulty be consecrated to our country, our every step in advance be made with a motive. Thus, sturdily, hopefully, pushing on our stubborn path, and gathering strength with each new trial, let us look forward to that goal of a suffering peoples' holy ambition—the ultimate restoration of our country's liberty.

A CAR DRIVER, named *Timothy M'Carthy*, was brought before the magistrates at the Police Office on yesterday morning. It appeared that through negligence he had left his horse and car on the stand the previous day, without remaining at the horse's head, the result of which was that the horse becoming wild dashed off through several streets, scattering the passers in all directions, and creating the utmost alarm and confusion. In Marlboro-Street, a woman named Mary Shine was knocked down, the horse and car passing over her and inflicting severe injuries upon her. She was lifted up by Constable Belton and conveyed to the South Infirmary, where it was first feared that her leg was broken, but ultimately it was ascertained that such was not the case, although she had sustained some very severe injuries. The horse continued to drag the car furiously through the town, smashing in a shop front in Paul-street, until, coming into collision with another horse and car, he fell down and was caught. The driver was arrested by Constable Belton and brought before Mr. Roche, J.P, who committed him to the bridewell for the night. The magistrates on yesterday morning agreed to take bail for his appearance until the poor woman who had received the injuries was sufficiently recovered to attend court.

Recreated from The Cork Examiner, Cork, January 1, 1851.

LARGE PIGS.

HAVING obtained two of the finest specimens of the above animals, for which I last week advertised, I invite public attention to them as models of Irish Produce. One of them is the largest to be had in Ireland, and is computed to weigh 8½ cwt. net. I intend exhibiting its hams at the Great Exposition of the Industry of All Nations, in London, next May; and have little doubt that they, with the Medium Hams and other Articles which I will have on show, and for the prime quality of which I am justly celebrated in the London Market, will sustain my well-known reputation, and defy competition.

On to-morrow only, the Public can have an opportunity of seeing these fine animals alive, as on Monday morning they must be slaughtered for the coming Exhibition.

EDWARD M'VEY,
James's-street.

3rd January, 1851.

Reprinted from The Nation, Dublin, January 4, 1851.

BELFAST EXHIBITION OF PAINTING AND SCULPTURE.

In resuming our notices of the works in this exhibition, we are happy to state that, notwithstanding the unfavorable weather prevalent at this season, the attendance from day to day continues numerous and respectable; and so far from being confined to the upper walks of society, that it includes many of the middle and working classes—those, in fact, for whose peculiar benefit and encouragement the exhibition has been devised. The daily attendance averages upwards of one hundred persons; and, as the exhibition will be open for several months to come, it is not too much to predict that, before it closes, its treasures of art will be inspected by every intelligent individual in the community.

No. 111 "Captives in a Harem," Richard Rothwell, R.H.A. This is a highly meritorious production, but the subject is one which somewhat needlessly offends the eye of taste. Two females are "discovered" as the dramatists say, *en deshabille*, in a chamber of the harem, open to the sunny glimpses of a garden, and surrounded by the gorgeous details of oriental luxury. They seem to be preparing either for the bath, or the toilet, for one of them, apparently a fair Circassian, is wholly nude, while the other, a darker beauty—more than brunette—who seems to have more regard for decorum, is loosely girdled, enough to convey the impression. They seem to be recalling the memories of their childhood's home, by the serious and innocent expression of their features; and if so, wherefore such a needless display of *abandon*? The colours are very brilliant, the flesh tints *Titantic* and the whole composition very highly wrought.

No. 136. "Female Head." Thomas Henry Illidge. Though in a bad light, near the ceiling, this picture has attracted our favourable notice. The subject may be inferred from the lines of Drummond of Hawthornden, which form its epigraph—

"By my bed methought a virgin stood,
Her head a garland wore of opals bright,
About her flowed a gown of purest light,
Pure amber locks gave umbrage to the face;
'How long wilt thou,' said she, 'estranged from joy,
Paint shadows to thyself of false annoy?'
Oh, leave thy plaintful soul more to molest,
And think that woe, when shortest, then is best."

The artist has well realized the poet's idea.

No. 128. "Landscape." Hugh Frazer, R.H.A. A beautiful river view—the silver stream, between its richly wooded banks, gradually narrowing itself from the front foreground to the middle distance, where it glides over a mill-weir, the perspective revealing a luxurious mass of forest, and a mellow, half-clouded, afternoon sky smiling all over. This we conceive to be one of the finest landscapes in the exhibition.

Recreated from The Belfast News-Letter, Belfast, January 6, 1851.

EXTENSIVE AND RUINOUS FIRE AT SUMMER-HILL.—DESTRUCTION OF MESSRS. HUTTON'S COACH FACTORY.

We have to record with deep regret the occurrence of a truly disastrous event, which has inflicted serious, and at present incalculable loss on our much-respected and deservedly-esteemed fellow-citizens, the Messrs. Hutton, the well-known coach factory proprietors; and has also, at one blow, suddenly deprived of employment (at least for the present) over three hundred individuals—artizan coach-makers, painters, smiths, coach-trimmers, and accessory labourers, who have, up to this period, derived the means of a comfortable and independent subsistence in the several departments of this once extensive and splendid establishment, which now (or the greater part of it) unhappily is reduced to a heap of smoking ruins.

The dreadful fire which has caused the wholesale destruction of this noble factory, and of many thousand pounds worth of property contained within its walls may be said to have commenced at about an hour after midnight on the morning of yesterday, Sabbath. The hour and the time at which the conflagration broke out are the more remarkable by reason of peculiar circumstances connected with the internal regulation of the establishment. In the first place the rule of the factory was, that no work should be done on Saturday evening after dusk, so that no lamps or candles could have been used in any part of the premises on last Saturday evening, unless in disobedience to that rule; and it is further clear that such was not the case, as Mr. L. Hutton (son of Mr. Thomas Hutton) remained on the premises until long after dark, and no late work could have been going on without his knowledge. Again, on other nights, when it was customary to have work proceed with by gas or lamp light, the watchman of the establishment used to make his rounds of the entire concern; but on Saturday night, there being no necessity imagined for such precaution, this duty of the watchman was not required. These facts were recalled when it was sought to account in some way for the probable cause of this doubly afflicting accident, and the supposition hazarded by some that the watchman, in going his rounds, might have dropped a spark from his lantern, was at once negatived by the statement of clerks and porters, that the watchman did not go round at all on Saturday night. The fire first appeared in the loft adjacent to and above the forge of the factory, and perhaps the truest, at least the most feasible, source to which the dreadful result of yesterday morning can be attributed is the slow ignition of one of the loft beams near the forge flue, and the gradual smouldering of the ignited timber until the fire caught the dry wood work of the flooring of the loft. After the closest inspection, and on comparing every account of the *locale* of the outbreak of the fire, this would seem to be the conclusion best sustained by fact as to the cause of this calamitous destruction of the premises and property of our esteemed fellow-citizen.

The idea of the conflagration being the result of malicious intent is at once negatived by the fact of the well-known enthusiastic regard entertained for the Messrs. Hutton by all in their employment, if, indeed, the sad and desponding looks of the crowd of artizans on yesterday, and the weeping of their wives and children, did not afford full proof of their participation in the heavy loss sustained by their kind and liberal employers.

It is of course impossible to calculate now the enormous loss which the firm of Messrs. Hutton have incurred by this calamitous fire, but from estimates made on ascertained grounds by parties authorised to speak on the subject, we learn that the computed loss is far beyond £30,000. The premises are insured in the National and Patriotic offices to the amount of £10,000 only.

Recreated from The Freeman's Journal, Dublin, January 6, 1851.

VISIT BY THE LORD LIEUTENANT TO ESTABLISHMENTS IN THE CITY.

On Saturday his Excellency the Lord Lieutenant visited the extensive distillery of Messrs. George and Henry Roe, Thomas-street. His Excellency was accompanied by Sir William Somerville, the Hon. William Ponsonby, Major Ponsonby, Captain Barry, Mr. Corry Connellan, and Captain Bernard, A.D.C. The viceregal party arrived at one o'clock, and were received at the entrance of the establishment by the members of the firm, as above named, and by whom they were conducted through all the principal departments of this most spacious and complete concern. Nearly an hour was occupied in inspecting the various buildings and highly improved apparatus for the distillation of spirits.

Having expressed himself highly pleased with all he had seen and the explanations afforded him, his Excellency and suite, with Mr. George Roe, proceeded to visit the vast establishment of the Right Hon. the Lord Mayor and his respected father, Mr. Arthur Guinness. The party arrived at the brewery, James's-gate, at two o'clock, and, entering by the front gate, were received at the entrance of the office by the head of the firm, Mr. Arthur Guinness, with his partners, and Mr. Sutton, the Lord Mayor's secretary. His Excellency and the gentlemen accompanying him were conducted by the Lord Mayor and Mr. Purser over the immense and interesting concerns of this, one of the most eminent breweries in Europe. The first place visited was the malt store, a pile of great magnitude, and containing tens of thousands of barrels of the necessary material. The brew-house was next inspected. Here the process of brewing was at the time in full operation in four huge boiling coppers, one of them containing no less than 47,000 imperial gallons, and weighing upwards of 20 tons, being considered the largest vessel of the kind in the United Kingdom.

The hop stores were then visited, then the vat house, the latter constituting a most remarkable feature of the establishment. This building contains 55 vats, all of them of enormous dimensions, and constantly kept filled with brewed drink. One of them holds 115,600 imperial gallons. After this the cooperage was seen; here upwards of 80 men are daily employed, 50 of them as coopers, the remainder being engaged attending to the cleansing of the casks, &c., &c. The work of cleansing is performed through the agency of heated air, by means of a patented and very ingeniously contrived machine, worked by a small steam engine, 30 men being constantly required to attend about the machine. The visitors on leaving the cooperage were shown through the offices into the dwelling-house, where, in one of the spacious reception rooms, they were entertained at a splendid lunch. His Excellency and the gentlemen in his suite expressed in the most unqualified terms the high gratification they derived from their visit, and took their departure at a quarter to four o'clock.

Recreated from The Freeman's Journal, Dublin, January 9, 1851.

ROBBERY.

On the morning of Tuesday the house of Mr. Somers, Michael-street, was entered by the back way and a small box which contained notes and silver to the amount of twenty-one pounds stolen. The thieves walked out through the front door deliberately, and left a half-crown behind them. On Wednesday, Constable Horan brought up before the magistrates four well known characters named Coady McNally, alias the peeler, and Healy, alias Ballyhale, also two ladies of the pave, Ellen Cody and Mary Moore, on suspicion of the robbery having tendered a £5 note for goods which they had purchased on Tuesday in Mr. Tobin's shop. They were remanded for further examination.

Reprinted from The Waterford News, Waterford, January 17, 1851.

IMPERIAL PARLIAMENT.

HOUSE OF LORDS—Tuesday, February 4.

The *Times* makes the following observations; but in the other papers we do not find any remarks of a like character:—

Yesterday the fourth session of the present imperial parliament was opened by the Queen in person.

The weather being singularly fine for the season of the year, an immense concourse of persons was attracted to St. James's Park and Whitehall, to view the royal procession.—Her Majesty, who left Buckingham Palace shortly before two o'clock, was received by her loyal subjects with unwonted enthusiasm throughout the line of route. The Queen acknowledged the continued cheering of the crowd with her usual grace and courtesy. Frequent cries of "No Popery!" during her Majesty's progress indicated the continued existence of the popular feeling which has been so generally manifested.

The Duke of Wellington arrived about one o'clock. His grace, who wore a Field Marshall's uniform under his peer's robes, looked hearty and well, but appeared to be prevented, by his increasing deafness, from entering into conversation, and contented himself with exchanging a casual remark or salutation with the peers who passed near him. The duke however, made an exception in favour of Baron Brunow, the Russian Ambassador, with whom he held a short colloquy. His grace appeared to shrink from the attention and respect of which he was the object, and it was observed, as a proof of his indifference to fatigue, that although frequently importuned to take a seat, he steadily refused, and continued in a standing posture until her Majesty's departure.

Among the earlier arrivals were Lord Gough, the Archbishops of Canterbury and York, the Bishops of Oxford and Hereford, Lord Chief Justice Campbell, Chief Baron Pollock, Lord Cranworth, the Earl of Cardigan, the Earl of Carlisle, Earl Grey, the Dukes of Devonshire and Buccleuch, the Marquis of Clanricarde, Earl Granville, and the Earl of Minto. The Bishop of Exeter, who entered the house late, seemed much enfeebled by illness. About half past one the Duke of Cambridge arrived, and was received, upon alighting from his carriage, with the honours due to his rank. The judges occupied their usual places between the cross-benches. The *corps diplomatique* attended in considerable numbers, and their uniforms, sashes, orders, and decorations, gave variety and picturesqueness to the scene. Among the more distinguished members of the upper house whom the eye sought in vain, might be mentioned Lords Stanley and Brougham.

At two o'clock the boom of canon was heard above the buzz and hum of conversation, which was instantly suspended at the announcement that the Queen had set her foot within her royal palace of Westminster. In a few minutes the prevailing silence and suspense became almost painful, when her Majesty, led by Prince Albert, and attended by her great officers of state, entered the house and took her seat upon the throne. Her Majesty, who looked exceedingly well, wore a tiara of diamonds, and was dressed in a robe of the richest white satin. The Prince Consort wore a field marshall's dress with black crape upon the arm; he took his usual place upon the Queen's left. The Duke of Wellington, with the sword of state, stood upon the left of the throne. The Duchess of Sutherland, as Mistress of the Robes, and the Marquis of Winchester, with the cap of maintenance, stood upon her Majesty's right, as also did the Marquis of Lansdowne, bearing the royal crown.

Every one rose upon her Majesty's entrance. The spectacle now presented has been often and powerfully described, under different adjuncts of time and place, and it will not speedily fade from the memory of those least able to convey a vivid idea of its grandeur. The chastened splendour of the gilded roof and the burnished canopy of the throne—the scarlet and ermine of the peers' robes—the gaiety of the tints of the female costumes, and the rich light of the stained glass windows, made a *coup d'oeil* which constituted a feast of colour and the perfection of form and outline.

Her Majesty, having taken her seat, bowed to her assembled nobles, and by a courteous gesture intimated her wish that they should resume their seats. The Queen next commanded the attendance of her faithful Commons, who attended at the bar, in the usual form, preceded by the Speaker in his gold robe of office. Lord John Russell occupied a front place upon the Speaker's right hand. Some amusement was as usual created by the somewhat disorderly and tumultuous manner in which the representatives of the Lower House appeared in the presence of royalty.

The LORD CHANCELLOR, kneeling, then presented her Majesty with the royal speech, which the Queen read (and which we have already published).

Her Majesty delivered the royal speech in a clear, musical, and happily modulated tone of voice. She was distinctly audible in every part of the royal speech, except in the first paragraph, which she began before the noise, occasioned by the arrival of the Commons, had quite subsided. Having finished this opening sentence, she suspended the further reading of the speech for a few instants until silence was restored. When the paragraph relative to the Papal aggression was commenced there was a general and suppressed cry of "hush!" and the most intense interest was evinced. We think a slight sensation of disappointment was felt throughout the body of the house when this paragraph was read, and there were some who, drinking in every tone of her Majesty's voice at this instant, thought she was conscious of this disappointment, and sympathised with it. This impression may have been the overwrought fancy of the moment, but we own that when her Majesty closed the paragraph with the words, "It will be for you to consider the measure which will be laid before you on this subject", we shared in the belief that her Majesty would have been glad to have enounced a more definite conclusion. It was also noticeable that the Queen, raising her voice, uttered with marked emphasis her resolution "to maintain the rights of my crown and the independence of the nation against all encroachment, from whatever quarter it may proceed."

Her Majesty, having finished reading the speech, handed it to the Lord Chancellor, who received it kneeling. Then, giving her hand to Prince Albert, and attended as before, the Queen, graciously bowing to the peers around her, left the house with the same formalities which had marked her arrival.

Their lordships then adjourned during pleasure.

Recreated from The Freeman's Journal, Dublin, February 6, 1851.

MEETING AT LORD STANLEY'S.
(*From the Morning Herald.*)

All the circumstances connected with the meeting of the members of the House of Commons at Lord Stanley's yesterday, are matters in relation to which we may congratulate every loyal and Protestant subject of her Majesty.

The noble lord declared that this was not a time for piecemeal legislation or for half measures in reference to the aggressions of the Popedom—that it was not a time for factious antagonism with regard to any means to be proposed by the existing government for the purpose of meeting such assaults upon the prerogatives of the crown and of the religion of the country. Lord Stanley maintained that if the measures of the government were sufficient they should be supported; but that if the premier flinched from the duty he had undertaken, he was no longer worthy to govern the British nation. Half measures, urged the noble lord, would but lead to further assumptions, further aggressions, further insults, and additional agitation.

Recreated from The Freeman's Journal, Dublin, February 7, 1851.

THE NEW PENAL LAW.

Lord J. RUSSELL rose, in pursuance of the notice he had given, to move for leave to bring in a bill "to prevent assumption of certain ecclesiastical titles in respect of places in the United Kingdom." The noble lord spoke as follows:—

The house, I am sure, will readily believe the anxiety with which I approach the important subject which I promised to bring under their notice, the deep interest which is felt in this country by all classes of persons, the numerous petitions that have been presented to this house, praying the house to resist encroachment on the part of a foreign sovereign, the addresses presented to the crown—all making it a matter of deep responsibility to undertake the task of bringing such a question before the house.

In the present state of affairs, with the great uncertainty which still prevails as to what was the intention of the measure that has been taken by Rome, whether it is the prelude to further measures, or whether it is merely a blunder committed on the sudden which will be retracted or amended—in this state of uncertainty I think it far better on the one side not to relax any power which you can now maintain by law and on the other not to propose any substitute which would of itself be the cause of further debate. I come, then, to the immediate question of the assumption of titles, and I think it is useful upon this subject to refer to that which was declared as the reason of a clause which is now contained in the Roman Catholic relief act. Sir R. Peel, in introducing that great measure, spoke to the following effect:—"A practice has occasionally, of late, prevailed in Ireland which is calculated to afford great, and I may add just, offence to Protestants—I allude to the practice of claiming and assuming, on the part of the Roman Catholic prelates, the names and titles of dignitaries belonging to the church of England. I propose that the episcopal titles and names made use of in the church of England shall not be assumed by bishops of the Roman Catholic church. Bishops I call them, for bishops they are, and have, among other privileges, a right to exercise the power of ordination, which is perfectly valid, and is even recognized by our own church; but I maintain it is not seemly or decorous for them to use the styles and titles that properly belong to prelates of the established church, much less publicly and ostentatiously to assume them, as of late. This will be prevented in future." Accordingly, that provision was inserted in the act, and I find that in the following year there was a pastoral address from the Roman Catholic archbishops and bishops to the clergy and laity belonging to their community throughout Ireland. The address spoke in very warm terms of the kindness which the legislature had shown in passing the act. It is worth while at the present time, when the language which has been used by Archbishop Cullen is not quite so respectful to the legislature and to the Sovereign of this country to recall a little to mind what was the universal sentiment of 26 archbishops and bishops of the Roman Catholic church in the year 1829.

It seems to me, therefore, if such were the provisions of the relief act, if these provisions were passed without objection on the part of the Roman Catholics themselves, if they were received with that submission and obedience by the Roman Catholic bishops in Ireland, that we certainly should be fully justified in proposing provisions of a similar nature with regard to the recent assumption of titles in this country. For I consider that whether the assumption be that of the title of the Archbishop of Canterbury, with the jurisdiction and authority possessed over every part of the archdiocese of Canterbury, or whether it be that of Archbishop of Westminster, with a new diocese carved out of that which is under its present Protestant bishop, is immaterial to the question—that it is an assumption of supremacy and of sovereignty which ought not to have been committed by the Pope of Rome cannot be denied (cheers).

It is believed, and I think not without foundation, that one reason for the change from vicar-apostolic, under which titles the Roman Catholics have enjoyed the free expression of their religion, and with which for 200 years they have been satisfied; and to make them bishops with a new division of the country is not merely to place them in the same degree with Protestant bishops, but it is also for the purpose of enabling them to exercise, by the authority of those names, a greater control over all the endowments which are in the hands of certain Roman Catholics as trustees in this country. I don't think it would be fitting that we should allow that control to be exercised by virtue of any of those titles which we propose to prohibit. If, therefore, the house should give me leave to bring a bill upon the subject, I propose to introduce a clause which shall enact that all gifts to persons under those titles shall be null and void (hear, hear), that any act done by them with those titles shall be null and void (hear, hear), and that property bequeathed or given for such purposes shall pass at once to the crown, with power to the crown either to create a trust for purposes similar to those for which the original trust had been created, or for other purposes, as shall seem best to the crown (cheers).

What I propose is, in the first place, to prevent the assumption of any title taken, not only from any diocese now existing, but from any territory or any place within any part of the United Kingdom (cheers). That provision is in conformity with a proposition which was made by the Bishop of London, in answer to one of the addresses which was presented to him. He said that he thought that not only we ought to prohibit the assumption of any title or rank already existing in this country, but any title derived from any place in the United Kingdom. Therefore I have agreed with that suggestion. Perhaps I may mention that when I informed the Archbishop of Canterbury that it was not intended to institute a prosecution, he said, "I did not expect that the government would institute a prosecution, but what I do expect is, that some legislation should take place upon this subject." I think, therefore, in this respect we prevent that which I consider to be an insult to the crown of this country (cheers), an interference with the rights of the established church of this country, and an attack upon the independence of this nation (loud cheers). By the other clauses to which I have alluded I think we shall obtain security against any person obtaining possession under these titles of any trust property to which I have referred. I have now stated the effect of the bill that I propose to introduce.

I am for the fullest enjoyment of religious liberty (cheers); but I am entirely opposed to any interference on the part of ecclesiastics with the temporal supremacy of the realm (renewed cheers). Whenever I have seen in other bodies—whenever I have seen in my own church—a disposition to assume powers which I thought were inconsistent with the temporal supremacy that belonged to the state, I have not been slow in urging myself, and inducing others to urge, strong and prevailing objections to any such measure. I may perhaps say that in the course of the very last year, when the proposal was made—which was plausible in itself, to give to the bishops of the English church a power which I thought would give them a control over the temporal existence and well-being and property of the clergy of the church, that proposal, because I saw in it a dangerous principle, was resisted, and successfully resisted, by my colleagues, in the place where it was proposed (hear, hear). But, if that is the case with regard to Protestants who have expressed the utmost attachment to freedom—if that is the case with regard to a church which, like the church of England is, I believe, of all the established churches the most tolerant of the difference of opinion, the most consonant with the freedom of the institutions of a country like this—if that is the case, shall I not far more strongly object to any attempt on the part of the church of Rome to introduce her temporal supremacy into this country (cheers)?

Recreated from The Freeman's Journal, Dublin, February 10, 1851.

The Cork Examiner.

MONDAYE VENING, FEBRUARY 10, 1851.

THE MEASURE AND THE MAN.

The groaning mountain is at length relieved of its burden, and lo a mouse! After all the yelling and hooting and howling on the platform, the ruffianism of the streets, and the blasphemies of the pulpit,—after bigotry has been lashed into madness, and every evil passion has been stimulated into frenzy,—after all the degrading and disgusting uproar of the last three months, the PRIME MINISTER of England pompously asks leave to bring a bill, his great measure of redress and remedy. Prefaced in solemn phrase, ushered in with ominous warning, introduced with a fearful air of responsibility, the miserable juggler, scared by the demon he has conjured up, and bewildered by the thickening consequences of his rashness, lays before the house and the country his mighty two-fold proposition. Willing to wound, but yet afraid to strike, he merely irritates where he desires to injure, and disappoints where he wishes to satisfy. He sounds a fierce trumpet-blast, summoning Protestantism to the fight, in the name of loyalty and liberty, and against the POPE; and when this appeal has rallied vast multitudes under the banner of intolerance, and they await the moment of battle, their leader attempts to gratify their ardour by aiming an ineffectual blow at the enemy, which is powerful enough to despise its feebleness, and strong enough to resent its insult.

Lord JOHN RUSSELL introduces his measure in a speech quite in keeping with his notorious letter to the Bishop of DURHAM, full of bitterness, full of bigotry, and full of slander; and after having scandalised the listening Ambassador from the United States, and elicited the thanks of the Representative of the University of Oxford, the noble lord asks the house to assent to two propositions. In his own words, the bill is—"*to prevent the assumption of any title taken, not only from any diocese now existing, but from any territory or any place which is subject to the authority, or belongs to, the United Kingdom.*" Also, "*to cause all gifts made to Roman Prelates null and to introduce clauses by which the object of those gifts shall de facto be vested in the Crown, to be applied to such uses as the donors shall direct, or to be appropriated as the officers of the Crown think fit*." This is the bill in its compound form, and with its double object.

We admit the measure is puerile in the extreme, at least so much of it as aims at the titles of the Roman Catholic Bishops of the United Kingdom, especially of Ireland, who are comprehended in this penal law, of course, with the design of cementing the political bond of union between the two countries; but though it is puerile, and, if passed, will be inoperative, it is not to be less execrated, or its author less despised, on that account. It is the hand of the pigmy which affects to smite, and not the sword of the warrior that deals the blow; and therefore the insult is the more odious, and the outrage the more unpardonable.

Now the whole mystery is cleared up. The Synod of Thurles is at the bottom of it all. Because the Irish Bishops assembled in solemn council to deliberate on questions which vitally affected the well-being of the Catholic people of the country, namely, their faith and morals, and because, after mature deliberation, they pronounced certain opinions on a subject which preeminently concerns the Church to consider, therefore those Prelates are to be made the objects of a dastardly revenge, and involved with their brethren in England in a contemptible and puerile persecution.

Reprinted and recreated from The Cork Examiner, Cork, February 10, 1851.

THE PAPAL AGGRESSION—LORD JOHN RUSSELL'S MEASURE.

At length the veil is lifted—the veil of silver tissue which kept the mystery of the Premier's political countenance hidden from popular curiosity—and what do we behold? A miserable, shrunken, fleshless skeleton, more than enough, like the visage of the Persian prophet, to excite the contempt of the phlegmatic, and appall even the most credulous believer in Whig honesty.

From our lengthened report of Lord John Russell's speech, explanatory of his "measure" against the Papal Aggression, our readers will be enabled to judge how far short of his magnificent promises falls his performance. Lord John himself has given the best description of the feat. When the blow was struck by the Pope, the Queen's minister stepped back a single pace—raised his arm to parry the thrust—and did nothing more. So have we seen the schoolboy who has received the "coward's blow," and whose prudence has forestalled his pluck. He looks big and assumes a scowl; attitudinises for a moment; cries out "Do that again, if you dare," looks around for applause, but takes good care *not to fight.*

It is useless to say that the "measure," whatever may be the details, which are not given, will disappoint the nation. It will do more. It will offend—disgust—exasperate it. It bears no proportion whatever to the vast bulk of highflying Protestantism, and what the Americans would call *Britishism*, of the speech. In that respect, it is like Sir John Falstaff's "penny-worth of bread to an intolerable deal of sack." Let us measure its full length and breadth. One sentence will suffice for the purpose. The bill to be introduced will forbid the assumption, by Roman Catholics, of any ecclesiastical titles, taken from any territory or place, within any part of the United Kingdom. The only penalty attached to the infringement of this statute will be the rendering void any acts done by any parties under those titles, and the annulling of any bequest made to them, which bequest should at once fall into the power of the Crown, to be administered under its discretion. This is, literally, the sum and substance of the great measure by which the Premier expects to appease the indignation and alarm of a unanimous Protestant people, during a ferment which he, himself, by means of his letter to the Bishop of Durham, so greatly helped to excite. It is with this paltry fragment he imagines he will repair the breach made by the Pope in the ramparts of the British fortress. It is with this fragile reed he hopes to repel the "insolent and insidious aggression" of a foreign ecclesiastical power upon the supremacy of our Queen and the independence of her people!

Lord John Russell virtually admits that this measure will be inoperative, for he assumes that it is only a temporary one, and liable to be frustrated by evasion. He feels that he is only aiming at the shadow, while the substance remains untouched. He has hopes that it may prove effective, and that, by it, Cardinal Wiseman may be induced "to reside in Rome," and no longer cross the path of a bewildered minister; but, if it should not have that effect, why—the struggle must be commenced *in earnest.* This is the tone adopted by the minister, apologetic, hesitative, timid, deprecatory; and his "measure" agrees with it; for, as Mr. Roebuck smartly observed, let Cardinal Wiseman only subscribe himself "Archbishop *in* Westminster," instead of his assumed title, "Archbishop *of* Westminster," and though his dignity will be taken down a peg, nothing is to hinder him from enjoying the full benefit of his masters rescript "from outside the Flaminian Gate."

The measure, while it gives no satisfaction to Protestants, will, certainly, not offend Roman Catholics. It seems to have been specifically framed to secure *their* civil and religious liberties, at least, as far as it goes; for if it have any avail, it will save their charitable trusts from the grasp of the *Propaganda*.

Recreated from The Belfast News-Letter, Belfast, February 10, 1851.

FROM OUR LONDON CORRESPONDENT.

London Saturday.

The debate last night was totally devoid of incident; every man knew how the division would end, and no man seemed to take any interest even in that. Of course most of the Irish members who voted *for* the government *when the government was in danger,* and needed friends, voted *against* the government last night when it was in *no danger,* and could afford to dispense with friendly votes.

The numbers who voted for the introduction of the penal measure were 395; the numbers who voted against were 63, leaving the government a clear majority of 332. A few votes more or less they could well afford to disregard, when they could command such a majority. In this miserable minority of sixty-three, there were but 38 *Irish members.* It is worthy of note that *the* twenty men who voted no confidence in the No-Popery cabinet on Thursday night, *were all at their posts* on Friday night to vote against the introduction of the penal law. Not so with the men, who, confiding in the Russell policy, have confirmed in his hand the sword of persecution. You will be pleased to see the names of Bright and Cobden, and Gibson, and Walmsley, in the minority. Those men are acting nobly.

I have the most satisfactory reasons for believing that the votes of the twenty Irish Liberals have "put the fear of *man*" into the hearts of the ministers. They verily did not believe till that night that an Irish member was a *man.* I am not, however, at liberty to state as yet all that I have heard on the subject; but of this be assured, that if the Irish church and Irish institutions are saved, to these twenty men will the whole credit be due. *The very morning after their vote the* TIMES *began to lower its colours.* But I must not enter on a subject which I am not at liberty at present to discuss. Support the policy of these men, and all may be yet well.

Recreated from The Freeman's Journal, Dublin, February 17, 1851.

ROBBERY BY A SON AND NEPHEW.

A man named Sullivan, living in a remote part of the county Kerry, was robbed on Thursday last by his son and nephew of the sum of £9 1s. Sullivan came to Cork yesterday, and, after making some inquiries, he heard that they were on board a hooker on their way to join an emigrant vessel at Passage. The plaintiff, accompanied by two policemen, went with a boat in pursuit of the hooker, and, when alongside, and after they had attached the boat by a rope, the rope was cast off, the hooker made sail, and the boat was sent adrift. Constable Duross, whose duty it is to watch the quays, heard of the circumstance, and, seeing the hooker sailing down the river, called out to the captain to come to, but the captain told him "he might go be damned", and set him at defiance.

The constable then leaped into a boat, and pursued the hooker down the river, but, as he came alongside, one of the oars unfortunately broke, and he was compelled to abandon the chase. The Royal Alice, Captain Cameron, was coming down the river at the time, and after the constable had hailed him, the steamer was stopped, the constable got on board and related the circumstance to the captain.

The Royal Alice steamed after the hooker and came close alongside in a short time, when Constable Duross, after arming himself with a bayonet which he got from one of the Queenstown policemen who were in the boat, and directing another policeman to follow him, jumped into the hooker and called on the captain to lower his sails. A cry of "throw them overboard" was immediately raised in the hooker, and the hostile appearance of those on board seemed as if they intended to carry their threat into effect; but Constable Duross immediately ran towards the man at the helm, took the helm from him, and ran the boat ashore at Foaty, opposite Blackrock Castle.

A number of boats immediately put off from Blackrock and Silverspring; and, in the meantime, after an active search amongst the emigrants, who amounted to several hundred, the active constable found the prisoners, and had them conveyed ashore. On the person of the elder lad, the nephew of Sullivan, he found a passage ticket for two to New York, for which £7 hade been paid, and the balance of the money taken.

The prisoners were brought up at the Police-office this morning, and remanded until to-morrow, for the purpose of enabling them to appear as witnesses against the men of the hooker, Sullivan having declined to prosecute either his son or his nephew. The Bench expressed its approbation of the intelligence and great activity exhibited by Constable Duross, and hoped such qualities would shortly lead to his promotion.

Recreated from The Cork Examiner, Cork, February 19, 1851.

HIGHLY IMPORTANT.

We have this morning seen a letter to a very respectable gentleman in this city, from Mr. Keating, our honest county member, stating that a compact body of Irish Representatives met at the residence of Cardinal Wiseman, in London, on Tuesday evening, and came to the unanimous resolution of voting against Ministers on *every occasion*. Many of the Irish Seceders attended the meeting.

To-night this gallant Brigade will oppose the Minister on the Income Tax, when, it is expected, he will be beaten. We hope that our County and City Members will, to a man, vote against these vile persecutors of our religion and country.

If Government is defeated, there will be a dissolution, so our constituents had better look out. It is now acknowledged that the Irish Brigade hold the keys of office.

Reprinted from The Waterford News, Waterford, February 21, 1851.

DEFEAT OF THE MINISTERS!

"Coming events cast their shadows before." Ministers have sustained a defeat—just to begin with—but not such a one as will induce them to resign. Mr. Locke King brought forward his annual motion to assimilate the county franchise in England to that of the boroughs, by giving a right of voting to occupiers of tenements rated to the annual value of £10. Lord John Russell resisted the motion, and, on a division, was beaten by a majority of 48, the numbers for being 100, and against it 52. On this the *Times* observes very *naively*:—"It is useless to conceal that government is losing weight both in the house and out of it. There are rocks ahead of all sorts." Such is the consolation of the *Times*, after having contrived to get ministers into the difficulty for which they are now upbraided without pity. Ministers have sustained the first of their defeats, and at an earlier period of the session than ever before had befallen them. They are likely, unless they retrace their steps, to incur similar and far more important disasters.

Our readers will understand from the smallness of the numbers who divided that this was not one of the great occasions of the session, and that ministers have sustained the present mortifying discomfiture more from the contemptuous indifference of their friends than from the strength of their opponents. Still the defeat is regarded by the London journals as ominous of what was likely to happen on last night when the division on the income tax was likely to take place. We regret to say that some Irish members are lingering in Dublin who ought to have been present last night to make good the blow. Absence upon paltry excuses, or now upon any excuse, will be regarded by the country as treason, not less decided only more cowardly, than if the vote were openly given to the ministry. Above all things we cannot understand how any of the twenty to whom the country has been willing to award so much honour can now absent themselves.

Recreated from The Cork Examiner, Cork, February 22, 1851.

THE FALL OF THE RUSSELL CABINET.

Like a shout of triumph, let it ring through the land—*The Whigs are out!* Amidst the scorn of all honest men, and by the weight of its own infamy, the Government of Lord JOHN RUSSELL has fallen to pieces.—Execrated for its apostacy, detested for its tyranny, laughed at for its financial absurdities, this miserable administration has tumbled to the ground, overwhelmed with scorn and derision. The formal announcement of this glad tidings is thus given in the *Times* of Saturday:—

"Lord JOHN RUSSELL has tendered his resignation to her Majesty, and only holds office till another Government can be formed. The extensive loss of Parliamentary confidence, or rather Parliamentary sympathy, which his Lordship and his colleagues have evidently suffered of late, has probably prepared most of our readers for this result. In the face of so much resolute opposition from so many different quarters, and with so much irresolute support—in the face of such divisions as those of yesterday week and last Thursday, Lord JOHN RUSSELL could not expect that the present Cabinet would safely ride thro' the many delicate questions pressing upon the attention of Parliament."

It is now clear that it was the vote on the motion of Mr. DISRAELI that killed this Whig Cock Robin. The majority on the motion of Mr. LOCKE KING was but a mere bagatelle, which any staple government might afford to despise. Even the budget of Sir CHARLES WOOD, contemptible piece of finance as it is, could be managed one way or another. But the defection of the Irish Members was a home thrust that no possible dexterity could parry, a crushing blow that no amount of ministerial management could ward off. In the article of the *Times* there is not the slightest allusion to the real question upon which Lord JOHN RUSSELL has been declared politically insolvent.

It is utter nonsense to suppose that the question of Protection or Free Trade had anything whatever to do with the stranding of the shattered hull of the Whig administration; it was the deliberate abandonment of his own policy, in reference to the once-sacred principles of civil and religious liberty, that shook his Cabinet from base to top. It was the daring aggression on the Catholic Church of the empire that caused him that "extensive loss of Parliamentary sympathy," so delicately alluded to in the *Times*, which compelled him to tender his resignation, and give way to some ambitious rival.

Recreated from The Cork Examiner, Cork, February 24, 1851.

FALL OF THE WHIGS.

The cabinet of Lord JOHN RUSSELL has fallen—fallen before the resistance that their treacherous attempt upon religious liberty has provoked from the people of Ireland. Twenty Irish representatives, usually supporters of ministers, had the courage and decision to strike the first blow. Never was public act hailed with such a welcome of public acclaim as that act has been welcomed with in Ireland. The next blow would have been struck by fifty—fifty men who usually vote with ministers, and whose adverse votes now would make a difference of one hundred on a division. Rather than await this blow, ministers have resigned. Some of the London journals affect a mysterious knowledge on the subject of the resignation, and reason learnedly on the delinquencies of the budget. Mystification is a great resource in diplomatic emergencies; but this is a plain case, and its merits are palpable to plain men. Stories about personal jealousies, and theories about the incidence of taxation, are mere babble which nobody heeds, or in his heart believes. The religious liberty of Ireland was assailed by the Whigs,—the spirit of Ireland has resisted, and the assailants are overthrown. This is the beginning, the middle, and the end of the matter, and except for the purpose of keeping the simple and instructive truth clear of all insidious shroudings, there is no more to say.

Recreated from The Freeman's Journal, Dublin, February 24, 1851.

STOP PRESS.
THE MINISTERIAL CRISIS.

FREEMAN'S JOURNAL OFFICE,
Tuesday Morning, Quarter to Seven.

We have just received, through the Messrs. Smith and Son, the following important communication:—

FROM OUR LONDON CORRESPONDENT.

London, Monday, Four o'clock.

All is yet in confusion. The Whig satellites who were so confident at this hour yesterday are now in utter dismay.— Lord John Russell is said to have found it impossible to reconstruct his cabinet and to have declared that he abandons the task. Sir James Graham and Lord Aberdeen are still at work to try to reconcile matters and arrange terms for a reconstruction and coalition. Lord Stanley still holds the commission to be in readiness to construct a cabinet, in case the negociation for the re-construction of the cabinet fails. The alleged retirement of Russell would seem likely to place that duty on Stanley.

The excitement and uncertainty is beyond anything ever remembered in former "crises." The *Morning Herald* has published *five* editions to-day, each containing matters new, and apparently contradictory; but all reconcilable by the facts I give you above.

Lord John Russell's retirement I have heard from a party likely to be well informed. His dining at the Whig clubs seems to be a confirmation of the rumour.

BY EXPRESS AND ELECTRIC TELEGRAPH.

We have received through our Liverpool correspondent, and by electric telegraph from our London correspondent, the following summary of the proceedings in the House of Commons last night, from which it will be seen that all ministerial projects are at an end.

The Whigs are out—finally out. The Irish Catholic phalanx have broken one ministry; how many more may they not disperse?

HOUSE OF COMMONS—MONDAY.

The SPEAKER took the chair shortly after four o'clock. When the house had assembled,

Lord J. RUSSELL rose, and in brief terms moved the adjournment of the house till next Friday. He did so because from the various votes which had been given in the house since parliament had been called together, antagonistic to the government of which he had the honour to be the head, he was induced to believe that her Majesty's present advisers had not the confidence of that house; and, therefore, he moved that the house be adjourned till Friday, in order to allow of a new administration being constructed (deep silence). Whoever might be the leading member of that (the new) administration there was one rumour abroad which he was anxious to correct. It had been reported that Lord Stanley had been appointed to the office which he was about to vacate; but nothing could be more unfounded; for that nobleman (Lord Stanley) had declined to undertake the responsibility of that duty (hear, hear).

Mr. B. D'ISRAELI denied in emphatic terms the statement made by the noble lord, that Lord Stanley had declined the offer of accepting the responsibility of forming a cabinet. The noble lord must be labouring under a mistake.

Lord JOHN RUSSELL assured the house that Lord Stanley had refused to organise a ministry.

Mr. ROEBUCK addressed the house upon the then position of ministers, and contrasted their acts as the advanced Reformers when out of office with their "finality" policy when in; and after warning all future governments against interfering with the civil and religious liberty of the subject, concluded a telling but short speech amid the applause of the house.

A short desultory conversation then ensued, and the house adjourned at an early hour.

From the Sixth Edition of the Morning Herald.

Matters are still in a thoroughly undecided state, and it is not believed that Sir James Graham can form an administration which would be acceptable.

Mr. Gladstone, who might have been expected to arrive to-night, will not be in London until Wednesday.

It is ascertained that, should Sir James Graham be able to form a ministry, Ireland will be omitted from the provisions of any measure he may bring in with reference to the Papal aggression.

Reprinted from The Freeman's Journal, Dublin, February 25, 1851.

THE MINISTERIAL CRISIS.
RESIGNATION OF LORD STANLEY.

Lord Stanley has abandoned the desperate task of constructing a Cabinet on his lordship's principles of restriction in trade, and persecution in religion. This might have been anticipated from the moment the duty was imposed upon him of carrying out in practice the principle which he has so recklessly asserted in speech. As to his protection principles, he was ready to place them in abeyance, in order to secure the support of men who might help to float him and his Cabinet to sea. Indeed, of these principles he had for some time past been rapidly disencumbering himself, so that this part of his proposition for office probably came sufficiently easy to him; but his declarations on the subject of the Catholic persecution had been too recent, his protest against even the bill of Lord John as shortcoming and insufficient, too passionate and emphatic to be easily escaped from. He could get none of the abler statesmen to join him in the task of destroying religious liberty, and more especially, in the attempt to govern this country on the old principle of Catholic Penal Laws. So Lord Stanley has once again in his life been shipwrecked on the coast of Ireland, towards whose shoals and rocks he seems to have an invincible attraction.

As to the precise hour at which Lord Stanley abandoned the reins authorities differ. Several of the London journals state that an authoritative announcement of his immediate intention to do so was made at White's at six o'clock on Thursday evening, while the *Morning Herald*, the organ of his lordship's party, came out on Friday (yesterday) morning expressing, though, with a wavering confidence, its trust that he would have his Cabinet formed that day. If, however, the concurrence of all the other London journals had left any slight room for doubt that his lordship had failed, even that is removed by an announcement in a second edition of the *Herald*, dated twelve o'clock yesterday (Friday), and telegraphed to us by our London Correspondent, which proclaims the fact in these words—"Lord Stanley has resigned."

(*From the Morning Herald.*)

Until past five, p.m., yesterday afternoon it was currently believed that Lord Stanley was making rapid progress in the formation of a government. The bulk of his followers were in the highest spirits, and the bare probability of a failure was scouted by his organs in the press. They were in the very height of their exultation, when a noble earl, known to be in Lord Stanley's confidence, suddenly walked into White's, and stated that he was desired by Lord Stanley to mention that he had failed in the attempt to form a government. The announcement was received with doubt, and the authority was disputed by eminent Protectionists, but there can be little or no doubt by this time of its truth. Various specific causes are of course alleged for the failure, but the only wonder to our mind is that Lord Stanley persevered so long.

The current belief is that some Whig combination is on foot. We firmly adhere to our original opinion that no administration will stand which transgresses the genuine principle of toleration. It is all very well to say that the No-Popery feeling of the English nation must be indulged; but let those who use this language state how they propose to govern Ireland upon their theory. A civil war will be inevitable if the Roman Catholic hierarchy is assailed. It may be a misfortune for a Protestant Great Britain to be linked with a kingdom containing five million Papists; but a wise statesman will not aggravate the evils of such a situation by enacting or enforcing penal laws against a religion of the majority. Again, we say, all hope of a stable government is not over, until both Lord Clarendon and Sir James Graham, alone or jointly, have failed in forming one.

Recreated from The Waterford News, Waterford, March 1, 1851.

CALLAN TENANT SOCIETY.

This body held their weekly meeting in the Town Hall, on Wednesday evening, MICHAEL LYNCH, Esq., in the chair. In consequence of the feverish curiosity of the people to have no person in the next Board of Guardians but stern adherents to the Tenant League, who are prepared to fight every inch of the ground with the *ex-officios* in the Board Room and out of it, the meeting was a very crowded one. The Committee were delighted to learn that the same determined preparations are being made in the Unions of Kilkenny, Castlecomer, Thomastown, and Urlingford, to get rid of landlord tools and the "no religion" men.

The secretary read the minutes of the last meeting, also the report of the last meeting of the Castlecomer Society. It was stated that the sound of the crashing crowbar was heard for some days in Maxtown, within half a mile of Callan. One side of Newtown road, for nearly a mile, from where it diverges from the road leading to Kilkenny, is strewn with the ruins of demolished houses. The inmates, some of them wretched widows, were seen that day collecting their ragged starved children under the cover of the old thatch thrown up again on the rafters, which were laid horizontally on the unroofed walls. The property belongs to the Rev. Mr. Hunt, of Cavan, a minister of the Gospel of Mercy. This tale brought fresh again to every mind the horrid memory of the demolition of Toomevara last year, by the Rev. Massy Dawson.

The lands are said to be cleared to consolidate the entire into one farm, in order to hand it over to the notorious land-jobber here, on whose dusky brow the "widow's curse," like the lightning of heaven's vengeance, is dancing. There is another person spoken of as the future tenant; but if it be at his bidding this work has been done, he belies all the antecedents of his family and his own. A report was ordered for the next day of meeting of the number of houses levelled and the number of individuals set adrift.

Recreated from The Nation, Dublin, March 1, 1851.

STOP PRESS.

FREEMAN'S JOURNAL OFFICE,
Seven o'Clock, a.m.

THE MINISTERIAL CRISIS.
RESTORATION OF THE WHIGS.

We have just received, through the Messrs Smith and Son, the following summary of the proceedings in parliament last evening:—

BY ELECTRIC TELEGRAPH.
HOUSE OF COMMONS—MONDAY NIGHT.

The Speaker took the chair at four o'clock, and shortly after five, on the motion for the reading over the order of the day for the second reading of the ecclesiastical titles assumption bill,

Lord JOHN RUSSELL said he would state what had occurred since he last addressed the House of Commons on Friday, promising that he would make no remark upon Lord Stanley's explanation elsewhere, except that his lordship (Lord Stanley) had full power to form an administration, and that no request which he could reasonably make to the Sovereign would have been refused. Late on the preceding evening her Majesty had received a communication from the Duke of Wellington. Yesterday (Sunday morning) he (Lord John Russell) had been admitted to an audience with the Queen, at which it was signified that the Duke's opinion was, that the late ministry should be recalled (hear, hear). This had been done (cheers). He would therefore propose that public business should be postponed until Friday next, when he proposed to proceed with the bill respecting the assumption of titles by Roman Catholic prelates. On that evening Sir G. Grey would state the alteration which it had been determined to make in this measure, and, at the same time, the days for proceeding with the other government measures, including the budget (hear and partial cheers).

Reprinted from The Freeman's Journal, Dublin, March 3, 1851.

CASE ON BEHALF OF THE CATHOLIC ARCHBISHOPS AND BISHOPS OF IRELAND.

Counsel has herewith a copy of a bill intituled—"A bill to prevent the assumption of certain ecclesiastical titles in respect of places in the United Kingdom," and is requested to consider its provisions, and advise:—

How, and in what respects, if passed into law, it would affect the Roman Catholics of Ireland in the exercise of their religion, and the free observance of the discipline of their church?

How, and in what respects, it would affect the management and continuance of their existing trusts and charities, and the creation of such trusts and charities hereafter, regard being had to the usual mode of providing for the administration and devolution of such trusts and charities in Ireland? And counsel will please state the grounds on which his opinion may be formed.

OPINION

I have carefully examined the provisions of "The Ecclesiastical Titles Assumption Bill," and considered their probable influences on the Catholic hierarchy and the people of Ireland.

As I understand the discipline of the Roman Catholic Church in Ireland, the provisions of this bill, if rigidly carried into execution, would be wholly inconsistent with the free action and practical existence of the Catholic hierarchy. It forbids the "assumption or use of the name, style, or title of archbishop, or bishop, or dean of any city, town, or place, or of any territory or district (under any designation or description whatever) in the United Kingdom," by any other persons than archbishops, bishops, and deans, of the established church, and proposes to inflict on the person offending, by such use or assumption, a penalty of £100. Now, the Catholic prelates of Ireland are not bishops *in partibus*—are not vicars apostolic—but members of an episcopate, regulated by the settled law of the Roman Catholic Church, which requires that each bishop should be the bishop of a particular see in Ireland, and have a peculiar local jurisdiction.

According to that discipline, each of them has his own local title, and must use it in discharging the functions of his office. If the contemplated enactment takes effect, he cannot discharge those functions, as his predecessors have ever discharged them, and as the constitution of his order requires them to be discharged.

The second clause annuls all deeds or writings made, signed, or executed by a Roman Catholic archbishop, bishop, or dean, under any name, style, or title which the law forbids him to assume. According to the usage of the Irish Roman Catholic Church, many episcopal acts are completed by writing, and this clause must operate to nullify such acts in law.

I come to the third section, which is framed with extreme ingenuity and astuteness, to render the endowment of Roman Catholic archbishoprics, bishoprics, deaneries, in any way, impossible. It provides, that all property which is given or "expressed, or intended" to be given, "directly or indirectly," for the endowment of such archbishoprics, bishoprics, or deaneries, instituted as of any place—or for any purpose,—all such property shall vest in the crown, "without any office or inquisition whatever."

The fourth section of the bill is designed to make evasion of the preceding provisions impossible.

These are the observations and suggestions which have occurred to me in considering the provisions of this bill. I might have illustrated them by many references to particular case. But I have thought it more desirable to continue my opinion to the possible and probable effects of the measure generally, as conflicting with the discipline of the Catholic Church in Ireland—incompatible, if effectually enforced, with the maintenance of the Irish Catholic Hierarchy in its old integrity and freedom, according to that discipline—and interfering injuriously not only with Catholic trusts and charities hereafter to be created, but also, with those which already have existence.

Thomas O'Hagan

GREAT MEETING IN MEATH—THE PENAL LAWS.

On Saturday last, a numerous and influential meeting was held in Kells, to protest against the proposed Penal Bill of Lord John Russell. The meeting was held in the Catholic Church of that town, and the large building was crowded in every part.

On the motion of Mr. Landry, the chair was taken by the Very Rev. Dr. M'Evoy, P.P., Kells.

The Very Reverend Chairman said—Men of Kells, and of the surrounding districts, from my heart I thank you for the distinguished honour in calling me to preside over this most respectable, influential, and important meeting, embracing, as it does, so much of the wealth, talent, the respectability, and the intelligence of the ancient borough of Kells. (Cheers.)

Using your constitutional right, you are here to-day assembled for the lawful, and let me say in time, a glorious purpose—(hear, hear)—of adopting a petition to Parliament praying the rejection of the penal measure that is now under its consideration—(hear, hear)—a measure directed, not as that bill falsely professes, against the titles merely of your venerated hierarchy, but directed against the very existence of the Catholic Church in these United Kingdoms. (Hear.)

You are assembled to-day for the purpose of declaring your indomitable, your uncompromising determination to stand by that church, aye, even to death—(vehement and prolonged cheering.)—in spite of pains, and penalties, and persecutions, aye, and even of legal enactments, too. (Renewed cheering.) Men of Kells, I am proud of you, and have I not reason? (A Voice—You'll always have reason, and loud cheers.) I cannot find language adequate to express my feelings of delight and gratification at the earnestness and zeal, and enthusiasm with which I see you congregated around this sanctuary, for the purpose of offering constitutional resistance to this penal law. (Hear, hear,)

Yes; though hunger and cold, and nakedness have emaciated the forms of some amongst you, still your unprecedented privations have not extinguished your undying devotion to the faith of your fathers—the faith that has descended to you upon the crimson ground of their blood, and the faith in which you are, every man of you, determined to die. (Loud cheers.)

My Lord John "Mummery" (groans) thought, in his unparalleled wisdom, that he had devised an effectual means whereby to sever the ties that had so long and so indissolubly bound together the faithful Irish people and their devoted hierarchy and priesthood. He introduced a bill directed exclusively against the princes and priests of the Church, while he left the laity still to enjoy all their honours. (Hear, hear.)

Yes, he thought by this means to throw the apple of discord amongst us—to disunite us, and, in our disunion, to accomplish the easy degradation, enslavement—aye, and in the phrenzy of his folly, the utter destruction of the Church of St. Patrick. But, my Lord John, little indeed did you know the nature of the ties that bind together the Irish priesthood, and the Irish people. (Loud cheering.)

Recreated from The Nation, Dublin, March 8, 1851.

BURNING OF LORD JOHN RUSSELL IN EFFIGY.

The inhabitants of the principle town in the county of Kerry, following the example set to them in Killarney, Ennis, and elsewhere, burned Lord John Russell last evening (Thursday) in effigy, in the presence of a mob of at least 2,000 persons, and under the windows of her Majesty's Judges in Denny-street. It appears that two persons were tried and acquitted in the morning, before Mr. Justice Ball, of being concerned in a riot which took place in the town of Killarney some weeks back upon the occasion of a similar display, and the result of the trial was to give their lordships a personal opportunity of witnessing another demonstration of confidence in the Prime Minister. The mob, who was accompanied by a band of local musicians and a strong body of torch bearers, marched through the principal streets of the town several times during the evening, shouting and firing off squibs, pistols, &c., to the great consternation of the various inhabitants; and, having nearly exhausted their indignation against Lord John Russell, about ten o'clock they terminated their proceedings, by burning a figure of his lordship opposite to the judges' lodgings amidst roars of laughter and shouts of execration.

As soon as the effigy was consumed they dispersed, and in a short time the streets resumed their usual tranquil appearance. Several bodies of the constabulary patrolled the town until a late hour to preserve the peace; but their assistance was fortunately not required, as the unanimity of the inhabitants had the effect of keeping order.—*Saunder's Correspondent*.

Recreated from The Waterford News, Waterford, March 22, 1851.

PROVIDENTIAL ESCAPE OF THE EMIGRANT SHIP "FAVOURITE" WITH TWO HUNDRED AND FIFTY PERSONS ON BOARD.—About two o'clock, Thursday morning, the night watchman in charge of Mr. E. Burke Roche's demesne, of Trabolgan, was attracted by loud cries and lamentations, which appeared to come from some vessel a short distance off the coast. On hurrying down to the shore, he found that the cries proceeded from the people on board a large vessel, which was drifting in on the rocks. Lights and assistance were immediately procured, and after a short time it was found that the vessel was the *Favourite*, St. John's. She left Liverpool on the 28th February, and became leaky on the 17th March, and made for Cork harbour. When off Ballycotton, a pilot was taken on board, but he was incapable of getting her into Cork, and in consequence she drifted towards the shore, at Trabolgan. A despatch was sent to Queenstown, and several boats having arrived succeeded in conveying the terrified passengers (250 in number) safely to shore, where they received that hospitality for which the Irish are so proverbial. It is feared the vessel will become a total wreck.—*Limerick Examiner*.

Recreated from The Freeman's Journal, Dublin, March 31, 1851.

A RUNAWAY APPRENTICE.

Richard Gleeson, who was brought up to receive the sentence of the court, being convicted on a former occasion, appeared to be a rather *knowing one*.

Mr. Power, (Solicitor) informed the bench of the facts which were proven against him, and stated the present occurrence for which he was about to receive their judgement, was the fifth or sixth time he had deserted from his master, Mr. Thomas O'Brien, of Patrick-street.—He [Mr. Power] also informed their Worships that they had it in their power to sentence him under either of the two acts of parliament which he had just read, and prayed that the bench would have the kindness to add hard labour to its judgement.

Mr. Tabiteau having addressed the prisoner on his very bad conduct in leaving his master so frequently, and informed him that they had it in their power to imprison him for three months.

The Mayor informed him that he should be sent to jail for one month, with hard labour.

Prisoner—Put the three to it.

Mr. Tabiteau—This is another instance of your bad conduct by your disrespect to the court. You think that you are now a very fine fellow for doing this, and that you will earn the approval of your associates by it.—You shall get the three months you require, for on the expiration of the month you will be sent back again, and so repeated until you receive the full period.

A CASE OF CABBAGE.

Patrick Mullally was charged by Mrs. Judy Fleming, of the yellow-road, for having *cabbaged* a quantity of that vegetable, a few days ago, the property of complainant.

Judy Fleming sworn—After a very lengthened display of her oratorical powers in detailing the facts of the case—she stated that, having missed the cabbage, on the morning of Tuesday, she had brought "that young man there—No. 43," to the house of Mullally, where he had found it.

Mr. Phelan [Solicitor] exhibited a *plant* of cabbage, which he stated was one of those that had been found with the prisoner, although complainant described it as being fit for use.

Mrs. Fleming—Oh! my God! Do you hear that 44? will you say nothing for me?

No. 44 cautioned her to be silent.

Mr. Power [Solicitor for the prosecution] explained the case from which we gathered that a misunderstanding existed between the parties as to the rightful owner of the property.

Bench to Mrs. Fleming—How long are you in possession of the garden?

Mrs. Fleming—Nineteen years next 15th of August. I recollect it very well, for it was on that day I was married to my poor man [laughter].

It was agreed to return the case over to the petty sessions court, when the proper party should get the value of the cabbage, which the Constable was ordered to have sold, being, as Mrs. Fleming described it, a "perishable substance."

The parties then left the court, and we could see that Mrs. Fleming was anything but pleased by the decision, and looking as if she believed the bench had really *cabbaged* her out of her "early York."

EMIGRATION FROM WATERFORD.

On yesterday the fine ship *Orinoco*, Captain Burke (the first passenger vessel that left this port) glided down river, with a full complement of passengers, nearly all of whom were of the middle class of farmers, and farm servants. The *Orinoco* looked well as she "walked the waters" with her portion of the "bone and sinew" of our poor old land. Immediately after the sailing of the *Orinoco*, Ald. Forristal will have his other three vessels in readiness for the same destination. To Irish emigrants it is not only a boon, but a great saving, to have ships sailing from their own shores; and hence we would suggest to the persevering Alderman the propriety of chartering some ships for New York, after his own shall have departed.

The *Medina, Jenny Lind, Amazon* and *Ann Kenny* (all successful ships) are, as will be seen by advertisement, also preparing for the "land of Liberty."

Recreated and reprinted from The Waterford News, Waterford, March 30, 1851.

NEW DISCOVERY OF A RACE OF CANNIBALS AT BORNEO.

The Colonial Church Chronicle of April contains an important letter from Mr. Macdougall, the missionary of the Borneo Church Mission at Sarawak. He gives an interesting description of his new edifice raised for public worship, and also a curious account of a race of cannibals lately discovered in Borneo, the latter of which we subjoin:—

"We have had here for sometime an interesting Dyak from a long way in the interior, he says a fortnight's journey from this. He left his tribe on account of a skin disease, 'which,' he says, 'gave no peace, and puts him to shame in his tribe, as the other men have all clean skins.' He heard I could cure it, and came to ask me to do so; but the case is too inveterate, I fear, for poor Koosoo ever to be cured. He is an intelligent fellow, and gives a most enchanting description of his country, in which, he says, there are large lakes and fine mountains, and which abound with wild cattle, deer, and other game, in abundance. But his account of a race of Kayans, who border upon his tribe, is very remarkable, and forms the reason for mentioning him.

These people are cannibals, and of all the androphagi I ever heard of they seem the worst, and we may well assert of them what old Herodotus says of the cannibals of his time, that *agriolaia panton anthropor cchiousi ethea*. They are perfect gluttons in human flesh, and prefer it to any other food.— They carry attached to their sword-scabbards a sharp skewer of about eighteen inches long, which, when they have killed a victim, man, woman, or child, they introduce into the flesh, and pass it along the bones of the extremities and spine, working it so as to divide all the muscular attachments from the bones. They then take off skin and flesh together, beginning at the soles of the feet, and carry on the operation from below upwards, doing it so rapidly that, in a few minutes, nothing but the bones and viscera are left. They take out the brain and cook it slightly in a particular kind of leaf, and consider it the great *bonne bouche* of their abominable feast. When they have cooked and eaten all they want, they cook and smoke the rest as the Dyaks and Malays do boar's or deer's flesh, and will eat no other flesh while it lasts—Koosoo says, when his tribe go to war some of these people always come to eat the bodies of the slain. They never kill their friends for food, but always eat an enemy when they can get one; eating all indiscriminately, men, women, and children. But, with the exception of this horrible taste, Koosoo describes them as a very good people, and as more civilised and clever than the Dyaks. He has lived amongst them once and again, and has always found them kind and hospitable to strangers, and honest in their trading transactions. He is quite sure they would not eat white men, but would be very glad to receive them as friends, and would take great care of them. This narrative, which I quite believe, from the perfect simplicity and artlessness of the man, establishes the existence of cannibals here, a fact long disputed. These cannibals are a numerous and powerful nation, governed by a Rajah, but religion seems to be at a lower ebb amongst them than even amongst the Dyaks. I am trying to get a vocabulary of his language from Koosoo; it is very different from that spoken by our land Dyaks."

Recreated from The Freeman's Journal, Dublin, April 3, 1851.

SPRING FASHIONS.
MY BLACK CLOTH WALKING COAT,
in various shapes, at 30s.
This is a Standard Article – Cut, Quality, and Trimming.
The above in Superfine, Plain, and Elastic Cloths, at 35s.
Trouserings and Vestings in variety.
J. M. ROONEY,
MERCHANT TAILOR,
82, UPPER SACKVILLE-STREET
(Above the Gresham Hotel).

Reprinted from The Freeman's Journal, Dublin, April 3, 1851.

DR. FREW IN TROUBLE.

Dr. Frew, a notorious quack, and his wife *Bella Frew*, were this day brought up on the charge of assaulting Ann Montgomery, their landlady, on Thursday week. When the Doctor, who appears to be a very ignorant man, was brought to the Police-office and searched, a quantity of pills was found in his pockets, composed solely of bread, with which he is in the habit of gulling the parties that call upon him for professional advice. In appearance, the Doctor was more like a nailor or shoemaker than a professional gentlemen. He was much excited during the proceedings, and seemed as if he was just recovering from a fit of *delirium tremors*.

Ann Montgomery having been sworn said—The prisoners live in my house. On this day week I went up to them to ask for some rent. Mrs. Frew drew a knife upon me and swore she would stick me. She pulled the shoe off me, and struck me two or three times with it, and attempted to stab me. Some time ago the Doctor struck me with a poker. He did not strike me on this occasion.

Mr. TRACY.—Prisoners, what have you got to say to this complaint?

Dr. Frew observed that all he had got to say was that the complainant, on the day in question, came up to his room and called his wife out of her name. She had been drunk for the last month, and was drunk at the present moment. Because he would not give her whiskey, she swore that she would settle with his wife, that she would swear that Mrs. Frew threatened to stab her. The complainant, he said, kept an improper house, and was so desperate an old villain that she ought to be hanged. His wife was an honest woman and would not defraud any one of a penny—she was "a real game one." (Laughter.)

Mr. SEEDS.—Is not the complainant a game one too?

Witness.—She is in some respects. (Laughter.)

Mrs. Frew requested to be heard. She said that this woman came into her room on the day in question with four infamous characters, and demanded drink from her husband.

Dr. Frew.—Exactly so.

Mr. TRACY.—Why did you draw the knife upon her?

Mrs. Frew assured his worship that nothing of the kind occurred; that her husband had got one shilling's worth of drink for her, and had given her 4s. for rent; she asked for more drink and her husband wanted her to go and get it for her, but she refused. The complainant then stamped her foot and swore she would be revenged upon her.

Mr. TRACY addressing the complainant said when obtaining the summons against these parties you swore that the husband struck you at the time the wife threatened to stab you. Now you tell a different story. I must dismiss your complaint; and Doctor I would advise you to go into some other locality, and not squander your professional earnings as it appears you have been doing. (Laughter.)

Jane Byrne, an old woman who had got liberty to come into the house of Catherine Scott, on Wednesday, to warm her hands, rewarded her by stealing from her a quarter of a stone of flour. Mrs. Scott missed the flour, and followed the prisoner, and gave her in charge of a constable. The prisoner was committed to the Quarter Sessions for trial.

Jane M'Mullan was charged with stealing a blanket, the property of Mary Carr. The prisoner had been in hospital, and after she came out she was so naked, that the prosecutrix took compassion on her, and gave her a gown. The return she made for this kindness was to steal the blanket which she pawned and afterwards made fun of the prosecutrix about it. The prisoner was ordered to pay a fine of £1, Irish, or in default to be imprisoned fourteen days in the house of correction.

No other case of any interest came before the court till its rising.

Recreated from The Belfast News-Letter, Belfast, April 4, 1851.

DINNER TO LORD STANLEY.

Lord Stanley's political supporters in the two houses of parliament feted him at Merchant Tailors' Hall on Wednesday, when his lordship took occasion to address them at considerable length on the policy and prospects of the party. Great interest seems to have been attached to this demonstration, men not unnaturally expecting that when a chief and his followers met, the plans of the future campaign would be distinctly traced. In these expectations, however, they were destined to disappointment. The noble lord scrupulously avoided details and dwelt only in vague generalities, such as are not likely hereafter to be brought up in judgement against him. He would give relief to agriculturists, but added, "how that relief may be afforded this is not time to consider." It might not be the time to "consider," for it ought to have been considered long since; but surely the noble lord, who prides himself on his frankness, will not say that the meeting of his parliamentary supporters, on what he himself described almost in terms as the eve of an appeal to the country, was not the time, above all others, on which he ought to have frankly declared his views and plans, for the advancement of which he aspired to the government of the country. His lordship was little less vague when he came to speak of his projected duty on human food. He would have "*moderate* duties" to afford a "certain though *moderate* check" to the "unlimited influx of corn *when not required in this country*." The duty that one man would think moderate another might deem immoderate. Lord Stanley should have told us what he thinks a "moderate" duty, and what tribunal has to decide whether the breadstuffs were not required in this country, if the demand in the public market is not deemed the best evidence of their being required. If the corn be not required there will be no demand, and the importer will cease to introduce it. But we must not quarrel with his lordship for being consistently and successfully indefinite. It was his object to be so, and he has achieved it.

Another question occupied a not inconsiderable portion of his address—it was the so-called "Papal aggression." On this his lordship was not quite so indistinct. He is dissatisfied with the government measure of penalties, and promises that he will endeavour to render the bill equal to the requirements of fanaticism. "I shall not be satisfied," says the Chief, "if I do not see that which the government proposes to make effectual, shall, really and effectually, be effectual." What he will *do* he does not tell: he only says he will not be "satisfied."

One fact we gather from the speech, or rather spell out of it; it is this—Lord Stanley will not take office without at once dissolving parliament. This he does not think distant, and the Irish electors should be prepared to meet it when it shall come.

Recreated from The Freeman's Journal, Dublin, April 4, 1851.

A FEMALE PUGILIST.

On Monday morning last a woman of the name of Honora Dogherty, from the county Tipperary, bought an old shirt for one penny, from a woman of the name of Kate Downey. The husband, who is a pensioner, was coming towards the door, saw the shirt converted into a bag to collect yellow meal in the country for herrings, at once caught the woman who purchased the shirt, and said she stole it. The "Tipperary lass" moved up towards him and said, "you lie, you old ruffian, I bought it honestly from your wife," and at the same time taking one step to the rere, giving him a "clip" over the eyebrow, and tumbling him into the water-course, and told the sheepish dog to rise, that she would not strike him down.—After rising he made at her with double fury, and in coming to close quarters, she caught him by the collar and elbow, gave him an upset in the channel. The police soon arrived and took both of them into custody.

Recreated from The Waterford News, Waterford, April 5, 1851.

MILITARY INTOLERANE IN THE GARRISON OF DUNGARVAN.

Dungarvan, April 2nd, 1851.

Sir,—Your Correspondent deplores the cause by which he is actuated on this occasion to inform you, and an enlightened community, of the intolerance, and bigotry of the commanding officer of this garrison. A lay-brother of the Franciscan Order, from the diocese of the " Lion of the Fold, of Juda," visited this town last week, to solicit the bounty and generosity of the Roman Catholics towards the erection of a suitable place of worship, to offer up to an Omnipotent Being, prayers, adoration, and thanksgiving; in expiation for the sins, and iniquities of a deceitful and corrupt generation. He visited this garrison with all the meekness, and humanity for which he is characteristic, to ask for the "widow's mite," from the Catholic soldiery, and they like christian men contributed 8s. 4d., and in handing this to the servant of the Lord, orders were issued to have the " Popish ruffian put outside the gate, and to give no money to such roving beggars for the propagation of Popish idolatory and blind superstition." This lowly and humble man received but one shilling, and bowed with due respect and submission to the mandate issued by this hair-brained fanatic of Exeter Hall school, which is based upon the principles of false philosophy, hypocricy and dissimulation. And all such characters are only fit for the scorn of wise men, and the admiration of fools.

Yours, &c., &c.,
VERITAS.

Reprinted from The Waterford News, Waterford, April 5, 1851.

POLICE OFFICE—MONDAY.

A DARING RUFFIAN—STEALING AND DRINKING MILK.

Pat Brien (a young man with an awful black eye) was charged with stealing a quart of milk from a young countrywoman, in John-street, on Sunday morning.

The young woman stated her complaint—she said prisoner and four others came up to her and told her to take down her can and give him a drink of milk; and he would pay her; witness did so, being rather afraid of prisoner; when he drank the milk he went off and would not pay a farthing.

Brien (looking daggars)—Now did I take de milk from you agin your will, did I? sure I ax'd you for it, and tou'ld you I'd pay you, and you wouldn't take the money.

Young Woman—Oh! your worships, all he's sayen' is lies; she called for the policeman to take him.

Policeman (with a black eye too)—Your worship he assaulted me.

Constable Barrett—He took the great coat off the policeman, your worship and knocked him down.

Policeman—Your worship he assaulted me.

Mr. Tabiteau—Oh, *you* are always complaining of being assaulted; you never arrest any one that does not assault you (laughter.)

Brien—Oh! the villains; was there ever a man so wronged as I am?—the peeler says I struck him, knocked him down, tore his coat, and blackened his eye—and that *lady* there (pointing to the milk girl) says, I broke her pitcher and drank her milk. In the expressive words of an *ould* poet well may I exclaim—

"O! save me from my enemies."

Brien was then sent to the quarter sessions for trial; from which place he had been acquitted for a supposed offense, on the previous day.

Recreated from The Waterford News, Waterford, April 5, 1851.

THE MARQUIS OF LANSDOWNE AND HIS TENANTRY.

From our American correspondent (E.K.):—
Several thousand Irish emigrants arrived here last week, many of them in a more wretched condition than it would be possible to describe. The streets of the vast city are crowded with them. On Saturday last, as I was passing by the Emigration Officers' office in the Park, I observed a more than usual number of living skeletons, just arrived from Liverpool in the ship *Sir Robert Peel*—many of them having passed as many as 60 or 70 summers in poor old Ireland,—and, on enquiring, I learned from them that they had been tenants on the county Kerry estates of the noble and philanthropic Marquis of Lansdowne, the *humane* President of the Council of her gracious Majesty, Queen Victoria, of England's ministry,—that they had been turned out, and their houses levelled—and that they had been shipped in the aforesaid ship, without a cent in their possession,—all under the directions of the aforesaid noble lord.

They had spent the hey day of their lives in cultivating the land from which they were thus inhumanely driven off, when their physical energies are so prostrated as to unfit them for even one day's toil. I never beheld such pictures of misery, despair, want, and disease.

Some of them died on the passage, and as a natural consequence, were thrown into the sea; while those that reached here, only lived long enough to be buried in the strangers' land. Good God! How long will the people of Ireland continue to allow themselves, to be thus peacefully, legally and constitutionally "murdered?"

A YOUNG OFFENDER:—A very little boy named Morris—one of the 'tipping' school—was charged with stealing 2d worth of bread on the previous day.
Policeman—Will you ever steal bread again?
Boy—Not till I'm hungry, sir.—Discharged.

Recreated from The Waterford News, Waterford, April 12, 1851.

THE CENSUS.

It is a painful and heart-rending consideration for us now to dwell on the *real* object which has induced the government of the country to institute the present enumeration of the population of Ireland. It is merely to know what we have suffered during the last few years from starvation and its horrible concomitants — the emigrant ship, &c.; just as a general after battle would direct a poll of his remaining men, to learn the number of "killed and wounded."

EMIGRATION OF 600 FARMERS.

We have heard that 600 persons connected with agriculture, residing in and about Bannow, county Wexford, are preparing to emigrate to America. These emigrants held small farms or patches of land in that locality. We understand that Mr. Boyse is advancing a sum of money to pay all expenses, the *half* of which is to be repaid to him afterwards by the people of the districts in which these emigrants reside. This plan is considered to be better, more respectable, and *cheaper* than to allow those poor, but honest, persons to tumble into a poor house, in which they —whilst alive—should be supported; and when dead, buried at the expense of the ratepayers.

A MODEL PAUPER!

A Correspondent informs us that the poor law guardians of the South of Ireland will neglect their duty if they do not send over one of their model paupers to the great London Exhibition. He says it is but right to do so, in order to shew the visiters from other nations the maternal care with which England watches over our people.— 'Tis, we admit, rather unfair that foreigners should see nothing but the *bright* side of the picture.

Reprinted from The Waterford News, Waterford, April 25, 1851.

IRISH EMIGRANTS LEAVING HOME.—THE PRIEST'S BLESSING.

Reprinted from The Illustrated London News, May 1851

EMIGRATION.

The rage for emigration knows no limits. The people are leaving the land in myriads. From Tipperary the emigration continues to an unexampled extent; and from Clare the best of the population are hurriedly betaking themselves to the other side of the Atlantic; whilst of Kerry, Cork, and Limerick the same may be said with perfect veracity. As an instance of the feeling by which the more comfortable class of persons are actuated, a fact has been communicated to us on authority which we cannot question, and which relates to the emigration movement in Clare:—A comfortable farmer of the name of John Keating, of Kilbaha, purchased a farm about a fortnight since for his eldest son. He laid out a large sum of money on the purchase; and everything seemed to prosper the commencement in life of the young man, who is of excellent character and most industrious habits. The day after the farm was taken, the son, accompanied by his eldest sister and others of his family, abandoned the newly taken farm, proceeded to Limerick, took shipping for New York, and are now at sea on their voyage to the free shores of America.

Recreated from The Freeman's Journal, Dublin, May 1, 1851.

ATROCIOUS ATTEMPT AT ASSASSINATION.

We feel doubtful whether we should not head this paragraph "murder" as, in all probability, the unfortunate man, whom we saw a few hours ago weltering in his blood, has now ceased to exist. The hour at which we go to press compels us to be brief, and besides the general circumstances connected with the outrage we are about to relate, are of that nature upon which it would be difficult to speak with certainty at present. At one o'clock on Friday, the inhabitants of Dundalk were thrown into a state of great excitement by a report that a murder had been perpetrated in this neighbourhood. On hearing the report we instantly repaired to the place assigned as the locality of the outrage—namely, Shortstone, which is situated within about three miles of this town on the road to Crossmaglen. The report, though not strictly accurate, proved to be but too near the truth. Stretched on a pallet in his parlour we beheld the individual upon whose life a murderous attempt had been made a few hours before. His name is Samuel Coulter. He held a farm of about one hundred acres of land. His head presented the most dreadful appearance which the eye could witness. On one side it was bruised in, and yielded to the slightest pressure, while all over, and especially in the back region, it was covered with deep wounds, which continued to drip blood. On the other parts of the body there were no marks of violence discernible. Several of the wounds were evidently inflicted by a bayonet—it would be difficult to say how the remainder of them were inflicted. One of the ears was nearly torn away. The face was untouched. Dr. Pollock was in attendance, and had dressed the head; but human aid was then manifestly of no avail, and every hour Mr. Coulter was expected to breathe his last. He was quite insensible—nor did he speak a word which could afford a clue to the perpetrators of this fearful outrage. The following particulars we were enabled to gather from parties on the spot. About nine o'clock on Friday morning, Mr. Coulter left his residence, on horseback, for the fair of Crossmaglen, having in his possession the sum of nine pounds. Shortly afterwards an alarm was given that he was dead on the road. Some persons having proceeded in the direction of Crossmaglen, he was found in a state of insensibility lying upon a stone ditch. The gap was loosely built with large stones, and he appeared to be leaning across the stones with his head to the field and his feet towards the road, as if he had been apparently dragged into that position. It would appear that the first attack was made about thirty yards from this spot, and in a place which we shall presently describe. The road between both places was sprinkled with blood, and in such a manner as if the person from whom it had come staggered along. A struggle appeared to have taken place on the scene of the first attack, and it would seem that Mr. Coulter made an attempt to return home, but that he was overpowered in the place where he was found. On examining the back of the hedge near this spot, traces were discovered as if two persons had been secreted there. It would appear as if two parties had lain in wait for him, one in each of the places alluded to, and that, having escaped from the first attack, he fell under their united forces at the place where he lay. Here the stones, some of which had rolled into the field, were quite covered with blood, and upon one of them was some hair. A brass pistol and an old bayonet were found here, the one broken in the stock, as if it had been used in striking the victim; the other was covered with blood. There was also found the lock of a gun and a leaden bullet. The place of attack was about a mile from Mr. Coulter's house, and where the road has a lonely appearance. On both sides there are high thorn hedges, and on the side where the attack was made the

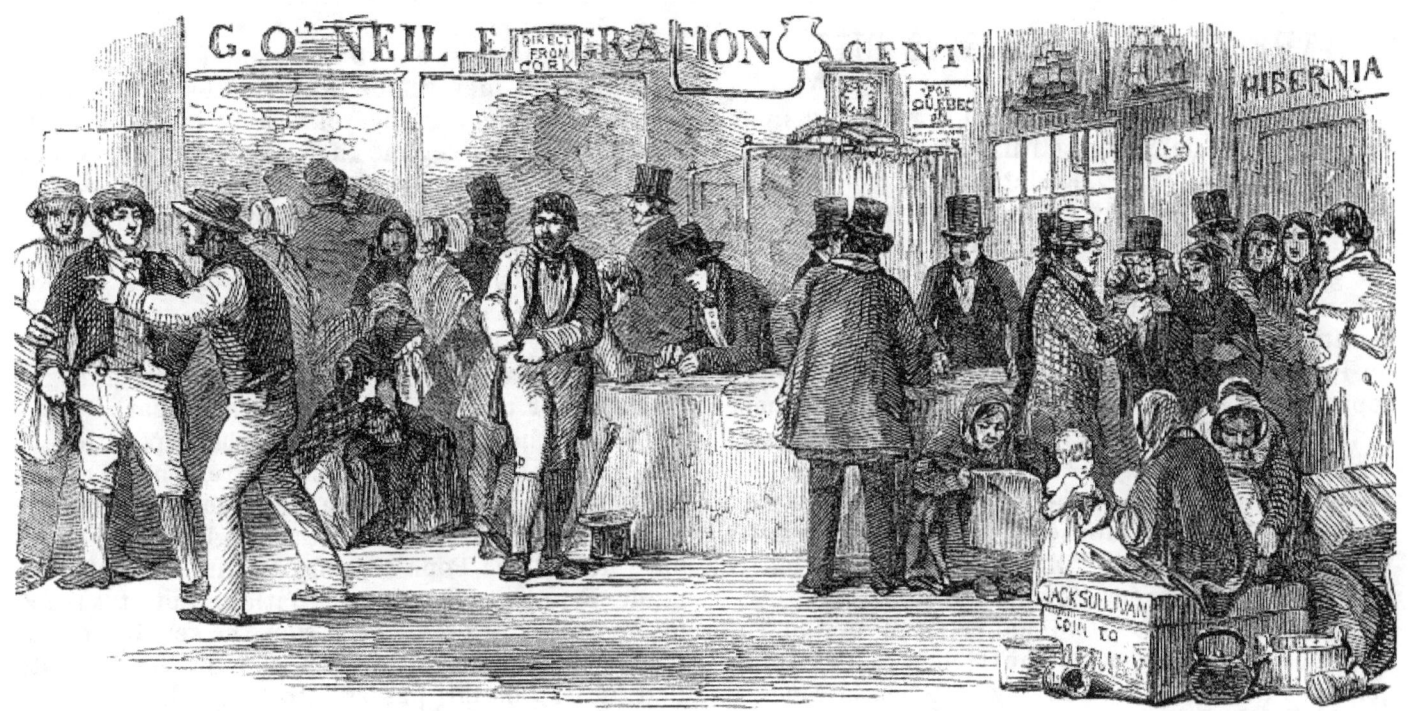

THE EMIGRATION AGENTS' OFFICE.—THE PASSAGE MONEY PAID.

Reprinted from The Illustrated London News, London, May, 1851.

hedge is backed with large whin bushes. On a rising ground at about two hundred yards, there stand two houses; and a short distance further on is a clump of cabins. Owing to a slight bend in the road there would be a difficulty in a person at the first house seeing what took place, but shouting could easily have been heard. One fact is particularly deserving of notice—his money was not touched. As far as we have been able to learn, this outrage had its origin in an agrarian cause. Mr. Coulter was agent to some property in the neighbourhood, and some time ago he had served notices to quit on some of the tenantry. He was a married man, and had two children. Mr. French, R.M., and Mr. Bigger, J.P., with a party of police, under the command of Sub-Inspector Hill, were quickly on the scene of the outrage. *Louth Advertiser.*

A correspondent of the *Daily Express*, writing from Dundalk on Friday evening, at eight o'clock says—

"The unfortunate gentleman received, in his struggle for life, five bayonet wounds. Hope exists no longer, and it is his medical man's opinion that he cannot live an hour longer. Circumstances have transpired to lead to the probability of the discovery of the assassins."

Recreated from The Belfast News-Letter, Belfast, May 5, 1851.

THE MINISTERIAL JEWS' BILL.

With what we may justly term a pernicious pertinacity, Lord John Russell has again forced upon the attention of the Legislature and the country the question of admitting Jews to seats in Parliament. The second reading of the bill, which, under the general pretence of relieving the conscience of several classes of her Majesty's subjects, has, in reality, for its sole objective, the legislation of Baron Rothschild's claim to sit amongst the Christian representatives of the Christian people of these realms, was, on Thursday night, carried by a majority so small—only twenty-five—as to foreshadow the ultimate fate of the measure when it comes up before the Upper House—a body which, from its very constitution, must inevitably reject it on its religious, or rather irreligious, merits.

The question has two aspects, in neither of which can it appeal with confidence to the indulgence or favour of the country. The one is general, the other is personal. Taking it in a view irrespective of Lord John Russell's exigencies or Baron Rothschild's individual qualifications, and wholly as a matter of national concern, the objections to the measure are, in our mind, of an insurmountable character.

Admit the Jew, and you break down for ever the barriers which hitherto preserved the Christian character of the House of Commons from the invasion of the enemies of our creed, and, consequently, of all the national institutions regulated by the spirit of its doctrines. But you do more. You endanger the Christian character of the House of Lords, whose acts are intimately connected with those of the House of Commons. Suppose the whole legislation thus debased by heathenism and infidelity, what security remains for the Christianity of the Monarch? If we are to be legislated for by Jews and infidels, on what principle can it be denied that we may yet be *governed* by a Jew or an infidel? Not very many years ago, in the days of the monarchical regime in France, the idea would have been scouted with indignation that a Jew should ever hold the destinies of that country in his hand. The French admitted the Jews to seats in their Legislature. A revolution ensued, and we find a Jew—M. Cremieux—a member of the supreme Provisional Government which hurled the French Monarch from his throne. The unchristianising of the French Legislature created more mischiefs than this. It effected the separation of the National Church from the State. That Church, had it preserved its nationality under the fostering care of the monarchy and the Legislature, might have defied the Pope and the Jesuits—might have made France a Protestant nation. But it turned for succour to Rome, and is now the servile tool of Ultramontane ambition. Will it be otherwise with Britain, if this bill passes into law? What followed the third reading of the Jews' bill of 1848? Petitions from the Puseyite clergy of the Church of England, praying that, if the bill passed into law, *the Act 17 Henry VIII, as to the appointment of bishops, might be repealed*. This is a serious matter for consideration, and should act as a warning how we tamper with that glorious principle in our constitution, its foundation on the impregnable basis of Christian doctrine.

The personal aspect of the question is equally unfavourable, to the extent of its importance. Baron Rothschild's last exhibition at the bar of the House of Commons proved that he was as much of a Jesuit as a Jew. He tried to obtain his seat in defiance of the rules of the House by a fraudulent shuffle—by a tricky alteration of the context of the oath; and he endeavoured surreptitiously to obtrude upon the Speaker a spurious qualification paper.

Even the late Daniel O'Connell, when opening the doors of Parliament to his Roman Catholic fellow-subjects, scorned to resort to such a pitiful artifice as this. He manfully declared his objection to the oath at the table of the House, and would not filch by a quibble what he demanded as a right. We say nothing of the private leanings of the Premier, and the obligations he is said to be under to the rich Jew, who seems determined to have his "pound of flesh," according to the bond, and no mistake.

Recreated from The Belfast News-Letter, Belfast, May 5, 1851.

BRUTAL AND SAVAGE ASSAULT BY RIBBONMEN.

(FROM THE CORRESPONDENT OF SAUNDERS' NEWS-LETTER.)

Dundalk, Monday, 5th May, 1851.

In the fresh outrages perpetrating in and about this immediate neighbourhood are to be seen the consequences of those sanguinary and blood-thirsty doctrines propounded and received as truths by the deluded peasantry of this unhappy country— doctrines and opinions, which, if permitted longer to be instilled into the Irish mind, will, decidedly, eventuate in acts of barbarous aggression on the one side, and in judicial and legal sacrifices of life, on the other. Scarcely had the public mind calmed into repose from the painful excitement produced by Mr. Coulter's murder, than its feelings are again roused by the perpetration of a fresh outrage on the life of a farmer and his wife. On Saturday night a party of eleven armed ruffians entered the house of a farmer living between Castleblayney, in the county of Monaghan, and Redy, in the county of Armagh, and beat him and his wife unmercifully, inflicting severe wounds on the old man's head, and telling him, that if he did not give up the land he had lately taken they would return and kill him.

A neighbouring farmer, who heard the cries, ran to the Garragh police station, a short distance off. The party promptly arrived, but found the villains had fled, leaving the old man weltering in his blood. The police heard the barking of dogs, and at once proceeded to the place whence the barking came. Upon arriving at the bog, close to where the omnibus driver was lately fired at, they saw light in a house. They went to the window and looked in, when they saw eleven ruffians in the act of swearing the man of the house, who was on his knees. The police, though few in number, at once entered, just as the oath was administered, and at once arrested the eleven men. They were handcuffed and conveyed to the old man's house, when he and his wife at once identified seven of them as being the persons who broke into their house and nearly murdered them. I conceive this to be a most important arrest.

It will, I trust, deal a death-blow to the infamous Ribbon system now in vigorous operation in this locality, and, as I am credibly informed, for miles round. One cannot but feel painfully satisfied as to the efficacy with which the principles of rank Communism, in reference to the tenure of land, are operating on the peasant mind of Ireland when the history of these localities is recollected and analysed. Mr. Mauleverer's murder—the murder of the Clarkes (brothers)—the attempt to assassinate the omnibus driver—the dreadful tragedy of Friday, and the present outrage, all occurring within a circle of five or six miles. Since my coming down here I have driven for some miles around, and my different conversations with peasantry forced me to know that they imagine they ought to pay no rent at all.

The adjourned inquest on Mr. Coulter's body will be held to-morrow at the Police-office, Hackballstown.

Recreated from The Belfast News-Letter, Belfast, May 7, 1851.

AMERICAN PASSENGERS' ARRANGEMENTS FOR
1851.

NOTICE TO EMIGRANTS FOR 1851.
MICHELL'S AMERICAN PASSENGER OFFICE,
118, WATERLOO ROAD.

PASSENGERS can secure the best Cabin or Steerage accommodations to the United States by the following first-class, fast-sailing, regular American Packet-ships, despatched punctually on their appointed days, and noted for their short passages.

FOR BOSTON.
"TRAIN AND COMPANY'S LINE."
(Signal, Red Flag with White Diamond.)

Ship	Master	Tons reg.	To sail
GEORGE RAYNES (new)	PENHALLOW	1300	5th May
DANIEL WEBSTER (new)	HOWARD	1300	20th May
PRESIDENT (new)	COMINS	1200	5th June
JOHN H. JARVIS (new)	RICH	1000	20th June
PLYMOUTH ROCK	CALDWELL	1000	5th July
SUNBEAM	PUTNAM	1000	20th July
PARLIAMENT	SAMPSON	1200	5th Aug.
STAFFORDSHIRE (new)	BROWN	1800	20th Aug.

FOR NEW YORK.
"EAGLE LINE."

Ship	Master	Tons	
RIP VAN WINKLE (new)	BAKER	1500	
KNICKERBOCKER (new)	CONE	1600	Every
WILLIAM NELSON (new)	CHEEVER	1400	Fortnight.
SANTA CLAUS (new)	—	1300	

FOR PHILADELPHIA.
"M'HENRY & CO.'S LINE."

Ship	Master	Tons	To sail
MARY PLEASANTS	DECAN	1000	1st May
SHENANDOAH	WETT	1000	1st June
WESTMORELAND (new)	DECAN	1200	1st July
SHACKAMAXON (new)	WEST	1300	1st Aug.

Passengers by these Ships will be furnished with the following supplies, *every week*, during the voyage:—

Two and a half pounds Bread, five pounds Oatmeal, one pound Flour, two pounds Rice, half a pound Sugar, half pound Molasses, two ounces Tea, one pound Pork, *and three quarts Water daily.*

The reputation of the above Ships is well known; they are all first-class American-built Packets, celebrated for their quick passages, have spacious between decks, well ventilated; carry skilful Surgeons, and are commanded by favourite and experienced Masters, who bestow every attention on the health and comfort of their Passengers.

Passengers engaging by letter (addressed to the Subscribers) for any of the above-named Ships may rest assured of having the best disengaged berths reserved, at the lowest current prices, on sending at least one week before the day of sailing, with their names and ages, a Post-Office Order for £1 each; on receipt of which a Certificate of Passage will be returned, and the amount sent deducted from the Passage Money: by this arrangement all unnecessary expense and delay is prevented, and Passengers avoid the high prices invariably charged those who defer making their arrangements until they arrive at Liverpool.

Those intending to proceed to the interior of the United States or Canada, can have full particulars as to the most direct and economical mode of reaching their destination. Emigrants, or others, requiring information respecting the Prices of Passages, &c., will receive prompt attention, by addressing the Subscribers (if by letter post paid) as below.

D. P. MICHELL,
118, Waterloo Road, Liverpool; or,
E. S. FLYNN,
15, Merchants'-quay, Cork.

No other Passenger Agents in Liverpool or Cork are authorised to sell Tickets for either of the above Lines.

Passage by the Regular Line of Packets to NEW YORK, BALTIMORE, and NEW ORLEANS, can also be obtained, on application, as above.

N.B.—Those holding Certificates of Passage from America, for either of the above Lines should write immediately, stating which of the Ships they intend to embark in, so that berths may be reserved. When writing the number of the American certificate should be given.

*** Passengers for Ship "George Raynes" can leave Cork by the Steamer of Saturday, the 3d May for Liverpool.

TESTIMONIAL
FROM THE BISHOP OF BOSTON.

"BOSTON, JANUARY 22, 1849.

"I am happy to testify from personal knowledge, that the firm of Ship-owners in this city of Boston, under the name of ENOCH TRAIN & CO., is composed of Gentlemen of tried and acknowledged integrity, and that implicit reliance can be placed in their fidelity to accomplish all that they may promise to those who have occasion to make any contract with them.

(Signed)
"✠ JOHN B. FITZPATRICK, Bishop of Boston."

Reprinted from The Cork Examiner, Cork, May 9, 1851.

DEATH FROM STARVATION—VERDICT OF CORONER'S JURY — CHARGE AGAINST THE CALLAN BOARD OF GUARDIANS.

Under this heading, in the last number of the *Kilkenny Journal*, we have read with much pain a letter written by the Rev. M. O'Keeffe, C.C., to the Callan board of guardians detailing the evidence taken by the coroner at an inquest, on the body of a poor creature named Mary Kearney, which is of a fearful nature, indeed. The proceedings terminated by the following verdict—"*We find that Mary Kearney came by her death on Friday week at Somers' lane, Coolagh from the want of food; and that the board of guardians have not done their duty in withholding out door relief from the family of John Kearney.*"—What a consideration for the guardians of the Callan union!

Reprinted from The Waterford News, Waterford, May 9, 1851.

EXECUTION OF THE CONVICT CATHERINE CONNOLLY.

The execution of this unhappy female, with whose conviction for murder at the last assizes the public are acquainted, took place in front of the County Gaol, on Saturday. It is needless to say that the spectacle presented by the crowds of the lowest order of society who thronged every road and wall commanding a view of the prison was as horrifying as the occasion of any public execution exhibits. From an early hour of the day the Western Road, the Dyke, Sunday's-well Road, and every spot from which a glimpse at the hideous spectacle might be obtained was filled with spectators. Indeed very soon after eleven o'clock people had begun to take their places on the road and walls and in the fields just before the gaol. Something like order was preserved by a body of police under Sub-Inspector St. Leger, two troops of hussars, and a body of the 90th regiment on foot. During the few days preceding the execution the unfortunate woman had apparently given up all hope of life and seemed deeply penitent. She was attended by the Very Rev. Dr. Barry, the Rev. P. Begley, and by the sisters of Mercy, and she invariably joined in the prayers which they offered up with every semblance of fervour. All through she declared that she was innocent of the deed for which she had been sentenced to die, asseverating that she was "as innocent as the child that lay in its mother's breast."

On Friday she was attended for a long time by the Very Rev. Dr. Barry and Rev. Mr. Begley, and when they had gone the matron of the gaol, at her own request, joined with her in prayer. She also requested the matron during the night to lay her out in the coffin.

On Saturday morning the reverend gentlemen already named were with her at ten o'clock, and prayed with her until about one. She was then conducted into the press room, where she remained until half-past one, still engaged in prayer. She was then led out with the rope around her neck, being supported by the Rev. Mr. Begley and the nurse, and followed by the Rev. Dr. Barry, the Sub-Sheriff, and the Governor of the Gaol. When on the drop, which she ascended with firmness, the Rev. Mr. Begley read the prayers for the dead in which she joined with great earnestness. She then addressed a few words to the crowd in Irish, the purport of which was to reiterate the declaration of her innocence in the emphatic words which we have already mentioned. The executioner then attached the rope to the beam, the prisoner was left alone on the drop, and in a few seconds the bolt was withdrawn. The unfortunate woman struggled but for a moment. The crowd soon after gradually dispersed.

Recreated from The Cork Examiner, Cork, May 12, 1851.

The Duke of Wellington's Grand Ball.

The grand ball given to the diplomatic corps, the leading members of the aristocracy, and the illustrious visitors to the World's Fair, by his Grace the Duke of Wellington, at Apsley House, on Friday evening, was on a scale of unusual splendour. The magnificent *suite* of rooms and galleries, emblazoned with mementoes of his Grace's martial triumphs, from the dawn of his glory on the battle-fields of Asia, to the consummation of his renown on the plains of Waterloo, and decorated with the choicest gems of pictorial art, were thrown open for "the event." In the lofty banquet-room, adorned with *monumenta* and *opima spolia* of a deathless fame, were displayed the costly presents made to the Prince of Waterloo by the allied sovereigns on the Bourbon restoration, including the ruby Sevres and porcelain gifts of his Saxon Majesty, the superb Muscovite candelabra, pendent with silver frost-work, and the gorgeous service of plate, the product of auriferous Brazil, presented by the Portuguese Government. The massive shield, traced with exquisite artistic cunning, emblematic of Gog and Magog's sturdy protection, the appropriate gift of the Corporation of London to his grace, formed the "living grandeur" of the scene. In addition to the twinkling chorography of May-fair, the lyrical and orchestral arrangements of the ducal *fete* included the most brilliant professional talent.

Serious Accident to the Marquis of Anglesey.

We regret to announce that an accident which might have been attended with very serious consequences occurred, on Wednesday afternoon, to this gallant veteran. Lord Anglesey was riding down Grosvenor Street, at a sharp pace, when the pole of an omnibus was driven with considerable force against his lordship's horse. The concussion caused the animal to rear up and fall back. Lord Anglesey lost his seat, but, fortunately, disengaged himself from the stirrups, and rose unhurt—a circumstance the more happy, from the fact that the left leg worn by his lordship was always attached to the stirrup-iron by a small chain, which the force and weight of the fall providentially broke. The noble Marquis rode to Uxbridge House in a friend's carriage; and, in answer to inquiries on Wednesday evening, was described as a good deal shaken, but not seriously injured by the accident.—*Globe*.

Recreated from The Belfast News-Letter, Belfast, May 19, 1851.

THE MARQUIS OF LANSDOWNE'S TENANTRY.

It would almost seem that the deplorably destitute circumstances under which these unfortunate people left this country and arrived in America, will never pass out of public attention. We now learn that on the arrival of a large number of them, a few weeks since, in one of the Liverpool Packets, the Commissioners of Emigration refused to pass them, in conformity with a just and necessary regulation by which emigrants must at least show that they will not become immediate paupers in the land of their adoption. After a lengthened negociation the commissioners consented to compromise the matter by accepting twenty five dollars a head from the emigration agents by whom they were shipped from Liverpool as a sort of provision for their maintenance in the event of such a result as the commissioners anticipated.

Marriage a Lottery.—At an evening party recently it was proposed to dispose of the *belle* of the room by lottery. Twenty tickets were immediately sold at a mixed price. The joke ended not here. The fortunate adventurer has since married the lady.—*Aberdeen Herald*.

FILIAL AFFECTION.

A few days ago two little boys passed through this town having with them a coffin upon an ass's car. They seemed to have journeyed a considerable distance, and to have suffered not a little from the fatigue of travelling, the inclemency of the weather, and hunger.

Upon inquiry we ascertained that they came from Mayo, and that the coffin contained the remains of their mother, who, being a native of this county, had, previous to her dissolution, expressed a wish that her ashes might repose in the same grave with that of her father's; and these poor children had travelled a long and toilsome way, not in obedience to a positive injunction, but merely in accordance with a wish expressed by their mother on her death-bed. They were both destitute of that knowledge which is acquired in schools, and ignorant of the ways of the world but, strong in that filial affection which the heart teaches, which poverty cannot chill, and which is alike the ornament and treasure of the poor man's home, they had borne suffering and privation in order to perform their labour of love —to lay down the remains of one so dearly loved in their last resting-place—to plant the green turf above a mother's grave, and water it with their tears.

Their sad task performed, they returned to that desolate and poverty-stricken region from whence they came, cheered amid their sorrow by the gratifying reflection that they had done their duty in accomplishing the desire of their departed parent.— *Westmeath Guardian.*

Cardinal Wiseman boasts that he has a pocket list of 200 Protestant clergymen or more, ready to come over to Rome, if the stumbling-block of necessary repudiation of their wives could be removed.— *Scotsman.*

Recreated from The Cork Examiner, Cork, May 12, 1851.

WRECK SALE.

TO BE SOLD by AUCTION, (for account of whom it may concern,) on Wednesday, 4th JUNE next, at the NEW PIER, KILMORE,

The Hull, as it will then lie,
of the Austrian Brig "Liepa Zaritza," of Trieste, about 400 Tons Register, P. B. GIURICOVCH, Master, wrecked on her voyage from Lima to Liverpool,

And her Materials, consisting of Two Chain Cables, Four Anchors, Two Hawsers, (9 and 12 inch,) Sails, Standing and Running Rigging, Blocks, Chains, Masts, Spars, Two Boats, a quantity of Copper, Cabin and other Stores, &c.

Also,—To be Sold, in convenient Lots, about 40 Tons of
Peruvian Guano.

Terms—Cash. The Purchasers to pay the Auction Fees. Sale to commence at 11 o'Clock.

FRANCIS HARPER, Agent for Lloyds.
JOHN WALSH, Auctioneer.
Wexford, 26th May, 1851.

DONKEY KILLING.

(*From our Dungarvan Correspondent.*)

On the evening of the 18th inst. a man, whose name I could not learn, killed *two Donkeys,* at a place called Shandon near this town. This steel-hearted man committed this wanton and cruel act by beating out the brains of these harmless animals with stones, and in the course of a short time skinned them, and sold the hides to a "Rag and Bone" merchant of the town for the sum of 2s 6d. He was taken by the Police on the 19th and lodged in our bridewell to await his trial on next Saturday.

Reprinted and recreated from The Waterford News, Waterford, May 30, 1851.

PRIVATE THEATRICALS AT DEVONSHIRE HOUSE.

Last night the first performance for the benefit of the "Literary Guild" took place in one of the drawing-rooms of the Duke of Devonshire's residence, which was fitted up as a theatre for the occasion. As only the representatives of the daily press were allowed the privilege of admission, we are compelled to postpone criticism upon the comedy. Shortly after eight o'clock a brilliant company began to pour rapidly into Devonshire house.

The Duke of Wellington was the very first to arrive. As the audience appeared, they were conducted up the grand marble staircase, a circular flight of great beauty, into the gallery, fitted up as a temporary theatre, and which abuts upon the landing place. This gallery, along the walls of which are arranged a collection of the ancient masters, is fitted up in rich Louis Quatorze style, elaborate with gilded panellings and richly decorated cornices. The audience portion was furnished in front with chairs for a favoured few—further back, with comfortable benches. Upon the left hand, looking towards the stage, was fitted up a royal box, calculated to contain several persons, and canopied by gold fringed and tasselled curtains.

The proscenium of the stage was cleverly decorated in harmony with the embellishments of the room, the adaptation being so complete that it might have been supposed that the original purpose of the gallery was the dramatic end to which it was applied last night. Before nine o'clock the audience portion of the gallery was completely crowded and shortly after the arrival of her Majesty, who was, of course, conducted to her box by the Duke of Devonshire, the performance commenced.

The *Times* says it is a piece more of character than plot, and that though there are several strong situations, they are not closely connected by a continuous interest. The language is often brilliant. The amateurs performed better, probably, than any other amateurs who could be collected together, and the decorative artists produced a spectacle which could not be exceeded for completeness.—*London Weekly News* of Saturday.

O'CONNELL—INGRATITUDE.

Let us contrast the conduct of the people of an English town, with that of the population of the Irish nation. O'Connell is now four years dead, and not a stone has been placed above another to do honour to his memory. It is true that in the last few years of his life, numbers had taken exception to his policy and fled from his ranks, and that the nation was divided respecting that policy, when he was called from amongst us. But what of all that. He was a great man, the greatest that Ireland has ever seen. No one can deny this: for even his greatest enemies admit that his abilities were commanding, and his powers to wield the strength of the nation without parallel in history. And yet the nation which he emancipated from an unjust ascendancy, the nation which he liberated from the infliction of a cruel penal code, has not contributed half the sum (£8,000) which Liverpool has collected to do honour to a borough magistrate.

Ireland has been ungrateful to her public men. No doubt she has had many bad ones, many who betrayed her when the hour of trial came, but she could not say that of O'Connell, for he could not be purchased by the enemy, and it is ungrateful in Irishmen, not to honour his memory by the erection of a monument on which to describe his victories for freedom.—*Dundalk Democrat*.

Recreated from The Waterford News, Waterford, May 30, 1851.

The EXHIBITION—
DIAMONDS & THEIR VALUE.

Mr. H. T. Hope, of Picadilly, exhibits a casket containing a blue diamond, weighing 177 grains, mounted as a medallion, surmounted by brilliants, and supposed from its size and colour to be unique.

We may observe that the diamond, when in its purest form, is transparent and colourless, and consists of pure carbon. When it has colour it always contains some foreign matter, such as the oxides of metals which exist in it in very minute proportions. If it were practicable to liquefy pure charcoal and allow it to crystalize in cooling, we should produce diamonds artificially, but no efforts of art have yet accomplished this.

The value per carat depends upon the quality of the stone, which is subject to great variation. The diamonds of the purest water are absolutely colourless. There are others which are tinged more or less with pink, orange, blue, yellow, and some are even black or rather a blackish brown. The most valuable of the coloured sorts are those of a rose or pink tint, which in some cases exceed in price the most limpid, though as a general rule the latter are most highly prized. There are but two districts upon the globe where diamond mines can be said to exist—India and Brazil—the former of which has been celebrated from the most remote antiquity as the country of diamonds. The principal mines are in Golconda and Vizapour, extending from Cape Cormorin to Bengal, at the foot of a chain of mountains called the Orixa, These gems are so dispersed in the soil where they exist that they are rarely found directly, even in searching in the richest spots, because they are enveloped in an earthy crust, which must be removed before they can be seen. This earth is washed in basins and spread out to dry, after which the diamonds are recognized by their sparkling in the sun.

Recreated from The Cork Examiner, Cork, June 4, 1851.

THE CROPS—The late fall of rain with which we have been favored, has done a vast amount of good to the country. The potato and cereal crops, in appearance, far exceed those of past years.—Such a good prospect of potatoes we have not had for many years. We understand that John P. O'Shee, Esq of Gardenmorris, has no less than 90 acres under oats this year; and a beautiful crop it is.

Reprinted from The Waterford News, Waterford, June 6, 1851.

THE CROPS IN THE WEST.
[FROM A CORRESPONDENT.]

CROOKHAVEN, MAY 30.—For your information I beg to state that I made inquiries of the farmers in general, of the state of the Potato crops in Kilmoe and Crookhaven; their reply is most cheering; that they look uncommonly well, and have every appearance of a most plentiful and abundant harvest. Wheat, barley, and oats are very promising and healthy—grass is growing well. The farmers are preparing the land for the turnip crops, as there is every facility afforded for their cultivation. On the whole there is no doubt but the result will prove satisfactory to the people in general.—A. O'DRISCOLL.

Reprinted from The Cork Examiner, Cork, June 2, 1851.

THE POTATO CROP.

SINCE the usual market note was written, accounts have reached us from a few localities, in which some appearance of blight has appeared. Of course, this is what might be expected; but we feel convinced that it is owing mainly to the late harsh winds and frost, and that the present rain will effectually restore the plant to health and greenness.

Reprinted from The Cork Examiner, Cork, June 6, 1851.

EMIGRATION.—
AN ADVICE AND AN ILLUSTRATION.

Mr. William Steuart Trench deserves to be regarded as an authority on questions connected with emigration. As an agent of the Marquis of Bath, he pledged himself "either to employ, or to emigrate, at the expense of the proprietor," every pauper fit for work, or disposed to travel; and so faithfully has he redeemed that, in his capacity as Chairman of the Carrickmacross Board of Guardians, he boasted, lately, that not 100 paupers were then chargeable to that fortunate property. Mr. Trench, does not say how many he employed, and how many he induced to travel; but the supposition is, that he liberally made over upon the United States of America the larger portion of those who once owned the Marquis of Bath as their liege lord, the earthly steward of their Divine Master. Strengthened in his conviction of the beauty of emigration, as a means of relieving overloaded estates of their human incumbrances, Mr. Trench respectfully calls on all proprietors, great and small, to follow his example, and walk in his footsteps. Not knowing the mode and manner in which Mr. William Steuart Trench carried out his benevolent intentions with respect to the paupers of the Marquis of Bath, we cannot say whether the adoption of his advice by the proprietors, great and small, whom he addresses, may be attended with felicitous results to the immediate objects of his benevolence. But, if the paupers of the Marquis of Bath have been disposed of after the fashion in which the paupers of the Marquis of Lansdowne have been provided for, we would hope, for the sake of humanity, if not for the honour of the empire, that the advice may be entirely disregarded. In the latter instance, Mr. Trench may not have had at his disposal sufficient means wherewith to gratify the wishes of his heart, and send out the emigrants in a comfortable condition. At any rate, the fact is, that a more miserable class of beings never crossed the Atlantic than the most of the paupers of the Marquis of Lansdowne, sent by his agent, Mr. William Steuart Trench. Take, for example, the history of a small squad of 50, who sailed, among other emigrants, in a vessel which left this port for Liverpool, there to take shipping for New York. These 50 human beings were in the last degree destitute, and their raggedness was only equalled by their emaciation. So utterly deplorable was their appearance, that the local emigrant agent was compelled to smuggle them on board "between the two lights"—that is, where the picturesque character of their garb could not be well appreciated; for the agent trembled lest the eye of the Captain should fall upon his unhappy clients, as he knew that he would be certain to refuse them a passage. Well, they sailed, did these happy emigrants; and the moment they reached Liverpool, they spread themselves over the bustling thoroughfares of that thriving port, and piteously begged for a morsel of food—for, it may be incidentally remarked, they then had not a pound of bread, or any other description of provision, against the voyage. How Mr. Trench forgot that a poor Kenmare man had just as keen an appetite as the Chairman of Carrickmacross Board of Guardians, we cannot imagine; but it must have been forgetfulness, sheer forgetfulness. At length, and after disgracing poor Ireland, and reflecting no extraordinary degree of credit on the foresight of Mr. Wm. Steuart Trench, these 50 miserables sailed for New York. What follows should be a warning to Emigration Agents in future wholesale transactions. No sooner were these 50 Irish emigrants landed, or arrived, in New York, than the authorities compelled the owners of the vessel to pay down 25 dollars for each emigrant—that is £5 a-head, or £250 for the whole lot.

This was done for the purpose of indemnifying the State against loss, as these 50 additional people had no visible means of living—in fact, because they were admitted paupers. This was not a pleasant predicament for the owners, who had only received an average sum of £3 5s. per head for their freight. The loss therefore on each—besides the total loss of passage money—was £1 15s. 0d. per head, or £90 on the transaction. The owners naturally looked for a remedy, and, in their simplicity, supposed that Mr. TRENCH, or the Marquis of LANSDOWNE, was responsible for the loss, and should refund them the £250. They asked, "is there no British law to compel the proprietor of an estate to send out his tenants in a good condition; or to prevent him from shipping them in a state of utter destitution?" Lawyers were appealed to, with what result may be supposed. The owners had no redress. The British law, that allowed a proprietor "to do what he liked with his own," did not condescend to trifles of such a nature, as the consideration of food and pocket-money for pauper emigrants, the "thinnings" of Irish estates. So the owners were compelled to endure the loss of their £250, and to place it in their books, against so much "experience gained."

We have only followed the first fortunes of the 50 of the LANSDOWNE paupers, while some 2,000 on the whole were induced to prefer a change of country; and, from the few facts which we have stated, we ask, if the proprietors, great and small, of the Carickmacross Union, would be acting as they ought to act, in adopting the emigration part of Mr. TRENCH's advice, and on the exact system practised by Mr. TRENCH in the case which we have detailed? We say not; but people will differ on such matters. If they do anything, let them adopt the "employment" side of the question; which may have been adopted on the estate of the Marquis of BATH, but which we have not heard of being yet carried out in the Kenmare estate of the Marquis of LANSDOWNE We expressed our regret before, and we do so again, that the vast sum spent in clearing the Kenmare estate by emigration, was not expended *in employment*; for while no gain, but much individual suffering, resulted from the former, immense benefit would have followed from the latter. The great pity is, that Mr. TRENCH has been bitten by the emigration mania; as it naturally follows, that when this system is carried out on a large scale, misery and suffering must be the fate of many of the emigrants; not by any means owing to want of humanity on the part of the proprietor, or his agent—but want of *adequate means* to supply those comforts which are required by those who are compelled to undertake a protracted voyage, and that means of temporary support which is absolutely necessary to those who must try and live in a strange country.

Recreated from The Cork Examiner, Cork, June 13, 1851.

THE WEATHER—THE CROPS.

CAPPOQUIN, JUNE 10.—We have had a visit from the blast or blight. But it has not done much harm. Three fields adjoining one another were attacked on the night of this day, two severely, the other only slightly, but they are now recovering. The rain has been very heavy and constant here since Saturday last; all our crops are much improved.—*Cork Examiner.*

NENAGH.—The country all around Nenagh looks beautiful, though it was much feared the harsh wind and slight frost, some time back, would have retarded vegetation; but the late rain has crowned all, particularly the potato crop. Altogether there is every prospect of an abundant harvest, under Divine Providence. But here and there is to be seen the blighting work of merciless men, in the uncultivated spots that once marked the homes of our peasantry, now alas! in the grave, in the workhouse, or in America.—*Limerick Examiner.*

Recreated from The Freeman's Journal, Dublin, June 13, 1851.

DEATH OF THE EARL OF DERBY.

We regret to announce the decease of the Right Hon. the venerable Earl of Derby, which took place at his seat, Knowsley Hall, Lancashire, on Monday last, in the 77th year of his age, surrounded by his noble and celebrated family.

The late noble deceased was the thirteenth Earl of Derby, having succeeded to the title at the death of his father, Oct. 21, 1834; he had been previously created (Oct., 1832) Baron Stanley, of Bickerstaffe. He was colonel of the Lancashire militia, vice-admiral of the coast of Lancashire, and president of the Linnean and Zoological Societies.

The family of Stanley, it is scarcely necessary to remark, is one of the most illustrious, as it is one of the greatest antiquity, in the peerage. Adam de Aldithley and his two sons attended Duke William of Normandy in his expedition to England, and had large possessions conferred upon him by the Conqueror.

The first Baron Stanley was summoned as such, in 1456, by Henry VI. He was Comptroller of the Household and Chamberlain to that King, and from his third son, Sir John Stanley, descends the present Lord Stanley, of Alderley.

The noble earl, although neither a soldier nor a statesman, was a most worthy representative of his illustrious house. His political career was noiseless and unobtrusive, but his predilections were consistently in favour of what was called the *Liberal* party of the State. His chief characteristics were hospitality and benevolence, and throughout a long life he ever maintained most scrupulously in his own good acts and deeds the family motto "*sans changer*."

The Lord Stanley is now fourteenth Earl of Derby; and again we have in the House of Commons, in the noble earl's eldest son, a Lord Stanley, who has already added no small distinction to the time-honoured name.—*Morning Herald.*

Recreated from The Belfast News-Letter, Belfast, July 4, 1851.

THE PAPAL AGGRESSION BILL.
(From the *London Morning Advertiser.*)

The recent aggression, the conduct and pastoral letters from Wiseman, the language of the Papists in Parliament, and the repetition of the Pope's insolence, are the recommencement of those attempts to encroach upon the liberties of the Crown, which our Roman Catholic ancestors repressed by penal statues. We are placed in their situation, and should be simpletons, indeed, if we did not avail ourselves of our power and superiority.

As the bill now stands, there are no bishops among the Roman Catholics, and consequently ordinations and all other official acts of persons assuming to be bishops by the Pope's appointment are annulled. Hence, by strict construction, all marriages performed or to be performed by the clergy are void, and the issue bastardised.

The country is deeply indebted to Sir Frederick Thesiger, both for making the bill efficacious, as far as that goes, and for enlarging the power of instituting prosecutions.

As to the difficulty of proving the act of procuring Papal bulls, that may be met by assuming it to have been done by the vicar apostolic, in whose diocese they are directed to be published. The assumption will be good because where they are pronounced, it is either on his application, or with his privity and consent.

CRUCIFIX OF MARY QUEEN OF SCOTS.—The crucifix that belonged to this unfortunate Queen, and which she is said to have held in her hands on the scaffold, is still preserved with great care by its present owners, a titled family in the neighbourhood of Winchester, and at whose seat I have frequently seen it. If I mistake not, the figure of our Saviour is in ivory, and the cross of ebony.—*Notes and Queries.*

Reprinted and recreated from The Waterford News, Waterford, July 11, 1851.

PASSING OF THE PENAL BILL IN THE COMMONS.—FIVE MONTHS' WORK!!

On Friday night this atrocious Bill—the venom and extent which very few are aware of—passed the House of Commons by a majority of 263 to 46!!!

The Bill was, on Monday, transmitted to the Lords, where, of course, it will have less delay than it had in the Commons.

For five long months the wiseacres of St. Stephen's have been toiling to pass this foul measure—a measure that, at once, not only abridges the religious privileges and opinions of millions of her Majesty's subjects, but strikes DIRECTLY at the very root of Catholicity itself. For instance, the Bill, as it now stands, prevents the reception into this country of any bull or letter apostolic from Rome, for the appointment of Catholic Bishops; and, if Bishops can't be (legally) appointed, surely Priests can't be ordained. Such, of course, was the intention of the framers of this ill-considered measure.

The Bill, moreover, gives the power to common informers to use their SKILL in "detecting", and swearing against, and prosecuting, Catholic Bishops! What sad days we have fallen on! What a state of things—after the destruction of thousands of our people—that the remainder will not be permitted quietly to kneel at their own altars, to say their prayers in peace with the world, without having Sir F. Thessiger's "common informer" to GUARD and watch over them.

What has Ireland done to merit this cruel treatment? In England the faction may raise the excuse of the CARDINAL; but, in Ireland, where there is NO CARDINAL, there could have been no excuse for the extension of a measure which would reflect discredit on a community of Hotentots.

Stupid and fanatic individuals may imagine that this Bill will have the effect of staying the onward, and to them alarming, progress of Catholicity in these countries. But, to men of mind, to all rational persons—to those who are acquainted with the results of religious persecution, we need not say that the penal measure will have the very *opposite* effect.

Taking it, then, in every point of view, never did England commit so great a mistake—so fatal a blunder to herself—as she did in the passing of this foul enactment.

And why? Because she has (by it) made millions of enemies for herself in every part of the civilised world—Catholics, who would split straws and break each other's heads on political questions, will, when their religion is treated with insult and sought to be trampled upon, stand like walls of brass against the tyrant who so attempts it.

But as to the Bill having an injurious effect upon religion, as some fanatic journals suppose, there never was so great an error. On the contrary, we believe it to be one of the best stimulants, one of the great auxiliaries that Catholicity could possibly have for its rapid extension. Just and honest men, though holding different or adverse opinions, will naturally say "there must be something extraordinary in this religion or Government would not think of crushing it"—And then they'll enquire what offense has it committed? When, of course, they will be told that it has done nothing more than sought the right to appoint *its* own Bishops and priests—to exercise its own religion, in fine, without seeking to interfere with the religion of any other person.

The faction Press need not gloat over this Bill as though they had gained a victory; for we need not tell them that, in these countries, 'tis no new thing for the Catholic Church to live in antagonism with the law. For the last 300 years the Church had to combat the Law., and now that we are in the 19th century, it is rather late for us to think of quailing before a Statute as false as it is despicable and unjust.

Shame, eternal shame on those who, while they cry out for religious liberty, and "freedom of thought" for themselves, will not extend them to anybody else.

Recreated from The Waterford News, Waterford, July 11, 1851.

GREAT ORANGE DEMONSTRATION IN BELFAST.

On Wednesday evening, the Orangemen of Belfast and neighbouring districts held a great commemorative meeting in the Circus, Wellington Place. It had been originally intended to hold a meeting for the purpose of inaugurating a Grand Master for the County Antrim, in the room of the late lamented James Watson, Esq., of Brookhill, but as the Nobleman selected was unable to attend, in consequence of a recent serious accident, the inaugural ceremony has been necessarily postponed until some time in the ensuing Autumn. It was felt, however, that other grounds existed which rendered it expedient to hold a great meeting of the Orangemen of this and the adjacent districts at this time. Precluded, by law, from the ordinary mode of commemorating the anniversary of the Battle of the Boyne—that is to say, by public procession—it was but reasonable to afford the loyal and patient "Sons of William" an opportunity of giving expression to their principles, and of assembling in fraternal concord, and in such a manner as might best demonstrate their unwavering attachment to the Protestant cause, and to the memory of the illustrious monarch who effected the deliverance of these kingdoms from despotism, and secured to them the blessings of civil and religious liberty. Besides, inasmuch as the project of founding a great public building in Belfast, as a visible memorial of the strength of those principles, and as a centre of Protestant association in the province, has been most favourably received, and needs only some authentic stimulus from the collected Protestantism of the vicinity to be forthwith carried into execution, it was also determined that such an opportunity of placing it before the Orangemen of the North-East should not be neglected. With these objects in view the meeting was held, and certainly a more magnificent demonstration of its kind was never before witnessed in this, or perhaps any other town.

Recreated from The Belfast News-Letter, Belfast, July 18, 1851.

ENGAGEMENT WITH SLAVERS.

SANGUINARY ENGAGEMENT WITH AN ARMED SLAVER.—By advices from the Thetis, 38, Capt. A. L. Kuper, we learn that she was at Monte Video on the 24th of May. She left Rio Janeiro for that place on Good Friday (April 18), and whilst on her passage down, sighted a clipper vessel, showing Portuguese colours at the main, and Yankee at the fore, proving to be a slaver mounting no less than twenty guns. She was on the weather bow of the Thetis, lying on the port tack, and on the Thetis firing her bow guns did not heave to. "We," says our informant, "then gave her our starboard broadside, which she returned by her own, carrying away our rigging in some places. Another broadside from the Thetis set her on fire, and we had only time to save the remainder of her crew, of which fourteen had been killed and six wounded. We had four killed and fourteen wounded."

CAPTURE OF A SLAVE STEAMER BY THE CORMORANT.—A letter from the Cormorant, dated June 9, 1851, off Rio, says:—"You will be glad to hear of our having captured a steamer, with a slave cargo on board, at twelve o'clock this day. We were lying quietly in the harbour (having only arrived yesterday from a six weeks' cruise), when the steamer was observed going out; after she was about four miles outside the fort, we weighed and proceeded in chase, much to the astonishment of a large number of men-of-war of different nations.

As soon as she perceived us in chase, she 'bout ship, and tried to regain the harbour, but it was of no avail—Cormorant toddles too fast. When we were but a short distance from her, we fired three or four guns at her, but she took no notice of it, so we were compelled to take more effectual means of stopping her, which was quietly giving her our stern, which knocked both masts and likewise her funnel down on the deck. The plan succeeded, and she is now our prize. In the collision our jib and flying jibbooms were carried away. All of this time we were within range of Fort Santa Cruz—mounting about seventy guns in three tiers—and in full sight of the harbour. I believe that it is our captains's intention to send the prize after another vessel, of which we have information. The Plumper, screw-sloop, shares with us, as she was not far off."—*Portsmouth Herald.*

DREADFUL OUTRAGES IN THE COUNTY DONEGAL.—A correspondent of the *Derry Standard* thus describes the state of the country in the neighbourhood of Kilmacreenan:—We are suffering beyond description from the daring outrages almost nightly committed, by clubbed or banded ruffians, whose sole occupation is to plunder, and, if resisted, maltreat their more industrious, but unprotected neighbours around them. Since the month of February, not less then thirty-six robberies have been committed within two miles of this town, and not a single detection, save in one instance, although most of them were of a very serious and aggravating nature.

You cannot travel out almost any distance in any direction without meeting some party either going to the doctor to have their wounds dressed—to the local magistrate to lodge informations—or inquiring after some stolen property, horse, cow, meal, money, bed and back clothing, or other effects of which they have been plundered by these daring and heartless robbers. One man is lodged in Lifford jail at present for being one of eighteen who came by night to the house of an unprotected widow and her son, and, having gained an entrance through the roof of the dwelling-house, commenced beating with their weapons the aged woman, her son, and a relative who was servant in the house; and when the work was done (as they conceived), when they had broken down their strength that they could offer no further resistance, and that they might not recognise any of the party afterwards, they bound their clothes round their head and their arms with ropes, and threw them all into a bed, shutting the apartment. This done, they at once struck up their lights, kindled a fire, and collected all the butter, milk, eggs, and bread in the house, on which they feasted for one hour without any apprehension of danger, no neighbours being convenient. When this scene was over, then the work of plunder commenced.

One party collected all the linens—eighteen shirts, three suits of clothes of the son's, all the knives and forks, &c. Another party collected the sacks, and filled them with meal, not leaving one pound behind of a large quantity. Another party loaded their own horses first, and afterwards broke open the stable door, and took out a horse to carry of what remained. Here they left the widow's house a complete waste, herself, her son, and servant, bound with ropes, full of large wounds, bleeding profusely, and rolled up, as they believed, in their bloody grave shrouds, without a single article of food or raiment, should they ever require it.

Indeed, "so cruel," relates the aged widow, who as yet survives, though greatly disfigured from many large wounds on her face, and other parts of her person, "was the human monster, who inflicted on her all her sores, that when he had broken down her strength, that she could make no further resistance, and was in the act of binding her with ropes, he stooped down and chewed off part of her nose with his teeth." This is one of the acts of unparalleled cruelty perpetrated in this quarter of the country almost weekly.

AN IRISH JURY.—*The Cork Constitution* speaks of a coroner's jury who refused being empaneled, unless paid for their attendance, and on perceiving the coroner was determined to hand them over to the custody of the police, said they would compromise the matter, and take a pint of porter each. This being peremptorily refused, they at last submitted.

Recreated from The Belfast News-Letter, Belfast, July 28, 1851.

THE HARVEST—THE POTATO.

We are happy to have it in our power to state, that the potato still "holds its own"—to use a popular definition, and gives promise of returning to its old *status* in Paddy's Land—so far as health and soundness are concerned.—*Wexford Independent.*

The potato crop is perfectly safe in this part of Ireland; there is no complaint, and we have heard the opinions of farmers from every part of the country. The cereals never presented a more luxuriant appearance. The after-grass is very rich, and will turn up well to the grazier in the improvement of his stock at the next October fair. It is a glorious season of rejoicing to all, but especially to those poor creatures who have their little gardens sown, as they have a certainty of food during the winter.—*Western Star.*

Another week has passed, and we are happy to be in a position to state that our former conviction, that no potato failure will this year occur, has received additional strength; we have made the most strict inquiries, and the crops in several parts in this country have been viewed by a party connected with this office, and they all look healthy and blooming. It is considered that another fortnight will set all doubt on the subject at rest.—*Roscommon Messenger.*

Rumours of the appearance of the potato blight have been circulated during the week, not, we believe, without some slight foundation; but the very partial extent to which the crop is, up to the present, affected, permits us to indulge the most sanguine hopes that the vast proportion will remain perfectly sound. The harsh winds which recently prevailed affected the stalks and leaves of the potato and even the leaves of trees considerably, giving them a black shriveled appearance, many persons mistake this for the blight.—*Sligo Journal.*

Recreated from The Cork Examiner, Cork, August 1, 1851.

OPENING OF THE RAILWAY TO GALWAY.

On this day the railway will be opened to Galway, and thorough communication established between Dublin and the capital of the west. It is impossible to overrate the importance of this event, from which we may reasonably date the beginning of an era fraught with circumstances of the deepest moment to Ireland, and of equal, if not greater, good to the distant province whose resources have lain so long dormant and neglected.

In a few hours the traveler may be conveyed from Dublin to Galway, and the distance between the provinces of Connaught and the capital practically reduced to one-fifth. Regarding the Galway line in its effects on the prosperity of the west,—now, for the first time, the vast but hidden resources of Connaught are afforded an opportunity of development which must communicate its impulses to the rest of Ireland, and all proceed together on the highway to prosperity.

At the western end of the Galway line there is a field of undeveloped productiveness, of which there is now a fair, and not very distant hope of cultivation. We have seen specimens of Galway marble at the Great Exhibition—green, streaked with white veins, than which nothing could be more beautiful. We question whether a finer specimen than the green marble slab from Galway is to be found in the entire department of mines and minerals at the Crystal Palace.

Recreated from The Freeman's Journal, Dublin, August 1, 1851.

NOCTURNAL ROBBERIES.

Scarcely a night passes without our hearing of some new cases of robbery, in the city ; and every one asks, "What is to be done?" We answer that the only remedy is a night watch, of say 20 men. Without this body, every house in the city—at the present rate of plundering—may expect *one visit*, at least, from these daring villains.

DUBLIN: MONDAY, AUGUST 4, 1851.

THE LAST STAGE OF THE PENAL BILL.

The Queen has set her hand to the enactment prepared by her perfidious ministers, and passed amid the shouts of her bigoted parliament, to proscribe the faith of eight millions of her subjects, and abolish, so far as the power of Queen, Lords, and Commons can abolish, one of the essential elements of the religious organization of Catholicity in these kingdoms. Henceforth by *parliamentary* law the existence of the Catholic church, as a church, and the existence of the Catholic religion in its full and necessary development, are not only ignored but rendered penal in this realm. To be a Catholic bishop is a crime and high misdemeanour against the law. To act as a Catholic bishop is a penal act against which the law has authorised even the most infamous in the community to aid us in denunciation and demand the punishment of the episcopal

INGENIOUS MACHINE.—Mr. William Delany, of Jerpoint, in this county, a miller in humble circumstances, has invented an extremely curious and interesting machine, which is calculated to excite considerable public attention, and perhaps lead to important results in the military world. It is a most original piece of ordnance, consisting of six barrels disposed in the form of a wheel, which revolve upon an axle, and are loaded, primed, levelled at an object, and discharged alternately without the lapse of a moment between, so that the fire upon any point may be perpetually kept up without the slightest loss of time. The model, which we have had great pleasure in examining, is beautifully contrived and put together, and the machinery is perhaps as ingenious in its conception as we have ever seen.—*Kilkenny Moderator.*

Reprinted and recreated from The Freeman's Journal, Dublin, August 4, 1851.

PAUPER APPRENTICES TO THE SEA SERVICE.

A copy of an act of parliament which came into operation on the 24th, was laid before the Guardians, entitled " An act to extend the benefits of certain provisions of the general merchant seamen's act, relating to apprentices bound to the sea service, to persons bound to the sea service by Boards of Guardians, of the poor in Ireland ; and to enable such guardians to place out boys in the naval service."

[As the foregoing is an important act we give a few extracts from the clauses which bear directly on the subject.]

Clause 1.—The guardians may put out an apprentice in the sea service for not less than 4 years, to any British subject, being the master or owner of any ship registered or licensed in any part of the United Kingdom, any boy who has attained to the age of 12 years (and not more than 17 years), whose parents are receiving relief in such Union, until such boy has attained to 21 years of age ; or such other shorter period not less than four years as may be fixed and agreed on.

Clause 10.—If any boy not already in the merchant service who, or whose parents shall be receiving relief in any Union in Ireland be desirous of serving in the naval service of her Majesty, and be accepted or approved, and received by competent authority in such service, the guardians of the poor of such Union are empowered with the consent of the commissioners to allow him to enter into such service, and to pay out of the rates of such Union, or electoral division where chargeable to, such sum as may be required for out-fit and conveyance to the port at which the vessel shall be lying.

Reprinted from The Waterford News, Waterford, August 8, 1851.

HARVEST PROSPECTS
THE POTATO CROP.

The *Wexford Guardian* publishes the following report from Mr. Harte, now making an inspection of this union, on behalf of the Wexford Union Agricultural Society:—"I am sorry to say that the appearance of the crops is rather discouraging for all classes, particularly so for the rent-paying farmers. Wheat is, in my opinion, fully one-third lost; spring oats not free from disease, though it is, perhaps, better than last year; barley, in general, very good; winter oats fully equal to the most sanguine expectations of the producers. Now, for potatoes, all hope is dispelled of the success so anxiously looked for by all classes. It is beyond doubt that the further growth of this invaluable esculent is now completely checked; and as to the Swedish turnips, the way in which they have been this year attacked is very discouraging. I hope the general crop may not be so bad as present appearances exhibit it. Mangold and carrots are looking well."

Our reports of the potato crop are so conflicting that it is with difficulty we can form a proper estimate of its real condition. There can be no doubt but that it has, in various localities, received injury to a greater or less extent; but we still feel very confident that even after making a liberal deduction for the ravages of the disease, we shall have a very large, if not very abundant, supply of sound and good potatoes.—*Cork Examiner*.

The potatoes look most luxuriant, the blossom, where still out, having all the beauty and richness of the geranium. In many places we have seen the apple on the stalk, an appearance which, since the failure, has been wanting. We may now almost pronounce this crop safe.—*Kilkenny Moderator*.

THE POTATO CROP.—We had lately an opportunity of examining the state of this important crop, which, at the present time, excites so much anxiety, in a tour through several northern counties, and we regret to state, that the now too familiar disease has, undoubtedly, once more commenced its ravages. We have detected it not merely eating away the haulms, but rapidly, in some fields, corroding the full formed tubers. For so far the kidneys and the cruffles have been most severely injured, but the Ballygawley pinks and cups are also exhibiting diseased appearances in the stalks. In a few cases the progress of the disease has been exceedingly rapid; a field near Ballylesson, in which only some slight traces appeared on the evening of the 5th instant, was on the following day discovered to contain a great number of diseased tubers. A crop of the ash-leaf kidney variety has been almost completely destroyed. In Derry, Donegal, Antrim, and Down, our reports show us that the disease has fairly commenced.—*Northern Whig*.

We regret to state that within the last few days the most alarming reports have been circulated with regard to the state of this crop. Without giving full assent to the truth of these reports, we feel bound to state that in the main they are, unfortunately, but too well grounded. The disease of former years has appeared in several districts, and potato fields that a fortnight ago presented the most cheering promises are now blackened and withered—the tubers, too, are seriously damaged. A gentleman who travelled through the greater part of the county Louth this week has informed us that, in every district through which he passed, he perceived the most unmistakable evidences of the blight, and, on minute examination, he traced its destructive progress to a truly formidable extent.—*Newry Examiner*.

Recreated from The Freeman's Journal, Dublin, August 11, 1851.

ENGLISH EMIGRANTS TO IRELAND.

TO THE EDITOR OF THE TIMES.

Sir—I was surprised to see by the papers, that in a report called for by the House of Lords, out of the many English and Scotch purchases of land in Ireland under the incumbered estates bill, only one had become a resident; that being my case, I presume I am that one, and I feel called upon, as a duty to my countrymen, and to the land of my adoption, to give publicity to my experience, feeling certain that should any follow my example and advice both will be benefited.

A simple statement of facts is always most convincing. Driven from the army, in which I was a lieutenant-colonel, by illness, and seeking health by travelling in Ireland, I was struck by the advantages of purchasing under the incumbered estates bill. I found a property beautifully situated, but in a wretched state of farming, with a number of small tenants. I bought it at ten years' purchase. My first step was to get rid of the tenants off that portion of the land which I determined to commence improving and farming. There was half a year's rent due directly after the purchase; this I forgave them, paid their rents and charges, and bought their crops by valuation. From such as wished to go to America, I took their stock also by valuation; and for those who preferred taking other farms, I allowed their cattle to remain on my land until they found one. By these means I got all the land I wanted without any trouble, generally receiving the blessings of those who are represented in England as ready to murder under similar circumstances. Some of the smaller tenants still occupy their houses, work for me as labourers, and are well contented. I pay them 8d. a day, but most of my work is put out by the piece. I average 75 men and 50 women daily; the former are employed in draining, making roads, knocking down fences, and other general improvements; the latter in weeding, carrying turf, picking stones, &c. They are under the management of a Scotch steward, and are very amenable, but require much looking after, as they are inclined to be lazy. I purchased the land last autumn. I put in my spring corn principally with the spade, and my crops are now looking well. The lands of this country are most fertile, 40 to 60 tons of green crops per Irish acre are to be obtained by decent farming. Stones for drainage, brick earth, water-power for machinery, and turf are on the land, and my produce can compete (by water carriage) in the London market with those 100 miles off by rail. The rates and charges upon the land, if but a few English would come over with capital to employ the poor and improve the land, would dwindle into nothing.

I am living in a cottage without lock or bolt, sleeping on the ground floor, without shutters. I would not venture to live in England so little secured. I have received the greatest kindness and hospitality from all ranks. We have nine or ten neighbours within visiting distance. I have grouse, woodcock, snipe, and hares on my property; yachting close by. Geese and codfish are brought to me at 1s. each, large turbot 2s. soles 1d. each, fowls 1s. a couple, and everything in proportion.

Now, the Englishmen, who have capital, with intelligent active sons, think of land at 10 years' purchase, improvable to an enormous extent, doing good in your generation, and able to laugh at free trade. I do not advocate the purchase of lands without the intention of residence and improvement, but I am so confident of the advantages to be derived that I am intending to stake all I am worth in the venture.—

I am, Sir, your obedient servant,

CINCINNATUS.

P.S.—Should any be inclined to know more, you are at liberty to give my name and address.

Recreated from The Freeman's Journal, Dublin, August 14, 1851.

THE QUEEN'S VISIT TO THE NORTH.

Yesterday the arrangements for the reception and transit of the Queen, *via* the Great Northern Railway, were in a far advanced state of completion under the direction of Mr. Lewis Cubitt, the engineer, and Mr. Seymour Clarke, the general manager of the Great Northern line. It is now definitely arranged that her Majesty will arrive at the Great Northern Railway from Osborne at or as nearly as possible one o'clock on the afternoon of Wednesday. She will be received at the station in Maiden-lane, which will be decorated with emblematical devices in evergreens, dahlias, and other flowers suitable to the occasion. Mr. Denison, M.P., the chairman of the company, together with the directors, Mr. Lewis Cubitt, the engineer, Mr. Mowatt, the secretary, and Mr. Seymour Clarke, the general manager will conduct her Majesty and the royal suite to a magnificently furnished, although temporary, suite of apartments erected over the station under the direction of Mr. Cubitt. It is arranged that the royal train shall be in readiness at two o'clock precisely, in order to give her Majesty and her Royal Consort time to partake of the splendid *dejeuner* which is to be provided for her by the company on her arrival. The royal train will consist of twelve carriages, namely, three ordinary although entirely new first-class carriages; the three royal salons, one for her Majesty and royal consort, another for his Royal Highness the Prince of Wales, and the third for the royal suite; two break vans and four carriage trucks, for the conveyance of the luggage of the royal party and suite. The Queen's carriage will be surmounted by a splendid silk royal standard, four feet six by two feet, it having been ascertained that all the bridges and tunnels on the line will enable them to carry a flag of such dimensions and leave four or five inches to spare. The train will be preceded by a pilot engine for greater security, and will be drawn by an entirely new and powerful engine, driven by Mr. Sturrock, the locomotive superintendent. The royal carriages at present remain at the establishment of Mr. Williams, the railway coach builder in the Gray's Inn-road, but they will be removed at an early hour on Monday morning to the line, the directors having resolved to take them down on Monday on a trial trip as far as Peterborough. The royal salon carriages are quite in keeping externally with those of the ordinary first-class carriages of the line, being all constructed of teak wood, and not of Spanish mahogany, as erroneously stated in a daily contemporary. The length of the royal salon carriage is 18 feet 6 inches, by 7 feet 4 inches, in width. It is lined with white brocaded silk of Indian manufacture with raised scarlet flowers, and as an evidence of the texture and value of the material, we are assured that if it were made in England the cost would be at the rate of 3 guineas per yard. The windows are of the most beautiful plate glass, and the whole of the furniture, as well as the retiring room attached to the salon, are of walnut tree wood, the chairs and ottomans being covered with the same material as the lining of the carriage. The carriage is lighted from a lantern, with a powerful reflector, over the retiring room, and on the opposite side of the salon is a magnificent mirror reflecting the light back again, giving the apartment, for that the carriage really is, a most brilliant and elegant appearance. The only exterior distinction is a broad gold moulding round the carriage, with a splendidly gilt crown and coat of arms over each door-way, and the panels exquisitely painted with the orders of the Rath, the Garter, and the other orders of knighthood. The Prince of Wales's salon and retiring room is of equal dimensions, and equally elegant, with the exception that the lining is pure white brocade silk, instead of having any coloured flowers, and the salon for the royal suite is very similar.

Recreated from The Cork Examiner, Cork, August 27, 1851.

On Saturday evening a gingleman was driving a horse and covered car up Albert Quay, after leaving a passenger at the terminus, when the horse became suddenly restive and commenced to back in towards the Quay. The driver endeavoured to turn his head either up or down the quay, but the horse continued to back in towards the river, and the man had barely time to leap from the seat, when horse and car were precipitated into the river. The horse, which is the property of a poor man, was drowned, and the car broken almost to pieces.

Reprinted from The Cork Examiner, Cork, August 18, 1851.

ACCIDENT TO AN EMIGRANT VESSEL.

A large vessel, the Jacob Westervelt, carrying emigrants from Liverpool to News York was brought into Queenstown about three o'clock on Monday, by one of the tug vessels belonging to this river. She had lost several top masts, yards, and sails. It appeared that the vessel, which is 1,400 tons burden, left Liverpool on Sunday the 17th inst., with a crew of 35, and having about 700 passengers.

The wind was very changeable, and upon Saturday last it blew from the west, became squally, a very high sea running, upon which all the large sails were reefed, and the light sails were taken in. On Saturday morning, a very heavy gale came on accompanied by thunder and lightening, and shortly after two topmasts were broken bringing down sails and yards. Great difficulty was experienced in clearing away the wreck, and one of the sailors fell into the sea, and was with a great effort saved from drowning.

The ship was then off Cape Clear, and the captain determined to run for the nearest port. From Kinsale a pilot got on board, and on Monday the tug steamer took up the vessel and brought her into Queenstown. No loss of life or even injury resulted to any of the passengers or crew.

Recreated from The Cork Examiner, Cork, August 27, 1851.

ARRIVAL OF LORD GOUGH— IN KILLARNEY.

Lord Gough, his family and suite arrived here on Thursday from Mallow, by special coach, and was immediately driven to the Victoria Hotel. His lordship seemed to enjoy excellent health, and it would be difficult to recognise in the bland and gentle countenance of the venerable old man, the warrior who had charged and routed the Sikhs with such determined gallantry and saved India.

The news of the great man's arrival soon spread widely, and on Friday evening it was determined to testify in a public manner the general respect entertained for him. Large crowds assembled, a huge bonfire was lighted in front of the hotel, on the brink of the lake, and from a battery erected by Mr. Finn, the canon sent forth their mimic thunder, the echoes of which were taken up and repeated again and again by the surrounding mountains. The scene was extremely animated, but nothing could equal the enthusiasm, when the Hero of India made his appearance.

He was greeted with thunders of applause by those present, and by every mark of respect from numbers of tourists, staying at the hotel. He remained for a long time in the open air, and the beauty and majesty of the lakes and mountains, the ruddy glare of the fire reflected in the waters, the picturesque grouping of those assembled, and the booming of the guns, formed a scene not easily to be forgotten.

The firing continued at intervals to a late hour, and his lordship seemed much gratified and affected by his reception, and repeatedly expressed himself much pleased with the elegant accommodation, the comfort and attention afforded him at the Victoria Hotel.—*Cork Examiner*.

Recreated from The Waterford News, Waterford, August 29, 1851.

WRECK AT KILKEE.

KILKEE, SATURDAY MORNING.—A pleasure yacht has just been towed into Kilkee bay, by the fishermen belonging to this place. It is supposed a party of ladies and gentlemen had been enjoying an excursion at sea; for, in the cabin, ladies' bonnets and broken mirrors are all knocked about here and there; the blankets and sheets are marked 'R. M.' There was also a letter found in the cabin addressed "Robert Moore, Moorehall, Tallow." There is no name on her, as her stern and part of the deck are washed entirely away, she is coppered and copper-fastened and about 180 tons burden. There were bread and meat found in her cabin; the bread was quite fresh, and it is supposed that she was all right on yesterday morning. There was not a soul on board. All her rigging, canvass, masts, spars, &c., &c., were carried away. She now lies in the centre of the bay.—*Correspondent Munster News.*

The following is an extract from a private letter with which we (*Evening Packet*) have been favoured. It has been written by a passenger on board an American emigrant ship commanded by Captain Hein, which vessel fell in with the wreck, rescued her despairing companions, and safely landed them at Kilrush.:—

"In a few minutes after the captain thought he saw a flag up, about four miles to the leeward. On using the glass he said it was a flag of distress, flying from a wreck. My blood ran cold when I heard it. The captain at once bore down, and when he neared the wreck the most terrible sight presented itself to my view; the masts were all blown away, the bulwarks were smashed to bits, the rudder was gone, and her stern was a complete riddle.

It was indeed an awful sight to see human beings, including ladies, clinging in agony to the wreck, which every moment we thought would be imbedded in the sea, which then ran mountains high. Sometimes the sea broke over them, and we thought they were lost, while screams of agony burst from the wretched sufferers.

We at once lay to, to try and save them; but from the tremendous sea we dared not go close to them, for fear of running them down. Each time, as we passed, we tried to throw them a warp, but from the violence of the storm our efforts were in vain, and no boat dared to venture on such a sea. For seven hours the captain and crew toiled incessantly to get them off, but in vain; while the misery we suffered, seeing so many human beings so near a watery grave was intolerable. I remained lashed on the deck the entire time. It was now getting dark, and the captain was alarmed for the safety of his own ship, as in our efforts to save them we had gone very near the dangerous coast of Kilkee. We ran alongside them for the last time, and failed to throw a rope. A cry of despair burst from the poor creatures as they saw their last chance fail; but the brave Captain Hein, who is a Prussian, would not desert them, and determined, in spite of the awful storm and sea, to send a boat, bravely volunteering to be the first to go.

The chief mate, Thomas Larkin, however represented to him that the lives of all the passengers were in his hands, and that he would fail in his duty if he ran so great a risk. The mate Larkin gallantly offered to go himself, and four other brave fellows volunteered to go with him; the boat was lowered, and they committed themselves to the raging deep. They arrived safely alongside the wreck, which proved to be a private yacht, The Owen Glendower of 123 tons, belonging to Wm. Moore, Esq., of Moore Hill, Waterford, a gentleman of large property, who with his wife, Mrs. Massey and Miss Llewelyn, were on board. They were in a most exhausted state, having been on the wreck 30 hours without food.

The captain paid them every attention, and landed them yesterday at Kilrush."

Recreated from The Cork Examiner, Cork, October 1, 1851.

GOING BACKWARDS!

As regards quick communication, it is a fact very remarkable that the *nearer* railways approach our good city of Waterford, the *slower* is our mode of travel. For instance, when there was no *rail* in Ireland, a letter posted in New Ross this evening, could be had in Waterford on in two or three hours afterwards. But *now* it takes as many days. Again, when a person wants to write to Cappoquin, he must make up his mind that his letter will have to travel through the counties of Kilkenny, Tipperary & Cork, before he can hope it will reach its destination. One of our exchange papers was *three weeks* coming from Dublin a short time ago, it having been sent to Naas, through mistake. During the same time we had a letter from New York; published it, and had it on its way *back*. Last week we had the Paris *Constitutionnel* at the same moment that we received a Barony Forth (Wexford) letter, although *both*, letter and paper, were posted on the *same* day!

Surely this is too bad. Though depressed our trade is, if we allow this ruinous post office bungling to continue, it must necessarily be much worse. To every man it must be clear enough that government don't care for our position—they sympathise not with us—their look out is, to fill the coffers of their exchequer, totally disregarding when or how our letters come to hand.

Then, surely it is our business to spur them on to their duty.

Reprinted from The Waterford News, Waterford, October 17, 1851.

ACCIDENT TO AN EMIGRANT SHIP.

KINGSTOWN, OCT. 20.—The American ship James Wright, S. Clarke, master, with four hundred emigrants for New York, grounded on the Kish Bank at eleven o'clock this morning, two hours before low water. There was a fresh breeze on S.S.W., but fortunately no swell. The harbour master, Lieut. Hutchinson, R.N., proceeded to the ship in pilot boat No. 2, and, with a view to be prepared to give assistance if required at the pumps, he took a boat and 8 men in addition to the pilot crew of eight pilots. On arriving at the vessel it was found that she had been boarded by the master of No. 1 pilot boat, and as the ship did not strike with severity she was forced off with the aid of her sails before three p.m. Lieutenant Hutchinson, in order to satisfy himself, had the pumps sounded, when they found fifteen inches of water. The captain gave every assurance that he would put back if the vessel became leaky. The crew and passengers were in the best possible spirits and most obedient.

Reprinted from The Cork Examiner, Cork, October 20, 1851.

A CLIPPER.

The clipper ship Flying Cloud, commanded by Captain Cressy, had made a most astonishing trip to San Francisco. She left New York on the 2d of June, at 6, p.m., and arrived at San Francisco on the 20th of August, thus making the passage in the unprecedented short period of 90 days, the shortest by 6 days ever before made by sailing vessel. She made Cape Horn in 50 days, and the line (Pacific side) in 71 days. Her run from Cape Horn to San Francisco was made in 39 days. Her best run in 24 hours was 374 miles, the greatest run ever made by a sea-going vessel, averaging $15\frac{3}{4}$ miles per hour. While making this run she was carrying top-gallant sails, with the wind one point forward of the beam. She ran in three days 992 miles. On one occasion, during a squall, 17 knots of line were found insufficient to measure her speed. 40 miles were her shortest run in 24 hours. When ten days out she sprang her mainmast head, rendering the mast very tender the rest of the voyage.

Reprinted from The Cork Examiner, Cork, October 27, 1851.

FASHIONS FOR NOVEMBER.

DINNER COSTUME.—Robe of pink Irish poplin, the skirt with three deep flounces, each edged with a trimming of narrow black velvet ribbon, run on in an Egyptian pattern. The corsage is open in front, and half high at the back, the top being edged with the same trimming as that of the flounces. The open fronts of the corsage are confined by three bands of black velvet. Under the corsage is a chemisette of very beautiful lace, open and square in the front. The sleeves are demi-long, and finished at the end with frills, edged with velvet trimming, the same as that on the flounces. Loose under-sleeves of white lace. The bracelets of black velvet, with gold clasps. Head-dress composed of loops of pink ribbon, edged with narrow black velvet, with two ends flowing towards the back of the neck. Short white kid gloves.

The bouquet of flowers destined for the new winter bonnets are mounted in two different styles. In some, the flowers are disposed in drooping sprays; others are so arranged as to admit of bows of the ribbon employed to trim the bonnet, being intermingled with the flowers and foliage.

The winter mantles and mantelets which have as yet been prepared are very full round the lower part, and sit rather more closely on the shoulders than those worn in summer. Velvet will be the most fashionable material for cloaks in dress promenade costume.

The Parisian ladies are wearing black velvet corsages, or pardessus with cloth jupes, in riding costumes. The corsage of black velvet has a basque at the waist, and is usually buttoned up to the throat. Some, however, have the fronts of the corsage turned back in the form of revers, when a gilet or vest is worn under it. A broad-brimmed beaver hat, with a veil, is generally adopted. The colour of the hat may be black, dark grey, fawn, or chestnut-brown, and it may be trimmed with bows of velvet ribbon, or with a feather, of the same tint as the hat.

Recreated from The Belfast News-Letter, Belfast, November 3, 1851.

BELFAST POLICE COURT.—MONDAY.

YOUTHFUL THIEF.—A very small boy, named *Patrick Corrigan*, who had been only a few days out of jail, having terminated a second imprisonment of three months for indulging in similar practices, was charged with stealing a bottle of castor oil, the property of Mr. Dobbin, of North Street. The bottle was in a window, and the prisoner broke a pane and abstracted it, but was taken into custody by a constable shortly after, with the bottle in his possession. He was sent to jail for another three months, and to get a good whipping. [A more appropriate punishment, perhaps, would have been to make the delinquent swallow a good dose of the oil.]

INCORRIGIBLE DRUNKARD.—*Owen Christy* was brought up, for the 102nd time, charged with being drunk in Castle Lane the previous evening, and having used abusive language to Mrs. Trevor. The usual mitigated punishments having had no effect on this inveterate drunkard, and having on the present occasion exhibited an addition to his usual offence, the bench took advantage of the circumstance, and sent him to jail for three months.

LEAVING A HORSE AND CART IN THE STREET.—*David Corrigan*, a countryman, was charged with leaving his horse and cart in the street, on Saturday, when it took fright and endangered the lives of several people. Constable Williamson said, when he observed the horse first, it was crossing North Street, with no person at its head, and, before he could get hold of it, it got on the side-path, and set off at full gallop, scattering the passengers right and left, injuring many of them, and two women, in particular, very severely. He could not stop the horse till it had reached the head of the street. Corrigan, who was in a yard at the time, was fined 10s. and costs.

Recreated from The Belfast News-Letter, Belfast, November 12, 1851.

CASTLEBAR PETTY SESSIONS.

The magistrates attending those sessions on last Wednesday were, Dr. Dillon, chairman; Sir Samuel O'Malley, Bart., Wm. Kearney, and Dominick Browne, Esqrs.

DERRYHARRIFF AGAIN.

Major-General George Charles, Earl of Lucan v. Thomas Lavelle, sen., John Lavelle, Edward Lavelle, Mich. Lavelle, and Thomas Lavelle, jun., for breaking down a house and throwing out timber at Derryharriff.

Three of the accused were brought from the gaol by the police and placed in the dock—namely, the father and his two eldest sons. The other two, mere children, were not arraigned. The defense was conducted by Messrs. C. B. Jordan and Lewis O'Donel, attorneys.

Richrd Stanton sworn—Was appointed caretaker at Derryharriff by Lord Lucan over the timber of the houses that were pulled down last week; the defendants came to the house and began removing away the timber, saying it belonged to themselves; when I heard what was going on I ran to the house, and on endeavouring to prevent their removing the timber one of the sons struck me—but I must, in justice to the father say, he did all he could to prevent my being injured; they put the timber out in spite of me.

Cross-examined by Mr. Jordan—My own house was levelled with the others by Lord Lucan; the house I was put in as caretaker was that occupied by Lavelle for the last fifty years; the furniture in the house, I believe, belonged to Lavelle; there was a sledge there and I put it outside; there was also a scythe, harrow, and other farming implements, and some old timber on the loft; does not recollect if there were bed posts or sides in the house; those were part of the things they put out.

Mr. Young—Did they not pull out a beam that was across the house from wall to wall?

Witness—Yes, and it was when I attempted to stop their doing so I was struck.

Mr. Jordan—Your worships know that an old stick, used in a country cabin as a loft bearer for half a century, could be of no value to Lord Lucan.

Dr. Dillon—Yes, but you know they had no right to remove fixtures.

Mr. Jordan—The act only applies to fixtures set in stone and mortar.

Mr. Young—Lord Lucan would not press the case if he did not see there was law for it.

Mr. Jordan—Surely Lord Lucan does not place such value on a rotten piece of stick as to justify such cruel and harsh proceedings against those poor creatures?

Mr. Young—It is not the value of the timber, Mr. Jordan, his lordship looks to, but it is to put a stop to the crime of throwing down the houses! so prevalent in the country (ironical laughter, and oh, oh! in the midst of which Mr. Young resumed his seat, apparently much confused).

Mr. Jordan—I am glad to hear Mr. Young calling the levelling system a crime.

Mr. O'Donel—Yes, it sounds admirably coming from that quarter.

After examining the son of Stanton, who corroborated his father's testimony, Dr. Dillon announced the decision of the bench to be, that the three Lavelles be fined ten shillings each or be imprisoned for fourteen days.

Such, reader, is the mercy shown by the newly-created major-general in the British service, but who in Irish service ranks "General of the Crowbar Brigade," not by brevet, but by active service in the field of extermination.—*Mayo Telegraph.*

Recreated from The Freeman's Journal, Dublin, November 28, 1851.

MORE EVICTIONS IN CONNEMARA.

The Law and Life Assurance Company seems determined to give ample illustrations of the blessings of the introduction into Ireland of English capital, and English enterprise, and English spirit, and English modes of managing property. In a recent number of this journal we had to announce the extermination of upwards of three hundred persons, and the total demolition of the habitations in which they once dwelt.

The *Galway Vindicator*, which has just reached us, brings the following statement of the further progress of the Law and Life Assurance Company in improving the condition of Connemara:—

In our last number we called attention to the wholesale evictions which are now carried on by the Law Life Assurance Company, in Connemara; and we regret to find that we have, this day, to add SIXTY-NINE to the other victims of the depopulation.

On the 24th of November Mr. John Robertson, with his party of bailiffs, proceeded to the townland of Ballinafad, evicted two families, consisting of eight persons, and levelled their houses.

On the 25th, same party visited the townlands of Derryvickreene, Glencoaghan, and Letty, evicted TEN FAMILIES, consisting of 61 individuals, and levelled their houses.

When the people are hunted from Connemara, and no labour remaining to till the healthy mountain side, the Law Life Assurance Company will have a most valuable property in their possession!!

Recreated from The Freeman's Journal, Dublin, December 2, 1851.

SANATORY ASSOCIATION.

A report upon the proceedings of the committee of the corporation charged with the duty of abating nuisances, regulating lodging houses, &c., was submitted by Mr. Mulloy and Dr. Nalty. The report stated that those gentlemen had waited, as a deputation, on the committee above named, and that the latter had expressed a strong desire for the co-operation of the Sanatory Association in abating nuisances and improving the dwellings of the poor. The deputation approved in the strongest manner of the rules and regulations which had been adopted for sanatory purposes by the corporation, and they ascertained that under those rules, which had come into operation only a few months ago, about 1,600 cases of nuisances had been abated.

With respect to slaughter-houses, copious and detailed information was obtained by the committee, in order to enable the council to grant the necessary license or certificate. As to cellars and lodging-houses, there had been about 1,000 visited by Mr. Reid, the inspector, and upon his report 283 had been closed, and 67 lodging-houses had been registered.

The report concluded by expressing the satisfaction of the deputation at the amount of work which had been performed by the committee since the commencement of their labours, and the cordiality with which they offered to supply any information which the Sanatory Association might require.

REGISTRY OF BIRTHS AND DEATHS.

The Chairman referred to a passage in the address of Sir R. Kane, at the last meeting of the Statistical Society, in which he referred to the importance of a registration of births and deaths in Ireland. Sir Robert Kane had alluded to this matter as being important for statistical purposes, and he (Sir Edward Borough) did not, for a moment, deny the truth of this statement, but he believed, if a registration were important when viewed in this light, it was much more so when used for sanatory purposes (hear, hear). It was of the utmost importance that an act of parliament should be passed, providing for the registration of births and deaths in Ireland, and for the more effectual registration of marriages; and he trusted another session would not pass over without such an act being passed (hear, hear).

EARLY INTERMENTS.

Doctor Vance said that he had observed by the report of the corporation, which appeared in the papers of that morning, that it was intended to prevent interments in the cemeteries after the hour of twelve o'clock at noon. This was a very excellent resolution, and he was sorry to see that a member of the corporation, who was also a member of the cemetery board, had expressed his intention of calling a meeting of that board, with the object of getting a resolution rescinded which was favourable to the early interments. He trusted there would be a full meeting at whatever time it might be convened, and that they would not rescind the resolution, but confirm it; for he had no hesitation in saying that the practice of early interments, if carried out, would be most beneficial to the public (hear).

Having transacted some routine business, the meeting adjourned.

Recreated from The Freeman's Journal, Dublin, December 3, 1851.

EXTRAORDINARY CASE OF SUICIDE BY A LADY IN LEICESTER.

A most melancholy suicide happened in Leicester on Friday evening, the 21st instant. The victim of self-murder in this case was a lady by birth, connection, taste, and literary accomplishment; though she was destitute of pecuniary means. She had lately been attempting to gain a livelihood by the sale of printed poems, and appeared to have been a virtuous, refined, and gifted female, but possessed of overwrought sensibility. Her domestic history had been peculiarly unhappy; and recently her prospects were painful and discouraging, if not such as to create despair. Her name was Caroline Charlotte Veasey Gilldea. The inquest was held at the Fountain Tavern, on Saturday evening. The jury was sworn, and went to view the body, which was that of a female of forty, rather good looking, and with a disposition to fullness of figure. Her hair was brown, and braided over her forehead. Her features were regular and well marked, and her complexion was florid. She bore the traces of having been, in her earlier days, a fine looking woman. On the return of the jury from the examination of the corpse, the evidence to be adduced was taken.

From the evidence, it appeared that the unfortunate lady having been reduced to desperation by the state of her circumstances, had taken a quantity of prussic acid. She was still breathing when discovered. Mr. Buck, surgeon, was called in and used the stomach-pump, and also administered the usual antidote—ammonia—but without effect. She gradually became weaker, and in about ten minutes expired. Several documents in her handwriting, found in her room, were read at the inquest. They were written in a clear, firm, ladylike hand, and in a correct, grammatical and literary style, amongst which was a letter to Lady Peel imploring her assistance in her difficulties. The jury found "That the deceased poisoned herself while labouring under a temporary fit of mental insanity."

The body of the deceased was removed to the dead house in the cemetery on Sunday afternoon, for the purpose of being visited by any person connected with the family of the deceased, should they hear of her tragic end. In a volume published by the unfortunate lady, entitled the "Family Altar," containing prayers for every day in the week, to which are appended "Mahalaths," or sacred songs, is a "Private Prayer for a person in a state of poverty."

The following is proposed to be "added, when a person is under temptations to self-murder:"—"Let no temptations or trials so far prevail with me as to put an end to my being, but let me consider that I am thy creature, and that thou only hast a right to dispose of my life, and that it is my duty to submit to the greatest troubles with perfect humility and resignation, when thou seest fit to lay them upon me."—*Leicester Chronicle*.

Recreated from The Freeman's Journal, Dublin, December 4, 1851.

RELIGIOUS EXCITEMENT IN TUAM.

(FROM A CORRESPONDENT.)

December 9th.

An unusual degree of excitement has been called into existence in this town and neighbourhood in consequence of the importation amongst us of a few of these hireling missionaries commonly known as "bible readers," and their uncalled for efforts to pervert some Catholic families from their faith. The inhabitants of Tuam do not, it seems, require the aid of such men to teach them the ways of salvation. At least it would appear so from the very unmistakable manner in which they have welcomed them here. Whilst these bible readers confined their walks to the houses of the few Protestant families who live here, they were not molested.

But having intruded themselves into Catholic houses, uncalled for, and against the wishes of the occupants, a good deal of indignation was manifested. This got vent amongst the boys and children, who began to shout at them whenever they made their appearance afterwards in the street. To protect these intruders from having their ears regaled with such grating music, the resident magistrate of this town issued orders to the police to arrest and imprison any person found shouting "Jumper." In accordance with this order, which is altogether illegal and unconstitutional, two poor women were arrested in the market place on Saturday morning, and marched off to the bridewell of the town without a warrant or any written document beyond this verbal command. Several summonses were also issued by the same resident magistrate against a number of little boys for an alleged assault upon one of the proselytisers. These cases came on for trial at the petty sessions bench on yesterday. It was only in the court that the warrant was produced. It stated that these women were arrested for riot.

The evidence failed to establish the slightest semblance of a riot. One of the women was proved by the very policeman who arrested her to have been standing at her usual place in the market-square, selling her eggs. The only crime imputed was, that she shouted, and in consequence of orders from the resident magistrate, she was taken away from her stand and kept in prison for 50 hours. Another poor woman, also detained for 50 hours in prison, was only passing through the street with a pail of water, and she, too, in this condition was taken up and arrested for "rioting."

This conduct created the utmost indignation in the minds of all classes in the town. The immediate cause of annoyance given to the inhabitants is worthy of note, as it may tend to turn attention to the real agents in the present crusade.

The cathedral bell tolls in this town at morning, noon, and evening for the "Angelus Domini," and it seems that on Friday last, as one of the Catholic clergymen was responding to the bell, by repeating the prayer, these two Protestant clergymen, who happened to be passing by, were observed to laugh in derision at the priest. I merely give you the story as I find it rumoured about the town. In Tuam, where the Catholic priesthood are held in such respect, this conduct was capable of creating great annoyance to the people; and hence the feelings against the bible-readers became more intense.

The courthouse was densely crowded by the inhabitants, who were anxious to see the result of the trials. As not a semblance of "riot" or "assault" could be proved, the parties in prison were liberated, and the summonses dismissed by the unanimous verdict of the bench. It is worthy of remark that even the resident magistrate who signed them, made no objection to the dismissal of all the complaints and the liberation of all the arrested parties.—There is a rumour that an action for illegal arrest and imprisonment will be taken against the resident magistrate.

Recreated from The Freeman's Journal, Dublin, December 11, 1851.

POLICE CALLED OUT IN A CHURCH YARD.

On Friday last, whilst a young man named Edmonds, from this city, was being interred in Dunmore, the Protestant clergyman of the place came to read over the grave. The wife of deceased, and a number of persons who attended the funeral, objected to the service, as deceased had recently become a Catholic. The brothers of deceased, who are Protestants, insisted that the office *should* be performed—the people still resisted—the police were sent for.

A conference was then held between the police, the parson, and the people about sending for Sir R. Paul; but, after the minister had been satisfied (by an eye-witness) that deceased had become a Catholic, he withdrew in peace without reading prayers. Before this, however, the police refused to *act*, as their numbers being "too few," as they said, before so large a body of people. No one knows what the results might have been, only the minister very wisely did not go to the grave to "pray for the living."

A Christmas Dinner Gone!—On Wednesday night a little boy, who carried a pig's head in his hand up the Quay, incautiously let a young "tipper" examine its beauties; the latter, in an instant, ran across the Quay with it. The owner shouted in vain for his mother! whilst his head disappeared under the shadows of a lighter.—*Correspondent*.

Catholic Church.—Miss Easche, a lady of fortune, and who has moved in the best circles of society, has lately been received into the Catholic Church, at Farm-street, London, by the Jesuit Fathers.

We have also to inform our readers that Miss Massey Dawson, a grand-daughter of Lord and Lady Sinclair, has been received into the one true fold, at the Church of the Immaculate Conception, Farm-street.—*Tablet*.

Recreated from The Waterford News, Waterford, December 26, 1851.

ELECTRIC TELEGRAPH BETWEEN DUBLIN AND GALWAY.

The Directors of the Midland Great Western Railway have concluded and signed a contract on most favourable terms with a London company for the immediate laying down of the electric telegraph wires along their line from Dublin to Galway.

Reprinted from The Waterford News, Waterford, December 26, 1851.

On Wednesday, as a cart belonging to one of the milk-contractors of the city gaol was passing through Sunday's Well, the horse, affrighted by some object, broke away and dashed at full speed down the road. At the spot where the occurrence took place, the road is extremely narrow, and was very much crowded at the time with passengers, so that great damage even to life was caused and much injury might have occurred, but for the conduct of Constable O'Brien, of the Sunday's Well station, who ran down and succeeded with difficulty in seizing hold of the horse. Although he was dragged along the ground by the infuriated animal and received considerable personal injury, he still kept his hold, until he at length succeeded in stopping the horse and preventing any mischief that might have otherwise occurred. The constable received some severe bruises in the effort and had his clothes much torn.

An inquest was held on Friday, at the North Infirmary, before Mr. Jones, coroner, on the body of a man named Michael Newton, of Blarney Lane. It appeared, from the evidence of the mother of the deceased, that upon Christmas morning she went out at seven o'clock, and left deceased in bed with his son, a child of six years. There was a fire in the room, but no candle. When she returned at eight o'clock she saw a crowd round the house and perceived smoke, and on going into the room found deceased lying on the bed and all blackened, having apparently been burnt. He lived but for a short time, and stated that the fire was caused by his pipe, a spark of which ignited the bed curtains. It did not appear that the deceased had been at all affected by liquor previous to the occurrence. The jury found a verdict in accordance with the circumstances.

Reprinted from The Cork Examiner, Cork, December 29, 1851.

THE LOVER'S DREAM.

I dreamed a dream of home and love,
A summer crowned with flowers,
No thorns beneath, no clouds above,
To dim the laughing hours.

A dark change came upon our life,
It bade my vision flee,
But its beauty and its blessedness
Was for thee, love—only thee.

I dreamed a dream of power and fame,
Of royal rank and state,
Of nation that in homage due,
Should on thy bidding wait.

I joyed to think thy will should rule
The brave, the great, the free;
But the vision, with its pomp and pride,
Was for thee, love—only thee.

Recreated from The Waterford News, Waterford, January 30, 1852.

1852

Selected Headlines

THE IRISH PEASANTRY	333
LIGHTING ENNISCORTHY WITH GAS	334
MYSTERIOUS DEATH OF A FEMALE	335
DESTRUCTION OF LAGOS	340
PERVERSION TO POPERY	347
LOSS OF THE BIRKENHEAD	352
COMPLETION OF THE SUBMARINE TELEGRAPH	356
THE SLAUGHTER AT SIXMILE-BRIDGE	364
FUNERAL OF THE DUKE OF WELLINGTON	388
THE CROWBAR BRIGADE	392

SHEEP STEALING.

Patrick Navin having been charged by Mr. Kirwin, of Stradbally, with stealing two sheep, his property, on the 19th ult., and finding them in the possession of Thomas Croneen, butcher of this town.

The facts of the case having been proved by the parties, the Court granted informations against the prisoner, and returned for next quarter sessions.

LAMPS FOR DUNGARVAN.

Dungarvan, Dec. 30, 1851.

Our enterprising and spirited townsman, Mr. Michael Mahony, merchant, has purchased four splendid lamps for the use of the public, and has placed them in William-street. They were lit on the night of the 24th ult., amidst the cheers and acclamations of the people, who assembled on the occasion to witness so novel a scene in this town, where the eye of a spectator never beheld such a treat, during the dreary dark and dismal winter nights. There has been many valuable lives lost here these years past, in consequence of having no lights to guide the footsteps of the stranger, or the unwary traveller passing through the dirty and impassable streets, and obliged to remain inside doors, rather than endanger his life. This has not been the first kind act that this generous and noble-minded man has done to render a service to this town, and I hope and trust that the other merchants will imitate this good and humane example, to set up a few more in the other streets; most particulary on the Quay, where lives have been lost—and at all hours of the night persons are in imminent danger of walking over it, as there has been no precautionary measures adopted to preclude the possibility of any such danger occurring.

Reprinted from The Waterford News, Waterford, January 2, 1852.

MELANCHOLY ACCIDENT.—On the night of Saturday last, the roof of a house in the townland of Corragha in the parish of Clonallan, in the county of Down, which had undergone a new thatching a few days before, fell in. On removing the ruins, two of the family were found to be dead from suffocation, together with other injuries from the pressure of the timber. It is supposed the weight of the new thatch had been too great for the timber. An inquest was held on the bodies when a verdict in accordance was returned.

Recreated from The Belfast News-Letter, Belfast, January 5, 1852.

WRECK OF THE TOWN OF WEXFORD STEAMER.—HOLYHEAD, SUNDAY.—The Town of Wexford (s.), of Liverpool, is in great danger on the rocks in Holyhead Bay. The Anglia, railway steamer, with lifeboat in tow, went to her assistance, and has since returned into harbour (3:35 P.M.), crew and passengers saved, and landed at Infadog. Wind North by West, strong breeze, fine. This morning she has parted, and will be a total wreck. It appears she had become leaky on the passage from Waterford to Liverpool, so much so that cows and pigs, it is said had to be thrown overboard, as the fires were nearly extinguished in the engine-room. Several pigs, poultry, &c., have floated to shore here since.

PRIESTCRAFT.—The *Limerick Chronicle* has the following statement in reference to the decline of the incomes of the Romish clergy:—"In all the rural districts of this county the annual Christmas offerings by their flocks to the parish priest did not average more than half the amount contributed last year, as thousands of farmers and hard-working peasantry had emigrated to America during the season, carrying with them large sums of money. The Roman Catholic clergy sustain a severe loss and drawback in their pecuniary resources, in consequence of the tide of emigration continuing to roll unabated."

THE RIBBON CONSPIRACY AND ITS VICTIMS.

TURNING OF THE TIDE.—AN APPROVER!

We were on the eve of putting to press, when we were informed, on the most unquestionable authority, that a man, arrested by the Collon police, charged with the murder of the late Mr. Bateson, has TURNED APPROVER; admitting not only his complicity in the case of that barbarous atrocity, but also his being a party to the murder of Owen M'Integart. This person was conveyed to Dublin Castle, by the police, on Sunday last. Verily, "it *is* a long lane that has no turning!"

This is exactly what was most to be desiderated. The revelations of the informer will not only lead to the satisfaction of the ends of justice, in regard to the murder of Mr. Bateson, but will, doubtless, tend to, if possible, a more important result—namely, the explosion of the whole conspiracy to its remotest ramifications, the frustration of its machinations, and the arrest of its principal leaders. Should this prove to be the case, we need not say how unaffectedly we shall congratulate the country on its riddance from the most fearful moral plague that ever desolated a nation, and on its escape from the sad consequences of a virtual suspension of the Constitution.

We understand that the magistrates of the county Louth assembled on Tuesday at Dundalk, to consider what steps were necessary to be taken in the present circumstance of the district. Lord Bellow occupied the chair, and the whole magistracy of the county were present, with two or three exceptions. As their deliberations were strictly private, nothing has transpired as to the resolutions which may have been agreed to.

DETECTION OF BASE COIN AND COINING IMPLEMENTS, &c.—On the 2nd instant, Sergeant Dickson of the Constabulary, stationed at Middletown (County Armagh), had information given him by Mr. Nathaniel Grayson, a grocer, that a woman, named Jane M'Kenna, had passed two base 4d. pieces in his shop, at different hours of the preceding day, one to his mother and another to his wife. After some search, the Sergeant succeeded in arresting the woman, M'Kenna, who, after the usual protestations of innocence, at length admitted that she had received the base 4d. pieces from a man named George Hamilton, a rather comfortable farmer, with ten Irish acres of land, cows and horses, &c., &c., living in the townland of Crossdall. Sergeant Dickson, taking two sub-constables with him, went to Hamilton's house, and, after making him a prisoner, searched his person, and found two bad shillings and two 4d. pieces. On searching through the house, they found in a cupboard fifty-three base shillings, two 4d. pieces, and a base half-crown, and, in an old bees'-cap, they found a quantity of old brass, copper, lead, and a hard white metal which sounded like bell-metal, with utensils for casting the metal into when melted; also a crucible, &c., &c. The prisoners were taken before the magistrates, at Petty Sessions, on the 3rd inst., and were by them committed to take their trial at the Quarter Sessions of Armagh. It is not much more than three months since Sergeant Dickson and his party detected, in the same townland, a young man, named M'Guigan, charged with uttering, and having in his possession, base sovereigns, and who is now suffering confinement in Armagh Jail.—*Newry Telegraph.*

FEMALE EMIGRATION.—The committee of the Female Emigration Fund, under the auspices of the Right Hon. Sidney Herhert, have engaged the fine vessel *Euphrates* to convey a party of sixty women to Sydney. The emigrants sent out by this committee now number nearly 700, most of whom are doing well in the colonies, where the demand for servants continues to be very great.

Recreated from The Belfast News-Letter, Belfast, January 7, 1852.

THE NATION.

SATURDAY, JANUARY 10, 1852

THE TENANT LEAGUE.

The Council of the League meets on Tuesday to take measures to revive and invigorate the agitation. The time is, for many reasons, a critical one—one, which if it be well and wisely used, may be fruitful in great results to the country; and by the acts of which the agitation must either stand or fall, for it can no longer bide time while the people perish.

The war between landlord and tenant, after leaving the South unpeopled, the West a waste, the towns bankrupt, the priests, and professions in beggary, is growing into a bloody jacquerie on the borders of Ulster. Louth, once so peaceful, is defiled with the terrible stigmas of the Ribbonman's bludgeon. The same woeful Christmas eve that saw thousands of emigrants making their desolate way to the shore, and scores of houses tumbling round their wretched tenants, under the exterminator's crow bar—saw another still sadder, more awful, and more evil sight, one weak and unarmed man, a landlord, beset, in the daylight on a public road, and nearly mashed to death in a quarry pit. Two great agrarian conspiracies—the conspiracy of the people to slay their oppressors, by an abominable and cold-blooded system of bravoism—the conspiracy of the landlords to rid their lands of the people, and to defend themselves by establishing drumhead law in lieu of the assizes,—mark the horrible crisis to which this question is coming in the North. How can the country be other than cursed, when wilful murder and oppression of the poor so often cry to God for vengeance? England, half in triumph and half in terror, marks "the sorrowful departure of the millions of broad shoulders and stalwart forms, holding hearts which, with all their feverish ravings and tumultuous passions, were never known to be craven or untrue in the presence of a foreign foe." Ireland lies in a death-like coma, drifting to destruction, and makes no sign.

Reprinted from The Nation, Dublin, January 10, 1852.

IRISH BALLAD SINGERS AND IRISH STREET BALLADS.

This is Fair-day in our Irish market-town. On every road, pour in flocks of sheep, droves of cattle (many of them of the old country breed, small and rough), and pigs; the latter for the most part coming singly, with hay-rope to jerking hind-leg. At every convenient brook or hedge side, country girls don the shoes and stockings they have been carrying so far in a bundle: partly for economy's sake, partly because they can walk with more ease barefoot; mainly in order that they may enter the fair with undimmed lustre of black, and spotless white or blue.

At an outskirt of the town spreads the "Fair-Green," bordered with hovels; its expanse of mire thickly trodden down with hoof and brogue—men shouting, swearing, bargaining, where the moistened penny smites and re-smites the rugged palm; beasts lowing, bleating, bellowing, braying, neighing, and squeaking. Horses, with ribbon on neck, dash recklessly to and fro; multitudinous horns threaten, parried and punished by innumerable sticks. Who keep all these asses? Are they never curried? In good sooth they *are* ill-used. There are few whiskey-tents, but this is because people prefer to drink elsewhere; for many have "broke their medal"—in other words, forgotten Father Mathew—long ago.

Down the street, it is all a moving crush of carts, beasts, potatoes (not quite extinct yet), corn sacks, and human beings. There are men in blue coats, flat cloth caps, old brown hats; matrons, in blue cloaks, red shawls, a cloak or two of the old-fashioned red cloth, white caps, white kerchiefs on head, red kerchiefs; maidens, with hair of brown or sable Spanish gloss, or, more ambitious, in bonnets with fluttering ribbons and flowered shawls. Yet these, too, found their last mirror perhaps in Pie's Pool there above, coming thence no longer barefoot.

At all corners and points of vantage, apples are offered energetically to the public; at a few, cakes and "sweet-rock." Elevated on carts without horses, the auctioneers of old clothes, and the Cheap Johns of new apparel, make their appeals to the crowd, and their apparently ferocious verbal attacks on each other.

A more quiet company of merchants continue to pitch their tents hard by. The stannens (standings) are conveniently ranged over the gutter on each side of the street, with roofs of patched canvas, sackcloth, or motley counterpane, stretched on rickety poles, or rounded with osiers; whereunder are spread the dazzling treasures of cheap cutlery and jewellery; distorting mirrors in red frames; round pewter-cased ditto, capable of being propped up and folded artfully; *gallowses* (*i.e.*, suspenders) and broad belts of coloured web—deemed wholesome wear by country youths; little blue and yellow-covered song-books; lives of saints, mixed with spelling-books and *Ree-a-ma-daisies* (Reading-made essays); and, in a corner, three or four second-hand volumes—perhaps one of Urquhart's "Rabelais," Dublin edition, and two of "The Justices of the Peace, published in 1823," which latter the stannen-keeper recommends to your attention as "an entertaining romance;" and, on being, with some trouble, undeceived in this point, says he's no scholar (meaning that he can't read), but that's what he bought it for.

At our elbow, a ballad-singer, a young woman in old plaid cloak and very old straw bonnet, strikes up with a sweet Connaught lisp, and slightly nasal twang, "The Sorrowful Lamentation of Patrick Donohue"—with the words, "Come all you tender Christians!"—and soon summons around her a ring of listeners. She will sing *da capo* as long as the ballad appears to draw attention and custom, and then she will change it or move off to another part of the fair.

The hour of melody seems to have struck; for, not far away we discover a second circle united by Orphean attraction. And here our curiosity is raised by the comment of a man, who seems to be tearing himself away from the influence. The best ballad-singer this, he declares, that he has heard these twenty years! "In troth, it's worth a ha'penny to hear him go over it, let alone the paper." The minstrel is found to be a tall, sad, stooping man, about thirty-five; his song, to the very favourite tune of "Youghall Harbour," is about two faithful lovers; his vocal excellence consists in that he twirls every word several times round his tongue, wrapt in the notes of a soft, husky, tremulous voice.

Urging our slow way through the crowd, we come within ear-shot of a shriller strain, which proceeds from two female vocalists, standing face to face, and yelling down one another's throats. Agrarian politics this time, and not of the most wholesome sort.

The muster of ballad-singers, to-day, is above the average; for, see, here is another! A little elderly man, wearing a very large and extremely elderly hat—his warehouse. He accompanies his comic song with a fiddle, upon which he leans one of his red weazen cheeks, watching with twinkling black eyes the movements of his left hand on the strings. His fiddle is cheap-looking and cracked, and his bow is mended with packthread. When the harsh-chords cease, and he lowers the instrument slowly from his chin, you observe that what seemed to be a continuous self-satisfied smile is, in reality, the effect of a dint or muscular contraction near his mouth; and that his expression of countenance is most doleful. He stands helplessly with the fiddle under one arm, and the sheaf of papers in his hands.

Let us buy one of his; and then go home, and look over a certain sheaf of our own gathering, of publications in the same humble, but not all unimportant, department of literature.

Recreated from The Belfast News-Letter, Belfast, January 12, 1852.

THE IRISH TENANT LEAGUE.

A meeting of the Tenant League was held last night in the Lecture Hall of the Mechanics' Institute, Lower Abbey-street. The attendance was most numerous and respectable, every part of the hall being densely crowded. The platform was occupied by a large number of the Catholic clergy, Presbyterian ministers, and other advocates of the tenant-right cause, who had for the last two days been attending the general meetings of the council of the League.

At shortly before eight o'clock, on the motion of the Rev. Mr. Dowling, P.P., the chair was taken by Patrick Lalor, Esq., of Tinnakil.

The Chairman having thanked the meeting for the honour conferred upon him by placing him in the chair on so important an occasion, requested permission to offer a few observations in explanation of the object for which they had been called together. Unfortunately, though the League had been in existence for three years, some people were, or affected to be, ignorant of its objects; and it was, therefore, necessary to state what those objects really were. It had been seen by those who had a feeling for the destitution of the people that the land was untilled, that the rents were unpaid, that the population was fast dwindling away—some in the poor houses, some starved to death or thrown into holes through the country, and others obliged to fly from their native land as from a ship on fire; and in such a state of things the Tenant League sprung up, mainly through the instrumentality of a gentleman who was not a native of this country, but who evinced the disposition of the best Irishman—Frederick Lucas (cheers). The people of the country did not assist as they ought in so humane an undertaking; but it was to be hoped that their lethargy was at length shaken off, and that in future every man, from the highest to the lowest, would put his shoulder to the wheel, and use his best efforts to forward the good cause (cheers). There being no manufactures in the country, land was the only article which afforded a means of livelihood to the people; and the consequence was that the competition for it was frightful, and people, in order to become possessed of it, were tempted to promise rents which they could not possibly pay. Yes, and in those instances where tenants made improvements they were, at the expiration of their leases, compelled either to pay increased rents or to submit to be turned out; and leave others to reap the advantage of their outlay (hear, hear). The natural consequence of such a state of things was, that no improvements were made at all—the land, in place of getting better, retrograded—the tenants were sinking, and the landlords themselves became vastly worse from the inability that existed to pay them their rents (hear, hear). That was the condition of this country when the potato blight appeared, and since then the bad consequences of the system had increased so fearfully that they were now almost intolerable (hear, and cheers). It was to remedy this condition that the Tenant League was organised; and the remedies proposed were—first, that there should be a valuation of the property of the country—a valuation beyond which no tenant would be permitted to pay, and no landlord to enforce, by law (hear, hear); and secondly, that there should be, if not a perpetuity, something very like it, that any person who improved his land should not be dispossessed until the value of his improvements was refunded to him by the landlord (cheers). If the people only willed it, they could carry both of those objects (hear, hear).—They were now on the eve of a general election—the Whigs were about to retire from the political stage for many years to come (cheers); and he would entreat of the people to be true to themselves at the election which such an event would lead to (hear, hear). They had it in their power to return whom they pleased, and if they did not do so they would have no right ever afterwards to complain, or to lay the blame of whatever might happen to them to any one but themselves. The chairman resumed his seat amid loud applause.

Recreated from The Freeman's Journal, Dublin, January 15, 1852.

ARREST OF A POOR RATE COLLECTOR.

A policeman from Tipperary arrived in town this morning for the purpose of conveying Richard Stokes, the party arrested on suspicion by Constable Duross, to Cashel. It appears that the prisoner was a collector of poor-rates in the Cashel union, and is a defaulter to a considerable extent. Informations were received against the prisoner, preparatory to his transmission to Cashel.—*Cork Examiner*.

Reprinted from The Waterford News, Waterford, January 16, 1852.

PROSELYTISM IN MAYO.

We have received a very interesting account of the visit paid by Mr. G. H. Moore, M.P., to the Monastery of St. Mary, Partree, an institution to which he had some time since given the munificent donation of thirty acres of land, with the power to the rev. founders of selecting the site from any portion of his estate at Partree which they pleased. We have also received a report of the address which he delivered to the people of the surrounding district, who had assembled to meet him upon the occasion, warning them against the snares which the proselytisers had laid for them, and pointing out the absurdity and folly of placing any reliance whatsoever upon the promises of men whose objects were of a nature so extremely questionable, and whose power of even continuing the bribes to their miserable dupes depended solely upon the uncertain tide of morbid religious zeal in England, the ebb or flow of which was altogether beyond even their interested reckoning.

We regret the pressure upon our space prevents the appearance of the report in our columns this morning, but we hope to present it to our readers in our next.

Reprinted from The Freeman's Journal, Dublin, January 17, 1852.

CULLENISM.—ANOTHER ROW IN THE DRUMKEERAN CHAPEL.—On Sunday, the 11th inst., such of the members of the constabulary as profess the Roman Catholic religion attended the chapel in Drumkeeran. When they were some time seated in the gallery, the Rev. P. Trainor, C.C., directed his attendant or assistant to inquire if sub-constable Walsh was in the house. On learning that Walsh was present, the priest addressed him in coarse terms, and said that as he was a Freemason he must leave the house. Walsh replied that unless the priest himself was a member of that ancient and loyal fraternity he could not pronounce him (Walsh) one.

A tempestuous scene followed Walsh's reply, the priest, in great excitement, calling out at intervals "Put him out!" Many of the hearers attempted to obey; and prominent among them, it is said, was a certain poor law guardian. Constable Reynolds and his men stood firm, however, and the reverend gentleman, seeing that Walsh was not to be dislodged, said, "Good people, I cannot celebrate mass while a Freemason is in the chapel."

He then left the house, followed by almost all the congregation, to a distance of thirty perches, where he celebrated mass in the open air in the midst of mud and filth. When the constable saw that all was quiet in the chapel, he marched his men to the barracks. The above statement we give nearly in the words of our correspondent, who adds, that this is not a solitary display of the reverend gentleman's propensities—that similar treatment was given by him to Sub-Inspector Mullen, and adds, "In fact the Protestants of this neighbourhood fear much that he will disturb the long and steady good feeling that has existed between them and their Roman Catholic brethren." It is said that, during the discussion, his reverence stated that he would as soon have the evil one in the chapel as a Freemason!—*Fermanagh Reporter*.

Recreated from The Belfast News-Letter, Belfast, January 19, 1852.

RIBBONISM IN THE COUNTY OF GALWAY.—EYRECOURT, JAN. 13.—There was a large attendance of magistrates at the Petty Sessions of Eyrecourt, this day, to investigate charges of a very serious nature brought against a pensioner, named Duane, residing on Lord Clanricarde's property at Meelick, near this town. It appears that some tenants on the Meelick property having got deeply into arrear (owing from two to five years' rent), the excellent and respectable agent of Lord Clanricarde was compelled to have recourse, in some instances, to ejectments. Among the respectable and affluent portion of Lord Clanricarde's tenantry were persons of the name Killeen, who, with the sanction of the landlord, had purchased, at a very high rate, the good-will, or, according to modern phraseology, the tenant-right of the out-going former occupiers. An English gentleman, an officer in the army, had lately erected a handsome sporting lodge, and laid out a considerable sum of money on a part of the Killeen's farm. All this outlay of money by an Englishman, and the increasing prosperity of the Killeen family, awakened the jealousies of the midnight legislators. Inflammatory placards were taken down on the first of this month, by the police, from the pier of the gate leading to the Franciscan Convent of Meelick, and others attached to trees close by. In those placards Captain Windham and the Killeens were held up as objects of public reprobation. About this time a pensioner, named Duane, residing at Meelick, went to the house of Patrick Killeen, who keeps a shop in the village, and asked for drink. Killeen declined giving any, as he saw the man had already taken a sufficient quantity. Duane then asked if "Windham and the Killeens had got enough of land as yet." He further said, that "he himself wanted land for his son;" "that Windham and the Killeens ought to be shot," or words to like effect. This occurred a day or two before the Ribbon notices were posted at the convent gate. The whole case underwent a long and strict examination before the magistrates, who decided on taking informations against Pensioner Duane. Informations were then sworn by Robert D'Arcy, Esq., agent to the Marquis of Clanricarde, by Patrick Killeen, of Meelick, and by the constable who took down the inflammatory placards from the convent gate pier. The magistrates did not deem it advisable to have the placards read out in court, but, with the informations, they have been forwarded to Government.

Recreated from The Belfast News-Letter, Belfast, January 19, 1852.

SATURDAY, JANUARY 24, 1852.

"To create and foster public opinion in Ireland, and to make it racy of the soil."—CHIEF BARON WOULFE.

THE JACQUERIE AND THE HANGMAN.

Oyez! Oyez! A Special Commission has been issued in the name of "Our Lady the Queen," to try sundry offenders against the Rights of Property in the Counties of Monaghan and Armagh. There is open war between landlord and tenant on the Ulster border. Half a dozen of "the better classes" have been slain, and a full score threatened with sudden death. Thousands of "the lower classes" have been turned out of house and home to starve, or to beg, or to go abroad. And some of them madly usurped the Lord's red right of vengeance for oppression of the poor. So down go the Chief Justices, BLACKBURNE, the Striker of Terror, and MONAHAN, the arrayer of juries, with a full *tenue* of constables, panels, and hangmen, to make "examples," and "vindicate the law." A mortal leprosy devours the very life of the country; and our paternal Government contributes two black caps and a hank of hemp to deal with it.

It is the politico-economic fashion of the day to view English crime in a statistical contrast of Cause and Effect, and to quote murder and burglary as proportionals to ignorance and pauperism. We wish some expert actuary would undertake to show in figures the same connection between Ejectment and Assassination—for it exists—and to demonstrate the exact relative forces of the two great integers, the crowbar and the bludgeon. It is as true as any deducible of the Norwich Tables that in some districts of Ireland, and in the two great classes of landlord and tenant, life is regulated less by seasons or diseases than by the number of ejectments which the Quarter Sessions issue, and the area of clearance effected.

Reprinted from The Nation, Dublin, January 24, 1852.

THE IRISH PEASANTRY.
(*By Eliza Cook.*)

Eliza Cook, the great English poetess, moralist, and republican, has been making a tour in Ireland, during the past Autumn. She has been among the Corkonians and thus describes them:—

I have rarely seen a finer set of peasants than were assembled in the streets of Cloyne that Sunday. I do not pretend to discuss the question of race here; but to a certainty these people are altogether unlike the peasantry of England, or indeed, of the northern and eastern parts of Ireland itself. In Leinster, Ulster, and even in Connaught, you will find many fair people, red-haired, brown, or flaxen, with blue eyes; but here in Cloyne, the men and women were all dark, some swarthy, many even dusky, as you observe among the people of the south of Europe. Such beautiful women! with lustrous black eyes, finely arched eyebrows, long penciled eyelashes, and hair black as the raven's wing.

There is a grandness of gait, too, about these peasant girls, a freedom and ease, a dignified grace and witchery of manner, even though they be but peasant girls, which is infinitely fascinating. The peasant men were fine looking fellows, too, very swarthy and dark. There was an air of comfort and respectability about them greater than I have seen in any other district, and on the whole, there was a comparatively smaller sprinkling of beggars, though no Irish village, not even Cloyne, can be said to be free of such.

The language of the peasantry hereabout, and indeed, nearly all over Munster, is Irish, or Celtic; and though most of them know English, they speak it in a halting and imperfect manner, as if it were a foreign tongue to them.

The long cloaks of the women, and the great coats of the men, which they wear alike in summer and winter, were as common in many districts of Ireland three hundred years ago, as they are now. Edmund Spencer, the poet, refers to the dress at some length, in his "View of the State of Ireland," published in 1526; and he saw in the mantle a garment descended from a very remote antiquity. With most of the women, it is the principal article of their wardrobe, and it must be confessed that they wear it with both dignity and grace. An Irish girl shows as much art in the management and drapery of her mantle, and in the coy arrangement of her hood, as the Spanish donna does in the handling of her fan. And to see one of their hooded faces, set off by glossy black hair braided round a small delicately formed head, is indeed, a comely and fascinating sight. In Kerry, a district of Munster further west, the white linen is occasionally observed.—One day, we met a fine young woman, carrying a heavy wicker basket of stuffs upon her head, draped in one of these ancient mantles. Her feet were bare, and she was without bonnet or cap, but the folds of her white robe fell about her figure as gracefully as the drapery of a Grecian statue, and gave to the humble girl an inconceivably elegant look, notwithstanding her menial occupation.

Recreated from The Waterford News, Waterford, January 30, 1852.

LIGHTING ENNISCORTHY WITH GAS.

(*From the Wexford Independent.*)

On Monday last the Town Commissioners and other friends of social improvement resident in Enniscorthy, dined together at Nuzum's Hotel, in order to celebrate the interesting event of lighting the town with gas.

It is a gratifying reflection to the mind of the true patriot and philanthropist, that even this town—once the theatre in days long past, and we hope never to return, of stern political and sectarian strife—has now become an oasis in the moral desert, where men of every variety of sentiment can combine as citizens of the world and Christians, for the promotion of the public good, and the true interests of their naturally favoured, but alas too long neglected locality.

Thirty public lamps have already been lighted, and nearly all the people of business have introduced gas into their establishments. Nuzum's Hotel—where the public dinner took place, was brilliantly illuminated for the occasion—and a magnificent star composed of 470 lights, would have shed its lustre on the front of the building, but it blew nearly a hurricane the whole evening; and as gas figures of this nature cannot be protected by any glass shield, the Proprietors of the Works were compelled to extinguish it. At six o'clock, nearly sixty gentlemen sat down to dinner, the chair being ably filled by **THOMAS POUNDER**, Esq.

Recreated from The Waterford News, Waterford, January 30, 1852.

DUBLIN POLICE—YESTERDAY.

ATTACKING A BAKER'S CART.—James Cain was brought up in custody of Constable John Rourke, 197 A. The constable stated that between seven and eight o'clock that morning, in Lower Exchange-street, a crowd of upwards of one hundred persons consisting mostly of wretched-looking ragged boys, had stopped a baker's cart, or van, laden with bread, and were attempting to pull the baskets filled with loaves off it when he came up, and having secured the prisoner, who appeared to be the ringleader of the occasion, the rest scampered off in various directions.

The prisoner was sentenced by Mr. Magee, the presiding magistrate, to a month's imprisonment with hard labour in Richmond Bridewell.

Recreated from The Freeman's Journal, Dublin, February 3, 1852.

THE QUEEN'S SPEECH—OPENING OF PARLIAMENT.

The speech from the throne on Tuesday, last, being the production of LORD JOHN RUSSELL and company, as our readers are aware, contains little, if anything at all, to raise the hopes of unfortunate Ireland. Not one word of consolation for this portion of the united kingdom. Her Majesty's attention has been drawn to the state of crime in our northern counties, and will continue to be directed to that object with the view of repressing it by the prompt exercise of existing laws.

This, to be sure, is all very good; but is it not strange that her Majesty's attention would not, at the same time, be drawn to the impoverished state of the country, for the purpose of recommending salutary measures calculated to sustain its broken-hearted and skeleton population? *But* it is not strange that the allusion made to Ireland, to which we have referred, should be the only one in her Majesty's speech when we consider the quarter from which it emanated—from the cabinet of the "base bloody and cruel Whigs", with the father of the Ecclesiastical Titles Bill at its head.

Nothing to cheer the Irish subject on through his life of labour and unexampled penury. But the laws of Great Britain will be rigorously enforced for the suppression of crime which ill-advised legislation has mainly created.

Recreated from The Waterford News, Waterford, February 6, 1852.

OPENING OF PARLIAMENT.

Her Majesty left the Palace shortly after two o'clock, and having entered the House, delivered the following speech;—

MY LORDS AND GENTLEMEN,

The period is arrived when, according to usage, I can again avail myself of your advice and assistance in the preparation and adoption of measures which the welfare of the country may require. I continue to retain the most friendly relations with foreign powers. The complicated affairs of the Duchies of Holstein and Schleswig are continuing to engage my attention. I have every reason to expect that the treaty between Germany and Denmark, which was concluded at Berlin in the year before last, will, in a short time be fully and completely executed. I regret that the war which unfortunately broke out on the East frontier of the Cape of Good Hope more than a year ago, still continues. Papers will be laid before you shortly full of information as to the progress of the war, and the measures which have been taken for bringing it to a termination. I have observed with sincere satisfaction the tranquillity which has prevailed throughout the greater portion of Ireland; but it is with much regret that I have to inform you that certain parts of the counties of Armagh, Monaghan, and Louth have been marked by the commission of outrages of most serious descriptions. The powers of the existing laws have been promptly exerted for the detection of the offenders, and for the repression of a system of crimes and vice fatal to the best interests of the country. My attention will be directed to this important object.

MYSTERIOUS DEATH OF A FEMALE—CORONER'S INQUEST.

Yesterday Dr. Kirwan, one of the city coroners, held an inquest at M'Quaide-bridge, on the Grand Canal, Grand Canal-street, on the body of Jane Timmins, aged eighteen years. The circumstances under which it was very generally reported the deceased, an extremely good looking young woman, had come by her death had excited considerable sensation in the locality, so that notwithstanding the heavy rain that continued to pour without intermission throughout the day, dense crowds of persons remained congregated during the investigation in the immediate neighbourhood of the house in which the inquest was held. William Archer, aged about twenty-one years, a working jeweller by trade, and resident at 6, Pleasant-view, Irishtown, was present at the inquest in custody of the police under Mr. Inspector Reilly, of the B division.

A respectable jury having been sworn the following witnesses were examined:—

Constable Edward Hughes, 109 B, deposed that he was on duty on the previous night in that neighbourhood and round the basin of the canal; between one and two o'clock that morning he was coming out of Albert-street when he observed a man and a woman standing on the footway; he heard the woman say very distinctly—"You know well that I have no place to go to;" he did not well hear the answer made to this; they then walked away arm-and-arm and at a quick pace in the direction of the canal; they were in his view all the time till they came to this house (that in which the inquest was held), when they passed out of his sight for a minute or two; after that he heard a scream given; the scream seemed as if occasioned by fright or a blow; witness judged it to be that of a female; it occurred to him at the time that she was in the water; he ran

(cont'd)

as quickly as possible in the direction whence the scream proceeded; on arriving at this house he met the prisoner (whom he identified); he was coming from the water side; he did not seem to be much alarmed, though he should have heard the scream; no other person appeared at or near the place at the time; witness asked him where the female was who had come up that way in his company; the other then appeared a little alarmed and said, "Oh, policeman, come here and I will show you where she jumped into the canal;" witness went with him to where he pointed out a place at the rere of this house; there was a boat lying near the bank, on which witness got, accompanied by the prisoner; found a pole in the boat, and searched for the body with it, but without success; he then left the place, and as he had some suspicion of foul play, he took the prisoner with him to the station-house; having left him there, he again returned to the boat to make a closer examination; he continued searching from about two o'clock, a.m., till five, a.m., when he found the body within about two yards from the spot pointed out by the prisoner; the remains were placed on the bank, for the purpose of identification.

In answer to Mr. Inspector Reilly as to whether the prisoner manifested any feeling or anxiety about the drowned woman's fate, the witness replied, "Not the slightest."

In reply to a Juror, the prisoner positively declared he did not throw the deceased into the canal. She ran away from him, and leaped in herself. He had never seen her before that night.

To another Juror—He said he met her at the gate of the Railway Company's Works, and she told him that she lived in the town, but after they had walked as far as Sir Patrick Dun's Hospital, she said she lived at Beggar's Bush; he said that he would see her home, and they proceeded together as far as the canal, where she broke from him, and endeavoured to throw herself into the water, but was prevented doing so by a stone wall about four feet high, and which ran along the banks of the Basin for a few yards; he caught hold of her and pulled her off the wall, when she again broke from him, and, running along the bank for a short distance, threw herself in; he ran after her, and endeavoured to catch hold of her, she was, however, already in the water; he called out "Hoy, hoy," to try to attract attention of any person who might be passing by, and seeing a policeman on the bridge, he informed him of the circumstances; was sure that he addressed the policeman first.

Constable Hughes was recalled, and stated most positively that he had questioned the prisoner as to what became of the female who had been in his company before the prisoner said a word to him.

Prisoner—I spoke to you first, and then we both got into the boat.

Constable—It was I who spoke to you first; I am on my oath.

In reply to a question, the prisoner stated that the deceased, while in his company, had not made use of the expression "I have no place to go to;" he was not intoxicated at the time, but had partaken of some drink with his brother, in Abbey-street, before returning home; he was on his way to his lodgings when he met the deceased; the latter was then in a very excited state, and was sighing and sobbing all the time she was in his company, which was not altogether more than ten minutes.

Mr. James Clarke, 5, Nash-terrace, Donnybrook, deposed that the deceased had been in his employment as general servant for about one year and eight months; until within a short period she had been an extremely well-conducted girl, but about two months since he heard that she had made an acquaintance with a soldier named Prentice, a private in the 27th regiment, stationed at Beggar's-bush Barracks; from that period she frequently made excuses for going out; especially in the evenings when the family were engaged; she would on these occasions slip out by the garden; deeming it his duty to ascertain the character of the man with whom she had thus formed an acquaintance, and meeting the adjutant of the regiment one day in the vicinity of the new road, he spoke to him on the subject; the adjutant told him that the man was one of the worst moral characters in the regiment, and desired him to keep him away from his house; on his (witness's) return home he went to the kitchen where deceased and her mother were, and he informed them of the character he had received of Prentice; he then reasoned with deceased on the impropriety of her conduct, and begged her to break off his acquaintance; this she promised to do; since that she was frequently out at night, contrary to his express demands; on last evening he and his family remained up later than usual; on going up stairs his sister-in-law called to her (deceased), and desired her to make haste to bed; the other answered, and said she would; his sister waited for some time, and the girl not having come, she went back to ascertain the reason of the delay; on entering the kitchen she found that deceased had slacked the fire there, put out the candle, and gone out by the back door, which she had closed after her; supposing that she had gone out for a moment she retired to her bedroom, and sat there till about three o'clock, a.m., when thinking possibly deceased had passed the night in some of the neighbouring houses, she went to bed, but on awakening at six o'clock in the morning she repaired to his (witness's) apartment, and told him that the servant had not been in the house all night. He rose and went to the kitchen, and there on the table he found the following paper:—

"Mr. Clarke—I am sure that you will never have an opportunity of seeing me again, as I am intended to put an end to my life, and for the sake of James Prentice; God forgive him, for I have found out at last that he was a blackguard; and I am heartily sorry I did not take your advice. Tell my mother that I did not get out in time, or I would have seen her before I was drowned."

Mr. James Arnold Clarke (son of the preceding witness) deposed that he was acquainted with the deceased's handwriting; to the best of his belief, the writing in that paper was in her hand; at about half-past eleven o'clock on the previous night he saw her, and she then appeared to be slightly under the influence of drink; he had seen her intoxicated once before; that was on the Sunday before Christmas Day; he never saw the prisoner previous to this inquiry; he had never seen Prentice about the house.

Surgeon Porter stated that he had examined the body; no marks of violence appeared on it except a slight scratch on the left knee, and which might have been caused by the wall, against which she came in contact in endeavouring to throw herself into the water as described by the prisoner. In his opinion death had resulted from drowning. She did not appear to have at all struggled in the water.

The jury, after a lengthened deliberation, returned the following verdict:—

"We find that Jane Timmin's death was caused by drowning in the Grand Canal, near M'Quaid's-bridge, on the morning of the 2d February, 1852. Whether this was her own act, or that of others, we are not able to say, from the evidence which has come before us, but we entertain some suspicion that William Archer the prisoner now before us, was in some way accessory to her death. We therefore recommend his being sent for trial at the ensuing commission."

The Coroner at once granted a warrant for his committal accordingly, and the prisoner was removed in custody of Inspector Reilly, for the transmission to Richmond Bridewell.

Recreated from The Waterford News, Waterford, February 6, 1852.

THE SUBMARINE TELEGRAPH BETWEEN ENGLAND AND IRELAND.

We understand that the arrangements for carrying out this important undertaking are now nearly completed, and that there is no longer a doubt that Ireland will, in May next, not only possess the same advantages of internal electric communication as England, and Scotland, but also be enabled to communicate directly with all the principal towns in those kingdoms. Mr. Charles West, the engineer of the Irish Submarine Telegraph Company, has been in Dublin for some days—he has decided upon bringing the telegraph to Howth, in preference to Kingstown, or any other part of the coast. This selection is made in consequence of the advantage of a bold deep shore in that locality, and of its being out of the track of vessels anchoring, and the trawling of fishing boats. It was for some time a matter of consideration whether the Submarine Telegraph Company should carry their wires from Donaghadee to Portpatrick, but after carefully weighing all attendant circumstances, it was found that the advantage of a shorter sea distance was more than counterbalanced by numerous obstacles contingent upon that route. In the first place, from the nature of the soundings and the shelving shores, the wires would be less secure than they will be in the deeper water between Holyhead and Howth. This, of itself, would prove a fatal objection, even if there were not other difficulties in the way. Secondly, there is no railway within forty to fifty miles of Portpatrick, and there is no established line of telegraph within double that distance. Consequently, although the distance by sea is shorter, yet there must be nearly ninety miles of telegraph erected on shore, of which fifty are without the protection of a railway. These and other circumstances have decided the Irish Submarine Telegraph Company to cross the Channel from Holyhead, where the wires of the Electric Telegraph Company (with which the Submarine Company ia in exclusive connection), are already established.

The directors of the Electric Telegraph Company are also in negotiation for the erection of their telegraph along the various lines of railway in Ireland, and propose to have a central station in Dublin, in connection with the Submarine Company, with wire radiating to the termini of the different Irish metropolitan railways. Thus, when these arrangements are completed, Belfast, Londonderry, Coleraine and all the principal towns in the north, and Cork, Limerick, Waterford, and Clonmel in the south, will be able, as well as Dublin, to communicate direct with London, Liverpool, Manchester, Glasgow, and all the principal places of business in Great Britain. There is no question but that some port on the western coast of Ireland will ultimately become a North American Packet Station, and no circumstance is more calculated to expedite the event than the establishment of such a net-work of telegraph as is now described—for whatever differences of opinion may exist as to the saving to be effected from landing and embarking mails and passengers on that coast, there can be no dispute as to the speed at which intelligence can be conveyed to or from a western port by the telegraph. At the present time, when a packet arrives at Liverpool, London and all the principal towns in England, are at once, and simultaneously, advised of the state of the markets, &c., whereas Belfast, with its vast manufacturing interests, Cork with its corn trade, and, in fact, every town in Ireland, is now shut out from all such advantages, and has to wait for 24 hours after England has had, and *discounted* the news. The introduction of the telegraph will at once level this distinction.

The Earl of Howth has, in the most prompt and handsome manner already given his sanction to the company to make use of his land in conveying the telegraph from the shore to the railway terminus at Howth. The Directors of the Dublin and Drogheda Railway Company, have also expressed their desire to afford the Submarine Telegraph Company every facility and assistance in carrying out this national object.

Recreated from The Freeman's Journal, Dublin, February 7, 1852.

THE MISSIONARY POLICE—
DOINGS IN TUAM.

We regret to learn from the subjoined correspondence that the authorities in Tuam are still resolved on using the police force of that district as an auxiliary force in aid of the Exeter Hall missionaries who have invaded that locality in the vain hope of proselytizing the Catholic population.

The following is the communication to which we advert:—

(FROM A CORRESPONDENT.)

Tuam, February 5.

The emissaries of Exeter-hall are determined to leave no effort untried in seeking to annoy those parts of the country which have withstood, and are still resolved to withstand, their stupid, as well as insane, attacks upon the consciences of the famine-stricken poor. One would have thought that the disgraceful and damaging notoriety their proceedings have obtained here of late would have acted as a warning to these misguided men, and saved the poor from further trouble; but it seems they are resolved to persevere.

Some unpleasant circumstances have occurred here within the last few days which should be made public and exposed in their deformity. Notice was given last week of the intention of the Rev. Mr. (*alias* Captain) Dallas to preach a lecture in the Protestant church. Kind, but insulting, invitations to attend were issued to several Roman Catholics. Wednesday evening was the night fixed for this lecture. On the previous evenings placards and tracts of an offensive kind were thrust, I am told, into several houses without the knowledge of the occupants. In accordance with this invitation, a large concourse of people went in a body towards the church, where the stipendiary magistrate was found stationed with a body of some sixty policemen in military array.

As I was not present on the occasion, I cannot state with accuracy what occurred; but I am informed that, in consequence of some manifestations of dissatisfaction at this exclusion, and some groans against the Bible-readers, the resident magistrate arrested some of the children or boys present. This led to further symptoms of discontent on the part of the people. The result was, that the resident magistrate read the riot act.

'Tis not easy to say where this might have ended had not one of the Catholic clergy of the town speedily come up, at whose representations the people quietly retired to their homes. One of the Bible-readers struck a poor countryman who had nothing to do in the transaction a blow, from the effects of which he is suffering severely. Here is more of the skull-cracking in Tuam. Several persons have been arrested and imprisoned by order of the resident magistrate. As these cases will come on for trial on Monday next I will offer no observation.

All I will say for the present is, that in the opinion of every honest and thinking man in the town and neighbourhood, both Protestant and Catholic, the chief parties to blame in the present system of annoyance and excitement are the Lord Bishop of Tuam and the Rev. Mr. Seymour. What right have they to continue to insult, by offensive and intrusive placards, the feelings of the Catholics? And when smarting under the influence of these insults some of them hoot or groan obnoxious parties they are at once taken up and sent to gaol by a paid magistrate, who only seems too willing to lend his services. The government police force sent down here seem to have no other object than to aid in furthering the plans of Exeter Hall, and acting as a shield of defence to its emissaries. More of this again.

Recreated from The Freeman's Journal, Dublin, February 7, 1852.

ACCIDENTAL DEATH.

[From our Dungarvan Correspondent.]

On the 13th instant Mr Thomas Ahearn, of Ballymacarberry (poor-rate collector) was on his way home, when his horse became restive, and ran off with him.—One of his legs got fast in the stirrup, the horse ran at full speed, when the unfortunate man was dragged at a considerable distance along the road. When his body was found, next morning, so disfigured was it that his friends could hardly recognise it.

LIGHTING LISMORE.

We are happy to perceive that the people of Lismore are about establishing a Gas Manufactory, for the purpose of lighting their beautiful and picturesque town. When the project has the sanction of the Duke of DEVONSHIRE, and the active exertions of Mr. E. CURRY, there is no doubt but it will succeed.

In the name of wonder, what are the shopkeepers and people of Dungarvan about? Do they always intend to live in darkness? Why not burn gas as well as Enniscorthy, New Ross, Lismore, &c.

Reprinted from The Waterford News, Waterford, February 13, 1852.

THE GALWAY PACKET STATION.

THE PREMIER AND THE BELFAST DEPUTATIONS.—The following are the most important points dwelt on in the able statement laid before Lord John Russell, by the Belfast deputations:—We have the honour of addressing your lordship on behalf of the town council, harbour commissioners, and the Chamber of Commerce of Belfast, and of laying before you their opinions with regard to the establishment of an Irish Transatlantic packet station; a measure, as they believe, of vast importance, not only to themselves and to Ireland, but to the British empire. The first point to which we beg most respectfully to direct you lordship's attention is the telegraphic communication between the old world and the new. The sailing distance from Liverpool to New York is 3,045 miles; from Galway to Halifax, 2,160 miles; from Galway to Canso 2,006 miles. On the American side a telegraph is already in operation from New York to Halifax. In Ireland, the Midland Railway Company are laying down wires from Galway to Dublin; and a proposition is before the public to submerge them between Dublin and Holyhead; but whether this shall be carried out or not, it is determined to extend this means of communication from Dublin to Belfast, and thence to Scotland, by means of a submarine telegraph across the channel, thus transmitting intelligence from Ireland throughout Great Britain. By this means, and with Galway as an Irish Transatlantic packet station, a saving of four or four and a-half days might be effected in conveying news to and from Europe and the western hemisphere.

Recreated from The Freeman's Journal, Dublin, February 14, 1852.

DESTRUCTION OF LAGOS BY THE AFRICAN SQUADRON.

Her Majesty's steam-frigate Sampson, 6, Captain L. T. Jones, put into Lisbon on the 11th instant for coals, and transferred her despatches and mails to the Royal Mail packet Severn. She communicated the fact of the total destruction of Lagos by the boats of the African squadron. It is understood that these hostilities were undertaken in consequence of the refusal of the king or chief of that place to sign a treaty for the effectual suppression of the slave trade in his dominions. It was accordingly determined to attack Lagos, and, after two day's fighting, the object was accomplished, and the place destroyed, an immense number of the natives being killed. The chief or king has also been deposed, and another one substituted.

THE SEARCH FOR SIR JOHN FRANKLIN.—News has been received of her Majesty's ship Enterprise, dispatched in search of Sir John Franklin. She reached Cape Prince of Wales on the 3rd of July, where they found the Plover, much shaken from her third winter's sojourn in those regions. The Plover had not found any traces of Sir John Franklin. She brought back Assistant-Surgeon Adams, and the Seamen of the Enterprise who were left with Lieutenant Barnard at Port Michelouski, to inquire into the truth of an Indian report, to the effect that white men in distress had been seen on the source of the Darabin River, but they had heard nothing of Sir John Franklin.

Recreated from The Belfast News-Letter, Belfast, February 20, 1852.

THE HOUSE OF COMMONS denied, by a majority of 229 to 137, that the dealings of Lord CLARENDON with the press were of a nature "calculated to weaken the authority of the Government, and to reflect discredit upon the administration of public affairs." To that verdict we attach no moral weight, even though four representatives of this country were found amongst the majority, and three of the four took a prominent position in the debate. It was the verdict of partisanship, and not the pronouncement of conscience—in support of the grossest and most dangerous system of corruption, and not in the vindication of public morality. By that verdict Lord CLARENDON was "whitewashed," not absolved from guilt. It cannot make the slightest impression upon the conscience of the country, or blot out one tittle of the damning record which now belongs to the history of the administration of the law in Ireland by an English Viceroy. Let Lord CLARENDON be ever so embalmed in the praises of his admirers, ever so creditably associated with Practical Instructors, or industrial movements, still he is indissolubly connected and identified with flagrant and brazen corruption—corruption of the very fountain-source of public opinion.

On which side lies the truth? Fact, conscience, and common sense proclaim, that of the minority. Just remember the description given, by the counsel employed by the Government, in the Court of Queen's Bench, of the journal subsidised by the VICEROY. The journal was described as "an assassin press," and its conductor in language too painful to repeat. And Mr. ROCHE, who voted against the proposition, branded the paper as "an infamous journal." Nay, even so disreputable did Lord CLARENDON seem to view the whole transaction, that, after having given £1,700 to the journalist for his defense of "law and order," he paid, and out of his own pocket, it is now asserted, £2,000 more, as hush money, and to prevent the publication of letters which BIRCH had in his possession, and which, we are at liberty to assume, would have fully disclosed that hateful system which was indicated in the note of Mr. CORRY CONNELLAN, who practically edited the *World*, inasmuch as he constantly supplied it with valuable hints, as to what subject could best be turned "to account," and what person or party could be most beneficially attacked. "The *morale* of this might be well applied to MITCHELL and Co.," writes Mr. CORRY CONNELLAN, who on various occasion assures his "dear" friend Mr. BIRCH of the gratitude and admiration of his noble principal. Mr. BIRCH appears in the light of the confidential adviser of the Irish Viceroy, and the hand-and-glove associate of his official underling; and his journal is known to be the constant assailant of every man who entertains an opinion against the Government of Lord CLARENDON.—And when it comes out that all this had been a matter of bargain and sale—that Lord CLARENDON was the soul, the spirit, the mind, the very volition of this same journal, and the undisputed master of its nominal conductor—is the public to be told—or is the public to *believe*—that a transaction of this kind was not "calculated to reflect discredit on the administration of public affairs?"

Recreated from The Cork Examiner, Cork, February 23, 1852.

The Freeman's Journal

THE FALLEN CABINET.

Russell has fallen, and Clarendon has fallen, and the Whig cabinet now lies in Downing-street a despicable wreck capable of doing no more mischief to the country, and awaiting only the formal entry of its successor to be flung out to rot and perish. The news of the short-lived victory of corruption, achieved by government promises and court canvass, on Thursday night, had hardly reached this kingdom, and Lord Clarendon and his associates had hardly time to commence their revels at Dublin Castle, when the electric wires bid them hold—and announced that their hour of retribution had arrived.

It has come—and though it may bring months, and, perhaps, years, of trial and conflict for this country, we hail its arrival with joy—we gladly accept the penalty; and the country will cheerfully meet the trials it will have to endure under a Derby administration, and be borne through them all by the proud consciousness that by her have guilt, and perfidy, and treason, been signally punished.

Russell has fallen, and Clarendon has fallen, and they have fallen by Irish hands. To the Irish representatives is due the credit of avenging the wrongs of the past, and of vindicating the principle of religious liberty by expelling from office and from power the men who belied all their former promises, betrayed all their former friends, and laid violent hands on the very principles they had most solemnly sworn to defend.

Ireland has driven the Whigs from office. She has cast off that double-tongued Ligurian—Clarendon—and by maintaining the same attitude whereby this has been accomplished, she can defy the worst enemies that may arise, and in good time lay them, too, prostrate in the dust, if they take not warning from the fate of the base and treacherous Whigs.

Recreated from The Freeman's Journal, Dublin, February 23, 1852.

(*From an Extra Edition of the Dublin Telegraph.*)

LONDON, SATURDAY AFTERNOON.

The Russell Cabinet has been shattered to pieces by the cleverly devised tactics of Lord Palmerston and the Irish Brigade. By a majority of eleven votes the House of Commons declared, to use Lord J. Russell's own words, that "at a time of very serious import, and with regard to a very serious question," they had no longer confidence in his administration. One hundred and thirty-six members, including many old Whig allies, endorsed this damning admission; and the eleven of the Brigade, who turned the scale, and gave true significance to this vote, are the following:—M. J. Blake, Oliver Grace, Henry Grattan, John Green, O. Higgins, Robert Keating, Wm. Keough, Sir Timothy O'Brien, Anthony O'Flaherty, John Sadleir, Michael Sullivan.

When the House broke up last night all the Ministers went to Earl Grey's Mansion, in Carlton Terrace. They remained in consultation up to 12 o'clock.

It is said the Duke of Wellington was called to the counsels of the Sovereign this afternoon, and that he recommended her Majesty to send immediately for Lord Derby. After the Cabinet Council, which was held to-day at the Foreign Office, Lord J. Russell went to Buckingham Palace, and remained closeted with the Queen nearly two hours.

Recreated from The Belfast News-Letter, Belfast, February 23, 1852.

LORD DERBY TO FORM NEW CABINET.

LORD DERBY has had an audience of her Majesty, and has undertaken the formation of a Cabinet. This will occasion no surprise, as it has long been evident that some new Ministerial combination must be effected. The similarity which at first sight appears to exist between the present Ministerial resignation and the crisis of 1851 is only superficial and casual.

On both occasions, Lord John Russell threw up office suddenly, after a defeat, in a thin House, on a point of secondary importance.

On both occasions, also, the manner of resignation indicated a mixture of pique and management on the part of the Premier. But, last year, it was his object to anticipate Lord Derby's preparations, and to satisfy the Crown, the country, and the malcontent adherents of his own party, that no other combination than the old Whig league could, at the moment, conduct the administration.

The scheme so far succeeded that it led to the recall of the ex-Ministers, and to the exposure of Lord Derby's intrinsic weakness; but it failed altogether in rallying the Liberal majority of the House of Commons round their former leader.

The second resignation might be thought equally insecure, if the causes which led to it had been less obvious and substantial than they are. A return to office, at the present moment, would not shelter Lord Grey from censure, nor would it make the new scheme for enfranchising rotten boroughs popular or tenable. There was an evident convenience in resigning on a point which few have troubled themselves to understand, in which no important principle was involved; and a falling ministry seldom waits for defeat on a vital question. There can be little doubt that the withdrawal of Lord John Russell from office is, for the present, definite and final.—*Morning Chronicle.*

Recreated from The Cork Examiner, Cork, February 25, 1852.

HOUSE OF COMMONS—
MONDAY.

MINISTERIAL STATEMENT.

At five o'clock the body of the house was completely filled. All the members of the government were present, as well as the chief members of the Opposition. We noticed that Mr. Disraeli, Mr. Gladstone, and Major Beresford were particularly restless. They frequently left their seats and entered into conversation with political colleagues in different parts of the house. The entrance of Lord John Russell was a signal for loud cries of "hear, hear," and cheers. Lord Palmerston took his seat on the great bench past the gangway, but was not noticed on entering. The noise and confusion in the house until Lord John Russell rose was so great, that the members who took part in the discussion on private business were scarcely heard in the gallery.

Lord J. RUSSELL rose and said—Sir, after the occurrence of last Friday night the house will be prepared for the announcement I have now to make (hear, hear.)—At a meeting of her Majesty's servants on Saturday, we considered what course it was incumbent upon us to pursue ; it appeared to us that it was impossible to carry on satisfactorily the business of the government in this house after the events of the preceding night. We considered the alternative of advising her Majesty to use her prerogative of dissolving the parliament, but we considered that there were such grave objections to such a course, that we ultimately declined to recommend it to her Majesty. We, therefore, determined to lay our resignation before her Majesty, which I accordingly did in the course of the afternoon (hear, hear.) Her Majesty was graciously pleased to accept our resignation, and has since sent for my Lord Derby, who is understood to have undertaken the task of framing a Government (opposition cheers). We therefore merely hold office until our successors are appointed (hear, hear).

RESIGNATION OF MINISTERS.

LORD JOHN RUSSELL is out! We think we hear our readers clap their hands in joy and exclaim, "Thank God!"—*Catholic Standard.*

Reprinted from The Waterford News, Waterford, February 27, 1852.

ADDRESS TO THE LORD LIEUTENANT.

On Monday a deputation from the Council of the Chamber of Commerce waited upon his Excellency the Lord Lieutenant, to present to him the annexed address on his retirement from the government of this country—

TO HIS EXCELLENCY GEORGE WILLIAM FREDERICK VILLIERS EARL OF CLARENDON, LORD LIEUTENANT GENERAL, AND GENERAL GOVERNOR OF IRELAND.

MAY IT PLEASE YOUR EXCELLENCY.

We, the President, Vice-Presidents, and Council of the Chamber of Commerce, Dublin, approach your Excellency on your retirement from the government of this country, to express our grateful acknowledgements for the anxious zeal, and the eminent judgement with which your Excellency has endeavoured to promote the industry and trade of Ireland, during your distinguished and arduous administration.

Called to the high and responsible office of Lord Lieutenant at a period of unprecedented difficulty, you found the entire population of this country prostrated by a visitation unparalleled in the history of the civilised world; and, while with indomitable courage you encountered the great emergency, and endeavoured to alleviate distress and relieve destitution, you saw with the prescience of a statesman that under Providence, the regeneration of Ireland mainly depended on her own exertions.

Influenced by this conviction, your Excellency has constantly seized every occasion to inculcate the duties of self-reliance, of persevering industry, and of prudent enterprise—while you never omitted an opportunity of fostering, by your patronage, and promoting by your influence, every undertaking calculated to develop the resources and encourage the struggling energies of our country.

For services such as these your Excellency is entitled to the gratitude of every lover of his country.

In now respectfully taking leave of your Excellency, we venture to express an humble hope and a confident trust, that, though removed from amongst us, your Excellency will continue to regard with interest this scene of your honourable labours, and that we may still be permitted to recognise in your Excellency the friend and benefactor of Ireland.

Signed by desire and on behalf of the President, Vice-Presidents, and Council of the Chamber of Commerce of Dublin,

ARTHUR GUINNESS, President.
FRANCEIS CODD, Honorary Secretary.

ANSWER.

GENTLEMEN,—I am most thankful to you for this record of your good opinion and kind feelings. The highest reward to which a public man can aspire is the approbation of his fellow-countrymen, and to receive such a testimonial from the Chamber of Commerce of Dublin, composed as it is of men perfectly acquainted with the true interests of Ireland, and actively engaged in promoting them, fulfills every object of my ambition, and will always be remembered by me with mingled feelings of pride and gratitude.

On my appointment to the office, which I have had the honour to fill for nearly five years, the difficulties which beset the government were, doubtless, of no ordinary character; it was the will of Providence that Ireland should be afflicted by a calamity, unparalleled for its extent and duration, and unparalleled also for the patience and resignation with which it was borne; but widespread ruin, not unnaturally, engendered feelings of despair, and the national energies were paralysed and prostrated.

It then appeared to me that my official position be turned to useful account; and, although I had not the presumption to think that I occupied the chair of practical wisdom, which, according to the happy expression in your address, should be the seat of authority, yet I resolved to miss no opportunity of declaring, in the frank language of conviction, that the government and legislature might, and ought, to alleviate the sufferings of the people, but that the real and only remedy for the misfortunes of Ireland would be found in that spirit of exertion and self-reliance, which necessity seldom fails to evoke in manly minds, and the firm determination to overcome, and not be conquered by difficulties, however appalling. I had no claim to influence public opinion, but I hoped to turn public attention towards what I believed to be for the good of all. The advice which, as a friend, I took the liberty to offer, was received in a corresponding spirit; and it is to that rather than to any efforts of mine, that we now owe the satisfaction of knowing that the energies of Irishman have been roused, that the national resources are better developed, and that the industrial progress of the country is placed upon a sounder and more permanent basis.

DEPARTURE OF THE LORD LIEUTENANT.

This morning, at half-past seven o'clock, his Excellency the Lord Lieutenant took his final leave at the Castle, and, accompanied by the Countess of Clarendon and their children, proceeded to the railway station at Westland-row where they were received by Mr. Magee, Chairman, Mr. George Row, and several of the directors of the Kingstown Railway Company, the Lord Chancellor and Mrs. Brady, Sir Phillip Crampton, Bart., and a numerous assemblage of persons of the first rank in the city. A special train having been prepared, his Excellency was conducted to the carriage appointed for his reception, and at a few minutes before eight o'clock the noble Earl was on board the *Prince Arthur* steamer, and in a few minutes more was on his way across the channel to Holyhead, having bade farewell to many sorrowing friends, and this country, whose prosperity he had zealously laboured to promote.—*Dublin Evening Post of Yesterday.*—Joy be with him!

Recreated from The Cork Examiner, Cork, March 3, 1852.

CENSUS OF IRELAND FOR THE YEARS 1841 AND 1851.
SKIBBEREEN UNION.

County of Cork Electoral Divisions.	Area. A. R. P.			Population in 1841	Population in 1851
Aghadown, North	3110	0	1	1636	913
Aghadown, South	5080	0	36	3566	2188
Breedagh	4410	1	20	1785	1108
Caheragh	6033	1	29	1839	1164
Cape Clear	3889	3	3	2755	1916
Carrigbawn	5079	2	23	2071	890
Castlehaven, North	6447	1	33	4058	2209
Castlehaven, South	4596	0	9	2413	1698
Cloghdonnell	5738	0	13	2182	1308
Clounkeen	4642	1	19	1892	1034
Drinagh	4395	0	38	1278	671
Dromdaleague, North	6089	1	37	1015	526
Dromdaleague, South	5025	1	12	1852	1001
Gurranes	5259	3	29	1468	801
Gurtnascreena	6831	3	6	1972	1131
Kilfaughnabeg	2934	3	30	1892	1241
Killeenleigh	4251	2	9	1843	1101
Knockskagh	4964	0	7	2651	1196
Myross	3523	1	35	3307	2092
Streelane	4773	3	39	1812	1055
Skibbereen	9005	2	37	9557	8931
Tughall	4252	3	20	2516	1791
Woodfort	4628	0	8	2079	1318
Total	114,963	3	17	57,439	37,283

Census Office, Dublin, 2nd January, 1852.

Reprinted from The Cork Examiner, Cork, March 10, 1852.

PUBLIC MEETING IN TUAM.

We refer with unfeigned satisfaction to the proceedings at a meeting of the public-spirited inhabitants of Tuam, a condensed report of which appears in another part of our paper this day. The Catholics of Tuam feel the grievances under which they labour, in common with the rest of their fellow-countrymen, and hence they call on the legislature for a recognition of the rights of the tenant, as a measure of the most vital importance, one absolutely essential to the salvation of the country, and give expression to their congratulations on the downfall of the vile Whig cabinet, and to their abhorrence of the recreancy of those Irish members by whom that cabinet was for a moment preserved from its inevitable destruction.

But, in addition to those matters upon which the men of Tuam only feel in common with other honest Irishmen, there are grievances against which they have, in a special manner, a right to protest. Such are the offensive assaults made upon their religious feelings by the fanatics and their degraded instruments who are employed to work out the infamous proselytising system, and who are sustained and encouraged in their aggressions by the very authorities to whom the people should be able to look for protection. Most truly do the men of Tuam proclaim—

"That the Protestant establishment is the bane of Ireland's posterity, as well as peace—crushing the country by its enormous weight, and annoying its inhabitants, by the offensive bearing of so many of its ministers, who, not content to enjoy in silence the plundered revenues of the ancient religion, go about exasperating the people and provoking them to an infraction of the peace by their stupid and blasphemous handbills."

Recreated from The Freeman's Journal, Dublin, March 5, 1852.

MUTINY ON BOARD YORK— INJURIES TO CAPTAIN AND CREW.

LIVERPOOL, SATURDAY EVENING.—The neighbourhood of the Great Landing Stage and the surrounding localities were thrown into a state of the greatest excitement by the announcement that the seamen on board the New York packet ship Queen of the West, Captain Morse, bound to New York, had mutinied in the river; that recourse was had to deadly weapons, and that the captain and several of the crew had suffered very severely, and in some instances fatal injuries. Having repaired to the Central Police office, I was enabled to glean the following particulars:—

The Queen of the West, which had put back from Queenstown for the purpose of refitting and repairing some damage which she had sustained in setting out for New York some weeks ago, was about to sail on her voyage this forenoon; she therefore hauled out of the Wellington Dock about ten o'clock this morning. When in the river the crew was mustered by the captain, and 26 men answered to their names; whereupon one of the seamen remarked to the captain that they were short handed, and that the proper complement should be 30, and manifested symptoms of unwillingness to proceed to sea. On observing this the captain, it is reported, rather rudely pushed the man (George Freeman) aside, when he immediately rebelled, and the crew generally sided with him, and the captain was savagely assailed and knocked down. He went down into the cabin and having armed himself with a revolver pistol and a cutlass returned, accompanied by the first mate also having a sword. As soon as they made their appearance a dreadful conflict ensued. The captain snapped his pistol at the head of one of his men, but fortunately it missed fire. Another of the men seeing the bloody nature of the conflict which was going on jumped overboard, and on him the captain fired, but without effect. Both he and the mate then used their swords, and many of the men have been cut and mutilated in the most shocking manner. The battle raged with terrific fury for some time. At length the mutineers were subdued, and the captain in his anger had one of the men tied up and gave him a dozen lashes on the bare back, a punishment which greatly irritated the crew. In the meantime news of the *emeute* was sent on shore, and Mr. Superintendent Ryde set out with a large posse of police for the scene of the conflict, and on reaching the ship arrested eleven of the chief rioters. Their names are Thomas Brown, a Norwegian; James Blake, James Fowler, George Freeman, Henry Downs, William Party Eastwood, Alexander Jack, said to be the ringleader; John Drones, of Waterford; James Turner, James Thompson, and John Morton. They were all more or less cut up, and Captain Morse, who appeared to prefer the charge, had several bandages around his head. One of the crew has been sent to the Northern hospital with a dreadful wound in his arm.

The men have been sent to Birkenhead Bridewell, the riot having taken place on the Cheshire side of the Mersey. The case will be investigated on Monday, when I shall send you the particulars.—*Saunders*.

Recreated from The Cork Examine, Cork, March 10, 1852.

The Guild of Literature and Art netted as large a sum as £1,400 by their two performances at Liverpool. At Manchester Mr. Charles Dickens and associates were entertained by the Mayor and Corporation. At Liverpool they filled St. George's Hall ; a feat that even the Swedish Nightingale failed to accomplish. They have received a pressing invitation to return to Manchester in May.

The Duke of Newcastle (divorced from his Duchess) will shortly be married to a daughter of Mr. Quintin Dick with a million and half of money.—*Limerick Chronicle*.

PERVERSION TO POPERY.

The *Edinburgh Witness* says that "Lady Harris, a very beautiful young widow, only 26 years old, who perverted last year to Popery, has given over to the Jesuits her beautiful estate of Seacliffe, in East Lothian, her prospects of £10,000 a year from an old uncle (Mr. Sligo, of Carmyle,) and all the treasures collected in India by her late husband, Sir William Cornwallis Harris. She has been induced to forsake an aged grandmother and her mother, whose only child she is, and to retire into a strict convent at Grenoble, France, committing herself to the protection of the Jesuit priests."

FIRE.—On Tuesday evening, about eight o'clock, a fire broke out in Mrs. Magrath's public house in the Glen of Ballybricken, and in a very short time, the house, together with the two adjoining ones—all being thatched—were consumed. Harvey's and Mason's engines were soon on the spot, and rendered—as did the people—all the assistance in their power. It was a melancholy thing indeed to see three poor families thus suddenly left houseless when some of them were preparing to retire for the night. We understand that the fire originated in Mrs. Magrath's house in consequence of a lighted candle having fallen into a bed, whilst a child was being put to sleep.

We have heard that the property was not ensured.

AN EXTRAORDINARY PARENT.—A woman at Leige has just been confined of three children, making 24 in nine years, having had three at every *accouchement*. The husband, who is very anxious to perpetuate his name, is much disappointed at all his children being girls.

Reprinted and recreated from The Waterford News, Waterford, March 12, 1852.

ARRIVAL OF THE LORD LIEUTENANT IN IRELAND.

Another representative of the Majesty of England has arrived amongst us—another item has been added to the monotonous alternation of Whig and Tory governors of Ireland in the person of his Excellency Archibald Earl of Eglinton. The official announcement having been issued giving notice of the expected arrival of his Excellency, the usual preparations were made by the military and civic authorities for his reception. The advent of a new Viceroy used to be, in our recollection, a matter of no small moment—an event usually productive of considerable excitement amongst all classes of our citizens; but on this occasion, judging from the aspect of the city in the earlier part of yesterday, no indications were perceptible of any great popular interest. However, towards the hour of eleven o'clock numerous groups of respectable citizens of both sexes might be observed proceeding along Great Brunswick-street towards the Westland-row station of the Kingstown Railway, and the marching down in the same direction of a splendid infantry regiment (the 35th), with its colours, led by its colonel, and preceded by its finely-appointed band, gave some animation to that part of the city, and had the effect of collecting a number of people in its line of progress, and of crowding the windows with spectators. The arrangements provided by the directors of the Kingstown railway were excellent. Quarter hour trains were started regularly,

Reprinted from The Freeman's Journal. Dublin, March 11, 1852.

ARRIVAL AND SWEARING IN OF THE LORD LIEUTENANT.

His Excellency the Earl of Eglinton arrived in Dublin on Wednesday, to assume the high and honourable office conferred on him by her most gracious Majesty. The noble lord has met with a reception which, take it in every point of view, must be very gratifying both to him and to the Government with which he is connected. For some days past, it had been generally known that the new Lord Lieutenant and his amiable Countess would leave London on Tuesday morning, sleep in Holyhead that night, and come from thence to our city on Wednesday. From an early hour in the morning, Kingstown presented a most animated appearance—groups of people were to be seen proceeding towards the jetty—the various ships in the harbour were hoisting their gayest colours—the weather was beautifully fine—and all betokened the coming of such a reception as, with all their faults, the people of this country are ever ready to offer to a stranger, with even a character less celebrated for manly feeling and noble and generous spirit than that of Lord Eglinton. From ten o'clock, crowds continued to arrive in the half and quarter hour train; and by twelve, those who had not been fortunate enough to secure standing room on the pier, or the railway platforms,

Reprinted from The Belfast News-Letter, Belfast, March 12, 1852.

COUNTY GALWAY.
MANSLAUGHTER—CRUEL CASE.

Peter M'Intire was indicted for the manslaughter of John Leonard on the 23d of August last.

It appeared in evidence that the deceased was an infirm pauper, and prisoner was employed by James O'Shaughnessy, relieving officer, to bring deceased on a cart from Ahascragh to the Ballinasloe workhouse, which he undertook to do; however, the prisoner on the road got drunk, and was driving the car so fast that deceased complained of fatigue, and begged he would check the pace, but the prisoner becoming exasperated at being spoken to, attacked the man; he struck him with a stick, and along the road continued to assault him; the poor man was in such a state of exhaustion when he arrived at Ballinasloe he was obliged to be put immediately under medical treatment, and he died on the following day.

The prisoner was convicted, and sentenced to six months' imprisonment.

Recreated from The Freeman's Journal, Dublin, March 12, 1852.

EMIGRATION.

The following is the Prospectus of Mr. Vere Foster's benevolent scheme of emigration, which we noticed a week ago:—

IRISH FEMALE EMIGRATION SUBSCRIPTION LIST.

For the purpose of raising the condition of destitute families in Ireland, from extreme poverty to comfort and independence, by assisting the emigration to North America of one able-bodied member of each family, in most cases a woman, selected on account of good character and industrious habits, and therefore with the natural expectation that she will afterwards, from her earnings in America, extend that assistance to the remaining members of her family, in imitation of the notorious and very remarkable characteristic example of hundreds of thousands of the very poorest class of Irish emigrants, who have most affectionately and generously so acted within the last few years, with the least possible aid from their superiors in wealth and intellectual education.

It is hoped by this means, not only to benefit the individuals assisted, but also their families—the non-emigrating population, the tenant farmers, and the landlords—namely, the first obviously and directly. 2d. Their families, indirectly, through placing an able-bodied member of each in a situation where she will have opportunities of earning by her own independent exertions the means of assisting them. 3d. The non-emigrating labouring population, by creating a tendency through diminution of population, and therefore of competition among labourers to raise their wages. 4th. The tenant farmers, by a tendency to reduce the excessive poor law taxation to which they are present subject, and the continued pressure of which is now reducing them to emigrate themselves and their capital, thereby increasing the proportion of poor rates to be paid by those tenant farmers who remain, and by their landlords decreasing the employment of the labouring population, and therefore increasing the general distress. 5th. The landlords, by a tendency to reduce the pressure of excessive poor law taxation upon them also, by reducing the otherwise increasing motives for their still solvent tenants to emigrate, and by therefore checking the downward tendency of competition for farms, and therefore of landlord rents.

The expense of passage to Quebec, New York, or other ports, usually varies from £2 10s. to £3; from £1 to £1 10s. will be required for outfit and other expenses previous to embarkation; and arrangements will be made so that such emigrants as have no friends to meet them on arrival in America shall receive £1 each on landing, together with directions how to proceed into the interior of the country in search of employment.

Subscriptions of any amount from one penny upwards, in postage stamps, or otherwise, will be thankfully received.

N.B.—It is stated in the last Annual Report of the Irish Poor Law Commissioners that there were still 61,000 able-bodied women in the Irish poorhouses, a fact most glaringly discreditable to the wealthy portion of the inhabitants of this kingdom, and which it is to be hoped requires only to be generally known to be atoned for by increased exertions to relieve, and also to prevent destitution in future.

Number of subscribers to this date, 1,165.
Amount collected £92.

Vere Foster,
5, Whitehall-yard, London.

Recreated from The Nation, Dublin, March 13, 1852.

HOUSE OF COMMONS—Tuesday.

State of the North of Ireland.

Mr. Napier moved for a select committee to inquire into the state of those parts of the counties of Armagh, Monaghan, and Louth, referred to in her Majesty's Speech, the cause of crime and outrage there, and the efficiency of the laws for suppressing those offenses.

He drew a dark picture of the organized system of crime existing in that part of Ireland, describing the outrages of Ribbonism as the overt acts of a great confederacy against life and property, which, if not put down, would put down the law, overawing and intimidating the whole population, so that jurors were deterred from fulfilling their duties, criminals escaped, and Special Commissions failed of their effect.

Mr. Napier explained the state of the law in Ireland applicable to secret associations, and showed the manner in which the law had been brought to bear upon these confederacies, the mysterious organization of which he incidentally noticed, and the tyranny they exercised over the lower classes. He did not think that these outrages could be traced to the state of the law between landlord and tenant, though it might furnish topics for fomenting discontent, and it was his intention, at no distant date, to submit to Parliament a measure for simplifying this part of the law, consistently with the rights of property.

He gave details of some atrocious murders perpetrated, several in open day, within a comparatively short period, in not one of which had the law reached criminals, and he threw out suggestions for rendering the existing law more efficient in this fearful state of things.

Recreated from The Nation, Dublin, March 20, 1852.

GENERAL TURNER.

We understand, and not without feeling of regret, that Lieutenant-General Turner, who has been so long and so creditably connected with this city, is about leaving it on Friday next, having been succeeded in command of the district by Major-General Mansell, lately commanding in Limerick. It would indeed be an act of very great churlishness on our part, if we allowed that connexion, extending over a period of *thirty-five years*, to be severed, without some expression of the respect and regard which, in common with the inhabitants of Cork, of all classes and persuasions, we entertain towards that most deserving officer, and perfect gentleman.

General Turner has been so long a resident of this city, that his name has become a household word. So far back as we can remember, we have heard that name spoken of with the most affectionate regard—as that of a man whom all liked, and even loved, for his gentleness, his kindness, and his urbanity. It but rarely happens that men in high command, or entrusted with authority, are particularly popular; and indeed the manner and bearing of military men towards civilians are not always such as to propitiate good feeling, or inspire respect. But we have seldom known any military man, of any rank, more truly or more deservedly popular than General Turner, whose bearing towards the people of Cork has been the theme of constant praise.

He and his family have been associated not only with the amusements of this city, but also with its charities; and we are happy to say that no feeling of religious difference has ever held General Turner and his amiable lady from affording aid to charities which to some might seem of a sectarian character. This is a trait well worth recording in a country where prejudice often chills the warmest impulses of the heart, and bigotry often steps in between charity and its most deserving object. In the discharge of his professional duty, even in times of trouble, when harshness might seem to be but the evidence of a laudable zeal, General TURNER has been equally remarkable for his prudence and firmness, his humanity and good temper. And when property or life was placed in peril by the calamity of fire, no one could be more active in affording assistance. It was not enough with him that troops were at once despatched from the barracks; but he was immediately on the ground himself, to see that the assistance was real, and that nothing was left undone to save life from danger, and property from destruction.

These are services which have earned for General TURNER the gratitude and love of the citizens of Cork, and will retain the memory of his command long fresh in their recollection. It is quite impossible that *he* can cease to feel an interest in this city, in which the best years of his life have been spent, and in which he has reared up with the utmost credit a large and accomplished family. We cordially wish him every happiness, wherever he goes; and we trust that his successor will earn for himself the same reputation during his stay, and the same regret on his departure.

Recreated from The Cork Examiner, Cork, March 31, 1852.

EMIGRATION.

For the last fornight 150 families have left Cappoquin, Lismore, and the Old Parish (Dungarvan) for the land of freedom; each family having three children;—450 individuals left these localities. This whole-sale system of emigration will soon depopulate this unfortunate country.

Reprinted from The Waterford News, Waterford, April 9, 1852.

CENSUS OF SKIBBEREEN UNION.

ELECTORAL DIVISIONS.	Population in 1841.	Population in 1851.
Aughadown, North	1,636	913
Aughadown, South	3,566	2,188
Breadagh	1,785	1,108
Caharagh	1,839	1,164
Cape Clear	2,755	1,916
Carrigbawn	2,071	890
Castlehaven, North	4,058	2,209
Castlehaven, South	2,413	1,698
Cloghdonnell	2,182	1,308
Clonkeen	1,892	1,034
Drinagh	1,278	671
Droumdaleague, North	1,015	526
Droumdaleague, South	1,852	1,001
Gurranes	1,468	801
Gortnascreeny	1,972	1,131
Kilfaughnabeg	1,892	1,241
Killenleagh	1,843	1,101
Knockskagh	2,651	1,196
Myross	3,307	2,092
Shreelane	1,812	1,055
Skibbereen	9,557	8,931
Tullagh	2,516	1,791
Woodfort	2,079	1,318
Total	57,439	37,283

Reprinted from The Cork Examiner, Cork, April 7, 1852.

WATER CARTS IDLE IN THE MIDST OF DUST!!

We have had several complaints this week from many respectable and intelligent gentlemen, that though our water-carts and poor people are idle, our citizens and our shops are permitted to be enveloped in clouds of *dust*. On Wednesday, as our readers will remember, it became an absolute nuisance. We know that it is only necessary to direct the attention of the authorities to the matter, to have it rectified.

Reprinted from The Waterford News, Waterford, April 9, 1852.

LOSS OF THE STEAM TROOP SHIP BIRKENHEAD.

FOUR HUNDRED AND FIFTY PERSONS MISSING.

We announced in yesterday's FREEMAN, by telegraphic despatch, the melancholy intelligence of the loss of her Majesty's troop ship the Birkenhead, on the 26th of February, off Point Danger, near the Cape of Good Hope, with a fearful loss of human life. The following are the fullest particulars that have as yet been ascertained of this disastrous event:—The Birkenhead left Queenstown on the 7th of January, having on board the following officers and detachments of regiments serving at the Cape:—12th Lancers, Cornets Bond and Rolt, and six men; 2d (Queen's Royal) regiment, Ensign Boylan, one sergeant, and 50 men; 6th regiment, Ensign Lawrence Metford, one sergeant, and 60 men; 12th regiment, Captain Blake, one sergeant, and 14 men; 43rd Light Infantry, Lieutenant Giradot, one sergeant, and 40 men; 45th regiment, one officer, one sergeant, and 70 men; 60th Rifles, one sergeant, and 40 men; 73d regiment, Lieutenants Robinson and Booth, and Ensign Lucas, one sergeant, and 70 men; Lieutenant Colonel Seton and Ensign Russell, one officer, and 60 men; 91st regiment, Captain Wright, one sergeant, and 60 men; making a total (besides the crew) of 13 officers, nine sergeants, and 466 men. The Birkenhead carried four guns. She was an iron paddle-wheel vessel of 556-horse power, and was built by Mr. John Laird, of Birkenhead.

The first intelligence of the wreck reached Cape Town on Friday morning, the 27th instant, at half past nine a.m., Dr. Cullhane, of the ill-fated vessel, having, ridden up from the place at which he landed for assistance. Shortly after a statement made by him was published. It is, however, considered to be so inaccurate that very little faith can be placed in it.

The following report has been addressed to the commandant of Cape Town by Captain Wright, of the 91st Regiment, one of the survivors of the late mournful occasion:—

Simon's Bay, March 1, 1852.

SIR—It is with feelings of the deepest regret that I have to announce to you the loss of her Majesty's steamer Birkenhead, which took place on a rock about two miles and a half or three miles off Point Danger, at two a.m., on the 26th February.

The sea was smooth at the time, and the vessel was steaming at the rate of 8 1/2 knots an hour. She struck the rock and it penetrated through her bottom just aft of the foremast. The rush of water was so great that there is no doubt that most of the men in the lower troop deck were drowned in their hammocks. The rest of the men and all the officers appeared on deck, when Major Seaton called all the officers about him, and impressed on them the necessity of preserving order and silence among the men. He directed me to take, and have executed, whatever orders the commander might give me. Sixty men were immediately put on to the chain pumps, on the lower after deck, and told off in three reliefs. Sixty men were put on to the tackles of the paddle-box boats; and the remainder of the men were brought on to the poop, so as to ease the forepart of the ship. She was at this time rolling heavily. The commander ordered the horses to be pitched out of the port gangway, and the cutter to be got ready for the women and children, who had all been collected under the poop awning. As soon as the horses were got over the side the women and children were passed into the cutter, and, under the charge of Mr. Richards, the master's assistant, the boat then stood off about 150 yards. Just after they were out of the ship the entire bow broke off at the foremast, the bowsprit going up in the air towards the foretopmast, and the funnel went over on the side, carrying away the starboard paddle-box and boat. The other paddle-box boat capsized when being lowered. The large boat in the centre of the ship could not be got at.

It was about 12 or 15 minutes after she struck that the bow broke off. The men then all went up on the poop, and in about five minutes more, the vessel broke in two, crosswise, just abaft the engine-room, and the stern part immediately filled and went down. A few men jumped off just before she did so, but the greater number remained to the last, and so did every officer belonging to the troops. All the men I put on to the tackles, I fear, were crushed when the funnel fell; and the men and officers below at the pumps could not, I think, have reached the deck before the vessel broke up and went down. The survivors clung, some to rigging of the mainmast, part of which was out of the water; and others got hold of floating pieces of wood. I think there must have been about 200 on the drift wood. I was on a large piece along with five others, and we picked up nine or ten more. The swell carried the wood in the direction of Point Danger. As soon as it got to the weeds and breakers, finding that it would not support all that were on it, I jumped off and swam on shore; and when the others, and also those that were on the other pieces of wood, reached the shore, we proceeded into the country, to find habitation of any sort, where we could obtain shelter. Many of the men were naked and almost all without shoes. Owing to the country being covered with thick, thorny bushes, our progress was slow, but after walking till about three p.m., having reached land about twelve, we came to where a waggon was outspanned, and the driver of it directed us to a small bay, where there is a hut of a fisherman. The bay is called Stanford's Cove. We arrived there about sunset, and as the men had nothing to eat, I went on to a farmhouse, about eight or nine miles from the Cove, and sent back provisions for that day. The next morning I sent another day's provisions, and the men were removed up to a farm of Captain Smale's, about 12 or 14 miles up the country. Lieutenant Giradot, of the 43d, and Cornet Bond, of the 12th Lancers, accompanied this party, which amounted to 68 men, including 18 sailors.

I then went down to the coast, and during Friday, Saturday, and Sunday, I examined the rocks for more than 20 miles, in the hope of finding some men who might have drifted in. I fortunately fell in with the crew of a whale-boat, that is employed sealing on Dyer's Island. I got them to take the boat outside the seaweed, whilst I went along the shore. The sea-weed on the coast is very thick, and of immense length, so that it would have caught most of the drift wood. Happily the boat picked up two men, and I also found two. Although they were all much exhausted, two of them having been in the water 38 hours, they were all right the next day, except a few bruises. It was 86 hours, on Sunday afternoon when I left the coast, since the wreck had taken place; and as I had carefully examined every part of the rocks, and also sent the whale boat over to Dyer's Island, I can safely assert that when I left there was not a living soul on the coast of those that had been on board the ill-fated Birkenhead.

On Saturday, I met Mr. Mackay, the Civil Commissioner of Caledon, and also Field-cornet Villiers. The former told me that he had ordered the men who had been at Captain Smale's, to be clothed by him, he having a store at his farm. Forty soldiers received clothing there. Mr. Mackay, the field-cornet, and myself, accompanied by a party of men brought down by Mr. Villiers, went along the coast, as far as the point that runs out to Dyer's Island, and all the bodies that were met with were interred. There were not many, however, and I regret to say it could be easily accounted for.

Five of the horses got to the shore, and were caught and brought to me. One belonged to myself, one to Mr. Bond, of the 12th Lancers, and the other three to Major Seaton, of the 74th, Dr. Laing, and Lieut. Booth, of the 73d. I handed over the horses to Mr. Mackay, and he is to send them on to me here, so that they may be sold, and that I may account for the proceed.

Recreated from The Freeman's Journal, Dublin, April 8, 1852.

VICEREGAL VISIT TO THE ZOOLOGICAL GARDENS.

It having been intimated that their Excellencies the Earl and Countess of Eglinton would visit these gardens on yesterday, a grand promenade was announced, with the additional attraction of military music.

From an early hour in the afternoon the equipages of nobility and gentry continued to arrive at the entrance in rapid succession, and the gardens began to fill with gay groups of fashionables of both sexes. The weather was beautifully serene, and the promenade through these picturesque and tastefully laid-out grounds, constituted in itself a most refreshing treat. Two splendidly appointed military bands were in attendance and performed a variety of airs, overtures and waltzes. At about half-past three o'clock their Excellencies arrived at the gardens in their private chariot, drawn by four beautiful bays, and preceded by two outriders. The scene in the gardens at this period was brilliant and enlivening in the extreme. The circular lawn, carpeted with closely shaven verdure of the richest green, and surrounded by a belt of rich foliage and flowering shrubs formed a sort of silvan drawing-room, wherein was collected a crowded assemblage of the very *elite* of Dublin society.

Not only the centre lawn but every part of the grounds was thronged with ladies and gentry, and all seemed to enjoy heartily the summer's day and the brilliant scene around them. The Viceregal party inspected the not very large but still interesting collection of zoological specimens in the several departments of the gardens, and the Lord Lieutenant expressed his admiration of the excellent arrangements adopted by the society for the preservation of the different classes of animals, birds, &c. After remaining about an hour their Excellencies retired, the band playing the national anthem. The gardens continued thronged with promenaders until an advanced hour in the afternoon.

Recreated from The Freeman's Journal, Dublin, May 6, 1852.

MR. CHARLES DICKENS AND THE CORK EXHIBITION.

THE subjoined correspondence has taken place between the above distinguished novelist, and Mr. J. W. Bourke of this city, with reference to the object of inducing him and the other members of the Guild of Literature and Art to come to Cork, for the purpose of giving a dramatic representation in aid of funds of that institution. It is understood that an effort will be made to overcome the objection in point of time, to which Mr. Dickens refers:—

Office, 9, South Mall, Cork, 15th April, 1852.
SIR—I should do the world a wrong, if I trespassed inconsiderately on your valuable time.

I am sure you will not consider that I do so when you learn the purport of this communication.

Absorbed in your literary occupations, you may not possibly be aware, that an Exhibition will be held here in the ensuing summer, moulded on the principles and adopting the system of its greatest prototype, but designed solely to promote the arts and stimulate the industrial resources and enterprise of Ireland.

It has occurred to me, remembering how happily the past memorable season in London was inaugurated by the first representations at Devonshire House, in aid of the guild of literature and art, that if the founders of that noble institution meant to extends its benefits to the fugitive genius of Ireland, no more appropriate time could be chosen to enlist the sympathies of this country in its favour, than during the continuance of the Exhibition.

The commencement here of a series of your dramatic performances, would add a delightful feature to the brilliancy and attractiveness of our coming season, and I have little doubt would result in the realization of a large sum for the funds of the institution.

I should place this suggestion before the Executive Committee of the Exhibition, from whom, I am sure, a public invitation would emanate, but that I think it obviously desirable for all parties to ascertain previously through you, as the chief promoter of the guild, if the proposition would be acceptable to you, and its accomplishment practicable.

Soliciting the favour of your reply, I may be permitted in conclusion to add, that I augur far more than a passing benefit to Ireland, from the presence among us, at such a time and under such circumstances, of the distinguished and influential members of your "Corps Dramatique."

I am, Sir, your most obedient servant,

J. W. BOURKE.

Charles Dickens, Esq., London.

Tavistock House, London Saturday, 8th May, 1852.

SIR—I beg to acknowledge the receipt of your obliging letter, dated on the 15th of the last month, and to thank you, on behalf of the Guild of Literature and Art, for the obliging proposals set forth in it.

I regret to add, after considering the subject well, that the distance it would be necessary for the large body concerned to traverse, and the very great difficulties in the way of an absence from London prolonged beyond four or five days consecutively, combine to impose upon me the disagreeable task of declining the visit you suggest. I discharge the duty, I assure you, with great reluctance.—

I have the honour to be, Sir, your faithful servant,

CHARLES DICKENS.

J. W. Bourke, Esq.

Recreated from The Cork Examiner, Cork, May 21, 1852.

THE SUBMARINE TELEGRAPH BETWEEN HOLYHEAD AND HOWTH.

The announcement which appeared exclusively in the columns of the FREEMAN'S JOURNAL on Saturday morning, that the work of laying down the telegraphic cable between Holyhead and Howth had already *actually commenced*, created more surprise in Dublin, and elicited more expressions of incredulity than we could have expected under the circumstances.

Our information certainly was peculiar, and limited as we were in the portion that we had liberty to publish, the account may have appeared more meagre to the uninitiated than it did to us. We are now, however, enabled to place before our readers some further particulars, which will, at least, dispel all doubts as to the reality of the stupendous undertaking; but, before doing so, we may be allowed to acknowledge our regret that some of those little accidents and unforeseen delays which too frequently occur to mar the anticipated success of the best projected enterprises have prevented our giving either on Saturday or this morning the first message "BY SUBMARINE TELEGRAPH" to the Irish public, for which we had made every possible arrangement, and which we had every reason to expect we should have accomplished.

Reprinted from The Freeman's Journal, Dublin, May 31, 1852.

RETURN OF THE COURT TO BUCKINGHAM PALACE.—Her Majesty and Prince Albert, accompanied by the younger members of the Royal family, left Osborne for London, at two o'clock on Friday afternoon. Her Majesty and the august party crossed in the Fairy, from Cowes to Gosport, and travelled by a special train on the London and South-Western railway to London.

On Monday the 7th June the Court will take its departure from Buckingham Palace for Windsor Castle. Her Majesty and the Prince Consort will entertain a large circle of distinguished visitors during the Ascot Race week, and will honour the course with their presence on Tuesday and Thursday.

Reprinted from The Belfast News-Letter, May 31, 1852.

COMPLETION OF THE SUBMARINE TELEGRAPH BETWEEN IRELAND AND ENGLAND.

The FREEMAN'S JOURNAL was the first paper to announce to the Irish public that the telegraphic cable for the Dublin and Holyhead line was being laid down.

We have now the satisfaction to communicate the gratifying intelligence that the first message from Howth to Holyhead was transmitted at half-past eight o'clock last evening, and an answer instantaneously received. The Irish public will at once anticipate that that message was an

HURRAH FOR THE IRISH AND AMERICAN PACKET STATION!

The telegraphic communication being now, we may say, completed between London and Galway, the establishment of an American packet station on the west coast of Ireland cannot be long delayed. The mercantile necessities of the empire will now force on what every government has hitherto denied for the advancement of Irish interests.

But we must not to-day indulge in anticipations as to results. Our present duty is to detail the latest facts connected with the completion of the stupendous undertaking.

The Britannia and Prospero made their second start from Holyhead shortly after two o'clock A.M. yesterday morning, the Britannia "paying out" the cable steadily, and constantly testing, by the indicators on board and ashore, the perfection of the communication.

The voyage was unmarked by any incident of importance, and was, happily, free from any accident. The cable fell so straight, and sank so evenly, that only *three* miles more than the straight line across the Channel were payed out. This, in a course of *sixty-five* miles, was really extraordinary.

A few minutes after three o'clock P.M., the vessels were sighted by our look-out, and at eight o'clock P.M., the Prospero entered Howth Harbour, the Brittania lying outside near the island of "Ireland's eye," through the Channel near which the cable was subsequently brought to shore by boat.

The moment the Britannia arrived at her destination, and communicated the fact to Holyhead that the Irish shore was reached, the final grand test was applied to the telegraphic cable by connecting the wire with one of the ship's loaded guns, and passing the word, "fire!" to Holyhead. The answer was the immediate discharge of the gun on board the Britannia. The hour was then just half-past eight o'clock. The works had been performed in a little more than eighteen hours!

Messages were now rapidly interchanged, and a salute of the Britannia's guns fired from Holyhead. A letter arrived in Dublin, directed to a gentleman who had left for Holyhead by the mid-day steamer, and whose presence was immediately required in London. A message was sent to seek him out. Within half an hour he was discovered, and he responded, "I am here." "You are wanted in London." "I shall start by the next train."

Another hour and the cable was ashore, the connection completed with the land wires, and the indicators at the Dublin Terminus of the Drogheda Railway, in Amiens-street, were conversing with those at the terminus of the Chester and Holyhead Railway, in Holyhead. By this time all the parties connected with the now happily successful enterprise were quite worn out with fatigue, and further experiments were abandoned for the night.

We feel great pleasure in again expressing our obligations to Mr. Culverwell, Secretary to the Dublin and Drogheda Railway Company, for the kindness which we experienced at his hands, and the facilities which he afforded us to witness the completion of this arduous and magnificent undertaking.

Recreated from The Freeman's Journal, Dublin, June 2, 1852.

EMIGRATION—TRAIN'S LINE.

A very fine vessel the "Napoleon," Captain Hunt, has arrived in Passage West and will sail on the 10th inst., for Boston with 200 emigrants. The "Napoleon" has been chartered by the house of Messrs. Train & Co., who are carrying weekly hundreds of emigrants from this port and Liverpool to the states. This vessel, built at Boston 12 months since, of 700 tons burden, is one of the handsomest clippers that have entered the port of Cork. She is 8 feet between decks, and as an emigrant ship her accommodations are excellent. Her cabin is spacious, gorgeously fitted up, and affords accommodation for 12 passengers. Several spring sofas, covered with crimson plush, line either side of the saloon. The panelling is of Spanish mahogany. Columns of rose wood divide each panel, the column surmounted with a plain cap of pine wood, on which a pure statuary white is brought out with metallic polish. The rudder is worked in a novel manner. The wheel is attached to a powerful but easily worked screw, on which is a heavy box of iron, with a projecting arm. As the wheel is turned the iron box either advances or recedes, and the arm from the box places the rudder in the position desired. The object the inventor had in view, and Captain Hunt states it has been successfully attained, is, to keep the rudder in its position during the heaviest sea.

The "Napoleon" made the run from Liverpool to Queenstown in the incredibly short space of 25 hours! A medical gentleman connected with this county is going out as surgeon. Captain Hunt entertained several citizens, on Saturday, on board to dinner, which was got up most creditably, with almost every delicacy, claret, hock, sherry, brandy, foreign liquers, &c. The health of Captain Hunt and a speedy voyage to the "Good Ship" Napoleon, the house of Train and Co., were warmly drunk and responded to.—*Constitution*.

Recreated from The Cork Examiner, Cork, June 9, 1852.

FATHER CAHILL'S LAST EFFUSION.

The excruciating evidence taken before the Crime and Outrage Committee—evidence which directly implicates certain Romish priests in the Ribbon treason, in addition to its other very remarkable revelations—has elicited from the notorious Father Cahill an epistle dedicated to Lord Derby, which, if it be not the product of a madman, is certainly that of a person who must believe the great majority of his fellow-subjects idiots, if they accept it as sane disclosure.

Notwithstanding this, there is a sort of method in this man's frenzy which forbids us to deny him the possession of a large share of the craft and cunning for which his order is proverbial. This is manifest when we reflect that his untenable logic, his distorted facts, and his furious invectives are not meant merely for the perusal of the Government, to whom he appeals whilst he assails them, or to the educated classes, among whom a scholar, an ecclesiastic, or a respected public writer might desire to find an audience. No, the letters with which Priest Cahill inundates the Popish press, are, in reality, addressed to the ignorant masses of the Irish Roman Catholics, whom it is easy thus to inflame against British legislation—who are unapproachable by the avenues of knowledge and reasoning—who are strangers to history—and who have resigned their consciences, to the keeping of their priesthood. It is Father Cahill's express mission to effect that object by violent missives, which the Ribbonmen and their allies are endeavouring to accomplish by Thuggism, and which the Ultramontanists are trying to achieve by intrigue—the expiration of Protestantism from these islands, and the ascendancy of the Papal authority therein. This man, Cahill, does his part of the task cleverly enough, and if he assumes a species of insanity in his language, it is because he knows that lunacy is contagious, and his object being to drive his ignorant countrymen mad, he must be omitted to have made use of the most direct and successful method of attaining it.

Recreated from The Belfast News-Letter, Belfast, June 11, 1852.

LORD EGLINTON IN CORK.

VISIT OF THEIR EXCELLENCIES TO THE EXHIBITION ON FRIDAY.

Their Excellencies the Earl and Countess of Eglinton and *suite* visited the exhibitions at eleven o'clock on Friday. They first visited the Northern Hall, and were particularly struck by the work exhibited by the various Industrial Schools. They much admired the embroidered vestments contributed by the Kinsale school, and as they were about to leave the department, Mrs. Paul M'Swiney and Mrs. Sainthill requested her Excellency to accept a beautiful handkerchief made at the Cork Embroidery School—a request with which she graciously complied.

Among the many other contributions of which their Excellencies expressed their admiration were Edden's carriages, and Fletcher's and other cabinet furniture, and the marble altars of Daly, which particularly arrested their attention.

A beautiful door foot-brush, made by Mr. M'Carthy of this city, was selected by the Countess to be forwarded to the Castle at the close of the Exhibition. His Excellency also minutely examined the work of the inmates of the County Jail, particularly the garments manufactured from unsteeped flax, and expressed his approval of the conduct of the Governor in endeavouring to establish such manufactures there.

Their Excellencies spent an hour in the building, and before leaving it his Excellency, on examining the "Dead Christ" of Hogan, expressed his regret at having omitted to mention his name, as he had intended, in his speech at the dinner, when enumerating some of the gifted individuals this country had given birth to, and requested, if opportunity offered, the expression of his regret for the omission should be conveyed to Hogan.

EXCURSION DOWN THE RIVER.

A few minutes after twelve, their Excellencies, accompanied by their *suite*, proceeded on board the river steam Company's boat, the Prince Arthur, which vessel lay stationed a few yards from the Anglesea bridge. The vice regal party were received on board by his Worship, SIR WILLIAM HACKETT, and several members of the executive committee; and, immediately upon their arrival, the Prince Arthur cast off her moorings, and steamed slowly sown the river. Albert quay, Anglesea bridge, and Lapp's quay, were lined with people, who respectfully but somewhat coldly saluted their Excellencies, as they proceeded on the excursion.

After passing the Cork Steam Ship Company's office, the Prince Arthur was joined by the Juverna, and a short distance after her came the Royal Alice, despatched by the river Company, to afford the public generally an opportunity of witnessing the reception of his Excellency in Queenstown, which latter vessel was followed by the Princess, which was on her regular trip.

The Royal Alice and Princess were crowded, as closely as their space would permit, by fashionably dressed people, many of whom were disappointed in the expectation of being enabled to accompany his Excellency in the Prince Arthur. The appearance of so lengthened a procession of steamers, gaily decorated with flags and banners, accompanied at intervals by small craft of various kinds, decked out in their snowy canvass and tiny bunting, formed a spectacle novel and attractive. The principal vessels, belonging to the Cork Steam Company, the shipping lying in both channels, the dock yards of Messrs. Wheeler and Robinson, and the more prominent buildings along the banks of the river were gaily decorated with flags, and occasionally fired salutes in honour of his Excellency's visit.

Recreated from The Cork Examiner, Cork, June 14, 1852.

Communication with England,
VIA HOLYHEAD,
THREE TIMES EACH WAY ON WEEKDAYS,
Twice on Sundays, Sea Passage 4½ Hours.

THE time allowed for Single Journey Tickets is the day of issue and two following days. The Journey may be broken at Dublin, Holyhead, Bangor, or Chester. The Return Tickets to or from London, are available for Fourteen Days after date of issue: those to other Stations for Seven Days, and the holder may break the Journey at the same places as the holder of a Single Journey Ticket. A Second Class Passenger can travel in the Saloon and After Deck of the Steam Boats, upon paying 3s. extra. Second Class Passengers can now travel by the Day Express trains between Chester and London.

THROUGH FARES TO OR FROM Kilkenny with	SINGLE.		RETURN.	
	1st Class	2nd class	1st Class	2nd Class
	s d	s d	s d	s d
London,	70 0	48 0	105 0	72 0
Birmingham,	52 0	38 0	78 0	57 0
Manchester,	38 0	28 0	57 0	42 0
Liverpool or Chester	32 0	21 0	48 0	32 0

Children under Twelve, Half Fares.
Offices for Dublin—52 Westland Row, and Steam Packet Pier, Kingstown.

Reprinted from The Waterford News, Waterford, July 2, 1852.

AUSTRALIAN
GOLD REGIONS.

PORT PHILIP,

Will be despatched from **BARNSTAPLE**,
(to avoid the trying and tedious passage of the Channel,)
THE 15TH DAY OF AUGUST,
The Splendid Clipper Built Ship,

LADY EBRINGTON,

A. 1. at LLOYD's for Fourteen Years,
700 TONS BURTHEN,
GEORGE HARRIS, Commander.

THIS Vessel is built upon the most approved principles of Naval Architecture—expressly for fast sailing; she takes no cargo, and will be put in the best train for comfort and sailing; a very short and pleasant passage may be anticipated.

The Rates of Passage, including provisions of the best kind, are as follows:—

After Cabin, £30. Fore Cabin, £20. With a few in the Saloon on Deck, at £50, for a separate and convenient State Room; but if occupied by Two Persons, £40 each.

For further particulars, apply to
B. MOORE AND SONS,
28, QUAY.

Waterford July 4,

Reprinted from The Waterford News, Waterford, July 9, 1852.

THE TENANT LEAGUERS AT DROMARA.
ANOTHER DISPLAY FRUSTRATED.

A FEW days ago the Leaguers appointed Dromara to be the scene of their next display, and yesterday was the day fixed upon. It was doomed to the fate of the Waringstown one, not by the magistrates' proclamation, but by the following circumstances:—On a rising ground, at a point where four roads meet, Mr. Crawford's friends had erected a platform. The locality was most appropriate for an Irish row, the macadamizers abounding in shoals. Before one o'clock, the hour appointed, a crowd of some hundreds of Leaguers and oppositionists had assembled. Expressions and watchwords were flying about, which plainly indicated hostilities. On the stage of planks being completed, whereupon the Leaguers were to figure, one of the party called out, "I'm neither Orangeman, nor Thrasher, but Crawford's the man", striking the platform with his fist. This was replied to by cheers from the Leaguers. The friends of Lord Edwin Hill and Mr. Ker, taking this as a yell of defiance, made a rush towards the platform, stones began to be rattled about, and in a few moments to fall in showers amongst both parties. The Leaguers of the platform, being hotly beleaguered, gave way *instanter*. The whole erection was reduced to its native planks in an incredibly short time. Fortunately the magistrates of the district, knowing the divided feeling of the people, had a strong body of the county constabulary, under Sub-inspector Stafford, on the ground, whose immediate interference prevented the disastrous result which must have ensued. The police having been drawn up, with fixed bayonets, in a line between the belligerents, with some degree of order being restored, H. A. Boyd, Esq., J.P., stood up, and requested the people to disperse peaceably. Cheers were given for Mr. Boyd, and cries of "We'll go home" were sent from the crowd. A gentleman then elevated himself, amidst cheers for Lord E. Hill and Mr. Ker, and called upon those who had convened the meeting, and had caused the disturbance, to send home their followers, and the rest would disperse immediately. This was hailed with great cheering. Meantime, Mr. W. S. Crawford, Mr. John S. Crawford, Rev. Julius M'Cullough, Rev. John Rogers, and some priests, with a few of their friends, were holding a consultation at a public house, at a short distance from the stormy scene. The result was the following resolution:—

"That the intended meeting be postponed for the present, for the purpose of avoiding any further disturbance."

Out of the window of this house several appeals were addressed to the people, admonitions to keep the peace, and earnest intreaties to go home. One old gentleman presented himself, and began to harangue rather formally on the rights of British subjects to meet, discuss their grievances, and address their rulers. He was besought to desist, and then pulled in by Mr. John S. Crawford. At last it was proposed, as the best plan of dispersing the people, for Mr. Crawford to drive off. He did go off in a direction so as to keep entirely clear of the crowd, and the people, cheering on both sides, began to proceed homewards.

Recreated from The Belfast News-Letter, Belfast, July 9, 1852.

THE QUEEN'S VISIT.

The Queen, I am assured on trustworthy authority, will leave Osborne in the Victoria and Albert yacht on either Saturday or Monday, and arrive in Cork the following day. The visit will be a strictly private one, as I have already stated, and it is the royal wish, I believe, that no addresses, deputations, &c., should take place, as the Queen's object is to go like any private lady to witness the exhibition of the fruits of Irish industry as well as the beauties of Irish scenery.—*Correspondent of the Freeman.*

Preparatory to the arrival of her Majesty and Prince Albert, orders have been received directing that the moorings of H.M. Ships, lying in this Harbour, under Admiral Corry, are to be altered, so as to be anchored there in line, in the Man-of-War Roads, for the purpose of giving effect to the Royal Salute, and the manning of the yards.

Reprinted from The Cork Examiner, Cork, July 12, 1852.

THE TWELFTH OF JULY.

BANBRIDGE.—I am glad to say the Twelfth has passed off here in the quietest manner; and, although these are very exciting times, yet the Orangemen of this district have displayed a wise discretion on this day, and have manifested that spirit for which they have at all times been distinguished—loyalty to the Throne, and obedience to the laws.

LURGAN.—The anniversary of the Twelfth passed off as quietly as in the memory of the oldest inhabitant. A flag was exhibited in the tower of the Church, and the bell rung at intervals during the day, as in former years.

DOWNPATRICK.—Not the slightest manifestation of party feeling occurred here to-day. The members of the different lodges, dined together at their respective lodge-rooms, after attending to their business throughout the day as usual. Half a troop of dragoons arrived in town during the morning.

RIOT IN NEWTOWNARDS.—On Monday, a messenger arrived in Belfast, from Newtownards, for a body of constables to go there and put down an alarming riot that had broken out. A party of police, under Head Constable Kidd, got under arms, proceeded to the scene of this disturbance, and succeeded in inducing one of the contending parties to disperse. This might have ended the affray, but that a party of Ribbonmen re-erected a green arch which had been taken down, and which was the origin of the whole emeute. Another stone-throwing match was commenced and kept up til John Andrews, Esq., of Comber, arrived at the head of a body of constabulary. He deemed it advisable to send to Belfast for a company of infantry, but when they arrived the whole affair was over.

DREADFUL PARTY RIOTING IN BELFAST.

WE greatly regret to state that, since an early hour yesterday morning, there has been, in a portion of this town, serious rioting, and that bloodshed and violence have resulted from party animosities.

It appears that a good deal of ill-feeling was excited throughout the whole of yesterday, in the neighbourhoods of Sandy Row and Durham Street, the respective strongholds of the Protestant and Roman Catholic partizans in town, the two localities forming one line in the street, and pretty equally divided between them.

The origin of this ill-feeling was an attack made on the house of a man, named Ball, a Protestant, in Cullentree Road, in that vicinity—commenced, it is said, by the Romanist party—and which resulted in the wounding of three parties by the shots which were fired during the *melee*—two men, named M'Kenna, and a young woman, named M'Loughlin, who was shot in the back of the neck, immediately below the ear, and in such a manner that the slightest deviation of the ball from the direction it had taken would have caused immediate death. One of the men, Peter M'Kenna, fifty years of age, was shot through both bones of the right leg. The ball has been extracted from the neck of the girl.

Both were removed to the hospital, and are now, we learn, progressing favourably, though not out of danger. This affair occurred shortly after daybreak; and the circumstances kindled the spark which only wanted such an opportunity to cause it to break out into a flame. A party of constabulary, consisting of sixty men, under the command of E. C. Flinter, Esq., C.I., and Geo. Hill, Esq., S.I., had been stationed in the neighbourhood, and under directions to use unremitting vigilance, in order to prevent any breach of peace.

Recreated from The Belfast News-Letter, Belfast, July 14, 1852.

DREADFUL AND FATAL AFFRAY—ONE MAN KILLED AND A NUMBER WOUNDED.

(*From The Belfast Chronicle of Wednesday.*)

One of the most fatal affrays that have occurred in Belfast for a long period, took place yesterday evening—it was still more lamentable than the York-street riot, both in character and consequences. The origin of the affray seems almost unknown to any person, but, so far as we can learn it, arose altogether out of the circumstances of the previous evening in Cullingtree-road. A number of Roman Catholics and Protestants who inhabit that street had quarrelled; but, as referred to in a paragraph elsewhere, the matter seemed to have been quelled. The girl M'Loughlin, of whom mention is made in that paragraph, having been removed to an hospital, a rumour of her death was circulated among the Roman Catholic population of Barrack-street, and Cullingtree-road and round about Old Pound. Whether by pre-concert we cannot say, but almost in a mass they turned out and commenced to wreck the houses of the Protestant inhabitants in Cullingtree-road. This having reached the Orangemen of Sandy-row, they assembled at once to defend their friends, and the two parties meeting, a most fearful engagement ensued.—Both parties appeared to be prepared for a determined encounter, as a vast number of them were armed with guns and pistols. Those who were not so armed tore down brick-bats from the dead walls and gathered stones from every quarter.

The commencement of the riot was about eight o'clock in the evening, and it began so suddenly that, before the constabulary were aware, several thousands were fighting in Durham-street and up to Mill-street. The balls were flying like hail, and the aspect of the people was murderous. It was quite impossible for the constabulary to make head against the determination evinced on both sides, and, even could they have succeeded for a little, they would have been immediately overwhelmed by reinforcements that poured into the Roman Catholic party from Mullan's corner.

In the mean time, fighting was going on in Carrick-hill. The rioters were armed with grapes, pitchforks, spades, shovels, and every weapon that hand could be laid on. It was apparently the rioters in that locality that poured upon the police in Durham-street. The Mayor, Mr. Tracy, and other magistrates came on the ground immediately, they received notice of the encounter, and proceeded to read the Riot Act; but before this was accomplished, a section of what, we are informed, was the aggressive party, began an indiscriminate attack on every house from Durham-place to midway down Townsend-street, and there is scarcely a habitation that is not more or less injured, and some of them are completely smashed, the windows and sashes broken to atoms, and the frames beaten in.

It is with great regret we have to mention that a young man named Spence, a mill-worker, was shot dead by the rioters; and although it is impracticable to arrive at any conclusion as to the number wounded, in consequence of their being carried off as they fell, yet persons who witnessed the fight for some time estimate those wounded at between thirty and forty, but whether fatally or not is beyond conjecture.

After the riot act was read, the military, horse and foot, were called out, yet it was with the greatest difficulty that the rioters were dispersed. From the Soho Factory to Christ Church, the causeway sidepaths are almost impassible from the bricks and stones used by the rioters.

It may be mentioned that head constable Henderson found several guns loaded with balls in Roman Catholic houses, but the names of the occupiers we, for obvious reasons, refrain from publishing.

Recreated from The Cork Examiner, Cork, July 16, 1852.

On Yesterday evening there were very many bonfires lighted in various parts of the city.

Some of the landlords of this and the neighbouring counties are threatening extermination, the roadside or the poor-house on every tenant who does not vote as they like.

Reprinted from The Waterford News, Waterford. July 21, 1852.

LEAGUE INTIMIDATION AND OUTRAGE.—We were yesterday evening informed that a very large number of the tenantry of Mr. Price, of Saintfield, travelling on cars, *en route* from that town to Hillsborough, in the earlier portion of the day, were stopped at Ballymacbrenan, and maltreated by a mob of Mr. Crawford's Leaguers. We have also heard that the carriage of Mr. Mussenden was stopped, that the horses were greatly injured, and that the carriage itself, after being wrecked, *was burned*.

A correspondent tells us that, during the day, the approaches to Hillsborough were infested by League desperadoes, who assailed the supporters of Conservative candidates with stones, and every other species of intimidation which it was in their power to practice. This is freedom of election! Shortly afterwards the same cowardly rabble attacked another train of cars occupied by voters moving in the like direction, about two miles from Hillsborough, on the cross road from Saintfield, and attacked them with bludgeons and *bars of iron*. A large number of the cars boldly dashed through their assailants and got clear of them but those of the remainder were savagely maltreated. One of the cars was broken to pieces, and a respectable gentleman-farmer, Mr. Forde Campbell, a tenant on the Marquis of Londonderry's Barnamaghery estate, had his nose literally split open by the blow of a bar or bludgeon. The party had to fly across the country, and eventually reached Hillsborough, by Lisburn, without further molestation.

Recreated from The Belfast News-Letter, Belfast, July 23, 1852.

TOTAL ROUT OF THE LEAGUERS IN DOWN.—PROTESTANTISM, LAW, AND ORDER, TRIUMPHANT!

THE most important of the county elections in Ireland—we might say in the United Kingdom—terminated, on Friday evening, in a glorious majority for Lord Edwin Hill and Mr. Ker, and in the utter discomfiture of the League nominee. There has been no greater triumph achieved for—we shall not merely say the Derby Ministry—but for the sacred cause of religious truth and liberty, and the scarcely less sacred cause of social order, since the General Election commenced. It is not too much to say that the eyes of the whole nation were fixed upon the issue which the electors of Down were called upon to determine.

Regarded as the very citadel of Protestantism and loyalty in Ireland, Down would, indeed, have given a heavy blow and a great discouragement to the Conservatism of the empire, if its intelligent, industrious, and high-minded yeomanry had returned to Parliament the champion of communism, voluntaryism, Radicalism, and all the other *isms*, political and religious, which now menace the Constitution, the Monarchy, the Protestantism, and the property of these realms.

But Down, though maligned on League platforms—though solicited by all the temptations which republican socialist doctrines hold out to the restless and the ignorant—has nobly vindicated the proud character it has so long maintained; and in spite of that terrorism which the League demagogues, lay and clerical, have drafted from the South—in spite of Popish intrigue and Ribbon organisation—has, by one decisive victory, proclaimed the soundness of its own principles, and stamped with the brand of defeat and shame the monstrous combination of mischievous elements which attempted to debauch and pervert its population.

Recreated from The Belfast News-Letter, Belfast, July 26, 1852.

THE SLAUGHTER AT SIXMILEBRIDGE.

ADDITIONAL PARTICULARS.

Late in the evening a young man named Michael Glynn was conveyed by his father, mother, and sister on a car from Sixmile-bridge to Barrington's Hospital labouring under a severe bullet wound in the groin. The ball passed clear through the fleshy part of the thigh, without affecting the bone; hopes are entertained of his recovery, though his condition is not free from danger. The agonised state of his parents and family could not be described. It appears that he was standing at a distance from the crowd and soldiers when the firing took place; and he alleges that the only cause given for the firing was some stones thrown by a few women who had been weeding potatoes near the green of Sixmile-bridge when they saw the voters escorted by Mr. Delmege and a party of the 31st. All was quietness and good order up to that moment. A man of the name of Haneen died of his wounds about six o'clock P.M. The lives of others are despaired of. Another man, whose name we have not ascertained, with a compound fracture of the shoulder bone, was conveyed to the Clare Infirmary at Ennis.

After the *military execution* of the poor men in Sixmile-bridge, it was shocking to witness the glee and delight with which the soldiery amused themselves amid the dead, the dying, and the wounded by whom they were encompassed!!

Nearly all the people left the village soon afterwards, and the peace that prevailed was that of the grave!

The officers and soldiers of the 31st marched into Limerick without the slightest concern for what had happened.

It appears certain on all hands that there would be no firing—at least no sudden murderous firing—were it not for the order to prime and load given in the early part of the morning at Thormond-gate. If such an order is usual remains to be seen.

Two of the soldiery are said to have been hit with stones, and the musket of one of them splintered; but, in addition to this, there was no cause whatever afforded for the firing, and this was done by stones thrown by women.

Twelve shots were discharged in all, each of which took effect—nearly all deadly effect.

Mr. M. Canny, of Clonmoney, coroner, impanelled a jury about five o'clock, p.m., to hold an inquest on the bodies of the dead. The inquest was adjourned till to-morrow (Saturday), when several witnesses will be examined.

Sir Lucius O'Brien, Lieutenant of the County, and Sir E. Fitzgerald, nephew of Sir John Fitzgerald, one of the candidates, were present soon after the *battue*, and expressed themselves in the most indignant terms at the outrage. Sir Lucius declared that there was no cause given for the firing as far as he could ascertain, and called upon the magistrates present to state who gave the order.

All the magistrates declared that they gave no order. The officer in command stated he gave no order.

The licentious soldiers fired at a considerable distance from the women who threw stones after them, and at the top of the street. They fired, as we have above stated, in two directions; in each direction there was a wall, which completely enclosed the people, so there was no escape whatever, one way or the other, from the murderous fire.

Michael Maloney was brought into Barrington's Hospital this day labouring under the effect of a gunshot wound over the hip joint. The ball has not been extracted.

This morning Mr. Delmege's milk was all upset at the milk market, and the utmost excitement prevailed among the people.

Recreated from The Freeman's Journal, Dublin, July 26, 1852.

(*From the Limerick and Clare Examiner of Saturday.*)

The facts of the case, so far as we have been able to determine them, are these—The tenantry on the estates of the Marquis of Conyngham and Colonel Wyndham, in the parish of Meelick, had received orders from the respective agents of those landlords, Messrs. Crowe and Keane, that they must poll for Colonel Vandeleur. Many of them, it is believed, would have been well pleased to have taken their stand with the popular party, not alone refusing to vote for exterminators, but polling for the popular candidates. But as few of them were bold enough to use the privilege the constitution gives, they were willing to adopt the temporising course of remaining altogether away from the poll.

Under these circumstances, many of the electors in and around Meelick came into Limerick in the course of Wednesday last, and took shelter in the vicinage of Thormond Gate. Several of them were accommodated for the night in the temperance assembly room in that quarter. There was no pretense of compulsion having been used to bring them there, or of duress to continue them. They were unwilling to exercise their franchise.

On Thursday morning, one of the Messrs. Keane, brother of the agent to Colonel Wyndham, appeared in Meelick, to collect the voters and take them to the poll. Many of them it was found had wandered from their usual pastures; Mr. Keane set himself about collecting them. In this labour he called to his assistance a gentleman in the commission of the peace, Mr. John Christopher Delmege, of Castlepark. A company of infantry was next procured, and these were marched to Thormond Gate, where, as we have stated, the miserable electors of Meelick had taken earth, and thought to burrow during the election. The infantry formed part of the 31st regiment, and were under the command of Captain Eager—we have heard, we know not truly, that this gentleman is a member of the Kerry family of that name.

Having reached the place, the doors of the rooms where they lay were at once thrown open, and the electors brought to the light of day.

Cars were soon procured, and the electors were placed on them, and, surrounded by the escort of the infantry before-mentioned, they were marched in triumph to Sixmile-bridge to record their votes *free* and *unshackled* for Vandeleur. Previous, however, to the march of the party, Mr. Delmege, as the magistrate in charge, thought it his duty to order the military to prime and load. The cortege set out in peace and without interruption—they arrived in the same way at their destination in the village of Sixmile-bridge. Upon reaching the village—for it is no more—the party of military and electors proceeded towards the polling place. There were not many people then on the street; the principal portion of what were there consisted of women and children from 7 years upwards. It was the first time a polling ever occurred at Sixmile-bridge, and it was necessarily an object of curious interest to see the parties come and go. The voters and their guard approached quite close to the line of the people; the cortege consisted of first a long car, drawn by four horses, next to this followed six covered cars, and the file closed by a second long car like the first. Mr. Delmege and the officers of the party rode with the guard. No sooner was the party discerned by the populace than they commenced to groan "the convicts," as they scornfully designated the electors under coercion. As they came nearer other indications of disapprobation were not withheld; and, if one might conclude from what was done, to the motive for doing it, the object would appear to be to enable the coerced electors to escape in the confusion. At first sods were thrown from the sides of the way, which are little else than potato fields, with a few scattered cottages, and then, as a corollary, a

(cont'd)

few stones were flung indiscriminately at the electors and military, and flung, we firmly believe, with no desire to injure any parties.

Let it be remembered that the military were on the cars the whole of the way—they did not walk as with an escort. By this time the party had reached within about ten yards of the people, and suddenly, without any preparation or previous notice—without any order to disperse, or threat of having recourse to force—without any warning whatever—we are not aware, indeed, whether the soldiery even left the cars and occupied their ranks—when into the very breasts of the unarmed people a murderous fire was poured! The result was precisely what might have been expected—every shot took effect! It is said that not more then twenty shots were fired; and when we recollect that the military fire by sections in such cases, we think the statements likely to be true—and six men fell dead immediately—two were so badly wounded that one has since died, and the eighth, cannot survive! From eight to ten have been wounded, and the parish priest of Sixmilebridge, the exemplary Rev. Mr. Clune, was struck by a ball which cut his head, but fortunately having glanced, his life was saved. The reverend gentleman was on the outside of the crowd, and with his back to the party approaching, a sure sign that he neither witnessed or apprehended any attack upon the military which could warrant the taking away of human life.

The question arises—who gave the orders to fire? Upon this point the statements were various. As we have said, Mr. J. C. Delmege, J.P., was the magistrate in charge of the party, and as it is well understood that when the military act under a magistrate they have it in command not to fire without his orders, it was at once stated that Mr. Delmege gave the word to fire. This statement, however, Mr. Delmege positively denies in a letter (already given in the FREEMAN).

Recreated from The Freeman's Journal, Dublin, July 26, 1852.

THE *BLACK* NORTH.
(*From the Nation.*)

Shame on the north! It has betrayed and sold Ireland and itself. We have heard of treachery, and bigotry, and slavishness, and shame only from one province of Ireland in the election; and that was the province most solemnly pledged, most validly interested, and best able to make a triumphant struggle. Everywhere tenant-right members have been returned to parliament unless in the Tenant-right district. Everywhere the people have rallied with sturdy independence for their own cause, unless where "sturdy" and "independent" are the favourite and native epithets. "The north began, the north held on"—the north bragged and boasted; and left the cause in the lurch at the last moment. There is the truth. Clare, like a skeleton in rags, standing on the verge of its grave, rose up, and swore that its old historic name should not be blotted; and though bailiffs drove the voters to the hustings, and bullets whistled among the people, that an exterminator should never represent it in parliament. The Twelfth of July sent from the hustings of New Ross news that should sound like a challenge through the province—not the less because it was a northern who stood there to vindicate the principles of the conference. Along the Ulster border every single county and borough did its duty gallantly. Catholic Louth began by returning a Protestant northern Tenant-righter. Meath sent a Leaguer at the head of the poll. Westmeath, and even Longford, pledged their members specifically and unequivocally to Crawford's bill. Leitrim, whose representation had been in the nomination of aristocratic families for a century, rose in insurrection against the strongest influence in the county to return the candidate of the League. Wherever else, unless in Ulster a tenant-right candidate appeared, the people fought for the cause at every sacrifice. Almost every constituency in Leinster, Munster, and Connaught exacted satisfactory pledges from its candidates. But all Ulster—not one.

Recreated from The Freeman's Journal, Dublin, August 2, 1852.

THE HARVEST.

As harvest time approaches we are blessed with a continuance of such weather as must satisfy the most anxious and loquacious alarmists, and effectually banish long faces and fearful forebodings. The grain crops in the neighbourhood of this city may be all described as looking well, and the present days of powerful and brilliant sunshine will secure an early realization of the best hopes indulged in during the season. The only gloomy perspective that can be conjured up relates to the unfortunate potato. About this esculent the fears entertained are certainly not exaggerated, though the worst to be apprehended is a loss of about one-third of the crop.—*Kilkenny Moderator.*

THE POTATO BLIGHT.—It is with feelings of a painful nature, that we have to add our testimony this week to the rapid spread of disease in the potato fields in this district. The withered leaves and the shrivelled stalks, together with the offensive smell which assails the passer by, gives cause to well-grounded alarm for the safety of the crop. Within the past week the spread of the disease has been more rapid than in any season that has succeeded the memorable 46—so much so that the apprehension of a general failure is not ill-founded. We have visited within a few days the counties of Galway, Roscommon, Longford, through Westmeath and the King's County, and in all these a field unvisited by this calamity has but in few instances come under our notice.—*Westmeath Independent.*

We regret to learn that the potato blight has appeared rather extensively in the county of Limerick, and in Clare to a considerable extent, between Ennis and Kilrush and on to Kilkee.—*Limerick Reporter.*

We are very reluctantly compelled to state that the blight upon the potato leaves has progressed with an alarming rapidity within the last eight or ten days. Little or no damage, however, is yet done to the root itself. We have never seen the markets stocked with a more abundant supply of potatoes, nor of finer quality. The appearances of the disease are yet nearly altogether confined to the spot on the leaf.—We have not seen many instances of its extension to the stalk. From early tillage of the crop, and its advanced stage of maturity before being overtaken by the blight, we are in sanguine hopes that the loss will be only trifling.—*Tuam Herald.*

The fatal potato blight has once again made its appearance. The crops in this neighbourhood are, we regret to say, affected to a considerable extent, and the farmers are now digging out the early portion of them, and sending them to market daily. From all we could learn on the subject, however, the injury yet done has not been as great as that sustained up to the same period last year; and it is confidently hoped that as the breadth of potatoes planted this season has been much greater, the consequences may still prove trivial.—*Galway Vindicator.*

The potato crop in this locality is very much injured by the late blight. The stalks in some large fields are regularly shrivelled up and crumbling into dust. It is feared that the disease will be greater this year than it has been for many seasons.—*Roscommon Journal.*

We don't mean to say that the disease has vanished, or is about to vanish entirely, but what we really believe is, that it is almost as certain, as any nighly approaching event can be, that we shall have a plentiful supply of our much-slandered, badly-doctored, yet incomparable vegetable. If the weather continues as promising as it has been for the last week, we are sure of having an early and abundant crop of wheat. A large area is laid under barley, in consequence of the good price it brought last year. Oats will give, perhaps, the average yield. Turnips, mangels, and other green crops have been extensively cultivated.—*Leinster Express.*

Recreated from The Freeman's Journal, Dublin, August 2, 1852.

THE IRISH ELECTIONS—THE TENANT CAUSE.

(From the *Freeman*.)

The Irish elections have terminated, and though we have to regret the failure of the efforts made to secure Tenant Right members in the northern counties, the general cause has signally triumphed, and the new Parliament will contain a compact, able, vigorous, and earnest Tenant Right party, to which Parliament has been hitherto unused, and from whose uncompromising devotion and unceasing labours the brightest hopes may be entertained.

The Tenant Right party has undoubtedly suffered a serious loss in the non-election of Sharman Crawford; but we confidently hope that before the new Parliament will have been many weeks sitting some place will be found for a man whose labours have been so eminently useful, and whose presence is so essential to give weight, authority, and guidance to the cause of tenant-farmers. Apart, however, from the miscarriage in Mr. Crawford's case, the Tenant League party have had sufficient success to counterbalance all the less important failures that befell them in the recent conflict.

In the old Parliament there was but one apostle of Tenant Right—Mr. Crawford. There were many men who voted with him whenever he brought the question before the house; but there was no man, save himself alone, who, in absence of an agitation on the subject, and in the absence of a popular movement in favour of Tenant Right, would have moved hand or foot for its accomplishment—no man who, with or without these stimulants, would have become an apostle of the tenant cause. In the new parliament there will many such apostles—men who, through evil report and through good, stood by the people; who, when others were apathetic, laboured with unabated zeal and confidence, and who now go into parliament to introduce their same zeal and the same laborious and preserving efforts that characterised them as the organisers and moving powers of the Tenant League.

NO POPERY.

An investigation, ordered by the Poor Law Commissioners, has been held in Oaghterard Workhouse, by Mr. Burke, Assistant Commissioner.

The following facts were disclosed in the course of the inquiry:—A female pauper, named Margaret Kelly, who was registered as a Protestant, being in a dying state, asked to have the attendance of the Catholic Priest in her last moments. The Master of the Workhouse, acting in compliance with his instructions, despatched two messengers simultaneously, one for the Catholic Curate, the Rev. Mr. Kavanagh, and the other for the Rev. Mr. O'Callaghan, the Protestant Chaplain.

The parson reached the death-bed first, and proceeded to discharge his spiritual functions against the remonstrances of the nurses and patients present, who stated that the woman desired to be prepared for death by the Catholic clergyman. Mr. O'Callaghan persevered in his ministry, and was so engaged when Father Kavanagh entered the ward, and asked permission to enquire of the sick woman if she wished his attendance. After a long resistance, he was enabled to interrogate her, and found that she had sent for him, and desired to die a Catholic.

The Rev. Mr. O'Callaghan, who is one of the most notorious and active of the western battalion of proselytization, and himself an apostate Catholic, prepared to battle for the departing soul and knocked down the Priest as the most conclusive way of settling the dispute. The reverend warrior had first delivered himself of a foul attack on Pope and Popery, Antichrist and mummery.

The end of this disgraceful scene was, that Father Kavanagh administered to the woman the sacraments for the dying. It has been distinctly proved by the master of the workhouse, the matron, the wardmaid, and several inmates of the house, that Margaret Kelly had desired the attendance of the priest. The whole of the sworn testimony established that Mr. O'Callaghan forced his ministry upon her, and acted in the most violent and outrageous manner.

There is something truly horrible in a riot like this around a death bed. If the last moments of wretched paupers are to be disturbed by the violence of intemperate soul-snatchers like Mr. O'Callaghan, it would be far better to dispense with such a mockery of Christian ministry; or to provide separate poor houses—one for Catholic paupers, and one for Protestant.

We shall anxiously await the decision of the Poor Law Autocrats in this remarkable case. There is but small chance, we fear, that it has not already been decided in the *bureau* of the Orange Viceroy; and that the Reverend Gladiator, O'Callaghan, will be applauded for his vigorous repulsion of the emissary of "Antichrist."

Recreated from The Nation, Dublin, August 7, 1852.

THE CROPS—THE POTATO DISEASE.

MONAGHAN.—Since our last, the progress of the disease appears to have been arrested. Some few fields have, to a certain extent, recovered their healthy appearance, and the quantity in market would not lead us to suppose that farmers were obliged to dig out and bring to market in consequence of damage.—*Northern Standard.*

LOUTH.—We deeply regret to have to announce that the potato crop in this county is most seriously damaged. The blight came very suddenly upon it; we were aware of the circumstances a week since, but refrained from mentioning it until we had quite assured ourselves as to the nature and extent of the disease, and we have only now to say, that, from all we have seen, there seems no prospect of the crop being, to any great extent, either useful or profitable.—*Louth Advertiser.*

DOWN.—The potato blight is, we regret to find, almost universal in this district. The tubers are becoming affected, and it is much to be feared, this uncertain crop will not be better than in the disastrous year of 1846. The corn fields are beginning to assume the golden hue of ripeness. Already several fields of winter-sown barley have fallen under the sickle, and in eight or ten days reaping will be pretty general in this district. All the cereal crops promise to be abundant.—*Downpatrick Recorder.*

GALWAY.—The accounts of the potato disease from every part of the country are as gloomy as ever; but we hope that a remnant will be saved sufficient to prevent the possibility of anything like famine. During the last two days we have had occasional showers, which, it is feared, will not serve the crop.—*Galway Vindicator.*

CAVAN.—It is with extreme reluctance that, in the discharge of our duty, we are compelled to state that this week the potato crop in the county of Cavan has been visited with "*the* blight." So extensive and general is the disease that scarcely a field (as far as we know from personal observation and through correspondents) has escaped. Immediately after the terrific thunder storm recorded in a late number, the rot made its appearance, and ever since has rapidly progressed. The potato stalks are withered or are fast withering, and the tubers are decaying in the ground before they have attained half their usual size. This year a larger breadth of land was planted with the potato than in any year since the famine set in, and we much fear the destruction of 1852 will be little less than in the fatal year of 1847. The oat crop has suffered some, but, we hope, not extensive, damage. The other crops, wheat, &c., promise fairly, and that is the utmost we can say for them.—*Anglo Celt.*

Recreated from The Belfast News-Letter, Belfast, August 9, 1852.

DR. GRAY—SHARMAN CRAWFORD— LANDLORD INTIMIDATION.

(*From the Tuam Herald.*)

We are glad to perceive from several communications which have appeared in the FREEMAN, extracted from some of the leading Ulster journals, that the friends of tenant-right, though vanquished for this time, are not discouraged, but that, on the contrary, they are buckling on their armour and making active preparations for the next election campaign. Until the result of the late contest bared up the matter to the public view, we were not aware that the northmen were so thoroughly landlord ridden, as they have proved themselves to be; nor so wanting in the spirit of martyr endurance which characterises the Catholic peasantry of the south and west. We say it not in the spirit of vain boasting, but with feelings of regretful consolation, that the Catholic yeomen of Monaghan have done themselves credit by the fidelity with which they clung to the cause of altars free and "happy homes" at the late election. If the good cause was lost, it has not been by want of courage in the Catholic electors. For the mostly truthfulness with which Dr. Gray, though a Protestant, has avowed the real cause of his defeat, the Catholics of Ireland owe him a debt of gratitude. After the statements which have appeared in public, and uncontradicted, as well as in the Dublin journals as in the *Dundalk Democrat*, the *Northern Whig*, and other influential Ulster papers, there can be no further doubt of the extent and intensity of the intimidation brought to bear by the landlords upon the electors. Take the statement, for instance, of Mr. Girdwood, agent for Sharman Crawford's committee in the county of Down, made at a public meeting on Friday last. It may be briefly summed up in the following startling facts:—"The high sheriff, whilst having given tickets of admission to the court-house to upwards of 300 of the friends of Hill and Ker, could be induced to give only 12 to the friends of Sharman Crawford." Again Mr. Girdwood states "that cart loads of bludgeons were sent into town on the carts marked with the name of the Tory candidate; the military also were in favour of the opponents of Sharman Crawford." Talk of clerical interference after these notable examples.—The same course, it appears, was adopted against Dr. Gray in Monaghan. The leaders of the movement are not, however, it seems, prepared to die so softly. Another election is admitted, on all hands, to be not far distant. The course of intimidation pursued at the late contest demonstrates to evidence the antagonism which exists between landlord power and cupidity on the one hand, and the just claims of the tenantry on the other. The stakes at issue are so great that the tenantry of Ireland cannot and will not permit the game to be played with loaded dice by their antagonists. Landlord property for the landlord, and tenant property for the tenant, must henceforth be the hustings cry at all and every future election. It must now be clear to the men of Down, Monaghan, and Tyrone, that the profession of "Orangeism" will not save them from the gripe of their landlords. They will not be nearer to the legalization of tenant-right, if, to please the grandmaster of the Orange Lodge, they were to wade knee deep in Catholic blood. The late contest has blasted that delusion, at once, and for ever. The northmen should take warning by the fate of the tenantry of the south and west. Identity of religious principles with his landlord is no safeguard from eviction for the poor Catholic tenant. And so it is, and will be in the north.

A spirit has been awakened which will not slumber until the question of "free altars and security for tenant industry" is settled on such basis as will put an end for ever in this kingdom to landlord and sectarian ascendancy.

Recreated from The Freeman's Journal, Dublin, August 10, 1852.

THE MASSACRE AT SIXMILEBRIDGE.

CORONER'S INQUEST—FIFTH DAY.

Thomas M'Grath was called and examined—I recollect the occurrence of the 22d July; I heard shots fired and saw men killed; immediately before I heard the shots fired I was standing near O'Brien's corner at the opposite side; I was near the potato filed wall; I came along with the voters and army from Flannery's corner to that place; I was on the same side of the road the whole time; before we got into the lane I heard shouting, but saw no stone-throwing or rioting; I did not see the military abused or threatened; I got as far as the Bridewell wall before I heard any shot fired; there was a van there; the front car of all was a jaunting-car; with four men on it and a driver; I was on the right side of that car from the time we entered the lane; when we arrived at the Bridewell-lane I saw an attempt made to cut the harness; I saw a man take a knife and try to cut the reins and bellyband; I saw the officer come up with a drawn sword and the soldiers advancing with charged bayonets; the soldiers did no harm, and the people rushed away; up to that I saw no sticks used, no stones thrown, and no violence; stones might have been thrown in the rear unknown to me and there might not; no stones were flung at me as I passed up the lane; when I walked up four or five yards I saw a gentleman fire a shot out of a small pistol; that gentleman was quite convenient to me; I saw a soldier step out of the ranks, and he fired and shot a man at the left, near the barley field; the man when he fell attempted to get on his knees; he fell again and never rose; I heard his name was Casey; at this time I did not see any stones thrown; the circumstances created much confusion; the people rushed here and there; I could see O'Brien's corner then; between where I stood and the corner I saw no rioting, or violence, or stone-throwing amongst the people and the military; I stood where I was at the time; I remained for a couple of minutes; there were military before and after; in half a minute I saw three soldiers fire very quick one after the other; there were two men killed by these shots; these men also fell near the barley field wall; I saw the gentleman who fired the pistol shot come back to the rear guard and say "fire, fire, front and rear"; there were three shots fired behind me, and a man killed within a short distance of me at the same side; when I saw the man fall I left the place and got over the potato field; when the firing was all over I returned and saw the man dead; the man who fell at the same side of me was not quite dead; I heard he was a smith at Newmarket, in Sir Lucius O'Brien's employment; I saw afterwards on that day the gentleman who fired the pistol; I saw him in the court-house; it was about an hour and a half or two hours after the firing was over; there were a good many people in the court at the time; I spoke to him after he had spoken to me; he told me not to be staring at him; I was looking at him then; I replied that he was the man that was after committing all the slaughter; I said that openly; he said nothing in reply [identifies Mr. Delmege as the gentleman who fired].

SIXTH DAY.

John Kelly examined by Mr. Coffey—I live at Ballyourgell, about two miles from this village; I am not at present in any employment; the last person I worked for was Mr. Gabbett, I was here on Thursday, 22nd July; I heard shots fired that day; I was a little bit up from the corner of the bridewell; immediately before I heard the shots fired I was standing close to the potato field; I saw the military that came on that way the time the shots were fired; the first place I met the military was down at the bridge; I accompanied them from the place I first met them to where I have described; I walked along with them all the time; I recollect having seen cars with the military; I was convenient to one of the covered cars for a while; I think it was one of the last cars; I did not continue walking by the side of that car from the time I entered the lane until I came near the bridewell wall; I walked with the cars at the left hand side until I came

(cont'd)

seven or eight perches over from the bridewell wall, and I then went to the right side; up to that spot in the lane I saw people on each side of the road; there were men, women, and boys; I saw them from the time I entered the lane to the time I stopped; some of the boys were big and some small; I saw "gorscons" and grown men there, from the time I entered the lane to the time I heard the shots; I saw stones thrown; I observed stones thrown first near the houses at the right hand side, near the bridewell lane, coming up to the court house; I think there were about from five to seven cars in the procession, but there might have been more; I did not see the persons who threw the stones; they were thrown from behind over me; I was passing down the lane; the lane is narrow and there is not much room for a crowd besides the military and cars; the breadth of the road at that place is about twelve feet, to the best of my belief; it is perfectly impossible that a dense crowd could have congregated between the car-wheels and the wall at either side of the road; I saw the place since several times; I think that 100 or 120 people could be crammed in the space between the cars and the wall; I am supposing that the people were closely packed, but they were not on this occasion; they were walking along with the military; I do not know the length of the potato garden wall; as I walked along I did not see people in the potato field or the barley field, nor did I notice any sitting on the wall; I took no notice of them, nor did I look to see; the cars were passing along when the stones were thrown; the stones could have hit the people as well as the military; upon my oath they were as much exposed to the stones as the military on cars; I was between the cars and the military; I was as much exposed to danger as the military; I did not see whether there were any military in the front or rear; some of the stones came out over my head; I believe the people who threw the stones were indifferent as to whether they struck a red coat or a frieze; I didn't see the stones strike any person, but I saw them strike the cars; the cars continued moving on while the stone throwing was kept up; I did not see any danger to man or horse from what stones were thrown; I did not consider that my life was in danger; If I did I would have left the place; as far as I can judge I heard about twenty shots fired; there might be a few less, or there might have been more; I did not go out of the lane until they were done firing; nor did I see the military go out; I went back towards the chapel for a time; and when I returned to see the people dead the military had left the lane; I got shot myself in the collar of the coat and shirt; I was standing seven or eight yards at the chapel side from the bridewell wall, towards Dalton's house, and about two yards out at the time I got shot; there were two shots fired so close one after the other, that it appeared the same as if a double-barreled gun were discharged; the wadding of both struck me in the side of the head, I thought it burned my hair on my head, and it actually burned the collar on my coat, made a hole in the front of my shirt, and struck against the potato field wall; it did not touch my skin; I did not know the soldiers who fired; from the manner the shot struck me I did not think the person who fired could have been more than the length of the musket from me; I was stunned, and when I recovered myself I saw a man shot through the temple, with his brains on his trousers and on the wall, the man was up against the wall, about four or five and a half yards from where I was hit myself; I crept on by the wall a short distance; when that shot was fired which hit me, and when I saw the man with his brains blown out against the wall, the stone throwing had ceased; if there were stones thrown, or if there had been any rioting at the time or place I would have seen it; I am quite positive there was no fighting or stone throwing when I was hit by the ball; I do not believe there was any; I would not believe any man who would swear there were stones flung, and a man knocked down; I saw one stone of a middling size pass out by a voter's head, but whether it struck him or not I can't say; upon my oath that was the only stone I considered of any consequence.

EIGHTH DAY.

Mr. Bolton Waller was examined by Mr. Graydon—I am a resident of Castletown, in the county of Limerick, and am a magistrate in that county; I remember the morning of the 22d July; I joined the military escort that accompanied voters at Wellesley Bridge; I went as far as Meelick, and waited there until the military returned; I accompanied them to Sixmile-bridge, where the military got off the cars; I saw Father Burke at the corner of the village; he was walking along addressing the people on the cars; he had a whip in his hand; there were people following him; I was in care of one car on which the voters were, about the fourth in front; Father Burke made several attempts to get up to the car; he shoved me and I shoved him, but we did not strike each other; the mob had considerably increased near the chapel; I was enabled for some time to keep the Rev. Mr. Burke off until the crowd pressed too much, and I called on two soldiers who were near to remember the orders they got from their officers—to do their duty and keep off this gentleman; Mr. Burke said he had a right to interfere; I did not get into the narrow part of the lane until after the shots were fired; the people did not get between the car and the soldiers before that; when the shots were fired I was two or three yards from the corner of the barley-field; as far as I could see the lane was crowded; I saw people standing on the wall of the cornfield; there were a few stones coming about us, and I saw some coming from the people on the wall in front; I saw a great number of them; when I heard the first shot fired I pushed forward as fast as I could towards the firing; I thought I might be of some use, but when I saw the nature of the *melee* I pushed on to get out of the way; the soldiers and the people were mixed up together, each man fighting for himself; the soldiers' ranks were broken, and there was stone-throwing of a dangerous character going on; I saw a large number of people in the barley-field; on the road, along the wall, and in the field, I should say there were, on a very moderate calculation, three hundred people; I saw stones thrown in the direction where the firing took place, but I cannot say whether the lives of the party were in danger, or whether a necessity for firing existed; the stones were calculated to endanger the lives of those at whom they were thrown; I was not at the place where the first shot was fired when it was fired; I saw Mr. Burke after the first shot was fired, and I heard him cry out to hold firing; he stooped low, and ran away.

NINTH DAY.

The following is a summary of the examination of Lieut. Henry Hutton, 31st regiment: I am nearly nine years in the regiment; served with the regiment in India, and was in active service; I have been in four general engagements and an affray; I was with the party that left Limerick with voters for Six-mile-bridge on the 22d July; we met at Wellesley-bridge; and took up some voters there; we came on cars to Six-mile-bridge; when we came into the village we continued our route straight on towards what I now know to be the chapel green, on from the police barrack; there were a great number of people collected there; we were received with hooting and groaning; the people followed us, and almost immediately commenced stone throwing; it continued without intermission on to the chapel; the mob pressed on us very much; I spoke to them several times as a way of remonstrance, but they only went on worse; they called the voters convicts; while this was going on the character of the stone throwing was very violent; I was struck three times with stones; also, several of my party; I heard the stones rattling off the bayonets; my view of the front was much impeded by the cars and people; I did not see the front guard, but I saw connecting files; about the time firing commenced, I think the front rank must have been in the lane; I was near the chapel at the time; before the shots were fired, the excitement was very great, and the stone throwing most violent; about the time I heard the first shot fired, or I think after it was fired, I ordered my men to load in presence of the people where we were; after loading, I marched the men on again, and notwithstanding the attack was renewed; the lives of all were in imminent danger at this time.

Recreated from The Nation, Dublin, August 14, 1852.

PRIZE FIGHT.

One of those disgraceful and demoralizing exhibitions, fortunately of such rare occurrence in this country, came off on Monday morning between six and seven o'clock, at Rathcoole, Naas road, between a man named Moore, "the Black Diamond," and another named Murphy, for large stakes the amount of which we could not learn.

Nearly three thousand people were present, interspersed with a large sprinkling of betters, and favorites of the "ring."

Two of th: A division of the metropolitan police, and eight of the constabulary were present, who made every exertion in their power to disperse the crowd and arrest the combatants, but to no available purpose, and the fight had to go on to the finish. Fifty-two rounds were fought, in which tremendous blows and falls were exchanged, when the Diamond was declared the victor, Murphy not being able to come to his fight, being regularly *hors de combat*, and frightfully mutilated.

The unfortunate man was conveyed to the Richmond Hospital, where he now lies, no hope whatever existing of his recovery.

EVICTIONS.—Over one hundred and twenty nine persons were evicted on last Monday, in the immediate neighbourhood of Galway. The property formerly belonged to Lord Oranmore, but was recently purchased in the Incumbered Estates' Court by Mr. Barton, the late Candidate for the representation of Clonmel.—*Galway Vindicator*.

THE DEFENCE.

If no potent accusation is hidden behind the evidence already produced for the defence the defence is palpably a complete downbreak. The slaughter could only be paliated by a formidable attack, and the presence of the people in such overwhelming numbers as to imperil the lives of the military. But it is confessed there were "breaks" in the thin line of people who stood along the potato and barley field; and the untrodden condition of the crops in each, the narrowness of the road and the space covered by the cavalcade, showed that the crowd could never have been very considerable. The vehicles and military filled the lane-way almost as a bullet fits in a barrel; and the margin beyond the walls, in one place being narrow, and in the other just *nil*, there was not standing room for an overpowering crowd.

The estimate of Mr. Waller is three hundred of all ages and sexes, in front and in rear, on the right hand and left, and those distributed along the train of cars. some in extreme youth, some in old age, some entirely quiescent, and others, if hooting, non-combatants in fact—the escort could not have had, each for himself, or all in a body, to encounter assailants hard to subdue. If the lane were Thermopylæ, and the three hundred of all ages all Spartans, the "pass" might have been perilous to the military party; but near a reserve force, backed by civillians, backed with stout freeholders to call upon, and against so few combatants, none of whom had a pistol, the escort must have been the weakest and worst soldiers that ever fixed bayonet, if they could not have repulsed the "crowd" with that weapon.—*Limerick News*.

Reprinted from The Waterford News, Waterford, August 20, 1852.

SIX-MILE BRIDGE—The Verdict.

After fourteen days investigation, it will be seen that the verdict of "willful murder" has been found against the soldiers who killed the people at Six-Mile Bridge. A great deal has been said as to the provocation the soldiers received; but then, we ask, where are their killed?—where are their slain? Nowhere. Not a single soldier was killed after this desperate fight, or "riot" or anything else you like to call it, on the part of the people. It is a satisfaction to the country, at all events, that these butcher soldiers should be put on their trial.

Read Mr. Coffey's remarks at the conclusion of the inquest:—"There was a fact in this case which all the ingenuity of man could not get over—the lane was narrow—there were seven vehicles in the lane, four horses under one of them—there were voters in the cars, and forty-two soldiers by their sides, and though they must have been closely packed, and though stones were falling like hail, where were the casualties and injuries received? One soldier admitted he was seriously hurt, but the rest of the assertions were all a farce; and among the public men wherever all over Europe this transaction shall become known, there could be but one feeling of strongest disgust against these *brave* men who raised their loaded muskets against flying men, and hurried six men into eternity under the savage fire of a savage soldiery."

The Coroner made the following remarks:—"Soldiers deserve no protection from their position as soldiers, unless they acted in firing under the order of their officer; they stand in the same light as any other subject would who, being molested in the performance of a lawful duty and in danger, have a right to defend themselves. Unless you believe that their lives were in real peril, and that they felt them to be so, that soldiers under the command of a brave and experienced officer, and also in charge of a magistrate, who should be supposed to be close to that officer in the moment of danger, should fire loaded guns amongst their fellow creatures without the orders of that magistrate given through their officers, the moment they did so they acted in the capacity of citizens defending themselves from real or imaginary danger."

Having delivered his charge, and after some discussion as to points of evidence, the Coroner directed that the jury were not bound to specify the particular men who fired the shot by which a particular man was killed.

The Coroner then put to the jury the issues they had to try, and said it was for them to consider whether their verdict should be one of manslaughter or justifiable homicide.

Mr. Coffey.—Suggested that a verdict of murder was within the range of their consideration.

The Coroner.—With respect to murder, the circumstances of the case and the provocation received, whatever it was, must do away with that, the provocation has been admitted.

The jury retired to their room shortly after three o'clock. At about twenty minutes to five, the jurors returned into court, and stated, twelve jurors had agreed to their verdict. The foreman here handed the issue paper to the Coroner—containing the finding as follows:—We are satisfied that John C. Delmege, J.P., John Gleason, (first), James Postings, William Banners, John Thompson, John Dwyer, James Sharpe, Thomas Clarke, and Corporal John Carter, soldiers of her Majesty's 31st Regiment are GUILTY of the WILLFUL MURDER of Jeremiah Frawley, on the 22d July last. This verdict exculpates Isaac Weston and William Whitebread.

The military against whom the verdict was returned, have been removed in custody of the Dragons, and lodged in the County Gaol, at Ennis. It is rumoured, we know not on what authority, that Mr. Delmege has left for the Continent.

Recreated from The Waterford News, Waterford, August 20, 1852.

America—Letter from an Emigrant.

By the last mail we received a letter from a respectable young Irish girl, who sailed from this port per the *Orinoco*, for New York. The following is but an extract from it:—

"NEW BEDFORD,* State of Massachusetts,
"July 31, 1852.

"When we began to recover from sickness, we danced and sung the whole passage. We had a very good violin player on board. I was so comfortable that I did not care if I was sailing since. The Captain (Knox) was very kind to me—he is a very kind man, and so were the two Mates, really civil men. We arrived at Staten Island in the evening; but the Captain did not like to let the passengers go up to New York till next morning. "This is a good place for girls when they once get settled. The Yankees don't like to take a *green horn* when they can get old hands; but once a person gets in they are all right. This is a fine place; it is not one bit warmer than the old country. There is not a wholesomer place in the States. It is a small town, about as large as Carrick-on-Suir. I never enjoyed better health in my life than I do now. The sea made me really healthy. I don't feel home sick. If I was at home again I would come out here. There are some prospects for a young person in this country. Servants have from one dollar to two and half dollars a week, and their board of the best kind. I would not like to live in New York, it is so much crowded. The girls don't eat with their masters, and they say "sir" and "mam" as they do at home. There is Mass here only every second Sunday. There are very bad Catholics here; but there are more good ones. "ELIZA."

* New Bedford is about 400 miles from New York.

☞ Great numbers of labourers are now employed on the Kilkenny Railroad; and the county was never known to be in so peaceable a condition. So much for employment.

Think always of eternity, and temptations shall cease to allure.

THE SIX-MILE-BRIDGE VERDICT.
(FROM THE TIMES.)

The Coroner's jury have returned their verdict at the Six-mile-bridge inquest. Fourteen days have been consumed in the mockery of an investigation which might as well, for the purposes of justice, have never taken place. The verdict is one of "Willful Murder" against the unfortunate soldiers, who simply endeavoured to save their own lives and those of the voters under their charge from the ruffianly savages who were pressing on them from all sides, and had well nigh succeeded in carrying their murderous purposes into effect. The investigation was as perfect a mockery as ever disgraced the walls of a room which by any abuse of arguing, we must speak of as "a court of justice!" The jury went in determined to find the men guilty—no matter what the evidence might be—no matter how impudent and transparent the perjury of the Irish witnesses—no matter how flagrant the contradiction between their respective statements—no matter, in the case of each witness, how irreconcilable the first with the concluding portion of his testimony—no matter how clear and consistent the depositions of the witnesses upon the other side, or how much in accordance with the progress and result of the whole affair. They did not go to execute justice, but as blind agents and ministers of the fierce passions which actuated the gang of savages by whom the Queen's troops were attacked in the simple performance of their duty. It is obvious enough that although the jurors may have forgotten their duty as citizens, and as men of common honesty and character, not the hair upon the head of any of the soldiers ought to be injured. Things have not come to such a pass yet that we will deliver up to the fury of a vindictive mob, a number of men who have committed no greater crime than that of defending their own lives, whilst engaged in the discharge of a duty which they had no choice but to perform. Let them take their trial by all means, but not before a Six-mile-bridge jury. The first step must be to remove the soldiers to some part of the country where they may have a fair trial; we do not mean any hotbed of Protestantism or Orangeism, or any otherism, but to some spot where the witnesses and the jurors shall not combine together to carry out their private revenge with all the solemnities of public justice, and by any amount of perjury that may be necessary to carry their purpose into effect.

Recreated from The Waterford News, Waterford, August 27, 1852.

EXTERMINATION BY A BISHOP.

By reference to our Poor Law Report, it will be seen that the Right Rev. Dr. DALY, Bishop of Cashel, &c., has, on the 13th and 16th of August, used the *crowbar* instead of the *crozier*, in the eviction of "several persons" off his property. This fact we have on the written testimony of Mr. O'GORMAN, relieving officer. In our next, we shall, we hope, be in a position to give the names of these several persons with other particulars relative to the "Tenant Right," which his Lordship practices towards his poor people.

When Bishops of the Church—meek and humble followers of CHRIST, who carried his cross to show his humility—are banishing the people, can we wonder that hard-pinched landlords resort to harsh means? Only think of a man, with his many thousand pounds a-year for the *cure* of souls, falling back upon the *crowbar !!* in the midst of a potato blight !!! Oh! God help us !

Reprinted from The Waterford News, Waterford, August 27, 1852.

CARRIAGES.

FOR SALE,
AT
STEPHENS'S COACH FACTORY,
41 BISHOP-STREET,
(Established A.D. 1800.)

A Pilentum for a pair of horses.
An Open Mail Drag, London built.
A light One Horse Open Phaeton.
A Pony Phaeton, equal to new.
Two cheap One Horse Phaetons, in good order.
An excellent Covered Car, price 15 guineas.
A light Covered Car on four wheels.
A Sociable Car equal to new,
An Outside Car and Harness, &c.

☞ A remarkably light Open Albert Phaeton, well worth the inspection of persons wanting a commodious One Horse Carriage.

FOR SALE
AT
ROBERT E. GRADY'S COACH FACTORY,
38 DAWSON-STREET,
Opposite the Mansion House Gardens,

A handsome Victoria Phaeton.
A light Brougham.
A Pilentum with side lights.
A Clarence.
A light-running London-built Tilbury.
A fashionable Domestic Phaeton, equal to new.
A Coach Car.
A strong Outside Car.
A fashionable Outside Car in excellent order.
A light Phaeton, with head and removeable seat.
A Park Phaeton.
A Stanhope Gig.
A Whitechapel Tax Cart.
A Dog Cart.

☞ Carriages to let with option of purchase.
New Outside Cars, Pony, and Park Phaetons, Clarences, &c.

Reprinted from The Nation, Dublin, September 4, 1852.

DUBLIN CASTLE.

HIS EXCELLENCY THE LORD LIEUTENANT has been pleased to appoint WILLIAM VALENTINE, 92, GREAT BRITAIN-STREET, Italian Warehousemen to his Excellency. Dated this 28th day of August, 1852.
ADMIRAL MONTGOMERIE, Comptroller.

Reprinted from The Nation, Dublin, September 11, 1852.

INSOLVENT DEBTORS' COURT—Sept. 13.

The sittings of this court were resumed this morning by Mr. Commissioner Law, who disposed of the business set down for hearing in all the courts.

In re George Henry De Strabolgic Neville Plantagenet Harrison.

This insolvent, a tall, military-looking personage, was described as above, and known as Prince de Plantagenet Harrison; then as General Harrison; then as Marshal Plantagenet; then as George Henry Harrison, formerly of Jermyn-street, St. James's; then of Mexico; then of Peru, a General officer to the Peruvian army; then of Monte Video; then of Corrientes, in the Argentine Republic, a general officer in the army of the Republic of Corrientes and Uruguay; then of the Rio de Janeiro, in Brazil, Ambassador from Corrientes to Brazil; then of the United States of America; then of the Falls of Niagara; then of the Island of Cuba; then of St. Domingo; then of Venezuela; then of New Grenada; then of Curaçoa; then of Hayti; then of the United States; then of No. 3, Verulam-buildings, Gray's-Inn, London; then of Horsmonden, in the county of Kent; then of the kingdom of Denmark, a general officer in the Danish army; then of Sweden; then of Frankfort-on-the-Maine, Lieutenant General in the army of the Germanic Confederation; then of the kingdom of Sardinia; then of Rome; then of Naples; then of Vienna; then of the kingdom of Saxony; then of Hanover; then of the Hague; then of 3, Verulam-buildings; then of Paris; then of Madrid; then of Grenada; then of Gibraltar; then of Morocco; then of Lisbon; then of Holstein, a general officer as aforesaid; then of the kingdom of Prussia, a prisoner; then of Gloucester-place, Hyde Park; then of North-bank; and now of the Queen's Prison, in no employ or occupation.

The only assets stated in the schedule consisted of a claim on the Government of the Republic of Corrientes for £3,000 on account of expenses incurred while ambassador to Brazil.

Reprinted from The Cork Examiner, Cork, September 17, 1852.

DEATH OF FIELD MARSHAL THE DUKE OF WELLINGTON.

DOVER, TUESDAY, 5 P.M.

His Grace the Duke of Wellington was seized with illness this morning, and expired at Walmer Castle at a quarter past 3 this afternoon, after a succession of fits.

A young seaman, scarcely 19 years of age, belonging to the frigate La Fort, who was sentenced to death by court-martial for striking his captain with a sabre, was executed at Brest on the 6th inst. His youth, and the marks of repentance he exhibited on his trial, led to the belief that his sentence would be commuted, but in consequence of his previous bad conduct, and the necessity for making an example, the law was suffered to take its course.

Reprinted from The Belfast News-Letter, Belfast, September 17, 1852.

AGRARIAN OUTRAGE IN COUNTY ANTRIM.—On Sunday, the 12th instant, about three o'clock in the morning, the inhabitants of Kells were aroused by the cry "Fire!" and found an entire range of houses in one burning mass along the eave. Fortunately, the morning was quite calm; had it been otherwise, the entire village might have been consumed.

There is no doubt the fire originated from the hands of an incendiary, as in *five* distinct places matches had been set to. The fire was discovered by a young man returning from the neighbourhood, who aroused the inhabitants, and with much difficulty got it extinguished. Fortunately it was discovered at that moment; had it not, there is no doubt four families must have perished in the flames. This is the second time the proprietor of these premises has been visited by incendiaries. His corn mill and kilns, with a large quantity of grain, was burned down a few months ago by those agrarians who infest the neighbourhood. A few weeks ago, a most respectable farmer, who lives convenient to Kells, had his hay thrown down on Sunday morning, and scattered all over the field, and afterwards threatened, by letter, "should he offer a reward to find out the guilty party, his premises would be burned."

MALICIOUS OUTRAGE.—On the night of Saturday the 11th or early in the morning of Sunday the 12th inst., some person or persons unknown, entered the corn field of a farmer named Samuel Mercer, of Lisnacarren, near Hillsborough, and maliciously threw down forty stooks of oats, and loosed the sheaves thereof and scattered the oats through the field. Mercer has been always considered an inoffensive person, and no cause is given for the outrage, except that he rendered himself obnoxious to some of his neighbours—supporters of Mr. Crawford—by voting for Lord E. Hill and Mr. Ker at the late election. Others say that he was employed to distribute the money allowed to some men who acted at the election, and a dispute arose as to the manner in which he divided the amount allowed. Mercer has served the necessary notices to apply for compensation at the next Special Presentment Sessions to be holden at Dromore, for the loss and injury sustained by him, which will amount to £4. As soon as the occurrence was made known to that vigilant officer, Head-Constable Francis Murphy, Dromore, he proceeded to the scene of outrage, and there is every reason to believe that he will be able to bring to justice the perpetrators of this wanton outrage.

Recreated from The Belfast News-Letter, Belfast, September 17, 1852.

THE DUKE OF WELLINGTON IN THE IRISH HOUSE OF COMMONS.

The first act of his life was eminently, and so to speak, *prophetically* Irish—of course we speak of his public life. He was a Member of the Irish House of Commons in 1792 and '93—and he had the singular good fortune to move the Address to the Crown, in answer to the Lord Lieutenant's speech. That speech contained a paragraph about the advisability of relaxing the Penal Laws against Catholics, and, in coming to this paragraph, the young *Aide-de-Camp* was most vehement and emphatic in his panegyric on its policy. This man, in his old age, was the Prime Minister in whose administration the final measure was consummated.—*Evening Post*.

PUBLIC NOTICE.

MESSRS. TRAIN & CO. beg to inform parties who may intend coming to Cork to engage for their BOSTON PACKET of the 5th OCTOBER that, through the kindness of their Irish Friends in Boston, that Ship is now full of Persons paid for by relatives in that City, and none but those can have a Passage by her.

To prevent the disappointment and delay incident to this, Messrs. TRAIN & Co. will dispatch the Magnificent Extra Packet Ship,

CLARA WHEELER,

Captain NELSON—2000 Tons Burthen.

ON THE 12TH OCTOBER, PUNCTUALLY.

The Clara Wheeler is one of the Finest, the Largest, and the Fastest Ships in the Transatlantic Trade, and will be fully fitted and found in the best possible manner.

For particulars apply to

TRAIN & Co.,
121, St. Patrick Street, Cork.
W. NEIL CONNOR, *Manager*. [244]

Reprinted from The Cork Examiner, Cork, September 17, 1852.

WE, this day, record with feelings of regret which will be shared in by the entire population of this vast Empire, the death of the Duke of Wellington, which took place yesterday afternoon, at Walmer Castle, at twenty minutes past three o'clock. His grace took his usual exercise on Monday, and retired to rest in perfect health; but, between six and seven o'clock yesterday (Tuesday) morning, he was seized with a sudden illness of so alarming a character that it was deemed necessary to send immediately for medical assistance. Drs. Macarthy and Hulke, of Deal, promptly attended, and soon afterwards the Duke had a violent fit, which continued for some time, and was followed by several others. At nine o'clock, he became insensible, in which state he remained until the time of his death, which occurred, as we have stated, shortly after three o'clock. The only members of the family present were Lord Charles Wellesley and Lady Wellesley.

His grace completed his 83rd year on the 1st of May last. The greatest captain of the age—the victor in an hundred fights—the pacificator of India—the liberator of Europe from a fierce military despot—the honest and high-minded statesman, whose sense of duty was paramount to all considerations of party, and whose patriotism rose superior to all political influences—the man whose fame for nearly half a century has been blazoned over the civilised world, is no more; and it is in no extravagant spirit of eulogy that we say of him "we shall not look upon his like again."

Arthur Wellesley, Duke of Wellington, third son of Garret, second Earl of Mornington, and of Anne, eldest daughter of Arthur Hill, Viscount of Dungannon, was born at Dangan Castle, county Meath, Ireland, on the 1st of May, 1769. His education commenced at Eton, and he afterwards studied at the Military College of Angiers.

At the early age of eighteen he was appointed to an ensigncy in the 73rd Foot, and was shortly afterwards made lieutenant. When barely of age he was returned to the Irish Parliament for the borough of Trim, which was in the interest of the Mornington family, and it was, doubtless, owing to the same influence that his military promotion was so rapid, as we find him in 1793 appointed to a lieutenant-colonelcy in the 33rd Foot. In the following year he was first ordered upon active service, and with his regiment joined the Duke of York's army in the Netherlands, the operations of which are merely a disastrous record of brave exertions ineffectually struggling against ill fortune. Colonel Wellesley was intrusted with the perilous task of bringing up the rear guard during the retreat, and gave striking evidence of activity and intelligence in the manner in which he accomplished this duty. On his return to England he was ordered to the West Indies, but the fleet was repeatedly driven back by unfavourable weather, and finally returned to port. Before it could put to sea again, a change of orders sent Colonel Wellesley and the 33rd to India, where he landed in February, 1797. At the storming of Seringapatam, Colonel Wellesley commanded the reserve in the trenches, and was subsequently appointed commandant of that fortress. In July, 1799, he received the command of the provinces of Mysore and Seringapatam; and here he first gave evidence of that energy and decision which distinguished him in after life, in the repression of military disorder, and the promptness and rapidity of his movements, which enabled him to surprise and cut off the formidable robber chieftain Doondiah. In May, 1800, he was offered by his brother the command of the Batavian expedition; but, at the urgent request of Lord Clive, who could ill spare him, he gave up what would have proved a lucrative and honourable post, and sacrificed his private interests to the exigencies of the public service. He was prevented from joining another expedition against the French by an attack of intermittent fever, and soon after, as Major-General Wellesley, we find him entrusted with very extensive civil and military powers in the district of Poonah, where his local knowledge, and the personal influence he had acquired over the Mahratta chiefs, were found to be extremely valuable. His first exploit was the siege and capture of the fortress of Ahmednuggur; and on the 23rd of September following was fought the memorable battle of Assaye, in which the determined courage and discipline of between 4,000 and 5,000 men, aided by the advantageous position selected for them by their general, effected the signal defeat of between 40,000 and 50,000. This was General Wellesley's first pitched battle; and although few military operations have been more discussed and cavilled at, the inevitably disastrous consequences of a retreat, and the moral effects of the blow, which was felt throughout India, abundantly justify the bold and decisive course adopted by the young and energetic commander. So highly was this service estimated by the inhabitants of Calcutta, that a monument was erected to commemorate it, and a sword, valued at 1,000 guineas, presented to General Wellesley. The officers of his division presented him with a service of plate, valued at 2,000 guineas, on which the word "Assaye" was engraved, and he received, in addition, the thanks of Parliament, and was made Knight of the Bath.

It is needless to refer to the rapid succession of important events which led to the battle of Waterloo, and the final overthrow of the power of Napoleon. The return of the French Emperor, after his voluntary abdication, was the signal for a combined and determined movement on the part of the leading powers of Europe, as arranged at the Congress of Vienna, to put an end to French aggression, at whatever cost. On the 18th of June, 1815, after some preliminary contests, in which the Prussians were compelled to fall back, the allied forces, under the command of the Duke of Wellington, met the advancing French army on the plains of Waterloo, and after a sanguinary struggle, which lasted till sunset, the simultaneous advance of the allied troops and the Prussians, who had just arrived on the field of battle, effected the total rout and disorganisation of the French, while the occupation of Paris, and the convention which followed close upon it, attested to the important moral and political results of this signal victory. With the exception of the part the Duke took in procuring the restoration of the works of art which had been taken by the French from the different Continental powers, and the deep stain which attaches to his character for obstinately refusing to interfere to save the life of Marshall Ney—an act which his warmest friends and admirers have never fully justified—his military career ends here.

His political parliamentary career may be said to commence with the famous declaration which he made in 1819, and which was so frequently referred to when subsequent events had given it additional significance and importance, that Roman Catholic emancipation was impossible without some security for the Protestant religion, of which he saw no reasonable prospect.

The Duke's personal habits were extremely temperate, if not abstemious. He slept little, and, whether from old military associations of for health's sake, used a hard mattress and a camp bed. He appeared to avoid display in his dress, equipage, and attendants, preferring horse exercise to the state and luxury of a carriage; and even when increasing weakness rendered it a task of some difficulty to sit erect upon horseback, day after day he was still to be seen ambling slowly down to the House of Lords, touching his hat to the crowds assembled round the entrance to catch a glimpse of the veteran warrior. His household was said to be a model of good order and good management. He incurred no debts; punctual and precise in all his dealings, he was always just, and frequently—though privately—very generous. His Waterloo banquets, which for many years drew around him all his surviving companions in arms in this his last glorious field, were the only exceptions to his usual indifference to display.

Recreated from The Belfast News-Letter, Belfast, September 17, 1852.

THE SERVICES OF WELLINGTON.
(*From the Times.*)

We believe we should best describe the national feeling at this remarkable period by saying that no one can yet fully realize the loss which the country has sustained. The Duke of Wellington, for generation after generation, had lived among us so long, and had so adapted his presence and capacities to the changing exigencies of time, that it requires some effort to look back on more than the last stage of such an eventful life. For most political characters it would be distinction enough to say that they had been appealed to for nearly twenty years, in every crisis of the State; but these twenty years would not carry us even to the Duke's own Ministerial career, and this career itself did not commence till a military life of prodigious celebrity and duration had finished. Even Lord Grey's premiership now wears almost an historical aspect, but the great Duke was Premier before Lord Grey. He was the contemporary and colleague of Liverpool, Melville, Sidmouth, Castlereagh, and Bathurst—names which have long been consigned, with various remembrances, to the pages of the past. Though not absolutely a member of the Administration, he exerted a material influence on the policy of England when existing ministers were in their cradles. He was a powerful and energetic mover in times which the present generation can only reach by study, and can scarcely comprehend without an effort. The great Duke's actual span of life was extraordinary, but it acquires almost a character of immensity when we think of the events it embraced. Into the fourscore years of Arthur Wellesley were crowded the revolutions and wars of two ordinary centuries, and the course and consummation of these wars and revolutions were controlled in no small degree by his own achievements. The great Duke had been in the confidence of Cabinets who were little less despotic than the Cabinets of Austria and Naples, and yet he survived till the days of Disraeli and Cobden, and was not a protectionist.

Recreated from The Belfast News-Letter, Belfast, September 20, 1852.

THE DUKE'S TITLES.

The Duke was Duke, Marquis Earl, and Viscount Wellington, Marquis and Baron of Douro, in the United Kingdom; Prince of Waterloo in the Netherlands; Duke of Ciudad Rodrigo and a Grandee of the first class in Spain; Duke of Victoria, Marquis of Torres Vedras, and Count of Vimiera, in Portugal; a Knight of the Garter; Privy Councillor; Commander-in-Chief of the British army; a Field Marshal in the services of Great Britain, Russia, Prussia, Austria, Spain, Portugal, and the Netherlands; Colonel of the Granadier Guards; Colonel in Chief of the Rifle Brigade; G.C.B.; G.C.H.; Knight of the Golden Fleece in Spain; the Black Eagle in Prussia; the Tower and Sword in Russia; Maria Theresa, in Austria, and of many less distinguished orders. He was Constable of the Tower, Rangers of St. Jame's and Hyde Parks; Chancellor of the University of Oxford; Commissioner of the Royal Military Academy; Master of the Trinity House; a Governor of King's College, and of the Charterhouse; a Trustee of the British Museum, and a D. C. L.

Reprinted from The Waterford News, Waterford, September 24, 1852.

THE FASHIONS FOR OCTOBER.
(*From Le Follet.*)

Autumn is already sufficiently advanced to cause much thought and invention for the approaching winter; and the singular mixture of materials and costumes visible at the between-seasons gives scope to the imagination as to what is likely to be the "mode." The melange of rich and light materials—gauze and satin velvet, and tulle—produces graceful and pleasing effects. Among the novelties for bonnets, scolloped velvet, with application of straw, mixed with tulle or blonde, is much admired. Velvet is used in various forms, sometimes forming a fanchon; at other times flat bands, placed according to fancy on the crown and front of the bonnet.—Some of the capotes are made of velvet drawn on the bias, with the crown entirely of velvet, and a light design in straw ornamenting the whole, having the appearance of gold lace. We have been able to judge of the effect of this novelty, having seen one that had just been produced by one of our artistes. It was of black tulle bouillonne, scolloped at the edge; bands of velvet, also scolloped, were placed to separate each bouillonne of tulle, and ornamented at each side of the crown with a bunch of maize and violet velvet flowers. The inside was trimmed with a triple row of blonde round the face, and a bunch of maize placed high on each cheek, the same style of capote in green and black, or pink velvet and tulle, with an application of straw work.

The trimmings for bonnets are composed of wreaths of velvet foliage, mixed with very small ostrich feathers—garlands of satin volubllis, or bunches of satin flowers, which take the place of the ribbon bows formerly used on the capotes.

A very pretty capote is formed of black tulle, with deep points of blue velvet reaching from the crown to the edge of the bonnet, trimmed with blue daisies and brown foliage. A simple capote is composed of three papillons of blonde, over which are fastened bands of narrow velvet ribbon. This capote may also be made of some light-coloured taffetas, mixed with blonde lace, caught over at intervals with narrow velvet ribbon.

Large cachemire squares, embroidered with silk and gold, will be very fashionable this winter, and are brought to great perfection in the manufactories in Lyons. We have seen some beautiful robes of fancy taffetas, trimmed with a single deep flounce, having at the bottom a wreath formed of exquisite narrow ribbon, in raised designs, appearing like shaded moss.

Recreated from The Freeman's Journal, Dublin, October 2, 1852.

THE EXODUS.—From all quarters the cry is still the same. The population is flying by wholesale, and, unless some unforeseen obstacle interposes, the next census will show a more startling result with respect to the decrease of the old race than the official return of 1851. The *Clare Journal* thus mourns over the exodus of the people:—All parties among us are seemingly turning their faces to the far west—the home beyond the deep. Old, middle-aged, and young are on the move, leaving the old country, where there seems to be no hope, for the young, where hope is budding with the certainty, in their imagination, of bearing good fruit. It is really distressing to contemplate the changes that a few years will effect in Old Ireland if the desire for leaving that now agitates the people shall continue. Before this period of the year until the present all idea of leaving for America was deferred until "spring returned again." The season for emigration closed at the beginning of our harvest, and the people never thought of facing the wintry blast before the coming spring; but now spring, summer and autumn are alike. The streets are daily crowded by families on the move. It seems to them as if they had only to travel a hundred miles, instead of thousands. And why is this? There is now one great inducement in addition to that which before induced them, and that is, there people are there before them. The old-remembered faces that disappeared a few months since are waiting, with the blush of hope, to assist them to leap ashore on the land of their adoption, and to sleep once more under the same roof with son or daughter, that they never hoped to see on this side of the grave. This is now a great cause for the long-continued stream of emigration. Yesterday, nearly the entire day, the street was crowded with cars, waiting for families to complete their arrangements with the emigration agent. They are gone, and the numbers are sufficient to leave a blank in the parish where they resided, that will not be easily filled.

Recreated from The Nation, Dublin, October 2, 1852.

EMIGRATION ACT.

The new emigration act came into force on Friday last. It enacts with regard to every emigrant ship proceeding from any part of the United Kingdom, to any place out of Europe and not within the Mediterranean sea, that she shall not, under penalty of seizure, clear out without a certificate from the emigration officer, and a bond given by the master to the crown for the performance of the provisions of the act. To every adult passenger (*i.e.* over fourteen years of age), twelve square feet must at least be allowed, if the vessel be not intended to proceed beyond the tropics, not less than fifteen otherwise; two tons of registered tonnage must be allowed for each adult—in all cases two persons under fourteen to be considered as one adult.

All unmarried male adults, too, must have separate sleeping accommodation in the fore-part of the ship; in no case shall more than two persons be permitted in the same berth; no two adults of different sexes to sleep in the same berth except husband and wife.

Every passenger ship is to be properly provided with an hospital, necessities, proper ventilation, life boats, life buoys, fire-engines, &c., and must not carry as a part of the cargo any horses, cattle, gunpowder, vitriol, lucifers, guano, green hides, or any other commodity to which the emigration officer may object; no part of the cargo to be carried on deck, without the consent of the emigration officer. The berths are to be left up for forty-eight hours after the arrival of the ship unless the passengers all leave the ship previously of their own free will.

The following provisions are made for the length of the various voyages:—To North America (except west coast), sailing vessels seventy days between January 16 and Oct. 14—eighty days during the rest of the year—steam vessels forty days in the first instance, forty-five in the second; to Western Australia, sailing vessels 120, day steam eighty-five. Emigration officer to certify as to the goodness of the provisions—penalty for bad stores £100.

A dietary scale is regulated by the commissioners, for the master of each ship, of provisions which he must carry in addition to that brought by the emigrants themselves—to be issued at two o'clock daily. Each ship to carry a passenger steward, cooks, a medical man, if the voyage exceeds eighty days, and the passengers, fifty in number, or if the passengers exceed one hundred, with less than fourteen feet for each adult, or in any case if the passengers exceed five hundred, sick passengers may be landed at any port of the United Kingdom with their families, and passage money shall be refunded.

If a passage be not provided according to contract, the passage money must be returned and compensation for the loss of convenience. If a ship does not sail on the day contracted, subsistence money at the rate of one shilling per day is to be paid to intended passengers, or they are to be maintained on board. If the delay exceeds seven days there must be additional provisions taken in.

In case of any disaster at sea the passengers are (as far as is possible), to be provided with passage in another ship, and to be maintained in the meantime. Governors and consuls may send on shipwrecked passengers, and charge the owners of the ship with a crown debt. The Queen in council may make rules for preserving order on board ship. Rules are to be posted up in conspicuous places on board. No person shall sell spirits to any passenger under a penalty of twenty pounds, and not less than five.

Recreated from The Freeman's Journal, Dublin, October 5, 1852.

WHAT EMIGRATION IS DOING!

(From the London Weekly Standard.)

We are augmenting by hundreds of thousands—almost by the million—the population of the great Transatlantic Republic;—and we not only thus thin our own population to an extent that, when dispassionately considered, must appear positively alarming—but we engender hostility in that nation from whose natural rivalry we have so much to apprehend. We are driving away a people whose race we revile, and whose religion we persecute, and by one and the same operation we diminish our population—the *first* element of national greatness—and throw into the arms of our most dangerous maratime and commercial rival millions of hearts panting with hatred of Great Britain and longing for an opportunity to make us little.

Against America we must ultimately contend for maratime supremacy,—and therefore for our commercial ascendancy;—and this lamentable crisis—for deplorable it will be, whatever the issue—we are hourly precipitating by our infatuated conduct towards Ireland. Every cargo of emigrants that quits our ports for New York or Boston, carries with it mischief to Great Britain.

Reprinted from The Waterford News, Waterford, October 8, 1852.

ELOPEMENT IN HIGH LIFE.—Information has just reached London, by electric telegraph, that Miss Blair, a ward in Chancery, and a rich heiress, possessing between £800 and £1,000 a year, eloped this morning from Taunton, with Garratt O'Moore, Esq., of Queens County, Ireland. The young lady, who was residing with her mother and step-father, Capt. Meaher, and who is extremely beautiful as well as highly accomplished, is only 17, while the fortunate gentleman is verging on 40. What could have induced the parties to elope cannot be imagined, as the mother and step-father were favourable to the match. The only assignable reason for the flight to Hyman's altar is the dread that the Lord Chancellor would not consent to the marriage, which, under existing circumstances, will no doubt deprive Mr. O'Moore of any life interest in the property beyond that of his wife's, as it will, according to the usual rule in such matters, go to the children, should Mr. O'Moore survive his wife.

Recreated from The Cork Examiner, Cork, October 8, 1852.

To the Editor of the Waterford News.

THE POLICE OF CARRICK-ON-SUIR.

Sir,—We have in this town a stipendiary magistrate, a chief of police, a head constable, and two constabulary barracks, one at either side of the river. With all this force it is impossible to walk the streets, even during the day, without having our pockets picked. Thieves, young and old, assemble every two or three hours, at the Cross, to divide the spoil, while a fine fat peeler looks on with apparent indifference, quite heedless of the "petty larceny act," or "vagrant act."

Should these slight-of-hand companies get up a sham fight to collect a crowd, no policeman can be seen there to bring the combatants to bridewell. The only places our gallant constabulary attend regularly are the suburbs of the town where they amuse themselves "sending" honest females from the paths of virtue.

Nearly all our street prostitutes have been first ruined by the police. There are three of the force "protecting" a Protestant Parson, at Mothil, since '48, and they have bastardized that locality so much that they were denounced from the altar of the parish last Sunday week, by the Catholic Curate the Rev. Mr. Fogarty. What does Colonel M'Gregor think of this immoral conduct?

VERITAS.

Reprinted from The Waterford News, Waterford, October 15, 1852.

POLICE OFFICE—Yesterday.

A FEMALE PICKPOCKET.
[Before the Mayor and Mr. Tabiteau.]

Bridget Fitzgerald, a well-dressed country girl from the County Clare, was charged with having in her possession a silver watch and other silver, for which she could not satisfactorily account.

Sub-Constable Hargan said that on Wednesday evening a lady called his attention to the prisoner, and said she was one one of a gang of pickpockets who frequented the shops that day, and on searching her found the watch produced, nine shillings, and some crochet work, which she endeavoured to conceal.

A young man from the shop of Messrs Tullis and Lumsden stated that he saw a woman put her hand into a lady's pocket in the shop; but she did not succeed in taking anything out of it—the prisoner is not the woman.

Prisoner refused to give any account of herself.

Mr. Tabiteau—Let her be remanded; she has the cut of a pickpocket.

Prisoner—I'm obliged to your worship! you're very complimentary (laughter).

Reprinted from The Waterford News, Waterford, October 22, 1852.

Portable Gas Light for Every House.

SEE THE PEERLESS SELF GENERATING GAS LAMP, a new invention of great practical value—a rival to coal gas.

Wicks, Glass, Chimneys, Smoke, and attention avoided.

A brilliant light at half the price of oil or camphine. Governable as gas by a stop tap.

No clock-work, springs, or other machinery, but simple, portable, safe, and durable, 30,000 have been sold and approved since patented.

This unique apparatus can be had for 6s. each and upwards, adapted for every purpose where a cheap and pleasant light is a desideratum.

It may be seen and prospectuses and engravings procured of R. Holliday and Co., 128, Holborn hill, London Turn-bridge Works, Huddersfield; and at Lampdealer generally.

MORE EXTERMINATION IN TIPPERARY.—We regret to learn that certain landlords in the North Riding of Tipperary are pursuing a very harsh and unfeeling course towards the tenants who had the temerity to uphold independence of thought, and to vote for the popular candidates at the late election. Within the last few weeks several hundred families have been evicted in the Nenagh Union, from the Toler, Henry, and Dawson estates; and the model agents are enforcing their claims with all the asperity of former years, heedless of the reduced demand for agricultural produce, and the evils which have fallen on the tillers of the soil.—*Limerick Reporter*.

Reprinted from The Nation, Dublin, October 23, 1853.

STATE OF THE STREETS—IMMORALITY.

The systematic manner in which public morality is outraged in the streets and on the quays of this City, has at last become insupportable. It has long been a crying scandal, disgracing and depraving our citizens; it has at last arrived at such a climax that no person can venture a yard from his own door without being obliged to witness and listen to the coarsest and most disgusting obscenity! Such of our citizens, male or female, as possess sufficient hardihood to enter the streets after nightfall must make up their minds to have their delicacy shocked at every step by the *ostentatious* and unchecked blackguardianism of depraved creatures who have lost all sense of shame, and who are permitted to amuse themselves as grossly and publicly as they please.

Verily, the prostitutes and vagabonds who honour our city by periodic visits are very powerful! They enact a despotism which no monarch or government that has ever ruled this country has been able to accomplish. They have proscribed the rank, the beauty, the virtue of the industry of this city. Let us do homage to their High Mightinesses, the vagabonds and Papbian nymphs aforesaid! they are the most potent *Authorities* that Waterford has ever seen; for they will not tolerate our presence in our own streets! They have voted delicacy and decency a punishable nuisance, and have accordingly banished them from the salubrious promenades which, in happier times the smile of a beauty brightened, and in which harassed industry sought health and relaxation without fear of encountering the pollution of vice.

Are there no means by which obscenity may be compelled to retire within its dens, and the reign of public decorum restored? Shall the only occasions in which we can be made aware of the existence of Police, be confined to the periods in which we are called on to disperse heavy sums for their support, or when they prove their efficiency by their promptness in dragging objects of charity and victims of social injustice to the punishment which society decrees to poverty and misfortune?

Let us know if we are to be longer abandoned to this species of despotism; for if we be, we must speedily organise some special mode of reconquering our public places from the empire of bestial depravity.

Recreated from The Waterford News, Waterford, October 29, 1852.

SYMPTOMS OF PROSPERITY.—The *Downpatrick Recorder* draws a glowing picture of Irish agricultural prospects, chequered in some measure by the fact of the "transition state" of the country continuing until the emigration drain shall have completely exhausted itself:—"No one," says our contemporary, "who observes attentively what is passing and scans the signs of the times can fail to see that, while this country is on the way to prosperity, in trade, commerce, manufactures, and industrial enterprise of several kinds, the present state of agricultural remuneration is gratifying, and its prospects cheering. Prices of grain, butter, live stock, &c., are all on the advance. Rents are well paid. The late Falkirk Truste tells a practical tale, as to the Englishmen and Scotchmen that have come lately to reside in Ireland. It is stated that 100,000 head of sheep and black cattle were brought there, to be sent over to Ireland to English and Scotch colonists. These breeds will do good, as well as their owners. The fact of the purchase may also convey a useful hint to Irish farmers. As we have observed already, prospects are encouraging, and the farmer should not fail in his part, to realise them to the fullest extent."

AN OASIS IN THE WEST.—The *Sligo Journal* thus reports the state of that county:—The improved state of the country is, thank God, becoming more marked, and everywhere one goes, and in every dealing one has, it is plain to see that the people are more comfortable than they have been for years. Two circumstances contribute mainly to this most desirable state of things— first a splendid harvest gathered in in the finest weather; and next the admirable prices which every sort of farm produce now brings. At the quarter session just past the landlords had no business, the tenants had all paid their rents, and at no sessions for years were there so few disputes on this vital matter between two such important classes, the landlords and the tenants. Land is now in this country well worth the rent paid for it, and, if it pleases Providence to grant us a few more such seasons, Ireland will be a different country.

Recreated from The Nation, Dublin, October 30, 1852.

CELEBRATION OF THE FUNERAL OF THE DUKE OF WELLINGTON IN CORK.

THE only indications by which the citizens of Cork were reminded that an event that has excited so vast an amount of pomp and parade in England was celebrated yesterday, were by the flags of a few coasting and foreign craft, lying at the quays, which were hoisted half mast high. No funeral bell pealed its solemn farewell; neither closed shutters nor shop fronts spoke of such an event in the ordinary way that respect or regret is testified by these means; and the only recognition of the fact that the funeral of the great Duke of Wellington was proceeding to be found in the streets of Cork, was by the flag, half mast high, which floated from the flagstaff of Mr. Sam. Haynes, of Patrick-street.

Reprinted from The Cork Examiner, November 19, 1852.

FUNERAL OF
THE DUKE OF WELLINGTON.

The 18th of November, 1852, will ever be remembered as the day when the British nation committed to the tomb the last remains of Arthur Wellesley, Duke of Wellington, a general whose name will be recorded in history to the latest posterity, and in whom shone, in the most brilliant manner, "the glorious results of military valour, the conduct of armies, the siege of fortresses, the capture of towns, the passage of rivers, spirited attacks, honourable retreats, prudently selected encampments, obstinately fought battles, enemies vanquished by force, dispersed by strategy, worn out and scattered by wise and enduring patience." Nowhere can be found so many and so striking examples of those achievements as in the recorded actions of him who was at once wise, discreet, liberal, and patriotic, combining obedience to princes with devotion to his country's service—great in adversity by his endurance, great in prosperity by his forbearance, great amid difficulties by his prudence, and great amid perils by his courage. If this be a true delineation of the character and conduct of the late Duke of Wellington, who could doubt but that all England would delight to honour such a man, and pay him the homage and the respect which were so pre-eminently his due? No greater mark of attachment could be manifested than that of according to him a public national funeral—placing the "greatest military by the side of the greatest naval chief" who ever adorned the annals of any country.

A scene at once so sacred and solemn, so awfully impressive, and so appropriate in every point of view, to the grand but mournful occasion, was perhaps never before presented to the admiration of the metropolis of any kingdom in the world.

Never were the feelings of the public more deep and general. Last night the inhabitants of London could have had but little repose. In every street through which the procession was to pass, parties were preparing to take possession of places; and persons remained around the Horse Guards all night. Long before daylight all the streets leading to the line of route presented an animated appearance, large crowds of parties proceeding to those various positions whence they expected to view the *cortege* pass along. Elegantly dressed females were seen parading through the streets, braving the uncomfortable atmosphere of early morn; but while the police arrangements were of so admirable description, that the utmost possible facility was afforded, alike to ladies and gentlemen, in gaining access to the seats which they had previously engaged, whence to witness the mournful procession dragging its slow length along to St. Paul's Cathedral. It would be impossible to estimate, with anything like accuracy the very many thousands who witnessed the procession from the various houses on its passage from the Horse Guards to the Cathedral; but this can safely be affirmed that nothing like the dense mass of human beings, with intense desire to gaze upon a public spectacle, were ever congregated before, and probably never will be again.

The procession then slowly advanced up the Mall, and the rest of those who had the privilege of taking part in the procession having passed, the chief interest of the scene was now felt to be approaching, and in a few moments was to reveal to the eyes of the assembled thousands the colossal car with its magnificent decorations, and the coffin containing the remains of that great hero whose exploits had filled the pages of history, who had secured the nation's glory, and who had consolidated her liberties on a firm and secure basis. To the remains of such a man—the hero of a hundred fights, the warrior, the statesman—a grateful country were now assembled to do honour, and by their presence, orderly, respectful, and decorous, to offer a last tribute of their respect to his services to his country.

A few minutes of anxious expectation were passed, and the car was drawn forth, and to say that it was imposing in the extreme would but faintly convey an idea of the magnificence of its general appearance, and the elaborate nature of its details. No sooner had it emerged from the tent, drawn by twelve horses, than the greatest interest was simultaneously manifested; every head was uncovered, and the thousands gazed in silent reverence at the object that now met their view. The hero of the Peninsula, of India, of Waterloo—whose fame had resounded through all quarters of the globe—was now laid prostrate in death on the small space which had been allotted for it on the bier. No one could gaze on it without being duly impressed and struck with the truth of the phrase, "*sic transit gloria mundi*". It proceeded towards the Mall at a very slow pace, when an accident occurred which for some time stopped its progress. In consequence of its great weight, the earth nearly opposite the steps leading to the Duke of York's Column gave way, and the wheels became completely embedded, and resisted the efforts of the powerful exertions of the horses by which it was drawn. At length some ropes were obtained, and being attached, a body of police by their united strength succeeded in extricating the vehicle from this temporary difficulty. The spectators who crowded the steps viewed the whole matter with considerable anxiety, and fears were entertained that this unfortunate incident would mar the whole proceedings.

As the procession advanced towards Buckingham-palace, the crowd began to increase in numbers, drawn together, no doubt, from its presenting a view along the entire length of Constitution-hill, as well as during its progress up the Mall; but even here the best order prevailed.

Her Most Gracious Majesty, the Princess Royal, and the Prince of Wales occupied the centre window of Buckingham Palace, and her Majesty was noticed, as the body of the illustrious Duke passed the spot, to pay a deep and marked attention, and to point it out to the juvenile branches of the Royal Family. Her Majesty was noticed by the crowd with a respectful but silent demeanour, but without any attempt to disturb the solemnity of the scene by any other demonstration. Here the procession was joined by his Royal Highness Prince Albert, wearing the uniform of a Field Marshall, and drawn in a carriage and six. He was immediately recognised by the assembled crowd, and respectfully bowed his acknowledgements to their salutations.

The procession was also increased by several other carriages of the Royal Family, immediately after which was an object that riveted general attention—it was the horse that had so long been ridden by his Grace, led by a groom, bearing his boots with spurs attached, which were placed in the stirrups reversed.

At a few minutes past one Prince Albert entered the Cathedral, and, as he proceeded to his position, seemed much affected by the solemnity of the scene which had just burst upon his view, as he looked to the right and the left.

At six minutes after one the body entered, and the choir immediately commenced the musical part of the service, proceeding while singing, at a very slow pace, towards the dome, and followed by the body of the late Duke.

The Dirge being concluded, the Dead March was performed: during which the body was deposited in the vault, by means of a block and pully standing over the narrow space underneath which lay the gallant Nelson, and down which, by an ingenious adaptation of the pully and windlass, the body of England's hero was safely lodged in its final resting place.

Recreated from The Cork Examiner, Cork, November 22, 1852.

DUKE OF WELLINGTON.

Our country has rendered her last great public tribute to her foremost citizen and her most illustrious military commander. The mortal remains of Arthur Wellesley, the great Duke of Wellington, were on Thursday consigned to their final resting-place in St. Paul's Cathedral, amidst the pomp of one of the most magnificent and solemn pageants recorded in history. No attainable element of impressive splendour was wanting to this great national ceremonial. All the resources of our modern art in decorative and heraldic illustration were lavishly employed to honour the dust of our hero; the Princes of our Royal Family accompanied him to the grave in mournful procession; military representatives from almost all the great States of Europe testified, by their presence on the occasion, the sense which their Governments still entertain of the services which he rendered to the peace and independence of Europe; the British army which he had so long commanded, and which, on so many a desperate field, his genius had made invincible, accompanied him here again in thousands, but accompanied him no longer to victory; our Senate assisted in a body at his obsequies; and, to complete the impressiveness of the scene, the people congregated to witness it in multitudinous masses, which would of themselves form no unimpressive spectacle, and such as the world, no doubt, has never seen since the triumphal marches of Rome's Imperial conquerors. Over all this throbbing life, however, there reigned the deep solemnity of death; and all this stately array but served to close the earthly glories of him who led the fiery charge of Assaye and the murderous shock of Waterloo.

Let the reader who did not witness the spectacle endeavour to picture in imagination the stately pomp of the military pageant passing in long column along the spacious avenue of the Mall, and then winding up Constitution-hill, while thousands upon thousands of spectators, in respectful silence, witness its progress. Let him fancy the departure of carriages and mourning coaches, broken at intervals by marshalmen, messengers of the College of Arms, trumpeters, pursuivants, and heraldic standard bearers. The strains of music, martial, yet solemn in its character, rise, die away, and are taken up again at intervals, and at length the moment has arrived for the funeral car to move forward. As it formed by far the most magnificent and interesting feature of the procession, some account of its general design and most prominent details will not be out of place. The whole lower part is of bronze, supported on six wheels, and elaborated with an amount of skill and artistic feeling which deserve unequalled praise. Above this metallic framework rises a rich pediment of gilding, in the panels of which the following list of victories is inscribed:— Ahmednuggur, Assaye, Argaum, Gavilghur, Roleia, Vimiera, Douro and Oporto, Talavera, Busaco, Torres Vedras, Fuentes d'Onor, Ciudad Rodrigo, Badajos, Salamanca, Vittoria, Pampeluna, Pyrenees, St. Sebastian, Nivelle, Nive, Orthes, Toulouse, Quatre Bras, Waterloo. On the sides of this pediment were arranged lofty trophies of arms, including spears, muskets, bayonets, swords, and flags, and surmounted by Ducal coronets and batons.

A similar trophy stood in front, rising behind the arms of the deceased, cast in bronze, and surmounted by his heraldic badges and honours, including the tabard magnificently wrought and embroidered. Over the bier and its bearers, the gilded handles of which protruded from beneath, was arranged the sumptuous velvet pall, powdered with silver embroidery, bordered with laurels in silver, and showing the legend round it, "Blessed are the dead that die in the Lord," and terminated by a magnificent figure of silver two feet deep. The coffin, with the Duke's hat and sword resting on it, surmounted the bier, and from four great halberts rising at each corner was suspended a magnificent canopy, with pendent cords and tassels of the richest and most costly description. To this gigantic vehicle, twenty-seven feet long, ten feet broad, seventeen feet high, and weighing from ten to eleven tons, twelve of the largest and finest black horses that could be procured were harnessed three abreast. They were completely covered with rich velvet housings, having the arms of the deceased splendidly embroidered on them, and with heads surmounted by nodding plumes they looked quite elephantine. Such was the funeral car as it fell into the line of procession, surrounded by a swarm of undertakers' men, and on each side five colonels on horseback, bearing the bannerols of the Wellesley family.

Recreated from The Belfast News-Letter, Belfast, November 22, 1852.

POLICE OFFICE—Yesterday.

A wretched looking woman was charged by Mr. Cary of Ballynamona who attended personally this day to prosecute her for stealing a small quantity of field turnips from the lands of Ballynamona. The turnips were taken from her and prisoner kept until the aid of a policeman was had to bring her in. One month's imprisonment.

Sporting Intelligence.

LORD WATERFOD'S HOUNDS
WILL MEET

Nov. 27, Newtown Chapel, Co, Waterford,
" 30 Kilmegany.
Dec. 4th., Castle Morris.

THE FAITHLEGG HARRIERS
WILL MEET

On Monday, 29th Nov., at Belle Lake.
On Thursday, 2d. December, at Kill St. Nicholas

Reprinted from The Waterford News, Waterford, November 26, 1852.

CHRISTMAS DAY.

Whilst many of our readers are making themselves comfortable and happy at their warm firesides, and enjoying themselves over their good dinners, with their wonted appendages, &c., on to-morrow—Christmas day—we hope they will not forget the poor, upon whose vitals, we are sorry to say, penury and disease, to a considerable extent, still feed. Time was—and we are old enough to remember it—when no one need feel cold or hunger on Christmas day. Well, may we hope that a similar tale may be told of to-morrow? But we fear not. With an expensive poor law, a decimated population, and a daily emigration, still we fear that we shall have numbers of our population to whom to-morrow will be anything but a " happy Christmas." And, we moreover, venture to say that we shall have our domiciles besieged, and as great an amount of wailing and crying that day, as if a tax-man had never gone on his rounds! But, what can the afflicted do?—it is more their misfortune than their fault. All can't be rich; and if all were rich, there would be no contrast, and very possibly no comfort in affluence. In the name of God, then, let us not at this holy season forget the devoted children of travail and penury; and at the same time, let us express our ardent hope that, by this time twelve-months, both our readers and our country may be more happy and prosperous than they are to-day.

Reprinted from The Waterford News, Waterford, December 24, 1852.

NEW EXTERMINATIONS.

"Throughout the entire extent of Connaught," says the *Galway Mercury*, "a very great and alarming change is now taking place in the occupancy of the soil. The purchasers under the Incumbered Estates Court vie with the old landlords in effecting the depopulation of their properties. Once a small holding becomes vacant, no man can have it again upon the old terms, however solvent he may be. The dwelling house is forthwith levelled with the ground—the boundary marks are obliterated—the fences are removed; and several acres are thus formed into one large field, destined to form a portion either of a sheep walk, or of a large farm constituted out of a number of these smaller tenancies. This is the system now adopted throughout nearly the entire of this province. There are, of course, occasional exceptions, but they are rare."

THE CROWBAR BRIGADE.

Notices have been lately served upon Mr. Cullen, relieving officer for the Galway district, of the eviction of no less than thirty-eight families, comprising about 160 individuals, at Bridge-street, in this town, most of whom will be obliged to seek refuge in the workhouse. Notice has also been served upon the same officer of the eviction of all the families living upon five townlands in the electoral division of Barna, and three townlands in the electoral division of Carrabrowne, forming part of the property lately the estates of Lord Oranmore, by Mr. Murray, of the Provincial Bank, on the part of an English Insurance Company. Mr. Flynn, another relieving officer, has likewise received notice of the eviction of all the occupants of two townlands on the property lately owned by Lord Oranmore, in the electoral division of Bellville.—*Galway Mercury.*

THE PROVINCES.

Mr. Wynne, the Government Inspector for Railways, has reported favourably of the portion of the Londonderry and Coleraine line already constructed, and the railway will be opened on Monday next, between Derry and Newtownlimavady, for passengers as well as goods traffic.

The terminus of the Ennis and Limerick Railway will be at the Limerick side of the Shannon in the immediate vicinity of the Limerick terminus of the Waterford and Limerick Railway, and for which purpose a bridge will be thrown across at Corbally, near the Salmon weir.

This last week our town has been inundated with emigrants *en route* to America. Bianconi's big cars to Waterford are seldom empty, and three days, at least, each week, do we hear the cheers of those who remain behind, encouraging their friends who are going to the land of promise and hope.—*Clonmel Chronicle.*

The tide of emigration flows on in this part of the country with a rapidity almost incredible. Day after day we see shoals of the better class of peasants moving off to a distant but better country. On Monday last no less than eighty-seven young men and women left this locality. The two villages where they resided are quite deserted, except here and there an old man or woman may be found. These parties had kind and indulgent landlords, but nothing could induce them to remain in Ireland.—*Roscommon Journal.*

EMIGRATION FROM GALWAY TO AUSTRALIA.—The rage for emigration to Australia has not been confined to the towns and cities on the Eastern sea-board. Hitherto the emigration from Galway was Westward, but its tide is now setting in for Australia. Seventeen highly respectable passengers from Galway sailed on Friday from Dundee in the El Dorado.—*Galway Packet.*

LOSS OF TWO BELFAST VESSELS.—It is with regret we learn that information has reached town to the effect that two large vessels connected with this port—the Sobraon, Belonging to Messrs. Fitzsimmons, Sinclair, and Coates, and trading between San Francisco and Hong Kong, and the Chippewa, belonging to Lemon and Co., have been lost. The particulars have not reached us. The registered tonnage of the former vessel was 1,280 tons, and that of the latter 746.—*Banner of Ulster*.

IRISH INDUSTRY.—A new branch of industry has recently sprung up in the province of Ulster, in the shape of shirt making for London houses. Last week, one agent alone of a London house in Coleraine, took in 177 dozen, or 2,124 shirts, all ready for giving into the hands of the laundress. The material for making them was given out at various periods during the last few weeks. We are within the mark, in all probability, when we say that no less than one thousand dozen shirts are made every month in this district for wholesale London houses.—*Coleraine Chronicle*.

AUSTRALIA.

GENTLEMEN about Emigrating to Australia or the Colonies, are particularly invited to leave their orders with

M'COMAS and SON,
2 LOWER ABBEY STREET,

as from their extensive connections in Australia, and constant communications with the Colonies, they are able to offer advantages which will insure a very large saving to the Cash Purchaser.

Their present stock is one of the most extensive and fashionable, and their OUTFITTING DEPARTMENT will be found well worthy of inspection.

By Special Appointment,
DRAPERS AND TAILORS,
To His Excellency the Earl of Eglinton.

SHIP HOTEL, TAVERN, AND DINING ROOMS
5, LOWER ABBEY-STREET,
SACKVILLE-STREET,
(Rere Entrance, 14, Sackville-Place.)

	s.	d.
A Table d'Hote daily, from 5 to 7 o'Clock.		
Dinner, Fish, Soup, Joints, &c., &c.,	1	0
Ditto, Steaks, Chops, or Cutlets,	1	0
Lunch, ditto., ditto.,	0	8
Ditto, off the Joints, hot or cold	0	6
Breakfast, Tea or Coffee, with Eggs,	1	0
Ditto, Steak, Chops, or Cold Meat,	1	3
Oysters, Fresh from the Beds every Morning, per Dozen	0	6
Bread and Butter,	0	
Kidney, Bread and Butter,	0	5
Glass of Ale and Sandwich,	0	4
Fine Old Sherry, per Bottle,	4	0
Ditto, Pint	2	0
Old Crusted Port, per Bottle	4	0
Ditto, Pint	2	0
Jameson's Prime Old Whiskey, per Tumbler,	0	4

Jamaica Rum, Cognac Brandy, Liqueurs, Lemonade, Soda Water, Ginger Beer, &c., &c., charges equally moderate.
BEDS, per night, 1s.

Craven, the Celebrated Irish Harper, plays his popular and much admired Airs every Evening.

The *London Times, Bell's Life, Illustrated News, Punch, Liverpool Journal, Saunders, Freeman* and NATION Newspapers, taken in, and may be had for half-price the day after publication.

LEECHES.

WE beg to inform the Medical Profession, that we import both French and German Leeches every week, thereby ensuring them fresh and of best quality.
JOHN GEORGE BOILEAU and Co.,
Druggists and Manufacturing Chemists,
Wholesale Dealers in Druggists' Sundries, Surgical Instruments and Medical Appliances,
26 MARY'S-ABBEY (Capel-street), Dublin.

Recreated and reprinted from The Nation, Dublin, December 25, 1852.

Gerald Reilly is the author and editor of this anthology.

His previous work, *Things Change, a reflection on the 70's, now and tomorrow thru images of Boston*, was written with his daughter, Alanna, in 2013.

Mr. Reilly lives on Cape Cod, Massachusetts, near Buzzard's Bay.

www.ingramcontent.com/pod-product-compliance
Lightning Source LLC
Chambersburg PA
CBHW080050190426
43201CB00035B/2155